Aria

Novels by Brown Meggs

ARIA   (1978)
THE MATTER OF PARADISE   (1975)
SATURDAY GAMES   (1974)

Aria

BROWN MEGGS

Atheneum NEW YORK 1978

Who's Who in America is a registered trademark of Marquis
Who's Who, Inc.

Library of Congress Cataloging in Publication Data

Meggs, Brown.
  Aria.

  I. Title.
PZ4.M4915Ar   [PS3563.E34]   813'.5'4   77-5188
ISBN 0-689-10832-X

Published simultaneously in Canada by McClelland and Stewart Ltd.
Manufactured in the United States of America
by American Book–Stratford Press, Saddle Brook,
New Jersey
Designed by Kathleen Carey
First Edition

IN MEMORIAM

Norman and Nancy Ellett
29 DECEMBER 1976

Robert E. Myers
12 MARCH 1976

Anna Victoria Wasser
4 APRIL 1977

Nota bene

No living person appears in this book. Though I have come recently from a record-company background, this narrative is entirely an invention. Harry's company, Melos-Doria, is imaginary, as is the cast of Harry's *Otello*, the Rome Opera, the businessmen and lawyers, especially the ladies. The Consortium is not CBS or DG or EMI or Philips or any other real conglomerate. This is a novel, not a memoir.

I am indebted to Herman Gollob, Ned Brown, Paul Hirschman, Ines LaBonté, Marvin Schwartz, M. J. Snyder and George Sponhaltz for their generous contributions to the manuscript.

Brown Meggs

Pasadena, California
August, 1977

Contents

PRELUDE   HOLLYWOOD/ZUG: *April*   1

ACT ONE   FLINTRIDGE/BURBANK: *April*   9

ACT TWO   PARIS/LONDON: *April-May*   63

ACT THREE   GENEVA/NEW YORK/MILAN/
          MUNICH/MARSEILLES/COTE D'AZUR: *May*   181

INTERMEZZO   HOLLYWOOD: *June*   281

ACT FOUR   ROME: *August-September*   293

ACT FIVE   FLINTRIDGE/BURBANK:
          December   401

The Consortium

```
                    ┌─────────────────────┐
                    │   Globelektron AG   │
                    │       Zürich        │
                    │    (Secretariat)    │
                    └─────────────────────┘

┌─────────────────────────────┐   ┌─────────────────────────────┐
│                             │   │  Leisure Time Industries,   │
│  Hampstead Record Group,    │   │          Inc.               │
│           Ltd.              │   │ (Melos-Doria Records        │
│          London             │   │        Division)            │
│                             │   │     Burbank, Calif.         │
└─────────────────────────────┘   └─────────────────────────────┘

┌─────────────────────────────┐   ┌─────────────────────────────┐
│                             │   │                             │
│        Apogée SA            │   │   Dischi La Cima S.p.a.     │
│          Paris              │   │          Milan              │
│                             │   │                             │
└─────────────────────────────┘   └─────────────────────────────┘

┌─────────────────────────────┐   ┌─────────────────────────────┐
│                             │   │                             │
│ Spitze-Schallplatten GmbH   │   │  Itadaki Music Co., Ltd.    │
│          Munich             │   │          Tokyo              │
│                             │   │                             │
└─────────────────────────────┘   └─────────────────────────────┘
```

CHAPIN, HURSTON ELIOT, II, record co. exec; b. Darien, Conn., Oct. 9, 1932; s. Hurston Chester and Bette Cortlandt (Milne) C.; B.A., Harvard, 1954; M.A., Yale, 1956; m. Margaret Louise Beach, May 11, 1957; twin sons, Hurston Eliot III, Beach Hurston. Masterworks dept., Columbia Records div. CBS, N.Y.C., 1957; asst. repertoire mgr., Melos-Doria Records, N.Y.C., 1957, creative services mgr., 1958, producer, 1959, artists and repertoire mgr., 1962, v.p. artists and repertoire, 1967, v.p. and gen. mgr., 1970; v.p. and gen. mgr., Melos-Doria Records div. Leisure Time Industries, Burbank, Cal., 1973–. Recipient Grammy award Nat. Acad. Rec. Arts and Scis. Mem. Record Industry Assn. Am., Nat. Acad. Rec. Arts and Scis. Composer: Woodwind Quintet, Trio for Flute, Piano & Bassoon. Clubs: Harvard (So. Cal.) Annandale Country. Home: 10 Wendover Road Flintridge CA 91103 Office: 6300 Olive Ave Burbank CA 91505

Who's Who in America

Prelude

HOLLYWOOD/ZUG: *April*

a·ri·a (är′ ēə) n.
1. An accompanied elaborate melody sung (*as in*
   opera) *by a single voice*

Observing a lifelong habit, he waited until the last possible moment to give Ponti the bad news about the *Requiem*. This moment was midnight Thursday, April 21st, Hollywood time, which was eight the next morning by the Lake of Zug, near Zürich.

". . . Is that you, Gian-Carlo?"

"*Allô?* Who is calling, please?"

Harry's timing was apparently less than propitious. The usually dulcet vox humana of Gian-Carlo Ponti smoldered with impatience.

"It's I, Gian-Carlo—Harry Chapin. Please forgive me for disturbing you at such an early hour, but we're about to go to bed here and I was afraid I'd miss you later on, because of your rehearsal."

"Dear Harry. Of course, this is most understandable. I am pleased to hear your voice, as ever."

"I'm afraid I have bad news, Gian-Carlo."

"Oh, yes?"

"It's the *Requiem*. I'm afraid we must postpone."

"What is this you say?"

"The London dates. I regret, Gian-Carlo, that the existing dates are no longer good for us."

"But it is all arranged. I have the dates in my book. It is beginning, I think, on the twenty-third day of August."

"We shall still do it, of course, Gian-Carlo. But there are problems for this year."

"Because your business is not good? I have seen your remarks in *Time* magazine."

"Actually, Gian-Carlo, I was misquoted. No, the problem is—another commitment."

Gian-Carlo uttered a sharp gasp.

"Did you say something, Gian-Carlo?"

There was no immediate reply: only a muffled rustling, as of bed-clothes.

"Hello? . . . Are you there, Gian-Carlo . . . ?"

"You must please excuse, dear Harry. We are for the moment—indisposed. . . ."

Not the sovereign *we*, but the *we* of female companionship. Harry might have anticipated such indisposition. Gian-Carlo Ponti, forty-four years of age—after Bernstein, the most glamorous conductor of the day—was reputed, among sopranos at La Scala in particular, to have a foot-long prick. Maestro Ponti employed a very short baton (something he had learned from Ormandy) and the Bulgarian mezzo Milash-Drozny had let it be known somewhat publicly (during piano rehearsals for Scala's new production of *Un Ballo in maschera*, to be precise) that Ponti's prick was longer than his stick. This charge, disseminated with characteristic dispatch by an interested lady columnist of *Corriere della Sera*, Milan's leading daily, accounted, some said, for the Maestro's extraordinary success with ladies of the Friday-afternoon subscriptions. Whatever the truth of the matter, the celebrated Florentine was perhaps even now demonstrating his prowess.

". . . Ah, we are here again, dear Harry. A thousand apologies for this interruption. Can you repeat?"

Harry started again. "To be perfectly candid, Gian-Carlo—Mme. Cavalieri is coming out of retirement."

"Can this be true?"

"Yes, quite true. Edith has informed us that she wishes to resume her career with the *Otello* which, as you probably know, we committed to her some years ago. Unfortunately, the only dates convenient for her are the ones we've set aside for the *Requiem*. Our number-one crew cannot be in two places at once, and, regrettably, she requires the same hall—and of course Kunz, the Otello."

"And who is to conduct for the great lady?"

"Again, Gian-Carlo, I must ask for your understanding. Naturally, when Edith informed me that she was ready to work again, I instantly put forward your own name as the ideal maestro—given the great success you had with *Otello* at Scala. But I'm sorry to say that the lady insists upon her own regular conductor, Passafiume."

Gian-Carlo laughed. "The lady has not performed anywhere in the world for almost a decade—yet she has a 'regular' conductor? Do you not think this humorous, dear Harry?"

"Believe me, Gian-Carlo, I don't look forward to undertaking such a long and expensive project with a gentleman who has already celebrated his eightieth birthday. But Passafiume studied with Toscanini, and Edith has always had it in mind to record her Desdemona under his baton."

"But you see, dear Harry," Gian-Carlo oozed with his special charm, "if I may say so, I have warned you of just this problem. These singers are merely spoiled children. It is truly *jeux d'enfants*, this business of opera—it is not serious work for men like you and me. In Bach and Beethoven one does not find these childish games. One's art remains pure."

"Gian-Carlo, off the record I must certainly agree with you. And your art *will* remain pure. We will eventually do the *Requiem* and of course the Beethoven and, really, anything else that makes artistic sense for you. But right now . . ."

"I can see that it is a difficult commercial decision for you, dear Harry. Naturally, you must place the greater value on the greater, what do you say, commodity?"

"You are *not* a commodity, Gian-Carlo. You do me an injustice to suggest that."

"Please accept my apology, dear Harry. It is only that I am upset. Forgive me."

"Gian-Carlo, I can say to you without reservation that I hold no other conductor of today in higher regard—none."

"Dear Harry, I accept fully the pain that you must now feel. But I must ask myself—perhaps I am wrong to renew my contract with Melos-Doria? Perhaps it would be better for us to go in our separate directions. What do you think?"

"Gian-Carlo, I think such talk is ridiculous. We are still at the beginning. Naturally, there will be occasional setbacks, occasional rough spots in the road. But let's not forget our ultimate objective, to build a permanent catalog of great recordings—a monument, not to be too grand about it, to your own exceptional artistry. And, looking on the bright side, please remember that whatever work we do from now on will be covered by the new contract, Gian-Carlo—meaning the new royalty rates and, most importantly, the tax advantages of Swiss law."

"For which I am most thankful, dear Harry. But what am I to do in August—in the time that I have put aside for our *Requiem*? I have passed over a great many engagements—a great many profitable engagements—to be free to make records for Melos-Doria."

"I'm just this moment working on that, Gian-Carlo. I leave for Paris tomorrow evening and then go on to the Consortium's annual repertoire conference in London. As soon as I'm finished there, I shall come to see you. Really, I've got some exciting new ideas. I think you'll share my enthusiasm."

"You speak of new ideas?"

"Well—the Beethoven, for example. With the Third already on the market—and doing very nicely, I might add—and the Fifth scheduled for January release, I intend to propose in London that we complete all nine. What would you think of that?"

"I—I would be most grateful, of course, dear Harry."

"And perhaps a record or two with some of our better young soloists. Both of the Brahms concerti, I was thinking, with the young American girl Diana Kaufman."

"I would like to hear her, of course."

"And opera, too. After witnessing your work at Scala—well, what would you say to some Puccini? A complete *Bohème*, perhaps? As a matter of fact, we owe Del Campo a *Bohème*."

"Del Campo? Ah, but only for the Musetta, dear Harry. Surely you are not speaking of the Mimì?"

"Well, if you're not high on her, Gian-Carlo, let's think of something else."

"I would be interested only in *Manon Lescaut* or *La Fanciulla*. Perhaps the *Trittico*. Nothing else."

"Fine. Our catalogs could certainly use all three, though of course the competition is very strong for the *Lescaut*—Caballé and Domingo, you know. But I'd love to get a *Trittico* from you."

"You know I have done it at Rome many years ago?"

"Yes. But the Schicchi—what would we do for a Schicchi?"

"Hah, there is only one—but he is not available. That is Benno Toggi. He is an old man now, but he is the best."

"Well, we'll talk about that, too. Look, the possibilities are endless. Let us think things over."

"Of course, dear Harry. I am in your hands, as always."

"That's it, then, Gian-Carlo. I look forward to seeing you very soon."

"Dear Harry, there is someone here who wishes to say *allô*."

"Oh?"

". . . Harry? Surprise—it's me, Marianne."

"Marianne—well, *hello*. This *is* a surprise."

Or perhaps not. How did she think he knew to phone Ponti at Otto Kunz's villa in Zug? For Marianne was Mrs. Otto Kunz, wife of the well-loved tenor, who was probably asleep at that moment in their Manhattan apartment, dreaming of the Texas Company's forthcoming Saturday matinee broadcast of Bizet's *Carmen*, in which Herr Kunz was to sing his fifty-third Met Don José.

"Have you seen Otto lately?" she asked blithely. "How is he?"

"Saw him, oh, two weeks ago. He's fine. Matter of fact, he's doing the Met broadcast Saturday. I was invited to appear on the intermission quiz, but I'm off to Europe tomorrow—Paris and then London. Otto's finally going to do *Otello* with Cavalieri, which is what Gian-Carlo and I have been chatting about. I guess you didn't know."

"How would I know? We're so isolated out here, Harry. Oh, we saw the item in *Time*. It was so like you. Just *loved* what you said about tits!"

"Yes, well—sometime I'll explain."

"We miss you, Harry. Why don't you come see us? We're only minutes from Paris. We'd love to see you, Harry."

"Sure. Love to see you, too. As soon as the meetings are over . . ."

"Got to run now, Harry. Love and kisses to Otto . . ."

She replaced the receiver without giving Gian-Carlo a chance to resume. "Harry's awfully nice, isn't he?"

But Gian-Carlo didn't seem to care: had begun to caress her again—was, in fact, kissing the soles of her feet.

"Did you like what I did for you? While you were talking *business?* That's the first time I've ever done *that!*"

"*Cara mia,* I am grateful, as always. And did you understand what dear Harry has said? *All* the Beethoven symphonies. *Two* Brahms concerti. Perhaps even the *Trittico!* Your Gianni is becoming one of your superstars, don't you agree?"

"Oh, men," Marianne said, sliding her perfect pink ass to the center of the bed. "If you're going to kiss something, superstar, kiss *this,*" pulling him by the ears like a puppy, feeling his tongue soon enough.

The *Time* thing was ruining him. Two issues back, Mr. Luce's successors had run an asinine piece on the record business, and naturally they'd asked Harry Chapin, powerful boss of Melos-Doria, to comment on classics. Just to be whimsical (he now guessed), he had said: "In today's record business, classics are about as useful as tits on a mule." Had he meant to say bull? A mule is the offspring of a donkey and a horse, is it not? He didn't know. But he knew about classics: so-called "serious music" had less than a five-percent share of market, according to the latest industry report. The Age of Rock, eh, *Monsieur?* Unfortunately, *Time*'s fabulous circulation among influentials had brought response to his whimsy from half the people who'd ever passed through his life, including one hundred percent of former girl friends. Girl friends. The very words made him dizzy.

"You forgot to ask for charges."

What was the name of this one? Heidi—latest in a long line of unsatisfactory, unsatisfying temp-secs, a bad-tempered twenty-five-year-old who had reluctantly shared her bed with him on perhaps a dozen occasions over a two-month period, and who now, lying nude beside him, watched with soulful gaze as he searched for his shorts. "Look," he said remorselessly, "when you get the phone bill, I'll pay you back, okay?"

"I still don't understand," she whined on, "why you waited so long to tell him. You've known about the *Otello* thing for weeks. And should you promise him all that Beethoven? I thought you said he didn't sell that well. . . ."

These young women of the office who help their bosses through each business day—was it so unreasonable to ask them for help through the night? "You're probably right," he said, looking for his suit.

"Do you *have* to go?" she persisted. "Wouldn't you like to try again? Maybe if you'd just relax—not think about business . . ."

He certainly didn't need this bitch to remind him of his mortality. "Not tonight," he said, pulling on his trousers. "Just not in the mood, I suppose. . . ."

Not then and not ever again, with her.

Act One

FLINTRIDGE/BURBANK:
April

Rejoice! The Moslem pride is buried in the sea;
ours and Heaven's is the glory!

Boïto-Verdi, OTELLO

1

Harry Chapin, 170 days short of his forty-fifth birthday (eyes puffy, original sharply etched features submerged in unwanted flesh: harvest of excessive Bordeaux consumption and other forms of suburban debauchery), awoke in pain and despair, member all dressed up and no place to go. Share your good fortune with the lovely lady there by your side? Well, hardly.

Ouch. Heart seemed to flutter: jolted him with unlikely pain on the left side. More of the same when he took a deep breath. But not a heart attack, he reassured himself. Only last Monday old Pope, the GP who looked after Maggie and the twins among other distinguished clients, had told him he had the heart of a sixteen-year-old girl: a girl weighing, however, 188 pounds. The old codger had instantly started Harry on a 750-calorie diet, and these latest pains, he now estimated, came from his stomach, which cried out from unaccustomed emptiness.

Ouch again. Who *was* this middle-aged woman asleep at his side? My God, none other than Miss Stanford Cheerleader of 1955. What's *happened* to her?

Ouch yet again. Ah, this one stemmed, he supposed, from painful memory of the night just passed. He had returned home at 2:10 A.M.; the sheriff's deputies arrived shortly thereafter. "Three false alarms in six months," the friendly officer said. "Next one's a misdemeanor."

They were talking to *him* about misdemeanors? "Thank you, Officer. Got to get the damned thing fixed." His life, he meant. "Dog sets it off, you know." He couldn't seem to remember the burglar alarm's infra-red beam. A moment's forgetfulness and you had L.A. County's finest right there in your living room, guns drawn.

Maggie's gun drawn, too. "We're going to have a little talk, Harry."
"Hey, not *now*, huh? In the morning, okay? If you don't mind . . ."

He eased out of bed and padded into the bathroom, dropped his
pajamas and let them lay. His piss had gone deep yellow, his head
ached, he felt a fool: everything normal. He collapsed onto the crapper,
but got right back up: no magazines. He walked naked through the
living room, remembering for once to shut off the goddam alarm and
looking for something less intellectual than *Smithsonian* or *Archaeology*,
which lay in Maggie's chair. Doing a little late-night reading, was she,
while he was out, what, gallivanting? The living-room curtains were
open, exposing a magnificent sweep of plate glass. He paused to admire
the ice plant in front. Tak, their arthritic Japanese gardener, had recently added six flats of *Delosperma alba* to fill in a new animal path:
deer and coyote coming down at night to drink from the swimming
pool. Big surprise for the animals this morning: naked man with
residual hard-on in living room. But no fear of other witnesses: the
Chapins' remote cul-de-sac, shared only with the Burgesses, would see
no further traffic until the mailman came at noon, the newspaper kid
having long since vanished in his Day-Glo bug.

He found *National Geographic* in the front hall—it was either that
or *Time*, and he was permanently off *Time* after what those bastards had
done to him. He headed back to the bathroom, member in retrograde
mode now, ears catching the morning roar of trucks and early com-
muters on the distant freeways. The Chapin house ("Fabulous Family
Living, superb 5 bdrm Mediterranean w/pool & detached studio/guest
cottage, dream kitchen, wet bar, ½ acre, space for tennis court, 3850 sq.
ft., immaculate & private, offered at $295,000") stood atop a ridge on
the Pasadena-Flintridge border, and the San Gabriel Valley creaked and
groaned at their feet. Ideal location, really, except during the week
before New Year's when the Goodyear blimp and rehearsals in the Rose
Bowl made the place unbearable. Still, it had never occurred to Harry to
live anywhere else on the Coast. His father had spent his whole life in
movie advertising, first with BBD&O and later with JWT, meaning that
the family could live only in New York, which meant Westport or
Darien or Greenwich, or in L.A., which meant Pasadena. A boy raised
within narrow life-style parameters, this Chapin . . .

A distant rasp: the muted telephone. On the third ring the answering service got it. A call at this time of morning could only be bad
news: he would wait, ask for messages later, when he felt more like
fighting He threw a switch and out came KFAC-FM, its signal
even more distorted than usual. One of the bathroom speakers had
developed an annoying buzz: make a note to have Electronic Mainte-

nance repair the thing while he was away. He stepped bravely into the shower and gave himself a lukewarm blast: ah, life starting to make some sense. . . . Fire Heidi first thing (sketching the day's agenda behind closed eyes, as on a blackboard). . . . Don't put it off until he returned from Europe; do it now, like a man. . . . Also, sound out Maggie, again, on the separation idea. . . . But don't push it unnecessarily. He had been stalling on that a dozen years or more; another two weeks wouldn't make any difference. . . . Mmmm, the patient was showing such improvement that a test of his mighty *Heldentenor* was in order. . . . No annoying buzz *there* . . . smote the air like a sword—*Siegfried* this morning, the magnificent diatonic steps, each more heroic than the last, climbing, ever climbing, steely and bright (eat your heart out, Otto Kunz), power on top of power—

". . . Harry? *Harry!* Do you *hear* me? If you have no consideration for me or the boys, I wish you'd think of the Burgesses. . . ."

What time was it, that Maggie should be up hitting on him already? If the Burgesses—who lived at least a hundred yards away—didn't like it, they could move. You didn't hear singing like this every day. . . .

Toweling off, he watched Maggie in the bathroom mirror: the Compleat Forty-three-Year-Old-Woman, hoary veteran of the Cellulite Wars, exponent of what did they call it, jodhpur thighs? Saddlebag buttocks? Maggie's current passion was Richard Hittleman, the lean yoga stud on Channel 28, with whom she was now sharing her morning workout. "A strong, lithe figure," the *Stanford Daily* had reported during her track days. She'd been something of a middle-distance runner—had a fifteen hundred meters in 4:17:05, she liked to remember. But that was in the '50s, let us not forget.

Now, still in obscene black leotard, she sat on the bed and drank her coffee and watched him in that not-quite-believing-what-I'm-seeing attitude of hers. "Did you reach your precious Gian-Carlo?"

"Yes, fine."

"Where did you call from?"

"The office, naturally."

"I tried the office. You weren't there."

"Who said I wasn't? That old guard—"

"They looked all over the lot and they couldn't find you. You were with one of your little friends. Which one was it? The new one, I suppose. Heidi, is it?"

"I'm not going to discuss it."

He had to dress under the reproachful eye of Maggie's father, framed in wedding-gift silver on their communal dresser. All females he had ever known kept their fathers in the bedroom. He pulled from his wardrobe the best of the three new suits from Saks, a summer-weight gray stripe. He'd wear it straight onto the plane that evening and have it pressed in Paris. Damned thing already didn't fit: the trousers had been let out to thirty-eight inches, but there was no more material in the waist or seat, and forty inches was what was required nowadays. Well, he would skip lunch and maybe eat nothing on the plane—eleven bleak hours without repast—and then have a good meal, a great meal, even, with Solange. A promise of reward to carry him through the day.

He couldn't seem to find a tie he liked.

"The blue one," Maggie said. "I'm surprised you didn't spend the night at her place—call me up with one of those stories of yours, how you'd had too much to drink and didn't want to get stopped for drunk driving. You haven't used that one in months."

He settled for an old foulard: pattern too subtle for the suit, but he couldn't very well accept a recommendation from her.

"I don't see how you could be so stupid as to walk into the alarm again. I suppose you really *were* too drunk to notice. You snored for hours."

He slipped on his Gucci loafers, which needed—he now saw—a shine. Shining his shoes was all the boys had to do to earn their allowances and they didn't do even that.

"She must be quite a girl. Does she do something exotic? Something you specially like? Why don't you tell me?"

"Dear, there's no point going through the whole thing again, is there?"

"Why don't you call me by my name?"

Mostly he called her "Dear" or referred to her, when talking to the boys, as "Mother." As near as he could tell, she hated both words. "Maggie, then."

"I suppose you'll be seeing them on your trip, won't you? Who is it in London? I've forgotten her name. Shows you how ridiculous this has all become."

"Maggie—"

"And the one in Paris. Dionne, isn't it? We haven't had any love letters in such a long time. I suppose she'll be waiting for you at the airport."

Solange, not Dionne. Dionne was several seasons ago. But she brought up a good point: he would have to cable Solange and ask her not to meet him at Charles de Gaulle after all. His good friend Jean-Luc Barraud of Apogée would be meeting him instead.

"Really, Harry, I don't know what they see in you. You're not particularly good-looking. Your hair is beginning to turn gray on the sides and you're putting on fat. What *do* they see in you, Harry?"

He had wondered the same thing without establishing any real hypothesis.

"Is it that they understand you, Harry, while I don't? You're not falling back on that cliché, are you?"

"I don't think so, no," he said.

"Well then, *why* do you involve yourself? You're bright. You have a good mind. I know you *know* better. You never seem to *want* them once you've had them. Do you eventually treat them the way you treat me? I suppose you must."

She was crying now.

"Look, Dear, how do *I* know? I'm not a fucking analyst."

"Don't use that word in this house."

"Sorry."

"You bastard," she said, adopting his style. Her voice actually hissed.

"Dear—"

"Don't *call* me that! Call me by my *name!*"

"Margaret, then."

"Call me Mag, the way you used to."

"Mag, then."

"You *bastard*."

"Look, hey—you're excited. I'll be home early—we'll talk it out when we've both calmed down."

Trouble was, he already felt calm.

"Why do you say things to hurt me?" she cried.

Hitting him right where he lived: emotion-tipped bullet straight to the animus. Fuck you, he wanted to say, but such expressions were not permitted in this house. "Look, Mag," quickly, before she knew what was happening, "maybe we should think about, well—a separation kind of thing. Trial separation. Maybe you would be happier."

The front of her leotard was wet with tears. "Why do you say things to hurt me?" she repeated. "What have I ever done to you?"

Good point. He didn't know. Just stupidity on his part, he supposed. Which was small consolation.

She lay in wait for him in the kitchen. She had fixed her eyes and changed into her school outfit, a formless gray jumper affair with a Volunteer patch on one sleeve. "Oh," he said, "school."

"It's Friday," she shot back.

One Friday too many, my girl. Maggie worked two days a week at a school for deaf children. He was sick of being treated like some kind of mute himself: "I might as well be speaking to one of the children," she would say. "Here—look at me when you talk to me"—as though she needed to see his lips to know whether he was telling the truth.

Mutt, Harry's white bull-terrier bitch, was also waiting for him in

the kitchen. They exchanged warm greetings, to which Maggie took
immediate exception. "You saw what Mutt did?"

"What?"

"In the yard?"

Harry moseyed to the window, cocked one eye, saw what she
meant: dichondra scraped all to hell. "Mmm. Probably smelled a
gopher." Mutt was only a dog, after all. Tak, that lazy swine of a Jap
gardener, could make repairs.

"I don't know why we keep that dog. She's yours, but you don't
feed her, you don't clean up after her, you never do any of the work
associated with owning a dog. Do you want orange juice or cranberry?"

"Doesn't matter."

He drank the juice without noticing which kind it was; took his
vitamin C tablets (no time to be getting a cold, with Paris just
around the corner); sipped his coffee in normal silence. The bacon
smelled good, but that was for the boys, who gulped things down at the
last minute after Mom and Dad had done their fighting. (Boys of
fifteen were not quite so dumb as parents made out.) Speaking of
which, sounds—terrible sounds—emanated from the piano in the living
room. "What's gotten into him?" Harry said, just to be talking.

"It's Beachie's *lesson* day. You don't pay attention to anything that
goes on in this house, do you?"

You call this a sports section? L.A. *Times*, lousiest paper in
America.

"I'm sure this won't interest you, but Mrs. Wallace"—Mrs.
Wallace was the Tuesday and Friday piano lady—"thinks that Beachie
is one of the most musical children she's ever had."

"My condolences to Mrs. Wallace." What did they pay the woman
for making such judgments? Eight, nine dollars an hour? Or was that
what he paid Perry Lyle, his tennis pro?

"He *does* come by it naturally, Harry. It shouldn't *surprise* you."

"Oh?"

"You know perfectly well that my mother was practically a concert
pianist. That must count for something."

"I thought acquired skills weren't, uh, inheritable."

She failed to take the bait. "I think you should have a serious talk
with Beachie. He respects you. You should let him know you think he
has talent. It would mean a great deal to him. To have, for once, an
encouraging word."

Harry couldn't help humming "Home on the Range." He hummed
it in F, the key in which he'd first learned it, for assembly at Darien
Elementary School, what—1939? "I don't think he's got any talent.
None that I've noticed, anyway. As far as I can tell, his talent—and
Heck's too—is limited to riding his Honda and asking me for money."

What an unoriginal thing to say. Maggie was bringing out the very worst in him: reducing this distinguished Man of the Arts to a mere clod.

She had begun to cry again, not dramatically, but enough for even a clod like Harry Chapin to notice. "It won't be long," she said between shudders, "before they're gone and we're having all our meals alone."

"What?"

"When they go to college, you don't see them anymore. Midge was over last night while you were out—playing. It's already the end for her. They hardly ever see Scotty."

"Scott goes to Amherst, doesn't he? They can hardly expect to see him at meals."

No rebuttal. "Besides," he went on, "the boys are only sophomores in high school, aren't they? We'll see enough of them, I'm sure, before they get to college. Assuming any college will take them, with their grades . . ."

"This is so typical of you," she said, shaking her head sadly. "You can be just as superior and blasé as you want about Scott Wheelock. But I'm talking, Harry Chapin, about your own *flesh and blood.* I should think that just once in your life . . ."

More Maggie crap. God, these Frisco girls with the Upper-Middle-Class Upbringing could sure go sour on you. "We still have some time, is what I'm trying to say in my inadequate and labored way," he said. "You're dripping," he added. "On your uniform."

She blotted her eyes ineffectually with a potholder. "There's something else I want to show you," she said with renewed spirit.

Now what? Mutt do pee-pee on the sofa?

"I found these in the boys' room. Under the bed."

She handed the stuff over. A pack of rubbers. Hadn't seen those in years. All the girls he knew were on the pill. And what's this? Ah, small tweezerlike device: roach-holder, he believed it was called.

"Well?" she accused.

"Maggie, look—they're growing up. They've got to learn about these things sooner or later."

"Is that your *attitude?* Is that what you really *think?*"

He didn't know.

"They're *your* boys, Harry."

His wonderful boys. Yes, you must be very proud. The boys were fifteen: it was time to talk about birds, bees and roach-holders. Till now he hadn't been able to get up nerve—the boys seemed so, well, *advanced* in that department. And what did *he* know? He had made a mess of the whole thing himself, as was clear even to the boys. "I'll talk to them tonight," he said, surrendering.

"Why don't you do it now?"

"Tonight is soon enough. I've got a lot on my mind this morning."

"When's your plane?"

"Ten thirty. I'll try to get home by four, four thirty latest." Then, the zinger: "I've got Deering." Confrontation with the boss. Got to have a clear head; can't be messing around with a pair of adolescents at a time like this.

"Do you want me to cut your hair?"

Cutting his hair: the only physical act they shared these days. He was in no mood to give Maggie such a forum: twenty minutes of uninterrupted lecture. "If I need one," he said remotely, "I can always get it in Europe."

Mutt wanted to go out: scratched at the back door until Harry got up and did his duty.

"The only person you care about in this house," Maggie said, "is that dog."

Her tears were more or less continuous now. Harry refused to look her way and give her another chance to read his lips. "Yes, I love my dog," he said.

Poor Mutt. He really did love Mutt. His only real regret at leaving home would be leaving Mutt, who'd cost $600 and had AKC champions on both sides of the family. The breeders had called several times begging Harry to let them have Mutt back for a season or two of shows, just long enough to get Mutt's own championship points so that the great blood lines wouldn't be interrupted. But Harry wouldn't have it. Harry wanted Mutt right there with him, for when the going got tough. Like now.

He drained his coffee; made a neat pile of the paper for the boys, sports on top; stood up to go. Felt almost like tipping: very good service in this establishment.

Maggie, breaking eggs, said, "I may not be here when you get home."

"Oh?"

"I'm going to see Brad this morning."

"Brad?" Brad Snow was their lawyer.

"He'll know what options I've got. I'm bound to have *some* rights." Maggie, headed for pure melodrama.

"All right, Dear," spoken with groaning sarcasm, "what do you want me to do?" Whining. She liked it when he was reduced to whining.

"I wonder what Mr. Deering will say when I tell him we're getting a divorce."

She would never call Deering in a million years. She hardly knew the man; talked to him maybe twice in her life, at studio functions. Still, it would be awkward if she called. "I would appreciate your not calling him," Harry said wearily. "No matter what happens to us, we're going to need money. And Mr. Deering is the only source of income we've got."

"Don't you think I've *considered* that? Don't you think I've considered *everything*, Harry? God, you've given me plenty of nights to think about such things. To think about the years I've thrown away on you, while you're out making a fool of yourself . . ." Weeping again.

He'd had enough. He pulled on his $3300 eighteen-karat-gold Rolex (say what you would, Otto Kunz gave fabulous Christmas gifts to people he liked); prepared to strap himself into his $21,400 Mercedes 450-SEL sedan; made a brush-kiss feint toward his weeping wife—only item of impedimenta he'd actually paid for himself.

"Don't *do* that."

"I've got to go."

"You should have your car washed. It's filthy."

"If I have time."

"Oh, Harry," she cried.

"I've got to go."

"Sometimes I think nothing good has happened to us since the twins. Fifteen years . . ."

She watched him march resolutely toward the living room. Finally, she called after him:

"Aren't you going to kiss the boys?"

He diverted smoothly back toward the twins' quarters. The boys were fifteen years old. Wouldn't they go to school without his kiss?

2

  Friday morning on Forest Lawn Drive, perceived now through incipient smog. Harry shared his route with the other regulars: horsemen from Griffith Park (horsepersons, too, jugs flopping up and down in equine rhythm), joggers in their sleek warm-up suits puffing along the banks of the concrete-channeled Los Angeles River, uniformed cyclists in plastic yellow crash helmets, endless streams of Porsches and Mercedes zapping toward Hollywood and points west.

  Passing the Toluca Lake Tennis Club, he remembered his 7:00 A.M. tennis date with Brad Snow and the boys—which he'd forgotten to cancel. Rushing the Europe trip had probably been a mistake: how many other things had he forgotten? But he had panicked at the idea of appearing on yet another Met broadcast intermission quiz and had moved up his entire timetable: get out of the country, only acceptable alternative for brave Harry Chapin, whose current three-year employment contract with Leisure Time Industries, Inc., parent company of Melos-Doria Records, of which Harry was general manager, would expire on December 31 (quick slant into the right-turn lane, cutting off some poor slob Cadillac), providing, he now reasoned, a sweet measure of poetic justice. For, depending on how good a lawyer Brad Snow turned out to be (they'd never used him for anything more serious than the drawing of two as-yet-untested wills), Harry's marriage of almost twenty years to Margaret Louise Beach Chapin would expire at about the same time—meaning that Harry would be footloose and fancy-free, no job and no wife, for the first time since 1957. Hurrah.

* * *

As tourists know, Leisure Time Industries, Inc., boasts a fabulous location, sprawling across forty-some acres of what would otherwise be choice Burbank residential property. Once the home of Pentatron Pictures, LTI has been declared a "Major Southland Attraction" by the Los Angeles Chamber of Commerce. Its most prominent neighbors are MCA, Warner Bros., NBC and Disney. When LTI acquired Pentatron in the late '6os, LTI's chairman, Leslie Deering, who had maneuvered the principals and plotted the take-over bid, decided, for purposes of image, to preserve the old "lot," including the Western Town and a tangled network of street scenes and half a hundred pink stucco bungalows and six massive but obsolete sound stages, even though motion-picture production had long since ceased (some of the early Buster Keaton one-reelers were shot here, in the days before smog) and even though the major structures, built in the '2os, failed to meet the city's earthquake code—meaning that someone from Finance had to make a payoff to somebody downtown once a year, an item which even today was buried in the LTI annual report under "community relations."

Old Max, the cop on the front gate, gave Harry the usual cheery wave, but Harry was too preoccupied to respond. Settle the Heidi thing right off—no, first have her call Deering's office for an appointment, and pick up his plane ticket, and do his banking. He was scheduled to have lunch with Sorenson from *Newsweek*, but have her cancel that: dieting. And give his assistant, Maury, a list of things he wanted done by the time he got home, so that Maury, a lazy bastard, wouldn't sit around for three whole weeks doing nothing. Lots to think about this morning.

Everything at LTI was measured with reference to the Executive Bungalow, or EB, which was Front Lot. The more important your division, the closer you were to EB. Film & TV, Music (which meant LTI's galaxy of pop labels—Honeybee, Tramp, Gold Bag, Scrimshaw, Fools Gold) and B&B (bowling & billiards) were right up front; Culture Group (which was mainly Melos-Doria) was Back Lot. This arrangement was not entirely to Harry's dislike. Geographic remoteness tended to give Melos-Doria the low profile appropriate to artistic endeavors, and the lot in general wasn't a bad place to work, especially when compared to Harry's pre-LTI quarters, the musty brownstone belonging to Melos-Doria's long-departed (but wealthy, thanks to Leslie Deering) founders, Mr. and Mrs. Leonid Strauss, on 49th Street just off Third Avenue in deadly Gotham.

In the parking lot a familiar behind blossomed before him. Just his downfall: smallish female with bad skin and big tits. He had known those boobs intimately since early in the Second Quarter. "Well, *hello*," he said, smiling.

"Thought you were in Europe."

"Leaving tonight, as a matter of fact. Want to come along?"

"I wouldn't go anyplace with you again even if you *paid* me," she said and then ducked left, down toward Accounting.

And another one: Terri MacMillan, gliding gracefully along the same path. "Morning." Noncommittal now.

"Well, *hello*," this one said with warmth. "That weekend in San Francisco . . . Still waiting," she cooed.

Naturally she would weekend with him. He had never met a girl in business who wouldn't give herself to any man if the weekend was attractive enough: a nice dinner, a good hotel, a minimum of social embarrassment. "Just off to Europe tonight. . . . As soon as I get back . . ."

Altogether too many girls. I am some new kind of sexual pervert. For me, the only illicit sex act is making love to one's wife. . . .

Heidi was already at her desk; had a sounder constitution than he; had drunk less of the wine; hit him with accusations the instant he fell into his chair:

"Mr. Snow called. He was *very* upset. You had tennis this morning. They waited for you until they finally lost the court."

Mmmm. The bitch had turned somber under his careful tutelage. "That wasn't this morning. They must have the date wrong."

"Well, they're *very* upset."

Yes, you said that. No mail on his desk, no appointments list, two of the sherry glasses on the sideboard still dirty from yesterday. But it was hard to be overly critical when you'd left the lady's bed only hours ago.

"They tried to reach you at home, but they couldn't get through the service."

Which was the whole idea of the service: surely she understood that? "I'll talk to Snow later. Call Mr. Deering's office, will you, and say I'd like an appointment? Remind that girl of his—Dorothy, is it?—that I'm going to Europe tonight and there are some things I must review with Deering before I leave. . . ."

Beethoven's Sonata No. 23 in F minor, Opus 57, "*Appassionata*," suddenly engulfed him: walls of the bungalows were papier-mâché from Buster Keaton's time. Harry picked up the phone and buzzed Com #2.

"Yeah, boss?"

"Who is that? Sounds like Serkin."

"Hey, you know your apples, huh?" This from Maury Wiseman, Harry's latest management trainee, a twenty-five-year-old brass player out of UCLA.

"Rudi's leaving CBS and coming to Melos-Doria?"

"Not that I know, boss. Just timing him against Donny."

Donny Kurtz, Melos-Doria *Wunderkind;* callow youth already tackling the *"Appassionata,"* a work that Serkin still found intimidating. "And?"

"Serkin's slower."

"I believe you mean Donny is faster. One generally uses as his reference point the greater—or at least the earlier—performance."

"Maybe. But Donny's got a few ideas of his own, you know? You want a dub? Maybe give a listen?"

"Thank you, no."

"Hey, boss, I've got an Urgent folder here that never stops. If I don't see you before you go, we're both going to be in a lot of trouble."

"Five minutes. Give me five minutes and then come straight in."

In longhand, on a yellow pad, he drafted the cable to Solange:

REGRET SLIGHT CHANGE IN PLANS STOP BEING MET BY BUSINESS ASSOCIATES STOP WILL PHONE YOU INSTANT ARRIVAL RAPHAEL RE DINNER STOP LOVE HARRY

He tore the sheet in half and put the message in his wallet. They would go to Fouquet's, he decided. Solange liked the place—she could gawk at all the Americans from down the street at the George V—and he would order them a terrific Burgundy.

". . . It's Mr. Snow again. Do you want me to say you're out, or what?"

It was absolutely ridiculous, putting up with this nasty female.

". . . Oh, Brad? . . . Look, I'm *very* sorry about this morning, but, candidly, we've had kind of a crisis at the house. . . . No, no, everybody's fine, in terms of health. You're going to get a call, probably, from Maggie. . . . Yes, and since I'm off tonight—Europe, usual spring conference—I wanted to alert you. All I ask, Brad, is that you take what she says with a grain of . . . No, no, nothing specific. It's more a time-of-life thing for both of us. The twins, after all . . . Right . . . I feel better, knowing that you know. . . . And again, about this morning, I'd rather have been playing tennis, believe me! . . . Great, and many thinks . . ."

Brad's response had been totally predictable: two swell kids like Harry and Maggie, got to stick it out, remember the twins, bullshit, bullshit, bullshit. But Brad was smart enough to realize where his next retainer was coming from—from Harry, not Maggie—ergo, dear Brad could be counted upon to hold the fort until Harry returned. After that? He had no idea.

"Is there no mail today?"

"It just *arrived,*" spoken with major annoyance. "I'm bringing it *in.*"

"And hold the calls, okay?"

"Mr. Moss is here and would like to show you something."

"Fine. Send him in. But no other interruptions."

". . . Greetings, O Chief of Commerce. What occupies your time?"

Burt Moss, wisecracker from Advertising. He and Harry had come together at the time of the LTI take-over and hit it off principally on the grounds that they were both Ivy Leaguers and both mordantly sarcastic in meetings. "I'm about to cut out for Europe, actually," Harry said.

"Ektually, are you? Already practicing up on your veddy U.K. accent, ektually? You wanna maybe okay this little louvring?"

Louvring was Burt's word for artwork. "Mmmmmmmm," mused Harry, holding the piece at arm's length. Moss had talent but no ambition. While Harry had climbed high into the corporate tree, Burt was content to languish among fellow poorly-paid simians on lower branches; life a lot more pleasant down there, he maintained. Still, Burt was something of a celebrity at Melos-Doria, having recently published a pair of pornographic novels, scandalizing his prominent Eastern family and putting a stop to invitations home for Christmas. Fiendishly clever, this Moss.

"Wonderful, Burt, as always. But isn't Schneider's name misspelled? Isn't it 'e' before 'i' . . .?"

"Except after 'n' maybe? No, you're probably right, in that you're the boss. I'll check with Editorial. Otherwise, how do you like it?"

Artist's name misspelled. Typical of the state of affairs at Melos-Doria these days. These young chaps didn't *care* the way people had when Mr. and Mrs. Strauss were still active. "The line 'newly recorded' —that will be stickered on the shrink-wrap, I assume."

"No, right in the plate."

"I don't want that. No sell-copy on the cover—that's a rule. People shouldn't have to read advertising copy after they've bought the damned thing and gotten it home."

"Sticker's another three cents, Harry. Maybe five, with plant charges and all."

"Don't care. Use a sticker. Now, if that's all, Burt . . ."

"Going, going. Got a nasty letter from your esteemed stick-waver Freddie Sax, but won't bother you with that."

"Saying what?"

"Hates the Watteau you picked for his Mozart Forty."

"Wants a photo of himself instead."

"He talked to you?"

"No, they all want photos of themselves instead. Stick with the Watteau. . . ."

". . . You have a lunch reservation at The Bistro, one o'clock."

Heidi on the com. Com should be one-way: boss to girl, never girl to boss. "Cancel, will you? Tell Sorenson I'm leaving for Europe earlier than expected—I'll phone him when I get back."

Lies and more lies. He was supposed to be persuading *Newsweek* to do a full take-out on Kurtz, the Melos-Doria *"Appassionata"* whiz, but his heart wasn't in it. Typical Chapin stunt: set the date, then cancel out at the eleventh hour, preferably the fifty-ninth minute, having known from the start that something crucial or petty or nice (in a skirt) would come along to provide an excuse for moral laxity. "What else have I got?"

"Mr. Bloom at eleven thirty."

"I don't want to see Bloom." Rosco Bloom, the Junk Man. A great scavenger of other people's recordings, who'd made a fortune in the budget business selling LPs by the ton: execrable pressings, no liner notes, terrible printing, obscene "pop art" covers. Even knowing how Harry felt, the rascal never ceased pestering Melos-Doria for surplus repertoire.

"You *told* me to give him an appointment."

"I've changed my mind. I don't want to see him."

"He called yesterday to *confirm*. Mr. Wiseman talked to him."

"Mr. Wiseman can see him, then," whining the way he did to Maggie. "Yes, set Maury for the eleven thirty."

"You have Mr. Blankenhorn at four thirty. Will you see *him?*"

Incredible sarcasm in a mere hired hand. "Of *course* I'll see him." Joe Blankenhorn, Vladimir Slonimsky's attorney, a very important man in this business; not someone to palm off on a Maury Wiseman.

"I've set you at three with Mario."

"I don't want a haircut."

"According to your calendar, it's been four weeks. You look shaggy."

"I'm not going to have time. Cancel."

"Mr. Batchelder says he needs five minutes—the budgets go to print while you're away."

"Four o'clock, then. But tell him I'm pressed for time."

"Do you want to make *another* lunch reservation?" Knowing how Chapin operated.

"No, staying in today." He was dieting; couldn't she tell? What had he eaten at her place? Nothing but almonds and Bordeaux, or had she forgotten? "Has my expense check come yet?"

"Accounts Payable is sending it over in the next delivery."

"I'd like you to take it to the bank when it comes."

"I *know*," she said in her bitchy way.

"And Heidi?"

"Yes?"

"Hold the damned calls, will you?"

"I *am* holding the calls."

No, no, not just outside calls: *yours*, too. But he lacked courage, naturally, to say it.

I I

Mail full of crap. On top, an invitation to visit Montreux in September to accept a *diplome d'honneur* from the Prix Mondial du Disque people for "*services rendus à l'art du disque*" during his twenty-year career with Melos-Doria. Better not count on Harry Chapin, messieurs—probably be in the lawcourts with Maggie in September.

Hmm, the weekly computer sales print-out. Nothing much selling, as usual. The top item was Córtez's *Rossini Overtures*, which had just crossed the 12,000 mark: more a tribute to Rossini than to Córtez. Ponti—where is Ponti? Ah. For a guy who got such good reviews, Ponti was sure running behind in the popularity polls: his Beethoven Third showed a miserable 2200. A Beethoven Fifth with this gentleman would be lucky to clear 7500 in its lifetime. Horrible.

Another plea for funds from Harvard. Christ, hadn't he just *sent* them something?

Finally a letter worth reading: from Hilary Cairns, boss of the Consortium's U.K. company, the Hampstead Record Group, Ltd., and Harry's best friend among the Europeans:

> . . . Your remarks in powerful *Time* magazine (including, you'll be happy to hear, the European Edition) were most salubrious and amusing, for which we all thank you. It is nice to know that someone in our poor little business still commands international attention, and it is most fitting that that someone should be you.
>
> Flew into Munich on my way to Salzburg for the endless Easter celebrations of our esteemed Herr Dr. Adler, who spoke of you with warm affection. The good doctor was surrounded

by luminaries of the international jet set, including all of our most despised competitors, each of whom made a more outlandish financial offer than the next. I was the only Consortium representative, as all others were in Paris holding Mme. Cavalieri's hand and pledging undying support for her forthcoming Desdemona. My hat is off to you for your achievement in bringing this lady out of her usual retirement.

We are expecting you for supper chez Cairns on the final day of the Conference, by which time we shall both require a carefully orchestrated collapse. I am taking the liberty of inviting a lady whom you will find, I believe, charming, witty, and intelligent. She is Lady Amanda FitzMaurice, her famous actor-husband having been banished from her bed several seasons ago, so I do hope you will not be disappointed.

Anyway, dear Harry, we are off to France for a short holiday—frankly I can't take any more. Penny sends you her love.

Decent man, Cairns. Decent and considerate—qualities not often found in these twentieth-century music men. Lady Amanda—already he experienced a childish hankering after another phantasmagorical female; random seeds of yearning to be plowed under not a moment too soon.

"This just came," Heidi said. "I haven't opened it yet." She handed it over, an angry-looking envelope stamped in red, "ATTORNEY-CLIENT PRIVILEGE," from Davis Bull, LTI's imperious chief counsel. But disappointing: simply another warning of possible Justice Department interest in all these Swiss contracts that Harry and his overseas colleagues were getting themselves into. Which reminded him: he owed his fellow Consortium members a detailed report on last night's conversation with Melos-Doria's latest Swiss-contractee, Maestro Gian-Carlo Ponti. "Take a letter, will you please, Heidi. . . ."

TO:	Repertoire Directors
	The Consortium
FROM:	H. E. Chapin II
	Melos-Doria, USA
SUBJECT:	*Gian-Carlo Ponti*

Gentlemen:

Since making our first contract with Sr. Ponti in early 1970, we have all endeavored to support this estimable artist in our respective territories, despite his natural proclivity for repertoire of less than ideal commercial appeal. We have in fact counted on the Verdi *Requiem,* scheduled for recording in London in late August with an all-star quartet of soloists (Kunz-Pascoli-Mosbacher-Lichine) to provide Gian-Carlo with the natural "breakthrough" that his talent so richly deserves.

Unfortunately, we now find this plan impossible of execution, thanks to the winds of change that seem to blow constantly around Mme. Cavalieri. . . .

He explained the latest problem with an admirable blend of incisiveness and tact, listing all of dear Gianni's future repertoire aspirations and concluding with the sentiment that "despite disappointing sales to date, we have every confidence in the ultimate success of this fine, serious-minded conductor. . . . P.S. Sr. Ponti's new contract shall be, for the usual reasons, with Globelektron (AG) Zürich, instead of directly with Melos-Doria (USA). Hence, intra-Consortium pressing fees will be reduced to 3% on new recordings; catalog LPs however will remain at 7%. . . ." It never hurt to mix a little commerce with art, in Harry's experience.

"Will that be all, Mr. Chapin?"

Mr. Chapin? My, my—we *are* a bit cool this morning. "On second thought," he said to his apprehensive helpmate, "make me a lunch reservation, will you? St. Germain, table for two, twelve forty-five? That's all for now, Heidi. Ask Maury to come in, if you will."

"I have something to say."

"Oh?"

"Yes. I've decided that I'm not going to see you anymore. Out of the office."

"Ah. I'm—shocked, obviously."

"Well, that's it, and I wanted you to know now, before you made any more plans."

"I appreciate your candor."

What had she gotten out of the silly relationship? A few good dinners, a trip to San Francisco, a night at the Disneyland Hotel complete with monorail ride and cotton candy and a chance to try out that keen new diaphragm just like the married ladies used, after the pill made her skin break out. Her present declaration would make it easier for him. She still had the Ponti letter to type up. Perhaps just before lunch . . .

" Ah, young Beethoven."

"I don't get you."

"The Stieler oil? From 1819, wasn't it? Very good likeness, Wiseman—the eruption of curly hair hinting at a part in the middle. Very poetic—I'm sure you could pass."

"Hey, boss, if you object—"

"Not at all—just funning at your expense. By the way, what about joining me for a little luncheon? I want your views on several topics bound to arise at the Conference."

"Whatever," without enthusiasm. This was the trouble with Wiseman: already an intellectual sloth. Instead of lunching elegantly with Chapin, he would prefer to sit around the commissary sharing Bob Dylan stories with his cronies from the pop side.

"Now then, what are these matters of great urgency?"

"For starters, Ponti. How'd he take the news?"

"With comparative equanimity. I suggested Diana for both Brahms; this is a possibility. Also, maybe some Puccini. He likes the *Trittico*. But he does not like Del Campo."

"He doesn't want the *Bohème* with Didi?"

"No. The only Puccini he likes is *Manon Lescaut* or possibly *Fanciulla* or maybe the *Trittico*."

"Shit."

"Yes, isn't it? But, as you'll learn, this is the nature of the beast. On the positive side, Gian-Carlo loves anything having to do with Beethoven, for which we must be grateful. So I told him that now, with the Third on the market and the Fifth in the can, we shall probably be interested in going ahead with all nine. Naturally, he was ecstatic. So prepare a formal proposal, will you, covering the complete set? And get that off to London yet today."

"You're *kidding*. A complete set from *Ponti*? Who would buy an expensive bomb like that?"

"Maury, really, I'm not feeling that well this morning—just do as I ask, please. Costings, sales estimates, the whole thing. If you want to check format, look in the files for our proposal on the Adler set."

"You're the boss."

"That's right, I'm the boss. And you should be taking some notes, shouldn't you? To aid your wonderful memory? Here, let me give you a pencil."

Accepted grudgingly. "Speaking of Diana, she's into a thing with the management at Alice Tully Hall."

"A thing?"

"She says she's not going to wear a bra. At the recital."

"So?"

"So Alice Tully is talking about maybe no recital."

"But the nude cellist—"

"Not at Lincoln Center. You go to Town Hall or Carnegie for the nude stuff."

"She's not that big, is she? Would anybody notice?"

"Hey, boss, you know her better than I do. But Norman says we have the specter—his word—of the stagehands marching out and shutting the lid on the keyboard."

"I'm coming back through New York—maybe I can see her, assuming she's in town, and talk some sense into her." The girl's bosom had never impressed him. Perhaps bralessness would help sales. "What else?"

"Your pal Barraud called yesterday from Paris. There's already a problem with Cavalieri."

"Another problem?"

"The lady demands a Rolls-Royce limo the whole time she's in London—Cadillac or Mercedes unacceptable. Also, a per diem of two hundred and fifty dollars, which she says you okayed, plus three first-class round-trip plane tickets, London–New York, for herself, her cook and her hairdresser."

"But the lady lives in Paris."

"Yes, but, according to Barraud, she's going to be in New York before or maybe after the sessions, and that's part of the package as far as she's concerned. And since it's a Melos-Doria project, Barraud wants your okay before he goes ahead and arranges for the tickets. And the Rolls."

"I never agreed to the Rolls, and her demands for New York tickets are outrageous." The usual blackmail. "But tell him okay."

"Hmmm. So that's how it's done."

"Yes, that's how it's done." Another chapter for Maury's Ph.D. thesis on Management in the Arts. "Next?"

"Your boy Laframboise."

Melos-Doria's great black hope, Ezekiel Laframboise: refugee from the Philadelphia Eagles, loudest tenor in the history of the sport, Zeke by nickname: The Great Black Raspberry. "And?"

"We need some repertoire decisions."

"Where do we stand on the contract?"

"Three years firm plus four one-year options. Now in the second year. One LP per year minimum, 'repertoire to be mutually agreed,' " read with relative ease from the data brief by this curly-headed Master of Arts.

"And we've already done two LPs?"

"Yes—the *Trojans* excerpts and the scenes from *Samson et Dalila*."

"What else has been suggested?"

"We've proposed him to the Consortium for *Masked Ball* in place of Kunz, but nobody's keen except the Germans—Zeke's getting a reputation in Düsseldorf and places like that."

"Fine. I'll push *Masked Ball* at the Conference. Meanwhile, what about another solo LP? More excerpts?—what our German cousins call a *Grosser Querschnitt?* Maybe something with Del Campo?"

"The thing closest to Zeke's heart, you may remember, is an aria record. Usual stuff, from 'Celeste Aïda' through 'Vesti la giubba.' Could be done cheap as hell with one of the second-line German orchestras. He likes the German orchestras, so we can give him the Bavarian Radio, for instance, and he's happy."

"Maybe."

"Although, now that I think about it, he probably won't go along— he'll want the *Ballo* for sure. Norman saw his manager—"

"Gravinius?"

"—right, Gravinius, a week or so ago, and Gravinius says Zeke's about to break into the big time, which means complete-opera sets. Zeke's in Paris, by the way—maybe you can stop in and see him, since you discovered him and all."

Perhaps. The boy had a certain rough charm. "And what do we owe Didi?"

Flipping to another file folder: "One complete opera—the same old *Bohème*—and the usual two recital LPs. Mutual approval on reper- toire—meaning we can stall her indefinitely, if that's what you have in mind."

Young Beethoven was catching on; would undoubtedly acquire his Master of Commerce degree in short order, under Herr Chapin's rigorous instruction. "Yes, temporize," Harry said with admiration. "I do believe that you're learning some of the rules of this game, Mr. Wiseman. How long has it been now, that you've been in our employ?"

"Seven months—going on eight."

"Well, perhaps you're a quick study. We must hope so. What else have you got?"

"Mandelbaum."

"Yes?"

"Wants the Mendelssohn postponed. Says he caught his bowing hand in a cab door. Says it's all swollen."

"Bullshit. Did you talk to him?"

"Talked to Gravinius."

Gravinius again. These *Wunderkinder* all had the same nasty New York attorneys. "That's bullshit. He's decided he doesn't like Córtez. He wants another conductor. Tell Gravinius we require a letter from his doctor."

"You want me to *tell* him that?"

"Yes, tell him we need it for the union—or else the union will file a grievance. Better still, tell him we're going to charge Mandelbaum for the canceled session."

"*Really?*"

"Sy's been around. He knows the games these kids play. God, Heifetz in his sickest day never canceled a session. Who the hell does Mandelbaum think he is?"

"He thinks he's our only viable fiddler. He thinks we need him more than he needs us."

"We shall see. And tell Sy I better not hear that young Mr. Mandelbaum is appearing on the Tonight Show or playing any concerts with that damaged hand of his. Make sure Sy understands what I'm saying. How much more of this crap have you got?"

"Tons—most of it pigshit that can wait. But there's one thing I *know* you don't want to talk about that I *gotta* have a decision on. Promise you won't get mad?"

"Nonsense. I reserve the right to get mad, as always."

"Rosco Bloom."

"I don't want to hear about it. *You* see him. Didn't Heidi tell you?"

"Boss, I've got to know what to *tell* him—what our *policy* is."

"You know my policy."

"What he wants isn't really that much—mainly those early concerto things done by Slonimsky at St. Louis. All mono, but he'll mock them up for stereo, maybe even quad. *Slonimsky Plays the Great Romantic Concertos,* he wants to call it. There's a Brahms Two, a Beethoven Three and the Schumann."

"No."

"The masters are just sitting in our vaults, boss—and Bloom's offered some nice advances."

"The Schumann was never passed—does Bloom know that?"

"Maybe we could get Slonimsky's permission. Or maybe Bloom could?"

"*Never.* I've told you before and I'm telling you now—for the last time, please. No records for the Junk Man. Nothing. This bastard lives off the carrion of great men, and we won't be party to that. I don't *ever* want Slonimsky on low-price. If we're going out of business tomorrow, I don't want Slonimsky on low-price."

"But from a business point of view—"

"Damaging a great man's reputation is not my idea of business. Slonimsky never passed the Schumann because he knew it wasn't up to his own standards. Isn't that rather easy to comprehend?"

"But, boss, as you yourself told me, the *public* can't tell. What's the harm in—"

"*Fuck* what I've told you. I can tell. *Slonimsky* can tell. That's enough. So make our policy clear when you see Mr. Bloom. And don't raise the subject with me again. Understood?"

"Understood. But—"

"You say one more word on this subject and you'll be eligible for unemployment compensation. . . ."

I I I

Bolstered by visions of St. Germain's roast of lamb and Burgundy to suit, Harry found sufficient reserves of energy and moral rectitude to apply himself to *l'affaire Slonimsky.*

"Get me Norman Rose on the WATS line, will you, Heidi? If there's going to be a delay, go straight through."

Vladimir Ivanovich Slonimsky: "Vova" to intimates like Harry. Always in retirement or just coming out of it—similar to Edith in that respect—and even now about to make his fourth "historic return." The man was only seventy-seven, not old for a grand master of the piano: same age as his lifelong rival Horowitz but younger than others of his artistic rank, past or present: Rubinstein, Rachmaninoff, Hofmann, Paderewski (his teacher). Spectrously thin, six feet four inches tall, with a great head of glistening white hair—there was still nothing like him in white tie and tails, which he insisted on wearing in this day of turtle-necked glamour boys. A man of enormous charisma and charm when he wanted to display it, which was seldom. A recluse by nature, he was bound to outlive them all because of his personal habits: no pain, no strain, no meat. A lifelong vegetarian and yoga devotee. Never a gram of meat—or fish or fowl even—had passed his thin purplish lips: went straight from mother's milk to some sort of vegetable gruel. Now, in his Fifth Avenue apartment, he had become America's greatest living exponent of Beethoven, Brahms and the Waring Blender, which Melos-Doria had presented to him more or less as a joke. Vova's dedicated wife, Angélique (twenty-five years his junior and magnificently preserved herself), blended every damned thing to a fine liquid pulp, which Vova then drank in hearty, noisy gulps, relishing every vitamin, every mineral.

And now—Vova was back. Or at least Harry thought he was back. Norman would know more. Where was that call? "Heidi?"

"It's going *through.* If you can just *wait* a minute . . ."

Bitch. Yes, dear Vova was back and good old Melos-Doria, his label of almost three decades, would be there, microphones in hand—only this time with the wrinkle of quad: capture the bastard's Steinway with four different mikes, catch every clinker for posterity's sake, show what a lousy technician this "Poet of the Steinway" actually was. Only this wasn't true either: they'd fix every clinker, every blur, in the Melos-

Doria edit rooms, and everybody—critics included—would say what a
great technician this Slonimsky was. There was no way to win in this
rotten game.

". . . Mr. Rose is on the line."

Such a relief to have an adult to talk to, after Maury.

"Good afternoon, Norman. How's your weather?"

"Raining and bleak, as usual, Harry."

"Be thankful—nothing but depressing sunshine out here. I've spent
the morning with Maury—forgive me if I seem totally uncivilized."

"He means well, Harry. Or at least that's my impression."

"I accept your judgment on faith. I want to talk about Vova, but
first I must bring you up to date on Ponti. And I need a favor or two. By
the way, your Paris arrangements are made?"

"Yes. I'll meet you at the Raphaël Tuesday evening."

"If I'm not in my room, try the bar."

"I intended to. And how did Gian-Carlo take the news?"

"Badly. Until I started talking about Beethoven. Norman, did you
know that Gian-Carlo's prick is longer than his stick?"

"I don't think I'd heard that. Is it true? That would explain a great
deal, I suppose—his penchant for vocal music. Sopranos and that sort of
thing."

"Just a rumor, but probably true. Anyway, I'd like you to get hold
of our singers and tell them that the *Requiem* is postponed. And why.
In your most charming manner."

"Really, Harry, you've waited until an unconscionably late moment
to break the bad news. It's not fair to—"

"Norman, for God's sake, do you think I *like* canceling projects?
You know this business as well as I do." At times Norman could be
unbearably self-righteous. "Anyway, you can skip Otto—he knows,
obviously—and if the others squeal too much, talk to them about another assignment—something small, Norman. Something we can live
with in the future—or, rather, something we can cancel. Pascoli—she
may be difficult. Tell her we're still thinking about her for the *Bohème*."

"But the *Bohème* is promised to Didi."

"Yes, yes, but if that doesn't work out—it doesn't *hurt*, Norman, to
have these ladies thinking they may get a role. Now does it?"

"You know my views."

"Yes, but just this once . . ."

Poor Norman; how often he'd lectured Harry on the evils of
double-booking—committing the same role to several artists and then,
at the last moment, canceling all but the most desirable. But this was

the real world, not a university campus. "Anyway," Harry plowed ahead, "enough of the *Requiem*. Tell me about Vova."

"Well, I had supper *chez* Slonimsky last evening, as scheduled—just the three of us, with Angélique in absolutely top form, very witty and full of compliments for you, Harry. I really do wish you'd been present—I think you might have gotten Vova to sign on the spot."

"Sorry I couldn't be there—I wasn't getting many compliments where I was. But go on."

"Quite clearly, Vova wishes to re-sign with Melos-Doria. He feels at home with us and, as I've said many times, he especially values the personal relationship you and he have developed down through the years. He trusts your judgment totally, and he wants to continue artistic collaboration with you on his new program."

"So what's the catch?"

"The catch, of course, is terms. Blankenhorn has been shopping him around very aggressively, Harry, and it now appears that both CBS and RCA have offered terms substantially better than our package."

"I find that hard to believe."

"Apparently it's true. We're all talking six LPs over five years with an advance of sixty thousand per year against a royalty of twelve and a half percent. But on top of that the other companies will throw in ownership of masters at some future date to be mutually agreed. That's the difference, Harry."

"Well, that's a deal-breaker as far as I'm concerned."

"Oh, I hope you don't mean that, Harry."

"I do."

"It's just that he wants something tangible for his old age—something on which he can take capital gains."

"He's already *in* his old age."

"He's seventy-seven, Harry—a very youthful seventy-seven, musically speaking."

"What else? Besides ownership of masters?"

"Remember, I told you that he was adamant on retaining at least one contractual 'out' to record for somebody else? Maybe a concerto with Ormandy or Mehta?"

"Yes?"

"Well, he's gotten over that. He's now talking about absolute exclusivity with Melos-Doria."

"Wonderful. But ownership of masters is still a deal-breaker. I'm seeing Blankenhorn this afternoon—I'll tell him. Hey, wait a minute—the last royalty figure I approved was *ten* percent, wasn't it? Not twelve and a half?"

"Sorry—I meant to explain that. Somehow Vova's heard that

Apogée pays Fuchs twelve, and purely on ego grounds Vova must have more."

"That's a deal-breaker, too, of course."

"Again, Harry, I hope you aren't serious when you say this. As an artist, this gentleman is—well, unique."

"We'll see. Look—I'll be in New York anyway in what, three weeks? You and I will sit down with Vova and apply the old Chapin-Rose magic and we'll come away with a deal, we both know that. . . . What about Edith? Have you talked to Mme. Cavalieri of late?"

"Yesterday morning, as a matter of fact. She's in good spirits and looking forward to seeing you with great anticipation. She's another member of the Harry Chapin fan club. You haven't spoken to her yourself? In recent days?"

"No. What's to talk about? She's ready and we're ready. As usual."

"Then I don't suppose you've heard about poor Mann."

"Fritz? What about him?"

"He's been arrested. At the Berlin Airport—on the way to see Edith."

"But *why?* What's he done?"

"Illegal currency transactions. Apparently he's been carrying more in his music case than music. He's in jail awaiting trial. The bail was set at some incredibly high figure—a hundred thousand marks, I think."

"My God. How awful for his wife and boys. Is there anything we can do? As a company?"

"I'm afraid not, Harry. It's a very serious offense. But you haven't heard the best part."

"There's more?"

"What Edith said when she heard the news."

"What?"

"She said—I'm quoting, Harry—'And now we have no accompanist. . . .' "

His tax attorney, Taylor Smoot, came at ten-thirty: disagreeable stump of a man smelling of cigars and loopholes, an odorous tyrant who told you how to live and scolded you for your excesses: reminded Harry of wretched Sister Charity, who lay in wait in fifth-grade cafeteria and knuckle-wrapped his forlorn ten-year-old psyche out of shape with cautions and threats and exhortations: "No more potatoes, Hurston—such a greedy little boy!"

"Can't do that."

"I don't think I understand."

"Can't have it both ways. Take it this year, take it next, but can't take it both."

"Then as you think best."

"As for those shares you're tendering . . ."

"Oh, yes?"

"That's ordinary income. No capital gains. You're going to be in a very rough bracket this year, Harry. I suppose you realize that."

That was the idea, wasn't it: to make as much as possible? "Well—"

"We're looking at a base of a hundred, plus another thirty for the shares, plus the Christmas bonus, assuming you have one."

Another twenty thousand, probably, for the likes of Melos-Doria's chief executive officer.

"See for yourself, Harry."

"The tax-shelter thing, then . . ."

More terror from Smoot, who was forever putting together reprehensible tax-shelter schemes designed to keep Harry and his fellow white-collar criminals off Federal prison farms. This latest one was something to do with condominiums up near Monterey, a deal that offered the most wonderful interest and depreciation benefits. Smoot would meld a batch of overpaid corporate hacks like Harry into an investment group; have everybody ante up $20,000 a share; and then for the next ten years they would take paper losses, claim all kinds of deductions, beat the IRS at its own game.

"Are you in, Harry? Or do you want to suffer the consequences?" Smoot's normal once-in-a-lifetime offer.

"And if I don't come in?"

"By my estimates, you'll owe Uncle Sam at least eighteen thousand, over and above what we're having LTI take out of your checks. If you value my advice . . ."

"I guess I'm in, then."

"That's a good boy," and the bastard rose; departed with a hateful smirk on his weasel's face; dropped ashes all the way to the door and beyond.

I V

When he got to Deering's office, Judas Goat was blocking the entrance: five-man punk-rock band, of course—even Harry had heard of them. Biggest thing on the Honeybee label since Ground Zero, said *Rolling Stone.*

"Ah, Harry," Deering called out, "give us just a second, can you, like a good chap? Youth must be served, wot?"

Deering was Canadian by birth—the way he said *aboot* for *about* gave him away—but he tried to sound as much like a Knight of the Garter as possible, to the point that the water-cooler crowd, behind his back, called him Sir Leslie.

Harry stood aside; let pass the longhairs plus manager plus Honeybee's staff photog, Lindsay, who soon had his principals mugging mercilessly at the feet of their corporate mentor, Chairman of the Board and Chief Executive Officer, Leslie T. (for Thorneycroft) Deering.

"That's it—now everybody *frown*," cried Lindsay, who could hardly be heard over the din of the loudspeakers: the latest Judas Goat single, naturally.

"Marvelous tune, eh, Harry?" shouted Deering, one well-shod foot tapping in wild opposition to the group's insane rhythms.

"Very catchy," said Harry, whistling. "Mozart's key. Very nice."

"Don't getcha, man," said the group's leader, an evil-looking twerp in denim suit with leather trim.

"E-flat?" Harry suggested. "Usually considered Mozart's favorite key? Three of the four horn concerti? The Symphony Number Thirty-nine . . ."

"We don't play that way, man."

"Ah. Three flats, then? B, E, A?"

Glimmer of recognition from the bass player: "*Yeah*, man. Dig you now, man."

"Where *are* my manners?" said Deering with pain. "Gentlemen, may I introduce the head of our classical operation—the Melos-Doria label? Mr. Harry Chapin . . ."

The longhairs froze momentarily, then laughed as one.

Deering looked sorely disconcerted. "Harry? Ah—"

"Haw," said the bass player, waking up. "Must be a *different* one."

"Fuckin' right," said the leader. "'Cause we *know* the real Harry Chapin."

The famous one, yes—the powerful pop balladeer.

"Must be a common name, huh, man?" said another of them.

"Very common in my own family, as a matter of fact," said *this* Harry Chapin.

Deering broke under the strain. "If your publicity needs are satisfied, Lindsay . . . Gentlemen, I must ask you to excuse us—the pressures of time . . ."

". . . Frankly, Harry," said Deering, feet no longer tapping, "I find it most rewarding—interfacing with our artists in this way. But then you are a master yourself."

Artists? We're a little careless about the way we use that word around here, eh, wot? True: every illiterate rockhead who graced the pop department was automatically given the title.

". . . You saw the older chap? The manager? Cap'n Jack?"

You mean the busker in smartly tailored Levi's; briefcase of finest morocco leather hand-crafted in Paris; buckles and snaps all in eighteen-karat gold; boots for shoes, highly polished and exotic of cut with 2½-inch heels; superior smile punctuated—could be echt English—by palpably bad teeth, browned and broken and growing in askew and akilter with some inferior-metal (silver?) bridgework to keep the kernels of enamel in place? Do you mean *that* Cap'n Jack? "The manager? Yes indeed."

"That man, you should be aware, Harry, presently contributes over seven million dollars to LTI sales each year. More, may I remind you, than all of your classical endeavors added together."

Well, isn't this great fun. "Remarkable," said Harry, biting his tongue.

"About your trip . . ."

"You have my itinerary."

"Paris, isn't it?"

"And London, yes. The annual repertoire conference."

"How long will you be away?"

"Two, three weeks at the most," Harry replied. "If I can wind things up earlier, I'll be back earlier, of course."

"Good. I want you here for Board Meeting on the thirteenth in any case."

"May thirteenth," said Harry. "That shouldn't be any problem."

"There may well be some difficult questions at Board," Deering said. "I don't have to tell you that there is pressure, sizable pressure, to do something about operations like yours—that is, operations which do not cover their full share of overheads, never mind contributing to profits. . . ."

God, not *this* again. Did Harry have to repeat his lecture? Classics was a club, remember? A private club with very special membership requirements: knowledge, taste, thousands of hours of critical listening, study, study, study. With rock, anyone could belong: very little talent required to *perform* it and none at all—no education, refinement, critical faculties—to listen to it. "I'd be happy to answer such questions," Harry said with vigor, "at Board or anywhere else."

"Of course," said Deering. "And I sympathize with your point of view. But this is a business, as we know, and we must expect to hear dissident, even severely negative comments at Board. Indeed, your own remarks in *Time* magazine . . ."

"As I've explained, Leslie—"

"It is no secret, Harry, that several directors take a very dim view indeed—and I don't mean to be unnecessarily rude—of these operatic patchwork quilts of yours, where there seems so little possibility of profit. . . ."

A profit from *classics?* Quite ridiculous, old chap.

". . . Whilst I know you are doing everything in your power to improve results, I must demand greater performance—even *unreasonable* performance. . . ."

One of Deering's most annoying habits, Harry had always felt, was his use of *whilst* in place of everyman's *while.*

". . . No good having genius or talent or whatever you wish to call it, unless the results can be successfully packaged and sold. . . ."

Obvious point, old chap.

". . . Unfortunately—and I say this in all sincerity—our film people tell me this means sex, violence, gaudy surface excitements. . . ."

Ah, tell me more.

". . . Our audiovisual people even go so far as to predict a great future market for pornography—the stuff of our videocassette business, if you can imagine. . . ."

He could try; he would try.

". . . Cultural shock, nothing less—damned hard on people like you, Harry, damned hard on serious artists. . . ."

Thank you, but no thank you.

"Which brings me to the point, I'm afraid. . . ."

And what might that be, sir?

". . . Classics are today bringing us neither profits nor exploitable prestige, and we've always agreed—since the very day of LTI's acquisition of your little company from Mr. and Mrs. Strauss—that we must have one or the other, and preferably both."

Play Slonimsky first; keep back Cavalieri for the final hand. "I fully appreciate what you're saying, Leslie. And I believe, to some extent at least, I have anticipated you."

"Oh? Have you, now? In what regard?"

"Nothing to compare, I tell you in front, with Judas Goat—but, in its own way, very exciting. I've mentioned to you our continuing interest in the great Russian pianist Vladimir Slonimsky."

"Yes, yes. In retirement, didn't you tell me?"

"He has been, yes. But now, after months of arduous negotiation, Leslie, we are on the verge of being able to announce the signing of Slonimsky to a new long-term exclusive contract with Melos-Doria."

"And—he sells well, does he?"

"His past sales have been excellent, yes. An album of Beethoven sonatas is, in fact, the best-selling LP in the history of Melos-Doria— over a hundred thousand. But the prestige alone, Leslie—"

"Prestige, Harry, is bottom-line profit in the LTI annual report. Really, I don't mean to sound crass, but—"

"I understand. But prestige has *commercial* value, too, Leslie. News of this kind can spark our entire sales effort. Really, re-signing Slonimsky can be of great importance to Melos-Doria—and, ultimately, to LTI."

"Yes, of course. I don't wish to minimize your contribution."

Time for the ace: if anything, he had waited too long to play it. "But I have other news—even more important news, Leslie."

"Indeed?"

"You will understand that this is still *extremely* confidential. Edith Cavalieri, whose very name helped establish this label in its infancy— Edith has at last agreed to come out of *her* semi-retirement. My principal mission in Europe will be to complete arrangements for her first operatic recording in ten years."

Deering produced a warm smile. "My boy—this *is* good news. A true achievement. You are to be congratulated."

"I haven't wanted to say anything about it, Leslie, until final details were set. We expect to make formal announcement next week with as much panache as our publicity people can muster. We're creating history in the bargain, as the vehicle for Mme. Cavalieri's return will be the first quadraphonic *Otello* ever recorded."

"Isn't this fine! Isn't this *excellent!* The Board—"

"Yes, I was going to suggest that perhaps the Board would be interested—especially, Leslie, since we expect that recording to be issued by all companies of the Consortium no later than next March, which will give Melos-Doria maximum financial benefit in the new fiscal year."

"My boy, you shouldn't hold back good news when you have it! Isn't this a coincidence—I believe there was a tidbit about Mme. Cavalieri just this morning on the Today Show. . . ."

Harry was aware of his own sweat: underarms dripping, collar soaked in back. He would be entitled to a *very* fine Burgundy at lunch.

"Isn't she, ah, *involved*, should I say, with one of the big auto people? In Detroit?"

"A long-term arrangement," said Harry, voice with greater lilt now. "A gentleman committed, I believe, to furthering Mme. Cavalieri's film ambitions."

"You know, Harry, you spark an idea." Eyes wet and glistening now, like a big dog's. "Film. What would you think of *filming* your production? This *Othello* of yours? *Simultaneously?*"

He pronounced it *sim*, not *sime*, in the English manner, and of course got the piece wrong: they only had *Othello* at McGill, knew nothing of *Otello*.

"I see," said Harry, not seeing at all. Ludicrous: the idea that Edith

Cavalieri, who required an hour with the hairdresser before venturing out even to market, could come to the recording studio in condition to be *photographed*. "Quite an idea," he seemed to be saying: mind and tongue not connected at just this moment.

"Oh, you'd be surprised," said Deering, pacing now behind his enormous mahogany desk. "You creative people find it hard to believe that we mere businessmen—"

"No, no—"

"Yes, you do—don't deny it. You think it inconceivable that a man like me—just a glorified bookkeeper, really—should have *artistic* ideas. The film peoople treat me the same way. Hah! Videocassettes, Harry. I tell you now, this is going to be a *business*. Broadway shows, plays—yes, even operas. Remember our *name*, Harry—our business is *leisure* for the mass market. Never forget that."

"No. Of course. Yes."

"But more of this at Management Committee. You will be in attendance, I presume?"

"Of course." The monthly MC meeting at 5:00 P.M.—which he had planned to skip.

"Good. Meanwhile, as for your *Othello*, very promising—*very* promising. At an appropriate moment, be sure that I'm brought personally into the project. Let's apply the full prestige of the Chairman's office to this vital undertaking—perhaps have our pictures taken with Mme. Cavalieri at the contract-signing—something of that nature. Good for our image. Good for *your* image, too, Harry. Don't see nearly enough of you in the press—except for the *Time* magazine thing and that was terribly negative, don't you think? Perhaps a large cocktail party—invite all the major LTI shareholders—hold it right here on the lot at the time of the Annual General Meeting in the fall. Yes, many possibilities. Keep me informed, that's a good chap. . . ."

"I've taken up enough of your time. . . ."

"Oh, one other matter. I've had a call from this fellow Bloom. He says we're being unnecessarily difficult about giving him old records—our 'deleted catalog,' I believe he said—for reissue at low price? For which he will pay us, I believe, very nice advances?"

Harry sighed. "I'm afraid that's not quite the situation, Leslie."

"No?"

Naturally, Deering wouldn't understand the implications. "You see, he wants to dump on the market, in quite reprehensible pressings, recordings by our top artists. Slonimsky, for example. I've told him that we simply won't agree to it. We can't afford to have our top artists ruined in exchange for a few advances."

"What sort of advances?"

"Well, practically nothing. A thousand dollars per master. A thousand dollars for a complete concerto by Vladimir Slonimksy. And of course Bloom won't give us a correct accounting. He'll send us the thousand dollars and then go on selling the record, terrible quality and all, for the rest of the century. It's really out of the question, Leslie."

"I see. Well, given our financial problems—*your* financial problems, Harry—please let us not stand on niceties. Even a thousand dollars helps offset costs. And if the masters will otherwise lie fallow in our vaults . . ."

"Leslie, *believe* me—we can't afford to cast these particular pearls before a swine like Bloom. Really, it would ruin Melos-Doria's reputation in short order."

"I understand your position, Harry. But I'm also suggesting that giving a master or two to this fellow Bloom may not be injurious—and, indeed, I've told him just this morning that you will do everything possible to make available to him a reasonable amount of material. Please don't let me down on this. . . ."

Deering stood, leaned across the wide expanse of polished wood, shook Harry's hand. *"Bon voyage."* The great man's hand was pink and smooth, like his face. "And, Harry—*bonne chance,"* his free hand already moving to the telephone.

Heidi's eyes were puffy from crying. "It's John Morley's birthday," she said bravely. "There's a luncheon at the Smokehouse."

"Say I can't make it. The Europe trip. Et cetera."

"It's his fortieth birthday."

"And?"

"You know how important that is. For men."

Stupid woman. John Morley was a contemptible ass, as far as Harry knew; no reason to change his opinion at this late date. "Just say I can't make it."

"They've invited his wife. You'll be expected to say a few words. In your inimitable style," spoken with lethal contempt.

"Maybe I can stop by for dessert," knowing he never would.

He let Heidi make excuses to Morley's secretary, then called her back into the office.

"You're twiddling," she said.

"What? Oh—sorry." When preoccupied or nervous, he had the habit of playing with his hair: twisting and untwisting it maddeningly, until the girl he was with made him stop. "Let's face it," he began, hoping to say the whole thing in one uninterrupted speech, "I've spoiled everything between us. I realized that last night. One more aspect, really, of what we've both been thinking. And of what you said this morning."

She said nothing; generously made no comment on his incredible clumsiness.

"Anyway—I've thought about all aspects of it"—suddenly hung up on this word *aspects*—"and I think it's obvious that we can't go on with this arrangement. At the office."

"Do you mean I'm *fired?*"

"I just don't think we can continue. I'm sure there are other positions open. I'll call Personnel—"

"Don't bother. I'll be leaving." She turned and walked out.

Later, when he buzzed, Alix Stern, his best friend at Melos-Doria (not counting Norman, who worked out of New York), came on the line. "I'm taking over for Heidi," she said. "Temporarily."

"Oh, fine. Great. Thanks."

Alix had already moved her gear out of her private cubicle, where she functioned as an "administrative assistant" after ten years as a secretary (typical Melos-Doria token promotion), and reverted, quietly and efficiently, to her former role. "Do you want your calls held?" remembering his bad habits.

"Yes, please."

Within seconds she was bringing him hot black coffee. Fabulous secretary, Alix; hadn't really wanted her "promotion" except for the money, she'd admitted. "If you don't mind, Harry—some of us are going to take Heidi to lunch."

"Of course. And charge it to me, all right?"

"I was coming in to borrow a credit card."

He'd always found it easy to talk to Alix—confide in her, even—probably because she was the one female at Melos-Doria he'd never hit on. Not that she wasn't attractive; she definitely was, in a patrician, off-putting way. But she'd always had the knack of keeping stray males at arm's length, especially married ones, which was the kind mostly found around Melos-Doria.

"Here—take Master Charge. Oh, and Alix—bring me back a receipt, would you please. . . ."

Careful man with a dollar, H. E. Chapin II—though none of his girls ever had reason to think him miserly, and none ever would.

3

"Boss, you sure know your *vino*."

"*Vin*. In here it's strictly *vin*."

"Whatever," slurping it down.

"And please, Maury, as a personal favor—stop calling me 'boss,' all right? I would appreciate it. . . ."

"Sure. No offense meant."

"And this is nothing but the house white. . . . Modest Mâcon to whet the appetite. The real drinking comes later."

Le St. Germain was Harry's favorite restaurant in Los Angeles— favorite in America, even—and he thought it appropriate to introduce Maury to the place, Maury being in many respects his protégé and— hopefully—philosophic heir apparent.

Ah, Camille, and not a moment too soon. "Is the lamb . . . ?"

Perfect, as always. Well, then, to begin . . . "*Salade de champignons* awfully good here, Maury, or if you like pheasant, a really superb pheasant *pâté* . . ." For himself, the *salade* St. Germain (both mushrooms and endive) with just a slice of the *pâté* on the side (at Camille's insistence), followed by the *carré d'agneau à l'estragon*, pink, please . . .

"And for you, monsieur . . . ?"

Maury would have the same, thank you; whatever the boss was having was more than good enough for him.

And the wine? Nothing less than a '67 Romanée-Conti, which Harry had ordered before they sat down. They were here to celebrate, were they not? What, his trip? Maury's first eight months with the firm?

Or perhaps the new contract with Vova. "A toast, my boy . . . To Vladimir Slonimsky and all his kind . . ."

Mmmm, fabulous nose, superb fruity essence; done and done again.

"So as long as we're getting personal," probed young Mr. Wiseman, tongue now well lubricated by the grape, "do you mind my asking how a guy like you—being a composer and all, huh, Harry?—how you got into this funny business?"

"Ah." Not how, but why. "Nothing especially scandalous about it, I'm afraid," Harry heard himself saying; then told his life story, short version, between delicious mouthfuls of the ruby red:

". . . Studied music at Harvard, as you know. Got my B.A. and thought I'd burn up the track as a composer. Even then it wasn't possible to make a living writing music, but I didn't know that. Didn't want to go into teaching, which was where my training was taking me—and which was the only thing I was good for, I now realize. My senior year I got to conduct one of my own pieces—something about the atom bomb, as I remember, atom bomb being hot stuff in those days—my own 'Threnody for the Victims of Hiroshima,' à la Penderecki, you might say—and Hindemith was in the audience, and I ended up going down to Yale for the M.A. program there, not realizing that I either lacked real talent or else had nothing to say, or both. This was the musical highpoint of my life, it now appears. I used to play pretty good piano, could sight-read anything, which is useful for contemporary works, and actually for a while there—at Harvard still—sorry, getting out of chronological sequence—I was pretty popular with the other would-be composers around Boston because I could play their stuff with a certain bravura and it all sounded better than it was.

"But that couldn't last. Got the M.A. and the best wishes of Hindemith—really a sweet man, by the way—and thought it might be fun to be addressed as 'Dr. Chapin,' so accepted the honorable post of TA—teaching assistant—oh, but of course you know that, having been one yourself—at Berkeley, where I started work on the Ph.D. that never was to be and got a part-time job as program director for a small classical station there, KBX-FM, now defunct, with the idea that I'd lecture and write music during the day and play records at night. We ran six P.M. to midnight, which turned out to be the most thorough grounding in classical repertoire that anybody has ever had before or since. I had a nice little apartment just off the Cal campus, and that was my downfall—my wife's too, really—met Maggie, who was studying for her M.A. in philosophy after being campus queen at Stanford, and all our academic ambitions went down the drain in the second quarter—let's see, this would be 1957 by now—when I let myself get lured away to

New York by the promise of six hundred dollars a month and the chance to work as a management trainee under the fabled Goddard Lieberson at CBS. Sure, you don't even know the name, but Goddard was the greatest executive in the history of classical records—put Masterworks on the map all by himself, practically. The next thing we know, Maggie and I are settled down in the Village in a really ratty walkup, and Harry Chapin's 'Career in the Arts' is formally launched. Six months or so later, Mr. and Mrs. Leonid Strauss, beloved founders of Melos-Doria, were looking to expand their tasty little label, which they operated from their dining-room table—early works of Purcell and late ones of Scriabin—and Herr Professor Hindemith put them on to one Harry Chapin. The rest, as they say, is History. I know it doesn't sound like much, but if you'll check *Who's Who* . . . Here, let me pour."

"Fascinating," said the devoted Mr. Wiseman. "Did you ever think of going back for the Ph.D.? With your credentials . . ."

"Pipe dream. Yes, at times I've thought of it. Getting back on campus. Envy you your recent connection, actually. But no. It's too late for that, isn't it? All the guys in my class who stuck it out have tenure now—make the big campus money, such as it is. Bad timing on my part. A man chronically in the wrong place at the wrong time, doomed to wander the earth, I like to think, making unwanted operas with impossible casts. . . ."

"Don't look now," cautioned Maury, "but aren't those ours?"

Heidi and Alix and the farewell-luncheon gang from Melos-Doria, just now arriving. Was this the only restaurant in Los Angeles open on Fridays? Harry nodded, even attempted a smile as they swept past; the thin one—name was Gail, wasn't it? Not that he was interested. Not going to be interested in *that* ever again.

"I suppose we should talk some business," from Maury, without enthusiasm. "While I still can."

"If you insist," Harry said. "You saw Bloom?"

"He really wants those Slonimsky masters. Upped his advance to fifteen hundred a title."

"The answer is no."

"He says Deering—"

"If he calls again while I'm in Europe, stall—tell him only *I* can act on it and I'll be in touch when I get back."

"Deering rough?"

"A most gentlemanly discussion, actually."

"We're in trouble, huh?"

"He expressed some anxiety about our profit contribution, yes. But he was most impressed with our plans for Mme. Cavalieri's return. In what he persisted in calling *Othello*."

Ah, the lamb—and pink as a baby's bottom. Gracious, where had all the Burgundy gone? "Camille? I'm afraid we're going to need another of these. . . ."

"Speaking of *Otello*," Maury went on, "do you mind if I ask another question? Sort of delicate?"

"Be my guest."

"So how did it happen? How did the whole project get so screwed up?"

With the second bottle, Harry put poor, ignorant, besotted Wiseman in the picture.

"Yes, screwed up, if you like. But understandably so. In 1965 Mme. Edith Cavalieri, leading diva of that day—who had already been a top Melos-Doria artist, mind you, for over a decade—signed a new and extraordinary contract specifically for *Otello*, receiving from us an advance of forty thousand dollars, unprecedented in the industry then as now. From that moment to this, the Cavalieri *Otello* has been an albatross around the Consortium's neck—if I may be pardoned a somewhat fanciful metaphor. We and our partners in crime—Hampstead, Apogée, Dischi La Cima, Spitze-Schallplatten, Itadaki—have doled out further advances, set up recording sessions, spent endless moneys on limousines, arranged the most fabulous birthday parties—and ended up with nothing on tape. Edith has been singularly successful in frustrating this project and others through 'indisposition' stemming entirely—in my humble opinion—from her widely-publicized liaison with the automotive gentleman from Detroit. This gentleman is, unfortunately, Catholic, married and the father of a large family. Edith had been waiting, presumably, for her lover to buy himself a divorce at Rome—he has an immense private fortune. But now she has accepted that he will never be free to marry her—or, indeed, to do anything more than make a final, very generous 'settlement' on her—including, as my friends at Apogée tell me, her fabulous Paris apartment, a new Rolls (the lady is crazy about Rollses) and his continued pledge of 'lifelong fidelity'—whatever the hell that is.

"So that today—having frittered away the best years of her working life in self-imposed retirement—having abandoned the opera stage and the recording studio at the very height of her powers—Edith finds herself free to resume her career, beginning—and this is where you and I come in—with the *Otello* that has been on the shelf all these years.

"There, now, is everything clear? And if you could see your way to passing me that bottle . . ."

"Oh—sorry. Hey, let me pour, for once."

"Thank you. . . . By the way, what are *they* drinking? Can you see?"

Maury had a good view of the farewell table. "Nothing. Or maybe a Coke."

Typical females. A gesture was in order. "Camille . . . ?"

A nice bottle of Cordon Rouge was soon making its way to the lovely ladies. "Can't let the girl simply slip away unnoticed. . . ."

"You wouldn't mind"—Maury a bit past it now—"if I asked a couple *more* questions, would you? Long as we're on the subject?"

"Fire when ready, Wiseman."

"So why Kunz, for example? He's finished, right? And the Iago—Florescu? You hear his aria LP—the thing he made in Germany? And shit—Passafiume. Same age as Verdi, that guy! So what kind of *Otello* is this supposed to be?"

Sour as hell, this boy: didn't know he possessed such depth of feeling. "Let me explain. Of course Kunz is tired now. Fabulous long career—you'd be tired, too. Agree with you—no charisma, no star quality, no sex appeal. But *interpretively*—you get me? Interpretively the best since Vinay. Yes, I say so. Florescu? Agree. Beautiful, charming boy. Diamond in the rough, maybe. Wrong timbre, maybe. No style yet, maybe. But Edith wants him. These are things you will learn. Passafiume? Eighty-one years old. Studied with Toscanini. Authentic style. Past his best work, maybe. But—authentic. So, you see, there are reasons. There are always reasons. . . ."

Hmmm. The champagne was obviously a big hit: Heidi herself smiling, telling stories. "Camille? . . . If the ladies should require another bottle . . ."

"Dig you," sullenly from the UCLA boy. "Dig what you're saying. But—"

"But what? What for dessert? Camille . . . ?"

Both settled on something simple, just a few raspberries covered in Kirsch, nothing too heavy, got to work this afternoon. And see what the ladies will have, okay? Time of celebration.

"Nope," Wiseman was now muttering between sips of the Kirsch. "Wrong. Bad idea . . ."

"You find the raspberries wanting?"

"Not *this*—this is fantastic. No, I mean the *Otello*. I can't help thinking. Harry, what you *ought* to do."

"We. What *we* ought to do. You're part of this, too, now. What?"

"We, then. What we ought to do—is make ourselves a whole new *Otello*. Getting ourselves, for starters, a new Otello."

That's right, these new boys always came with their own ideas. "Really? Who?"

"So what do you want, anyway? In a tenor?"

Oh, shit, one of those discussions. Harry had indulged in them

himself when he was a sophomore. "Ring. Power. Weight. Breath control. A fine legato, no seams. Scale even from bottom to top. A C-
natural. Or B-flat, at least. So?"

"So we've got him here on the label—that same guy you're de-
scribing."

"You're joking."

"Laframboise."

"Zeke? As Otello? Out of the question."

"I *saw* him do it, I told you—Munich, the summer after UCLA.
An absolute sensation. His 'Esultate' *murdered* the Krauts. I'm telling
you, Harry . . ."

Maury followed all the opera houses of the world. It was his
hobby—knew all the up-and-comers, always had a hair up his ass for
some new soprano, new tenor. But Zeke? Harry feigned indignation.
"You're trying to sell *me* on Zeke?"

"Right—he's your ace of spades, isn't he? Then you already know.
And wait till next season, after his debut at the Met. Falling-down
smash, I guarantee."

"Camille? . . . That special coffee . . . with the brandy?"

"Hey, no brandy for me!" cried Maury with alarm.

"In the coffee. Not to worry . . ."

Harry took a good close look at this Wiseman—bright, ambitious
Jewish boy already trying to pull the strings behind the WASPs—selling
Harry Chapin, of all people, on Zeke Laframboise. Harry Chapin, who
had *discovered* Laframboise and signed him as an absolute nobody to
the distinguished Melos-Doria label. Laframboise, the great football
star at Andrew Jackson High, New Orleans, Louisiana, and would-be
Harvard freshman. At that time he was more Harvard than any white
boy: button-down collar, gray flannel slacks, blue blazer, the works.
Except for the size 17½ collar and rolling black voice (nobody then
would have guessed that he was a tenor), Zeke might have passed
unnoticed in the Yard. Harry, as a favor to a classmate in the Harvard
Club of Louisiana, had appeared at Zeke's high school and lectured on
the benefits of a Harvard education: presented something called *The
Harvard Book* to the school's Outstanding Senior, who happened to be
Ezekiel Laframboise, All City and All State linebacker. Even then—
1965, as Harry remembered, when Zeke was seventeen and Harry an
aging thirty-two—Harvard wanted desperately to shore up its failing
football fortunes. But Zeke hadn't responded: another story.

"I know as much about Zeke Laframboise as anybody in the
world," Harry summarized for the benefit of his yawning assistant, "and
I say this. A singer of some talent and promise, yes. But Otello, no. Out
of the question. Not for another twenty years, at the earliest."

Zeke was only twenty-nine even now. And you didn't rest a $90,000 project on the shoulders of an unknown tenor, however black. Cavalieri, over the hill or not, would sell records even with a tired German has-been like Otto Kunz in the title role.

"Just an idea, boss," from a repentant Wiseman. "Yeah, Zeke *is* kinda young."

Forgiven. It costs nothing for the Maury Wisemans of this world to make such suggestions. Harry, too, had put forward ridiculous schemes when he was twenty-five. That was why, at forty-four, they paid him over $100,000 a year *not* to make such suggestions. This is a public corporation: Mr. H. E. Chapin II has fiduciary obligations, after all. Wiseman here may have the right instincts for classics, but his basic ignorance makes him dangerous, too. Let's not forget that, eh, Chapin?

"Suppose we oughta think about gettin' back, huh, boss?"

"Suppose." What time was it getting to be? *Good God!*

Harry signed off and they struggled to their feet.

"Wanna say hello?" Maury suggested.

Why not? "So how's everybody?" Chapin offered giddily.

Heidi was not speaking to him, but the others were remarkably gay and bubbling.

"Give anybody a lift back to the lot?"

But no takers: word on Harry Chapin had gotten around.

I I

Ah, Batchelder lurking outside Harry's door: the four-o'clock budget meeting, which he'd forgotten.

"How old were they, Bob, when your boys started beating you at tennis?"

These grim financial types were fish out of water when it came to anything nonprofessional: instant fear clouded the Batchelder irises. "Difficult to say, Harry. Twelve? Thirteen? I'm guessing. I'm not that good, as you know."

"I think my boys are retarded or something—fifteen and I can thrash either one of them—or both at the same time, for that matter. Me, forty-four and completely shot. Six-one, six-love last weekend—killed Beachie, and he's the coordinated one."

Batchelder eyed him warily. "Perhaps you'd like me to come back another time, Harry. . . ."

"No, no. Sorry—just letting my mind wander."

Silly thing to ask Batchelder, really: Batchelder had two sons (different ages, like normal people) and both were good athletes, made the school teams, gave their parents something to be proud of.

"About your budget, Harry . . ."

"I really won't need to be involved further, Bob. If you could show the final draft to my assistant . . ."

"Maury's awfully young, isn't he? Inexperienced?"

"Yes, but this is how we learn. . . ."

For momentary relief of nagging headache, Harry strolled out back to the Art Department to see his New York buddy Sidney Jonas, Melos-Doria's art director. In addition to art, Sidney knew about life. Harry especially liked talking to Sidney because Sidney had actually *done* it: made the trip across the dreaded River of Starting Over, found out what it was like on the other side. This brilliant Easterner, having fathered three amiable children and messed up the life of a nice New Jersey girl over a period of seventeen years, one day opted for separation, leaving the lady and brood in East Orange and moving west with Melos-Doria. Immediately he got himself one of those super bachelor pads two minutes from the office and hard by a swimming pool, Ping-Pong table and other *divertissements* of the swinging-singles set. All of this at the advanced age of forty-seven, maybe forty-eight.

Sidney really went at it. His full-time occupation was dating. His most urgent problem today was a date for the evening after next—tonight and tomorrow night having already been booked. He had an absolutely marvelous arrangement with his wife; it was like being divorced, only without the expense. No lawyers to pay, no judges meddling in your personal affairs, but the same blessed apartness, the ideal mental and geographic separation. On major holidays like Christmas (which Sidney didn't celebrate, being nominally Jewish) he could still trot out a full-fledged family. But if a young lady asked him, "Are you divorced or what?" he could truthfully say: "We're separated—wife and kids live in the East." The absence of wife and kiddies was all any self-respecting young lady demanded these days. Sidney would spin his yarn over the first candlelit dinner and the girl would inevitably go home with him and get straight into the sack. At the height of Sidney's operation—two weeks ago, as Sidney now related—he had had sexual relations with five different young ladies in a six-evening span—the seventh being reserved for laundry.

Ah, but is this the *answer*, Harry was now moved to argue. Because if you asked Harry, the early spring had gone out of Sidney's step. Five in six nights might just be more than Nature intended, Jewish or no Jewish. A steady diet of carnal bliss could give a man, perhaps, a bad case of phallic gout. "Gout," Harry warned, shaking his finger. "A disease of excess. Five in six nights. And all different."

"Ah, but they're *not* all different," wailed Sidney. "That's the trouble. They're all the *same*. They're all like early Hannah," Hannah being Sidney's lawfully-wedded in East Orange. "All fucking females are after the same thing. They'll humor you, suck your cock, do anything you want, just to get what *they* want. And what do they want? They want to get hooked into some poor bastard like you and me who'll father their nasty children, pay for the orthodontia and see to them in their respective old ages, which along the way they hasten in the coming. To you, Harry—an old friend, despite your rank—I admit that I have no solution. The swinging bachelor, I tell you from experience, is much like everybody else, only more so. Because the only thing worse than knowing the woman you're going home to each night is *not* knowing her. With these damned single ones—these girls we have here underfoot in all these horrible pink bungalows you've got us living in— with these secretaries so intent on *matrimony*, you must live up to some mythical standard of sexual performance. Yes, don't laugh; I do not exaggerate. It is unacceptable just to have a young woman up to your apartment for a quiet drink, some good conversation. No, she understands that we are speaking here of human ritual. We are speaking here of a *rutting dance*. She watches, she *judges* your performance of this dance. Indeed, she can be counted on to *review* your performance, in detail, with one or more of her girl friends—most of whom, may I remind you, also inhabit a horrible pink bungalow somewhere on this lot. 'First he said this, and then he did that . . . put his hand under my dress . . . pretended to be surprised I had no bra . . . his cock this size or that . . . but he came too soon, I had to finish myself off . . .' Oh, yes, all the gamy details right there on the table. And if you didn't do well that particular evening—being tired, maybe, from all day at your drawing board—woe be unto you! Because the next day, when you see that girl, or one of her cronies, they will quickly let you know, as all the world must know, that you are nothing in the sack. A fine world we live in, is it not?"

Harry lacked conviction in the matter. Perhaps it was unwise to visit Sidney so late in the day—or so late in one's marriage. "I've taken enough of your time," Harry said, rising.

"I envy you Gay Paree," Sidney retorted. "Bring me maybe a gift? French tickler to improve my performance? You want to borrow my Polaroid, shoot some filthy pictures?"

"Thank you, no. I'm not in the mood right now, Sidney. Feeling just the slightest bit depressed, to be honest about it."

"You feel bad *now*, huh? Well, take my word for it—don't ever get to be fifty years old."

Harry stopped short. "You're kidding. Tell me you're not *fifty* years old!"

"That's right, shout it all over the lot, so I'll never see a nipple
again. These walls, Harry—papier-mâché . . ."

III

". . . Vova loves symmetry. Twelve and one half for the U.S. and
twelve and one half for U.K."

Joe Blankenhorn, final appointment of the day, to be followed by
Management Committee and then he could go home.

"I take your point, Joe, but I simply can't pay that much—not even
to the great Slonimsky, as much as we love that gentleman around here.
What about ten and ten?—ten being in some ways even more symme-
trical."

Blankenhorn, bifocaled Wall Street lawyer of some repute, was not
amused. "Twelve and one half for the U.S. and Canada is a requisite,
Harry. Perhaps I can persuade Vova to take less in U.K., but I don't
think so. Is this truly a deal-breaker for you? Let us be candid, to save
each other's time."

"Yes, it is. Yes, definitely. I simply cannot pay twelve and one half
in U.K."

"I shall note your position."

"Are there any other open points? Besides ownership of masters? I
think not."

"And you remain adamant? How regrettable."

Precisely, you asshole. "There is simply no way in the world, Joe,
that I can give away ownership of masters for which I will have paid
hundreds of thousands of dollars in advances."

"Perhaps our friends at RCA will take a different view."

"Perhaps—though I would seriously doubt it."

"All record companies being, in my view, fungible."

God, he detested this son of a bitch. Was a new contract with
Slonimsky worth such indignity?

"Your money is no better than RCA's," Blankenhorn went on.
"Yes, his catalog is here—that's an advantage you have. But maybe you
also take him for granted. A new label would not. Of course, there is
also your special relationship with Vova. He likes you, Harry, which
complicates my job. I can only give him my best advice and counsel. If
he chooses to ignore it—fine, that's his prerogative. But right this
minute, if asked, I would feel compelled to recommend the RCA deal
over yours. Money means something even in these days of recession,
inflation, whatever you wish to call it."

Which was the trouble with these pompous bastards: most dishonest people in the world, lawyers. Blankenhorn was interested in ownership of masters because later on, when title passed to Vova, Blankenhorn could expect fat new fees for peddling the tapes elsewhere. But this was Harry's strength: he'd had long experience with these bandits and knew a few tricks himself.

"Well, then. Nothing more to discuss," Blankenhorn said, rising grandly in his elegant gray flannel: very nice, but then these tall, slim chaps—like Deering—did so much for their clothes. "As always, Harry, it's been nice chatting with you." Big smile.

"A privilege for me," not kidding anyone.

"I can find my way out."

"Have a nice day."

Fucking Blankenhorn. Harry knew what he had to do: get Gimpel into it. True, Harry had a special relationship with Slonimsky, but in his experience it never paid to go directly to the artist. Artists, being fundamentally insecure, tended to hear only the last words spoken, and Blankenhorn had Vova's ear far more frequently than Harry. No—the trick here was to get to Gimpel. It was Stash Gimpel who controlled Vova, not Blankenhorn. Harry would simply call Stash, with whom he'd done business for a decade, and tell him how difficult and—yes, *amateurish*—this fucking Wall Street greenhorn was being; suggesting, in a nice way, that, as much as Harry loved Vova, Melos-Doria would never be able to make a deal so long as Blankenhorn remained in the picture.

". . . Alix? I want to speak to Stash Gimpel. First try his office in Gstaad, Switzerland, will you?" The beautiful thing about Alix was that you didn't have to spell Gstaad.

"Harry? It's two o'clock in the morning in Switzerland. Perhaps when you arrive in Paris . . ."

"Of course—how stupid of me," which he could say to Alix but never to Heidi, who would have agreed with him. "Anyway, I'm off to Management Committee. If I'm not out by six, send the Marines."

". . . Let me begin again," spoken with horrible disdain, "now that Culture Group has deigned to join us . . ."

Late to MC, which was simply not tolerated. Deering glowered with professional skill; Harry skulked similarly.

". . . Diversification, gentlemen, with a capital D . . ."

Worse, the only empty chair around the directors' table was next to the Chairman himself, which all the good little on-time boys had left vacant. Harry tiptoed the length of the board room, making silent gestures of helplessness and apology to his dozen reluctant colleagues (r.

to l. from the Chairman, just like the annual-report photo): B&B
(bowling, billiards), Vehicular Rec. (snowmobiles), Sporting Goods,
Film & TV, Music (the pop people), Field & Stream (fishing rods,
mostly), Aluminum Products (canoes), Aquasport (scuba, plastic
boats), Culture Group (Harry, of course) and back to the Chairman.

". . . So that by 1985, if we are to maintain our present ten-percent share of what will then be a five-billion-dollar industry . . ."

Bloxom, oafish chief of Field & Stream, slid Harry a copy of the
A&P binder (agenda and program), ghastly orange affair festooned with
the LTI logo in silver stamping. Today's presentation to be made by
LTI's A&D man (acquisition and diversification), a loon named Ben-
jamin, recent acquisition himself.

". . . Well aware of our plans for expansion of the Camping Department . . ."

These sessions were healthy for him, Harry reasoned, because they
reminded him of where he stood in LTI's scheme of things: movies and
TV up near the top, followed by Honeybee and the other pop record
labels, followed by baseball bats and tennis rackets and catcher's mitts
and golf carts and ice skates and bows-and-arrows and billiard balls and
sleeping bags and—right down there at the very bottom—classics.

". . . Familiar as you are with our recent unfortunate setbacks in
Firearms . . ."

Too bad about Firearms—profits unacceptably poor, what with
people these days being generally opposed to the killing and maiming of
wild animals. Hmmm, nice employee discount, Harry noticed, on a
discontinued line of .308-caliber self-loading big-game rifles: $100 for a
weapon that listed at $495. But what would he do with a big-game rifle
in Flintridge, where—upon completion of one more stretch of free-
way—the deer and coyotes would be totally isolated and would thus
starve to death before Harry and his neighbors could bring them down
with a few well-placed copper-jacketed hunting loads from their trusty
.308s? No; pass on that.

". . . Whereas, for the same capital investment, far greater return
in other fields—fields in which LTI does not today hold significant
positions. I am thinking particularly of bicycles. . . ."

Harry agreed. With the inevitable gasoline shortage, who wanted a
snowmobile anyway? But bicycles . . . No, can't do bicycles—Japs
sending in cheap ten-speed bikes by the boatload.

Indoor ice rinks; hockey to be America's sport of the future. Nylon
fishing line and Ping-Pong balls, but that put you back into the Jap
problem, didn't it? Medicinal flea-killing dog collars, but not truly "rec-
reational" or "leisure," do you think? Except tangentially? Swiss skis,
tennis rackets from Australia. All sounded good to Harry; but must act
now or the Japs will get in ahead of us; Japs the principal bogeymen

these days; everywhere you turned, a lustful Jap with a stranglehold on the American market.

". . . It would seem we are agreed, then, that further study is required. . . ."

Chairman's closing remarks. (Thank God, Deering had forgotten about Cavalieri's *Otello.*) Brief excursion into cameras (if only Kodak and Polaroid hadn't gotten there before us) followed by spirited reaffirmation of LTI's traditional posture: stick to what we know—movies, TV, records and the rest—and spread our wings cautiously in these uncertain times, eh, gentlemen? Bearing always in mind LTI's rightful share of the 1985 market, with appropriate return on investment for our shareholders . . .

Of course by 1985, Harry reckoned, there would be nothing left to hunt or fish, no free space and no way to drive there anyway, and Harry Chapin himself would be long gone—wouldn't *have* records in those days, there being no petrochemical industry from which all records derive; indeed a pretty picture—or, more appropriate to his present line of work, a lovely final cadence. Agreed, agreed, all nod. All rise with the Chairman.

"And, gentlemen—next meeting, Toys and Games. Let's do our homework, shall we?"

He found on his desk a neat packet of materials: yellow pads, several kinds of pencils and pens, expense-report forms, his plane ticket and passport. Dear Alix, as efficient as ever. "Heidi wanted to say good-bye, but she finally had to run. She said to thank you for everything, and she hopes you'll have a good trip. Also, Maureen in Public Relations stopped by to say that she'd like to interview for Heidi's job."

Didn't take long for word to get around. Maureen? No—he was well aware of Maureen, Irish lass of recent memory; too dumb even for bed.

"Oh, and here's your Master Charge card, Harry, and the receipt from lunch—you'll want it for your expense report."

Dumbly he accepted the wrinkled carbon, evocatively spattered with St. Germain's delightful vinaigrette.

$131. Lunch for six girls, $131. What had they *eaten?* Wasn't the champagne on *his* check, not theirs?

$131, including tip. Oh, God—the *tip.* Immediately he did the arithmetic: it came out eleven percent. How could he ever show his face again at St. Germain? When he got home, he would write Camille a letter—maybe send a check. . . .

4

He could tell that Maggie had opened the Book-of-the-Month Club package in the front hall by the spoor of spongy white plastic nodules that all shippers use to protect their merchandise from the U.S. Postal Service.

". . . Impossible to get that stuff out of the carpets—don't know why you can't wait until you find a wastebasket. . . ."

But nobody listened to him around here anyway.

He fixed himself a strong rum Collins at the wetbar in the family room and put Dr. Hans-Hubert Adler's recent Brahms Third on the turntable. During the first measure Mutt began to howl in the kitchen. Mutt hated Brahms—something about the thick harmonic structure, all those blaring horns. "Mutt?" Harry called. "Come on, Mutt." The dog came to him. "Take it easy, poor dog. I know you don't like all those horns. Come, sit by me. Good dog . . ."

Maggie soon joined them. "Why do you *talk* to that dog, Harry? It's a *dog*—it's not a *person*. You talk to that dog more than you talk to *me*. Don't you know that it doesn't understand a single word you say?"

"In that respect, Mutt's not alone."

Which was really telling her. Harry made himself another rum; took off the Brahms. A flick of the switch gave him FM—Chopin, *Les Quatorze Valses*, the hateful No. 7 *en ut diese mineur*, opus 64, no. 2, gracing the airwaves. One thing about Harry Chapin, he knew what he disliked: it was one of Slonimsky's early efforts for Melos-Doria—who else could recognize both composition and performer in less than four bars? And a composer he'd learned to distrust in pubescence at that.

"I packed your bag. You'll have your old blazer and the other two Saks suits, plus the one you've got on. Will that be enough?"

"Fine. Thanks."

"I'm such a fool."

"Mag—"

"I suppose you don't want anything to eat."

She knew his travel routine as well as he did; had packed him off a hundred times. He never ate before long flights, expecially with Paris the first stop.

"Are you sure you don't want me to cut your hair?"

"I'll have it trimmed in London."

Where was the sparkling cocktail-hour conversation advertised for these bedroom communities? It wasn't her fault, he understood. Naturally, this Phi Beta Kappa of his (a girl once famed for brilliant extemporaneous lectures on Schopenhauer, Kierkegaard, Spinoza, Kant) could no longer make decent conversation: she spent most of each day in the company of an evil-eyed black woman named Lulu, who was supposed to do the cleaning, and, by late afternoon, two fifteen-year-old boys. After tailoring her conversation and mentality to their needs, naturally, when he got home tired and rebellious, she wasn't good for much.

"When was the last time we made love, Harry?"

"I don't know—week ago? What's the point? Say, do you want me to make you a drink?"

"A *week* ago? My *God*, Harry, I hope you haven't talked yourself into *believing* that. It's more like a *month*."

What the hell did she think he was, some kind of *mechanical* man? Some goddam *humanoid?* Nothing but an instrument of her own pleasure?

"Are you ready to talk to the boys?"

"The boys?"

"About those things I found in their room?"

The rubbers, the roach-holder.

"And while you're at it, Harry—we have another little problem, and that is the Burgesses."

"The Burgesses?"

"They may be progressive, Harry—modern, you would say. But Sheila called this morning to report on your fine sons. . . ."

He listened in agony: a grave new offense against decency, details fresh from their considerate neighbor "who knew you'd want to know." A less sensitive person might have called the police. This, added to yesterday's rubbers and the roach-holder, was indeed too much.

Immediately, Harry called the boys to his studio out by the pool:

what previous owners had used as the maid's quarters, but where Daddy now did his composing. (A woodwind quintet every five years wasn't too bad, was it?)

Harry sat at the work table, caused his offspring to stand. "Boys?"

Sullen stares from both Heck, the bright one, and Beachie, the athlete.

(No, these were unwarranted simplifications. Heck—five minutes older than his brother—was bright, sly, devious, a politician and not very nice. Beachie, Mother's pet because he carried her family name, was docile, polite, moral, dull and easily led astray.)

"Boys? Your mother has told me about the swimming pool incident. That Mrs. Burgess found you in the pool without your bathing suits. With Betty-Lou, is it? The new girl? From down the street? And she had no suit on either?

"You have nothing to say? Either one of you?

"It isn't right, you know. Your mother deserves much better than this.

"Did you *do* anything? You know what I mean. I hope to God you didn't."

Signs of life: from Heck initially, then Beachie. "We *didn't,* honest," together.

"What did you have in mind, then? What was your idea in going into the pool—*our* pool, where we face total liability—with a young lady, and none of you wearing your suits?

"Do you think that's a very nice thing to do? To have your mother come home tired from her volunteer work and hear from a neighbor that the two of you have been swimming naked with a girl from down the street? Is that fair, do you think, to your mother?

"Well, I think I know what you had in mind."

"But we *didn't.* I *swear* we didn't!"

"Heck, I would like to believe you're telling me the truth."

"She *wanted* to do it."

"What? What did she want to do?"

"Go for a swim."

"Without your suits?"

"We were just fooling around, Dad. We didn't *do* anything."

"Heck, Beachie—I realize now that I have been somewhat lax about your sex education. This is my fault. Still, you should have enough common sense to realize that having relations—don't interrupt—having intimate relations, just touching even, with a girl like that, naked in our swimming pool, can have serious consequences. What if—God forbid—this girl should make accusations? Tell her parents that you—the two of you—*forced* yourselves on her? What then?"

Tears now: first (surprisingly) Heck, then Beachie. They looked almost like men, big feet, coarsening features, but they were still little boys—except, of course, in the groin.

"She won't *tell*," from Heck, regaining his natural composure.

"Oh? And how can you be sure?"

"It was *her* idea—taking off our suits."

"I see."

"And that's the *truth*, Dad," from Beachie, not imaginative enough to lie.

"In any case, your mother and I shall discuss the matter further and let you know our decision. As to your punishment."

Glum now. The usual parental retribution about to descend.

"For starters, I suggest that you each sit down—as soon as your homework is finished—and compose an appropriate letter of apology to your mother, who has been very much hurt by this episode. Is that understood?"

Disgruntled sighs: huffs and puffs of frustration.

Fine, another lesson learned. "You may go to your rooms now and get cleaned up for dinner."

But still—better their course than his. Harry had vowed from the start to send the twins to a coeducational school: not the one-sex academies he'd been subjected to. Oh, the trouble *that* could lead to: just ask Harry Chapin, who'd married the first girl he asked, had first sex with the girl he married, and spent all the rest of his life (to this moment) chasing after others to find out what he'd missed. It was moments like this that made him happy they'd never had any more children. "We keep trying for another," Maggie used to tell the most-recently-met stranger at a cocktail party, "but Harry can't seem to find the mark."

The company limo arrived promptly at eight. Harry's last act was to turn over the checkbook to Maggie with a caution as to the current balance and reassurance that his salary checks for May 1 and 15 would automatically be deposited for him by Payroll. Also, the mortgage payment would be mailed by Alix on the 1st; so Maggie had nothing to worry about.

"And don't concern yourself about the incident in the pool," he said at the front door. "The boys and I have reached an understanding."

But Maggie retreated in tears toward the bedroom before he could explain about the boys, and it remained for Mutt to see him off.

He knew the driver reasonably well—Lars by name, a bright young blond fellow who intended someday to have his own limo service and, if possible, steal LTI's business away from his present employer: ambition that Harry had always lacked and never envied. "No particular rush, Lars—ten-thirty flight."

"To Paris, huh, Mr. Chapin? Wow—what I'd give to change places with you."

"You're welcome to it," said Harry with energy unusual for so late in the day.

"Yeah, saw what you said in *Time*. Guess every job's got its problems, huh? If you're gonna make some calls, let me close the partition—give you some privacy."

Make a note to add a particularly nice tip to the invoice. The electric window rose silently.

Sight of the mobile telephone had produced a puckering sensation in his mouth—metallic, like the taste of copper. Why not try Alix at home? Ask her to meet him at the airport—maybe pretend to dictate a letter, enjoy a moment's honest companionship, share a quiet drink or two?

"Alix? It's me, Harry."

"Harry—oh, thank *heavens*. I just tried to reach you at the house, but you'd left."

"Really? Well, what—"

"The night switchboard man called—there's a cable from Mr. Barraud in Paris."

"What's the problem?"

"I'll read it:

MEETING YOUR FLIGHT WITH GREATEST PLEASURE STOP MUST ADVISE LADY TODAY ANNOUNCES DESDEMONA NO LONGER SYMPATHETIC TO VOICE THUS REQUESTS CANCELLATION AUGUST SESSIONS STOP OFFERS INSTEAD ROLE OF MARSCHALLIN REPEAT MARSCHALLIN STOP WITH PROFOUND REGRETS STOP JEAN-LUC BARRAUD APOGEE PARIS.

"Does that make sense?"

"Yes, fine," he said blankly.

"Oh, I'm glad. Well—have a wonderful trip."

"Yes, thanks—for everything. I'll phone you from Paris."

It was only then that he realized he'd forgotten to ask the twins about the rubbers and the roach-holder.

Act Two

PARIS / LONDON: *April-May*

Iago: Well, Roderigo, what are you thinking?
Roderigo: Of drowning myself.
Iago: Stupid is he who drowns himself for love of a woman.

Boïto-Verdi, OTELLO

1

Arthur Godfrey: that's who the fellow in the window seat looked like. The same lovable redhead, rosy face wrapped in a smile, husky frame all done up in a terrific pinstripe. And what's this? Listening to Channel 3 of the inflight stereo system—the classical channel.

Harry wrestled with the hateful plastic earphones. Ouch—dedicating ourselves this evening to Schoenberg's *Verklärte Nacht*, lousy piece of third-rate movie music. Godfrey here seemed to share Harry's view: pulled off the phones and made another stab at the fat Gore Vidal in his lap. But that didn't last long either; Vidal not very helpful on long airplane rides. Godfrey banged the book shut with a sigh—hammy piece of stage business—then turned to Harry and announced in the most beautiful baritone:

"We've both failed, haven't we, Mr. Chapin—with the Muzak and me with this 'literature'? How would you feel about a little conversation? My name's Dell, by the way—Hoyt Dell. Delighted to meet you, finally."

"You have me at a disadvantage—"

"Sorry, yes—had the pleasure of hearing you speak, year or so ago, at one of those Washington cultural banquets. Record Industry Association, wasn't it?"

"Ah—"

". . . And just the other day thoroughly enjoyed your witty remarks in *Time*. Yes, my advantage indeed—looked forward to meeting you for some time now. . . . Your greatest living fan, I suppose you might say! . . . Just *love* that little company of yours. . . . Yes, from the very start—even knew the Strausses a bit. . . . Mutual friends . . .

Envied you all, doing something worthwhile with your lives . . . while
I—mortified to say it—nothing but a merchant. Got some money and
nothing else. . . ."

Thank God, the champagne. Harry failed to recognize the brand,
but saw the magic word Rheims. Pour, my girl, and keep pouring until
we see the lights of Paris.

The champagne gave him a few seconds in which to compose
himself. "Well, I'm afraid you're being overly generous. . . ."

"No, I mean it. A life in the arts. I'd have given anything. But
lacked the talent, obviously. Glorified salesman now . . ."

Harry didn't have to say a word—only nod at reasonable intervals.
Between glasses two and six it all came out. This Dell could really spin
a yarn. Born at Chicago on "Black Tuesday," October 29, 1929, day of
the Wall Street crash. Son of a prosperous building contractor who saw
to it that young Hoyt received the formal schooling that Papa Amos had
never had. Stayed in one school or another until he was thirty, gaining
ultimately a Ph.D. in Romance Languages from Columbia to go with
his M.S. in Electrical Engineering from Rensselaer Polytechnic Institute
and his B.A. in Philosophy from the University of Chicago. And let's
not forget his avocation—music, of course, including keyboard instruction at the professional level from Dame Myra Hess ("a beautiful
woman") and a stint at composition with Darius Milhaud in California.

The saga became more incredible by the glass. "My only real connection with Vova . . ." Oh, yes—had once played for Slonimsky, at
Hess's suggestion. ". . . So kind to me, and so generous. 'You have
talent, my son—but are you prepared to sacrifice all for your art?' If
only I had listened to that man . . ."

They began to serve dinner. Harry would eat only a salad, he now
resolved, perhaps a roll with a bit of the brie, half an apple: a light
repast which in no way would spoil his appetite for Paris—or for
Solange. Would they make love, then go to Fouquet's? Or go to
Fouquet's, then make love?

. . . So old Amos, who had no patience with the music thing,
provided Hoyt with a modest grubstake—Amos having retired to Florida
by that time, where he became a real-estate tycoon—and Hoyt made his
start with small, one-man franchised hotdog stands built on the corners
of parking lots in cities of 50,000 to 100,000 population. The first stand
gave way to a dozen, then a hundred, then—well, there were fifteen
thousand now, and multiplying with each tick of the second hand.
Europe, too—and soon (purpose of this trip) Behind The Iron Curtain.
Even the Russians had come to understand the wisdom of the hotdog;
hoped to have a string of stands from the Black Sea to Vladivostok by
1980, God Willing. . . .

Traded on the American Stock Exchange; "all different now that we've gone public"; millions in equity, but just not the same old fun. Still, a comfortable life: pied-à-terre in Manhattan, a place in the Hamptons, the new condo down at La Quinta. "Incidentally, the apartment in New York—feel free to use it at your convenience. We're hardly ever there except in the fall when Bernie—Mrs. Dell—goes on her annual shopping spree. Really, we've got to get you and Bernie and—yes, Maggie—together. I just *know* you kids will get on like a house afire. . . ."

Kids. Dell had this wonderful ability to encompass all age brackets: be your father at one moment, your brother at another, yes, even your admiring son.

". . . Victoria, she's the oldest—fourteen now, with all the raw talent in the world—she'll be class of Eighty-four in college. Bernie's hot for Radcliffe, where she went, but I'm campaigning for Juilliard or Curtis, someplace more *creative,* don't you know . . ."

Orwell had it all wrong: 1984 was going to be a lot worse than anybody imagined.

". . . Which is how, of course, I came to meet Donny—asked him for his advice on schools, which he was most generous in giving. . . ."

Dell knew them all—or said he did: Pinky and Barry and Donny and Danny, all of today's trendy post-teenage music-makers, the arrogant who had inherited the earth. God, Harry wished for a telephone: like to call Pinky or Barry or—yes, Vova—and show this Dell up for the great impostor he was.

"White, sir? Or red?"

He had succumbed—with greatest reluctance—to a single slice of the Chateaubriand, Paris being still many hours away; so, naturally, he opted for the Bordeaux, and Dell concurred. They were very close now, sharing the same tastes, living their lives in art.

". . . A loving observer at best. Not at all the professional and no hope to be . . . hence my envy. . . ."

"No envy justified, actually," Harry said, getting a word in edgewise.

"But *knowing* the people you do—*working* with these talented young artists. Such a privilege. Yes, envy . . ."

Time to set this yokel straight. "Donny and Barry? Whom you know?"

"Hardly know them at all, in *your* sense. Very fine beef, wouldn't you say? Not Charollais, but it will pass."

"Mmmm. Pass. Donny and Barry? Two very talented youngsters— who know nothing."

"Oh, but surely—"

"Bullshit. (Pardon my French.) Rookies—modern-day Katzenjammer Kids, life one big frolic, record companies providing all the laughs." Wry humor, the Chapin trademark. "Example. Gian-Carlo Ponti—you know him, too?"

"Met him—only briefly. Such a genius. Oh, you are so—"

Fortunate, yes. "Ponti, then. Older than Donny and Barry and the rest, but young for a conductor. Cannot broaden his repertoire to save his life. Still plays the same pieces he learned at the conservatory. Takes on maybe one new symphony a year, maximum. Knows Brahms One and Three, never heard of Two and Four. So when you say to him, how about a complete set of Brahms symphonies, you produce a crisis— *crise de nerfs* in his lingo.

"Mandelbaum, the same. Twenty-two years old and already tired of the violin. Sees a great career for himself as a conductor. Agitating to make a record with his pal Donny—Brahms First Concerto, a work that intimidates *Rubinstein*. Who would buy such a thing?"

"Ah, but the youth movement—renaissance of interest in the classics—"

"Baloney." (Ah, thank you, *Mademoiselle*, and don't forget my friend here—so many fine *châteaux* in Bordeaux.) "These trendy *Wunderkinder* love to *talk* youth movement, but as near as I can tell— working, understand, with the distinct disadvantage of having the sales figures on my desk—today's youth generation couldn't care less about classics. You want a generation gap? I'll show you a generation gap."

"I had no idea . . ."

"A perversion of Mr. Edison's and Mr. Berliner's invention, of course. Originally, records were a library function. We would capture for posterity the world's greatest scores as interpreted by fine old gentlemen who had spent lifetimes in determining inner truths. This was art, not commerce. But today—"

"Money, yes—I feel the same."

Shut up, Hotdog King, and let Chapin finish, will you? "Today we have this enormous, insatiable commercial pipeline to fill. With what? With *product*. Not art—*product*. What are the two most important words in American business? Surely you know them well: new and improved. New. A new Brahms Fourth even though the catalog is already filled with worthy ones. Improved. After acoustical, electrical. After electrical, high-fidelity. After high-fidelity, stereo. And now quadraphonic. A fraud. A sham. Am I boring you to death? Suppose I must be. . . ."

"Not at all! Not at all! Fascinating stuff for the likes of me. Please, don't stop!"

Never had an audience like Dell: rampant sycophancy built on an hour's conversation. "This Ponti I've spoken of? Maybe has talent, maybe doesn't. But we shall never know. He is forty-four years old, but already—thanks to World War II—he is in demand in every country of the free world. Entire generation of music-makers wiped out in the war, so that today we are left with these children—intellectually speaking. How can one have sufficient humanity in his heart to interpret great music until he's practiced his craft for, say, fifty years? All the great old men are dead—Szell, Beecham, Walter, Munch, Toscanini, Reiner, Ansermet, Cluytens, De Sabata, Klemperer—the list is endless."

"Harry, I had no idea of your, well—burden."

"Burden, yes. For I am part of the problem. I encourage these long-haired Donnys and Barrys and Dannys and Zubies, who find themselves stepping straight from the conservatory, with their student scores marked up the way their professors told them, directly into the concert hall and recording studio, there to spout back the lessons learned by rote. Any one of these young fellows—Ponti is a perfect case—can find himself appointed general music director of one or two or three major symphony orchestras in as many countries simultaneously, and his biggest problems in life are finding a convenient place to live—usually in Switzerland, because of the taxes—and arranging to get copies of scores he's never heard in time to play them for the ladies of the philharmonic on Friday afternoons."

"Surely you exaggerate. Things couldn't be—"

"And I help perpetuate this hoax. I help tell the consuming public, such as it is, that these new records by these new artists—*artists?*—are worthy of permanent encapsulation in vinyl. I help put these unformed fetuses into our museums.

"Which is wrong. Morally wrong. Can we truthfully say that there is an honorable business to be made from preserving the artistic insights of a callow youth of, say, twenty-two? If not, why on earth am I killing myself to put together a recording program for young Mr. Mandelbaum? What does Barry Mandelbaum know of the Brahms Violin Concerto except what Felix Balsam, his teacher, has just finished telling him? Better we should preserve the interpretation of *Mr. Balsam,* who is at least sixty years old! But the public does not want Mr. Balsam. Or at least that's what the concert impresarios tell us. . . .

"No, this is madness of a particularly nasty sort. For we, the professionals, are chronically confusing the judgment of the lay public, and that can have lasting damage. Who in the public can *really* say whether a piece is well or badly played? Ninety percent of the public, including most music critics, cannot read music: they merely know what they don't like. A cruel and savage business. An unworthy business for men of conscience—or even thoughtfulness . . ."

"A little cheese, gentlemen? And we have some nice apples. Or perhaps you would prefer a fresh pear? Or a nice fruit compote? A liqueur? Anything at all?"

Everything. Everything at all. For me and my friend here. My enthralled, adoring friend, from out of the blue . . .

Over Greenland, Harry woke up from his brief after-dinner nap. The Hotdog King by his side snored gently, giving Harry a much needed opportunity to do some homework in privacy: *l'affaire Cavalieri*, not something Harry wished to share with Mr. Dell.

He got out the *Otello* file and ran through the yellowing early sheets. The original proposal was dated April 1, 1964:

PROPOSAL No. R-19407

Composer	Work	Artists
Verdi	*Otello*	Edith Cavalieri, Desdemona
	(3 LPs)	Otto Kunz, Otello
		Robert Merrill, Iago
		London Philharmonic & Chorus
		Tullio Passafiume, conductor

Sales Estimates

USA	12,000 sets
	5,000 highlights
UK	6,000 sets
	2,000 highlights
Germany	15,000 sets
	7,500 highlights
France	5,000 sets
	5,000 highlights
Japan	5,000 highlights
Italy	3,000 sets
	3,000 highlights

Estimated number of sessions: 12.
To be recorded London, July–August 1965.
Mme. Cavalieri requests round-trip first-class air fare, London-Rome, plus $50 per diem general expenses, plus limousine at disposal during sessions. London hotel: Ritz.

Scribbled at the bottom, in Harry's youthful scrawl, was an addendum:

Project postponed to June 1967. Conductor possibly Mehta. Mme. Cavalieri indisposed.

Then, in red ink, another:

Postponed to September 1969. Conductor Passafiume. Iago uncertain: Merrill no longer available. Mme. Cavalieri indisposed.

Then, in blue again, another:

Project postponed—indefinite.
See Legal File #45632: "Action for Cause."

There would be no point in adding further addenda until he talked to the lady face to face. Another delay was simply impossible: everything was again set—her conductor (regardless of what Signor Ponti thought), her Otello (poor Kunz—one more postponement and he would no longer be able to sing the part), her Iago (some goddam Rumanian boy Harry had never heard, or heard of), her hall (Walthamstow, which favored aging vocal cords). He would now persuade her in the one language that all *prime donne* understood: money.

Let's see, the great lady, according to her original contract dated January 1, 1954—which was negotiated, let us not forget, by our dear founders, Mr. and Mrs. Leonid Strauss—gets a paltry 5 percent proportional on 85 percent of sales-less-6½-percent-packaging-deduction. Ah, but Leonid had sweetened that in late 1957, when the lady's records had begun to sell, as an inducement to make a *Barbiere di Siviglia* that she didn't want to make—and, indeed, never did make—by adding, on complete opera sets only, an extra 1 percent.

But all of this was ancient history (papers making more sense as he progressed through the file), for in 1965 Leonid had sweetened the deal even further, advancing the famous $40,000 (which, fortunately for Melos-Doria, was collateralized by Edith's entire catalog, not just the unmade *Otello*, so that Melos-Doria got its money back years ago) against a royalty rate of 7½ percent, with no further bonuses.

Meaning what, in money? If Desdemona's singing time, including duets and ensembles, was, say, 20 percent of the total playing time, then Edith would actually receive 20 percent of 7½ percent of 85 percent of $7.98-less-6½-percent, per LP. Whipping out his trusty electronic calculator, he soon had the number he was looking for:

$$.2 \times .075 = .015 \times .85 = .01275 \times 7.98 = .101745 \times .065$$
$$= .0066134. \text{ Then } .101745 - .0066134 = .0951316$$

Nine and a half cents per disc for a recording that promised to sell maybe 12,000 sets and 5000 highlights—41,000 discs in all—which would mean to Edith Cavalieri, in cash, eventually, say—$3900.39.

God, was that *all?*

That plus the Rolls, the Ritz, the gossip-column items, the attention of royalty in London—and the scathing reviews, inevitably, when the critics heard the test pressings. No wonder Edith wanted to do the Marschallin: anything to avoid Harry Chapin's $3900, which would hardly cover a year's hairdressing.

But *no*, you dummy—boy, champagne could really slow down the mental processes—he had forgotten *foreign* sales.

Ah, yes, *much* better—since foreign estimates amounted to another 29,000 sets (87,000 discs) and 22,500 highlights—a total of 109,500 LPs—Edith might expect to receive (years later, foreign royalties being notoriously slow to come in) a grand total of . . . $109,500 + 41,000 \times .0951316 = \$14,317$, give or take a penny or two.

Mmmm. Still not a significant sum by her standards. Perhaps he could persuade his colleagues at the Conference to increase their sales estimates. The market for Edith Cavalieri was bound to be bigger now than it was thirteen years ago—although 12,000 sets seemed high, for the U.S. *Otello* wasn't *Aïda*. If not that, what about increasing Edith's share—give her 10 percent proportional instead of 7½? What would that be, another $5000? The rest of the package wasn't that onerous. Kunz was surprisingly cheap, the Rumanian boy could be paid in potatoes, and dear old Passafiume would take a flat fee—not more than $800 or $900, plus expenses. London orchestras worked quickly and gave excellent results, rental of the hall was practically nothing, and the chorus got peanuts and sang the best Italian in the world. So what was he worrying about?

He was worrying about Jean-Luc Barraud's cable—words that reduced his dream castle to rubble:

. . . DESDEMONA NO LONGER SYMPATHETIC TO VOICE . . .
OFFERS INSTEAD ROLE OF MARSCHALLIN . . . WITH PROFOUND
REGRETS STOP

Yes, stop.

II

Air France 002 set down at Charles de Gaulle at 1830 hours Paris time Saturday evening, temperature 12° Celsius and raining. Harry made the usual mistake: exchanged business cards with Dell and said goodbye in the plane, then had to stand around awkwardly with his greatest living admirer while they waited for *le bagage*. If he'd had a token—*jeton*, was it?—he'd have phoned Solange. Only that wasn't necessary, because *there* was Solange, standing just beyond the Customs gate, not ten paces from Jean-Luc Barraud and the Apogée driver.

" Welcome, Harry," said Jean-Luc with warmth.

"Bonsoir, Harry," said Solange without warmth.

"My cable . . . "

"Cable?" Solange replied in disgust.

She hadn't received any cable, which wasn't strange because he had never gotten around to sending it—see, had the draft right here in his wallet.

Jean-Luc, splendid chap that he was, took them all in tow—Dell, too, who had no limo of his own, which Harry found disillusioning—and soon had them crowded like pups of a litter into the narrow back seat of the Apogée Citroën.

Traffic was gruesome—an accident or something up ahead—and it took more than an hour to reach the Etoile. Solange was characteristically annoyed; she remained silent all the way in, staring out at the scenery as though she'd never seen it before—she who had never been farther from Paris than Calais. She looked tired and thin and smoked continuously, straining the Citroën's air-conditioning to the limit.

Dell insisted that they go straight to the Raphaël rather than drop him off first at the George V: "Just your ugly American," he laughed, "and, besides, your time is more valuable than mine—far more." He helped them out, got them a porter as though the car were his, helped Solange up the steps to the Raphaël's lobby, hoped "you kids" would have a ball in Paris and what about a drink up in his suite tomorrow— say about five—and then some dinner on the town? Maybe L'Archestrate, which everybody says is now the best?

Harry would have to think about it, maybe phone Dell in the morning, what with business meetings and all . . .

Jean-Luc remained the most sensitive and discreet of men. "You will be exhausted from your long flight, dear Harry. I shall leave you now, and perhaps tomorrow—over luncheon, if you feel up to it—we can have a word about Mme. Cavalieri. Mademoiselle, a pleasure to meet you," spoken in Jean-Luc's sweet English, beautifully modulated and refined.

Which Harry was unable to match when Jean-Luc had gone. "Sorry about that—mix-up at the office. Damned secretary was supposed to—"

"Don't," she said. "It's not necessary."

"You look terrific. Come upstairs while I unpack and then we'll get some supper."

"I've had my supper," she said. She lighted another cigarette; blew out the smoke with effort.

"When did you start smoking again?" Hating the sound of his voice. "Most people are trying to stop."

"I don't remember. After you left the last time. It gives me something to do with myself. When I don't hear from you."

Telltale circles of wetness under the arms; poor kid was nervous. Obviously, this little tête-à-tête meant more to her than it did to him. "Well—I'm a poor writer. As we know." He tried to laugh, but failed. "Come upstairs. You can at least be comfortable."

"I don't feel like going to bed," she said, getting the smoke all over him. "I'll wait in the lounge. I've come to tell you goodbye, Harry."

They were all bitchy like this when you didn't answer their letters. "Suit yourself."

Meaning what? That he would sleep alone his first night in Paris?

He had stayed at the Raphaël perhaps two dozen times in ten years: it was just steps from the Champs-Elysées and within reasonable jogging distance of the Bois de Boulogne, where he would run in the morning. They gave him his regular suite overlooking the Avenue des Portugais and the old Majestic Hotel, where an end to the Vietnam War had been negotiated. On the sideboard he found a chilled bottle of Krug Brut '69, Private Cuvée. He opened the bottle and drank a first glass. Very fine. He found the card: "With the compliments of Leisure Time Industries, Ltd." Alix had arranged it, of course. He wondered, briefly, what it was costing him. Still, it tasted fine. Nothing wrong with fine champagne, whatever the source.

Maggie had done a superb job with his bag. Wonderful little woman you've got there, Chapin; going to make someone a fine wife. The right number and colors of shirts; his favorite ties; his jogging shoes carefully wrapped in polyethylene bags. Even washcloths for steaming the face before shaving: European hotels didn't seem to know about those. He poured himself another glass of the Krug, began putting away the underwear and discovered, under the neat row of rolled-up socks, a handwritten letter:

Dear Harry:

Today I'm going to write down some of my thoughts and try to keep them from evaporating before you get home.

First—please know that I appreciate how hard you work; and I am always impressed by how much you are admired by the men you work with; and I'm pleased that the woman you've chosen to come home to is me.

But for all these years that we've been together, we've only been *playing*—there hasn't been a truly serious commitment between us. Last spring and summer, only habit kept us together.

While I was in Brad Snow's office today, he asked me why I sometimes talk like a little girl. Automatically I answered that I probably hadn't grown up yet. Thinking about that, it seems to be exactly true. It's almost as if you and I, the parents of teenagers, are ourselves just getting through a grotesquely long adolescence and are about to become grownups at last. I am ready for it now—aren't you?

Harry, I think we can have a marriage of the highest quality. And that is the only kind to settle for.

Maggie

How could she *do* such a thing to him? But then she'd always known how to make him ashamed.

One of the telephones set up an annoying clatter.

"Yes? What is it?"

"Monsieur Chapin? The young lady inquires—"

"Tell her I am ill. Tell her I will phone her tomorrow. Or if she would come to the telephone now . . ."

No, that was not necessary; the young lady understood.

He finished his unpacking; finished the champagne, too. There was no TV and the radio didn't seem to work. He soaked in a hot tub for an hour and then, dressed in one of the white terry-cloth robes supplied to guests, he buzzed for the *maître d'hôtel* and ordered a bottle of Courvoisier.

After two glasses, he felt quite drunk. From one of the writing tables he took a pad of cablegram forms and began to draft a response to Maggie's letter. But words—thoughts—would not come, and after one more try at the radio he lay down on a divan in the sitting room and fell asleep, dreaming of women.

2

The jogging shoes remained in the closet: no unnecessary movements possible until he'd had his *café complet.*

Jean-Luc Barraud came at 11:30. Harry opened the French windows; the rain had stopped and he and Jean-Luc drank their Tío Pepes to the pastel hues of a Parisian rainbow. A Sunday procession of Catholic laymen moved resolutely down Avenue Kléber, followed shortly thereafter by a troop of World War II veterans in uniform. This colorful scene and a second Tío Pepe improved Harry's mood so dramatically that he ordered a bottle of champagne, Taittinger in contrast to last night's Krug.

"Your cable came as quite a blow, Jean-Luc."

"I was sorry to send it, dear Harry, but I thought you should know as soon as possible."

"And you think she is serious? About the Marschallin?"

"I believe so. But you will be able to judge for yourself. I have set our appointment for tomorrow morning at eleven."

"Fine. But the Marschallin—what would possess her—"

"My personal opinion? I think it is Herr Otto Kunz. You know they have always been very close, from the earliest days of her career— even before the man from Detroit. And now they see a great deal of each other and he encourages her. They talk together of her return to the stage. But now they talk of German roles. Of *Der Rosenkavalier,* as I have said."

"A role she's never performed on the stage—am I correct?"

"Perfectly correct, dear Harry. But then she will say to you, 'Well, what of Callas, who had not done Carmen on the stage but who has made the best recording?' She has answers for every question, dear Harry."

Jean-Luc: intelligent, perspicacious, sensitive. The Man in the Cardin Suit, always immaculately tailored in the peak-shouldered style of the rue du Faubourg-St.-Honoré. Jean-Luc came from a wealthy family near Tours and worked not because he had to, but because of the service his family had always performed for the arts; his father and grandfather had themselves been pianists of reputation. A graduate of the elite École Polytechnique, Jean-Luc spoke excellent English, having lived for a time in London; but still he lacked confidence, asking always, "Have I used the correct word? Am I being idiomatic?"

"So what then, Jean-Luc, remains for us to discuss with the lady? If her mind is already made up . . ."

"There are a number of topics, dear Harry, of great interest to the lady, if not to us. For example—she never again wishes to sing Puccini or Verdi or Mascagni or Leoncavallo or Catalani or Bellini or Donizetti —the list is very long. She has outgrown these composers."

"The composers who have given her her career and her fame."

"The very same."

"Ridiculous."

"Instead she feels that she is now ready—now 'artistically mature,' I think she will say to you—to undertake the German repertoire."

"Beginning with Strauss?"

"Strauss, yes—then Weber and finally Wagner."

"She *is* crazy."

"She believes in Otto, and Otto tells her that she can be the very best of all German sopranos."

"Why would he say such a thing?"

"He has been tutoring her in the German language, and he says that today—in the absence of real German stars—she can be at the top. Also, dear Harry, Otto has ambitions for himself."

"Oh?"

"Yes, to finish out his distinguished career by becoming a director and producer of opera. That opera will be, of course, German, the language of his birth."

"And what of *Otello*?"

"I think—and, again, this is only my personal view—I think Otto is perhaps realizing that he cannot go on forever—that his voice is not, shall we say, what it once was? And perhaps he has even contemplated —correct word?—that he is now past Otello. That he can no longer sing the role for records."

"I'm appalled."

"As are we all—we, your colleagues in this endeavor."

"You don't think I can talk her out of it? The German idea? And back into Desdemona?"

"You have great charm, Harry, and the lady thinks most highly of you. But there is Otto, always Otto—and he has appealed to Edith on grounds not available even to you."

"Ah . . . There is romance, are you saying?"

"Romance, yes—together with the lady's true respect for Otto as artist. Otto has come forward with this new Ochs of his—an Australian of the name Noble Morris. I have not heard the gentleman, but I understand that he will make his debut at Covent Garden next season. Otto wishes to direct and produce a new production for Covent Garden, with Edith as the Marschallin and Morris as Ochs. In addition, he wishes to make a film of the production, in the manner of Karajan."

"God help us."

"But I am telling it badly. Tomorrow the lady herself will make a far superior presentation and—who am I to say?—perhaps you will be persuaded."

"Not likely."

They finished the Taittinger in silence. Harry preferred Krug, he decided, but Taittinger was also very fine.

"There are several other aspects," said Jean-Luc at last, "but perhaps you would care to discuss them over luncheon?"

"I would," said Harry, getting up to dress, "or not at all."

Jean-Luc suggested restaurant Paul Chêne on rue Lauriston, which he knew to be one of Harry's favorites. Harry had the noble *boeuf bourguignon*, as he usually did, with boiled potatoes and fresh asparagus and a bottle of young Chiroubles, the best Beaujolais.

"To Edith, then," Harry toasted. "And to Desdemona."

"*Santé* . . . Do not be surprised tomorrow, dear Harry, if the lady asks us to stay for luncheon. Regrettably, her new chef is a Maltese and the cooking quite unforgivable."

"Then let us cancel the engagement. I have not come to Paris to suffer Maltese—"

"I speak only in jest, dear Harry. In point of fact, it is quite essential that you see the lady."

"You are obviously concerned, Jean-Luc. Is there another problem—beyond the question of repertoire?"

"Please forgive my perhaps—humorlessness? Is there such a word? There are, yes, other problems of a serious nature."

"Tell me, good friend. Perhaps there's something I can do."

"This is precisely my thought. I shall explain. . . ."

Harry topped off their glasses and listened with greater sympathy than he normally mustered in such affairs.

"Edith has for some time been under the care of a spiritualist. Yes, this is the correct word. She is convinced—she has told me this personally—that her recent vocal problems are not at all physical, but merely the reflection of certain well-known emotional—illnesses. Thus, she has retained an Indian gentleman—I cannot recall the name, though she has told me—who has prescribed a course of therapy. Including, I believe, some measure of hypnosis."

"My God."

"All quite proper—I am told. This same gentleman has treated, I believe, quite a number of opera singers and obtained very fine results. From what Edith says."

"The poor woman. She's obviously psychotic."

"What I tell you now, dear Harry, I would not tell another soul. I must violate a confidence to do so, but I feel I must share this—responsibility—with another person who cares as deeply for this lady as I do. . . . Edith has, only four weeks ago, attempted to take her own life."

"You're not *serious?*"

"Perfectly serious, dear Harry. This is why I cannot make light—correct?—of her present conduct."

"But *why?* What would drive her to—"

"Oh, it is well known—the source of Madame's present distress. The gentleman in Detroit. Are you aware, for example, that he has now sought other companionship? After so many years by Edith's side? It is true. A young woman who is now a celebrated American television personality. A lady, I am led to believe, who appears at the breakfast table each morning in twenty million American homes."

"I don't keep up with the gossip columns, Jean-Luc—no, I had not heard. And you think—"

"To have wasted the last ten years of her life in vain hope of marriage, and now . . ."

Harry signaled for a second bottle of the Chiroubles. A bona-fide nightmare—and he had thought of his visit to Paris as little more than a paid vacation.

"There are two further items, dear Harry. . . ."

"Tell me."

"First—the lady has not been entirely honest with us."

"What do you mean?"

"We find, dear Harry, that the lady is secretly planning to make recordings for another company."

"I don't believe it."

"It is quite true. Yes, beginning with an album of American 'pop-songs.' "

"Just *incredible*. But what label?"

"Unknown. British, it is thought. With enormous advances and high royalty. So I am told."

"Then she is through, of course. It's all over. Finished."

"You anticipate my final point, dear Harry."

"Oh?"

"In truth, Edith can no longer sing."

"Her famous vocal problems. Well, even in her prime, Jean-Luc, the voice was not perfectly produced—"

"No, no—I am saying this badly. Please forgive me. What I am attempting to say is that the lady cannot sing *at all*—not for records and never again for the public."

"But how do you know? How can you be so sure?"

"I have taken steps to secure verification. You and I, in fact, shall hear for ourselves. Tomorrow night, at Salle Vauban. The lady has booked the hall for a private rehearsal, and I have prevailed upon an associate of long standing—the gentleman who is the source of this sad news—to admit us. Quite confidentially, of course. It you are will-ing . . ."

It was all a fantasy. Harry drank down his wine, poured some more. On the one hand, the lady was committed to *Otello* and demand-ing *Rosenkavalier*. On the other, the lady could not sing and yet was making an album of popular songs for another label.

"Upon further reflection," Harry said, "perhaps a brandy would be in order. . . ."

"And may I recommend, dear Harry, the *charlotte aux framboises*? I think you will find it absolutely ravishing—correct expression?"

II

Jean-Luc's car next morning was a Rolls Camargue, as Harry had re-quested. Edith would expect a man of his position, a *directeur des artistes*, to have a proper automobile waiting downstairs; and who could tell, perhaps she would permit them to take her for a drive or even go to a restaurant or have a bottle of champagne at the Ritz. But this was unlikely: the woman lived like a hermit.

Edith's empire was situated at 30 rue Franklin, overlooking the Palais de Chaillot and the Parc du Trocadéro, with only the Cimetière de Passy separating her from that other retired lady, Mme. Callas. Per-haps all the aging beauties would end up here in the Sixteenth Arrondissement. Even for the Sixteenth, Edith's was an exceptional residence. Mr. Detroit had installed his *amour* in a veritable palace, a four-story affair of incredible splendor. Originally four apartments, the building had been converted in 1966 into one large town house with Edith's living quarters on top, the kitchen and several dining rooms below, the staff's quarters below that and, on the ground floor, a large reception hall and two acoustically isolated studios, each equipped with a ten-foot Steinway, so that Edith and another artist of her choosing—most recently Otto Kunz—might rehearse independently. *Paris-Match* had judged the value to be in excess of one million dollars, which, for Mr. Detroit, was not a serious sum of money. As frosting on the cake, the gentleman had recently provided a trust fund guaranteeing the lady approximately 400,000 francs per annum for the rest of her life, sufficient to cover taxes and upkeep and enable her to retain necessary staff.

Their ring was answered by Harry's long-time acquaintance Toto, Edith's butler and chauffeur, who came down in the ancient wrought-iron lift to receive them. "Madame is expecting you in the grand salon, messieurs."

"Why don't we walk?" said Harry. Jean-Luc, who had ridden the lift before, agreed. Toto looked perplexed, then irritated, then resigned; finally led the way. Very polished fellow, Toto: a Spaniard of some education, he seemed to Harry a kind of latter-day Valentino, gliding from room to room, a shadow rather than a presence, devoting his life to Edith's every want and pleasure—body servant, weren't they called, in India? "Oh, what would I do without my Toto?" Edith would exclaim. Here she was, a normal woman—mad as sin, but "normal" in a physical sense, Harry supposed—trapped without a man—*her* man now gone off to other capitals of the fantasy world with some video queen, leaving Edith with—Toto.

"Sherry, messieurs?"

Tío Pepe at eleven o'clock: no accident, for Edith was meticulous about observing other people's habits and life-styles. In her way, Edith was the most thoughtful of women, and the least considerate.

Suddenly they might have been in church. Toto's eyes sought the floor, head bowed. Jean-Luc rose instantly, as did Harry. Silence reigned. Harry—who had known the woman for fifteen years—could not speak. He had absolutely forgotten the drama, the *power* of Edith Cavalieri.

Breathtaking. No doubt about it, the most beautiful opera singer in the world, as advertised: tall, queenly of bearing, all pink and white in some kind of floor-length morning gown. White satin slippers, golden hair upswept and held in place with diamond clasps, face unnaturally smooth and even-toned. Of all fifty-year-old (or more) women in the world, she was unquestionably number one. *La prima donna assoluta,* Edith Regina.

"Well, Harry? Do we not kiss any longer?"

He kissed both cheeks, as did Jean-Luc in turn. She smelled of—
paradise.

"The Tío Pepe? Is it to your taste, Harry?"

"Perfect, as always. May I say, Edith, that you look quite marvelous
—and shame us all at this hour of the morning."

"You are still, dear Harry, the only man worth knowing in your
trade. Besides Jean-Luc . . ."

His trade. How precise. A woman with total command of the
language; not just English, but the human language, which she spoke
with unparalleled ease and accuracy, never an unneeded adjective or
wasted syllable.

She seated herself upon a nineteenth-century divan in the Egyptian
style, an authentic museum piece like everything else in the room. Harry
recalled attending a midnight supper for fifty persons in this same salon
following Edith's return to the Opéra almost a decade ago: gold flatware, Baccarat crystal, the entire affair produced by Maxim's, which
closed for the evening so that staff could move its operation from rue
Royale to rue Franklin. There had never been such a dinner before or
since.

"And have you seen the Strausses recently, Harry? How is Leonid?
His heart—I hope it is not worse."

"Leonid is very well—as is Sylvia. No, no further trouble with his
heart. They both ask of you constantly, of course."

"Leonid has always shown his devotion. Please give him my love."

But not Sylvia? Ah, the old tension. "I shall, with pleasure. . . ."

She said nothing more, waiting for Harry to commence hostilities.
Well, then, m'Lady . . .

"Jean-Luc has told me," he ventured, "of your current apprehension, Edith dear—"

"It is not apprehension, Harry. Let us be quite candid."

"Of course. Let me begin again. As pleased as we are, Edith, that
you have consented to go again into the studio—"

"You act, Harry—you and Jean-Luc and *everyone*—as though I
have been in retirement and am just now attempting a *comeback*. I
have never retired, Harry, as you know. I *do* wish the press would clarify
this. You have influence—I wish you would use it on my behalf, with
your friends at *Time* magazine, for instance. . . . I am *not* the only
prominent singer who has experienced vocal problems. . . . Problems
which have necessitated a regrouping of one's forces, a momentary
pause in one's career . . . So you see, it is not at all extraordinary that I
should now say to you, dear Harry, that I am interested in pursuing a
new and different path in my travels. . . ."

She was very beautiful, but there was now a flaw: her speaking voice, especially toward the end of these speeches, was shockingly thin, pale and ill-produced. But he would not be prematurely critical: perhaps she was merely saving herself for the big aria in the second act.

"The Marschallin. Yes, Jean-Luc has—"

"I know you will laugh, because in this respect you are the conventional male, Harry. You doubt my German and you have a hundred other objections, I know without even asking. . . ."

"You do me a profound disservice, Edith—"

"Please don't interrupt. Otto and I have worked long and hard in his language, and I think it unfitting and even unkind of you, Harry, to doubt, without hearing a note, that the Cavalieri interpretation will be in any way inferior. . . ."

"My dear Edith—"

"As we mature, we demand works of greater intellectual content. Frankly, I am sick to death of the Violettas and the Normas and the Mimìs and, yes, even the Turandots. I am sick to death of Puccini and I am sick to death of Signor Verdi—not that I am ungrateful, for these two gentlemen have provided many rewarding moments in a career which, I believe you'll agree, has seen its share of triumph. But now . . . I am ready for new challenges. . . ." Fading again. The voice reedy and unsupported.

Privately he might have agreed with her. What had *his* masters always taught *him?* The only great composers: Beethoven, Schubert, Mozart, Bach. Maybe Haydn, but no others. Edith was right for once: have nothing to do with Verdi or Puccini or any of those.

"Most understandable, Edith, and we—Jean-Luc and I, on a personal basis—would have no trouble in accepting these new interests. Even the Marschallin, which, as we all know, poses really enormous problems. However—"

"Oh, I do hope, Harry, that you are not going to be tiresome in a business way, because, frankly . . ."

"If I am tiresome in any way, dear Edith, you will throw me out."

"Yes, that is so. I must say I do miss seeing you, Harry—why don't you move to Europe? How can one possibly conduct a classical business from Burbank, California?"

"I agree. Please consult my boss. In the meantime—"

"Jean-Luc, have you told Harry of our discovery? Our new Baron Ochs?"

"Madame—"

"He has a most amusing name, Harry. Noble Morris. Very English, or Welsh, I think. From Australia, where all operatic Englishmen seem to come from these days. And he sings like an angel. I don't know

why you record companies always fail to find real talent. What would
you do if I didn't find your new singers for you?"

"We would all go out of business, dear Edith, as you know. He is
really fine, is he?"

"He is miraculous and he shall be our Ochs. Otto says he has never
before heard such an Ochs, and thus our plans for a new production,
Harry—which I'm sure you can arrange for Covent Garden or perhaps
even New York, though I think we shall prefer to begin here, in one of
the smaller houses. Otto favors Munich, but the two of you will make
your decision, and Noble and I shall abide. And film, Harry—Otto is
certain that our Austrian friend will wish to make one of his films of our
production, and thus we shall have a great success and you will sell
a great many millions of records."

The chimerical world of Edith Cavalieri: he had forgotten the
breadth—and depth—of Edith's self-deception. He found it now quite
frightening. He stood up, placing his sherry glass on the lovely marble
mantel. "Do you mind, dear Edith, if I stand while I talk? And will you
promise to *listen* for a moment—without comment or interruption?"

"I have been a naughty girl," she said, "and Papa will now discipline me for my excesses." She gave Jean-Luc a delightful wink.

"I shall not be tactful, Edith. I shall be candid, as you have suggested."

"Yes, Papa."

"The Consortium does not now require a new *Rosenkavalier*. Our
catalog contains a perfectly respectable—"

"Oh, but that one is *scandalous!* Otto has himself said—"

"*Please*, Edith. Our catalog contains a perfectly respectable recording, albeit getting on in age now. And even if this were not the case, I
seriously doubt whether we would be of a mind to invest over a hundred
thousand dollars—which is what such a recording would cost today—in
a work which, sorry to say, has never sold, irrespective of cast or conductor. This is point number one."

"My—Papa is angry indeed," pouting.

"Point number two. The Consortium *does* require a new *Otello*—
namely, the Cavalieri-Kunz *Otello* which has been in our recording
plans for many years. Naturally, as voices age—*all* voices, Edith, not
only yours or Otto's—technical difficulties may become more pronounced. And believe me when I say that such considerations apply
more even to Otto's role than to yours. However—fortunately for us
all—amazing things can be accomplished these days, both in the studio
and in the edit rooms afterwards. So that, should you be worrying
about a particular passage—a particular note, even, which is no longer
comfortable for you—it is not unheard of today, dear Edith—I might
even say that it is almost *routine* for us to indulge, in the interests of

absolute perfection, in some discreet 'overdubbing.' Adding a bit of voice here and there, fully beyond detection by any listener or critic. So you see . . ."

Edith, too, was standing at this point. "And you imagine that I would stand for such—*deception?* You would use this 'overdubbing' to put another voice over *mine?* Is that what you are saying, Harry Chapin?"

"I'm saying that such techniques—"

"Really, Harry, I cannot think why you should offend me in this way. The instrument may not be all that it once was—I am, after all, approaching fifty years of age—yes, I am not ashamed to say so—but it is still superior, dear Harry—especially, as I should have thought you in particular would know, in the middle range as well as in chest tone—to all other voices of which I am now aware."

"My dear Edith, you need not persuade the persuaded—"

"I am only sorry that I cannot demonstrate for you this instant— but it is quite impossible. The instrument must be warmed interval by interval, especially following such—such a sabbatical, shall we say. . . ." Wan smile, generous motion: colleagues, yes, three professionals practicing their art in this shared moment of privacy.

How had he let matters get so out of hand? "With respect, dear Edith, to Desdemona—"

"I know what you are thinking, Harry. You are thinking, ah, Edith is no longer happy *technically* with the Venetian lady and is thus fleeing to another role. But I assure you that you are wrong. *Emotionally* I am no longer Desdemona. Let us admit—which I am willing to do here, before two very close personal friends—that our past vocal difficulties have been a matter of emotional stress. . . ." Her eyes went briefly to two richly framed photographs atop the piano: Otto Kunz on the left and a smiling business executive—Mr. Detroit—on the right. ". . . But that stress is no longer felt. An artist must be at peace with herself, as I am today. And with peace has come a renewed desire to work. I am singing every day, Harry, and with each session the voice is stronger, more pliable, yes, more beautiful. . . ."

"For which, dear Edith, we can express only the most profound happiness. But—and again I ask your indulgence—I must speak as a businessman on this occasion. I must speak of harsh realities. Frankly, Edith, the Consortium cannot go on scheduling and rescheduling, canceling, booking, always canceling, in the face of the substantial costs of such 'indispositions.' On the strength of your most recent commitment—made to me, as I'm sure you remember, as recently as the Christmas holidays—we have once again made *every* arrangement, including reservation of Walthamstow Town Hall. We have contracted for the services of the principals and conductor of your choice. And now, Edith,

to hear from Jean-Luc, in what can only be regarded as the eleventh
hour—when matters are simply beyond canceling except under the most
onerous financial conditions—that you no longer find Desdemona to
your taste . . .''

She took a step nearer to him; glared with shocking emotion. "Oh?
And what of your *insurance*, Harry? Have you not gone behind my
back, as I am told, and asked Lloyds of London to insure your ridiculous
Melos-Doria against what you have the *nerve* to call my 'failure to
perform'? Or would you call this an Act of God? That your dear
Desdemona is no longer suited to the Cavalieri voice?"

Ah, *now* we are seeing the *real* Edith Cavalieri: no more of the pale
and ladylike imitation, but the true bitch come out from behind her
masking cream. Note the shaking hands, the heaving breast.

"That is untrue, of course," said Harry evenly. Technically untrue,
at least: Hilary Cairns had made the inquiries, not Harry.

"I have my sources."

"Your sources, then, are in error."

"But what is the point . . ."

"The point is, dear Edith, that we, like the legendary Cecil B.
DeMille, have our army of extras in place, the cameras are rolling and
we await only the arrival of our star. Except that now, as I understand
it, our star is asking us to change to another script."

"Perhaps you would prefer another star."

"Not at all. Our interest in *Otello* is solely a reflection of our
interest in Edith Cavalieri and Otto Kunz—"

"If Melos-Doria no longer values my services, perhaps another
company . . ."

"This gets us nowhere, Edith—"

"I still have my public, Harry. Or perhaps you do not agree?"

"Of course you do; your unique popularity is not at issue. It is only
because there *are* other voices to be heard on record these days,
Edith—"

"You refer to Sills, no doubt. Yes, I have seen the paid publicity,
which Melos-Doria has been so reluctant to provide in support of my
own career. Still, I do not consider *L'Assedio di Corinto* at the Metropolitan to be a career, do you, Harry?"

"But surely, Edith, you're not serious. Why, the lady has sung in all
the great houses—Scala, Covent Garden—"

"Then perhaps you will wish to ask Miss Sills to be your
Desdemona, if you are such an admirer."

"Edith, my dear—we have known each other for, what is it, fifteen
years now?"

"Which is why, Harry, I am more than a little surprised—yes, and
hurt—that you should treat me in this way."

"Not at all—"

"If I were someone you had discovered yesterday in one of those bargain-basement opera companies, Seattle or Dallas . . ."

Ah, the veiled reference to Mme. del Campo, who had been known to work such towns.

". . . But I had rather supposed that my own position *vis-à-vis* your company . . ."

"Your position, dear Edith, remains unique."

"Above even that of your precious Didi?"

"Mme. del Campo is your greatest fan. She is most grateful for the assistance you have given her career over the years."

"She displays her gratitude only through mischief. The rumors she has spread of my 'farewell' tour, if you can *imagine* . . ."

Meandering down yet other paths which would lead them nowhere. "Edith, my dear, it occurs to me—rather tardily, I'm afraid—that Jean-Luc and I have perhaps chosen a less than ideal moment for this discussion. You are working tonight, I know, and your mind must of necessity be consumed by far more important artistic considerations. We are under no obligation to resolve our differences today. Why don't we arrange to see each other later in the week when we have had an opportunity to think further?"

Chapin's Law: When in doubt, temporize. Do nothing and the problem will normally go away. But probably not now; not with this lady.

"Yes, perhaps you should think further," Edith said. "In the meantime, we work—and progress is made. I only regret, dear Harry, that I cannot invite you to come with us this evening while we rehearse. But it is something which, as you will appreciate, is of the most private nature, and which I cannot share even with you."

"I wouldn't dream of imposing, as much as I would cherish such an experience. Perhaps another time . . ."

"And you will forgive me, I hope, for not asking you to stay to luncheon. Piero, our chef, has not had good fortune in the markets."

"Perfectly understandable."

"You've heard about poor Fritz? To lose one's accompanist at this stage . . ."

"A tragedy. The boy has such talent."

"But of course I still have Toto, who is making great strides each day. I don't know what I would do without Toto. . . ."

Toto succeeding Fritz Mann as accompanist! The world was completely mad. Car, bed—now even piano. Bravo, Toto!

III

Edith's beautiful blue Silver Shadow eased into Salle Vauban's inner courtyard promptly at 7:00 P.M. Harry and Jean-Luc, watching from a dingy bistro across the street, gave the lady fifteen minutes—and themselves a second Calvados—then went to the side entrance, where an old friend of Jean-Luc's met them with whispers and hand signals: lady and accompanist at work in the main auditorium, nobody else in the building.

Jean-Luc led the way downstairs to a network of passages beneath the auditorium floor. As they stumbled along—Harry holding on to Jean-Luc's jacket—they could hear the piano above them, but no voice. They walked the length of the hall and emerged at the other end, climbing another staircase to the stage itself, which was also in total darkness. The main curtain was closed, but through a peephole Harry could see them: Toto seated at a piano in the middle of the auditorium, Edith leaning over him to examine some point of the score. The only source of light was a single naked bulb hanging from the ceiling.

"Psst," from Jean-Luc, calling Harry to another vantage point. Unfortunately, the stage was littered with scenery and props, and Harry immediately kicked over some metallic object—a music stand?—which fell with a crash.

"I hear you," said a coy voice: Edith. "Someone is back there. Come out, come out, whoever you are. . . ."

Edith sounded relaxed and in good humor: not at all the tigress of their morning adventure. Harry and Jean-Luc froze in place, Harry praying that she would not come after them—or, worse, send the all-purpose Toto.

"Come out, come out, whoever you are," she repeated. "Or we shall send for the *gendarmerie*."

How to explain? Impossible. She would be mortally offended.

"*Personne que moi, Madame. Pierre. Je vous en prie de m'excuser. Je suis tombé dans l'obscurité.*"

Jean-Luc's friend the caretaker! Such relief. Such joy! Even in the dark Harry could see Jean-Luc's smile. With infinite caution they took seats on a sturdy bench near the lighting board.

Edith showed no further concern. "Then let us begin," she said to Toto. It took Harry several bars to determine the language, but he recognized the melody at once: "Oh, What a Beautiful Morning!" In English but with most of the consonants swallowed and thus indistinguishable—and with horrendous accompaniment by poor Toto, who had obviously never heard the song before except in Edith's rendition.

Poor Spaniard, having to sight-read Rodgers and Hammerstein: a cruel occupation, eh, *Señor?*

When the initial shock had worn off, Harry listened to the singing. . . . Mmm—the old *squillante* bite up top . . . And the foggy middle with lots of chest tone: that lasted till the very end, he supposed. . . . Oops—upward portamento not so nice. Not much in the way of dynamics—not much volume, either. Nothing very *bella voce* about this lady; but that had never been her forte. . . . Drama still there—but he hadn't remembered all that breathy gushing. . . . Ouch!—nothing above the staff, please—that was meant to be what, a B-natural? He wanted to hum a scale of his own, to be sure of his place, but there was no point in taking such risks. . . . Yes, key of G, he was sure enough. Next time try it in E: a woman of fifty, after all—or even more. Old for an athlete. Dear Edith, you haven't been keeping up the daily dozen—got to exercise, any novice knows that. After all, what was a voice, any voice, but a set of carefully trained and controlled muscles? With no exercise the muscles became flabby; the miraculous electrical connections between brain and throat developed unpredictable short-circuits, resulting in unpredictable . . .

Broken off now in mid-phrase, the voice dry and dead-sounding: no ring at all even here on the perfect resonating board of the Salle Vauban. After a short pause, they began again—this time *"Pioggia,"* beautiful little song by Respighi, one of Harry's favorites. . . . But not for you, dear Edith, no, not any longer; though you retain your marvelous sense of style and your winning histrionics, the instrument itself has deteriorated—never again to be restored. . . . Control gone now; sustained notes sagging in pitch or collapsing into a breathy wobble; the top octave completely unsupported . . .

"Have you heard enough?" Too sad even for Jean-Luc, who had never been quite the fan that Harry was.

Yes, quite enough. The most exciting singer in the world—turned into a self-indulgent, self-deluding, middle-aged woman. To think that so great an artist should have fallen thus to human passions—victimized by hopeless love of some idiot auto-maker. The very stuff of tragedy . . .

I V

Norman Rose arrived from New York the next evening. Harry had never been so glad to see anybody in his life. He wouldn't even let Norman go up to the room, but rushed them into a taxi and raced over

to Harry's favorite bar in the world, the Espadon of the Ritz, there to
have a chilled bottle of Roederer Cristal and a complete ventilation, as
Deering would have said, of *l'affaire Cavalieri*.

"She *is* crazy, of course," Norman agreed. "Remember when she
asked us to have *Domingo* make a test? Domingo, who could, even
then, have any part he wanted with any opera company in the world?"

"One can't be too careful. What do you think—of the champagne?"

"Magnificent. Did you really go jogging in the Bois de Boulogne
this morning? Very chi-chi stuff, Harry."

"A losing battle. Do you realize that I have gained seven pounds
since last Friday? Where will it all end?"

"Doesn't Jackie Kennedy—or Onassis, I guess you call her—doesn't
she jog there, too?"

"All the best people, yes."

"The Marschallin. And you think Edith's serious?"

"Perfectly serious."

"Entirely Kunz's work, of course."

"*Der neue deutsche Svengali.* Except that this aging Trilby can no
longer utter a squawk. Yet, cheerful swine that he is, Otto tells her she
can still sing anything she wants better than anybody else. No morals. I
wish the Ritz served nuts."

"You know, Harry, she *could* sing again—"

"Never. Believe me, never. I am a witness, remember."

"If she will only avoid the G-A-B area—never touch any role with
an A above the staff. God knows, there *are* pieces. Carmen, perhaps.
Santuzza. If she could be satisfied . . ."

"A woman never satisfied. Like all women. Even without nuts, I
believe this to be the finest champagne I have ever drunk."

"Mmm—superb. I went over the score again on the plane—*Otello?*
There are obstacles, of course."

"Yes, yes—as in real life."

"Don't suppose she can still float the *dolcissimo* high A-flat at the
end of the 'Ave Maria,' for one thing. Never really very strong up there,
even in her prime. (Yes, thanks, don't mind if I do.)"

"I offered a solution to that. We'll get some bright young thing
from the chorus, dear Edith, I said—girl with a soaring gorgeous top—
girl like you, dear Edith, twenty years ago. You, my dear, do the best
you can at the sessions—make whatever noise it is you now make—and
then we'll bring in Miss X and plant her eggs directly over yours—do a
little fast and fancy cross-fading at the board—*voilà*, a perfect performance."

"She refused, of course. Well, good for her."

"Norman, don't be an ass. *Not* good for her. The lady would undoubtedly like us to do it, but she would like not to *know* about it. Or, rather, not to have Otto know about it. My opinion."

"Cynical man, Chapin."

"Is that English oratorio girl still around? The one we used in the Cherubini that time?"

"Watson," said Norman, who never forgot a voice. "Lucille Watson. Yes, I think so. Married now, I believe, but still able to sing."

"Could do high A-flats all day long, no?"

"Oh, yes. Watson could knock the spots off Desdemona."

Then why the hell didn't they record *her*? one might have been tempted to ask. Except that Miss Watson, or Mrs. Whatever as she now was, weighed three hundred pounds and couldn't act a lick and had the charisma of a turtle and undoubtedly wanted nothing more than to have the usual ten kids and a rotten summer place at Brighton.

"Well, it's an idea," Harry said. "Anyway, let the dogs bark. The caravan shall pass."

"You're as pissed as I am. I think I'm getting pissed."

"Excellent. Finish up. Can't order another till we finish this one. What about Didi? Did you see her?"

"Certainly."

"And?"

"She wants her aria record."

"Don't they all. Of course, nobody buys them. Did you tell her that?"

"Also, wants another photo session. Doesn't like any of the stuff they did on the Coast. Decided she wants Helmut Newton."

"The *Vogue* guy? Charlotte Rampling in the nude? People living out their fantasies?"

"Bizarre and erotic—yes, that one. Or else Scavullo. Oh, and she hates the tracks she did with Martoni. Wants them scrapped—wants to remake the whole session."

"Fuck her. First she learns to sing—*then* we think about remakes. Did you tell her—"

"Told her nothing. As instructed. Oh, and she's planning to get married. Groom unidentified and something of a mystery."

"You're *kidding.*"

"Serious."

"You *must* be kidding."

"Does it *bother* you, Harry? You and she—you're not . . ."

"Love that girl, but no, we're not. A less gentlemanly fucker than I might, on hearing such insinuation, blacken your eye, Norman."

"My apologies. No peanuts or pretzels in this place?"

"Monsieur? . . . This time, the Heidsieck Diamant Bleu, *s'il vous plaît* . . ."

"Do you know that man?"

"Where? Oh, shit."

Hoyt Dell: what, you here at the Ritz? Chubby little rascal—why not join us?

"Knew exactly where to find you, Harry! Only the best places! I don't believe I've had the pleasure . . ."

"Norman, meet Hoyt. Hoyt, this is Norman. Only fucking decent record-producer in the business."

Dell sat down, drank the final glass of their Diamant Bleu. Before Harry could order more, Dell said he had an idea: why not come back with him to his new hotel? George V just unbearable now, since the change in management—sold out to English people! So he'd moved into L'Hôtel, fashionable spot on the Left Bank, near the Ecole des Beaux Arts. Why not have some supper with him—great place for laughs!

Harry couldn't think of any reason not to. Norman did whatever people said. Harry had stayed at L'Hôtel in '68, soon after it opened; had slept in Mistinguett's bed, which seemed the main attraction in those days: whole room done in white fur or something. The thing he remembered best was the little refrigerator in the bedroom, fully stocked with champagne, spirits of all kinds, soda, anything one wanted. And downstairs, in the lounge—there wasn't any restaurant, as he remembered—you ate in individual alcoves on the main floor. And wasn't there a monkey cage?

The place was jammed. Even Dell had trouble getting a table. Finally they asked another party—was that *really* Ava Gardner?—to consolidate, thus freeing a very nice alcove with its own bar and a table for at least eight. The food wasn't much, Dell advised, but they served a perfectly acceptable *entrecôte* and the wine list was exceptional. Harry nodded; prepare his *entrecôte au point, s'il vous plaît.*

Oh, but this is such a shame, Dell felt: should make a *party* of it! Perhaps call some friends?

Harry laughed: he had an idea.

First, did they have any of that champagne in the clear glass bottles? (Memory left behind at the Espadon.) Yes, of course, Louis Roederer Cristal! Served at once, for what looked like $55 a bottle, but Dell signed the tab before Harry could be sure. Mmmm. Finest in the world. Dell agreed. Norman agreed. A girl from around the corner— Ava's party overflow?—agreed.

Ah, yes, now this idea of yours, Harry . . .?

They brought a phone to the table, plugged it into the wall, gave him the operator. He got straight through to Solange. Solange had never heard of L'Hôtel—Solange, who had been *born* on the Left Bank. But after only the slightest resistance, she agreed to come—and, what's more, to bring a friend called Huguette. Harry was flabbergasted: more of the old Chapin magic, eh, Messieurs? Or perhaps the poor girl simply hadn't had her supper yet.

So. Things picking up, eh, Norman? Dell made Harry order the wine, a Chambolle-Musigny from a shipper of repute. And *entrecôtes* for the girls, too, who would arrive any minute now. All girls liked *entrecôtes*, in Harry's experience.

Hold on, wasn't that—Tony Perkins or Warren Beatty, which? He always got them mixed. One of the two, certainly. And the *ladies*—this Dell had pretty good ideas.

Still no girls for them. While we're waiting, Dell said, come up and see the room. Norman stayed behind, to watch out for *les femmes*. Harry brought the Roederer with him. The hotel was built around a central well, like the core of a medieval tower—you could look up and see all the circular passageways on each floor, or look down and see the edges of the little dining rooms and the ground-floor lounge. Oscar Wilde died right here, Dell kept saying. Harry missed the name of the guy who'd actually had Dell's room; somebody famous. Dell showed Harry the little refrigerator, just like the one Harry used to have, in 1968 was it? Harry finished the Roederer, and sat down by the telephone. He wanted to phone Alix in L.A. Dell was the kind of fellow who wouldn't object. But then the phone rang: it was Norman, who was stuck with two girls.

Dell seemed partial to Huguette, so they put her next to him, with Harry on the other side, then Solange, then Norman. Norman had to shout to be heard, but he wasn't saying much anyway. The *entrecôtes* were all *bleu*, which nobody had ordered, but nobody seemed to mind. Solange never stopped smoking; most people are trying to stop, Harry heard himself saying again. She looked very tired, but she was in pretty good humor, for her, and she allowed Harry to hold hands with her under the table. Sitting close to her, Harry could see one of her nipples. He thought of buttoning the top of her blouse, but nobody else could see anything, so why spoil the fun?

After the Chambolle-Musigny they sent for Clos de Vougeot. You had one great Burgundy, you had 'em all, Harry's motto. This Dell sure laughed a lot. Mick Jagger! No, really? Well, it sure *looked* like him. Where was everybody going? Huguette made Dell take her into the living room, or whatever they called it, to see the monkey. Yes, there *was* a monkey cage in the living room, as he had remembered. Harry wanted to kiss Solange, but Norman would be embarrassed—Harry squeezed her hand instead. Solange whispered something to him in French, but he didn't get it. She looked very thin; her breasts had been fuller the last trip. Maybe it had been her period the last time, he couldn't remember. When Dell came back, he bent over and whispered to Harry, too: he said, hey, if you kids want to go upstairs, to Mistinguett's bedroom, why not? What for? Harry said.

The girls must have been hungry: ate every bite of their steaks, even the gristle. For the third bottle, they stayed with Clos de Vougeot, which Norman said was better than the Chambolle-Musigny. The guy they thought was Tony Perkins stopped by with his terrific-looking girl, who seemed to know Huguette: Harry couldn't quite make out the conversation. The Tony Perkins one was very nice, very polite. When the Tony Perkins one left, the owner appeared and hoped they were enjoying themselves. They said they were. And then a bottle of Pol Roger came, with the compliments of the Tony Perkins one. Harry did not ordinarily drink champagne after Burgundy, but tonight was an exception, being a celebration. He couldn't think of what. He poured another glass for Solange, who asked him why he was crying.

Harry left them. He sat at the Tony Perkins one's table and had a sip of the great-looking girl's drink, which he didn't like. Could it have been bourbon? In the living room he found the monkey's cage, but the monkey was gone, probably visiting in one of the alcoves. Not Solange's, he hoped, because Solange said she hated the idea of animals being cooped up in cages. He went into the cage and sat down. There was a regular chair inside, which the monkey used. A waiter asked him if he required anything and Harry said yes, a telephone. The waiter brought one at once.

Harry said he was Mr. Dell, but the operator said no he wasn't, because Mr. Dell spoke French with no accent. She took his call anyway, and while he waited, the Tony Perkins one's great-looking girl saw him and got him a bottle of Pol Roger, charged to Mistinguett, and two glasses.

"*Monsieur Chapin? Voici Los Angeles au téléphone. Ne quittez pas, Monsieur.*"

"Harry?" said Alix.

"Good morning."

"It's afternoon, Harry. Where are you? What's that noise?"

"I'm in a cage."

"In a what? I can hardly hear you, Harry. Have you seen Mme. Cavalieri? What did she say?"

"Fuck Mme. Cavalieri."

"You've been—drinking, Harry."

"Of course. Alix? I love you."

"You should go to bed, Harry. You'll feel much better in the morning."

"Alix? Alix?"

"I've got to go now, Harry."

They disconnected him. The monkey had come back and wanted to sit in the chair. Harry couldn't seem to stand up. Then Norman and Dell and Solange and Huguette came by. They wanted him to come upstairs. When Dell began to pull on his good Saks suit coat, Harry hit him as hard as he could in the face.

They put him to bed in the room where Oscar Wilde died.

3

"With your standards, Harry," Norman said, "you're going to have a lonely old age."

"Did I hurt him? Was he cut or anything? Tell me what to say—how to apologize, Norman. For Christ's sake, help me."

"If I were Mr. Dell, I would be very angry, Harry. You expect too much of people. You don't have much small talk, Harry, that's your trouble. You gave him a bloody nose."

"How did I get back here?"

"I brought you. Hoyt took the girls home. He's really an awfully nice fellow, Harry. You *do* owe him an apology. He got blood all over a very expensive suit."

"I'll buy him another one."

"You won't buy him anything. He's extremely generous, and he's got loads of money."

"Fuck him, then. That phony."

"Yes, Harry, you are going to have a lonely old age."

After more coffee, Harry sent Norman away. For once in his life, he couldn't stand the idea of lunch. Instead, he lay down and took a nap. He dreamed of a conference. The hotel was the Schiphol Airport Hilton at Amsterdam. He liked that hotel—it had an indoor swimming pool and sauna and nice little restaurant—and had always meant to go back with some appreciative young thing sometime when there was no business to occupy him. Now—in the dream—he was attending repertoire sessions and naturally saw himself unprepared, whereas all the others were primed to annihilate him with overwhelming figures, negative estimates, career-destroying facts and figures; which they did, leaving him to shout himself awake at the rasp of the telephone.

It was Norman. "What are you doing, Harry? Right now?"

"I'm in bed. Why?"

"Good. Don't get up."

"Shit."

"I mean it. I'm going to tell you something and I don't want you to get excited. How's your head?"

"I'm just fine, Norman. Am I the first person in the world who's ever had too much to drink?"

"I've just been talking to Maury. Maury Wiseman."

"What does he want?"

"Now don't get upset. He's right here. In Paris. At—the Ritz."

"You must be joking."

"No, I'm serious. And, you know—I think I like this boy more than ever."

"What the fuck's he doing here? He's on his own money, I presume."

"He's heard about Cavalieri. Alix showed him the cable from Barraud. He's come to save our ass, as he explains it."

"God, Norman, I hope you're making this up. Because if that bastard is actually *here*—"

"He's here, Harry, and I think it's a good thing. He has some ideas and I think we owe him an audience. When do you think you'll feel like talking?"

"Right this minute, if that bastard's actually here."

"Why don't we say thirty minutes, your place? . . . Harry? Are you there?"

"I'm here, Norman. But barely . . ."

He ordered up a French beer, Kronenbourg, and drank it in the shower. He felt marginally better. He put on clean underwear and his bathrobe and slippers and lay down on a divan in the sitting room. Norman and Maury arrived moments later.

"Hi, boss," Maury said, extending his hand in greeting.

Harry did not reciprocate. "We'll save the hand-shaking for later. Call the waiter, Norman, if you want something to drink."

Norman ordered Scotch; Maury said he would try the Kronenbourg. Harry agreed, without enthusiasm, to another beer. "And what brings you to Paris?" spoken acidly to the boy wonder. "Vacation, I assume."

Maury looked uncertainly to Norman.

Norman nodded. "Go ahead, Maury—don't be bashful. It's your meeting."

"Now, boss, I know you're mad—"

"Call me that one more time—"

"Sorry—Harry. Look—I know that my coming here like this may seem a little presumptuous—"

"A *little* presumptuous? Be aware, Mr. Wiseman, that the only reason you're still on the payroll—temporarily—is that Mr. Rose here is a much more mild-mannered and reasonable gentleman than I ever hope to be. But go on—don't let me interrupt."

The Kronenbourg was working; the yellow-green feeling in his stomach had gone to gray; with each modest burp, he felt relief.

". . . Now that Cavalieri has taken herself out of the package— well, I've got an idea"—Maury working now from a large file folder in which he had apparently gathered all elements of his scheme—"on how we can go ahead with the *Otello* that the Consortium expects you to deliver—and make ourselves a strong commercial package for the U.S. market at the same time. . . ."

"You couldn't tell us this on the phone? Save the expense?"

"Come on, Harry—give him a chance," from an unusually compliant Norman, who'd never had much use for the boy before, as Harry recollected.

"Forgive me. I stand corrected. Go on, Mr. Wiseman. And just how do we work this miracle?"

"What I'm proposing is—we junk the rest of the old package: Kunz, who's past the part anyway; Florescu, who was a mistake from the start; and the old man, Passafiume, who—you told me this yourself at lunch the other day, Harry—was just another of Cavalieri's hang-ups."

"Replacing all these misfits with—what? Who? Whom?"

"Okay. Now this is the plan. First—we dump Otto."

"Thus buying a lawsuit. Be sure to include that in your budget, Maury, because that much is certain. You cut Otto out of *Otello*, which he's had in his contract for about ten years now, and you meet him in court."

"With all due respect, Harry, I don't agree," said Maury.

"What Maury is saying, I think, Harry—"

"I *hear* what he's saying, Norman. But, with all due respect, I suggest that *I* know Otto Kunz a hell of a lot better than Maury Wiseman does—or even you. But—who am *I*? Go ahead, Maury. Finish your pitch. We can tear it apart later."

"I was about to say that I think we can avoid a lawsuit by giving Otto a substitute. And not necessarily this year. Promise it to him for next year, or the year after. *Lohengrin*."

"*Lohengrin?* Which costs even more to record than *Otello?* Five LPs instead of three?"

"I've worked out some estimates, Harry. And by careful scheduling of the sessions . . ."

"Okay. Let's not worry about details now. Go on. Instead of Mr. Kunz—who?"

"Laframboise. Like I told you at St. Germain, Harry . . ."

These young fellows never seemed to learn. "Put Laframboise aside for the moment," Harry said, his tone reasonable, even friendly. "What about Desdemona?"

"Again—and I only ask, Harry, that you keep an open mind until you've heard the whole package—"

"Anybody want anything else to drink? I think I'm going to switch. What would you say to some wine? A little Bordeaux?"

Norman stuck to Scotch; Maury would join Harry in Bordeaux. Harry asked the waiter to bring up some chips, too, and some olives, if they had any, or perhaps some hors d'oeuvres—yes, even better. "I appear to be coming back to life," he said sotto voce to Norman. "Go on, kid—tell us more."

"The logical candidates have all recorded the part for other labels. Freni, Jones, Tebaldi, even Rysanek. Caballé would be perfect, but she'd never follow Cavalieri into our set. Zylis-Gara? Good, but no box-office. Jurinac? I love her, but over the hill. Scotto, Crespin, De los Angeles? Not really, if you think about it. Callas, Schwarzkopf? Too late. Which leaves us with who?"

"Whom," said Harry.

"Whom, then? A lot of ladies can do it, but are they really first-rate—and will they sell records?"

"Lorengar?" said Norman tentatively. "Heard her in Berlin, 1969 or '70—really quite convincing."

"Or what about Carlyle?" said Harry, warming to the exercise, knowing it was going nowhere. "Remember—we saw her at Covent Garden? What, '66? '67?"

"I am thinking, gentlemen," Maury went on impatiently, "of the most obvious and the most *logical,* from our point of view, of all the ladies who now sing the role."

Really, this boy could be most irritating. Most obvious? Oh, now *wait* a minute, he didn't mean—

"You disappoint me—you two high mucky-mucks of the classical business. What about our very own Didi del Campo? What about the most gorgeous cunt in all grand opera?"

* * *

An imaginative piece of casting: unorthodox and just a mite hokey. Didi del Campo, all bust and ass and thirty-six years of total female experience. More to the point, already under contract to Melos-Doria. Commercial? Indubitably! Young Mr. Wiseman had the early *People* article as well as the recent *Playboy* spread ("The Met's Swinging Diva Gets It Altogether") there in his file. Didi was known the world over by laymen and opera buffs alike as the horse-riding, Bennington-schooled singer who, a few seasons back at Santa Fe, created a sensation in a new production of *Otello*—yes, *Otello*—playing the death scene in a filmy nightgown and ending up nude to the waist, *quel scandale!* She'd received the usual critical crap about too-much-too-soon—the Met at twenty-two, all those guest shots with Johnny Carson, a red-blooded "Star-Spangled Banner" at the Super Bowl—but nothing seemed to bother her. At Bennington she'd been captain of the debating society as well as field hockey: even then she was famous for her big mouth, which she'd learned to put to other uses, everybody knew, after yet another piece in *Playgirl* or *Viva* or *Oui*—Harry couldn't remember which one.

Too much woman, really, for Harry. Five-nine, 140 or more and heavy upstairs. The voice, when one got around to such things, was not extraordinarily large, but it was even over the entire range and clean and pleasingly girlish in timbre. Obviously, she didn't practice enough—like most people of natural talent—but when would she have time, a girl with her range of interests? God (casting an eye over the *Playboy* stuff again), she had nothing to be ashamed of in the tit department. "Great nipples," Mr. Wiseman concurred. But the point now was the lungs behind those nipples—the lungs of Desdemona?

"Norman? You're the vocal expert. What do you think?"

"Well, yes, Harry, she can *sing* it. Easily, in fact—plenty of range. The voice is smaller than it should be—impossible to hear, for example, in San Francisco. But that needn't bother us in the studio. Mind you, I have serious reservations about her *ever* making a proper Desdemona on the stage. Still . . ."

"The point is, Norman, can she sing it on records?"

"The voice is naturally thin above the staff. But I don't suppose anyone cares about such things anymore, so why should I? Certainly, she can sing it on records."

Maury looked relieved.

Wonderful, wonderful, thought Harry: everything going just fine: got everybody, even Norman Rose, abandoning his principles. "How do we know she'd be interested? Or available? Undoubtedly booked."

"She's free—itinerary right here," from Maury, who had covered all bases.

Hmmm. Holes from mid-August to October 1. Last job at Tanglewood on August 11, *Barbiere di Siviglia*. Fat lot she knew about singing Rossini. Or Verdi. "Looks possible, I suppose. If not desirable."

"No harm in asking her, is there?" from Maury.

"There can be, yes," said Harry with sublime patience. "Especially if the lady agrees and you later decide, for one reason or another, not to do it—or to use somebody else." Using people, his specialty. "But let's go on. The Iago?"

"There simply haven't been any Iagos," said Norman, "since Gobbi and Merrill."

"Boris Makhov," said Maury in a tone of voice that suggested an end to further discussion.

If only the boy displayed even an *ounce* of humility. "You've *heard* Makhov?" asked Harry.

"Only the aria LP in which he does the 'Credo'—and it's magnificent."

"He was murdered, of course," interjected Norman, "at La Scala."

"Not so," said Maury. "The *singing* was praised. It was his stage manner they hated—the critics accused him of playing Boris Godunov. He sang in Russian with the rest of the cast in Italian, but he was *learning* it in Italian. He must know it by now."

Makhov, star bass-baritone of the Bolshoi, supposedly the greatest singing actor since Chaliapin. It would be something of a coup to draw this celebrated artist into a Western recording studio. But—there were so many imponderables in this *cacciucco*. "And what conductor?" Harry asked.

Maury smiled. "Now, boss—I'm *sure* you know the answer to that one."

He did. Who but Gian-Carlo Ponti, current Chapin protégé? Had Gian-Carlo not complained bitterly to Harry just days ago that he, Ponti, should be doing the Cavalieri *Otello*, not Edith's creaking old Passafiume? Wasn't *Otello* one of the very few operatic scores that Ponti considered worthy of his talent?

Harry ticked off the obvious problems. "Gian-Carlo is, one, a notoriously slow worker in the studio, meaning that he could absolutely ruin us in a so large a project. Two, he has never undertaken a complete-opera recording. Three, he would ask two years' preparation time. Four, he would never accept any of the singers we proposed. Five, he's a pain in the ass."

"Six," said Norman with spirit, "he now cohabits with Otto Kunz's wife and we are talking about dropping Kunz from the project."

"Seven," said Maury, "all the critics love him and say he's the greatest Italian conductor since Cantelli, maybe even Toscanini."

"Eight," back to Harry, "all the delegations on the Committee would support him except the Germans, who hate him as a result of his Berlin debut, where he made an ass of himself conducting Beethoven and Brahms the way he conducts Respighi. Oh, God, *must* we play this game? Isn't anybody else hungry around here? What the hell time is it? What do you say to a little dinner, on ol' Harry Chapin?"

II

He walked them down the Champs Élysées to Fouquet's, lecturing them along the way on the glories of eating on the terrace; but it began to drizzle, and they had to settle for a corner table in the upstairs dining room.

"Now then," said Harry after a glass of the house red, "I suppose, Mr. Wiseman, that you will wish to tell us about Mr. Laframboise."

Harry and Norman swapped smiles; watch now, this is going to be fun: brilliant young long-haired coke-sniffing revolutionary departmental assistant will now tell two famous old hands how to run their business. Sure, he's got no shareholders asking *him* embarrassing questions at the Annual Meeting; thus easy to say, fine, dump Cavalieri (who, let's face it, had already dumped *them*), dump Kunz, dump Florescu, dump Passafiume, dump everybody in the name of Art and Youthful Exuberance; make the fucking *Otello* with a bunch of people who look good on paper and may, given a sufficient number of miracles at session time, produce acceptable noises from their throats and balls and cunts and elsewhere.

". . . Ezekiel Woodrow Wilson Laframboise, twenty-nine years old, of New Orleans, Louisiana, is going to be, gentlemen, the next great star tenor of the world."

"The Great Black Raspberry, I prefer to call him," mocked Harry, "having known the bastard since my cradle. Since *his* cradle, actually."

"I say we give him *Otello* now," persisted Maury, "while he's cheap, instead of later when he'll be expensive—very, very expensive, given the laws of supply and demand."

"And end up," said Harry, "with an *Otello* featuring a totally unknown tenor; Didi del Campo, who's not really a serious Desdemona; maybe this Russian baritone, whose Italian is awful; all under the guidance of a Swiss ascetic named Ponti who's never made a complete-opera recording before in his life, because, among other things, he hates opera and nobody is dumb enough to put up money for such a venture. Except maybe *us*, you're saying? I tell you, Norman, UCLA Masters of Arts ain't what they used to be. . . ."

"Pay no attention, Maury, he gets this way," Norman counseled. "Go on—the idea intrigues me."

To hell with them both. Harry would enjoy his wine now, say no to the project later.

"What sort of voice is it?" asked Norman. "I've not yet heard him in the opera house. A pushed-up baritone, is he, judging from the *Trojans* excerpts?"

"Kind of, yes," Maury began.

"*No!*" Harry protested. "Definitely *not* a pushed-up baritone. Jesus, Maury, you don't know what you're talking about. All right. Let *me* tell you about Zeke Laframboise. . . ."

Like Verrett and Treigle, Zeke was born in New Orleans, where his mother was a soprano for the Ephesus Seventh-Day Adventist Church. Zeke began as a boy soprano, but Mama got him out of the chorus soon enough—temptation there to sing louder and higher than anybody else, which could ruin your threads, which was what Zeke called his vocal cords; got to preserve the threads, man, he liked to say.

Mama was the major influence in Zeke's life. His father had run off when Zeke was a baby. Zeke never was certain how the family survived in those early days, but he had suspicions that Mama ran a house for rich honkies in the French Quarter. Whatever Mama's occupation, the family never went hungry, even though Zeke had seven sisters and four brothers, some younger, some older. Mama saw to it, in those early years, that Zeke entered as many competitions as she could find, singing someplace every week, getting lessons from an old black woman, Mattie Bush Carter, who had something of a reputation, and taking as many prizes—usually a bag of groceries—as he could. At Andrew Jackson High School he became the regular assembly singer, doing the National Anthem and various hymns and becoming, on the side, All City and then All State linebacker, which brought him to the attention of that famous Harvard football recruiter, Mr. H. E. Chapin II.

But Zeke passed on Harvard, preferring to accept a full scholarship to Grambling in Louisiana, where he made All American two years running: a great ham-handed black bugger with the voice of an angel: Black Angel Ezekiel, the New Orleans *Times-Picayune* once called him. Grambling was good for him because it gave him back his confidence. Just after high school—against the wishes of Mattie Bush Carter—Zeke had entered the Met Auditions, singing in those days as a high baritone, and had lost: frozen at the last minute, scared to death by the unfamiliar dry acoustics of a hotel ballroom. For three months he wouldn't sing a note. On the football field he got back his strength and his nerve.

When he made All American the first time, he decided to be a tenor, stretching his high baritone that final third, because that's where the money was. He would come down to New Orleans by car every Saturday (except in football season, when it would be Sunday) and spend two hours vocalizing with Mattie Bush Carter. Reluctantly, she showed him his first operatic scores; played him his first records—Caruso and Martinelli and Melchior and Bjoerling. Right away Zeke thought he sang better than all those folk—just a matter of time before he put them to shame.

During Zeke's senior year at Grambling he was scouted by the Philadelphia Eagles. He brought bad knees and a terrific ego to training camp, and they tried to make a guard out of him. Unfortunately, Zeke was too small for the pros—six-two and 240 pounds in those days, which was fine for Grambling but puny for the Eagles. One good pop in the second game of the exhibition season put Zeke out of pro football for good.

Harry next saw Zeke at Curtis Institute, also in Philadelphia. Harry was in town to have lunch with a friend on the Curtis faculty, and there was Zeke in the hallway—now maybe 265 pounds and a full-time tenor. Zeke appreciated what Harry had done in trying to bring him to Harvard, and they began to correspond irregularly. Zeke was not happy at Curtis. They made him study piano, theory, harmony, counterpoint, solfeggio, musical dictation, history of music: he hated everything but "studio," which meant singing. His principal tutor wanted to make him back into a baritone so that he could sing Porgy and be a second Paul Robeson—except that, in addition to having a nice warm baritone's middle, Zeke had this silver-sword top, all the way to B and even C if he was feeling right. They also tried to make him sing softer—not worry all the time about how *big* the voice sounded—but nobody could get through to him. Like most young singers, he thought he had all the time in the world; so that, fresh or tired, well or sick, he sang all-out on every occasion. They told him—as had Mattie Bush Carter—to mend his ways or he would have nothing left at thirty, much less fifty. This constant criticism, plus his natural aversion to language study—terrible German, awful French, even bad Italian—put him out of Curtis without a degree at the age of twenty-four, a "finished" singer, ready to conquer the world.

At first it looked like he would. While he was still at Curtis some local impresarios booked him, sight unseen, for a *Pagliacci* in Düsseldorf—his first professional appearance as a tenor. That led to a *Lohengrin* in Mannheim, which was canceled in rehearsal when the Germans heard his German. After that, in Germany, he was known as Ezekiel Laframboise, the French tenor. Following an ill-advised but well-paid *Carmen* in Strasbourg—the first black Don José in the history of that house—he was known in France as Ezekiel Laframboise, the Italian tenor.

Although he found reasonable amounts of work, Zeke was astonished to discover that the operatic world didn't fall at his feet. So he did the only thing possible: got himself a new vocal coach, the illustrious Donofrio Zito, a third-rate baritone who—while others were away at war—had served the Metropolitan briefly and none too well in the seasons 1942–43 and 1943–44. Signor Zito told him not to worry—"Anybody can pronounce the words correctly, but God lets only a few *sing* them as you can"—and introduced Zeke to dozens of scores, German, French and Italian, the language making no apparent difference. Zeke's fortunes seemed, again, to be on the rise.

For one thing—in 1975—Zeke's old friend Harry Chapin came forward with an offer of work: three LPs in three years, beginning with excerpts from *Samson et Dalila,* which Zeke had just performed with success at Frankfurt. His European activities eventually got him work in America—American Opera Society at Carnegie; duets with another young singer at Tully Hall; soloist with an orchestra here and there (mostly Verdi *Requiems,* which he could toss off with fantastic aplomb—a most dramatic black man in evening dress); summer opera at Aspen, that circuit. How many dramatic tenors were abroad in the land? Not many. For volume, there was no other tenor in the world like him. In 1976 Zeke did a Manrico at the Maggio Musicale in Florence, and after the "Di quella pira" there was a twenty-minute standing ovation. Zeke never really had to worry about engagements after that.

". . . His powerful black voice smote the air, rending the orchestral fabric like a silver sword. . . ."

The reviews were increasingly full of nonsense. So that after five years on the Continent, paying his dues at places like Aachen and Münster and Lübeck, singing every kind of shit (as he called it) in three different languages sounding all the same, he had finally reached Paris and was ready to go home again: ready to *destroy* the Met, which had never let him finish higher than third in their stupid auditions and which could have bought him for peanuts two seasons ago but which would now pay him $3500 per night for his Manrico, a black-assed troubadour who would cause the ladies to wet their panties at the matinees.

Oh, yes, unquestionably the Otello of a lifetime—even got the color right for once. . . .

". . . In short, Norman, voice of unusual timbre and production. Steely on top or when pushed—a little like Roswaenge, perhaps. But warmer below, with a strong chest register and a nice baritone quality down to maybe the low B. More powerful than Domingo, but less beautiful too. Not cold steel like King, but tempered like Bjoerling. Somewhere between McCracken and Vickers, maybe. But more lyric than either. A hard voice to describe."

"So I gather."

"So why don't we just go *hear* him?" from the exasperated Wise-man.

"Where?" from a startled Chapin.

"The Opéra. Tomorrow night. *La Juive.*"

Black man playing an old Jew, the Caruso role. When this Wise-man sets you up, he really sets you up. "We probably couldn't get tickets this late—"

"I have the tickets. Right here." Tossing the hateful ducats down between cheese and wine.

"Is there anything *else* we should know?" said Harry. "To save our time? You haven't signed him to a new contract, have you? Already *given* him Otello? Nothing like *that?*"

How far, thought Harry Chapin, I might have gone, with this boy's nerve. Drink your Burgundy, old man, and keep your mouth shut.

"It seemed logical, boss. . . ."

Well, my fine-feathered friend, you are most assuredly in the wrong business, if it's logic you want. "Well," Harry muttered, "we'll see how we feel tomorrow. No point to it, probably. Meanwhile . . ."

They stood together on the Champs Élysées, the usual fine drizzle in effect. Across the wide boulevard Harry could see the neon-draped façade of a theater playing a delicious semi-porn epic he'd been meaning to catch. Maybe later—when the boys had gone.

Wiseman made it easy for them: said he wanted to get some sleep.

"I know where *he's* going," said Norman as the boy faded into the darkness.

"Where?"

"*Le Crazy Horse.* Never seen the real Parisian striptease. He asked me to join him, but I declined."

"Why didn't he ask *me?* I'd have gone."

"There are some things one doesn't ask one's boss."

"*This* kid? With *his* nerve?"

"He *is* bright, Harry. Perhaps too bright."

"Meaning?"

"Bright and ambitious."

"Naturally. He's twenty-five. Even *I* was ambitious at twenty-five. So?"

"So it's easy for him, Harry, to put forward risky propositions."

"Like Zeke?"

"Because he's not taking the risk. You are."

"Hey, I get paid for taking risks. No one's making me do anything against my will. You don't really think we're going to make *Otello* with Zeke, do you?"

"Oh, well, fine. Then there's no problem."

"Hah! There's nothing *but* problems, Norman. Which is why we must do nothing. You know my motto."

"Yes, temporize. I agree with you. A policy that seems to make more sense all the time . . ."

I I I

First thing in the morning, Harry phoned Jean-Luc at the Apogée offices and got a line on Zeke. As Harry might have guessed, Melos-Doria's fugitive linebacker was staying at the Grand, across from the Opéra, and was to be found by midday at the Café de la Paix, where he took an early luncheon. Harry waited till noon, then headed over by taxi—disregarding his own advice, temporize.

A young and nubile lady reporter working one of the bush-league opera houses in Ancona or Bologna had, as early as 1971, christened Mr. Laframboise *"il più gran tenore del mondo."* Do not think that the general public was very much impressed by this as a singing title, but it meant a lot to Zeke—who took her to mean greatest rather than biggest, this being in the days before Pavarotti. Harry had no trouble in finding *il più gran tenore del mondo,* for he was sitting—a *jeune fille blanche* by his well-padded side—at a prominent table on the terrace along the boulevard des Capucines. Harry did not recognize the girl— late twenties, blonde, animated—a fan, perhaps, who had asked for the great man's autograph. The quality of patronage at the Café de la Paix had sadly declined: American tourists, mostly, noisy with their cameras and exclamations, schooling around the terrace like mackerel; cold-blooded creatures in total disregard of the great Laframboise.

My, the boy looked heavy. Very heavy. *"Come va?"* Harry said.

"Va bene, va bene, così sempre," said Zeke, rising ponderously, an ironic smile revealing one gold incisor in a mouthful of ivory.

Followed by an unexpected *abbraccio:* yes, this Andrew Jackson High School boy had been working the European circuit long enough to pick that up. Great soft hands, heavy and wet to the touch; nice smell, too.

"Now that we have exhausted each other's Italian," said Harry, "may I join you?"

"How *be* you, brother?" making room for his kin Harry Chapin. "Say greetin's to sweet sister Claudia here. Been readin' about you, great *Hahvud* man, in ol' jive-ass *Time* magazine."

"How do you do? Yes, well—"

Sweet sister Claudia was not smiling; looked hostile, in fact; kept both hands under the table.

"Maybe you know Claudia's old man," said Zeke. "Bevilaqua? You dig him?"

"Well, yes, of course," said Harry, drawing his chair up to the action. "*Great* pleasure," he tried again with the white chickie. Ramón Bevilaqua, Harlem's Poet of the Revolution; seen a little *Time* magazine himself, had he not? Burn, baby, burn: one of Ramón's more memorable lines.

Claudia had to go; whispered in Zeke's ear; got a fistful of francs for her trouble; took off.

"Always buyin' stuff," Zeke explained. "You like?" with a lascivious nod toward her fast-disappearing rump.

"Very nice."

"Split from Ramón, who's a pretty bad dude. Makin' the grand tour with dis here *Número Uno.* But how *be* you, brother? Been *missin'* my white cousin."

"Been missing you, too, Ezekiel. May I?" Pointing to Zeke's tempting carafe of red wine.

"Hep yo' self, brother."

Zeke's special dialect, put on for people he liked; but uttered now without much spirit. Unless he took pains, Zeke tended to talk like everybody else, with hardly a trace of his bayou upbringing. For a man who was supposed to sound like burnished brass (among other metals), Zeke had a most unimpressive speaking voice. In fact, like most of these rare animals, he hated to talk at all; felt that talk was bad for the voice; used a muffled whisper, really: had an irritating, hesitant quality that made his listeners want to clear their own throats and say to him, "Speak up, speak up!"

Harry poured himself a half-beaker of the red.

"Little *acqua?*" said Zeke.

"No, straight's just fine. I'm not in training."

Zeke grunted in approval—or disapproval, Harry didn't know which. Zeke was having his usual pre-game meal: a couple of steaks, a green salad, a pitcher of red wine, a bottle of soda water, a loaf of French bread to clean the palate and soak up the acids. Like most of this breed, Zeke drank nothing but red wine, preferably Italian (part of the mystique, like hockey players hitting the goalie's pads with their sticks before each period), which he cut fifty-fifty with soda water, producing the most vile drink imaginable. Sipped wine and water all day long, stuffed himself with vitamin C, never went to the movies, stayed out of public places—surprised he was here on an open terrace, though of course he wore his muffler; only man in Paris that day wearing a muffler—praying always to God that when he tried it out (as he constantly did, driving everybody mad), the voice would still be there.

But not looking much like an invalid. Deep-brown corduroy slacks with flared bottoms, blood-red silk shirt under a heavy leather jacket, the black wool muffler, nice Italian boots. Heavy mutton-chop sideburns plus the Afro made Zeke look like some wild-eyed preacher on an educational TV channel, maybe heading up the community's addict-rehabilitation program.

"Well, now, Ezekiel—cheers and *buona fortuna.*"

"Same to you, man. *Salud.*"

Harry drank; Zeke sipped.

"You look a little heavy, Ezekiel."

Zeke smiled deprecatingly. "Two eighty, maybe ninety," whispered.

"That's a little over your playing weight, isn't it?"

"Not for *Otello,* brother," said oh-so-smoothly: broad smile this time, exposing the soon-to-be famous larynx.

Looked manageable, but had some smarts; the old story. "*Otello?*"

"Little birdie pissed in my ear."

Mmmm. Little Birdie named Maury Wiseman, who had thus outlived his always questionable usefulness. "About *Otello?* That would seem unlikely."

"Don't give me no fuckin' jive talk, Mr. Harry Chapin," spoken loudly now, with massive indignation. "I know you toadies are going to be out there tonight giving your brother an *o-di-shun.*"

"An evening's entertainment, Ezekiel, nothing more. Surely none of us—who, I remind you, had the good sense to sign you to a recording contract some years ago—none of us would consider it necessary to *audition* Ezekiel Laframboise, a distinguished artist in his own right."

"Shiiiiiiiiiiiiiiiit."

"No, really, Zeke—and I'm speaking now as a friend, not as your business associate. To speak of auditions at this point in your career is—ridiculous. My young colleague—Mr. Wiseman, I assume we're talking about—may have given you the wrong idea, for which I now apologize. *Otello*—well, it's no secret that we've been planning for some time to do an *Otello* with Cavalieri and Kunz. And that project—that project has been postponed, again, for reasons which would only bore you. No, we're simply casting around now—testing, in principle, some new ideas. We still owe the piece to Kunz, of course. But—always thinking ahead, as we must in this business—it seems reasonable for you and me—being in the same city, as we are—to have a discussion. See how things stand with you. Find out what your own desires are. Test the temperature of the water, as it were."

"Jive talk. Nothin' but jive-ass fuckin' cop-outs."

"Hey, look—"

"I thought we were going to be *honest* with each other, brother. Didn't you tell me that? Didn't you say, Ezekiel, you got any problems, you come straight to me, honest Harry Chapin, and I'll level with you? Jive talk . . ."

"Which is why I'm *here*, Zeke. If this *Otello* matter bothers you—"

"Hey, baby, *Otello* don't *bother* Ezekiel. It's going to be Ezekiel's free ride—you *know* that."

"I've not actually heard—"

"What about your *ass-sistunt?* He was at Munich—what did *he* say?"

"He says you were quite marvelous. But that's not the point, Ezekiel. The point is—"

"I'm talking too much. I can't talk today. I'm working tonight."

"Don't talk, then. Let me talk. The point is this. Of *course* we admire your Otello. I don't have to hear it to know what you can do with that role. You'll be the best in history—better than Tamagno."

"So get to it, baby—the good part."

"So—we want your Moor. But not right this moment. You have plenty of time, Ezekiel. You shouldn't rush it. Later, when your voice takes on weight—"

"*Shit*, man, my voice is heavy *now*. You'll hear tonight."

"We want you singing for years to come, Ezekiel. Not simply for one season."

"Bullshit. I'm not thirty years old. Man, I'll be singing *Otello* when I'm *fifty*. How old is Vickers? He's still doing *Otello*, ain't he? How the fuck old is *he?*"

Very rough mouth for a man raised by women; Mama Laframboise and old Miss Carter would be mortified, all their Christian sentiments buried now under Grambling and the Eagles—and Curtis, which was the roughest of them all.

"Vickers is over fifty, yes, Ezekiel. But I think you'll find that he didn't cut his teeth on *Otello*. And even today he severely limits the number of performances he gives in a season."

"Fuck-all. You're trying to tell me I can't sing Otello because I'm not *old* enough? *Bullshit*. I've already got six *Otellos* for next season, and my manger's hardly even tried yet. But you ain't *heard* it, brother Chapin, so how can you *know*? You're going to make *Otello* with old Kunz when you can be doing it with *Laframboise?* Then you ain't got no fuckin' brains, and I don't care what *Hahvud* says about you. . . ."

"You're going to tire yourself," Harry said. "And there's no reason to. Of *course* we want your Otello. I'm willing to commit Melos-Doria to it right now. But there *is* the question of timing. I'm simply suggesting that before we rush into something we both may regret later on, we give the matter further thought. There's no real urgency—"

"Shit, man, I'm *doing* the piece all next season."

"But that's in Germany."

"Germany, fuckin' right. And I've got Manrico at the *Met*—doesn't that tell you where Ezekiel's going?"

"Yes, of course. I'm aware of the *Trovatore* and that's quite marvelous—"

"Because, brother Harry, when I make my debut in *that* house—you hear what I'm saying?—my price is going *up,* man. Up to the *roof.* Ol' Melos-Doria ain't gonna be able to *afford* Ezekiel's Otello after next February twelve, you dig?"

More sipping, Harry's own throat dry now from all this gentlemanly shouting. History and time on the boy's side, of course. God favored tenors over all other men—gave the voice to maybe ten percent of the whole, and only one in every million had any kind of *singing* voice, and only one in, what, a *billion?* had a voice like this big black bugger sitting across from him in what had always seemed, before, a perfectly nice restaurant.

"Ezekiel—say we *were* going to go ahead with *Otello.* What would you require—from a business point of view?"

"You know my man in New York?"

"Gravinius, yes. Know Sy very well."

"He's my man. You want me? You go see him."

"Our present contract—"

"No way, man. There's no way I'm going to sing *Otello* for that kind of bread. New contract, man. Whole new contract."

"Well—to save time—have you *any* idea of terms? Generally, as you know, we start with the idea of a six-percent royalty—"

"See the man," Zeke repeated. "But what we are talkin' about, brother Harry, is some good advance money so I got somethin' in my jeans, and a royalty as good as you give anybody, white or black. Is that terms enough? Yeah, and we are talkin' 'bout *three* pieces—not just *Otello.* We are talkin' about a Manrico, which I got in my throat today, and we are talkin' about another good piece—I don't know which one right now, but maybe *Cav-and-Pag* or maybe *Andrea Chénier,* which I'm studying this summer because they want me to do it next year in Cologne."

Incredible. Harry had been thinking of a standard contract, just the one role, six-percent proportional royalty, at most a $2000 advance. But now—*three* complete-opera sets? "This alters the picture even further, Ezekiel. Such a commitment—"

"Right on, brother—which is how come Ezekiel's tellin' you up front."

"Obviously, Ezekiel, from a personal point of view, I would like nothing better than to proceed with the *Otello*. And in timely fashion— perhaps as early, even, as this summer. But this requirement of three roles—if it *is* a requirement—well, it's simply beyond our capacity. About which I am most regretful."

"I read you, brother. Fuck-all, I dig you for the good things you been sending my way. Dig you, too, man. But I'm passin' this way only once, as my mama says, and I've got to make the most of what I got. The Krauts kinda dig me—maybe *they* got bread for an *Otello*. No harm in talkin'."

Except for that poor tired throat which, tonight, is scheduled to bellow some Halévy. "Again—these terms," Harry persisted. "There's no room for negotiation? The number of roles? It strikes me, Ezekiel, that we're talking here about an extraordinary income. I'm sure you've thought of the tax consequences. . . ."

Stupid, feeble argument, which Zeke immediately jammed down Harry's own tired throat:

"Awful big income for a *black* man, you mean?"

"That's not at all what I meant—"

"Hear me good, Mr. White Man Harry Chapin. Ah may be sepa-rate, but ah ain't equal, you dig?—'cause o' dis windpipe I got heah. . . . Got me the best fuckin' threads in dis game—else, how come de great white plantation-owner Massa Harry Chapin, he come callin' on dis low-down niggah? No, Massa Harry, dis is now mah game, and ah intends to collect mah share o' de winnin's. . . ."

But the real Mr. Laframboise soon took note of Harry's condition; came quickly to order. "I'll let you go now, brother—I don't want to *bore* you. But the time for singing 'Ol' Man Ribber' is over, Mr. Chapin, sir. You're not looking at Paul Robeson or Roland Hayes or any of those boys who couldn't get steady opera work because of their skins. No spirituals for Zeke Laframboise—this is something I learned from the Eagles. No little lieder recitals on Sunday afternoons in my mama's church because that's the only game in town.

"My old daddy—just found this out, brother, and I'm still thinking on it—my old daddy picked up garbage for you nice white folk in the city of New Orleans all his life, and right now this man is a cripple, with white man's arthritis, in a black home near where he was born in Charleston, South Carolina. Out of my first million dollars, brother Harry, which I'm on my way to getting, I'm going to take maybe a hundred big ones and give my daddy a decent place of his own and the right doctors, and he's going to spend the rest of his days in white man's comfort, thanks to what's in here, brother Harry"—big mushy black hand wrapped around that black-silver throat—"and what you white folks are willing to pay for it. I'm going to be rich—rich like Domingo and Corelli and Pavarotti and Gedda. Richer, 'cause I'm black and they ain't. . . ."

Short goddam list, which was the trouble: you couldn't fill all the opera-house seats in the world with that goddam short list. Harry nodded. "I hear what you're saying. In the unlikely event that I need to talk to you further—about the *Otello,* that is—how can I reach you? Next week, say?"

"Easy as pie, brother," with his best smile now. "Care of Ezekiel Laframboise, the Opéra, Paris, France. That'll get it. Don't need no ZIP to reach Zeke Laframboise in Paris, France. Soon won't need no ZIP to reach him anyplace in the world!"

"Just remember who signed you to your first recording contract—when that day comes."

"Right on, my man."

Ah, the poet's wife returning in the distance, packages in hand. Harry rose.

"You want my chick, brother? For tonight?"

"Thanks—but I try not to mix business and pleasure."

"Hey, man—that's your *trouble,*" said Zeke, genuinely concerned. "If you ain't got no pleasure, what's the point of de biz-e-ness?"

Harry went away, mulling that over. Brother Tamagno here sure knows his onions. . . .

I V

As soon as the final curtain descended on Jacques Fromental Halévy's nineteenth-century masterpiece, *La Juive,* Harry Chapin, Norman Rose and Maury Wiseman repaired to Harry's suite at the Raphaël, not pausing even to pay respects to their contractual artist Mr. Laframboise lest they lose the ring of his voice in their ears.

Harry ordered a bottle of the Roederer Cristal; Norman had his Scotch; Maury had a glass of Harry's champagne.

"Norman, you want to go first?"

This was a safe bet, Harry figured, because Norman knew more about singing than anybody else in the trade.

"Of course, Eléazar is nothing to compare to Otello," Norman began.

"Understood—but just give us, for now, your general impressions."

"Well. He has the right basic weight for Otello, and the right timbre. Resonant at the bottom, full in the middle like a good baritone, steely and ringing at the top."

"How high would you say he goes with comfort? Was that an interpolated C in Act Four?"

"I would judge the boy's range to be a full two octaves and a third. Yes, right up to the C—certainly down to the low A. Not to say that the whole of the range is equally well produced. The final third—well, frankly, he's got no business going above the A-flat. Also, the D-E-F passage gives him trouble—I'm sure you noticed—especially in descending figures."

"So he has the Otello range, top and bottom."

"Oh, yes, with lots to spare. But—and I hope you'll excuse me if I indulge a personal taste here, Harry—to my ears there can be a metallic *buzzing* to the voice at the top. Not all the time, but often enough to irritate—especially on records. I think we can get around this if we have enough working time, and if he has enough endurance. But it's something we must think about. I like his intonation, though—seems right on the money."

"Musicianship?"

"Hah, another matter altogether. Fairly rough-and-ready, I'd say. Sings around the notes when it suits him—probably lazy and doesn't vocalize nearly as much as he should. Fair agility, but can't do much with fast passage work. The voice is awfully big. His phrasing is about average for this stage of development—not great, not terrible. He makes the obvious points and he gives the music a moving-forward quality, which is nice for a change. He's not afraid to sing ahead of the conductor, as we saw in the big aria, if he thinks the old boy's going too slow. And he tends to save up for the high notes, naturally—they all do it at this age. . . . Mainly, Harry, I'd have to say that he needs a good coach, he needs to be told to slow down, and he'll be a good deal happier with the role—Eléazar and, I suspect, Otello—in another ten years or so."

"Ten years, huh?" from a fascinated, disbelieving Maury. "You mean you want him to wait ten more years before singing the part?"

"Another hundred stage performances, if you prefer." Norman, into his second drink already, was warming to his task. "For so young a singer, he's already picked up an astonishing array of bad habits. What are the teachers *teaching* these days? Sliding, scooping, taking everything from below—and that god-awful aspirating, like Di Stefano. I could also point to his terrible abuse of portamento and the tendency to sing everything either fortissimo or with that crooning pianissimo of his—*most* unfortunate falsetto at that, very woolly and unpleasant, to my ears at least. And nothing of the subtleties—nothing of *messa di voce*, for example, no use of head tones for variety—well, the list is endless. I don't mean to be unnecessarily harsh on the boy—because, despite the flaws, it's quite a marvelous instrument, isn't it? With training, as I say—well, there are no limits. But now—as he's presently going, keeping nothing in reserve—he makes everything sound loud, dull, monotonous. *That's* going to be your problem with this boy, Harry, in my opinion. . . ."

I believe you've made your point, Norman: Wiseman here about ready to cut your throat. So the boy is not precisely anybody's definition of a bel canto tenor, fine; we must make room for other kinds. Bel canto: "Heavy cream pouring from a jug," somebody had said; but the cream here is just skimmed milk, non-fat except for its container.

"Correct me if I'm wrong," Harry said, trying not to take sides in front of the rest of the faculty, "but I hear this boy as, eventually, a *Heldentenor*. Am I wrong?"

"I think you are very right," Norman said. "In another five years this boy's Siegmund is going to be something to hear. And Siegfried, too, later still. Not to overlook Lohengrin. He is essentially lyric in his approach and manages an exceptional legato—his Lohengrin could be very beautiful.

"But not, of course, if he starts doing Otello. That's the *real* problem for him right now, at his age. He shouldn't even *think* about doing Otello—we all know that."

"*Bullshit!*"

Ah, Wiseman: thought perhaps you'd gone to sleep. "What Norman means, Maury—"

"I just can't *believe* what I'm hearing. As though there were some *doubt* what this boy can do. Didn't you *hear* him? Didn't you *see* that audience . . ."

"What Norman *means*, Maury, is that *no* tenor should really do Otello till he's—what, fifty, Norman?"

"No tenor who wants a long career should sing Otello till he's fifty, no," said Norman, speaking only to Harry. "A half dozen *Otellos* in one season and the voice will no longer produce legato. If you don't believe me, ask Del Monaco. Ask McCracken. Ask Vinay. Ask—"

"What about *Vickers?*" demanded Maury.

"Vickers," said Norman, "it is true, learned Otello as a student and even recorded it, in 1960 when he was thirty-three, I believe. However, he is a *very* intelligent singer—the exception that proves the rule, I would say. And he puts a limit on himself. No more than eight *Otellos*, as I remember, each year."

"This is not really a unique situation, is it?" added Harry with sweet reason. "Do we want this boy to be another Rosanna Petri? Start with a rush but then have the career aborted during take-off—the voice burned up in two seasons? Or do we want him to have something left for his old age?"

Wiseman still wasn't getting the point. "Harry! Norman! How do I get *through* to you guys? This black son of a bitch is a *great fucking* Otello! He's the *best in the world* right this minute! And you guys are arguing about his old age?"

"If you think by simply raising *your* voice, Maury—"

Poor Norman. After such a distinguished career, to have to put up with a Maury Wiseman. "What Norman is saying"—explaining now for the third and final time—"is simply that, operating in a vacuum— given our druthers—we shouldn't be encouraging Zeke Laframboise to sing Otello so early in his career. You can't argue with the principle. Otello *can* ruin a tenor's voice. Otello is too low and too loud and the houses today are too big and a man's vocal cords are too small. I agree with Norman. If this were a nice world, we'd never ask Zeke to do it. We'd say, Zeke, how 'bout some *Pagliaccis* and some *Trovatores* and a *Forza* or two and maybe even *Aïda* but no *Lohengrins* and positively no *Otellos*. But this is the real world, as Mr. Deering likes to remind us, and we have little to choose from: either Mr. Kunz—to whom we owe the role, let's not forget—or Mr. Laframboise, who is perhaps a potentially great Otello. Haven't I stated the thing correctly, Norman?"

Nod of agreement from Norman, now into third—fourth?— Scotch.

"I hear what you're saying," Maury persisted, "but I still say *bullshit*."

"Maury—"

"Sorry, but that's the way I feel. Sure, it's easy for you to sit around talking about Zeke's old age. But try putting yourself in *his* place. He finds out he's got this voice, and it's like finding out you're seven feet tall like Abdul Jabbar or you got great natural speed like Muhammad Ali or you got great muscles in your ass like Henry Aaron so you can hit a zillion home runs. He'd be a *fool* not to take advantage of his gift, wouldn't he? And for him, today, that means singing Otello.

"Here we are, we've got the greatest fucking tenor in the world in our hands, and you guys want to wait maybe ten years before cashing in! You guys kill me, you really do. . . ."

Yes, my son, I know precisely how you feel. But you, too, will be middle-aged one day. Or perhaps not. Cure for middle age probably found by then.

Well, Zeke's no Tamagno, see. Tamagno? The original Otello? In 1894? Never *heard* of him? Oh, well—doesn't matter. Look, kid, this Laframboise ain't no Golden Age singer. But who knows? Maybe *this* is the Golden Age. Ever think of that, Chapin?

A circus act, that's what it is. Like tight-rope walking between the towers of Notre Dame: they pay more the higher you go. Modern-day houses—the new Met, for one—demand only two things, volume and altitude. If you are loud and high you can fake the rest. Skate over the sixteenth notes in "Di quella pira" if you like (as Zeke does), but for God's sake hit the final C fortissimo—which of course is the only way anybody who still has his *cojones* intact can reach high C from the chest.

It's crazy, the fatal shortage of these empty-headed animals with the high, loud voices. Where was God when it came to passing out the high notes: mankind mightily deficient in the high-note department, wouldn't you say? And you can't send your kids to school to learn tenoring, either: either they have the voice or they don't, and nothing you can do, including cutting off their balls (which has been tried), will produce the modern kind of tenor.

Selective breeding is probably the only answer: line up a whole batch of males and females with short thoraxes, long diaphragms, big head cavities, and set them to fucking. Immediately weed out the inevitable baritones and basses and the regular folk with their one-octave voice boxes, and start the remainder to fucking again. Eventually end up with a whole string of Giglis and Pavarottis and Carrerases—and still not find an Otello in the lot!

But stuck now with the present hit-or-miss system: no time, really, for all that breeding . . .

". . . A vote, then, gentlemen?"

Options few and painful. Dull old Otto baby, who has the piece in his repertoire and in his contract, or go with the black kid here, twenty-nine years old, with balls weighing a pound apiece.

"I vote go-for-broke," said Maury. "Zeke all the way."

"Norman?"

"I agree that the boy will—can—make a fine Otello eventually, assuming that he doesn't ruin his voice in the meantime. Now? No, Harry—I feel it's terribly premature. I would have to vote no."

"Then it's up to me." As he had known all along. "The total package being Laframboise, Del Campo, Makhov if possible, and Ponti?"

"Right on!" cried Maury.

"A package, ah, which"—Norman stuttering badly now, from the Scotch—"will *never* be accepted by the Committee."

"Bullshit! The Committee can be *sold!*" Maury barked.

Yes, Wiseman—but it's Chapin here, remember, who's got to do the selling. "It would be suicide, of course," Harry mused, "to appear even the least bit tentative in front of those wolves."

"But you've got the *goods*, I'm telling you," screamed Maury.

"Selling U.K., for example," Norman went on obliviously, "a tenor they've never heard of? For a set costing eighty, ninety thousand dollars?"

"By this time next year," Maury countered, "Covent Garden will be *dying* to get this guy. He's already *got* the Met, for God's sake. How famous do you have to *be*? Look—I'll say it again. I'm betting right now—any amount you want to bet—that this guy is going to be the next great star tenor of the world—bigger than Corelli, bigger than Domingo, bigger than—"

"And just what have *you* got to bet?" said Norman, no smile seen to grace his craggy countenance.

"I'll bet you *this*," Maury spat back. "If Harry sells Laframboise to the Committee—you guys will let me go to the sessions in London this summer. If not—Harry can fire me on the spot. *That's* what I've got to bet. So put up or shut up."

A nervous laugh from Norman; nothing more.

"I like that bet," said Harry. "Yes, I like it very much. Shall we take him up on it, Norman?"

"It *is* tempting," said Norman. "Very tempting."

"Then a bet it is."

"But you've got to *try*," said Maury, thinking now. "Really *try* to sell Zeke. Or maybe you'd like me to come along to London now and *I'll* sell Zeke?"

"Not necessary, Maury. Believe me, I shall do my very best."

And who knew more about flesh-peddling than Harry Chapin?

When Maury had gone, Harry held Norman back for one last drink. "The kid has chutzpah, huh? He certainly feels more deeply about this project than I do."

"Yes, isn't it amazing?" said Norman. "But youth . . ."

"Yes, youth."

"You're comfortable, Harry? With the idea? Laframboise?"

"I hate it."

"But I gathered—"

"The personal side of me hates it, Norman. The professional side—assuming there's any left—says we must do it. Take the risk."

"Ah . . ."

"Zeke shouldn't be doing Otello yet—you and I *know* that. But Zeke wants to do it. I talked to him this morning. He *will* do it, too—with or without us."

"Then no guilt—if that's the right word—attaches to you, Harry."

"Wrong. The guilt—and, believe me, that's the right word—very definitely attaches here. Because we make it possible. We put up the prizes. We convert his labor into cash."

"You're being unfair to yourself, Harry. The boy presumably has a mind of his own. And, as you suggest, if we don't put him on tape, somebody else will. And who knows? If he sings the role only four or five times a year—"

"But he won't, Norman—we *know* that. He'll start off saying he's only going to accept six a year. Then those wonderful offers will start coming in from all the goddam houses, the Colón in Buenos Aires, Vienna, the Met—they'll want *eight* a year for themselves—Frisco, Chicago, Dallas, Covent Garden, a dozen places in Germany because they think he's already the next Slezak there. Everybody telling him how marvelous he is and offering him the same five-thousand-a-night that Sills and Sutherland and Pavarotti get. And that will be that. A short life but a merry one. Two seasons of that and he'll have no legato left, meaning no more lyric roles, only Otello. And then his top will start to go and he'll keep forcing and soon he won't be able to make an acceptable noise anymore, and then what's he going to do for a living? He never finished college and the Philadelphia Eagles just may not want him back at guard. So what's he supposed to do? Spend the rest of his days telling his mulatto kids—because he'll marry some white chick, Italian, from Philly, and give her a few *bambini* before they split—how great their daddy's Otello was? The best since Tamagno? Got any answers, Norman, for any of this crap, hey, my man . . .?"

4

Norman crossed the Channel early Saturday morning to weekend with friends. Maury wanted desperately to hang around with an old Paris hand like Chapin, but Harry would have none of it and banished the beggar back to Burbank. Which left Harry free to drive out to Fontainebleau with Solange, their relationship having been slightly reawakened, if that was the word, by the disaster of L'Hôtel: man never quite so appealing as when passed out at his mistress's feet. He thereupon spent Saturday night in Solange's bed; couldn't do it on cue; and got sent packing early Sunday morning with absolute finality: she made him take his old Dunlop tennis racket, which he'd kept in her closet for two full seasons.

Attired in blue blazer, chino pants and loafers, and carrying the Dunlop, he caught the 1:00 P.M. Air France 727, which provided champagne, *l'entrecôte marchand de vin* and a very nice Pommard all within the fifty minutes before Heathrow. He ate and drank everything within the allotted interval and even had time to make a more or less successful pass at a sixteen-year-old American called Mimi, who carried only a tourist ticket but got put in first class beside the famous Harry Chapin because some frog ticket agent had overbooked steerage. Mimi was from Minnesota; had two enormously long black pigtails which she could sit on; strongly rejected U.S. politics and morals; was desperate for the latest TOP 40 news, which Harry didn't have despite being in the record business; had been to Paris to see her brother, who was drummer in a rock group passing through; wore a ratty-looking fur coat (beaver?) over her Levi's, passport sticking out of her hip pocket; and had no luggage—only a big leather handbag, which made it easy, she said, to get through Customs. Harry found her naïve but nice (she was hardly older than the twins) and decided to take down her phone number—she lived in a commune of former U.S. draft-dodgers and local drop-outs in Chelsea—and ponder her kind invitation to drop by for some very fine Algerian weed. Ah, to be young again. Ah, to rid oneself of an unwanted erection before Heathrow . . .

Her Majesty's Passport Control Officer was stout and mirthless. "Purpose of journey?"

For once he was tempted to say "Pleasure." But men with his cast of eye, men with such tired physiognomies (despite their tennis rackets), could never bring off such a lie. "Business," he sighed.

"Length of stay in the United Kingdom?"

"Just a week."

The clerk seemed satisfied; banged Harry's document with the official purple stamp. "Enjoy your stay in the United Kingdom."

Down more stairs, this time to Baggage Claim. Mimi went merrily by, blowing kisses in the air—yes, no baggage, how clever. Harry Chapin, getting some smarts in his old age, found courage enough to deposit the slip of paper with Mimi's address and phone number in the first available trash barrel. Sixteen, indeed.

The Hampstead Group driver was waiting for him with a small slate chalked: MR. CHAPIN. But as Harry introduced himself, a third party—a slim, ravishing creature in long white leather boots and red burnt-cork hair, almost hip-length like Mimi's—interrupted. "Hello and greetings from Mr. Teedee McEvoy," she said proudly. "I'm Frankie. You *are* Mr. Chapin?"

How like Teedee. "Yes, I am."

"You won't be needing the Hampstead car. I don't know why they sent one—we *told* them we would be handling your arrival."

The Hampstead driver was most understanding. "For your trouble," Harry said, slipping the man an American five-dollar bill. "And please thank Mr. Cairns for his thoughtfulness."

The car provided by T. D. McEvoy & Associates, Public Relations Counselors, was a gleaming white Rolls-Royce Phantom. "This is so like Teedee," Harry said.

"You are very old friends, I understand," said the lady, who could not have been over twenty-one herself.

"Classmates. Not *that* old." The tennis racket, see? "But how did he know—about my trip?"

"Quite by accident. We telephoned your office in California and your secretary gave us your itinerary."

Dear Alix. "And how is Teedee?"

"As always, I should think. Can I give you something to drink? Some champagne perhaps? Teedee says you know all there is to know about wines and such."

"The champagne would be fine, yes, thank you. . . ."

They had not seen each other in over three years, but Teedee acted as though they were still roommates. Even the business connection was tenuous. Honeybee used Teedee's firm to handle U.K. tour publicity for some of the label's major rock stars, but Harry's own press department had assigned only one Melos-Doria artist to McEvoy & Associates—Cavalieri, of course, who never sang in the U.K. anyway—and Harry, going out of his way to avoid any suggestion of the Old Boy Net, had never agitated to give Teedee more. Teedee McEvoy, Class of '54—but, unlike Harry, a will-o'-the-wisp: adventurer who had conquered many continents and who now ran a trendy flackshop-cum-restaurant in Chelsea. Funny how some of these history majors turned out.

"I understand you're a frightfully good tennis-player," said Frankie.

God, what a creature. Light as a bird and with that purest of pure English skin you sometimes saw; also gorgeous long legs, nicely modeled bosom and the breathtaking red hair, thick and full and long-long-long. All the Anglo-Saxon virtues rolled into one modest-seeming package. "Oh, I used to play," said Harry. "But nowadays—"

"I'm just mad for the game—after four lessons," she laughed. "I'm unforgivably bad. Will you be in England for Wimbledon? Teedee can get tickets."

"I'm afraid I won't—sorry. Love to go, otherwise."

"Teedee can get tickets to anything. But then you know all about Teedee. Oh, I believe someone is trying to catch your eye."

"What?"

There in the taxi alongside—sweet Mimi from Minneapolis. Harry waved back in royal fashion. "Just a fellow passenger," he explained to the bird in hand. "From Paris."

"How nice."

"While I think of it, where would one find a game—tennis, I mean? If one were free to play of an afternoon?" Hardly on British soil twenty minutes and already speaking the language.

"Are you *serious?* Why, Teedee has hordes of tennis friends. He can get you into any club you like. When would you like to play?" She got out pad and pencil and prepared to write down his every desire.

"Well—I haven't got a partner. I don't suppose you'd be free?"

"*Me?* Oh, you wouldn't want to play with me. Truly, I'm quite awful."

"Not a match or anything. Just for the exercise. Really—I'd love to. If you could arrange it."

She thought for a moment. "Grass or clay?"

"Well, I'd prefer grass—we don't have it anymore in America. That would be a real treat. But any surface you've got. Any time."

"Let me arrange something, then," very serious now.

"Terrific. I shall look forward to it."

And why not? Tennis with this sweet young thing, all milk-white skin and burnished red hair: such opportunities did not arise every day. How bad could her game be?

"We all loved that bit about you in *Time.* Teedee has sent clippings all 'round. Very good publicity, of course—for Melos-Doria."

"Do you work on our account? Classical, I mean?"

"Not really. I'd love to, but mostly I'm rock."

"Have you been with Teedee long?"

"Only eight months. I was doing publicity for Pinewood and Shepperton—films—but that's dried up now. There's very little work to be had in PR. I was lucky to catch on with Teedee."

"Well—we must talk to him about having you assigned to Melos-Doria. Perhaps you could come out to see us—in Burbank?"

"Oh, you're teasing."

"Not at all."

"Someday, perhaps. California—that's my dream. But I don't suppose it will ever happen."

"Don't say that," said Harry. "You never know how things will turn out. Believe me."

"I should like to," she said with a smile he'd already learned to love.

According to *Nicholson's London Guide,* Teedee's Place is a "convivial bistro on the King's Road serving better than average Continental food with several outstanding Basque specialities not found elsewhere in Chelsea. Good guitarist after 9:00 P.M." No mention of T. D. McEvoy & Associates, Public Relations Counselors, upstairs. Frankie escorted him to the second-floor reception area and introduced him to another young lady, this one severely brunette with heavy eye-shadow and purple clothing and accessories. "This is Tish, who runs things," Frankie said.

And then, to his absolute horror, Frankie bade him farewell, saying she still had things to do for a press party being given that evening for one of her pop clients at Annabel's. "Goodbye," she said formally, extending a delicate hand. "It's been nice."

"*Au revoir,*" Harry said with feeling.

Tish did not seem unduly delighted to see him. "You can leave your bag and the racket here," she said. "Teedee's been delayed. Would

you like a magazine?" She took him into Teedee's office and offered him
a chair. "If you need anything, ring that bell over there and one of the
girls will come in. There's champagne in the fridge—help yourself."

He was getting his post-luncheon champagne-in-the-Rolls headache
anyway, so he helped himself to another glass. The office was like any
other PR man's, Harry supposed, except for an ancient MG roadster
which had been filled with earth and turned into a planter along one
wall, and an enormous aquarium containing one large fish—a bass,
Harry thought. The room was very large, with a nice view of the King's
Road; the furniture was leather-covered and comfortable-looking. The
usual artist photos adorned the walls, including one of Mme. Edith
Cavalieri taken fifteen years ago and signed "With sincere best wishes,
Edith Cavalieri," but addressed to no one in particular. There was also
an eight-by-ten black-and-white glossy of Teedee's wife, Priscilla, whom
Harry had known as well as he cared to during college days. Her photo
was signed "With love, Prissy" and was also addressed to no one in
particular. Prissy was the source of all this magnificence: strong-tongued
bitch worth maybe ten million dollars, daughter of an Oregon lumber
fortune. Her ax-wielding father had given Teedee the PR agency as
Prissy's dowry, the agency having originally been headquartered in Portland, where her old man owned the country club and the Junior League
and a few other baubles of interest to his only daughter. Prissy still lived
in Portland—or had three years ago when Harry last made contact. "I
drink your health, dear Prissy," Harry said aloud—because it was certainly Prissy who had paid for the leather armchairs and the bass in the
aquarium and the Basque chef down below in the kitchen and even this
very fine champagne right here in Harry's glass. In fact, it was dear
Prissy he remembered with pleasure and even some affection, who had
taught them both—Harry and Teedee, two rubes when it came to
spending money—to drink champagne and who had later shown Harry
and Maggie, in that now fuzzy decade after Harvard, how to make ice
cream out of Dom Pérignon.

He moved closer to the aquarium. Besides the one bass, Harry now
saw a mini-school of smaller fish. Minnows? Anchovies? Baby sardines?
Harry knew astonishingly little about fish for a man who had eaten so
many of them in French restaurants. His suspicions were confirmed: the
bass was periodically *eating* the smaller fish. The smaller fish were, in
fact, dinner for the bass, as the bass would no doubt be dinner later on
for a patron downstairs in Teedee's Place. This McEvoy wasn't such a
nut after all. . . .

Ah, at last—Theodore Dawes McEvoy III.

". . . Frankie having done her best, no doubt, to snare you for her

silly party at Annabel's, which you quite rightly declined—McEvoy
having made other arrangements for your entertainment this evening . . ."

Caesar having graduated prep school in the late '40s: great one for
the ablative absolute, old Teedee, and that swell trick of referring to
himself in the third person. "She didn't," Harry said, clasping Teedee's
bony hand. "Invite me to her party, I mean. For which I shall never
forgive her. Anyway, you mustn't go to any trouble on my behalf.
Really, sending the car—"

"It is not a question of *trouble,* Harry. How often do you find
yourself in London? McEvoy and Associates are regretful that you did
not see fit to advise them of your arrival, but no matter. Obviously,
companionship this evening is required, and, knowing that you would
wish to be spared the gaucherie at Annabel's, McEvoy has taken the
liberty of arranging Fiona. I trust that you will not disapprove. . . ."

"Fiona? No, of course not. But—"

"Yes, you will be given supper here—joined, if you have no objection, by McEvoy and his present companion, one Tish. Have you met
Tish? She is really most efficient."

"Yes, fine—we just met. Seems most charming. But—"

"Fiona will come by at eight. Try to be on time for once, Harry—
you know how Fiona likes a good meal. A business expense, of course,
which McEvoy and Associates will eventually bill back to you by way of
Mme. Cavalieri. And how is the lady? I understand that you've been to
Paris. . . ."

"She's—"

"Things are changing in Britain, Harry. Have you noticed?"

Mustn't forget Teedee's way. Extraordinarily short attention span:
just went through the motions, asked the socially-expected questions,
but had no patience for the answers.

"Devaluation of the pound, you mean—"

"Not merely the *pound,* Harry. Such a bourgeois concept. This is
not Los Angeles. One is speaking of gross national *Angst.* The smell of
gloom, apprehension, perhaps even rebellion. The trade-union movement in Britain is not the mythical beast encountered in *your* country,
Harry—not a unicorn, not a dragon, but a hyena set to devour even the
bones. The stench of pessimism—does it escape your nostrils? Are your
senses so anesthetized that you cannot make it out? Have you been to
the docks, Harry? Seen the ships bound for America? Everyone to
America—all our best clients, Harry, are bound for America. . . ."

Like beautiful little Frankie, yes, he had heard. "Superficial evidence," he found himself saying. "But is it true that Caprice has gone
out of business? Prunier's . . . ?"

"Yes, Chapin has always seen life in terms of restaurants—how *marvelous!* Soon only Teedee's Place will be left. Nowhere to eat except Teedee's Place. May I offer you more champagne . . . ?"

My God, Teedee, what has *happened* to you? Physically he was much the same: spare and handsome in a weak-mouthed F. Scott Fitzgeraldish way, hair thinning just a touch but still straw-colored and cut short in the Charles River manner—Teedee had captained the JV crew his junior year. As bright and facile and charming as any Irishman was old Teedee—but charm wearing thin, charm on the verge of disaster. Still sporting those worn tweed jackets, the gray flannel slacks shiny at the knees, the penny loafers (still manufactured? where?), the club tie (Porcellian, best of his five clubs): the same outfit he'd worn in Eliot House. But there was something seedy about him now—seedy, not a nice word to use about someone you loved; unkempt like a man without a wife; a sweet boy grown now into a prickly man, graceless and harsh.

"About Fiona," Harry said. "It's been a year or so since . . ."

"Drinking and fucking," Teedee said, lazing back now, penny loafers on desktop. "The only real American pleasures."

He didn't *want* Fiona now—since Frankie. "How is Fiona? Still—acting?"

"Why ask McEvoy? She's *your* girl—find out for yourself."

Wonderful, the patented Teedee rudeness. And still smoking his pack an hour or so with the same manic-depressive edginess; as strung out at forty-four as he had been at eighteen, or at twelve. But Teedee was like a misunderstood older brother to Harry; you couldn't stop loving your brother, no matter how much you disapproved of his conduct.

"Loved your motor," Harry said. "Rolls just your style. Also loved your girl guide. And who is *she*, may I ask?"

"Hah! Little Frankie. Yes, McEvoy just *knew* you'd want her. Still got your pecker at the ready, as for a Wellesley mixer?"

Harry did not feel like laughing. "Getting old, of course," he said. "Forty-five about to come down on our heads, in case you've forgotten. . . ."

"You Americans. Age is all you ever think about."

"God, Teedee, when you move to a country, you really—"

"One must make a stand sooner or later, Harry. Even *you* should know that. Your asinine remarks in *Time* . . ."

"Mmmm. But you're not answering my question, Teedee. Who is this charming Frankie? And has she a last name?"

"Is that all you *do* now, Harry? Girls? And make those stupid recordings of yours? Her name is Tree, as in what a dog pees on. Frankie Tree. Frances, I believe her correct name is. She was most impressed by your mention in *Time*—these English girls are most provincial. If you play your cards right, Harry, I'm sure you can get into her panties without undue difficulty, you fucking bastard. . . ."

Teedee fed the fish, adding minnows from a small cardboard container like those used for take-out orders in Chinese restaurants. Harry watched in silence, sipping the excellent champagne, a soft Veuve Clicquot-Ponsardin, and pondering Teedee's unique ability to turn all developments to his own advantage. Teedee had always enjoyed feeling himself less fortunate than his fellows—even Chapin here, with whom he had marched through the years starting at Greenwich Country Day School in 1939, when they were both six going on seven. 1939! Prehistoric times. That the two of them should have ended thus: Chapin, with all his adolescent scratching about on music paper, now a Burbank, California, flesh-peddler; and McEvoy, whose Master's thesis had been on the War of the Roses, a London flack and proprietor of a Basque kitchen. Life was too hard.

"How do you know when it's eaten enough? Or does it matter?"

"Naturally, it *matters*. And it's not an *it*—he's a male named Tom. You can be so painfully insensitive at times, Harry."

"Sorry."

"No, don't apologize. To apologize spoils everything. They've told you, I suppose, about my citizenship?"

"No, I don't think so. What about it?"

"I've petitioned the Crown for permanent status."

"You can do that, I guess—dual citizenship, isn't it?"

"Not *dual*, Harry—you're not listening, as usual. I'm going to become a British subject. I have renounced my American citizenship."

Even for Teedee this seemed an extreme development. "I can see how there could be advantages," Harry said, trying to think of some.

"There are no *advantages*, Harry. My God, you are so *totally* predictable. So cynical, as you always have been. The only advantages, Harry, are *moral* ones. The United States of America fills me with revulsion. It and all its smug, totally immoral, totally obscene inhabitants. Living abroad gives one a whole new perspective. While you go on chasing the dollar, peddling those foolish bits of plastic of yours, some of us are drawing the line. You bastards. I don't mean you, personally, Harry. I'm sure you have very commendable thoughts from time to time. But you can, all of you, be so selfish. When it's generosity —can't you see that?—that's wanted . . ."

"I'm of the opinion," Harry said solemnly, "that, despite the charming Miss Tree, as in what a dog pees on, I made a serious mistake in not taking the Hampstead Group limousine."

Teedee laughed for the first time: his high, semi-hysterical laugh, not changed in frequency or effect since Third Form. Nobody knew better than Chapin how to dissolve these fine McEvoyian depressions. "You're the only one of them left, Harry—Americans—for whom I can

feel any love. So—isn't this fine? What would you like for supper? You
know Fiona—such a pig—she'll eat anything. And my Tish—eats practically nothing. But I shall prevail. We shall have a fine time."

Mad, completely mad. "Teedee," Harry said anxiously, "if you
don't mind, I'd like to go on to the hotel now and freshen up."

"Whatever you like, old friend. But please be back promptly at
eight. I wouldn't wish to disappoint Fiona. . . ."

I I

The Carlton Tower is in Belgravia, a section of London that Harry had
always liked. But now, in the rain, it seemed the dreariest place on
earth—and a stupid place to be staying, not handy at all to the Churchill, where the Conference was being held, in Portman Square. The
Germans, who were in the chair this year, thought the Churchill very
American, which they equated with modern and efficient.

He got himself unpacked and thought about making some calls: to
Norman, who stayed at the Grosvenor House; to Hilary Cairns, who, as
head of the U.K. company, was his host as well as his good friend; to
Maggie and the boys, who would be conducting their Sunday ritual of
breakfast beside the pool; especially to Alix, who deserved an apology
after his inane conduct at L'Hôtel. No—too difficult a program. Perhaps
later, after he'd had something hard to drink. Instead, he lay down and
watched a soccer game on the BBC, and then slept.

He awoke at 6:30, shaved and went downstairs. He was shocked to
see that the hotel had been taken over by Arabs; the lobby and public
rooms were filled with them. Wasn't there a *mosque* being built in
Golders Green, where Cairns lived? Oil. What was one to do without
oil? There were Americans, too, in the bar, where Albert, who remembered him from a year or so before, made a sensational daiquiri of fresh
lime juice, John Appleton Jamaica White Rum and just a little sugar—
the limes from Spain and quite fantastic. Harry had a second, and then
a third, within fifteen minutes. By this time not even the American
accents in the Rib Room bothered him. Say what you would about the
Arabs, they kept their voices down. He hoped he would recognize
Fiona—their last tryst had been two or three trips ago. Dark hair, big
eyes, a good body if somewhat coarse and big-boned, fairly decent tits.
She had been a gift from Teedee, like so many good things in his life.
She had been appearing in the London production of *Hair*, and
audiences tended to remember her because she was the one who appeared totally nude stage-front at the end of Act I. Harry had seen the

show as Teedee's guest, and Teedee had arranged an introduction. Harry and Fiona saw each other on several other evenings that trip, and even spent a Sunday together at Windsor Castle.

"Albert—if you would?"

He had a fourth, which he never did; Albert looked askance. But these are desperate times, Harry wanted to say; you see, my friend Teedee McEvoy has petitioned the Crown. . . .

He reported back to Teedee's Place promptly at 8:00 P.M. as ordered.

"Have you booked, sir? Otherwise, I'm afraid . . ."

There were tables in front, with hardly anybody at them, and booths toward the rear. "I'm Mr. Chapin," Harry said. "Friend of Mr. McEvoy's?"

"I don't seem to have your name on the list, sir. For this evening, was it . . . ?"

"Of course tonight. C-H-A-P-I-N. For dinner with Mr. McEvoy? Also, his—assistant? Tish? Also—Fiona?"

"One moment, please, sir . . ."

Never *heard* of Chapin around this place? He could hardly wait for Teedee to arrive—the great laugh they would have.

"Good evening, sir. I'm Eric, Mr. McEvoy's partner. I regret to say that Mr. McEvoy has not yet come in this evening. If you would care to wait . . ."

They showed him to a terrible table in back near the kitchen. He remained very cool, very polite. He ordered a daiquiri, which they couldn't make; no fresh citrus tonight, no rum either. He smiled; he would have a glass of white wine, then. No wine by the glass—a demi instead? He ordered a vermouth cassis, which apparently they could make: the boy moved off sullenly toward the puny little bar by the front door.

He sat and smiled and waited. He was very drunk, he knew, but not unpleasantly drunk, not violent or obnoxious or repetitive in any way. Just drunk enough to be very nice company. He fixed his mind hard on the image of Frankie Tree in her Rolls-Royce. Pity she wasn't there to enjoy his company. Girls traditionally loved him in this state. He was excellent company in this state, absolutely first-rate. Witty, told great stories, and pleasantly amorous in this state—admired all young ladies readily and romantically . . .

"Harry, luv?"

Fiona stood over him. He got to his feet and embraced her. "Fantastic," he said. "Fantastic."

"Hold on, can you, hun? I've got to use the telephone."

She bolted away. She was so much taller than he remembered, with lots of make-up. The dress was all feathers, and pink. He had forgotten what crooked teeth she had: curse of the English, all those rotten teeth—have a treacle tart, my dear? And her skin—not so blemish-free, either. Not at all the peaches and cream of little Frankie. Oh, Frankie . . .

"So kicky to see you again, luv. You've been a naughty boy, not watching your diet at all."

"Teedee's not here yet. He and Tish . . ."

"Oh, sorry, luv—they were supposed to tell you up front, but those boys can be so stupid. Teedee won't be coming, hun. He's not himself tonight—he knew you would understand. Why don't you give him a ring-round later in the week? I'm just *famished*. Have you eaten here before? Of course you have. What is that dish with the olives . . ."

"Can you excuse me?" Harry said. "The men's room—"

He had not been sick from drinking in many years; perhaps not since college days. When he came back, his forehead was still wet with perspiration.

"Well, *there* you are," she chided. "I was beginning to think . . ."

She had ordered for them both, knowing Harry wouldn't mind. "You're not much of a letter-writer, are you?" she said six or eight times.

They had a Fundador after the meal; as they drank it, she moved close to him and put her hand between his legs. Eric, the slim, dark chap in front who had identified himself as Mr. McEvoy's partner, got them a cab. . . .

Fiona hadn't moved since Harry's last visit: the same cold and bare apartment on the fourth floor of an ancient building in Eaton Place. She got out her usual foul Burgundy and put on the Beethoven Third which he'd given her two trips ago. "Can you stay until morning?" she said.

He didn't wish to offend. But after the rum and the Fundador . . .

"You don't have to," she added.

"I want to—you know that," he said lamely. "It's just that I've got to be up early—"

"I get up at six thirty now," she said. "Because of this new job I've got . . ."

She went to the bathroom while he locked the front door and hung up his suit coat in the front-hall closet. He placed his trousers and shirt and underwear on a chair beside her bed. The bed itself was icy, but the sheets had a nice clean starchy feel and he was relatively certain that no one else had slept between them since the linen was last changed. She undressed in the bathroom and as she stood naked in the doorway he shut off the bedside light so as not to embarrass her. For a girl who had worked so often in the nude, she was exceedingly modest.

She settled beside him in the bed and began to tell him about her new job, which was in an office overlooking New Bond Street but only temporary because she would soon be auditioning for a new musical. He was not at all interested, and finding himself suddenly very hot and surprisingly angry, even though the poor girl was still dry and unprepared, he forced himself upon her, making her cry out.

"You can be so nasty," she said afterward, turning away from him to the wall, and he agreed: she would think twice before inviting another impatient American to partake of her private parts. He daydreamed himself to sleep, thinking hard on Frankie Tree and Mimi from Minneapolis but not at all of poor Fiona, whose last name he could not remember.

5

The Conference's first business session began promptly at 10:00 A.M. Monday morning. Dr. Fritz Hopf, Managing Director, Spitze-Schallplatten GmbH, presided. "Welcome, gentlemen, and good morning," he said in English, which would be the language of the meetings. "If you do not object, I have instructed our young ladies that no cables or messages shall be given during our sessions. Please reserve your telephoning for the intervals, as at luncheon or during the tea and café times morning and afternoon. So in this way we shall maintain the pace of our deliberations. . . ."

There were seventeen gentlemen at table as Hopf banged the opening gavel: Hopf himself for Germany, Cairns for U.K., Chapin for U.S.A., Barraud for France, Quinzi for Italy, Ito for Japan, König for the Consortium's Zürich-based secretariat, Globelektron, plus ten aides and staff men including Norman Rose, who sat at Harry's left. On the table in front of each delegation was a miniature flag in a smart plastic holder. Poetically, the Axis had been reunited, with the Rising Sun of Japan, the gay red-white-and-green of Italy and the menacing black-yellow-and-red of the Bundesrepublik Deutschland all in a row. The U.S.A., U.K. and France sat opposite, with Herr König down at the end behind the neutral blue-and-white of the United Nations. Also in front of each delegation were three legal-sized yellow pads; two pencils and two ballpoint pens; a pad of RCA international cable forms; two bottles of mineral water, one Evian (*naturelle*) and one Vichy (*gazeuse*); and four sparkling-clean drinking glasses. The Consortium was a most beautifully organized business machine.

Harry had known his fellow delegates for some years. Even the newest member, Ito of Itadaki Music, was attending his fifth session, the Japanese firm having participated informally in the group's activities before achieving full Consortium status in 1974. Ito was a birdlike little man who commanded no language but Japanese, yet controlled the second-largest record market in the world. Appropriately inscrutable, he communicated only through a private interpreter, Mr. Watanabe, who had no personality of his own but existed solely as a mirror for his chief.

The other principals:

Dr. Fritz Hopf. Born in Austria, Fritz was now a resident of Munich, where he had organized Spitze-Schallplatten in 1946. A founding member of the Consortium, he was fantastically rich and a collector of fine motor cars and youthful wives. Current wife French, called Kiki. Fritz was very proud of her and had once—following the '72 meeting, which was held in Munich—taken Harry and one or two others to his palatial home in the suburb of Dachau and shown them, in the upstairs master bedroom, an extraordinary exhibit of life-size photo blow-ups of the lady without her clothes. A dirty old man worth perhaps fifty million Deutsche marks.

Hilary Cairns. Just turned fifty, slim and elegant, educated at Cambridge, a gentleman and scholar. Vastly underpaid by American standards, due for a knighthood, slightly pompous on occasion, but (very rare in Harry's experience) a genuine admirer of Americans. Terrifically nice wife, Penny (Penelope), and bright, handsome son, Spencer. Fine people.

Jean-Luc Barraud. Harry's pal from Paris—next to Hilary, Harry's best friend among Consortium executives. Didn't understand the English, hated the Germans, looked down on the Italians, was amused by the Japanese and remained distrustful of the Swiss.

Raffaele Quinzi, Classical Director, Dischi La Cima S.p.a., Milan. A brilliant, clever, multi-lingual lawyer from Florence, only thirty-five years old. Son of an immensely powerful Italian industrialist who had offered him control of Italy's second-largest (behind Fiat) industrial empire—declined by Quinzi on the grounds that he wished to play the viola and make classical recordings.

Finally, Klaus König, that useful Swiss. A schemer, in Harry's view, but artistically motivated. Handsome, in his late thirties, spoke all known languages, graduate of some highly rated *école* in Geneva; rumored to manage several important portfolios on the side. Curiously supportive of Harry's plans in the past, for no apparent personal gain.

Harry busied himself with his agenda packet. Each delegation head had received a large leather-bound notebook, almost a briefcase, with his name and company embossed in gold. Inside were market reports from

each of the territories for the past twelve months and a copy of each
company's repertoire program for the coming year. Norman had prepared the Melos-Doria material, which Harry hadn't yet read—being
certain that, like everything Norman did, it would be perfect in form
and not readily objectionable in content. Harry ran quickly through the
other companies' reports, which looked identical to last year's. There
would be no surprises except for those which Harry Chapin himself
would spring. He sat back and listened. He drank his Evian. He thought
about Frankie Tree.

Hopf's opening statement was admirably brief. Despite continuing
economic uncertainty in all territories, the Consortium's classical business had sustained itself and had achieved, in the overall, the financial
targets laid down at last year's Conference. This, despite Melos-Doria's
slight (five percent) decline in sales volume. Offsetting the American
experience were sales gains in other territories, although the increase in
Hopf's own country amounted to only ten percent against a target of
twelve. Business in France was extraordinary—up a full twenty percent—while that in Italy had improved marginally. Our Japanese
friends, despite the heaviest inflation experienced anywhere in the
group, produced an astounding *fifty-percent* increase in sales—Itadaki
now boasting the second-greatest sales turnover, falling only slightly
behind Melos-Doria. Conditions in U.K., on the other hand, were less
sanguine: turnover up twelve percent, but profits had declined as a
result of inflationary forces, labor difficulties at the Hampstead Group's
main plant, et cetera. . . .

The market reports and several new statistical studies developed by
Herr König occupied the members until almost 11:30. Hopf then called
a break to permit members to visit the "facilities."

Harry found himself standing at the urinals with Hilary Cairns.

"Business doesn't look so bad, then?" said Hilary.

"It will in a few minutes," said Harry.

"Your report on Mme. Cavalieri?"

"Among other things, yes."

"You may count on our support, of course."

"I wouldn't say that, if I were you—until you've heard the proposal. Devilish tricky business, as you English would say."

"Splendid. Matters awfully boring to this moment, wouldn't you
agree?"

"Agreed."

"By the by, Harry, you won't forget about Friday evening?"

"Supper *chez* Cairns—hardly forget such an event."

"Good. Penny's counting on it, as is Lady A."

"Lady A?"
"More later . . ."

". . . International advertising and promotion; packaging requirements in the respective territories; in-depth survey of competition,
with special emphasis on label image; and then, gentlemen, if time
remains, a full ventilation of current problems and recommendations as
to joint data-processing operations, including a special film, which I
think you will find most fascinating, from our good friends at ITT of
Germany. . . .

"But for now—to take us through to luncheon—I call upon our
dear colleague Mr. Harry Chapin to make for us his report on current
negotiations with Mme. Edith Cavalieri. . . ."

"Thank you, Mr. Chairman. As I believe most of you know, Melos-
Doria first signed Mme. Cavalieri to an exclusive recording contract in
the year 1954. . . ."

He took them through the painful saga, leaving out nothing—almost nothing—and reminding the members of the Consortium's long-
standing conviction that an exclusive association with the great lady was
worth almost any price, if only for its broad public-relations and label-
image benefits.

". . . Thus, the Cavalieri-Kunz-Florescu-Passafiume *Otello*, as proposed by Melos-Doria, was approved by this body as an expression of
fundamental Consortium policy. There were some misgivings expressed
last year as to the suitability of one or another of the supporting
artists—this young boy Florescu as the Iago, for example—or even
Signor Passafiume's ability, at his advanced age, to endure the severe
workload involved in such an undertaking. However—"

"In the interests of complete accuracy, Harry . . ."

"Klaus?"

"I would only wish to remind the Committee, in fairness to Dr.
Hopf, that our German colleagues have *always* had reservations about
putting so much of our common budget at risk where so undependable
an artist as Mme. Cavalieri is concerned—especially in view of her
periodic, shall we say, 'retirements'?"

"Mr. König makes a good point," Harry said amiably. "The project
has certainly been at risk from the very conception. However, the
Repertoire Committee has in the past given the project its unanimous
approval, and we have, indeed, taken sales estimates from all members
and the project has appeared viable."

"Quite correct," from Hilary Cairns.

"Which brings me, regretfully, to the present situation. . . ."

He laid it straight out. Cavalieri has again defected. The Cavalieri-

Kunz-Florescu-Passafiume *Otello* is dead. Mme. Cavalieri's new interest is *Rosenkavalier;* she wants the Consortium to arrange for a new stage production, with Otto Kunz as director, and she wants the Consortium to record it. She is not open to any other proposals at this time. She is studying German with Otto Kunz. Oh, yes, and the Consortium still owes *Otello* to Kunz, who will no doubt sue unless he gets *Lohengrin* as a substitute. . . .

"Gentlemen, gentlemen, gentlemen . . ."

Pandemonium. Even the Germans were offended, viewing *Rosenkavalier* as an effete poetical work of no commercial merit. As for Mme. Cavalieri's German lessons, those lessons were accomplished in bed, which everybody had known for months. ("German lessons" would thus become the joke of the Conference.) And *nobody* wanted *Lohengrin,* which was even less commercial than *Rosenkavalier.*

Dr. Hopf finally restored order. Before Harry could begin again, Herr König asked to speak. The time had come, König suggested, to consider legal action against the lady. After all, Melos-Doria had had a binding contract with Mme. Cavalieri, which she refused to honor, and her repeated cancellations and indispositions had now cost the Consortium significant sums of money, as well as irreparable loss of prestige.

Jean-Luc Barraud fumed at this idea, but said nothing.

Raffaele Quinzi, the elegant Florentine lawyer, spoke up on Jean-Luc's behalf. Bringing lawsuits against artists—especially world-famous and much loved stars like Mme. Cavalieri—was not a productive activity for companies that depended for their existence upon artists. "I can tell my pressing foreman to make more records," Quinzi said, "but I cannot tell him to sing. . . ."

Well said. Dashing fellow, Quinzi, with a lovely beard and mustache, full, black and luxuriant. Harry had wanted a beard once, too; tried to grow it, but the hairs tended to come in dirty gray and the effect was not one calculated to attract females.

"Have you another proposal, then, Harry?" from the always tolerant and helpful Hilary Cairns.

"I do. Gentlemen, if I may ask your further indulgence . . ."

It was one thing to come up with these outrageous schemes in a Paris hotel room when you've had too much to drink and are, in fact, at that moment still drinking; it was quite another to present such a package in a stuffy conference room in the Churchill Hotel, London, before an audience of knowledgeable, hard, sober businessmen.

Still, he had an edge, he felt. The men around him were essentially trained to say no, to conserve assets, to avoid unnecessary risk; while he—trained only to write a correct four-part fugue, with not a moment's *business* study to his name—was a close friend of risk, and actually knew no other path.

He spoke as quietly and as matter-of-factly as he could, making his listeners lean forward in their chairs to hear his words. Yes, Mme. Cavalieri has again let us down, which is the prerogative of great artists, one must suppose. But, looking on the bright side, when you lose Mme. Cavalieri's Desdemona you lose in the same breath the built-in liabilities of "her" cast: "her" Iago, the untried boy Florescu, whose career no longer exhibits its original promise; "her" conductor, the ancient Passafiume, who is perhaps no longer strong enough to endure the hardships of so major a project; and, in fact, "her" Otello, the redoubtable German tenor Mr. Otto Kunz, who—while still a beloved figure at the Met and in other great houses of the world—is past his prime and might find the Melos-Doria microphones too unforgiving at this stage of his distinguished career. . . .

Thus, gentlemen. Thus. (The segue here is a most difficult one, but a grand master like Chapin has the technique.) Thus, gentlemen, looking on this aforementioned bright side, I propose that we go back to square one (a favored U.K. expression guaranteed to win Hampstead Group approval) and approach the original problem—which, in case you've forgotten, is to fill a serious repertoire gap in Consortium catalogs.

(Strong round of nods here. Quite right, sir.)

Therefore, rather than give up entirely because of one unforeseen (or even foreseen, from the German camp) development—Melos-Doria has pleasure in proposing a brand-new *Otello* built around the following stars of tomorrow:

> EZEKIEL LAFRAMBOISE, *Otello*
> DIDI DEL CAMPO, *Desdemona*
> BORIS MAKHOV, *Iago*
> GIAN-CARLO PONTI, *conductor*

At first, absolute silence. The Committee is stunned. Not even Cairns and Barraud will look Harry in the eye. Then, heads of delegation consult frantically with their aides. Finally—the avalanche.

". . . We in France, while traditionally favoring new artists, must question the wisdom of . . ."

". . . The suggestion to abandon Herr Otto Kunz, the most distinguished Otello of this generation, is unacceptable. . . ."

". . . Would he accept Radamès, do you suppose, instead of Lohengrin, which, frankly, nobody wants . . . ?"

". . . I should have thought that our problem, Harry, was to find a Desdemona, not lose an Otello. . . ."

". . . Del Campo. Just because she sleeps about. And that travesty on Rome television—did you *see* it? A scandal, nothing less . . ."

". . . God knows, I never favored Florescu. But to trade a Rumanian for a Russian—what actually are we *gaining* . . . ?"

". . . With Ponti we would at least have a truly Latin *Otello*, as opposed to Dr. Karajan's, shall we say, Prussian approach. . . ."

". . . Poor Kertesz. You know, this project was originally for him. To drown while on holiday in Israel—God was out of sorts on that day. . . ."

". . . Thus, I can only reiterate—let us abandon the project for now and bide our time. Another *Otello* will, in due course . . ."

". . . Not to disagree, but have you the time? My stomach suggests that the hour of one approaches. . . ."

Dr. Hopf banged his gavel furiously.

"Gentlemen, gentlemen—if I may *please* have your attention. Herr König, as Committee Secretary, urges that we take sales estimates on Mr. Chapin's proposal. Reference number MD-four-zero-zero-nine is now assigned officially to this project. May we begin? The United States?"

"Fifteen thousand sets over five years. That is forty-five thousand individual discs, Mr. Chairman."

"Thank you, Mr. Chapin. Italy?"

"Two thousand sets with Signor Ponti. With a different conductor, I regret that we could not release. The Italian market . . ."

"Thank you, Dr. Quinzi. The United Kingdom?"

"I regret, Mr. Chairman, that until we can arrange for consultation with our marketing manager, who is regrettably absent today, we of the U.K. will be unable to make a commitment. We have no real objection to Mr. Laframboise, being fully ready to accept Mr. Chapin's professional evaluation of a singer who is as yet unknown to us. However, with respect to Mme. del Campo, we in U.K. face a more serious problem, perhaps, than is experienced in other territories—having to satisfy, or at least accommodate, a most difficult corps of critics, with whom, I must say, Mme. del Campo has, to this date, failed to establish any kind of rapport. Therefore, Mr. Chairman . . ."

"Thank you, Mr. Cairns. France?"

"Mr. Chairman, in view of the small market in our country for Italian opera generally, France will be satisfied to import a small number of sets from our associated German company, Spitze-Schallplatten."

"Thank you, Mr. Barraud. For Germany—I shall ask Mr. Dietrich, our marketing manager, to give estimates. Mr. Dietrich?"

"*Fünftausend komplete Aufnahmen und vielleicht noch einmal fünftausend grosse Querschnitte, insgesamt, lieber Herr Vorsitzender, sagen wir, zwanzigtausend Schallplatten.*"

"Mr. Dietrich has estimated twenty thousand LPs in total, being five thousand complete sets and five thousand of, what is your expression?"

"Highlights, Mr. Chairman."

"Yes, five thousand highlights. Thank you, Mr. Dietrich. Have we all estimates? No, I am sorry—from Japan? Japan? May we have your estimates, Mr. Ito?"

The two Japanese sat at the end of the Axis side of the table, as far removed from Chairman Hopf as possible, like two birds, Harry thought, out on a limb—rare drab parrots, perhaps, chirping away at each other in their curious tongue, catching only one English word in three (especially as pronounced by Dr. Hopf) and making, whenever asked, the most preposterous sales estimates for each proposal put forward.

"For Nippon," said Watanabe, "forty thousand sets."

Forty thousand sets. How nice, thought Harry. You *clowns.*

König leaned in the Japs' direction and repeated Hopf's question in French. Met with blank smiles, he repeated the question in pidgin English.

"Ah so!" said Watanabe at last.

"It doesn't really matter," Harry said to the others. "The estimates are not sufficient, obviously."

"The Japanese delegation wishes to correct its original figure," said König finally. "The Japanese estimate is *four* thousand sets. That would be twelve thousand LPs."

As Harry had said, it didn't really matter. His own penciled scrawls added up to 26,000 sets plus Germany's highlights—far short of break-even.

"The Secretary is requested," said Hopf, "to circulate a memorandum of profitability for Project Number MD-four-zero-zero-nine when he is able to obtain sales estimates from the United Kingdom. In the meantime it is proposed that the matter be tabled for further discussion at a subsequent time to be announced.

"It is now five minutes past the hour of one o'clock, gentlemen. Have I a motion for adjournment?"

Harry caught up with Norman in the Churchill lobby. "Well— what did you think?"

"I'm not surprised, Harry, if that's what you mean. I thought you did an excellent job under the circumstances. I'm only sorry that our young friend Mr. Wiseman wasn't present to witness the debacle."

"Battle's not over, Norman. Keep the faith, as our pop friends say. Incidentally, when you have a moment, I'd like profitability figures on a Kunz *Aïda*."

"Instead of *Lohengrin?*"

"Yes. Obviously, no one wants the Swan Knight, not even the Krauts. But all territories are willing to take another *Aïda*, so maybe we give Otto the Radamès and keep *Otello* for ourselves."

"*Otello?* Harry you're not still thinking—"

"Oh, hell yes, Norman. The *Otello* is far from dead, just you watch. This morning was merely the opening skirmish. . . ."

". . . Your party is on the line, London."

"Thank you very much, America. . . . You may go ahead, sir."

"Maury?"

"Jesus Christ, boss, I been *dying* out here. So what *happened?*"

"They hate your boy Laframboise."

"You've *got* to be kidding."

"I'm serious."

"Those *assholes*. They wouldn't know a great singer if he bit off their cocks. Shit—I'm sorry I wasn't there."

"Me, too."

"Though I'm sure you did a great job."

"I did what I could. But the boy's unknown outside of Germany, and the Germans prefer Kunz. That's the real problem—Zeke's not exactly famous, you've got to admit that."

"Yeah, but he *will* be."

"But he's not. Not today."

"So we'll get him a flack. We'll put him on TV—Andy Williams, Merv Griffin, Johnny Carson. He can be *famous*, Harry, in fifteen minutes. Don't those assholes know about the Tonight Show?"

"I don't believe it airs in Munich. But I take your point. And I agree—the boy can be made famous."

"You're thinking about our bet, huh? . . . Am I—fired?"

"Oh—not just yet. Let's let the chips ride awhile longer."

"Hey—terrific, boss. I'll make it up to you, one way or another."

"No need. Or perhaps you already have. About a flack for Zeke?"

"Yeah?"

"You spark an idea, my boy. Perhaps there is something I can do along those lines from this end. I shall keep you informed. . . ."

I I

The planned event for Night No. 1 was a concert at the Royal Festival Hall, to be followed by dinner at the Ivy. The program included Beethoven Symphonies 1 and 5, and the conductor was the distinguished Swiss-Italian maestro Gian-Carlo Ponti—the concert having been arranged by the Hampstead Group.

Gian-Carlo's thing was understatement. Stick shorter than his prick, etc. A bare twitch of the baton brought thunderous response from eighty-seven men and four women, each in perfect synchronization with the others. Fantastically studied understatement. The louder and faster everybody played, the smaller, shorter, less visible were Gian-Carlo's movements. In the end, only his eyes moved. His favorite stunt was to select the biggest, flashiest pieces, stuff with the most obvious and gimmicky finales, Tchaikovsky mostly (although his *William Tell* Overture was something to hear), and then, where Lennie or Seiji or one of the other glamour boys would be masturbating right there in public, Gian-Carlo would merely twitch his stick and the goddam roof would fall in.

Except that none of this worked in the recording studio. For that—orchestral musicians being the surly cows they are—you need a cattle prod with plenty of voltage: stick it up the ass of the concertmaster and the first horn and the rest of these nonvocal prima donnas until they play the piece the way you want it played—the way you are *paying* to have it played. An impossible task most of the time—which made Harry wonder, if only briefly, just why he was so hell-bent on saddling Signor Ponti with the world's first black Otello. . . .

At the interval, Harry and Norman rose to cheer with the others—best not to stand out in this particular crowd. "Too bad," Harry judged. "Hard for Gian-Carlo to out-reserve so reserved a work as Beethoven's First."

"I make it twenty-six minutes exactly," said Norman.

"Slow," said Harry.

"Still," said the older man, "we can get it all on one side. Which is the main thing." Unlike Harry, Norman was always on duty: had his stopwatch out before every downbeat, making careful notes in his priceless little black book. "Perhaps the Fifth will be more to your liking," Norman said.

"I doubt it," said Harry. "Anyway, we'll never know. We're leaving."

"Now? But really, Harry—"

"Now."

"And we're not going backstage? Oh, Harry, he knows you're in town—he'll be mortally offended."

"The entire Committee's going back—he'll never miss us. Anyway, I don't want to see him right now."

"Ah," said Norman, remembering. "Could it be his traveling companion, Mrs. Kunz, that you don't want to see?"

"For an old geezer, Norman, you can be pretty sharp at times. . . ."

The rain had stopped, so Harry walked them across Waterloo Bridge and up to the Strand to another of his favorite watering spots, the Savoy Hotel Restaurant. An ancient band of tuxedo-clad musicians offered dance music of the '30s. Lights on the Thames hung a cloud of *déjà vu* over the dance floor, where several elderly couples performed intricate steps with authority and grace.

"I spoke to Maury this afternoon," Harry reported. "Gave him the good news about his protégé, Mr. Laframboise."

"Oh, too bad. How did he take it?"

"Belligerently. He thinks the Committee is composed of assholes. His word. But then he's young. He'll learn."

"Perhaps."

"But then you've never been a fan, have you? Of Maury's?"

"I simply feel he's not above *using* you, Harry. That's the only reservation I have. He knows music. He's really very bright. In some ways, I find him most likable."

"But you don't *like* him—yes, I have the same feeling. He reminds me of Dustin Hoffman. Remember the great scene from *The Graduate*? —where some old crock goes up to the kid and says, kid, now that you're out of school let me give you one word of advice. That word is—"

"Plastics. Yes, I saw the film, Harry. But what's your point? That you and I are in the plastics business, too?"

"Something like that. Maury makes me feel *old*—I guess that's what disturbs me."

"Really, Harry—"

"Maybe it's because it hardly seems to matter anymore, Norman, what we put on the plastic."

"Hold on, sir. Just because the lowest common denominator turns out to be lower than anybody expected—this doesn't mean that you and I, for example, must abandon *our* standards. And we haven't, have we?"

Why was he constantly finding himself stranded up these back-waters of philosophical abstraction with so difficult a partner as Norman Rose? "I don't know, Norman. But our friend Hoffman—Wiseman—have you ever noticed how he looks at us? The disbelief? That old crocks like us are still running the business? The look of utter contempt?"

A wave of sadness distorted the older man's face. "To be honest, Harry—I've always taken that for respect."

Back at the hotel he thought again of phoning Maggie. But she would want to discuss her letter about making a new start, and Harry Chapin was clearly past making any new starts. Maggie, waiting at home, stuffing love letters—well, *wasn't* it?—into his traveling bags: horrors. Still, she was the best of them all when you got right down to it: zap—immediate champion, Margaret Beach Chapin, only one good for the long run, for lasting liaison, yes, for everyday use. Hence, their—what, twenty years together?

Twenty years on Wednesday of next week, it dawned on him. Her twentieth wedding anniversary, so naturally he was out of the country. Typical Chapin gaffe. Quickly remedied:

". . . Alix? It's me, Harry."

"Harry—what a nice surprise."

"First—about the other night—"

"Oh, don't worry about that, Harry. I—understand."

"You're kind to say so. Wish I did."

"How are the meetings? How is London?"

"Fine. Just great. And you? The office?"

"Oh, fine, Harry. Everybody misses you."

"Mmm. I wonder if I could trouble you for a favor."

"Of course. What can I do?"

"Next week is our wedding anniversary. Twentieth, believe it or not. I wonder if you'd mind ordering some flowers for Mrs. Chapin. For delivery on Wednesday."

"Certainly. How much should I spend?"

"Oh—fifty dollars? Whatever you think."

"And for the card?"

"Just say—'With love on our twentieth anniversary.' How does that sound?"

"Fine, Harry. I'm sure she'll appreciate that."

"How are things otherwise? Everybody getting on okay? No important calls? Letters?"

"No, everything's fine, Harry. Just getting along fine."

Everybody getting his work done for a change, she meant, with no interference from Mr. Chapin. "Well, fine, then. Talk to you soon—and thanks again, Alix."

"Good night, Harry. So glad you called."

It was stupid that he should find sustenance in these phone calls to females. Sustenance and appetite.

He got out the two volumes of the London Central Telephone Directory and, praying to himself, ran down the Ts. My God, she was listed: Tree, Frances A. In Marlborough Mews SW3. It was 1:15 A.M. She would be furious. Or, more likely, she would be out, comfortably settled in her young man's bed, getting a good fucking, which she no doubt deserved.

"Hello? Frankie?"

"Yes?"

"This is me. Harry Chapin?"

"Hello."

"You don't sound—too surprised."

"Should I be?"

"It *is* late. I'm sorry. We had a concert. Royal Festival Hall. How was your party—last night?"

"Smashing. Is this why you've called? About the party?"

"No. I'm calling—about the tennis."

"Yes?"

"You can really get us a court?"

"Obviously. Grass, as you asked."

He loved the way she said grass: grawss, very lovely, very sensual. "Grass," he said in the American way. "Super." Super: a word he hadn't used since college.

"What day are you free?" she said, all business.

"Any day. You pick a day."

"In the afternoon?"

"Fine."

"What about tomorrow, then?"

"Nuts—tomorrow isn't too good for me. The meetings, you know. What about the next day? Wednesday?"

"At what hour?"

"I could duck out at lunchtime."

"I'll send a map and directions 'round to your hotel."

"Fantastic! Should I dress in the hotel? Or there at the court?"

"Oh, at the club, I should think. Teedee will arrange a temporary membership."

"Oh—Teedee. Give him my thanks, will you?"

"It's getting late."

"Yes—and I do apologize, okay? Look—I'm *very* happy that you can play. You won't forget?"

"I won't forget."

"Well—good night, then."

"Good night."

Life was looking up.

6

Harry was in his chair at the Churchill by 9:15 A.M., arriving early in order to review the other companies' recording programs before being asked his opinions. Ten minutes' solid concentration just before class—a lesson learned at Choate—and Harry Chapin could give recitation with the best.

"Harry, may I interrupt a second?"

"Ah, good morning, Hilary."

"Say, old Terry's in town today and wonders if you could break away for luncheon. Promises you that the club claret is much improved since he's taken over as Chairman of the Wine Committee."

Sir Terence Goodall, K.C.V.O., Chairman Emeritus of the Consortium's Repertoire Council and once prime mover in the U.K. record business, as well as Harry's benefactor. Seventy-five or so, now, retired out to a cottage near Canterbury; still came to luncheon in London once a week; personal advisor to the Queen on matters musical; great financial wizard as well as top classics man. Old Terry had trouped all over Europe in the '20s and '30s with primitive wax recording gear, building a catalog of famous artists—catalog that the Consortium still lived on. A legitimate pioneer, now at well-deserved rest.

"Obviously, I'd be delighted," Harry said.

"Splendid. My girl will ring him your acceptance. One o'clock as usual, and we shan't expect to see you back much before four. . . ."

". . . The *ideal* Iago, gentlemen, if I may remind everyone, would be—alas—Signor Benno Toggi."

This from Raffaele Quinzi, Dischi La Cima's boy wonder, who, to everybody's surprise—especially Harry's—begged Dr. Hopf's indulgence in resuming a brief discussion of Mr. Harry Chapin's much-troubled *Otello.*

"Ah, yes," joined in Jean-Luc Barraud with traditional Gallic disdain, "no one would disagree, I am sure. But, as we all know, Signor Toggi is—shall we say—indisposed?"

"The presence of such a figure in your cast," said Klaus König directly to Harry, "would alter the situation most dramatically for all territories—would you not agree?"

No doubt of it. But poor Toggi, like Madame Cavalieri, had been enjoying an extended sabbatical—in his case, a ten-year sentence for felonious child-molestation, a third offense, involving two teen-age boys related by blood (Signor Toggi's very great misfortune) to Italy's last king, Vittorio Emmanuele.

"Is it your suggestion, Dr. Quinzi," from Hilary Cairns, "that the Committee give serious consideration to the participation of Signor Toggi in Mr. Chapin's proposed *Otello?*"

"I think this is not possible," said Quinzi with obvious anguish. "I have only taken the Committee's time in order to show that, speaking for Italy, we remain fully sympathetic to Mr. Chapin's proposals and would, given the opportunity, provide our traditional support to him."

"A view which we in U.K.," Cairns added, "share in full measure. My colleagues and I have had an opportunity since yesterday to discuss the matter with various executives of our sales and marketing organizations, and I wonder if the Chairman might grant us a few more moments—recognizing that we have deviated from the printed agenda—to explore several other casting possibilities."

"The Chair has no objection," said Hopf.

"In that event," said Cairns, "we would bring up the names Merrill, Gobbi and Milnes."

"Merrill? But has Merrill, in Europe, sufficient stature . . . ?"

"As for Gobbi, isn't he today more director than singer? And of course he has already recorded the part for RCA. . . ."

"Milnes has the voice, certainly. However, where subtlety and finesse are required . . ."

"We in France . . ."

"On behalf of Mr. Ito . . ."

"Mr. Chapin? Do you wish to comment?"

With a wonderful display of reluctance and modesty, Mr. Chapin would indeed comment. "Thank you, Mr. Chairman. As a matter of fact, gentlemen, we have considered in our own deliberations each of the aforementioned artists, any one of whom would be eminently acceptable in the American market. However—going back to something I said yesterday—at the heart of our concept is the idea of presenting truly *new* talent—as in the case of our Otello, Mr. Laframboise. And, in this regard, we persist in thinking that Boris Makhov—a leading Soviet artist who has already garnered critical acclaim, but who is largely unknown in Western markets—is a most deserving candidate. Mr. Makhov is the possessor of an extremely beautiful baritone, and it's my personal opinion that he will have a substantial recording career in the West—if not on Consortium labels, then surely on DG or Philips or . . ."

Oh, well done, Chapin. Anxious mutterings all over the room now. Makhov—yes, heard him in an absolutely marvelous *Don Carlo* at Rome. Mmmmmm . . .

But great victories are not so easily won. Dottore Quinzi now petitioned to address the Committee, and the chair consented.

With all due respect to our dear friend Harry Chapin, just what is there, gentlemen—the brash young Florentine wondered aloud in his bittersweet English—to commend such a recording to Italy?

Italy, which has never heard of Signor Makhov. True, he is a Communist and will find support in that direction. True, he has been one *stagione* at Rome in the new production of *Don Carlo*. But we are speaking here of *Otello*, not *Don Carlo*, and who in Italy will listen to the Iago of Boris Makhov who has heard the Iago of Benno Toggi?

Italy, which has never heard of Signor Laframboise. In many Italian households Signor Laframboise will be accepted as a French liqueur! Indeed, the record-buying public, which has never before seen his name on a record jacket, and which has never before heard one note of music from this American Negro gentleman, must assume Signor Laframboise to be a French singer—and what French singer has ever sold records in Italy?

Italy, which has never heard of Signor Ponti. Oh, yes, Signor Gian-Carlo Ponti has a fine Italian name. But Signor Ponti—it must be said with greatest sorrow and with all due respect to Signor König—is considered by the Italian record-buying public to be a Swiss, living often in that country and being "disengaged" from La Scala after only one season following a most unfortunate confrontation with the stage unions of that house.

Italy, which *has* heard, yes, of Mme. del Campo, who appears with some frequency on Italian television and in periodicals of a certain nature, very often with hardly any costume. Mme. del Campo, too, has a very fine Italian name, although, as all the world knows, she was born in Dover, Delaware, U.S.A. But, however charming, however *bella* the lady might be, could anyone seriously argue that she is the proper choice for the virginal "Salce, salce" of Act III?

And, added Dottore Quinzi with a cruel laugh, could anyone even *imagine* an *Otello* in which Otello and Desdemona sing with American accents while the Iago drowns his vowels in Slavic cabbage soup!

Bravo. In other circumstances, the delegates might have applauded; Harry, too. A brilliant exposition of the underlying weaknesses of Mr. Chapin's ridiculous proposal.

"Mr. Chairman, if I may . . ."

Klaus König's turn to kick the body. But no—he was only trying to be helpful: "I only wish, Mr. Chairman, to pay special tribute to our loyal Italian colleagues, from whom so many superb operatic recordings have come over the years—and to suggest, if it will be helpful in any way, that the Committee give consideration—in order to assign our Italian colleagues a greater role in what remains a potential source of significant revenues and prestige—to the idea of removing the *Otello* sessions from London to Rome—or, if Signor Quinzi prefers, even to Milan. . . ."

Bringing agonized shouts of pain from Hilary Cairns:

"Mr. Chairman, I must remind the Committee that our commitments to Walthamstow Town Hall for the period in question cannot be canceled at this time without incurring grave financial losses and, of greater importance in the long view, a severe rupture in relationships that have stood this body in good stead over a considerable period. . . . If indeed, primarily as a result of Mme. Cavalieri's regrettable and in many respects unconscionable withdrawal, we find, as now appears, that *Otello* is simply beyond reach, we have no recourse, gentlemen, but to arrange other artists and other repertoire for those same sessions at Walthamstow. To do otherwise would be to imperil a broad range of Hampstead Group activities. . . ."

For a further fifteen minutes the delegates maneuvered, rejoined, sympathized. Chairman Hopf then announced the consensus. The Committee could not, in conscience, abandon Walthamstow. If Mr. Chapin's *Otello*—for good and sufficient reasons—was impossible of execution, as appeared probable at the moment, other work would be assigned to Walthamstow to cover the time booked.

With specific reference to Mr. Chapin's *Otello*:

With four or five complete *Otellos* already in the world marketplace, including a potent one from Karajan, competition would seem too strong for the kind of "concept" casting that Mr. Chapin had proposed—meaning no disrespect to Mr. Chapin's estimable American artists, Mme. del Campo and Mr. Laframboise. However, if Melos-Doria wished to produce its set *without* the usual Consortium guarantee of worldwide release, then, depending on how the finished tapes sounded, perhaps Consortium members would elect at some later date to accept the album for their respective territories, reimbursing Melos-Doria through the customary "use royalty" of seven percent retail on gross sales.

". . . And so, gentlemen, the Chair must now ask the Committee to return to the order of activities specified in the printed agenda, as there is much still to consider this day. . . ."

I I

Sir Terry's club was the Indigo, occupying a fine Georgian building in St. James's Street. Sir Terry was in good form:

". . . And if you want my advice, dear boy, which you probably don't—never did when I was in your place—you'll forget about this Ponti. He's a child, thinks only of money and can't learn any of the damned pieces you want him to because, frankly, he hasn't got the brains, and, like most of these fellows, he's short on common courtesy."

"He does seem preoccupied with his tax set-up."

"Of course he does. What do they pay him these days? Four thousand American dollars for one concert? Furtwängler never earned that in his life! Today—and you and I contributed to this, we're to blame—today you don't hire Maestro Ponti, you hire a bloody corporation which engages the services of Maestro Ponti. Mr. Ponti's corporation then exports Mr. Ponti's fee to another bloody country where the tax rates are lower, usually Switzerland, where the bloody hills and valleys are crawling with these musical fellows. And if they change the rules tomorrow, why, Signor Ponti will move to Barbados or Guiana or Guernsey, for that matter, because these fellows don't care where they live just so you pay them at the highest possible rate and just so the currency remains Swiss.

"What do you say? Would you rate this claret above or below the former standard? Now be honest, boy. None of your record-company morals at a time like this."

"In truth—superior. Very soft, very round. A seventy-one? Don't tell me. Pauillac? Yes, definitely a Pauillac."

"You've a good nose, Harry Chapin! Yes, a Pauillac—though, to be absolutely correct, it is from the parish fields just to the west, St.-Sauveur. A seventy-one Château Fonpiqueyre, close by Liversan. Most marvelous place—given us a special bottling at a decent price. Only real benefit of the Common Market, prices more attractive now, praise be to God."

"I know you'll blanch when I say this, Terry, but—returning to

Signor Ponti for a moment—the Swiss-Italian gentleman covets, of all posts, Philadelphia."

"Unthinkable. You must do everything possible to block him. And what would he play after the second or third concert? How does he suppose Mr. Ormandy has made a career all these years? Playing the same five or six pieces? Absurd.

"But it's the rule now, isn't it? These chaps who are beautiful to look at get all the good guest bookings for two or three years, when the Brahms First and a little Mahler and two or three other bits and scraps will see them through—spend all their time on jet airplanes scampering back and forth, and finally after a few years of this nonsense they're finished, burned out. The public doesn't want them anymore and they go off to die in the conservatories or in some third-rate posting in South Africa or Cincinnati or one of those places.

"In an earlier day, of course, when I was just cutting my teeth on this business, it was all different. A young chap of promise would toil two or three decades or longer in some obscure German house, learning his business and developing a repertoire, so that by the time he got into his sixties or was even as old as I and we called him into the studio for the first time, he knew all the pieces there were to know and he played them from his heart and with a lifetime of practical experience in making the damned musicians play. All of it gone now. The old men all dead or dying. Nobody left but the Pontis and their ilk."

Not precisely the kind of talk Harry needed at the moment. "But, Terry," he said, "we *must* have new blood. Which accounts for our programs with Ponti and Sax and Córtez. We have only one remaining 'giant,' really—whom you signed, of course—dear Hans-Hubert."

"Ah, yes, Dr. Adler. Had a card from him recently—he'd heard I was ill and no doubt hoped for the worst! A fraud and a humbug—still trailing around that terrible Swedish woman, I'm told, soprano she calls herself. Sunbathing in the nude, her only real talent. Still making his films, I suppose?"

"Yes, more and more, at an ever increasing pace," Harry confirmed. "Wants us to videotape his performances in Vienna and sell them to TV, although we've been singularly unsuccessful in finding sponsorship. His latest rage is a complete *Parsifal.* Wants us to record it whole, film it, then persuade the Coca-Cola people or General Motors or somebody like that to put it on prime-time TV next Easter. So you see, Terry, the problems are not getting any easier."

"Which is the reason, dear chap, for a serious record man's ever increasing dependence on the region of Bordeaux. Drink up and I shall order another carafe. . . ."

At 3:10 P.M.—having already given up any thought of returning to the Conference—Harry submitted to Sir Terry the problem of *Otello.*

". . . And as you can imagine, Terry, I would find it impossible to justify to my own management the burden of financing—ninety thousand dollars at least—against only a vague hope that the other members will come in when we're done and bail us out. Our sales estimates for America would not, I imagine, exceed fifteen or twenty thousand sets, no matter what the cast. So you see . . ."

"You have asked my view, dear boy, and I shall give it. The entire project sounds bonkers to me. I never did think Del Campo could sing. You cannot have one of these Slavic fellows singing Italian. And your black tenor—never had them in my time—won't last two seasons. What tenor has begun with Otello? None, none at all.

"So it comes down, dear boy, as so many of these silly propositions do, to whim. If you want it, do it and don't give it another thought. Whole business hopeless, after all, ruined. Rules all changed, commerce to the fore, art take the hindmost. But then people at my stage of life must always view the present as disaster. Do as you will, dear boy. Do as you will. . . ."

Artistic hash that was commercially disastrous as well: a typical Harry Chapin production of late. But it was always wise to have a second opinion. . . .

He walked a few blocks to clear his head, then got a taxi. They had had two bottles of the Pauillac, followed by a superb brandy. At the Carlton Tower he took four aspirins and lay down. Moments later a cable was slipped under his door:

PLEASE CONFIRM BY RETURN CABLE THAT YOU WILL BE PRESENT
FOR LTI BOARD OF DIRECTORS MEETING FRIDAY 13 9:30 A.M.
PACIFIC TIME BURBANK CALIFORNIA.

M. GINGRICH, SECRETARY

Friday the 13th, eh? Meaning that Deering really had his hands full this time: dividend imperiled by the irresponsible meanderings of Mr. Harry Chapin, who has been called home from Europe, gentlemen, to explain his conduct. Perhaps the Board would like to apply itself to the matter of the Walthamstow Town Hall and Mme. Edith Cavalieri's most recent defection. They would no doubt make a better job of it than their appointed agent, Mr. Chapin. Any dullard would.

The next time he looked, it was almost 8:00 P.M. He got up and arranged his tennis gear on the extra bed so that he wouldn't forget it in the morning.

He yearned for the young lady; sorry to say so, but true. He argued against it for fifteen minutes, but lost: tried her telephone number.

"Hello?"

"Just checking—on tomorrow?"

"One o'clock sharp," Frankie said.

"What's your perfume?"

"Why do you want to know?"

"Can't tell. Oh, and what's your birthday?"

"Chanel Number Five and August twenty-seven."

"Splendid. Tomorrow, then—one on the dot."

Tried-and-true tactic from the Harry Chapin handbook of romance: first find out the perfume, then the birthday ("oh, a Virgo, how marvelous—perfect complement to a Libra like myself . . .").

He got dressed again and went downstairs. In his box was a message he'd overlooked when he came in: reminder that all Committee delegates were invited to drinks that evening at Hampstead House in Berkeley Square, headquarters of the Hampstead Group. That affair would still be in progress, with informal dinner arrangements sure to follow—no delegate ever wanted for food or drink during Conference week. But Harry yearned for a different kind of company. Instead of taking a cab to the east, he walked out to Sloane Street and started southwest, toward Teedee's Place. One never knew what one might find at Teedee's Place.

III

"Is he around? Mr. McEvoy?"

Now they remembered him. "Upstairs, I should think. Left at the top of the stairs."

First he looked in the bar. The place was moving at a certain pace already. Most of the customers appeared to be resident Americans. Army fatigue jackets were still in vogue; a bright new shoulder patch read "FUCK THE PEANUT." Harry ordered a glass of Danish beer, "chilled if you don't mind," and stood up to the counter to drink it. In a far corner a small band was setting up; thank God the guitars were acoustic. Harry felt some discomfort. His Saks pinstripe looked ridiculously out of place—there was *sawdust* on the floor. Steaks were being broiled in the kitchen, and now he felt hungry—surprising, in view of the late lunch. Maybe Teedee would give him supper. He drank up and paid. Upstairs and to the left . . .

"I hope I'm not interrupting," Harry said.

"My God, Harry—I didn't expect to see you again."

Teedee was alone with Tom, his fish.

"Oh? I'm no longer welcome?"

"In view of McEvoy's rather rude behavior last night . . ."

"Not at all. Fiona and I had a very nice supper."

"And yet—tonight?"

"Tonight—I thought I'd look in on my old friend Teedee McEvoy."

"Well, you might have let me know."

"I'm sorry."

"I have an engagement."

"Fine. Don't let me—"

"There are different kinds of rudeness, Harry. Sometimes—you make things so awkward."

"Look, Teedee—"

"I shall be back about midnight. McEvoy is making a speech, if you must know. On behalf of world disarmament, which should amuse you. A bit nerve-racking. Here, this is my key. Make yourself at home. I have rather a good library. Why don't you have supper downstairs? Yes, I'll arrange things with Tish. Spend the evening with Tish, if you'd like. Or perhaps you'd wish to call Fiona."

"Hey, Teedee—really, none of this is necessary. I'm just footloose and fancy free. I'm just—"

"*Please*, Harry. If you think anything of me at all—please accept my hospitality. It's not as though we see so much of each other."

"If it will make you feel better—"

"If I'm not here by midnight, go home. It means I won't be returning tonight. I'll tell Tish. There's a very good beef stew. Also, tell her which champagne you prefer. . . ."

Harry stood at the bar again while they prepared him a table. The place was almost filled now, the level of conversation unpleasantly raucous. He felt even more uncomfortable with the bottle of Krug in front of him: only man in the place with a suit, champagne and no female companion. He thought of asking Tish to join him, but she seemed particularly cold. Why risk further unpleasantness?

Poor Teedee. Forty-four years old, like some others Harry could name—but so desperate, so shockingly on edge. It was as though a brother were mortally ill. . . .

Oh, now *wait* a moment. Three more couples had entered: jam-up reaching an impossible level. But there was something about the way one of the girls shrugged her shoulders. . . . Of course—it was Mimi from Minneapolis, his recent travel mate.

He considered fighting his way over to say hello, but was put off by the look of her companions: everybody so *young* all of a sudden.

"Hey, Mr. Chapin! Mr. Harry Chapin!"

He didn't have to do a thing; they came to him.

"Isn't this *wild?* Isn't this *fabulous?* Say hello to Miles—the boy I told you about? This is Mr. *Chapin*—the same *one!*"

She kissed and hugged him with abandon. He pulled himself together and extended a hand to Miles. Miles, blond and sullen, was not much for hand-shaking. "How yuh doin', man?" The other two couples lined up for a similar ritual; gave back a similar response.

"So what are you *doing* here?" Mimi wailed. "And you haven't *called* me, you skunk! We've got this beautiful Algerian weed—now, you *must* come, tomorrow night and no fucking around. Did I tell you? Brain Damage got the gig? Tomorrow night. Afterwards we'll party . . ."

Harry took the drink orders: suds all around except one of the girls, who thought she'd like to try a "driver," which Harry took to mean screwdriver. In the poor lighting Mimi looked perhaps twenty, though Harry knew better. Didn't anybody ask for ID around this country?

"Wotzat?" the "driver" girl wanted to know.

"Oh? Just champagne, I guess you'd say," said Harry. Stupidity contagious around here; have an epidemic before we're through. "Like some?"

He poured like the gentleman he was, and then the others thought they'd try some, too—but pour it right in the beer, if he didn't mind. He poured what was left and quickly sent for another bottle. They came to get him for his table, but he was in no position to leave; let the table go, and another couple—also American, from their gestures—thanked him for his generosity by stopping by, en route to his table, to drink his champagne.

Two bottles wouldn't be enough. Responding to the nod of his sweaty brow, they brought a third. And then a fourth. People started saying they liked his suit. He sincerely hoped that Prissy McEvoy was paying for all this. Another sullen blond, just like Miles but lankier and even less communicative, was introduced as lead guitar of Brain Damage. "And how long have you boys been together?" Harry asked, imagining how his counterpart at Honeybee would act under the circumstances. "Got yourself a label deal yet?"

This was a serious mistake. "Got some tapes for you," the new one said—Billy, they seemed to be calling him.

"Oh? For *me?*"

Mimi came over and took Harry's arm. She was drinking Prissy's champagne at a pretty good clip. "Go get the tapes," she said to Billy. She had one hand, the one not holding champagne, wrapped around Harry's waist inside his suit coat, and he was trying frantically to smooth out the roll of fat on that side while at the same time leaning over to hear what she was saying, Mimi being five-feet-two with eyes of blue.

"What was that about tapes?" Harry said.

Instead of answering like any normal person, she pulled down on his neck and kissed him with her open mouth, cold with very fine champagne.

"Here they are," said sullen blond No. 2; right, Billy.

Harry accepted them with great pain: a pair of professional ten-inch reels marked BRAIN DAMAGE.

"We're gonna listen," Mimi whispered. "Come on."

She pulled him away from the others. When they reached the foyer, she stopped him and said: "First gotta find Tish. Gotta get the key."

"What? You mean upstairs? I have it."

"You're my honey!" She kissed him again, getting his sweat all over her cheek and neck.

I'm not believing this.

". . . We looked all over for you at Annabel's—the party for Cain and Abel?" ascending through the darkness. "Tish got us in. Miles knows all those guys. I told 'em I met this real heavy on the plane, like *owning* Honeybee and all. I don't think they believed me. . . ."

She had been to Teedee's office on other occasions; even knew where the light switch for the fish tank was. Teedee's tape machine was a European make that Harry had never seen before, but Mimi threaded it with ease. She switched off the overheads, leaving only the eerie green glow of the tank. "Now, my honey," she cooed.

Brain Damage seemed to be mostly percussion: highball glasses on the sideboard began to shake, rattle and roll. "Wait a minute," Harry said. "I think there's something you should know."

"Don't talk, honey. Just listen . . ."

He found it difficult to make himself heard over Brain Damage.

"Like," he yelled, trying to catch the informal rhythm of her speech, "like, I have nothing to do with Honeybee or any of our other pop labels. Like, I'm only *classics*," screaming now. "If I gave you the wrong impression on the plane . . ."

"You're a *boss*, aren't you? At the headquarters?"

"Yes—yes I am. But—"

"It's getting the fucking tapes to the right people that's such a drag, such a hassle," she said, her hands on his shoulders now, dancing him around the room. "Come *on*, man, like, you can *do* it. If you *want* to, you can make those A-and-R guys *listen*. . . ."

"I would like to help, of course. But . . ."

"At least you can carry the tapes to California, can't you? This is our whole trip, man. Like, Miles is wearing somebody else's *shoes*, man, 'cause he put all our bread into these tapes. . . ."

"It's just that . . ."

"Okay," she said, halting their dance. "I know what you gotta have, man."

She detached herself and moved to the door.

Oh, she locked it!

"Really, Mimi—I don't think—"

"Sit down," she said. "There—in Teedee's chair."

It had gotten warm. He took off his jacket and folded it carefully on the couch. *No lying on the couch permitted,* understood? God, he would horsewhip Heck or Beachie if he ever found them . . .

"Just so you won't freak out . . ."

She dropped Teedee's key into the fish tank.

Into the fish tank!

"Oh, Mimi, for Christ's sake . . ."

"Come on—sit down," she repeated.

He refused, but she kept advancing on him, backing him across the room into the windows overlooking the King's Road. He could feel the blades of the Venetian blinds digging into his shoulder blades. The red neon sign saying TEEDEE'S PLACE illuminated her silly sixteen-year-old face.

"Okay, then—don't sit down. Stand up if you want to. Either way . . ."

"Oh, no, Mimi—"

"Don't want me to *scream,* do you?"

It was too late for screams, except possibly his own. She slid gracefully to the floor and knelt between his legs, her surprisingly strong arms locked over his buttocks. With her teeth—yes, her *teeth!*—she pulled down the zipper of his best Saks trousers. *Incredible*—he had never heard of such a thing. She continued to work at him with lips and teeth, but Saks's best men's cotton shorts with snap fly proved too much. Finally she had to use her hands.

"Oh, *God,* Mimi—"

Too late now for anything but fear and trepidation and perhaps a small measure of ecstasy, for a sixteen-year-old runaway from Minneapolis, Minnesota, who knew his name and rank and the address of his company, was *copping his joint.*

Worse, those lovely deep-blue eyes looked up to him not with love or affection or distaste or any other emotion familiar to him—but rather with what he could only describe (later) as ultimate commercial fervor. . . .

"Now," she said resuming her normal height and attitude, "you *owe* me, huh, man? You *owe* me."

Such pretty, well-formed teeth—and to have swallowed him whole with no apparent disgust, no embarrassing regurgitation. His hands shook to the point that he could barely zip himself up. What was to become of him? Worse—what had he become? "Yes," he gasped, "I owe you. But, really, Mimi, you didn't have to—"

"Anyway, I wanted to," she said matter-of-factly. "I liked it." With further expert ease she rewound Brain Damage. "Here," she said. "When can you tell us? Will you phone from California?"

"Yes. I'll phone. As soon as I know anything. But—it could take, like, weeks. . . ."

"Here—I'll give you my number again, in case you lost it. If nobody answers, it means we're on the road, so call Teedee—he'll know how to reach us. You're really my honey, yuh know? Anytime you want to do this again . . ."

"Fine, fine—no, not necessary, really."

She kissed him again. He tried to reciprocate, but his lips would not respond. He was now their Burbank connection, and they were willing to take his body, his tired fat forty-four-year-old body, to get it. He would never be a free man again, so long as you both shall live. . . .

"And don't look so worried!" she admonished, reaching down into the tank for the key. "Who's gotta know, besides you and me and Tom?"

I V

". . . Had you a good evening in this delightful London?" asked Dr. Hopf. Fritz Hopf, whose first view of London had been through the nose of a Heinkel-111 night bomber.

"Oh, yes," said Harry. "Very nice. Went to bed rather early, actually."

Wednesday morning, May 4: Repertoire Council Session No. 3. Should be plowing through Instrumentalists, as near as Harry could tell. His tennis gear, including racket and bag full of shoes, shorts, socks, jock, shirt, sweatlets, and white vinyl jacket bearing the crest of the Annandale Country Club, Pasadena, California, lay in one corner.

"Feeling all right?" asked Norman. "You look a little pale."

"Fine," said Harry. "Tired, I suppose. Too much—high living."

"Sorry you missed the afternoon session. Got into some rather heated debate on the Adler program. Germany is inclined to go all-out, while most of the other territories . . ."

"Don't tell me we're still on Conductors?"

"Yes, appalling, isn't it?"

Dr. Hopf called the meeting to order at 9:35 A.M. despite the absence of Klaus König.

"Mr. Chairman?"

Dr. Quinzi, hand in the air, looking rather agitated.

"The Chair recognizes Dr. Quinzi, our distinguished colleague of Dischi La Cima."

"Gentlemen. I do not wish unnecessarily to prolong our discussions of the orchestral program. But—now that dear Mr. Chapin is once again available for our deliberations—I would like to ask that the Committee give somewhat broader consideration to the role of Signor Gian-Carlo Ponti in our affairs, and especially to his future development."

Heads nodded, including Harry Chapin's.

"Our good friend Mr. Chapin has suggested in his letters and proposals that, in the face of Herr Adler's tendency toward retirement and the failure or at least the very great initial disappointment we have all felt in the career of Maestro Sax—and the same may be said of Señor Jorge Juan Córtez—Mr. Chapin suggests that our star for the future may indeed be Signor Gian-Carlo Ponti. If this is so, Mr. Chairman, cannot we at least hope to settle this subject, once and for all, this very week—"

"Mr. Chairman," interrupted Jean-Luc Barraud, "while my distinguished colleague Dr. Quinzi has put onto the table this so very crucial subject of our future star, we in France would like to declare our enthusiastic and total support of Mr. Leonard Bernstein. . . ."

Harry did well, he thought. In one low-key, typically hard-to-hear dissertation, he at once supported Ponti and Adler and Sax and Córtez *and* Bernstein, asserting in conclusion and with patented Chapin wit that, in his admittedly narrow view, the problem of selecting conductors for worldwide exploitation demanded approach on a broad front, since "our God-given ears, gentlemen, unfortunately lack God's own infallibility in discerning in advance just which of the aforementioned maestri—excluding Maestro Bernstein, who had already proclaimed his arrival there—will ultimately attain Mount Olympus and the commercial acclaim attached thereto . . ."

Thus soundly applauded, Harry was able to return to his exceedingly painful reflections upon the likely application of English statutory-rape laws to foreigners traveling within Britain. Enjoy your stay in the United Kingdom. . . .

That cheerful Swiss, Klaus König, appeared just as the morning tea break was beginning and, to Harry's surprise, came directly to Harry's side. "Dear Harry, I believe I am the bearer of good news for you. If perhaps we might talk privately—outside?"

König did not mean simply outside the meeting room, but rather down the elevator to a quiet corner of the mezzanine lounge, where they were able to have coffee as they conversed.

"I hope, dear Harry, you will not mind my speaking to you on a most personal basis—that is, as one close friend to another, not just as business associates."

"No, of course not, Klaus. Please—"

"You see, dear Harry, it is very clear, from my own point of view as Secretary of the Committee, that the Harry Chapin *Otello*—if I may use an expression which is common among our colleagues—has failed to win enthusiastic support—and is even now tabled for want of a positive vote—only because, dear Harry, the project lacks any one ingredient of commanding artistic interest. Do you not agree with my evaluation?"

"I tend to agree with you. Of course the Committee, generally speaking, is unfamiliar with our Otello—this young tenor Laframboise. . . ."

"But you will agree, I think, dear Harry, that Mr. Laframboise is today—even with the strong support of our German colleagues, who have good knowledge of all these American singers who work along the Rhine—that Mr. Laframboise is a great commercial risk. To have Committee support, your project must include—to use an American expression which we understand well in my country—a much bigger 'box-office' name. Will you agree?"

"Yes. Mme. Cavalieri was just such a name."

"But Mme. Cavalieri is no more, dear Harry. Mme. Cavalieri, to use another phrase which I like very much from my travels in your country, is today a figment of her own imagination. She is not a singer, she is a personality—fine for your television 'talk shows' but not very amusing in the recording studio.

"Which is why, now, I have taken this liberty of speaking to you on a personal basis. What if I told you that a great box-office name could be made available to your project? Would this be of interest?"

"It would, of course. But I should first make clear that the Otello himself, Mr. Laframboise, is not subject to change. His contract is exclusive to Melos-Doria, and we have every reason to believe that he will become an important artist in the near future—especially following his debut at the Metropolitan, which is scheduled for February."

"I understand," said König. "It is not the Otello of whom I speak. It is the Iago."

"You have another candidate?"

"I do."

"Personally, I had hoped that the Russian Makhov would find support in the Committee. However—"

"The singer of whom I speak, dear Harry, is—to use another favored American expression—'light-years' ahead of Comrade Makhov. If you are agreeable, I shall arrange by telephone an appointment with a third party who is empowered to speak for the principals in this matter. May I presume to commit your time for such a meeting?"

"I shall be most grateful."

"Wonderful, dear Harry. And now perhaps we should return to the Conference before our absences are unduly noted?"

In the middle of the discussion of French pianists, König passed Harry a note:

The meeting is arranged for luncheon today. Please be prepared to leave promptly at 12:45 P.M.

But what, my dear Klaus, of Miss Frankie Tree and our 1:00 P.M. tennis date? Harry quickly scrawled a note of his own and passed it back up the line to König:

Luncheon today most inconvenient. Any other time acceptable.

König's second note left little room for negotiation:

Third party departing UK later this afternoon. No other time possible.

Harry nodded his assent; König again left the room.

"Problem?" said Norman.

"Not problem," Harry said. "Prob*lems.* Cover for me, will you, at lunch?"

König was waiting in the lobby; he had a private car outside.

"One quick phone call," Harry said.

But Frankie was out. She'd gone off to play tennis with a client, according to the switchboard at T. D. McEvoy & Associates, and was not expected back. Would he care to leave a message?

"It's *urgent* that she call Mr. Harry Chapin in the main conference room of the Churchill Hotel. Will you try to get a message to her at the tennis club? Somehow?"

"We'll do our best, sir," the girl said.

The utter stupidity of it all. What had *possessed* him—playing tennis with a goddam twenty-year-old English girl. This, after Mimi . . .

"Really, Harry," said König with agitation, "it is not wise to keep this gentleman waiting. As you will see . . ."

König's third party proved to be a middle-aged gentleman of severe expression and almost military bearing.

"Harry," König announced nervously, "I have the great honor to present Mr. Serge Schröder-Devrient."

"A pleasure to meet you, sir," Harry said.

Anyone who bore such a distinguished name, dressed in such formal attire, including bowler, umbrella and high collar with stickpin, and who was on terms of obvious familiarity with the *maître d'* of the Connaught Grill, would have little trouble commanding Harry's attention, despite latent images of Miss Frankie Tree in her tennis whites.

"I can't help commenting on your illustrious family name, Mr. Schröder-Devrient," Harry continued. "You are a direct descendant, I presume, of the great soprano who was Beethoven's Leonore."

Schröder-Devrient's severe expression softened immediately. "Ah, Mr. Chapin, you know your business, as we know ours. Yes, I am privileged to be of that line. We hope to perpetuate the name, but hyphens are so difficult for the bureaucracy. . . ."

The captain returned to take their orders. Harry decided on lamb; König and Schröder-Devrient preferred the Dover sole. Harry resigned himself to drinking white, but Schröder-Devrient proved surprisingly agile, supporting Harry's choice with a lamb of another color, a '64 Mouton-Rothschild, which would make even English mutton a memorable dish. "Well, thank you very much," Harry said. "An unexpected treat, to say the least."

Schröder-Devrient had little appetite for chitchat. "It is in all our interests," he said when the wine had been poured, "to speak of business before time slips by. Klaus has been kind enough to explain the difficulties surrounding your *Otello*, Mr. Chapin. It would be possible, under certain circumstances, to make available for your recording a supreme artist who, for well-known reasons, has been off the international market in recent years. I speak of Signor Benno Toggi."

"But we had understood—"

"Signor Toggi was only last week paroled. We have hopes, eventually, of a full pardon. For now, he is at home regaining his health and spirit after seven years of confinement. Naturally, work will play a vital role in his rehabilitation."

"This is wonderful news, of course," Harry said. "But recognizing that singing is both an art and an athletic endeavor—and in view of Signor Toggi's age—"

"On that score, dear Harry," König began, but Schröder-Devrient interrupted at once. "No, Klaus, Mr. Chapin raises a most legitimate consideration. During his life in prison—to maintain his sanity, if you like—Signor Toggi, who has always practiced his art on a most scientific basis, continued his exercises and performed, on occasion, at recitals for his fellow inmates. I can assure you that the voice remains. Naturally, it is not the voice of the forties or fifties. But for Iago, Mr. Chapin—as a singing actor, is there another artist in the world who can approach Benno Toggi?"

Toggi: a figure from Harry's youth. He could see in his mind's eye those beautiful glossy ten-inch 78-rpm La Voce del Padrone shellacs imported by Liberty Music and some of the other shops in Manhattan right after the war. Harry would go down on the train from Darien on Saturday mornings and spend hours browsing through the drawers— imagine, selling records out of *drawers*—settling on one, or at most two, to be bought from his allowance: $2.10 they cost, he could still remember that, and $2.62 for the occasional twelve-inch, when he felt like splurging. Toggi's "Largo al factotum"—Harry still had that somewhere, probably in the storage bin above the closets in his studio. Fabulous stuff—collector's items, every one of them. Toggi—it was like talking about Pinza or Kipnis or Gigli or Lauri-Volpi or De Luca: another generation of singers—not the Golden Age at the turn of the century or during the '20s, but the *real* Golden Age of recording, the late '30s and early '40s, just before the LP. Benno Toggi, a legitimate museum piece.

"The idea is breathtaking," Harry said. "To have Toggi—in a role for which he was so famous."

"*Is* famous, if I may be permitted a slight correction, dear Harry." König the real salesman here; not Schröder-Devrient, who seemed just slightly above such shenanigans.

"Assuming that the gentleman is still up to the demands of the role . . ."

Or even if he weren't—the idea was still breathtaking. A star like Toggi—the most famous Iago since Maurel—would absolutely ensure the commercial success of the recording. Without question, *every* member of the Consortium would guarantee release of the album; would *gratefully* share in the financing.

"What do you think, Mr. Chapin?" said Schröder-Devrient. "Have we a bargain?"

"I am inclined to agree," said Harry in his best executive manner. Now, then, Mr. Schröder-Devrient, as Mme. Tosca says in Act II, "Quanto? Il prezzo?" "As for the terms," said Harry.

"The terms," said Schröder-Devrient with total ease and savoir-faire, "need not be a matter of concern. There are still several problems to be solved, but none is insoluble. An unfortunate condition of Signor Toggi's parole is that he may no longer pursue a public career. However, our attorneys are of the opinion that, with persuasion of certain officials and with appropriate fees—no, you will not be asked to con-tribute—we shall, in the end, be able to make Signor Toggi available for your recording sessions, beginning, as I understand from Klaus, in mid-August. Steps must be taken to restore Signor Toggi's civil rights, which have been confiscated. But all of this can be arranged. And, indeed, our attorneys are at this very moment . . ."

"Please don't think me rude," said Harry, "but you have spoken of 'our attorneys.' Would it be possible to know just who are the princi-pals—besides yourself, of course—in these arrangements on Signor Toggi's behalf?"

Schröder-Devrient smiled broadly for the first time. "Why, I thought you knew. There is no secret. I am privileged to be the repre-sentative of the Count Stanislaus Gimpel, who conveys to you, through me, his warmest regards. . . ."

He should have known. Who else in the music world could arrange for the restoration of one's civil rights? In an instant Harry felt better—and worse. According to Harry's infallible chroniclers, *Time* magazine, the Count seldom left his luxury yacht, *L'Arlésienne*, which was normally moored at Marseilles. Yet, without ever stepping into another man's office, he controlled the destiny of all major classical under-takings. If there was a musical Mafia, then Stash—Count Gimpel, with whom Harry had had a thousand dealings, always by phone or mail—was the Godfather. And he looked the part—like a Vegas or Miami gambler, unnaturally slim in shiny black suits worn always with a dark tennis shirt, hair still black and slick and shiny, too: image derived entirely from the news weeklies, because nobody met Gimpel face to face unless Gimpel decreed it.

"I may tell the Count, then," concluded Schröder-Devrient, "that the proposition is acceptable to you?"

"Assuming that the financial terms . . ."

"The Count is pleased that he is able to assist your project. He gives his support as a personal favor, if you like."

"Assuming that the Count is able to do us this favor," said Harry, pushing his luck, "what do you think the Count will wish in return—on a personal basis?"

"You are most fortunate, Mr. Chapin, because you have it within your power to pay the Count his very modest asking price for this favor. But he will tell you of this himself. If we have concluded our business, gentlemen . . ."

They left the table, König running ahead to settle the bill and summon the car.

"You shall hear from us within a day or two," said Schröder-Devrient, "regarding a meeting between you and the Count. In the meantime, I would urge you to go forward with your arrangements for *Otello* as previously scheduled—but in Rome, Mr. Chapin, rather than in London."

"*Rome?* But our arrangements . . ."

"Oh, yes, Rome," said Schröder-Devrient. "A far better venue for an authentic *Otello*, wouldn't you agree? And absolutely a requirement, from Count Gimpel's point of view. Good day, then. Until we meet again . . ."

Harry sent König back to the meeting alone, going himself directly to the Carlton Tower to call Frankie. Perhaps she had gotten his message. Perhaps she had taken the bad news with admirable English grace.

There was a handwritten note in his box. It said:

> Dear Mr. Chapin,
> Stick your racket up your ass.
> Love,
> Frances Tree

He got Teedee's office number out of the book. "Miss Tree, please. . . . Hey, you're not going to believe what happened to me."

"Buzz off," and the line went dead.

He called back, but she wouldn't talk to him.

He waited fifteen minutes—not quite 4:00 P.M. yet, still plenty of daylight—and then tried again.

"Miss Tree is in conference and cannot be disturbed."

He still had time to get to Harrods.

Chanel No. 5, wasn't it? He bought a full ounce of the perfume and the largest-size dusting powder.

Then he returned to the Carlton Tower and had one of Albert's wonderful John Appleton Jamaica White Rum daiquiris, then another, then a third.

At 6:00 P.M. he went upstairs and tried Frankie's home number. No answer. He sat down in front of the TV and watched an English situation comedy about working-class people, dialing Frankie's number each five minutes or so.

At 6:40 P.M. she answered.

"Hey," he pleaded, "I *know* I'm a bastard for standing you up. But really—it was business—and very difficult business at that. I'll tell you all about it, if you'll give me a chance. Is anyone buying you dinner?"

Okay. But she was *furious* with him; had gone through endless difficulty to secure the court; wanted him to know how furious she was. Yes, he understood. Eight o'clock then? Where—a place of her choosing? La Parra, she said: small Spanish restaurant on Draycott Avenue in Chelsea, near Teedee's Place. I'll meet you, she added, by the photo of Fiona.

Fine. *Where?* But she was gone. Well, he would find it.

Typical Chapin ploy: could he have forgotten Mimi so quickly?

V

By God, *there* was Fiona—nude, on an album cover in the window of a small record shop next to La Parra. Nice picture, limbs all discreetly folded so that nothing really showed—taken, Harry judged, several years ago, when she was thinner. All these good meals tended to fatten the birds up.

Ah, Frankie—*Frankie!*

He grabbed her by the shoulders—their first physical contact, not counting the hand-shaking at Heathrow—and then kissed her.

She seemed fairly amused—not at all angry, in fact. "Would you rather be with her?" she said, indicating the photo of Fiona.

"Ridiculous!" he countered. "Come on, I'm starved. Have I got stories to tell *you.*"

The restaurant was downstairs under the sidewalk: simple white walls and grapevines and rustic Spanish furniture with waiters in Spanish get-ups and wine served from clay pots. They ordered gazpacho followed by chicken Marrakesh and an estate-bottled *rioja,* which the barman didn't have. Okay, they would drink the *sangría* the man kept recommending, and, surprise, it wasn't bad.

Halfway through—with Frankie looking more delicate and pink-white beautiful than he had remembered—she forgave him entirely for his past transgressions and allowed him to hold her free hand under the table.

". . . Always been an Army brat—Daddy's a colonel, but retired now. . . . Mmm, good chicken, isn't it? . . . In Brighton. Which is a resort town—oh, but you know England. . . . Am I bitchy? Spoiled rotten we were, my brother and me. Moving all the time. We've been everywhere there's a NATO base, I guess. I speak four languages fairly well. That's how I met Teedee—he wanted someone who could write letters in German for a new client. . . . My brother's the same. Kenneth. He's a photographer. Very *great* photographer, too. He's in America, isn't everyone? He does adverts now, but someday he'll only do portraits of rich and famous people. I'm good, too—with a camera, I mean. But I haven't got one right now. I'm trying to get Daddy to give me one for my birthday—in August, but I told you that. They're frightfully expensive, the kind I want. A Nikon, black body—in your money, oh, maybe three hundred dollars. I'm tired of being a glorified secretary. I know I can be a good photographer. Ken and I talk about having our own studio. But—could we have more wine, please . . ."

He got them a taxi without difficulty. "What's your address?"

She gave the man the address and told Harry how much to tip when they arrived. He had never seen an apartment quite so bare. There was hardly any furniture: only a kind of daybed in the living room, an unfinished bookcase, a floor lamp with a much-taped electric cord, and a great variety of wooden crates, some originally for fruit, some for heavy machinery. One, a huge thing stenciled 1 12 *HP Extra-Wound LCT 407* THIS END UP, had been made into a crude wardrobe closet; it contained a collection of frilly diaphanous blouses and tops and two or three dresses. Other crates contained books, mostly paperback, and tons of LPs—all hard-rock, from what he could see. "Any Beethoven around here?"

"In the closet by the door," she called to him. She came back from the kitchen with a tray of glasses and a bottle of brandy. "Those in the closet are Ken's."

Ken owned another hundred LPs or so, mostly classical. Beethoven Six, usually good in such circumstances. "And now, if we have a turntable . . ."

She put the LP on and gave him his brandy, allowing him to kiss her again, and then settling by him on the daybed. "My flatmate, Cindy, is away in Majorca this week. I'm sorry you couldn't meet her. Her boy friend's in the hotel business, and they get to stay places for nothing. She's very lucky. We meant to fix this place up, but we keep hoping to find something better, so we haven't bothered. We would move tomorrow, but where, on the wages Teedee can afford? You don't look comfortable. Would you like to go into the bedroom . . . ?"

Her bed was like a cot at summer camp. She undressed at once, leaving him to catch up as best he could. Trunks off, he came out of his corner like a wary middleweight (heavyweight, then), clinching as quickly as he could.

"I'm cold," she said.

He released his hold and she pulled down the covers, lying back on the icy sheets and making room for him. He lay on his side and helped pull her into the same arrangement: there wasn't enough room for them both to lie flat on their backs. *Aaah*—an icy hand touched his penis. He closed his eyes tight and kissed her neck and rose to his knees, tugging and pulling at her soft limbs, trying frantically to move her under him.

But no—"not yet" written all over her anxious mug; so he eased himself back to position number one and temporized. Oh, God, wilting already; how long did she suppose he could maintain himself? With enormous concentration he tried to think of something fabulously dirty and horrendous and utterly pornographic: five men with their things sticking into her in five different places; *anything,* Oh God, to avoid ultimate mortification.

Nothing worked. Well, what about a smoke then—her idea—while we relax? Girls were always telling him to relax, as though he were some kind of hypertense ballet dancer. "You're too uptight, luv. . . . Just try not to think of anything. . . ."

She went into Cindy's room and came back with her greatest treasure, a tin of "high-grade stuff," which he took to be marijuana. He decided against admitting that he didn't even smoke cigarettes, or that this was the first grass of his whole worthless forty-four-year life. You see, my dear, it's only in Pop that they have access. We in Classics . . . Such an admission would hardly enhance his image as a swinging record exec. He lay back and watched her. Such a beautiful female, with that opulent red hair and those lovely milk-white breasts. Her nipples were the same shade of pink as the soft clump of hair between her legs. She rolled them a communal joint, lighted it, took a drag and passed the confection over to Harry. He did his best to inhale without coughing, imitating her way of sucking in air around the joint. Very nicely done. His throat burned, which was good, as he understood it. He felt the smoke deep down in his chest, also good, and he felt fine, increasingly at ease. They took turns exchanging the dark-brown glowing tube. When she thought they'd had enough, she set the stump on an ashtray beside the bed.

He looked down and saw that he was erect—very erect. She was ready too, hot and gushy. He tried to keep his weight on his elbows and knees so as not to smother the poor child, which only made her cling up to him, pulling at him, wrestling with him to make sure he stayed in her. He had never been so hard in his life. It began to scare him. He wanted to come just so that she'd let him stop, but he couldn't seem to. "Oh, God, Frankie—I don't know how much longer . . ."

When he finally came, he screamed with relief. . . .

She had adopted the side posture; he luxuriated in the flat-on-your-back mode.

"You know what I'd like to do?" he said dreamily.

"What?" with suspicion.

"Give you a child."

"Oh, great God! I'm on the pill, thank you very much."

"No, really. A little girl, perhaps—like you, with lovely pink nipples."

"You talk such rubbish. Just like Teedee."

"Best friends, after all. Seriously—what's wrong with Teedee? Why does he seem so—unhappy?"

"He's just moody, is all. Like most men, I suspect."

"The other night—well, he seemed absolutely desperate."

"Teedee doesn't know what he wants. At times he wants everything, other times he doesn't want anything. Nothing that he already has, I mean . . ."

How stupid of him. Fiona, Tish—and this beautiful little Frankie was somewhere in that mob, too. But it wasn't like Teedee to be unhappy over a mere female.

"Change of life, I should imagine. He'll grow out of it."

That hideous phrase. These young girls knew so much more about their middle-aged men than the men themselves.

"This is the end of it," she said, indicating the makings of one more joint. "Got to get another supply this weekend. . . . *Really,* Mr. Chapin—we *are* eager, aren't we?"

She was speaking not of his smoking, but of further activity down below. It had to be the weed—he was simply not a two-a-day man under normal circumstances.

". . . And you know what else I've been thinking?"—talking now as he did it, just to show how a mature man made love. "I've been thinking . . . you really must have that Nikon . . . the black-bodied one . . . just as a small love token . . . oh, yes . . ."

Afterward he was startled by the sight of real tears. Frankie Tree, lady photographer—practically had her own studio, thanks to this itinerant and grateful American. The lousy Nikon was, what, three hundred, did she say? He had paid more for less. . . .

7

Thursday, final business session of the Conference, and Mr. Harry Chapin, representing the United States of America, is in love.

". . . And so, gentlemen," intoned Dr. Hopf, "except for this afternoon's quadraphonic demonstration, which has been arranged by our excellent hosts of the Hampstead Group, and tonight's final banquet, I believe that we have dealt with all items of the agenda."

"But, Mr. Chairman," cried Klaus König with frantic signals in Harry's direction, "our dear friend Harry Chapin will wish to speak again of his *Otello*. Is this not so, Harry?"

Oh yes, *that*.

"Thank you, Klaus. There has been, Mr. Chairman, a development of possible interest to the Committee. . . ."

He laid it out quickly and quietly:

Melos-Doria will be going ahead with its *Otello* after all—with or without guarantee of release from the other Consortium companies. The Iago, incidentally, will be Benno Toggi. . . . Yes, with the assistance of Mr. König and mutual friends who must remain anonymous at this time, we have been able to secure the great baritone's services. . . . Oh, yes, absolutely assured; sessions to begin, as previously scheduled, in late August. . . . Thus, gentlemen, Melos-Doria will go to market next spring with a world-class quadraphonic *Otello* built around the most famous Iago of the modern era, with the sensational young American tenor Ezekiel Laframboise in the title role and the popular sexpot, if you will, Didi del Campo as Desdemona—the entire enterprise to be given secure artistic underpinnings by the serious-minded Gian-Carlo Ponti. Oh, and there is one additional factor calculated to insure authenticity of style: a new recording venue. Yes, gentlemen, the Melos-Doria *Otello* will be taped in the Opera House, Rome. . . .

The war was over. There would be peace in our time, except possibly in Britain. The Axis Powers signaled immediate surrender; even the Oriental parrots at the end of the table chirped Harry's tune in unison. And there was no question of Melos-Doria's paying the bills and then hoping that the other companies would elect to accept the album for their territories; on the contrary, Herr König *demanded* that the Harry Chapin *Otello* be accepted now as a top-priority release by all Consortium members. Because the return of Benno Toggi was vastly more significant, artistically *and* commercially, than the return of an Edith Cavalieri, who would never return.

"But, Mr. Chairman, we of U.K. *must* protest the change of venue. . . ."

Mmm, yes, what of Walthamstow? What of the London Symphony? What of the Henley-on-Thames Children's Choir, which was at that very moment preparing Verdi's difficult score? Now be nice, Dr. Hopf: don't crush poor Hilary under the iron boot of Committee rule just yet.

Harry himself fostered a brief discussion of this ticklish point (no danger now, with these Gimpelian aces up his sleeve): indisputably true, London choruses sang better Italian than Roman ones; English orchestras were superior to any on the Continent, especially under recording conditions; London technicians worked with greater discipline and at cheaper rates; agreed, working conditions in Rome had deteriorated painfully since the '50s and '60s, when Harry had cut his own operatic teeth.

"But the fact remains, gentlemen, that unless this *Otello* is made at Rome, it cannot be made at all—Rome is *a priori* a condition of our contractual agreements."

In the end, even Cairns came around. The Committee awarded him a Cherubini *Requiem* in partial recompense, and all members were encouraged to find other work to cover rental of the hall and commitment to the orchestra.

"And now, gentlemen, if we may once again have sales estimates for Mr. Chapin's *Otello*—the same reference number to apply as before, but now with the cast headed by Signor Toggi . . ."

It was no contest. The United States, 20,000 sets, because Harry said so. Italy, 5000 sets, up from the previous 2000. United Kingdom, a reluctant 7500, depending on reviews. France, 5000 sets. Germany, 15,000 sets (Mr. Laframboise already an honorary *Staatsbürger*) and perhaps as many "highlights." And Japan—eventually—6000 sets plus 6000 highlights. There was no need to "do the sums," as the U.K. tribe liked to say: the project was profitable on its face.

"Then, gentlemen," crowed König the Swiss, "may we have, for the minutes, unanimous approval of dear Harry's venture?"

Approved by acclamation: hip hip hurrah for Mr. Harry Chapin and all his kind—he's done it again, given the world high art at a price which all can afford. Is there any higher calling, except maybe the priesthood?

"My hat's off to you, Harry," said old Norman, who should have known better. "I never thought you'd bring it off. But getting hold of Toggi—stroke of genius, really. How did you ever persuade him to do it?"

"Long story, Norman," said Harry with well-deserved modesty. "Ask me another time, huh? Meanwhile, how do you get a glass of sherry around this place? It's after eleven, isn't it?"

II

Hilary Cairns phoned Friday morning to cancel dinner. "Lady A's just rung round to say she's indisposed. Probably got the curse—just as well, eh? Rescheduling for Sunday—please say you can make it. . . ."

"Of course," said Harry with relief. He preferred Sunday anyway. This would give him unfettered Friday and Saturday nights to spend with Frankie. Perhaps they would take a short trip.

But now—there was so much to be done. First, got a cable off to Deering saying he would be unable to attend the Board Meeting on the 13th—vast Consortium crisis re Cavalieri, letter to follow. Then booked himself onto a flight Monday morning to Geneva, where Ponti had gone following his concert at the Festival Hall. With all the promises and commitments he'd made—to the Committee, to Ponti, to Laframboise, and indirectly to Gimpel and Signor Toggi—he would be needing lots of plane tickets.

Then sent Norman off to New York to see poor old Passafiume, who was about to go on the road with the Met's spring tour conducting a second-cast *Rigoletto*. Try to pacify him, Harry instructed, with a small—very small—"honorarium" to offset his disappointment at not being able to carry out Verdi's grand design; if necessary throw up a smoke screen of nebulous projects—chamber music of Puccini (was there any?), almost anything in the Italian line—projects never to see the light of day or sound of a single note in the recording studio. More importantly, go see Didi del Campo, give her the good news on

Desdemona and try to come to terms—something minimal to help off-set the heavy financial package that Sy Gravinius would demand for Zeke. And see Zeke, too, their budding Otello having repaired to Gotham after Paris for a few more lessons from the illustrious Donofrio Zito. Madness.

Then he gathered together all of the Committee's agenda documents and memoranda and packed them off to Maury Wiseman in Burbank with instructions to clean up the paperwork, have the sales estimates confirmed in writing and fill out the necessary forms for Finance. Oh—and most important of all, Maury—see that the enclosed tapes marked BRAIN DAMAGE go immediately to the A&R guys at Honey-bee—decision yes-or-no required with *great urgency*.

Finally, he called Frankie and said what about spending Friday and Saturday nights in some nice inn somewhere? See a bit of country, as the English said; do whatever it was lovers did these days? She stunned him with her response. No weekend of bliss possible for the likes of them: Mum and Dad coming up to town from Brighton and staying right there in the flat, expecting to take her shopping, make a family weekend of it.

Family weekend. What did it take to qualify as family around here, anyway? Had she already forgotten his promise of the Nikon?

Late Sunday afternoon, Hilary Cairns phoned to inform Harry that his partner for the evening would be picking him up in front of the hotel at 7:00: "Look for a willowy blonde in a blue sports machine—right up your street, I should think. . . . Female companionship aw-fully important at our time of life. . . ."

Hilary knew best, Harry supposed. The Englishman was only five or six years Harry's senior, but seemed even older—certainly more mature. Hilary's wife Penny, a lush north-of-England girl, was the daughter of a peer herself. Their son Spencer was now at Cambridge, where Hilary had taken a First in the late '40s. Hilary was a cultured man, chairman of the Elizabethan Society, a fine musician—piano and organ—and, like Harry (Harry liked to think), a businessman only because one had to earn a living, hadn't one? So how natural—given the closeness that had developed between them over the past decade—that Hilary, who knew Maggie and the twins from a summer vacation two years ago, should offer Harry a little mid-life companionship in the form of this Lady A, who, as Hilary told it, was a scholar in her own right (*Beowulf* and that period), had degrees in this and that, served as consultant to some research library and, to top it off, was a willowy blonde in a blue sports machine left over, no doubt, from her days with Lord Somebody. . . .

He wore his best suit, the French number, just in case. As an

identity badge, he carried a Melos-Doria pressing of Gian-Carlo Ponti's
Beethoven Third. Just in case what? he began to think in the lobby;
wondered if he'd have time for a fast daiquiri in the bar—but no, there
came a loud honking out front, to the distress of the doorman, who had
seen plenty of willowy blondes and blue sports machines in his day.
"Here we are, sir. Fine weather for a drive, isn't it, sir? Oh, thank you
very much, sir. . . ."

She leaned across from the right-hand driver's seat and extended a
gloved hand. "Oh, and aren't you clever," with a nod to the Beethoven,
making him feel not clever at all but stupid and obvious.

"I didn't know how else—"

"Frightfully sorry to be late, but this bloody machine—almost out
of petrol and had to stop to fill up. Are you related to the other one, by
any chance—the rocker? Watch that door—jagged edge just there. Have
you the time? Hilary will be furious—you know what a beast he is about
punctuality. . . ."

He stuffed himself in with difficulty: bucket seats practically on the
floor and the carpets damp to the touch—there had been rain. "Just got
down to the lobby, actually. Quarter to eight, I have. No, not to the
famous one—not that I know, anyway. What is this—Aston-Martin?"

"Lagonda. Bloody machine. Gift of my ex. Hilary will have explained?"

"He mentioned something—well, no, not exactly. Do you always
drive this fast . . . ?"

God, he hated these formidable women. Elegant yet informal,
what, gown? Expensive slippers, pierced ears, diamond earrings; long
blond hair swept back and pinned in place with more diamonds. Patrician nose, good complexion—warmer than Frankie's, cream rather than
milk—and a large, expressive mouth which seemed to be hardly ever at
rest. He put her age at thirty-seven, maybe thirty-nine: she had teen-
age children, Hilary had said, so late thirties wasn't out of line. When
she leaned forward to operate the gear-shift lever (which she did with
marvelous aplomb) Harry received an electric shock: caught sight of
the root—correct word? as Jean-Luc might have said—of her left breast,
where it began to burgeon (yes, correct word, Jean-Luc) off the well-
conditioned rib cage. The offending anatomy was covered soon enough,
but not before it had done its damage; got him yearning for more. He
hated to glimpse a perfect curve of flesh like that for fear the one delicious patch would lead on to two ideally formed pears (or whatever
you liked in your breasts) and thence to a hard, flat abdomen and onward to ideal thighs. He could tell already that this tasty peeress of the
realm was perfect from the ground up; would, if stripped, reveal one of
those detestably ideal bodies from which her basic formidability no

doubt sprang.

". . . Penny for your thoughts?"

"Oh, sorry," said Harry. "No thoughts, really. Just wondering how far to go. To Golders Green, I mean. Hard to tell where we are—in the dark."

"Is that all? I thought perhaps something was wrong. From the way you've been staring at my tits . . ."

While the men poured sherry, the ladies went into the kitchen to see after dinner.

"And what, then, are your initial impressions?" Hilary asked. "Very nice apparatus, wouldn't you say?"

Apparatus meant breasts in Hilary's lexicon. "Smashing, I guess the word would be over here. Oh, yes, she's already got me under her spell."

"The change of life . . ."

That awful phrase again. "Ridiculous, isn't it," Harry agreed, "all this unseemly catting around? But I seem to need it—require it, in a medical sense, like drugs. Or else why would I go through the agony—the just plain *crap* of it?"

"We all go through that, my boy, as I've told you. The key thing is not to lose perspective. For now, see how you and Lady A get along. One never knows. . . ."

"One thing I can tell you right now," said Harry.

"Oh?"

"It's such a pleasure to meet a woman who isn't twenty years old. Or, worse, sixteen . . ."

From sherry they moved to a '59 Beychevelle, the wine to be drunk with dinner, a favorite of Harry's—Hilary being the most considerate of men. Two glasses down, Hilary disappeared into the kitchen and sent Lady A back alone.

"Hilary likes to play matchmaker," she said. "I hope you don't mind."

"Not at all."

"Hilary says you've just come from Edith Cavalieri in Paris. What's she like? You know—the fan-magazine stuff?"

Like all you beautiful people, of course. "Oh, I don't know," he said. "Like all talented people, I suppose. Unpredictable? Isn't this good Bordeaux?"

"Can't tell one wine from another except that this is red and I like white. Will she ever sing again? One hears rumors . . ."

"One must hope. She has plans. . . ."

"Hilary says—sounds like a game, doesn't it, as though I get all my news from Hilary, which I do—Hilary says you're an important man in the arts in America."

"Hilary lies. As reds go, this is very fine."

"And you have twins. And a nice wife."

"Oh, yes, quite so. Have you noticed how Americans say 'quite' as soon as they've been in London a week?"

"I don't know many Americans."

"You're not missing a thing."

"I've caught you in a foul mood."

"Normal mood."

"Tired, then."

"Yes, tired. From two weeks of—crap."

"Personal or professional—the crap?"

"Both."

"Both? Sounds frightfully interesting."

"Why do English people say 'frightfully' all the time? And 'bloody'?"

"Because so much of life is frightfully bloody, I suppose. Which is why you're in this foul—sorry—tired mood."

"There was this sixteen-year-old girl, see. . . ."

"Are you bragging? Or seeking sympathy?"

"Both again. I could learn to like you, Lady A. Which is what Hilary calls you, in case you didn't know. I'm going to have another glass, if you don't mind."

"Call me anything you like. No, thank you."

"Amanda, then. Suits you. Very—superior."

"Ha. So I've fooled another one."

"Another American?"

"All right, I'm a liar. Known dozens of Americans. Notorious woman, so called. What did you say this was? Tastes horrid, to be truthful for once."

"Beychevelle. Very good Bordeaux, believe me. Everybody lies. Welcome to the club."

"I could learn to like you, Harry Chapin."

But Hilary came back before Harry could make anything of that.

Dinner was bloody awful, as Lady A might have said. English roast of some kind surrounded by boiled vegetables; only the Beychevelle—onto the third bottle now—saved the day for Harry. That and the vision, increasingly fuzzy, of Lady A across the table.

". . . Don't you think this girl should go to America?" Hilary was saying; Hilary, who liked Beychevelle as well as Harry did. "England a dying country, of course. Can't understand why anyone stays here except out of sheer necessity. But Amanda here—God, a girl of every conceivable talent . . ."

Harry was really not in the mood. He listened, but found little to say. He wished he hadn't booked himself onto the early flight to Geneva; wished he could wake up in Lady A's bed. U.K. was impossible for her now—her and the kids. As soon as the divorce was final . . . but who knew when that would be? And what would she do for a living? She couldn't very well live on what her ex was going to pay her in alimony. What about PR—the woman could write, after all? PR, you say: old Harry Chapin's got a friend or two in PR, ektually. Or maybe do interior decoration in Beverly Hills, Penny Cairns suggested, Amanda having such fabulous taste—just ask any of the furniture people in Sloane Street. Or editor, maybe, for a book publisher—oh, they don't have those in California? Or maybe write movies—very clever girl, and with the stories *she* knew . . . But no, Lady A wasn't having any. Bring the children up in *California?* Never. Needed British schooling, and Harry couldn't argue with that, knowing what he knew about the twins.

After dinner, Hilary broke out the brandy and retired privately with Harry to the study, while the girls—girls? these *mothers?* these practically *matronly* ladies?—busied themselves elsewhere.

"Just a word or two of business, if I may, Harry . . ."

"Of course."

"Watch out for Blankenhorn. We need him for Slonimsky now, but he's getting his teeth into Ponti, and he's controlling just about everybody we're interested in for America."

"As Gimpel does for Europe?"

"Oh, no—Joe is small fish, to use your expression—not at all in the same league as Gimpel. But important enough to make a mess of things for the likes of us."

Mmmm. Harry wished that he could pay attention to these business lessons, but really—with Lady A languishing where? In the kitchen?

"By the by, Harry, no hard feelings in the matter of *Otello.* Trust you understand that."

"Of course, Hilary. And as for Laframboise . . ."

"Your ears are enough of a recommendation for us, dear chap. If you say the boy's to be a star, then he will be a star."

"Did I say star? Suppose I did. Never can tell whether it's me or the wine talking. Don't suppose it makes any difference, really. . . ."

* * *

In the car, Lady A looked just a wee bit miffed. Harry couldn't blame her. Here she'd counted on an evening of the famous Harry Chapin ("oh, you saw the piece in *Time*, did you?") and mostly got just another English housewife, the very domesticated Penelope Cairns.

"Goddam business," he said. "Always spoils everything. I'd offer to drive, but we'd both be killed."

"I prefer to drive," she said icily.

"Look, I *am* sorry," he begged. "How can I make it up to you? Where can we go?"

No reply. No armistice. Yes, I know: stupid fucking Americans, always talking business, which makes them tick.

"We both know where we're going," she said, scaring him mightily. "So why not sit back and enjoy the ride . . .?"

"You're tired, we *know* that. Just relax. And stop talking about your 'performance'—such a filthy word."

Naturally, he couldn't *perform* now that he had a woman his own age (practically) in bed with him. Couldn't very well ask for grass, not under these circumstances.

"No, not there—the clitoris," she directed. "My God, Harry, you don't know much about pleasing a woman. . . ."

"I envy Sir William so much," he said in the whimper reserved for this stage of events.

"Why do you persist in calling him 'Sir William'? And me 'Lady A' for that matter? It's just Bill and Amanda, like ordinary people. I thought you understood—we're very common. I'm 'Lady' only because Bill got a knighthood for his work at the National. What do you envy him for, for God's sake? And don't do that—with your finger."

"Sorry. Getting you pregnant. I'd love to give you a child."

"My God, you *are* a bloody romantic, aren't you? That's precisely what I need at this juncture in my life—bear you an unwanted child."

"I'd want him."

"And if it were a girl?"

"Her, too. Don't you think we'd make an exceptional baby? Great high forehead, curly hair, long thigh bones. The world needs children of these qualities."

"I've had enough of this. If you don't mind, I'm going to the john. . . ."

Shortly after 2:00 A.M. Harry stared straight into those marvelous blue-green eyes and said with consummate sincerity:

"You know, I really *am* madly in love with you."

"I love you too, darling, but you're awfully heavy"—rolling him aside with ease—"and it *is* getting late. . . ."

Naturally he had assumed she would invite him to stay the night: probably get up early, insist on another attempt at love-making, fix him one of those marvelous English breakfasts of porridge with cream and ham and eggs and tea. The present turn of events staggered him. "My socks . . . ?"

She called him a cab. She had him up, dressed and out the door in less than fifteen minutes. Her last words were: "Be sure to brush your teeth."

Frankie came to the hotel at 9:30 A.M. to ride out to Heathrow with him in Teedee's Rolls. It was still raining, which suited Harry just fine: he had a really fantastic Beychevelle headache.

". . . And you won't forget—"

"Don't worry—black body, with the fifty-millimeter f-one-four lens. I'll pick it up at the Geneva airport as soon as we land."

"And about Rome—"

"Yes, yes—I'll phone you as soon as I've worked things out with Teedee."

Because somehow—in the ecstasy of the moment, or under the influence of her vile Algerian weed: there could be no other explanation—he had agreed to bring her to Rome for the *Otello* sessions in August, at Melos-Doria expense.

She clung to his arm until they reached Passport Control. There she kissed him passionately, to his great embarrassment, tears of gratitude (he supposed) streaming down her little-girl's face.

"I love you too, baby," he sputtered, and then mercifully he was able to escape into the duty-free shop where she couldn't see him any longer and where he could use the telephone, trying to reach Lady A, who didn't answer.

He bought a demi of Bollinger Brut at the bar and drank that, secure in the knowledge that he was emotionally bankrupt beyond redemption, not really caring about any of these transient loves of his life, not Lady A and not Frankie and certainly not Mimi from Minneapolis, a new record for callousness in the face of the enemy. . . .

But wait—he said to the champagne—what of Don Giovanni? According to Leporello's catalog, the Don had had 640 in Italy, 231 in Germany, 100 in France, 91 in Turkey and a breathtaking 1003 in Spain. Unfortunately, his present travels would not be taking him to Spain, *purchè porti la gonnella, voi sapete quel che fa* . . . Because if she wears a petticoat, you know what he does. . . .

Act Three

GENEVA / NEW YORK / MILAN / MUNICH / MARSEILLES / COTE D'AZUR:

May

> . . . *le plaisir délicieux et toujours nouveau d'une occupation inutile* . . .
>
> Henri de Régnier

Harry was met at the Geneva airport by Robert Maag, personal assistant to Globelektron's Resident Director, Klaus König. "We are honored, Mr. Chapin . . ."

The boy was about twenty-five, Harry guessed, and eager to please; he insisted on going off to find Harry's bags by himself while Harry waited in comfort in the limousine.

During the ride into town, Maag briefed Harry on events. Maestro Ponti had earned an ovation at last night's concert and was resting in his suite at the Richemond, where Harry was also booked. Maestro Ponti was not alone; his traveling companion was Mrs. Otto Kunz. Maag spoke of this "arrangement" with great circumspection, as though Harry represented Otto Kunz—which of course he did. The Maestro was leaving for Milan in mid-afternoon, there to conduct the Camerata della Musica Antica, which Ponti had founded. This was excellent news from Harry's point of view because, after concluding his business, he, too, would be able to leave Geneva, a dreary city at best. Maag was delighted to accept two assignments: book a first-class seat on the evening flight to New York and purchase (through advantageous Consortium connections) a black-bodied Nikon F2 with f/1.4 lens.

Gian-Carlo's suite was something to see: three great picture windows overlooking the lake, and a terrace besides. Marianne kissed and hugged Harry with gusto, which was her way; even normally-reserved Gian-Carlo gave him a brotherly embrace.

"We see so little of you, dear Harry," Gian-Carlo said. "In London, for example . . ."

"I must apologize, Gian-Carlo. Actually, I wasn't feeling terribly well on the evening of your concert at the Festival Hall. . . ."

Gian-Carlo remembered everything. He had the kind of persistent, nagging mind often possessed by successful men. In particular, he remembered unkept commitments and broken promises—Harry Chapin's stock in trade.

They led him onto the terrace, where an enormous brunch had been set out: eggs and fish and cold meats of various kinds, fruit and breads and champagne. Marianne waited on her men hand and foot, selecting foods and portions according to her intimate knowledge of each man's preferences. Harry got some of everything, but Gian-Carlo, who stood six feet or more and had the figure of a young matador, was limited to a piece of fish and half a melon.

"We also regret," Gian-Carlo continued, "that you have been unable to visit us in Zug. This fish that we are now eating—called in German *Rötel*—was taken only yesterday from the Lake of Zug and prepared to our order by the hotel."

"Isn't it marvelous," said Marianne, able to look Harry straight in the eye.

"Quite marvelous," said Harry, equally droll. If he were not a gentleman, he might have shared with Gian-Carlo memories of his own past visits to Zug, when he had consumed the delicate young salmon-trout under other auspices—in the days when Otto Kunz was in residence. In fact, the idea that Gian-Carlo now bedded Otto's wife in Otto's own villa struck Harry as the height of immorality.

"Not wishing to rush you, Gian-Carlo, but recognizing that your time is limited . . ."

"Yes, a concert. Always a concert these days, it seems. . . ."

"Norman will have explained to you the most recent change of plans—the distressing news about Edith and the London sessions?"

"This is so—we spoke last evening on the telephone. But I must tell you, Harry, in all honesty, that I am not at all happy about Mr. Rose's proposal."

"For myself, Gian-Carlo, I am obviously the most embarrassed person in the world. If we had had any *idea* that Edith—"

"Is it such a surprise that the lady has again changed her mind?"

"I only meant—"

"But this is no concern of ours. What, now, of Gian-Carlo Ponti? After cancellation of the *Requiem*—"

"Postponement only, Gian-Carlo."

"Postponement, cancellation, it is all the same. The fact remains that our preparations have gone for nothing. What choice had we but to accept other engagements in the period set aside for Melos-Doria? And now, for Melos-Doria to say, dear Gian-Carlo, we must change again, only this time we wish to record not the *Requiem* and not the Beethoven and not any of the other projects of which we have spoken, but a complete *Otello,* which requires not less than six months or nine months or even one year of preparation . . . Really, Harry, it is too much to ask."

Harry nodded pensively, ate some *Rötel,* drank some champagne. It was best to let Gian-Carlo rid himself of the venom. Marianne remained admirably silent throughout, giving Harry another sausage and filling his glass. She wore a fluffy pink peignoir, which he found most tempting.

"Admittedly, Gian-Carlo," Harry said at last, "preparation time is not as extensive as we might wish. But Melos-Doria is prepared to assist you in any way possible. As for these other engagements you have accepted for the period in question—a period dictated by availability of the Opera House—Melos-Doria will undertake to negotiate with the agents or sponsors involved for your release—even to the point of asking other Melos-Doria artists to substitute. . . ."

Gian-Carlo continued to shake his head sadly. "Dear Harry, it is quite impossible. Let me show you. . . ."

The Maestro absented himself from the table.

"Hopeless business," Harry said to Marianne, who had seen him in the same kind of discussion with Otto. "Maybe I should face up to the fact that I've got to find myself another conductor."

Marianne took his hand. "Don't be silly," she half-whispered. "You know Italians."

"But he's Swiss."

"He was born a Swiss, but, *believe* me, Harry, he's Italian. He *wants* to do it. I feel so disloyal telling you this. Ssssh, he's coming. . . ."

Gian-Carlo returned with his personal score of *Otello.* "Now you will see. . . . Look there. . . ." Each page was marked heavily in red: notes changed, accents eliminated, whole measures rewritten. "I have obtained, dear Harry, a facsimile copy of Verdi's own manuscript, which I am comparing bar by bar with the Ricordi edition. And what do I find? I find nothing but errors—*every page is incorrect!* Dynamics, phrasing—a whole new performing edition is required. And when have I time to make corrections? See here . . . We *know* from our studies that Verdi wanted phrase repeats performed, what do you say, uneven . . . ?"

"Asymmetrically?"

". . . *Sì,* asymmetrically. And yet the score—see for yourself. . . ."

"To help matters," Harry said, nodding and thinking about what Marianne had said, "we would be happy to make available to you a copyist—an assistant of your choosing, to help correct the parts. Recognizing the importance of this project, Gian-Carlo—and the beneficial effect that such a large-scale recording can have on your career—there is very little we *wouldn't* do to help. What more can I say, Gian-Carlo? Except, would I ask you to undertake such an enormously expensive project unless we had *total* confidence in your ability to produce a recording of the greatest possible distinction?"

Gian-Carlo closed the score with a gesture of despair. Marianne poured him another glass of mineral water, then peeled and sectioned an orange for him. Harry, too, accepted an orange. Not another word was said until both oranges had been eaten.

Harry made a point of looking at his watch—then pushed back from the table as though to rise. "You are right, Gian-Carlo. The project is probably impossible on such short notice. Unfortunately, we are committed to the singers, and to others who are now involved, and so we must proceed. Even though I, personally, shall be most regretful of turning such a venture over to another conductor . . ."

Marianne stopped peeling her orange and glared at him. Harry took the opportunity to study the shoreline of Lac Léman.

Finally, Gian-Carlo spoke. "I would undertake this project even now, dear Harry, but only under three conditions. First, the recording must be moved back to London and given to the orchestra of which I am principal guest conductor. Secondly, your tenor, Mr. Laframboise, must make a test, and if he is not in my opinion suitable, then another tenor must be engaged."

"And third?" Harry asked evenly.

"Thirdly," said Gian-Carlo, "we must find a replacement for Mme. del Campo, because this lady is quite impossible under any circumstances."

Harry couldn't help smiling. Yes, he motioned to Marianne, I will have another drop of champagne—in celebration, if you like. Because one thing was now certain: Maestro Gian-Carlo would be recording the Harry Chapin *Otello* at Rome with Zeke Laframboise in the title role and Didi del Campo of Dover, Delaware, as the Desdemona—just as Harry Chapin had proposed.

Dear Gian-Carlo. He was really not a bad fellow. Working with Gian-Carlo was like working with a priest: one tended to afford him endless respect, at least in his presence. Gian-Carlo was a man of ascetic notions, innumerable petty self-disciplines and the life-style of a monk— except in his dealings with the other sex. In this latter respect, his order apparently permitted an unbroken chain of liaisons, of which Marianne Kunz was the latest. For his part, Gian-Carlo was every woman's dream:

so virile, yet so soft and feminine, too, with a perfect aristocratic Roman nose, naturally curly hair with just a touch of handsome gray at the temples and sideburns: a dream vision in white turtleneck and soft French gray slacks, his body as spare as a long-distance runner's, his hands and fingers something out of Michelangelo.

Women aside, Gian-Carlo was a priest to his god, Art. He preferred to seek haven at his summer retreat in the Tuscan hills—there to study Bach—than to attend the fashionable parties at Rome, where all sensible musicians were to be found. With his looks and talent, he might have been the box-office sensation of the day—far greater than Mehta or Ozawa or one of those—but he chose not to be. He ignored ninety percent of the standard repertoire, learning as little new music as possible—new music being any score not taught him at the conservatories of Florence and Brescia, where he had learned his craft. He had the smallest repertoire of any of the active heavyweights—or light heavyweights, to be precise. The heavyweights were people like Karajan and Solti and Bernstein, who earned in excess of $5000 per concert. Gian-Carlo was in the next category—perhaps $3500—with Mehta and Giulini and Maazel and Böhm.

Still, Gian-Carlo was already a very famous conductor. He had risen above such stars as Boulez and Previn and Barenboim and Giulini and Davis. His "dramatic reserve" already earned him in excess of a quarter-million American dollars per year (paid in Swiss francs). He could have earned twice that amount, but refused to accept the necessary engagements, just as he refused to align himself permanently with any one orchestra. He could have had any of five prestigious orchestras in America, but in each case—despite the arrival of delegations on his doorstep—he declined. Increasingly, the critics likened him to Toscanini and De Sabata and Cantelli—best of the Italians—a sensitive artist with vast potential for ultimate greatness, if only he would broaden his horizons. For an artist who had played so few pieces in public, he had developed an amazingly devoted following. Without dispute, he was a serious artist—but one who painted on a very small canvas.

Now—finally—Gian-Carlo was showing signs of change: an awareness that his career would inevitably stall—especially as younger men came along—unless he sought new directions. At last Gian-Carlo was learning new scores—the Schubert Third, all the Beethoven overtures, an odd ballet of Prokofiev. Gian-Carlo had realized, perhaps, that he could no longer get by on his superb coiffure or the fine cut of his evening clothes. And in this realization, who was more important to his future career than his longtime benefactor and Consortium advocate—Mr. Harry Chapin of Melos-Doria Records, U.S.A. . . . ?

*   *   *

The sun had broken through the midday clouds with force; the terrace was uncomfortably warm; flies buzzed around the uneaten fish.

". . . And yet, dear Harry, to commit to such an unknown quantity as this boy Laframboise . . ."

"A boy who will soon be singing regularly at the Metropolitan," Harry said without undue stress, "and who is at this moment a great favorite at Munich and Bonn and other German houses. To ask Laframboise to test now—at this stage of his well-developed career—well, it is not something I would relish. For now, let me send you the recordings we have—very fine excerpts, by the way, from *Samson et Dalila*—and then let us speak again by phone."

"And what of this lady—Del Campo?"

"She has a substantial following in America," said Harry. "A good career at the Met, principally in lighter roles—and always with maximum publicity. Not having worked with her before, Gian-Carlo, you are naturally suspicious. But I can assure you . . ."

"One hears such terrible stories."

"Again, Gian-Carlo—let me send you her more recent recordings and you be the judge. We wouldn't want you to undertake such a monumental task with even the slightest reservation."

"And to work at Rome, dear Harry—where the players are without discipline, the management of the Opera House quite beyond reason . . ."

"In every project," Harry soothed, never raising his voice a decibel above normal, "there are ingredients which, if it were within our power to do so, we would change. In the present instance, I regret to say that the venue is a requirement. As are the principals of our cast. However, in every other regard—supporting singers, selection of musical staff, opportunity for piano rehearsals—in all these matters your own desires will be paramount."

"And if I should not be available for this recording, dear Harry— have you another conductor? Yes, of course, you must. . . ."

"Maestro Passafiume," said Harry gently.

"So you have your conductor and your singers and your orchestra," said Gian-Carlo with irritation. "Then I am wondering, dear Harry, why a busy man like yourself should travel to Geneva to discuss such a proposition with Gian-Carlo Ponti."

"Because, Gian-Carlo, it is my personal belief that an *Otello* under your direction will be great art."

"And what of business? Will it not be also great business?"

"Great business, too. But I didn't think you—"

"Do not be fooled by this face," said Gian-Carlo. "My father is a Florentine who cares only for art. But my mother is from a family of

Naples which has made its fortune in semolina, and I am my mother's son. When must we begin at Rome . . . ?"

I I

They took Gian-Carlo to the airport in Otto Kunz's Mercedes, Marianne at the wheel. Harry was stunned by the news that Marianne would not be accompanying Gian-Carlo to Milan. Further, Robert Maag had been unable to book Harry on a New York flight until the next day, meaning that Harry would be spending the night in Geneva.

As soon as Gian-Carlo disappeared into Passport Control, Marianne grabbed Harry's arm, maneuvered him into an alcove behind the newsstand and embraced him passionately, kissing him repeatedly and forcing her tongue between his lips. He was conscious of the onion garnish that had come with the *Rötel.*

"Oh, God, Harry, it's good to see you again—an *American.*"

He had the feeling that any American would have been acceptable. "Lovely to see you, too," he said with pain.

"What are your plans?" she demanded.

His plans—since Maag had failed him—were private, strictly private. He would go back to the hotel, rent a car and drive south across the border into France, to the town of Talloires. There he would have a magnificent dinner at Auberge du Père Bise, alone. His plans were for one person only. "No plans, really," he said.

"I don't want to drive back to Zug tonight."

As a gentleman, he had no choice. "Well, then. Why not stay here? With me."

"No, not at the Richemond. Everybody knows Gianni there."

"Ah. Well—"

"I've got a better idea."

He didn't care for her smile. "Oh?"

"Let's drive up to Lausanne. To the Beau Rivage—the hotel we went to that time?"

"Now? Without a reservation? Oh, I don't think . . ." He felt it slipping away: Père Bise, its Michelin three stars intact. "Besides, I've got to be back here by noon."

But she was already climbing into the Mercedes, on the driver's side. He hated being driven by women, and now it had happened to him twice in two days. They blasted away from the terminal with a great cloud of exhaust fumes and the squeal of rubber on concrete. "Hey, easy does it!" he cried.

But, like most women of his acquaintance, Marianne paid no attention.

Marianne asked for the center suite overlooking the lake—Noël Coward set *Suite in Three Keys* there—but a member of the Swedish royal family had beaten them to it. The substitute was almost as nice— across the lake they could see the mountains of the Haute-Savoie and, just appearing now, the lights of Evian.

"For dinner," he said, sketching his usual plans, "why don't we try La Grappe d'Or? Awfully good, the last time I was there. And maybe later we can have coffee at the Angleterre—that sidewalk café where Byron wrote 'Prisoner of Chillon' . . . ?"

"Oh, let's not go out," she said, emerging at last from the bathroom. "Can't we just send down for room service?"

She was naked under the peignoir that she now wrapped around her opulent body with studied innocence—tying the pink ribbons loosely in front so that her breasts remained largely exposed.

To order dinner from room service—a disgrace, with so many places of true excellence nearby. She was a lazy bitch, he remembered: would stay in bed all day long if you brought her her meals. How did Gian-Carlo, a man of such refined tastes, put up with her? For that matter, how did poor Otto? But then Otto hadn't—not for over a year.

"You have marvelous breasts, do you know that?"

"So I've heard."

"Did Otto marry you for your breasts, do you suppose?"

"I suppose."

"Well it would be worth it—really would. . . ."

But how long would all this admirable flesh remain a subject of interest? And what had Marianne ever seen in poor Otto? And why did Harry persist in thinking "poor Otto" when Otto was so very rich?

Harry had theories for everything. Marianne had married Otto to gain access to Otto's celebrity—he *was* a Met tenor—and his constant traffic among the beautiful people. This would be sufficient lure for any Cleveland-born clerk-typist in the Hurok publicity department—anything to move uptown, including marriage to the rotund, good-natured little brewmaster's son from Munich with the pushed-up *Heldentenor* and enough native musicality to fool some of the people all of the time.

Harry liked Otto—had even attended the wedding at the Jager House at 85th Street and Lexington Avenue and had been pleased that Otto had found himself a beautiful young American wife. It was really a very romantic story, of its kind. Like Hitler, Otto had been a corporal in the German army. He sang for the troops during the war and survived de-Nazification afterward. He came to America in 1945 and made a career for himself, first on the radio doing light music, and then at the Met. Marianne was born in 1940, when Otto was already a corporal. Otto married a German girl that year, when he was twenty, but she was killed during the war. Marianne, too, had been married—also at twenty and also disastrously: the boy ran away from all that flesh within six months and his parents obtained an annulment—spoiling off the goods, as her father so kindly put it, and sending her immediately into the job market.

Still, others had been worse off. Otto had made a lot of money with his singing, had invested it wisely, was now an American citizen and made very few demands on his wife—only a little company at mealtime. And he was generous by nature—Marianne would never want for the amenities of life, even now. True, he was a bit colorless as a performer, a terrible actor on the stage and not very romantic to look at. He was a simple man who laughed a great deal, made people happy and had become something of an institution in the Yorkville district of Manhattan. Harry knew from personal experience that Otto was simply not allowed to pay for a meal in Yorkville. Otto's only real problem in that respect was that restaurant-owners inevitably rolled out a piano at the end of an evening and wouldn't let him go home until he'd sung "Dein ist mein ganzes Herz" from Lehár's *Land of Smiles.* The piece was increasingly too high for him—especially after 1974, when he underwent something of a vocal crisis. Marianne, who was not a musician, hated the piece and stopped eating out with him—which may have accounted for their separation. That and the sex thing—because word had gotten around that Marianne had cut him off. Why? Because, of all the women Harry Chapin had ever known in this life, Marianne Kunz was *truly* a bitch. . . .

". . . Did you enjoy that?"

"Every minute of it," he said. He was surprised by his own enthusiasm.

"Aren't you going to ask if I did?"

"Oh, sorry. Did you?"

"Yes, I did. You've improved since the last time. I wonder why."

"Comes with practice, I guess," he said.

She laughed. "You absolute bastard. Okay, so who've you been practicing with? You can tell me, you prick."

"Oh—all sorts. Opera stars, mostly. You saw what I said in *Time,* didn't you?"

"You sounded like a horse's ass." She was smoking now, which he hated. "But I'm glad you mentioned that—because I want to talk business."

"Business? What business?"

"Otto's business. What you're doing to him. I don't mind you screwing me, Harry, but I don't want you screwing Otto."

"And what about Gian-Carlo? Am I screwing him, too?"

"Gianni can take care of himself. You heard what he said about the semolina factory. But Otto's different. You can't just take *Otello* away and give him nothing."

"We're not giving him nothing. We're giving him—well, *Aïda*."

This was the most ridiculous conversation he could remember. Just what did *she*, a former Hurok secretary, know about business?

"And *Lohengrin*," she said. "To be fair."

"*Lohengrin?* Who said anything about *Lohengrin?*"

Suddenly she grabbed his balls. "*Lohengrin*," she repeated.

"Hey! Not so rough, okay? What do you mean, *Lohengrin?*"

"We *talk*, Harry," she said, keeping one hand between his legs. "Just because Otto and I are separated doesn't mean we don't talk. Otto knows all about what you did to him in London. You'd have to give him both, wouldn't you, to be fair? After you've promised him *Otello* all these years?"

"Really, it's not something I care to discuss. It's very—*ouch!* Now, don't *do* that. Or I'll—"

She smirked. "You'll what?"

"I'll—" He could barely get his breath.

"I'll let go of your balls," she said, putting down her cigarette and climbing on top of him again, "when you let go of Otto's. . . ."

His flight was Swissair No. 112, which left at 1:40 P.M. Marianne got him to the airport by 11:00 A.M. and didn't wait to see him off, which was fine with Harry because Robert Maag was there, with Frankie's Nikon. Unfortunately, because of the recurring weakness of the dollar against the Swiss franc, the camera cost something over $500—for which, Maag gently chided, Harry might have had a far superior instrument, the Leica. Harry grunted in disgust.

"Well, then, *bon voyage*," said Maag, shaking Harry's hand vigorously. "*Au revoir.*"

"*Adieu*," said Harry with a vengeance—meaning *un dernier adieu* to Switzerland so long as Marianne Kunz remained within its borders.

2

A discreet bronze plaque now identified the Strausses' faded Manhattan brownstone as EASTERN EXECUTIVE OFFICES—MELOS-DORIA RECORDS DIVISION—LEISURE TIME INDUSTRIES, INC. This legend was not calculated to gladden the hearts of oldtimers like Harry Chapin. However, such pernicious LTI trappings were effectively offset by the continued presence of Miss Eunice Powell, originally Leonid Strauss's personal secretary and now office manager, a redoubtable lady of some sixty years who had looked after them all during those perilous early years when Mrs. Strauss herself cooked a hot luncheon each day for the tiny staff.

". . . Was the driver on time, Harry? But I must call you Mr. Chapin nowadays, mustn't I? . . . Was the suite in order?"

On arriving from Geneva the previous evening, he had been met by limousine and wafted away to the Melos-Doria apartment in the Sherry-Netherland, as a hundred times before. "Fine, Eunice. Driver on time, suite in perfect order, as always."

"It's so good to have you back, if only for these few days. . . ."

She quickly settled him into the visiting-VIP suite overlooking a small garden in back, silent and musty, with almost no hint of the traffic on Third Avenue just around the corner. The main room was spacious, plain, angular and filled with cubes: funny Italian furniture bought by the recently-discharged Director of Eastern Operations, who had let his expense account get the better of him. There was one nice piece, a couch covered in marvelous wine-colored corduroy, which Harry had always coveted: perfect for his office in Burbank. He had meant to broach the matter to LTI's Director of Property & Maintenance, but somehow it seemed slightly beneath his dignity—though, with his rank, he would most certainly have gotten it. Oh, and the portable bar in the corner: a teak cart on casters with a refrigerator in the bottom. And how nice: a chilled bottle of Mumm's waiting for him—dear Eunice.

"Will you be taking calls, Harry?"

"I'd prefer not to, Eu. Ask the switchboard to hold everything, why don't you, until I see what you've collected for me."

She came in with her pad and a bundle of message slips. "At Mr. Rose's suggestion, we've obtained for you a pair of tickets for tonight's *Wozzeck* at Lincoln Center. It's the visiting Hamburg Opera, and the curtain is eight o'clock. Mr. Rose, by the way, is in Burbank, recording Donny Kurtz. Also, reservations in your name have been made at Le Poulailler—two persons at eleven P.M.—in case you wish to have supper afterwards."

"If I feel up to it, Eu . . . Jet lag, you know . . . disruption of my circadian rhythms . . ."

"Mr. Cairns called from London to say that he will be in Munich tomorrow. If you need him on the Otto Kunz matter, he may be reached at the home of Mr. Bertil Ostrow—he says you have the number."

"Fine."

"Chatham Limousine will have a car and driver on call during your stay. I'm afraid you're going to need it, Harry—I've never seen so much rain for May, and you'll never find a taxi when you need one."

"Thank you very much—yes, I'll need the car."

"Julie Marx would like to stop in and see you with his client Miss Diana Kaufman concerning their difficulties at Alice Tully Hall. Perhaps you've heard . . ."

"Yes, but no—I don't want to get involved in that. Say I've gone to my sister's in Greenwich or something."

"Mr. John Wigglesworth wants an appointment at your convenience—he remarked that he's a classmate of yours. He wishes to discuss a Ford Foundation grant for the recording of some early Copland."

Old Wiggles, still playing at his game of giving away other people's money. Teedee would have a good laugh—or, rather, would bitterly decry Wiggles's Wall Street morality. "Again, Eu, make up something, will you? Tell him I'm just passing through and I'll be sure to see him on my next trip."

"Mr. Gravinius would like to come in this afternoon at three. He's sorry he can't offer luncheon, but the Coast was tardy, he says, in notifying him of your arrival."

"Fine."

"And Mr. Blankenhorn's office would like you to call."

"Later for that."

"And that's all I have—except to say that I've stocked the refrigerator, which I'm sure you've already noticed, naughty man. Now then, what can we do to help get you started this morning?"

Fabulously efficient, dear Miss Powell. "You've done wonders already, Eu. First, I'd like to talk to Didi del Campo's manager—what's his name . . ."

"Mr. Ferlinghetti?"

"Right, Giacomo Ferlinghetti. He's a slippery fellow—you'll probably have to call all over town to find him. Secondly, I'll be going over to see Otto Kunz later this morning at the Carlyle—call Otto, will you, and ask if eleven is all right? If so, tell Chatham to pick me up here at ten forty-five. And finally—and most importantly, Eu—get out two glasses and pour us some of that lovely Mumm's in celebration of Harry Chapin's return to this hallowed ground. . . ."

Hallowed ground it was. Leonid and Sylvia had interviewed him—sweaty-palmed Chapin still clutching the handwritten letter of recommendation from Hindemith—just down the hall in the second-floor sitting room, present site of Press & Information. Sylvia gave him Russian tea, the first of his life. He didn't like it then, he didn't like it now.

Theirs was a true American success story. Leonid, a German-born Jew of Russian extraction, came to America with a boatload of other refugees in 1938. Sylvia, daughter of a White Russian general, had already established herself in concert management: she and Leonid met in the foyer of Carnegie Hall. Leonid, who had been a printer of art books in Cologne, soon had himself a nice little printing business in Queens. But music was the Strausses' true passion. Leonid performed as violinist with chamber groups around the city; Sylvia, a pianist, joined him in sonatas.

In 1947, during the Strausses' first visit to Europe after the war, they ran into an old friend of Leonid's, a former bassoonist with the Berlin Philharmonic, who was then producing classical tapes and selling them at rock-bottom prices just to stay alive. The Strausses purchased an entire catalog—some sixty titles—for $300 cash, sailing back to New York with the tapes in their steamer trunk. Sylvia supplied a name for the new company: *Melos,* song, plus *Doria,* from the Dorian mode, implying music of Grecian simplicity and purity of form. The first six releases—primitive 78s pressed by a button-manufacturer on Long Island, with album graphics and liner notes printed in Leonid's shop—were offered in January 1948. Sylvia and one of Leonid's pressmen wrapped and mailed the albums by hand, and the initial runs of most titles, two hundred copies each, were gone before Easter. A year later they had done well enough to supplement the European tapes with recordings and artists of their own; Melos-Doria's first "star" was another Russian exile, Vladimir Slonimsky. Vova's recording of the Chopin scherzos became Melos-Doria's first LP, in 1950.

After that, the artist roster grew quickly in size and prominence. In late 1953 Leonid succeeded in attracting the then-blossoming Edith Cavalieri. In late 1957 the burgeoning label made perhaps its most important acquisition to that time (or so thought the future General Manager): for $575 a month and the title Assistant Repertoire Manager, Melos-Doria signed Harry Chapin.

In those early days the entire staff consisted of Leonid, Sylvia, Eunice Powell, an after-school mailroom boy, Leonid's younger brother Emil, who was the bookkeeper, and Harry. Even an unambitious Chapin was bound to rise in that environment: it was a "man and dog" record company, Leonid liked to say. Harry's rise paralleled those of Slonimsky and Cavalieri. From general repertoire duties (anything Leonid and Sylvia wanted done) he moved on to the post of Creative Services Manager (anything else Leonid and Sylvia wanted done). In 1959 he was officially appointed house producer, making most of the important recordings himself. As the release program grew from six albums a year to twelve and then twenty, Leonid reluctantly added staff and Harry became supervisor of the other producers. In 1967, on his birthday, the Strausses made him a present of the title Vice President, Artists & Repertoire.

Then, early in 1970, Leonid had his first coronary. Shortly thereafter he turned over all day-to-day operations to Harry, with the title Vice President & General Manager. Harry was happy as a chicken until that dreadful day in February 1973 when Leonid and Sylvia took him to lunch at Côte Basque and broke the news: a wonderful man named Leslie Deering, head of a major West Coast entertainment conglomerate, had made them an offer they couldn't refuse: bought little Melos-Doria, last of the cottage industries, for *five-point-three million dollars*, enabling Leonid and Sylvia and Leonid's brother Emil to finish out their days in well-earned luxury—namely, a nine-thousand-square-foot desert retreat outside Scottsdale, Arizona.

And what of the staff? Not to worry. The staff would be kept on—Deering had guaranteed this—although (appropriate lowering of the voice here) Melos-Doria's Senior Management (meaning Harry) would have to move to Burbank, California.

Oh, the pain. Oh, the *burden*. Leonid let it be known rather widely in the industry that he could never have accepted LTI's offer if it hadn't been for Harry Chapin. "This young man," Leonid said at the farewell party (Harry being then forty-one years of age), "has saved my life," kissing Harry as a Russian father kisses his son and heir. I bequeath to you, my son, Edith and Otto and Vova and all the others; I entrust to you my dearest love-child, my Melos-Doria. . . .

O Leonid, how *could* you . . .?

At 10:00 A.M.—7:00 on the Coast—he tried Norman Rose at the Beverly Hills Hotel.

". . . Harry? My God, what time—"

"Good morning, Norman. I made it—to New York, that is. Just thought I'd touch base. How are things?"

"Excuse me if I seem—disjointed. It *is* early out here, Harry. About Del Campo, you mean?"

"That, yes—everything."

"Well, there *are* problems, Harry. But I think we've got Del Campo."

"Excellent."

"That is, in principle, she's with us."

"But what?"

"But she wants a flat fee, Harry—doesn't care about a royalty."

"That's ridiculous. What did you tell her?"

"I offered her the usual five-hundred advance and six percent proportional. She said no. Actually, she said something more graphic than that—Didi being Didi."

"So what does she want?"

"She wants a flat fee of seven thousand five hundred dollars."

"Out of the question. We'll get somebody else."

"That's probably a good idea, Harry. Because there's another problem, anyway."

"What?"

"Only last week she committed herself to Salzburg—Susanna in *Nozze di Figaro*—and she could only be present for the second half of our sessions anyway, after the Festival. She'd have been singing Mozart for a month, and then we'd be asking her to put herself into a Verdian frame of mind, and it would legitimately be difficult for her. . . ."

"Shit, Norman, she sings Mozart like Verdi anyway—or vice versa, I forget which. What the hell difference would it make?"

"Understand, Harry, I'm on *your* side. I'm simply telling you the facts as Didi sees them."

"I'm not being critical of you, Norman—of Didi, yes. What do you think? What should we do?"

"Didi's got a mind of her own, Harry, as you most certainly know. She's got all the work she can handle right now, and if we want her we're going to have to pay her price."

It always came down to crap like this. "I'll be seeing her while I'm here," Harry said. "Maybe I can talk some sense into her. What about Zeke?"

"Zeke is fine, Harry—very confident, very optimistic. Of course, he thinks the world of you."

"Ponti wants him to test. Make a tape."

"Ah. Do you want my opinion, Harry?"

"What?"

"The boy won't test."

"He'll test or he won't get the part."

"Then you'd better go see Mr. Kunz and tell him it's on again—because Zeke won't test, Harry."

"I hope to see Otto this morning. To offer him *Aïda* in place of *Otello*. But I agree with you—I told Ponti that Zeke wouldn't test. Still—no harm in trying."

"You had me scared there for a minute," said Norman.

"Me, too," said Harry.

Predictably, Miss Powell could not locate Ferlinghetti, but Otto Kunz was perfectly agreeable to 11:00 A.M. So Harry headed uptown to the Carlyle to get that piece of bad news out of the way.

Otto answered the door himself. "*Mein lieber* Harry . . ."

Early in his Met career, when Otto still considered Zug his home, the cheerful little tenor had spent so many weeks each year at the Carlyle that he finally bought a spacious two-bedroom apartment in the place—an apartment which Marianne spent $50,000, it was said, in furnishing. Somehow Otto never looked at home in it—as at this moment. Resplendent in a heavily brocaded dressing gown (suspiciously like his Prince Calaf costume for *Turandot*), Otto had already lighted up a large Cuban cigar. After Kunz, Marianne would find Gian-Carlo refined indeed.

"And how goes it with Marianne?" Otto asked. "She has never liked this place, you know—Seventy-sixth street is too far from the action"—*achtshun*, in Otto's heavyweight declamation—"too far from the *Warenhäuser*—the big stores. She has preferred the St. Regis, the Gotham. But, regrettably, I already possess this *Wohnung* when we get married. She takes nearly five years to make it so. You remember how it was? And when it is finished"—desultory wave of the hand—"she goes. But this is no longer of importance. And how is the Rolex, *lieber* Harry? *Es tickt noch?*"

"Performs perfectly," Harry said, showing that he still wore it. "My most prized possession, in fact. As for Marianne? Marianne is—well, Marianne. You've not spoken to her—"

"I speak to her only last night. She says I am to be careful for myself and not to let you screw me. 'Screw me' is what she said! I told her not to worry for me, but for her boy friend, Herr Ponti. So she is very angry with that and calls me, you must pardon the expression, an old Jew. Which I cannot deny!"

"Not old, I wouldn't have said." Still, Harry saw Marianne's point. It was a shock to see Otto Kunz without his toupee.

"Fifty-seven years old," Otto said. "Make of that what you will."

They sat down on opposing sofas with an enormous marble coffee table between them, one of Marianne's happier inspirations. "I see by the *Wall Street Journal*," Harry said, "that you have out-foxed the Internal Revenue Service."

"This is so. We have had our day in the courtroom and I believe we are winning all our points. But it is the same everywhere—poor Edith, she is the same. We have contracts to these Caribbean corporations that exist only on paper, and your government—my government, too, as I am now a citizen—is very angry that we use their rules against them. I do not permit the Metropolitan to pay me money in this country because it is better for me that I have my money on some island which I have never seen."

Harry looked again to the Rolex. "Perhaps, Otto, we should discuss our business, however unpleasant—"

"Of course," said Otto. 'You are an important man, *lieber* Harry— I say this from my heart. And please do not be offended by what I tell you, *lieber* Harry, of Marianne's warning—that you will screw me. I have no worry where you are concerned."

"Thank you. But in this matter, Otto, please be aware that I must put my company's interest even before yours."

"*Natürlich.* This is only proper."

"Edith's most recent indisposition—"

"To save your precious time, *lieber* Harry—Otto knows more of this even than Harry Chapin. The only question is what you shall give Otto Kunz so that he does not sing the Otello in his contract—*nicht wahr?*"

"As usual, Otto, you have come straight to the point. Naturally, I, who negotiated your present contract—who wanted so much to have your Otello on tape—I regret the recent turn of events. However—"

"These lawyers, *lieber* Harry, they advise that we must begin a *Prozess*—a big discussion before the public—if Otto Kunz is not permitted to make this recording of his most famous role. But perhaps you will wish to make two recordings? One of Otto Kunz and one of this boy—Laframboise? You are serious—to record with this boy?"

"The sessions are already scheduled, Otto, for Rome."

"As I am told. Then, *lieber* Harry, let me speak again from my heart. This boy makes a very big name today, I know of it, in Europe. It is a novelty—this big black man who will be the Moor, as is written. He is not yet making his debut at the Metropolitan, but you run after him as if he is Caruso and Melchior and Slezak all in one body! He will have big successes in his life—bigger maybe than Otto Kunz. But it will be for a short time, *lieber* Harry—I think you know this. This boy is—tell me if I am wrong—not thirty years old?"

"Twenty-nine, I believe."

"Twenty-nine years old, *jawohl*—and he will already make a career of Otello? Otto Kunz is fifty-seven years old and did not sing this part, you will remember, *lieber* Harry, until nineteen-hundred-and-sixty-three when he was already forty-three years old!"

"Otto—"

"*Einen Moment, lieber* Harry—if you will permit. *Ja,* this season I have many engagements—see for yourself in my book. Stockholm, Wien, Paris, London. Why? Because the voice, even today, can do these three difficult things—Otello, Lohengrin and, *ja,* Radamès. Who is invited more often to the Metropolitan? No one. Otto Kunz is maybe not the greatest star, but they pay him three thousand dollars each night, *lieber* Harry, and this is not so bad in his class, do you not agree? He is not maybe, *wie sagst du,* 'glamorous' enough for opening night of the season. But he gives always value for money, *nicht wahr?* And I believe that the management even respects this Kunz a little—maybe even likes him *ein Bisschen!* They are fair to him and he is fair to them—each keeps the bargain. *Jaja, lieber* Harry—Herr Otto Kunz is maybe too old for his pretty young wife—but not too old for Otello and Lohengrin and Radamès. Otto knows how much voice he has each day, *lieber* Harry, and he spends no more than he has.

"But now this boy Laframboise, *der junge Herr Himbeere.* While I have not the good fortune to see this boy myself, I know from those very nice *Schallplatten* you so kindly send me from California that God has blessed this boy with the most *wunderschöne Stimme.* If I make a false analysis, please forgive me. But I say to you that he is more the *Hochbariton* than he is the tenor, which is very good for him because Signor Verdi has written this Otello too low for a real tenor. And when Herr Laframboise sings this wonderful role twenty, thirty times, he will truly be a *Bariton* again and he will be like poor Vinay, who was the best in the world and who had finished his career as *Basso.* . . ."

Harry kept his famous watch in view: now pushing 11:40 A.M. Unfortunately—just Harry's luck—this squat, bald little man was, in all essentials, correct. Poor Vinay. And poor Kunz, for that matter— Lohengrin actually too lyric for him now, after all that shouting as the Moor.

Harry eyed the sherry decanter on one of Marianne's exquisite antique sideboards. "Would you mind, Otto?"

"Of course, *lieber* Harry! I am such a bad host—in this Marianne is correct. No, not for me, *danke*—it is not allowed to my diet."

"*Prosit*," said Harry. "Mmmmm—excellent sherry—and, not to flatter you unduly, Otto, you have made an excellent analysis of the Laframboise situation. However, as we both know, such matters seldom obey the laws of logic—or even common sense."

"*Du hast Recht, mein lieber* Harry!"

"But getting back to our present dilemma—we would gladly record *your* Otello, Otto, if Edith were available for Desdemona. Unfortunately, she is not."

"Where does it say in my contract, *lieber* Harry, that I may sing Otello only if Mme. Cavalieri sings Desdemona?"

"And would you accept Signor Ponti as conductor?"

"*Jaja*, I think so. No, do not be surprised. Business is business, as we Americans say. I am not bothered that he wants so much my wife. Perhaps in the end he is *welcome* to my wife! But I hope he saves for the honeymoon a very large bank account!"

"Obviously, we want no lawsuits," Harry said. "But we also do not want two recordings of *Otello*—at least not right away. Which leads me to the idea of compromise. Are you open to compromise?"

"Maybe yes, maybe no. It must depend, Harry, on what it is you offer, *nicht wahr?*"

"Of course. Well, then . . ." First Harry poured himself a second glass of sherry. "What we propose is this. Despite its very great expense—and the fact that our catalogs don't really require a new recording at this time—we would be agreeable to substituting *Aïda*, which I know is very close to your heart, Otto, for *Otello*. And in place of the usual three-thousand-dollar advance—we would be able to offer five."

"But—this is *all?*" cried Otto. "This is *compromise?*"

"I'm afraid so—yes," said Harry.

"*Das ist nicht annehmbar! Nein*, it is no fair bargain."

"On a separate basis," Harry continued—mustering all possible earnestness now—"and trying as hard as we can, Otto, to overcome the present unfortunate stalemate—I would be able to offer one additional aria LP."

"*Nein, nein, nein!*" Otto punctuated his words by slamming his fist against the marble. "*Immer noch nicht annehmbar!* Again, *lieber* Harry—as much as I thank you for your personal kindness—this is still not a fair bargain for the loss of *Otello* which I have today in my contract."

Harry was beginning to feel annoyance with this smug little man with hardly any hair and an absentee wife who slept regularly in other men's beds. "Then I regret—" But he had no way to complete the sentence.

"Do not regret," Otto counseled. "Life is too short, *lieber* Harry, even for a young man like you. If this must end *so schlecht*—okay, we both do our best and it is bad luck."

"If there were *any* other way," Harry said. Damned sherry glasses were laughably small; and yet, to go a third time . . .

"So permit me," said Otto in a well-calculated *mezza voce*, "to say again what I say on the telephone to Marianne. No *Otello*? Okay, so then I must have the *Aïda*, which you are so kind to offer this morning, and I must have—yes, you will know that this has been in my heart also these past years—the *Lohengrin*. The *Aïda* I could do for you in summer nineteen-hundred-and-seventy-eight, the *Lohengrin* in summer nineteen-hundred-and-seventy-nine. And then I am finished. I will be then almost sixty years of age and that is enough. And maybe I also am lucky and find another company—maybe in Germany, where my success is better than here—to make with me *Otello*. And then I die a happy man. *Meinst du das nicht auch?*"

"I sympathize with your point of view entirely," Harry said. "But *two* complete operas—this is simply more than I can afford."

"More than the price, *lieber* Harry, of all these lawyers?"

"It is possible, Otto, to hire a great many lawyers for what it costs to record *Lohengrin*."

"This must be so. Forgive me for not understanding your business so well as I know my own. . . . But I have kept you already too long. . . ." With exaggerated politeness, Otto escorted Harry to the foyer.

"It is not allowed to my diet," the little tenor said, "to eat in a restaurant, or I would be happy to invite you—"

"Think nothing of it," Harry said. "Perhaps on my next visit . . ."

"And please to give my personal best regards to the charming Mrs. Chapin. . . ."

"Otto—"

"Yes, *lieber* Harry?"

The little bastard played it tough: you had to admire him for that. "As I say—if there were *any* further room for compromise—"

"I do not think so, *lieber* Harry. Unless—"

"Unless?"

"An idea that only this moment comes into my mind."

"Yes, Otto?"

"But maybe you would find it not acceptable."

"But then we might. The idea?"

"You shall make with me *Aïda* and *Lohengrin*—"

"As I've said, Otto—"

"—*but*, if I find this other company in Germany to make with me *Otello*—then I let you out of *Lohengrin. Was meinst du?*"

Harry didn't have to think twice. He threw his arms around the brocaded dressing gown. "Done."

"*Wunderbar!*" cried the beaming Otto. "Send around your man with the papers and we make a new contract! This proposition makes you happy, then?"

"Very happy," Harry said.

And why not? All he had to do now was get Consortium support for a new *Aïda*, which couldn't possibly cost Melos-Doria less than $100,000—and find another company willing to put on tape the legendary Otello of Herr Kunz. Home free and dry . . .

I I

". . . Trader Vic's it is," said the driver with admirable gusto. "Now, that's *my* kind of place. Expensive? Man . . ."

But Harry Chapin—visions of frozen Jamaican daiquiris dancing in his head—never made it to Trader Vic's; for upstairs in the lobby of the Plaza he ran into one of his oldest friends in the business, Herb Fink, record-reviewer and critic of *Music Week*, a fidgety little chipmunk of a man—vague resemblance to the middle-aged Mickey Rooney, Harry had always felt—who said: "The great Harry Chapin. How goes?"

"Terrible. Awful. Just had the most shattering experience."

"Wonderful. Buy me lunch and tell me all about it."

So, leaving the limousine out front, Harry and his pal Herb Fink strolled through a light drizzle down to Mercurio on 53rd Street, where they had often eaten in the old days, and where Harry still carried some weight.

"Reservation not required for you, Mr. Chapin. I have a nice corner table—come right this way. . . ."

Harry ordered a chilled bottle of Verdicchio; Fink agreed to go along, learn something about wines, which had always been, as everybody in the world knew, Harry Chapin's specialty.

"So what's the catastrophe, then?" Fink said. "Hey, you puttin' on a few pounds, or what?"

"A pound or two, yes—thanks for calling it to my attention. I've just come from Otto Kunz's place."

"Oh, yeah?"

"We've canceled Otto's *Otello*."

"Smart move, I'd say. You heard him lately?"

"This is off the record, by the way."

"*Toujours, toujours.* Background only—I didn't hear it here. So what'd he say? Pissed, huh?"

With some indiscretion but painful accuracy, Harry spun his tale of woe, ending with ". . . so, if you know anybody who's looking to make *Otello* with Otto Kunz . . ."

"Incredible."

"I repeat—*all* of this is off the record."

"And Otto didn't put Zeke down? Didn't rap him?"

"On the contrary. Otto says he's heard only good things about the boy—his only reservation being that the boy is too young. And operating in a vacuum, we'd probably all agree."

"He didn't mention *hearing* him?"

"Who?"

"Kunz. Hearing Zeke do it."

"Do what?"

"*Otello.* In Munich. They both work the German circuit, you know—Düsseldorf, Cologne, Bonn, Frankfurt, all those war towns."

"Hell, no. Are you *sure*? That Otto's *heard* Zeke in the flesh? In *Otello*?"

". . . Ah, gentlemen, today we have as the special . . ."

Harry ordered for them both. The antipasto (but no anchovies), followed by *gnocchi verdi*, followed by *insalata di funghi crudi*, followed by *petti di pollo alla bolognese*; a nice Bardolino to drink after the Verdicchio; and then, depending on their mood, the *zabaione* and *espresso*.

"Hey, Harry—how long you planning on us being here? I got a new girl friend I'm supposed to be meeting at five when she gets off work. But if we're going to eat all that—"

"You'll make it with minutes to spare. Now, what's this again— Otto *heard* Zeke in the role? What are you trying to say, Fink?"

"This is the way it went. I've got this on the very best authority, I shit you not. Otto, who's working the circuit, goes on a night off to Munich, and he hears this great new American fucking black *Wunderkind* Zeke Laframboise, and he thinks the guy's absolutely the greatest— this from a guy who's done what? maybe a hundred? two hundred *Otellos* himself.

"So he hears Zeke's maybe fifth *Otello*, maybe *third*, who knows? and he goes backstage, like all you great honchos do after the opera, and he sees Zeke, congratulating him, doncha know, in front of Marianne,

who's in those days still traveling around with Otto looking for action—
which she finds, but that's another story, which you know better than
I do.

"So later, privately, in a restaurant or someplace, Otto says to him,
hey, Zeke, you know you got a beautiful voice, really do, and you can
put on this beautiful show right now—complete with the color gimmick
and all. But really, Zeke, even Caruso, you know, the best of the best, he
wouldn't touch this fucking role even to the day he died—what? forty-
eight years old?—because he knew it would kill him.

"So don't do it, huh? Give it up now and go back to it later, toward
the end, okay? When your big career is behind you and you're coming
down the home stretch. Doing it that way, you can end up with a whole
new career—kind of the way Otto himself has done it—give twenty or
thirty *Otellos* in all the great houses of the world, and you go out with
everybody saying you were the greatest tenor of the age, all that shit.
. . . Hey, you know, whatever this is, this is fucking great."

"*Gnocchi verdi*—sprinkle some more of that cheese on it—spinach
dumplings. . . . So what happened? What did Zeke say?"

"So you know what this fucking great stud spade says to Kunz?
Now, I'm no great Kunz booster, God knows—never liked the timbre of
the voice and especially don't like that strangled sound he's getting at
the top now. But he's made a terrific career on what he's got, and he's
due some respect, wouldn't you say? So the great Zeke, whose big black
daddy hasn't even *made* him yet while Otto's out there in Berlin singing
for old Hitler, says to Otto: hey, Otto, what's the matter, you 'fraid you
won't get no more gigs once I start doing dis Otello o' mine?

"Now, I ask you, Harry—even for a callow youth like that, as we
used to say, that's a cheap shot, right? That's an illegal crack-back block
if I ever saw one.

"But you know Otto. Always the gentleman, he gets up in that
dignified way of his—he really *is* kind of a nice guy, you know?—gets his
hat to cover his shiny dome and he goes back the way he came, just
trying to be helpful to a real stupid linebacker. And the terrible thing is,
Harry—I saw this bastard, too, you know, on vacation, which is how I
happen to know all this crap—Zeke really looks the part and acts
enough to make the thing believable, and he's got this God-awful beautiful fucking voice up and down the scale, and when he strangles the girl
at the end you really find your hair standing on end and your arms are
all goose pimples and you wonder shouldn't somebody call the cops! The
guy's got all the raw talent in the world—he's musical, he's handsome
for a spade, and he's got the greatest goddam tenor voice anybody would
ever want to hear. But he's also got the same standard-the-world-over
tenor ego, you know? Gonads for brains. You ever heard of anything so

shit-for-brains stupid in your life, Harry? . . . What'd you say this was
again? Fuckin' tremendous chow, Harry Chapin—you've done it
again. . . ."

They walked back to Harry's limousine for exercise. "You ever been
to Rome?" Harry asked.

"Never have. Would love to go. Another good lunch? Count me
in."

"Just an idea. Stay loose, okay—end of August?"

Might not be a bad idea, really—have his old pal Herb Fink, who
already knew so much about Zeke and the others, come to Rome for the
sessions and do the album notes and maybe write some publicity hand-
outs, bios, what have you. Frankie had already picked up the publicity
assignment, of course, but it might not hurt to have somebody there
who could actually write. Maybe do an "appreciation" rather than a
review for his magazine, too. A little payola never hurt in situations like
these.

He was late back to the office. Gravinius, who had arrived promptly
at 3:00, met him with a gruff "Nice of you to come" and a sullen
glare.

"No damned cabs in this town. May I offer you something? Sherry?
Champagne?"

"Nothing."

It sounded so stupid, the way he offered drinks. But one never
knew about other people's habits. "Well," Harry said. "How's business?"

Gravinius & Greene, firm of disreputable lawyers, as far as Harry
knew. Simon (Sy) Gravinius and Schuyler (Sky) Greene: called Sy and
Sky in the music trade, which they mostly serviced: two of the less
distinguished products of the Harvard Law School. Someone had to be
at the bottom of each class.

"Business is fine, Harry. So let's get down to some, okay? I am not
at all amused by your recent conduct with my client Mr. Laframboise."

"Amused? I didn't realize that amusement was a requisite in your
line of work."

"Don't give me that superior crap of yours, Harry. You know what
I'm saying. You had no right to discuss terms with my client."

"You are misinformed, Sy. Or perhaps you would now prefer 'Mr.
Gravinius'? Your client proposed terms to *me*—if you can call them
terms. He merely said, in the course of an extended conversation on
artistic matters, that he expected a large advance, an appropriate royalty

and I forget what else. You sure I can't get you something? I'm going to have a glass of soda water, if you don't mind. . . ."

These skunks were all alike: hated having you talk directly to their clients for fear they, the hangers-on, wouldn't get a big enough piece of the action. Eliminate the middleman, Harry Chapin's motto.

"For one thing," Gravinius barked, "Zeke will *not* test for Mr. Ponti. Oh, yes, Norman Rose told me."

"This is no reflection on Zeke—"

"Furthermore, Zeke doesn't even want Mr. Ponti in the project."

"Well, I'm sorry to hear that," said Harry in his most reasonable tone. "Because there is nothing in Mr. Laframboise's present con-tract—and there can be nothing in any future contract with this company—which gives him that right of approval."

"Also, Harry—hey, let's cut out the bullshit, okay? and just speak to each other man to man?—also he thinks Didi's a lousy Desdemona. He saw her do it on Italian TV and he says, except for her tits, she stunk up the joint."

"Man to man, yes, fine," Harry said. "But again—Zeke simply doesn't have veto powers in the matter of casting. Beyond that, Sy, Didi sells records—you must know this, being her attorney and seeing her royalty statements as you do."

"She's a wiggy broad, Harry. So, yes, she sells records. But she's no Tebaldi. She's got no class."

"Never said she did. Just an innocent little girl from Dover, Dela-ware, far as I know."

"Shit. What else have you got—any Scotch? You've got a way, Harry, of driving people to drink."

Harry poured a stiff Scotch on the rocks for Gravinius and a glass of plain soda water for himself.

"*Look*, Harry," said Gravinius, his tone a touch more human now, "I *want* my guy to make a deal with you people. I really do. But you've got to be *fair* to him. He's only going around this track one time. When you're hot you're hot. And this boy's hot."

"Agree. Agree. So. Thus. The *Otello*. Fabulous opportunity for him."

"So what are you going to *pay* him? What's your *offer?*"

Harry leaned back in the plush visiting-VIP armchair, surveyed the space above Gravinius's head. "His current contract, as you know, Sy, calls for six percent proportional on operatic recordings, with an advance of one thousand dollars. We propose to maintain the royalty rate but double the advance."

"You must be kidding. Tell me you're *kidding!*"

"Not kidding."

"Hey, Harry, this is *me*, remember? Sy Gravinius? Let's not waste each other's time, okay? I *know* where you're coming from. You've promised a bunch of people there's going to be a new *Otello*—why, I don't know—maybe you've got a death wish or something. With Cavalieri out of it, you've got to unload Kunz because Otto can't sing the goddam piece anymore, and anyway Kunz without Cavalieri wouldn't sell ten copies. If Kunz wasn't balling Cavalieri, *she* wouldn't want him either—so let's not jack each other off, okay? You've got to get yourself another boy, and there's nobody else around except *my* boy. And you expect to pay him the same royalty he gets *today*, while he's still *nobody*? That's *unethical*, Harry!"

This swine wished to discuss ethics? "What terms did you have in mind, Sy?"

"I have in mind a fair deal. I have in mind a ten-percent royalty and a five-thousand-dollar advance on the first package—the *Otello*. After that, we go to seventy-five hundred on the second and ten-thousand on the third. That's what I have in mind. And that's a fair deal for this boy."

Laboriously, Harry wrote the figures down. Such ridiculous demands warranted a gesture of contempt, but he could think of none. "What can I say?" Harry said.

"So what bothers you?"

"What doesn't? These incredible advances. The very idea of three roles, when all we really wish to discuss is *Otello*."

"But you already *gave* him that! Three roles! In Paris! *Didn't* you?"

Splendid. Gravinius reduced to shouting. "I said we would certainly *consider* other roles. As follow-ups to *Otello*. But to say that—"

"You're welching. You're absolutely *welching!* I've never heard anything like this in my life. *Harry Chapin*—I can't *believe* it."

This from one of the great crooks of the business: albeit a crook who knew the value of his merchandise. "Let us say—for sake of argument, Sy—that we're willing to undertake three roles. *Otello* and two others to be mutually agreed—"

"He *told* you in Paris that one of the others has got to be *Trovatore* and the third is maybe *Cav-and-Pag. Didn't* he? Am I losing my hearing, or what?"

"Fine. For sake of argument, fine. But the point is, Sy, I can't pay more than I can pay. Obviously, you appreciate my predicament—you described it so well. We're talking here, Sy, about some very expensive manpower—Mr. Ponti, your client Miss del Campo, Mr. Toggi—who, parenthetically, thinks of himself as the star of *Otello*—et cetera. So you see . . ."

"Yeah, I'm touched. But look, as long as you're crying anyway, let me give you another point, and this one's a deal-breaker."

"*Another* deal-breaker?"

"He's got to have one let-out. Another label—don't ask me which one, okay?—Europe-based, which is maybe a clue—has offered Zeke a role—nothing you'd want to do anyway—and Zeke's got to be free to accept it. That's summer of seventy-nine, so it wouldn't affect *Otello* one way or another."

"But I find this most strange," Harry lied. "On the strength of Zeke's words to me in Paris, we are now in the process of setting up *Trovatore* for summer seventy-nine."

"No, that's impossible. Make that eighty. Or, better, eighty-one."

"Mmmmmm. It seems hopeless, doesn't it?"

"It's *not* hopeless, Harry. If you'll be halfway *reasonable*."

"And what do I get in return? Quid pro quo, as you lawyers like to say? For the let-out?"

"You get the deal. You get Zeke exclusively for three complete-opera sets—*Otello* and *Trovatore* and probably *Cav-and-Pag*."

"So—nothing for the let-out? Impossible."

"What do you *want*, Harry? Be *reasonable*, huh?"

"What about this? On the set that Zeke makes for the European company, Melos-Doria will take distribution for the U.S. and Canada—thus preserving his exclusivity to Melos-Doria here—and the producing company gets the rest of the world. We pay to the producing company, of course, the usual use-royalty on our sales here."

"No, he can't. He's already agreed to a world deal with the other company."

Ah, an error on Mr. Gravinius's part. "He *agreed?*" said Harry with mock outrage. "He's signed a *contract?*"

"As good as. Now look, Harry—"

"No, sir—I ask *you* to look. If I may remind you, Sy, Zeke is exclusive to Melos-Doria for a period of seven years from a year ago last July first—yes, I believe my memory is correct. You and I are talking now about a new contract, but, assuming that nothing comes of our discussions, Melos-Doria will most certainly take all necessary legal steps to protect the rights extended to it under the existing contract."

"Harry, don't get *excited*, okay? Look—sure, you and I know that the kid can't commit to anything. But he's, well, an unsophisticated boy from a very simple background. He's not *bothered* by contractual details, Harry. That's why he's got *me*."

"Fine. Well, one of the 'details,' if you like, is that we must have something in return for the surrendering of our exclusivity."

"Okay—so what do you *want?*" Gravinius moaned.

"How about one of *their* exclusive artists? A swap—how would that be?"

"Who?"

"Who have they got? On their roster?"

"I can't say or you would know the company."

"This is madness. How can we possibly negotiate in the dark like this? No, it's back to square one, I'm afraid."

"What do you mean?"

"I mean we wanted very much to use Zeke in our *Otello*. But at this price—with these conditions—it's impossible. We'll go with Kunz—or else we'll postpone."

"You're bluffing."

"We'll see."

"Then the German company—"

"German?"

"The other company, then—*they'll* do an *Otello* for Zeke."

"Fine. As long as they do it seven years from a year ago last July first."

Gravinius was instantly on his feet, gesticulating with his Scotch glass, which, fortunately, was empty. "You don't mean you would *hold* him to that? In the face of an offer for *Otello?*"

"*I* am making him an offer for *Otello*. Yes, we most certainly would hold him to his present contract—which you, I believe, negotiated."

"You *bastards*."

"Plural—or do you mean singular?"

"This is the most unethical—"

"Use that word one more time and this meeting is over."

"Okay, sorry. But *really*, Harry—"

"What about this? Two roles firm instead of three. And in return for the let-out, let's make the advances four thousand each, and let's make the royalty seven and a half percent proportional."

Gravinius sat down; Harry stood up. "Freshen that for you?"

"Had enough," Gravinius said. "Out of the question."

"Well, then . . ."

They want to play rough? Fine. He knew how to handle these Graviniuses and Blankenhorns, these parasites who bled their clients dry and always ended up on top, no matter what happened to the artists; boys with nothing to recommend them except a law degree and a lack of conscience. He had figured out, of course, who the other firm was. His rival for Zeke's affections was undoubtedly his old friend Dr. Udo Blinn, boss of DDRSch—Deutsche-Demokratische-Republik-Schallplatten, the boys from East Berlin. Trusty Jean-Luc Barraud had reported seeing Blinn and Zeke together in Paris shortly before Harry's arrival. And the piece was undoubtedly *Lohengrin*, which DDRSch had tabled last year when their house tenor Rosemeyer developed ulcers and went into early retirement. It was crazy: everybody making the same pieces, bartering for all the same singers. Harry would have to make a fast trip to Berlin to see Blinn, who made the business decisions. Blinn had an ancient

Kraut named Von Brauchitsch who handled the artistic stuff. This was Harry's mistake: trying, in the interests of economy, to combine the two: commercial and artistic decisions, which were often mutually exclusive. Tough bunch of cookies, the DDRSch people. There would eventually be a swap, the hated quid pro quo: something they wanted for something you didn't but which you had to swallow in the interests of "artist relations." What did DDRSch have that Harry might want? Nothing, probably. But if you bundled up enough nothings, you might have something. This was the beauty of opera: no such thing as a true zero in the opera business.

"Tell you what," said Harry in his most conciliatory manner. "Why don't we do this? Let's sleep on it—reconsider each other's position. Then, say, Friday, let's talk on the phone and see if we can't find some common ground."

"There *is* a time element," said Gravinius, very sour now.

"Something more urgent that Friday?" said Harry.

Mutter, mutter, mutter; no, Gravinius guessed not. "Really, Harry—I don't know what it is, but there seems to be a barrier between us. What's the problem? I like you—I really do. I wish there were some way—"

"My fault entirely," Harry said. "Friday—why don't we try again on Friday?" As though Friday were All Saints Day or something: day having special properties which would overcome the fabled Chapin obstinacy. "And please give my regards to Rachel."

"Rosalyn," Gravinius said with malice.

III

Thursday was devoted to Vladimir Slonimsky and his New York representative, Joseph Blankenhorn, Esquire. In the morning mail came a letter on the subject from Norman Rose, who was still in Burbank:

Dear Harry:

Trust you had a good trip back and aren't half so tired as I was on my arrival here. By the time you read this, I shall be making Chopin waltzes with your protégé Donny Kurtz—thank you very much!

Just a quick report on that other piano player, dear Vova, whom I saw briefly Monday night. In view of his decision to take up more or less permanent residence in New York (to be near Juilliard, etc.)—and since he continues to see you, quite correctly, as his principal sponsor and champion in the Con-

sortium—he would prefer to have the new contract made
directly with Melos-Doria (i.e., LTI) rather than with
Globelektron, assuming the tax benefits (Vova's Dutch An-
tilles corporation, etc.) can be preserved. I begged off—saying
you and Mr. Blankenhorn were better equipped than I to
discuss legal niceties. I have done my duty. . . .

Incidentally—or perhaps not so incidentally—I got the
distinct impression from Vova's manner, as well as his words,
that he pays very little attention to what Blankenhorn tells
him (except in the most technical aspects), and that, regardless of any view Blankenhorn might take of Melos-Doria, Vova
will sign if only to obtain the services—which he admires
totally—of one Harry Chapin! Thought you should know this
before your meeting.

And finally, the man illustrated various musical points to
me at the piano (you'll be happy to know that he's now on a
Scriabin "kick," as our pop colleagues say) and I can only
repeat what I'm sure you already know—namely, that this
gentleman plays the piano better than anybody else on earth.

Yours ever upward and onward in the Arts,

Norman

Noble sentiments, to be sure—but how, dear Norman, do we get
this talented old gentleman to sign the necessary piece of paper? How,
with Joe Blankenhorn—Harvard Law School, yes, but nothing like that
street scum Gravinius—standing in the way? (*Interposing* himself,
Blankenhorn would have said.) But then this—Harry reminded himself—was what he got paid the $100,000 for.

". . . The object of all negotiations being to confuse the judgment
and paralyze the will. Naturally, the orchestra capitulated."

He had forgotten what fun it was to take luncheon with Joe
Blankenhorn. Now, *this* was the law with some breeding, some wit. "Go
on, Joe— and then what?"

"Why, André said yes, of course. And the people in Pittsburgh
couldn't be more pleased."

André being Previn. "But wouldn't that have been a nice post for
one of *your* artists, Joe—say, Ponti? Or perhaps Córtez? You have such
a long list of distinguished clients—it must be hard to choose. Dear
Freddie Sax over there, even?" Said with a nod in the direction of the
illustrious young gentleman who was just now attacking his *pâté* several
tables farther back in the room.

"My, my, Harry—you are so charmingly naïve about these things.

Which is one reason I've looked forward with such anticipation to this luncheon. . . ."

Harry had been late in arriving, of course: it was best to keep these great men waiting, even in Caravelle, if you expected to have their respect or gain any advantage later on. Confuse the judgment, paralyze the will, as it were. But maybe not with this particular gentleman. Blankenhorn seemed so much more at home in Manhattan than in Burbank, California, for example. Still the slim-as-a-pencil pinstriped smoothie, but now totally at ease. Half the luncheon crowd at Caravelle may have wondered who the elegant masked man with the white horse and silver bullets was to command Table No. 1 just inside the big room—but the other half did business with him. Like young Freddie Sax over there, who was the sixty-seventh conductor on Blankenhorn's list and who said "Good afternoon, Mr. Blankenhorn" but "Hi, Harry, why the hell don't you answer my phone calls?" (Because, Freddie, I hate the idea of making records of little-known Schubert and early Liszt and unsalable Hindemith—though I love *you* because you're an unpredictable rogue with a considerable inheritance and even some talent and you give terrific Christmas gifts—see, I am carrying your fantastic Gucci briefcase right this moment.)

"I'm sorry, Joe—captivated by the menu. You were saying?"

". . . Entirely a question of timing—of striking at precisely the right moment in a career, neither too early nor—worse, far worse—too late. Mehta, for example . . ."

"God, yes, tell me about Zubie—the Philharmonic fiasco. Have you decided, by the way? I was thinking of the veal. . . ."

Their captain sensed precisely the right moment: neither too early nor too late; joined them for a brief critique of the *carte de jour.*

"The specialty today, gentlemen . . ."

But no—Blankenhorn's regimen permitted nothing more than a simple green salad and a small piece of sea bass, broiled—"dry, please— no sauce of any kind"—and nothing to drink.

Harry, cowering in the great man's immense shadow, accepted the very same choices, but with a second vermouth cassis. This would be his first luncheon without wine in—ten years? *Twenty* years, more like it.

". . . Oh, yes," Blankenhorn continued, "business as usual at the old stand. Goodbye, Pierre; welcome, Zubin. Surely no surprise, wouldn't you agree?"

Cheerful swine: easy come, easy go. "And no scandal?" Harry said, playing with his lettuce. "No juicy scenes?"

"Heavens no, Harry—not at all the style. Pierre had completed his mission: educate the masses of Gotham, jam all that modernism and erudition down our poor deprived throats. So now we can go back to basic pop: Tchaikovsky Four, Schumann One, Dvořák Old Number

Five. Goodbye to the avant-garde and good riddance. We've had enough Moderns around here—and enough empty seats—to last out the century. . . ."

Yes, again Harry remembered: you came away from a Blankenhorn luncheon stuffed not with Caravelle's superb French cuisine but with Joe's superb gossip. "And what about the Met? How long can Jimmy Levine keep it up? Tell me about the Met. . . ." Harry was like a schoolgirl, president of the local fan club: Tell me what Jimmy has for breakfast. . . .

By contrast, terms for the new contract with Slonimsky—when Harry was finally able to bring up the subject—seemed of little interest. "Royalty," Harry said. "We accept the twelve and a half for U.S. and Canada, but ten is our maximum for U.K., and half-rate elsewhere."

"We won't argue."

"Advances. Sixty thousand a year over the five-year period."

"Agreed."

"Product commitment. Six LPs, but no penalty if Vova can't deliver that number."

"Agreed."

"Packaging allowance. Ten percent on LPs, twenty on tape."

"We won't argue."

"Coupling restrictions. As now—only with Vova's prior consent."

"Agreed."

"Sorry to take time on such nits and lice, Joe—but better now than later."

"Entirely concur."

"And finally—ownership of masters. This gives us a problem, Joe."

"Vova is adamant, Harry. His tax people have expressed concern. Capital gains—you understand."

"I propose this. Ownership of masters to remain with Melos-Doria until such time as the applicable advances are recovered. Afterwards, masters revert to Vova."

"I like it. Let me put it to Vova. I think I can persuade him."

"Well, then—"

"There are two additional problems, Harry, from our side. The first is advertising. The second is audio-visual. Vova feels—and I concur—that he has never benefited from media exposure such as RCA and CBS have afforded Rubinstein and Horowitz. This isn't right. Vova will require a specific guarantee as to moneys spent on print and TV advertising. Say, twenty-five thousand dollars per release?"

"I'm afraid that's unacceptable, Joe. Unless you wish to make such costs recoupable from royalties?"

"Have Vova pay for his own advertising? Absolutely not."

"What about audio-visual?"

"Vova is of the opinion—shared by many of us—that video-cassettes or videodiscs will become a major business in the future. He wishes to retain all rights related thereto."

"We would propose to share such rights fifty-fifty," Harry said with no great enthusiasm.

"I doubt that Vova will find this acceptable. But again, let me put it to him. So—except for the advertising commitment, we are agreed?"

"And the audio-visual—yes, I think so."

"Excellent. It's such a pleasure, Harry, doing business with a man of your sensibilities."

"As always, Joe, the pleasure is mine."

They shook hands. True, Harry preferred this smooth son of a bitch to street scum like Gravinius, but the fundamental problem was the same: like Gravinius, Blankenhorn controlled an important segment of the Melos-Doria roster—Ponti, Córtez, Sax, Kaufman—meaning that he knew precisely what Melos-Doria could or could not afford to pay, and—again like Gravinius—the bastard wasn't above discussing one artist's terms with another, although this was clearly a conflict of interests and a violation of the New York Bar Association's canons of ethical conduct.

"We'll see you tonight, I expect," said Blankenhorn warmly, "at Juilliard's reception for Vova. Seven o'clock, I believe, at the Hampshire House?"

"Yes, of course," Harry said. "Wouldn't miss it for the world."

Unless something in a skirt came his way first.

But none did. Harry arrived at the Hampshire House promptly at 7:00, hoping for—what? The point of the reception was Juilliard's announcement that the legendary Vladimir Slonimsky would be giving master classes to advanced piano students in the fall quarter. Melos-Doria's Marketing Department had taken the occasion—and shared the costs—to announce a uniform edition of all of Slonimsky's past recordings, some fifty LPs in all.

"A little commerce with a little art," Angélique Slonimsky said to him in the receiving line.

"Not at all, Angélique," Harry replied, kissing the beautiful Parisian lady's hand. "A little commerce with a cornucopia of art . . ."

The Garden Room held something like two hundred people in comfort—meaning that the present crowd approached three hundred and was still climbing. Harry had to fight his way through a flock of Blankenhorns and Finks and Graviniuses before hitting his target, Vova, whose stooped six-foot-four frame had been backed into a corner by a covey of admiring ladies—an old jaguar treed by noisy hounds.

"Ah, dear Harry. If I may be excused, sweet ladies . . ."

Taking Harry's hand as an elderly teacher might take a young student's, Slonimsky said: "Do you suppose"—his rumbling basso flawed by uncertainty—"that we may find a moment's privacy? Perhaps another salon? Or would this be too impolite of me? Angélique always remarks . . ."

"Nonsense," said Harry, taking courage from the gentle giant's weakness. "They've only come to eat and drink at your expense anyway. Come . . ."

There was something terribly sad about Vova now. His limp was more pronounced—the disability that had been with him since an auto accident in the Paris of the '20s—and the great white-crested head seemed a burden almost too heavy to bear. Nonetheless, he remained an estimable figure, still favoring those elegant London-tailored double-breasted suits that had gone in and out of style a dozen times over the years but never seemed out of style on Vladimir Slonimsky.

"How is this, Vova? We won't be bothered here." They settled in a private alcove down the hall, where old ladies, Harry imagined, wrote letters to their grandchildren in the West. "You're looking well, Vova. The sea air agrees with you."

"Yes, I am still afraid of the flying, even at my age, when it would make no difference. But this new *Queen Elizabeth*—avoid it if you can, it is nothing to do with real ships. Poor Trixl, she was ill from the moment we left England. . . ."

Vova had never flown, even in his most active period, meaning that promoters had to measure time between concerts in terms of sailing schedules. For many years Vova had made his home in a great mansion on the tip of Lido Isle at Newport Beach, California, but the population explosion following World War II had driven him off, and he had settled with Angélique and his beloved dogs—always huge black poodles, the latest being Trixl and Tag—in London. But England, too, had proved too confining, its climate too harsh for an old gentleman who depended for his livelihood on the dexterity of his fingers, and they had come back to an enormous Fifth Avenue penthouse (Norman had reported) and the challenge of master classes at Juilliard.

"And what of your health, Harry? It's been over a year, hasn't it, since we talked? You look tired. Are you working too hard? Are you watching your food . . . ?"

"I'm fine, Vova, really. It's good of you to ask."

"And Leonid and Sylvia? They are well?"

"Fine, fine. Saw them, oh, two months ago when they stopped briefly in Los Angeles. They love Scottsdale, of course—all that sun. They seem to be very happy."

"This is wonderful to hear. They have earned their rest. Please give them my love when you see them next."

"I shall."

"And what do you think of this new scheme?"

"The Juilliard appointment? Quite marvelous for Juilliard!"

"I speak of these new records. This new contract. What is it you think I should do? I no longer hold so tightly to my opinions. It is a frightening thing—not to know one's mind. . . ."

"I understand from Norman Rose that you have renewed your interest in Scriabin. Perhaps . . ."

"Only a curiosity, nothing more. He is not for me, on records. The other fellow . . ." The other fellow was Horowitz. Vova detested reference to Horowitz—not because he feared competition but because he saw all artists as unique beings not susceptible to comparison. "In truth, dear Harry, I have no passions today. I shall do whatever you like."

Harry found the faraway quality of Slonimsky's musings most disturbing: could such a man lose his convictions overnight? "Norman told you of our basic idea? The six LPs over five years?"

"Yes, and I suppose it is a reasonable program. But I am an old man now, Harry. I do not know how much more I can do—or how much more I want to do."

"Well, as I told you in England, Vova, my idea is a simple one. Don't worry about the recordings themselves. Work on whatever repertoire pleases you. When you have something you think of interest, tell us and we'll tape it right there in the privacy of your apartment. If you like the results—the interpretation—then we can go into the studio and in a few brief hours put down the finished version. In this way, we shall build a savings account, if you like—from which we can select tracks for the individual LPs. Working like this—without the usual pressures, the usual commercial considerations—I think this is best for you. And we're not talking about a giant program. Don't be put off by the idea of six LPs. We are talking about a few Rachmaninoff preludes —your favorites—perhaps a little Chopin, Schumann of course, one or two of the Liszt things. Nothing more onerous than this. A modest program—as befits the greatest of players."

Slonimsky smiled for the first time. "In your own field, dear Harry—I believe you to be a great player, also. It is like the Beethoven. You have great powers of persuasion."

Their first collaboration in 1959—Vladimir Slonimsky, world-class pianist, and young Harry Chapin, novice record-producer. They had gone to Severance Hall in Cleveland and put down all thirty-two Beethoven sonatas in seventeen working days—an incredible feat then as now. The *"Pathétique"* disc alone, released separately, had sold over

100,000 copies. "As a matter of fact, Vova, Joe Blankenhorn and I had
luncheon today. I believe we are close to agreement. There are only one
or two ticklish points remaining."

"It is a problem for you?"

"Economically, Vova, I must be able to justify to my Board of
Directors . . ."

"Poor Harry—you have my sympathy. But do not worry about this
fellow Blankenhorn. If he becomes too big a problem, I am certain you
will know what to do. I speak of our friend in Marseilles."

"Of course," Harry said. "Please—I didn't intend to bring up business."

"Quite right, dear Harry. Never between us, the business. I only
request that you make this contract so as to be fair to us both. I count
on you for that."

"I shall do my best."

"But now—should we not return to our guests? Angélique says
always that I am rude beyond forgiveness. . . ."

He had determined to leave—until a vaguely familiar face and form
came into view.

"I understand that you don't like artist managers, Mr. Chapin."

"Oh? And who told you that? May I offer you a glass of champagne?"

"By all means—the least we can do is drink up Juilliard's champagne. My husband told me, of course. Or is it simply that you don't
like Joe?"

Joe Blankenhorn's nasty Smith-trained wife, Renée. When it came
to ambition and dedicated career-building, this lady had it all over poor
Joe. Unlike Joe, who had started with nothing but his Harvard Law
School diploma, this lady had begun life very well connected in the arts;
her Daddy, who owned banks and insurance companies, was one of the
Metropolitan's most liberal sponsors, and his money had gotten Renée
on all sorts of boards, including Juilliard's. About Harry's age, she was a
tall, thinnish woman with pretty good tits—braless now, in a very pretty
gown—Halston?—whom Harry had coveted once, oh, ten years ago.

"Not like Joe? On the contrary—if I were going to be an artist
manager, I would want to be just like Joe. It's the breed in general I
dislike."

"My, you *are* candid. Joe's been keeping things from me."

Harry cracked the famous Chapin smile. "Besides, artist managers
don't generally like record people—hasn't he told you that? Here
now—"

Chap with the champagne finally came their way: Harry got them both refills.

"I'm afraid I don't know many record people. Should I?"

"Well, I can think of at least one you should know." How many glasses had he had? If he was going to make an ass of himself with this powerful lady, might as well do a good job of it.

"Joe and I are giving a small dinner party this evening—just Vova and a few close friends. Did Joe tell you?"

"He did, but I have sent 'regrets.' I'm afraid I'm not at my best in groups, however small or distinguished. My strength, such as it is, is one on one."

"Really? How sad. I would have liked to continue our conversation—hear your views on managers' wives."

"The loss is entirely mine, dear lady. Another time, then—to be optimistic?"

"Perhaps . . ."

Oh, yes—definitely another time. And definitely one on one. . . .

IV

Friday. He walked in extraordinary sunshine to the Melos-Doria quarters, arriving at 10:00 in excellent spirits. "Any calls, Eunice?"

"Not yet, Harry. But lots of mail, I'm afraid. Still taking your coffee black, isn't that right?"

"Yes, Eunice, thank you. And if a Mrs. Blankenhorn should call . . . No, never mind."

The first cable was the one he was hoping for:

COUNT GIMPEL DELIGHTED RECEIVE YOU MARSEILLES 23RD MAY
FULL DISCUSSION TOGGI ETC STOP PLEASE INFORM IF CONVENIENT
STOP WITH GREATEST RESPECT STOP KLAUS KOENIG GLOBELEKTRON
ZURICH

It would be *most* convenient. "Eunice, if you don't mind . . ."

He gave her instructions for the reply and for his new plane ticket; there would be interim stops in Milan and Munich, but better leave the return open. . . . Also he would require another expense advance, "yes, another thousand, I guess."

The second cable was also good news:

PONTI WILLING ACCEPT LAFRAMBOISE WITHOUT AUDITION AFTER
HEARING PIRATED TAPES RECENT DUESSELDORF PAGLIACCI STOP

YOU ARE TO BE CONGRATULATED STOP DR RAFFAELE QUINZI
DISCHI LA CIMA MILAN

"Oh, and Eunice . . .?"
He dictated an immediate reply:

LAFRAMBOISE DELIGHTED PONTI DECISION STOP EXPECT SIGNED
CONTRACT THIS YEAR OR NEXT STOP REGARDS HARRY CHAPIN
MELOS-DORIA BURBANK

Giving the Italian lawyer something to puzzle over and preserving
Harry's reputation as a man of enigmatic wit.
The third cable was not good news:

FLORESCU REQUESTS DATES OTELLO SESSIONS LONDON STOP ALSO
REQUIRES FIRST CLASS TICKET BELGRADE LONDON NEW YORK
BELGRADE STOP PLEASE ADVISE STOP WITH COMPLIMENTS JEAN-
LUC BARRAUD APOGEE SA PARIS

Meaning that Herr König, whose business this properly was, had
not yet had the courage to inform Florescu that Signor Toggi would be
the Consortium's Iago in place of the Rumanian boy: inefficiency which
was most uncharacteristic of the useful Swiss—unless Signor Toggi's
participation was not the *fait accompli* that Mr. Schröder-Devrient had
described. A most worrying development—which Harry would investi-
gate personally in Milan.
So much for cables; he moved on to the letters. The first was from
Hilary Cairns, sent special-delivery and written in longhand on stationery of the Hotel Principe e Savoia, Milan:

> . . . Your participation in the Conference was most significant
> and, further, most refreshing for all of us tired Common
> Market functionaries. Won't you give serious thought to ply-
> ing your trade on our side of the Atlantic?
>
> By coincidence bumped into a great fan of yours, an
> American by the name of Hoyt Dell, who, whilst an amateur
> in the 19th-century meaning of that word, is a gentleman of
> some artistic attainments, coming well recommended by
> Maestro Adler. He seems to possess superb artist-relations gifts,
> should we ever be in a position to consider consolidation of
> those duties worldwide under one executive. Most regrettably
> he appears to be a man of vast means, president and proprietor
> of his own franchising scheme for your national dish, the hot-
> dog. . . .

Incredible! *Unbelievable.* What *was* Dell's game?
The next letter—a fat onionskin affair addressed in the florid hand
of Mrs. Marianne Kunz—was similarly irritating:

. . . So happy—and surprised!—to see you again, even so briefly, dearest Harry. Thank you from the bottom of your Marianne's heart.

Now in fairness to all concerned and especially Otto, who has always trusted you one hundred percent about his career—and notwithstanding our marital situation which, as you like to say, is immaterial . . . can only tell you in all honesty, dearest Harry, that Otto has given up many excellent dates—this I know to be a fact—to keep himself free for your sessions in London, and now to find out that you have gotten another singer . . . Otto not always the easiest man in the world to get along with—who was it who said that high notes adle the brain—am I spelling that right? . . .

Got to run now, dearest Harry, but am enclosing Gian-Carlo's itinerary which will give you some idea of the life I (we) lead. Dying to see you again very soon—you are so clever, why don't you arrange to have our paths cross more often?! Stay well, dearest, and think kind thoughts of your loving

Marianne

Once a tall, thin girl from the polluted shores of Lake Erie, now a fairy princess by the Lake of Zug. Ah, to be in show business . . .

He was about to have his first champagne of the day when the switchboard girl rang through:

"There's a call for you on line one, Mr. Chapin. A Mr. Fur-len—?"

"Ferlinghetti—yes, I'll take that one."

"Harry, dear boy? And to what do I owe this delightful surprise?" squeezed out with Giacomo's widely-imitated fag unctiousness.

"Good morning, Jackie. As a matter of fact, I'm trying to get in touch with your client—to sound her out on an artistic matter or two."

"My goodness, I don't think so."

"What do you mean?"

"Only this, dear boy—she's not in very good form appearancewise."

"I don't understand."

"Don't be dense, Harry—she's had one of her things."

"What things?"

"Surely you've heard?"

"No. What?"

"The things she does with her boys?"

"No. *What* things? *What* boys?"

"Poor darling—I guess you haven't heard. Which makes you the only one. Really, I'm *ashamed* of you," with giddy laughter.

"Frankly, Jackie, I'm a little short of time this morning—"

"All *right*, then. She finds herself three or four or even more, I can't swear, of these beautiful young boys, and very fetching they are, I can tell you, Negro boys usually, because Didi's into black, you know. And they go someplace very private—I let her use my own poor dwelling on one occasion, but never again, they broke absolutely *everything*. And she lets them do anything they want—absolutely anything— but nothing that leaves marks, of course, no welts or anything like that, because, naturally, of her appearance. But this time, last night or when- ever it was, matters got just the slightest bit out of hand, and she's given her pretty little self a bump and bruise or two—yes, even a nasty smudge on that pretty little face, which means no pix for a while and I wouldn't guess she'd feel very much like warbling for dear Melos-Doria either. . . ."

"My God."

"Yes, exactly. But don't burden yourself, dear boy—Didi's a fun girl, as we've always known, and one must accept an occasional rough patch among the smooth."

"Well—can I *see* her? Will she see me?"

"You can always try, Harry darling. Just tootaloo along, why don't you, and give her bell a ring. No harm in trying, as they say."

His Desdemona, so pretty and vivacious and reasonably talented— but, like most of them, programmed for self-destruction. Why did she abuse herself as she did? Obviously, she expected to beat the devil—but how?

And could not the same questions be addressed to you, dear boy?

V

The driver was delighted to have a destination in the Village. It was a warm spring day and Harry asked to have the electric sunroof opened. Traffic cops still frowned, but pedestrians moved with a lighter step and men carried their jackets.

"Del Campo—that's the opera-star one, ain't it?" the driver said. "I carried her a few times—that's a nice lively broad, ain't she?"

Harry hated it when people spoke deprecatingly of Didi. "She's a very nice lady," he said primly, and the driver raised the glass partition.

Didi's brownstone was off Eleventh Street. She and Edith Cavalieri had one thing in common: a man in the auto business. Didi's, however, was official: Mario Bucellatti, vice president of Fiat, had made her Mrs. Bucellatti. But now they were divorcing, the gossip columns said—now that her career had blossomed and she had her own money. Didi was only thirty-six, but she had already been at the Met for fourteen years. Counting concerts and her film and TV work, she must have been nicely into six figures. When Harry had first met her, back in the days when she was still Deidre Anne Ogilvie, her father ran a lumber yard in Dover, Delaware; perhaps he still did. There had been enough money to send Didi to Bennington and then to the New England Conservatory, where she sang in the women's chorus. The solo career came as a great surprise to Didi's classmates; she was a late bloomer. She had been very horsey, very athletic at Bennington, and had spent a great many football weekends at Dartmouth and Harvard and Princeton. In fact, it was surprising that she'd ever had time to learn to sing. The voice was essentially a *soprano leggiero*, quite flexible and of nice girlish timbre and moderate size: perfect for a women's chorus and very affecting in pieces like the "Esultate, jubilate" of Mozart, which Harry had included in Didi's first album, *Del Campo Sings Bach & Mozart,* dating from—oh my God—1966.

Didi had gotten into the Met in 1963 by way of some student-matinee *Madame Butterflys.* She looked terrific in her Cio-Cio-San outfit of those days; the nude-to-the-waist Desdemonas and other spectacular stuff came later. Mr. Bucellatti caught one of the early *Butterflys* when the Met was on tour in Detroit, where he had come to study Ford production methods, and soon thereafter Miss del Campo, as she was then called, began making regular trips to Turin. Mr. Bucellatti gave her a magnificent apartment in Rome to use while he obtained his divorce and Didi began her work for Radiotelevisione Italiana. They weren't married until January of 1970—Italian divorce laws weren't so easily circumvented in those days as now—and separated in late 1972, by which time Didi's Italian was flawless and her international career assured.

Today? The voice was a bit frazzled, last time Harry had heard it: just another pretty face headed for the inevitable vocal crisis. But still she turned in a marvelous Zerlina and a very funny Rosina and a very touching Adina and—well, there was hardly a lyric role in Rossini, Donizetti, Puccini or Verdi that she hadn't mastered, and for which there wasn't a bona-fide offer from some major opera house. She and all the rest: free-lancing like whores and singing every available performance as a hedge against the day, which would come soon enough, when the offers stopped. . . .

"This it? The big place?"

"Yes, fine. Wait, please—and if I'm not out by twelve thirty, please get yourself some lunch."

At least her old age would be secure. Harry valued the building and land at not less than a half-million dollars. There were four floors, with the downstairs devoted to an entry hall and kitchen; living room and dining area on the second; bedrooms on the third; and Didi's studio on top. Edith Cavalieri had nothing on this lady.

"Didi? It's me—Harry Chapin. May I come up?"

She received him in the bedroom. Her longtime maid, Carmel, had been applying an ice pack to a very bruised cheek. Didi wore a pretty blue housecoat trimmed with lace and ribbon, and she was barefoot: one ankle appeared swollen and discolored and—marked with the imprint of someone's teeth.

"Well, now," said Harry. "What have we here?"

"Oh, *Harry!*"—and then she dissolved in tears like the little girl she'd been when he first met her.

Carmel left to get more ice. "Also some alcohol or Bactine if you have it," Harry ordered. He studied her with care, as a doctor might have done. He was furious—to *think* of it—but resisted the temptation to scold. She might have been trampled by a herd of horses. There were still traces of blood on her upper lip and one side of her nose had begun to puff.

"What about—underneath? Any damage? You can tell Dr. Chapin."

The crying grew worse, but she shook her head—which he took to mean no broken bones, nothing that would require stitches. Carmel returned with the ice and a bottle of Campho-Phenique. "This is going to sting. . . ." He felt like Clark Gable; Vivien Leigh would recover, but there would be a long convalescence. "We'll be all right, Carmel. Thank you very much."

"There's sherry in the sitting room, Mr. Chapin," said Carmel, who knew him well, "and champagne in the kitchen." The black lady left.

He found the sherry and poured them each a half-beaker, adding some ice from Carmel's dish. "Cheers," he said. "And long life." She smiled for the first time, but the tears came again and he had to take back her sherry to keep her from spilling it in the bed. "Do you want me to call a doctor? Just to be safe?"

"Just trying to scare you," she said in her breathy speaking voice. "Jackie told you, huh? Basically, I'm a mess, if you want to know the truth. But who isn't? Basically—I've been fucked to death."

"Ah . . ."

"God, I can be crude. I seem to go out of my way to say horrible things. Ignore me, okay?" said with a series of small shudders.

"I'm a friend."

"Yes—yes, you are. You're about the only one I've got left, too. I think I've carried this image shit just about as far as it'll go, don't you? I need a vacation, you know?"

"Take one. Get out of here. Forget everything. Get some rest."

"I'm getting on a plane tomorrow—to Santo Domingo, of all places. Doesn't that sound romantic? Only I'm going solo, which is the whole idea. Then I'm going to the South of France. I can't tell you now—but later you'll understand. . . ." The shuddering started again and she couldn't talk. She lay back on the bed and wept furiously, hands covering her face. Her nose had begun to bleed.

"Oh, baby," he said to her. "Please—it's not as bad as all that. Tell Harry, okay?"

When she could, she told him. Jackie had exaggerated. There weren't three or four boys; there were two, and another lady, and none was black. They were simply people Didi knew in the Village. They had gone to the other lady's apartment to have a little innocent fun. One of the boys couldn't hold his liquor, and things had gotten rough—they had ripped up Didi's clothes and thrown them out the window. When they had finished with her, they let her telephone Carmel, who came and got her. End of story. Just another form of athletics for little Didi; a latter-day version of the field hockey in which she had excelled at Bennington. Sometimes the game got a little rough.

Minutes later she was up and laughing. "You still play piano?"

"Now and again."

"Let's do some songs later, okay? After lunch? You will have lunch with me? If you'll stay, I'll show you my new pictures. They're fabulous —please say you will."

"Newton or Scavullo?"

"Neither one—got somebody better right here in the Village, a divine boy called Ty Phelps. You'll stay?"

"Of course. Where am I going to find a better offer this late in the day?"

"Oh, I *knew* you would." She was like a little girl again. "Come on—we'll go get some champagne. But first—hold me, okay? Just for a minute?"

She felt very substantial in his arms—a feeling belied by her sobs. His shirt and tie were wet before she finished: he tasted the saltiness of her tears on his lips. But then—the moment passed.

"Okay, Buster," she said, limping toward the staircase, "let's get something to drink. And let's talk a little business, what do you say?"

They sat on high stools at a counter in the kitchen. "Shit," she said, "this is only 'Extra Dry.' I asked for 'Brut.'"

"It's fine, really. Cheers."

"So who's this Laframboise?"

"Black, loud and a real comer. You'll like him."

"You *knew* Edith would never sing again. Stupid cunt. Why do you waste time on her?"

"She's a great lady of the theater. Past her great days, perhaps, but still a great lady. Like you."

"You think I'm past—"

"Not for a moment. You are Desdemona—a lady at the peak of her powers."

"I like you, Harvard man."

"Any time you want to dump Mr. Bucellatti . . ."

"More later, as we say in the trade. And what about Toggi? Jiminy, I thought he was *dead*."

"Very much alive. I'm going to see him in Milan on Tuesday. The very greatest Iago of all time. Like Mr. Laframboise, you will love him."

"Yeah? And how about the asshole, then? Ponti of the great prick."

"You Bennington girls—very, shall we say, rough language?"

"They say he's an asshole. And he's fucking Marianne Kunz, right? . . . For 'Extra Dry' this isn't too bad, is it?"

"Very nice. He may seem a little—reserved—with people he doesn't know well, especially. But underneath . . ."

"Underneath he's got a foot-long prick, yeah, I know. Do you suppose I'm a nymphomaniac or something, Harry? Sometimes I wonder. With these sick ideas I've got . . ." She fingered her cheek and nose; could no longer stifle her sobs.

"Of course not," he whispered, holding her close again. "You're just—my own lovable Didi. . . ."

They lunched on cold salmon and cucumber salad, plus a pretty good Moselle. Afterward they climbed up to Didi's studio, where Mr. Bucellatti's Steinway was housed, and she made him sight-read a half-dozen Duparc songs which he hadn't seen in twenty years—she was getting ready, she said, for *Del Campo Sings French Songs*, an album Melos-Doria didn't want but which Harry had foolishly approved on another emotion-riddled occasion.

"You're in very good voice," trying to take her mind off the clinkers. "Oops, B-flat, sorry," but then mercifully she called the damned thing off.

"As your reward . . ."

She got out a huge portfolio marked TY PHELPS and covered the piano top with the most astonishing eleven-by-fourteen's in full color, first her Micaëla peasant outfit, then Thaïs in Act I, then totally nude.

"Oh—just magnificent," the catch in his voice making him sound like somebody else—maybe Joseph Cotten.

"Isn't that the most lovely bosom?"

"Breathtaking."

"Those last bits are for *Vogue*."

"Ah . . ."

"Not your average diva, huh?"

"Mmmm . . ."

"Ty's going to take off maybe another ten pounds in that one. Air-brushing or something."

"I love you."

"I know, baby," she said. "Isn't life awful . . ."

"Then you don't mind Rome?" Harry said with relief.

"I *love* Rome. Are you kidding? Rome's my town."

"Fine. What's this about Salzburg?"

"If you can get me out, great. Jackie said I had to do it. Fucking Mozart, which I hate."

"And Hollywood Bowl afterwards, early September?"

"Yeah, but leave that alone—that's good money and that's a good town, too. Producers and all—I can do some good in that town."

"Allowing time, remember, for a Melos-Doria reception, Beverly Hills Hotel, the works . . ."

"Whatever you say. You're the boss."

"Let me see what I can do about Salzburg. Worse comes to worst, we'll schedule things so that your scenes are done in the second week. But now, Didi—seriously—we've got to talk about these terms."

"Simple. Ten thousand flat. Send it to Sy, who will put it in the thing in Grand Cayman."

"*Ten?* I was told seventy-five hundred."

"No, it's ten now. Really, Harry, just this once—I *need* it."

"For one week's work?"

"Yes, it's criminal, isn't it? But I didn't invent the system."

"No, you didn't. I helped, I'm afraid."

"Hey, what about a *Traviata?* I'm really into *Traviata*. I play her, quote, thirtyish, bored with life and randy as hell, unquote."

"Where did you get that?"

"Out of a magazine. Charlotte Rampling said it, I think—about some movie. I dig her."

"So I've heard. But getting back to repertoire—"

"What's wrong with *Traviata?*"

"Don't need one. But we're thinking about a complete *Trittico* with Ponti. What about the Lauretta? Or maybe all three ladies—the Giorgetta would be perfect for you. Have you ever done it?"

"Yeah, once, in Portland. Hate it. Hate the whole idea. Why don't you give me something juicy? What about *Rondine?* I'm a sensational Magda—did it on Italian TV. I'll play it nude for you, if you want."

"Too late. Moffo's already recorded it."

"Who gives a fuck about Moffo? What about *me*, pardner?"

"Let me sleep on it."

"Which means that's the end of that. I know you, Harry Chapin."

"I'll send you some other ideas. Meanwhile—give some thought to taking a royalty on Desdemona instead of the flat fee, will you? Think of it as an annuity—something for your old age."

"I don't expect to *have* an old age—Christ, Harry, haven't I made that *clear?*"

"And on Laframboise—I'll send you his LPs. Try to accustom yourself to his timbre. Really very unusual."

"Whatever you say, teacher. As long as I don't have to suck his you-know-what . . ."

Perhaps it was all a mistake. There was no seriousness of purpose on her part, and he would be paying far more than he should to get her. Still, the girl was hot. And he had a funny feeling that the Laframboise-Del Campo chemistry might just provide the required miracle, especially in the Act I love duet.

It was a business of risks, after all. Done and done again.

V I

". . . We have Mr. Rose for you, Mr. Chapin. Line one, please."

"Thank you . . . Norman?"

"Good day, Harry. I trust all goes well."

"I've just come from Del Campo."

"She's ecstatic, is she, about Desdemona?"

"It's a flat fee, as you said, but the fee is ten thousand dollars, not seventy-five hundred."

"Astonishing!"

"Yes, isn't it. I'm seeing Toggi on Tuesday. Keep things together on the Coast, will you? I may be away another week or ten days."

"Of course. Don't give us a thought."

"And how's it going on your end?"

"It was a sad day, Harry, when you signed young Mr. Kurtz. He knows as much about Chopin as my cat."

"Fortunately for you and me, Norman, the public is just like your cat. . . ."

". . . Another call for you, Mr. Chapin. A Mrs. Blankenhorn?"

"Ah—I'll take that one, thank you."

". . . Harry?"

"Well, *hello.* This is a pleasant surprise."

"I called earlier, but you were out. I was going to ask you to buy me lunch."

"Oh, hell. Matter of fact, I was lunching with Didi del Campo—business."

"I'm impressed."

"As I say—business."

"And how's your time? Now?"

"Now? Ah—fine. No problems at all. Are you—free?"

"Until almost nine, darling—if you'd like a drink or something. I've got to meet Joe at Twenty-One for dinner. He's off to one of those tedious show auditions—some friends want us to invest. But the theater is such a bore right now."

"Well—what would you think about, oh, the St. Regis? King Cole Bar?"

"A little public, isn't it?"

"What about our suite—at the Sherry?"

"Daddy keeps a suite there, too."

"Ah. How would you feel about—here?"

"Your *office?*"

"More of a house, really. Nobody around but the cleaning ladies after five fifteen. And I'm looking at a most convenient bar as I speak to you. Mix anything you like, Ma'am—guaranteed to please."

"It's *different.*"

"Ten minutes?"

"Impossible to get cabs this time of day—I'm at Bloomingdale's. Why don't we say—five thirty?"

"I'll chill the wine. Mumm's all right?"

"Clever man."

It was almost 6:00 before she arrived: the rain had resumed.

"Well—isn't this elegant," she said, taking off her coat and gloves.

"It passes," Harry said. He shut and locked the door in a single motion. "It occurred to me that you might prefer Scotch—or bourbon?"

She settled onto his favorite sofa, the one in wine-colored corduroy. "Remember," she said, "I must be at Twenty-One on the dot of nine."

"No problem, dear lady," pouring with a practiced hand. "No problem at all . . ."

And within the hour, in the privacy of the Eastern Executive Offices, Melos-Doria Records Division, Leisure Time Industries, Inc., Harry Chapin found himself doing to Mrs. Renée Blankenhorn precisely what her husband had done to him so often in the past.

3

Alitalia's one-stop 747 to Milan didn't leave JFK until 7:30 P.M. Monday, giving Harry the full business day in which to clean up his affairs.

He told Gravinius yes, told Ferlinghetti yes, told Blankenhorn yes.

He called Quinzi in Milan and learned that the Toggi meeting had been set for Tuesday noon. Quinzi also informed him that Boris Makhov, the Soviet baritone, would be passing through Munich on Wednesday—would Harry be interested in meeting with that alternative Iago, if only for the cosmetic effect? Harry told Quinzi yes.

He called Frankie Tree in London and asked her to ask Teedee McEvoy to send her Wednesday to Munich for a meeting with Harry on publicity plans for *Otello*.

He got Eunice Powell to change his draft on New York Petty Cash from $1000 to $2000.

When all of this was accomplished, he called Maggie and told her that he might be away another two weeks. She did not seem unduly troubled by this news.

They circled in the Milanese fog for over an hour; it was 10:30 A.M. when the plane touched down. Il Dottore Quinzi met Harry at the head of the ramp and escorted him to La Cima's Mercedes. It would not be necessary for Signor Chapin to proceed through Customs with the other passengers; any friend of Dottore Quinzi's . . .

His suite at the Principe e Savoia had been pre-registered, his bags delivered upstairs and a chilled bottle of Krug ordered from room service. One could not fault La Cima's efficiency since the arrival of Dr. Quinzi.

"I bring you greetings of Maestro Ponti," Quinzi said. "There is the matter of a mezzo-soprano for your *Otello*—the Emilia."

"Oh, yes?"

"In particular, Maestro Ponti desires a young girl of the name Alberta Lisi-Mettler, who today makes her career in New York. Maestro Ponti would wish to audition. . . ."

Harry understood. Maestro Ponti's interests were not entirely musical. Even so powerful a Consortium executive as Dr. Raffaele Quinzi could be counted upon to apply himself to Maestro Ponti's personal needs. This was the Consortium's strength: perfect coordination of individual company efforts, with each of the senior managers serving always "the business" as priests served the temple in another time. "*Con piacere,*" Harry replied. He drafted a cable on the spot, which Quinzi promised to get off without delay:

NORMAN ROSE

MELOS-DORIA RECORDS BURBANK CALF

USA

UNDERSTAND ALBERTA LISI-METTLER EXCELLENT EMILIA STOP CAN SHE AUDITION FOR MAESTRO PONTI MILAN OR FLORENCE DURING PERIOD JUNE TENTH TO FOURTEENTH STOP HUROK OFFICE REPRESENTING STOP APPRECIATE MAXIMUM EFFORT STOP REGARDS

CHAPIN

"Signor Toggi is well?" Harry asked.

"Signor Toggi is an old man. He suffers the disabilities of age."

"But I had understood from Herr König—"

"Herr König, dear Harry, is not altogether an innocent party in this affair."

"Innocent?"

"Unbiased."

"Ah. Politics?"

"Herr König has ambitions—this is widely understood—to leave his post at Zürich and assume the managing directorship of an operating company. The larger the better."

"Oh, yes?"

"In fact, the largest on the Continent."

"Germany? But what of Dr. Hopf?"

"What indeed?"

"I see."

"Therefore, it is perhaps unwise to involve oneself in affairs managed by Herr König without first asking what is behind his efforts."

Harry was aware of Quinzi's animosity toward König, and of König's hatred for Hopf. But what had this to do with Benno Toggi or the Harry Chapin *Otello?* Quinzi's reservations were most disturbing. This brilliant young intellectual—just thirty-five, amazing—was sure to play a dominant role in Consortium future management, whereas König —well, the difference in quality was obvious.

"But now, dear Harry, if we are to keep our appointment . . ."

He was just a lonely old man—somebody's grandfather, perhaps, like those you saw in convalescent homes. He lay back in a large overstuffed armchair in one corner of the sitting room, making no effort to rise when they entered. The house was not his—he owned nothing now, Quinzi explained. Everything had gone to cover attorneys' fees, two divorce settlements, necessary bribes to officials of the penal system. A gracious patron had lent Toggi these temporary quarters "until the Maestro is himself again."

"Signor Toggi, I count it a very great honor, sir," Harry said in Italian, "to meet you on this happy occasion. The inspiration of your artistry over the years . . ." He had great difficulty in finding words formal enough for such a ceremony. His Italian was meant only for threatening recalcitrant studio hands, intimidating business associates, persuading lazy hotel staff. ". . . Even as a student, through such rare recordings as we were able to obtain . . ." But his attempts at grandiloquence soon petered out.

Toggi by contrast spoke in simple phrases, uttered in feeble half-voice and with minimal movement of the lips: "You are so kind to speak thus. Your reputation precedes you. You will excuse—these circumstances."

Harry was appalled. Toggi possessed a fey smile of great residual charm, but seemed far older than the stated sixty-seven. Big Harry— Harry's dad—was now sixty-nine, but seemed a boy by comparison: played eighteen holes of golf three times a week—but then had never been to prison.

"Your Figaro has, for me, been always the model," Harry began again.

"Figaro?" Toggi said with apparent alarm but no noticeable increase in volume.

Quinzi broke his silence: not to worry, dear Benno, but our American friend here simply means that he remembers your Figaro from before . . .

Everything now was labeled before or after the "indisposition." It was impossible for Harry to imagine that Benno Toggi had once represented Italy in the Olympic Games—two games, in fact, 1928 and 1932, and two events, discus and hammer throw. The once powerful physique, like the medals—one silver and two bronze, a very fine showing for Italy—was gone now, only a distant memory. He was bald except for wispy white strands behind his over-large ears. White-flecked eyebrows gave accent to an otherwise expressionless face. His cheeks were the color of pumice stone, lips thin and moist; laugh lines crowded around watery gray eyes. His skin sagged like that of a man formerly fat but now painfully thin. Like a marathon runner's, his veins and tendons were clearly visible: shirt collar too big for the drawn and wrinkly neck. Ah, but so *elegante*—velvet collar on a fine wool jacket, velvet trousers, Italian glove-leather moccasins, a gold watch. Not all his worldly possessions had been lost. . . .

Harry abandoned further attempts at gracious conversation and went instead to the business at hand. "Naturally, Melos-Doria is delighted to participate in your return to the operatic world—especially in a role with which your career has been so closely identified."

"It is the role of my debut at La Scala. But I have not sung it since the year nineteen-hundred-and-sixty- . . ." Toggi's teeth were exposed in this, his first display of interest: gums shrunken, teeth brown with age, spaces unnaturally wide between them.

Harry pressed onward. "I bring you greetings, Signor Toggi, from the lady who will be the Desdemona of our cast."

Toggi knew the name Del Campo, but had never heard the lady sing; his indisposition . . .

"As for our Otello, Mr. Laframboise, he admires your art most profoundly, and we are delighted at the prospect of this collaboration."

A recent recording, auditioned only yesterday: this was all Toggi knew of Laframboise. A very strong voice, without question. But in the matter of authentic Verdian style . . .?

Harry nodded agreement, stressing the contribution of Maestro Gian-Carlo Ponti, who would mold . . .

A very great maestro of the new generation, Toggi thought. No, he had not worked with Ponti, but his friends in the Opera House had said many fine words on behalf of the Swiss gentleman. . . .

Already Toggi appeared to be tiring. But sixty-seven is not *old*, Harry wanted to shout. He had considered asking Benno to sing something—there was a splendid Bechstein in one of the front rooms, and on this occasion Harry would have been delighted to provide accompaniment—perhaps a Neapolitan ditty to remind us of the old days, eh, *Padrone?* But this was clearly impossible. There was no telling when this legendary Figaro might call it quits for the day, so Harry hurried down his checklist: the dates for Rome, the piano rehearsals beforehand at

Maestro Ponti's home near Florence, the desirability of Signor Toggi's accustoming himself to the latest recording techniques by visiting La Cima's studios in Milan or in Rome, whichever was more convenient— and, again, Melos-Doria's sense of honor and privilege in bringing Signor Toggi's art once more to music-lovers around the globe. . . .

The old man nodded—gestured uncertainly—conveyed an ennui which Harry found contagious. "We've intruded long enough," Harry said with feeling. "All that remains for discussion, then, is the contract itself. The business terms?"

Met by still further gestures of helplessness. Harry appealed to Quinzi: "May we discuss terms of Signor Toggi's service? Perhaps I have not made clear my meaning."

But no, said Quinzi after brief consultation with Toggi, such a discussion would be inappropriate, all such matters having been delegated to Signor Toggi's trusted advisor, the Count Stanislaus Gimpel. And since Harry would be seeing the Count in only a few days . . .

Harry and Quinzi rose together. Toggi seemed relieved. The old man leaned forward to take Harry's hand and said with a smile, "*Questo Signor Lampone*," followed by a phrase—idiomatic expression?—that Harry could not translate, ending "*Così, Signor Mora, non è vero? Sì, sì, lo credo!*" punctuated by a shocking burst of black laughter.

"*Scusatemi, ma . . .*" It was merely a question of vocabulary. Over time one tended to forget these obscure nouns.

"It is only a joke," Quinzi explained without smiling. "Signor Toggi has suggested that your American Mr. Raspberry—*Signor Lampone*—is more correctly called *Signor Mora*. That is, Mr. Blackberry . . ."

4

He caught the 10:10 A.M. Lufthansa flight to Munich.

And what if Comrade Makhov, for one reason or another, *isn't* available, eh, Chapin? Do you *really* plan to rely on Signor Toggi? How could that frail, desiccated old man be expected to carry such a load? Verdi had considered naming the piece *Iago*, for God's sake! Surely König—and that evil man Schröder-Devrient, who had sold them this bill of goods—knew better. How was Signor Toggi expected, in his condition, to manage the final F of the "Credo," for example? "Credo in un Dio crudel": yes, correct sentiment at this juncture.

What was worse, Harry had nobody to blame but himself. He'd gone out of his way to audition Laframboise, who sang two dozen performances a year in major opera houses; he knew Didi could sing because, among other things, she'd just finished an LP for Melos-Doria; and he'd made sure that Edith Cavalieri *couldn't* sing by crawling around like a sewer rat under the Salle Vauban. Toggi? For Toggi, he'd violated a career-long rule: never rely on other people's ears. And what ears? Nobody but Benno's fellow prison inmates, so far as Harry knew, had heard the old baritone sing a note in seven years!

The flight over the Austrian alps was incredibly beautiful: heavy snows, sapphire blue lakes, millions of acres of unspoiled wilderness dotted with the most famous winter resorts in the world: Garmisch-Partenkirchen, Oberammergau, Innsbruck. Maybe he and Frankie would rent a car and make a weekend of it in nearby Salzburg, just getting to know each other again. They had never even played tennis— it was quite amusing. His immediate concern was the Bayerischer Hof:

would the hotel give him the suite he'd asked for, Number 504, with the double-sized bathtub? He dozed off, savoring the delicious vision of Frankie's slim frame spread-eagled wantonly beneath his rapacious bulk . . .

". . . Good day, dear Harry. Welcome to Munich."

"Dr. Hopf—a pleasure to see you again so soon. Makhov is here?"

"I regret to inform you that Herr Makhov is delayed. He will arrive now at one o'clock. In the interim—if you do not object—we have planned a short visit to our new offices, which you have not seen. . . ."

They made for Spitze-Schallplatten headquarters at high speed. In the car they gave him two messages: Miss Tree would be arriving from London at 4:15 P.M., and Herr König, on behalf of the Count Stanislaus Gimpel, had taken the liberty of adding Miss Tree's name to the list of guests who would be boarding *L'Arlésienne* at Marseilles on Monday.

"If you wish to reply by cable," offered Dr. Hopf with evident pride, "it is possible from this automobile."

"Very kind of you," Harry said. "Perhaps something like: 'To Klaus König, Zürich. Marseilles arrangement most satisfactory. Regards. Chapin.' "

His message was radioed within moments. Say what you would about these Germans, they understood the modern world. He pressed his face to the glass like an eager tourist. Munich seemed fabulously efficient and well-to-do. The lunch hour was approaching and rain had begun to fall: the streets were crowded with pretty young secretaries in miniskirts and plastic rain gear. So this is tomorrow. Very nice, very nice.

Spitze-Schallplatten's new headquarters was a huge mirrored cube set into a grassy slope near the 1972 Olympic village: the structure itself seemed to dissolve into the reflected slate-gray skies above. The lobby was white-on-white plastic accented by red-and-yellow logos (the Spitze-Schallplatten corporate colors) in anodized aluminum. Dr. Hopf and a large reception committee escorted Harry onto a tube-like escalator which carried them to the mezzanine. There, uniformed guards helped them board sleek electric carts which rushed them the length of the building in seconds and deposited them silently at the entrance to the Executive Suite.

". . . You have met, of course, Herr Dr. Ek, in charge of repertoire . . ."

"*Jaja*, all German tenors today are American! Cassilly, King, Laframboise, Thomas, McCracken . . . !"

A very good joke. Everyone here was a doctor—most wore white overalls and carried clipboards. It was hard to believe that these people made music.

". . . Now in progress, a meeting of the European Art and Advertising Committee . . ."

The conference room was circular and separated by electric doors from Dr. Hopf's private office. The red-and-yellow motif was repeated everywhere in aluminum and plastic. On the table: tea, coffee, little cakes, four kinds of mineral water and a canister of Dutch Mantanos.

". . . If Herr Dr. Chapin would honor us with a few remarks . . ."

Harry spoke to them in halting English: even *this* language seemed to have gone to pieces on him. ". . . The great strength of our joint enterprise . . . Proper presentation of Consortium image . . . Dominant presence in the marketplaces of the world . . ."

Strongly applauded, of course.

"But now, dear Harry, I believe it is time. . . ."

Makhov was shorter than Harry had remembered, and stockier, in one of those awful Russian square-cut suits, gray, with a very narrow tie, also gray, with a small pink Cyrillic monogram. Despite his dress, Makhov made a somewhat elegant impression—the manicured and glossy fingernails, for instance—and seemed friendly enough, smiling constantly, whereas his companion—some companion!—never ceased to frown. Boots—now, *those* were boots. Colossal white things, knee length, in very fine leather; she had never obtained *those* in Russia.

"Gentlemen," said the Amazon, "I have great pleasure in introducing the People's Artist of the Soviet Union and Hero of Socialist Labor, Comrade Boris Makhov."

They were led quickly to a VIP lounge on the second floor. Comrade Makhov's next flight, to Bonn, would depart in exactly thirty-five minutes. In keeping with Comrade Makhov's preference, glasses of orange juice were provided. The lady's name was Salome Weiss. She had recently been appointed, she said, Comrade Makhov's manager pro tem and she functioned as the artist's sole agent outside Russia. Her native language was German, but she spoke Russian and—hopefully, she said—adequate English.

"Quite wonderful English," Harry said.

But she refused to smile. God, she was a formidable beast—perhaps five-ten, 150 pounds? A certain caution was indicated.

Harry turned his attention to Comrade Makhov. "On behalf of Melos-Doria Records, I wish to express our company's great admiration—"

"Comrade Makhov prefers," the Amazon broke in, "that you address your remarks only to me. I shall then interpret."

"Of course. Well, then—we are, naturally, great admirers of Comrade Makhov's art. And we look forward to some future occasion when perhaps—"

Makhov and Miss Weiss suddenly exchanged rapid-fire bursts in Russian. Harry couldn't tell from their expressions whether Makhov was pleased or angry. After some gesturing, Miss Weiss turned to Dr. Hopf and spoke in German.

"Of course—it is understood," Hopf replied in English. And then to Harry: "Comrade Makhov wishes to discuss with you alone, dear Harry, a matter of some privacy. Therefore, I shall absent myself."

A matter of privacy? Harry smiled, turned palms up.

"Comrade Makhov wishes to thank you for your courtesy," Miss Weiss said when Hopf had gone.

"It is a great privilege for one such as myself, who has long admired Comrade Makhov's art, to meet the gentleman in person," Harry said, hating every word.

The Amazon translated and Makhov grabbed Harry's hand and shook it vigorously.

"Comrade Makhov appreciates your kind remarks," Miss Weiss said. "But now he wishes to speak to you of a business proposition."

The Russian spoke at some length. Harry tried to seem interested, but caught not a single word: apparently no cognates in Russian. Ah, except *Otello*—yes, *Otello* definitely on the agenda.

Finally, the lady in the great white boots provided a summary:

"Comrade Makhov is aware of Comrade Chapin's *Otello*, to be recorded this summer at Rome. There are no secrets, as we know, in the world of art. Comrade Makhov is honored that your Consortium has thought of him for the role of Iago. Comrade Makhov has appeared in this role in many cities of the world with very great success. He has done so in both the Russian and the Italian languages. . . . Of course Comrade Makhov and all singers everywhere have applauded the decision of Melos-Doria to offer the role of Iago to the very great Italian gentleman Comrade Benno Toggi. The whole world has applauded this as a 'sentimental' decision. However, Comrade Makhov, like Comrade Chapin, is a man of great experience in this business. And Comrade Makhov wishes to tell Comrade Chapin that if, for any reasons—the illness? the indisposition?—Comrade Toggi should be unable to participate in the recording sessions that Melos-Doria has planned for Rome, then Comrade Makhov would make himself available for such an engagement. And this proposition is therefore offered to Comrade Chapin this day by Comrade Makhov."

Harry smiled and nodded again in the Russian's direction. "Comrade Makhov is most kind and generous. And what business arrangement—what fee—would Comrade Makhov expect in this regard?"

Makhov did not wait for translation, but immediately gave the Amazon further instructions.

"*Ach, so.* This is most simple," Miss Weiss said, smiling herself for the first time. "There should be no fee for such an engagement."

"No fee? But surely—"

"When inside the Soviet Union, Comrade Makhov has no need of the customary moneys which are employed in your business. He is, as I have said, People's Artist of the Soviet Union and a Hero of Socialist Labor."

"And outside the Soviet Union?"

"Comrade Chapin is most—astute?—most *clever*, yes, that is the word I want. Comrade Makhov would request for such work only a very simple thing, which is a Mercedes sedan, the model to be the four-five-oh-SEL, which would be registered in Comrade Makhov's name, and which would be kept garaged for him in the city of Zürich, Switzerland."

Makhov smiled very broadly at the word "Mercedes."

"I see," said Harry, recoiling in horror. A $20,000 automobile—perhaps *more* in Switzerland—for a few days' singing at Rome. What had happened to the socialist ethic?

"You will understand," Miss Weiss continued, "that Comrade Makhov's recordings cannot be available to your companies in certain territories. The German Democratic Republic, the People's Republic of Albania, the Republic of Cuba, the Democratic Republic of Vietnam . . ."

"I am familiar with the list," Harry said. "Unfortunately, such a restriction of territories would inevitably reduce any terms that I might be able to offer. A Mercedes, for example . . . I regret that this would be far more than we could afford."

Miss Weiss translated.

Comrade Makhov scowled, then laughed.

"Comrade Makhov is most distressed," Miss Weiss said.

No less than Harry Chapin, dear lady. For now it was Toggi—or nobody—at Rome. "I regret Comrade Makhov's distress," Harry said. He did not mention his own.

"Comrade Makhov expresses his willingness to hear from Melos-Doria another offer. Another model of the Mercedes, perhaps . . ."

"I would not wish to waste Comrade Makhov's time, knowing as I do that any offer we might be able to make in this instance would be far short of his expectations." And then Harry had another idea. "On the other hand . . ."

Makhov barked further instructions.

"Comrade Makhov would express interest in this other hand," the Amazon said.

"Well, I was just going to say—having had many past dealings with Comrade Popov in the Ministry of Culture—perhaps Comrade Makhov would wish me to open negotiations on a more formal level—with the aim of furthering this cultural exchange?"

Comrade Makhov's orange juice went flying as he scrambled to his feet. He grabbed his startled companion by one shoulder and punctuated his remarks by jabbing a stubby finger into her broad chest. When he had finished, he executed a dramatic pirouette and stalked out of the room.

Oh, then you *don't* want me to tell the boys in Moscow about the Mercedes in Zürich?

Miss Weiss—rubbing at the target of all those pokes—blushed, then attempted to resume her duties as interpreter-translator. "Comrade Makhov advises that negotiations with the Ministry of Culture will not be necessary, as he finds that he is not available for such a recording because of—other commitments. Comrade Makhov bids you good day, sir."

Suddenly she seemed more likable. "Are you all right?" Harry said solicitously. "Did he hurt you?"

"I am not injured," she said, continuing to rub. "He is such a baby. . . ."

"Well, I feel badly—"

"No. You are quite correct. A Mercedes would be too much."

"I appreciate—"

"And will you be staying in Munich for some days yet, Mr. Chapin?"

"Regretfully, no. I am meeting a—business associate—and then we are leaving almost immediately for France."

"How unfortunate. I am staying myself two days."

Now Harry, too, was most distressed. A lady of such—power. "In case I should have a change of plans—perhaps you would let me know your hotel?"

"With pleasure," she said, brightening. "It is a small hotel—here, I shall write it for you. . . ."

Because one never knew. English ladies had missed airplanes in the past.

Miss Tree, however, did not miss her plane.

"What do you think of it?" he asked in the bathroom.

"What is it?"

"It's a bathtub, silly. Hermann Göring model. For two people."

"Oh, Harry, it's *awful.* . . ."

"Know what you need?"

"What?"

"A bath. You're absolutely filthy."

"I am *not*. Oh, you're fooling. . . ."

"Come on. What else have you got to do? Last one in's a—"

"You're *serious*. I don't believe it. Shouldn't you be at an office or something?"

"I told you—our Russian friend is gone. And no, I don't have to be at an office. What a ridiculous idea, that men should always be in offices." He began to run the water. "So come on—get out of those things."

Just then a maid appeared at the door and asked a question in rapid German, which he didn't understand. "No—everything's fine," he said anyway.

The maid looked blankly from Harry to Frankie and back again.

"She's trying to tell us something," Frankie said.

"No—*nichts*," Harry said. "We'll turn down the beds ourselves. *Alles ist in Ordnung. Danke sehr.* Everything's just *fine*."

With apparent reluctance the German lady closed the door.

"What if she'd caught us—in there?"

In some ways Frankie was a most conventional female. Harry liked that: it increased his own excitement. "You didn't bring any grass with you, I don't suppose?"

"Through the Customs? Not likely!"

He was first: tried a toe—*hot*—but eventually got seated, water already chest high. She followed, arms held tightly over her bosom as though he'd never seen her naked. "Oh, God . . ."

It was painfully hot. He ran more cold and opened the drain to keep the tub from overflowing. She had tied her long red hair into a knot atop her head, but the knot began to unravel and she was afraid to lie back. "I'm very uncomfortable," she said in her prim way. Her nipples looked hard as bullets. 'I don't think this is a very good idea," she said after several minutes.

"You may be right." He helped her stand and they clambered out together, splashing great quantities of water onto the bath mat.

Ah—*that's* what the maid had wanted: *Wünschen Sie Badetücher, bitte?* Did they wish any *bath towels*? Now he understood, because there weren't any.

"It's freezing!" she wailed. "What are we going to do?" A girl of mercurial moods, whose fair English complexion had just gone bright pink.

"You look like a boiled lobster," he laughed. "But that's fine—I like my women this color."

She got a glassful of icy cold water from the tap and flung it at him.

"Ooooooooooooooo! You—*bitch!*"

He chased her into the bedroom and pinned her atop the king-size bed. "And now, my girl . . ."

"You're scaring me, Harry. I'm—cold. . . ."

They got between the sheets. "What will the maids . . . Oh . . ."

Her insides were as hot as the bathwater. "I love you," he heard himself whispering.

"You *are* heavy," she replied. . . .

He felt much better after their first coupling. It was just Wednesday, and they weren't due at Marseilles until Monday. He was determined that they would enjoy the kind of long weekend that lovers everywhere dream of and seldom manage: meaning large amounts of sex for the man, lots of sightseeing for the girl.

They began with supper that evening. Rather than eat in the hotel, which had an excellent grill as well as its own Trader Vic's, he moved them out smartly to the Hofbräuhaus for sausages, sauerkraut, potato pancakes and liter mugs of dark Bavarian beer. Frankie was not impressed; she wasn't crazy about beer, she said, and she found the brass band at one end of the great seven-thousand-seat beer hall to be noisy and dull.

"Tell me about Teedee," Harry said, hoping to take her mind off the surroundings. "What did he say—about your coming here to see me?"

"Oh, you know Teedee."

"He didn't mind?"

"He didn't say."

"But—you did *tell* him?"

"Of course. Oh, he suggested that since I'll be working full time now on the Melos-Doria account you might wish to pay me directly in American currency—so I can benefit from the exchange rate."

"Well—I'd have to have our legal boys look into that. The tax consequences. But of course I'd like that very much. To have you—that much closer."

He didn't like the sound of it at all. What was Teedee up to? Trying to offload an unwanted employee; yes, the usual thing.

"This is called the *Schwemme*—literally, the horse pond—figuratively, the bar. Upstairs there's a regular restaurant."

"As frightful as this?"

It was all coming back to him: a similar ideal holiday taken—three years ago?—with the famous Marianne Kunz. A lovely drive to the Beethoven-Haus at Bonn, romantic dinner at Godesberg overlooking the Rhine, poetic meanderings up the Valley of the Ahr. Three glorious days accompanied by non-stop complaints and infrequent sex.

"*Fräulein? Die Rechnung, bitte*. You're right—it's much too noisy in here. Come on, I've got another idea. . . ."

They returned to the hotel. He had hoped to hold off a little longer before triggering maximum usable gratitude, but her general bitchiness necessitated a new timetable.

"Oh, don't *tell* me—not that ridiculous bathing scheme again . . ."

"Something even more exciting. Now sit down—and close your eyes."

"Harry—"

"Do as I say. It's not going to *hurt*. It's a gift, as a matter of fact."

He went to his suitcase and got out the camera and case and instruction manual and warranty slips and several rolls of Kodachrome; dumped the whole works in her pretty lap.

"Oh, *Harry!* You absolute *darling!*"

Yes, ecstatic, as he had foreseen. She jumped up and kissed him with great vigor—then abandoned him entirely in favor of her new toy. Within minutes she had read the booklet and was clicking off shots out their bedroom window—getting the neon signs, he supposed, on the Promenadeplatz.

Meanwhile he undressed. When she refused to take her eye from the viewfinder, he tiptoed up behind her and gave her a sudden kiss.

"Oh!" she said, seeing his condition.

"Why don't you put that down for a while?"

"Now? Again? Really, Harry—it's *indecent*."

Gently, he took away the camera, placing it on the dresser and pulling her down onto the bed.

"It's very hard getting undressed like this," she said, her annoyance tempered—he assumed—by frequent glances toward her beloved Nikon.

"We're going to have a magnificent weekend," he muttered between kisses.

"I don't know how to tell you this, Harry, but that just doesn't turn me on at all—what you're doing."

He was sucking her freshly exposed nipples. "This?"

"Yes, that. I mean, it's not one of my, what is it, erogenous zones? Now *please* . . ."

"All right. Well, how about this, then?" directing his privates toward her loving mouth.

"No—not now, Harry. Not after dinner."

"I promise not to come. . . ."

"*No*, Harry. I don't know where you got the idea that girls want to suck men's things—but, believe me, we *don't*."

"Just the slightest bit . . ."

"Oh, God . . ."

Soon enough he achieved his ends, his own muddled head *in nubibus*, hers somewhat lower down. She was a good child, really—spoiled, of course, as so many of these working girls were. But she accepted him on his own terms, ignoring (apparently) the catastrophic age difference—meaning that he could afford to put up with a certain amount of congenital bitchiness on her part.

"Your teeth . . . ah, not quite so hard . . ."

Giving him, finally, that instant of unworldly pleasure when she actually swallowed him. He'd have kissed her good night, a ritual to which she attached inordinate value, except that he disliked the taste of his own semen.

5

Thursday was a waste: Munich a dull town except during *Oktoberfest* and Frankie doing everything possible to stay out of the bathtub. No, she did not want to see Schloss Nymphenburg; no, she did not want to drive up to Salzburg. The spring rains continued, cutting down on her opportunities, he finally realized, to use the Nikon. Now, if only she'd had an electronic flash unit, she hinted . . .

Well, then, what about the heated rooftop swimming pool of the Bayerischer Hof? No. In fact, perhaps she had been wrong to come to Munich at all—suggested with the great seriousness that only a twenty-year-old English girl can display—since Harry had failed to sign Boris Makhov and there was thus no Melos-Doria business to be conducted in this city. Perhaps she should return immediately to London and begin preparations for *Otello*—collect the bios, set some photo dates, arrange interviews for the principals—and thus start earning the money that Melos-Doria would be paying her.

"And by the way, Harry, what will my salary be? And will I have my own expense account?"

There was nothing more infuriating than an employee who exhibited greater interest in his business than Harry did. "We'll discuss that another time, if you won't mind. Meanwhile—"

He had a better idea. What about getting out of Munich at the earliest possible moment and going straight to Marseilles, renting a car there and making a long weekend in Provence? Driving bound to be *much* better down there—weather likely to be absolutely gorgeous.

Yes, she said. These thin-blooded English girls reponded, in his experience, to anything having to do with warm weather. Instantly she was on the phone, seeing to the bookings. He felt good about himself for once, very clever.

"Nothing this evening," she reported, "but there's a ten-o'clock tomorrow morning with a stop at Paris."

Done. They would be going out of their way, but there was only a forty-five-minute layover at Charles de Gaulle, where, she reminded him, the duty-free shopping was fantastic. ". . . I need the flash anyway, luv —really, you can be an awfully nice man . . . most of the time. . . ."

Whereupon he attempted to parlay his slight advantage into something bigger—but she said no, firmly and positively. "I'm going to nap. Why don't you walk down to the Lufthansa office and collect our tickets—you can do with the exercise. . . ."

The flight to Marseilles was made in perfect alcoholic ease. In CDG they bought a nice Braun flash unit, only $95. The first picture made with it was one of Harry standing by the regal entrance to the Grand Hôtel Noailles on the boulevard La Canebière leading down to Marseilles's Old Port. Later they walked as far as the yacht basin and had supper on the quai des Belges, during which Harry said "I love you" about ten times, until Frankie asked him to stop as he was making her cry.

Afterward they went down to the quay and Frankie climbed over a railing and Harry took her picture, using the fabulous new flash unit, standing on the fantail of somebody's beautiful sailboat—a sleek catamaran the equal of anything Harry had seen at the Balboa Bay Club, where Big Harry kept his Cal 40. A uniformed attendant appeared on the scene, but Harry pretended to speak no French and the security guard—if that's what he was—waved goodbye to them, these foolish lovers, who were obviously having such a good time.

The Hertz man next morning gave them a bashed-up blue Renault, a selection of Michelin maps and an out-of-date *Fodor's France* and pointed them north to the Autoroute A7, warning them to watch for the A51, which would take them to Aix-en-Provence. Harry's basic idea was to go as far north as Orange—great Roman theater there—and then come south along the Rhône to Avignon, where they would spend the night at the Hôtel Europe, within walking distance of the historic Pont d'Avignon. Then Sunday they could see the Palais des Papes before moving on to Nîmes—more Roman ruins—and then Arles, "the little Rome of the Gauls," with its fabulous arena where Harry had watched the bullfights one summer. Then back to Marseilles in time to board *L'Arlésienne* Monday morning.

It was at this juncture—imagination fired by the exquisite detail of the Michelin maps—that Harry conceived yet another of his grand and ruinous schemes. Right there before him, in at least seven glorious colors, was the realization that they were now within easy striking distance of Saintes-Maries-de-la-Mer in the Camargue, the great marshland formed by the estuaries of the Petit Rhône and the Grand Rhône, on a sandy tip extending out into the Mediterranean—Saintes-Maries-de-la-Mer being the very city in which Jesús Vásquez, called El Vástago, had found refuge for these, his final years.

Excitedly, he told Frankie. "And not more than three or four hours out of our way. What do you think?"

Frankie, naturally, had never heard of El Vástago.

"Unbelievable!" Harry exclaimed, shaken. "In the music world today, a unique figure. Noble Spaniard of the old school—called El Vástago, which means sapling or descendant, because, really, he's the final link to Bach. I'm *sure* you've read about him. We have all his old recordings in our Heritage Series in the States, stuff made in the Twenties and Thirties—absolutely fabulous. After Falla and Casals he's the end of the line as far as Spaniards go. And we can actually *see* him. . . ."

No noticeable excitement on the part of Miss Tree. But was this surprising? Who cared about these living relics?—except maybe Chapin here—Chapin, who had been asked to do the new entry for Grove's:

vásquez, jesús (b. Cádiz 1886). Composer, conductor, concert pianist, organist. Renowned as "El Vástago," The Link, for his direct artistic lineage to J. S. Bach; i.e.: Vásquez studied with Henri-Paul Busser (1872–1973!), student in organ and composition of César Franck (1822–1890), pupil of Pierre-Joseph-Guillaume Zimmermann (1785–1853), student of François-Adrien Boieldieu (1775–1834), disciple of Charles Broche (1752–1803), student of Johann Christian Bach (1735–1782), student of his brother Karl Philipp Emanuel Bach (1714–1788) and his father, Johann Sebastian Bach (1685–1750). Vásquez became an exile from his native country in 1939 (with Casals, Picasso and others) following the victory of Franco. . . .

No, not a prospect of overriding interest to Miss Tree. But the fresh air and glorious sunshine of Provence had already infected him. Seeing the old man—getting his advice on art, values, one's role in society—yes, worth a pilgrimage any day. "We'll do it, then," he concluded.

"So what is it that makes him so great?" sayeth his partner. " 'Cause he's got to be ninety-one or something?"

II

They entered the Camargue by the road to Aigues-Mortes, the walled
city built by St. Louis in the thirteenth century. It was not yet eleven in
the morning, a quiet Sunday in the least commercial part of France, but
they had been part of a massive traffic jam for over an hour. "You *must*
have known," she chided him.

"I didn't know. I had no idea. And, besides, what's the rush? He
doesn't even know we're coming. . . ."

What irked him now wasn't her general nastiness and constant
bêtise, but the thought that Klaus König had invited the bitch to join
them aboard Gimpel's yacht.

"Listen to what it says. . . ." He had made the mistake of giving
her the *Fodor's France*, which she now used against him like a weapon.
"'. . . A wonderful land of French cowboys called *gardians*, of fighting bulls, of gray, muddy marshes, pink flamingos, vast plains, and thousands of mirror-like ponds . . . The great single point of attraction is
the town of Saintes-Maries-de-la-Mer—the Saint Marys of the Sea. . . .
It is not the Marys who have made the spot so celebrated, but the
Negro servant, Sarah. . . . Sarah is the patron of the Gypsies; and'—
are you *listening* to me?"

"Yes, yes—go on."

"'. . . And on May 24'—today is the twenty-*second*, isn't it?—
'Gypsies from all over the world gather here, enter the crypt of the
fortified Romanesque church where Sarah's statue stands, and carry it to
the sea for a ritual bath. . . .' May twenty-*fourth*. How *could*
you . . . ?"

It was entirely his fault. She would miss the photos of a lifetime—
photos she could have *sold* just like a real professional—because he had
not kept track of the gypsy calendar. There was nothing for her to shoot
today but this incredible file of automobiles—a million unemployed
Rumanians (or were gypsies nowadays Spanish?) en route to the sea.

They arrived at the town—a barren cluster of whitewashed stucco
cottages surrounding a gray stone church—shortly after three o'clock.
Frankie complained of a debilitating headache and announced that she
had no intention of visiting El Vástago—why didn't he go alone? He
quickly agreed. They made a bargain to meet at the car, which he
parked and locked in a just-vacated spot behind the church, in exactly
two hours. "You'll be all right?" he sympathized. "Alone?"

But she disappeared into the gypsy swarm without replying,
stopping every few paces to point her Nikon at some target of likely
interest to *National Geographic*.

The sea air was gusty and humid. According to a harassed

gendarme, El Vástago's house was no more than half a kilometer's walk along the largest of the drainage canals that crisscrossed the marsh. With each step the footing became softer. Soon water filled Harry's footsteps as his shoes left them: handmade English oxfords—like most of his things, from Saks. But this discomfort, the loss of an expensive pair of shoes, was something Harry could accept without regret. To say to one's grandchildren, yes, I had the honor to visit El Vástago in his home . . .

El Vástago's home was the least imposing of the stucco cottages. This came as no surprise, as El Vástago had been without funds for many years, refusing all offers of work in protest against the totalitarian regime of his homeland and being dependent, thus, upon benevolent musicians of France who made donations and arranged occasional grants and commissions for pieces that were never written.

Harry was met at the wooden half-door by a young woman of especially sour countenance. This would be María, El Vástago's current companion, a simple country girl of about Frankie's age, who fixed his meals and did other chores. "My name is Chapin," he said in French. "I have come a long way to pay my respects to El Vástago." He took from his wallet one of his business cards.

The girl's frown deepened. "You will have to wait," she said in Spanish. He detected no sound of music; only the buzzing of the mosquitoes which had followed him across the marsh. The late-afternoon sun reflected off patches of water surrounding the house; what of the tide, he wondered, which appeared to be coming in? He kicked at a stone in the courtyard to shake the mud from his shoes, without success. The mud was sticky, like clay.

"This way," the girl called to him. He ran after her, down one side of the cottage to another entrance in back. "Go in," she ordered when he seemed to falter.

". . . El Vástago?"

"Come out of the sun, why don't you? Have you brought money?"

He looked just like his album covers: a white-haired gentleman of ninety-odd years, his skin as cracked and brown as parchment.

"I ask your pardon, sir. My Spanish is not what it should be."

"The damned *money*," El Vástago said in English. "Have you brought money or haven't you?"

"I'm afraid I haven't, sir. I have come a long way. That is, I have been in France on business, and I have often thought what a great privilege it would be—"

"Damned nonsense. You see those records there—get 'em for me, can't you?"

Harry saw what the old man meant: under stacks of old magazines and newspapers, a dozen Melos-Doria Heritage Series LPs in pressings manufactured by Apogée.

"Scoundrels," El Vástago said.

"Sir?"

"All of you—scoundrels. Where are my royalties? Never see a dime. If they had any kind of judicial system in this backward country, I'd have you locked up."

"Sir, you have me at a severe loss. I am unaware of the situation. But I shall be pleased, on my return to Paris—"

"Don't bother. Government would only take it. Have you brought food? Drink?"

"I regret, sir . . ."

"Get out, then. Why do you trouble an old man? You belong in prison. . . ."

"Are you coming back?" the girl called to him from the barn.

"I don't believe so," said Harry. His shoes sank deeper into the grassy plain.

"That's good," she called to him in Spanish. She then repeated the phrase in French, to be sure he understood.

Frankie was waiting not by the car as arranged, but on the steps of the church.

"And how was your precious Vástago or whatever you call him?" she said in her charming way.

"I'm only sorry you didn't come along. Most fascinating experience. Very moving."

"It was worth the detour, then?" she said, now quoting the *Guide Michelin.*

"Oh, certainly. Why do you ask?"

"I just wondered if it was worth the cost, is all. See there."

Oh, yes. The usual climax to a Chapin pilgrimage. "We'd better find a hotel," he said with anguish. "They'll have a telephone."

Because the gypsies had made off with all four tires of the Renault.

6

They sat impatiently in the lobby of the hotel like school-children of different ages waiting for the bus.

"You're certain you got it right?" she said to annoy him. "It *was* to be Monday, wasn't it? Not Sunday? Or Tuesday?"

"I'd hardly make a mistake like that," he countered, fishing in his pockets for König's cable, which he couldn't find. "Monday, the twenty-third of May—I'm absolutely positive."

"After yesterday . . ."

Naturally she would hold him responsible for the Renault affair. The Hertz people at Marseilles had been hardly less unreasonable. If it hadn't been that Melos-Doria was associated with Apogée, a French firm, they would still be arguing in Saintes-Maries-de-la-Mer. "It's not quite eleven thirty," he said defensively. They were to be picked up at eleven and escorted to the harbor. "And I don't understand why you seem to feel that I—"

Ah, saved by a familiar face: the august Serge Schröder-Devrient, personal secretary to the Count Stanislaus Gimpel. "I must ask your indulgence, Mr. Chapin, Miss Tree. We have experienced minor difficulties with *L'Arlésienne*'s air-conditioning system, causing us to put into Toulon for repairs. We regret very deeply this inconvenience. But if you will come with me now . . ."

A magnificent midnight-black Rolls Corniche awaited them. Frankie's attitude remained gloomy. "You mean we're going to *drive*?"

"We shall be aboard *L'Arlésienne* within thirty minutes," Schröder-Devrient said.

"*L'Arlésienne*? A tribute to Bizet?" Harry suggested.

"A tribute to the first Mrs. Gimpel," said Schröder-Devrient. "She was born in Arles. Perhaps you are acquainted with the lady? Madame Olimpia Rossen?"

"Only by reputation," Harry said. Olimpia Rossen had been a great star of the Paris Opéra in the late '40s and early '50s. Unfortunately, hers was a soprano with the characteristic rapid vibrato of many French ladies, and thus not suited to recording. But her artistry was well received in Paris, and she had even appeared at the Metropolitan. Harry told all of this to Miss Tree, who responded by blowing cigarette smoke in his face.

Their destination was a small seaplane basin in the Old Port. "So you see," said Schröder-Devrient, "we shall complete our journey with the assistance of 'Mother Goose.' "

"Mother Goose" was an Italian Piaggio amphibian, a gull-winged twin-prop five seater bearing across its nose the legend: MA MÈRE L'OYE—L'ARLÉSIENNE—MARSEILLE. "Oh, no," Frankie protested, "we're not going in *that*. . . ."

Schröder-Devrient took note of her apprehension. "A most delightful craft," he said in his soothing Continental manner, "and most substantial. Are you not fond of air travel? I am the same. But I can assure you that *Ma Mère l'Oye* will speed us safely to our destination."

"*Ma Mère l'Oye*—a ballet by Ravel," Harry informed his reluctant traveling companion. "It must be said"—to the elegant Schröder-Devrient now—"that Count Gimpel is a most musical gentleman."

"That is quite correct," said Schröder-Devrient. "Even the captain of our ship is a musical person. His name is Waldteufel."

"A French composer of waltzes," Harry explained to Frankie.

"I *know*," she shot back. "I'm not *completely* stupid."

Oh, really?

Their first glimpse of *L'Arlésienne* was deceiving. From the air the glistening white hull did not look particularly large. "One hundred and ninety feet, according to Lloyd's registry," corrected Schröder-Devrient. "Her twin twelve-hundred-horsepower diesels permit a cruising speed of fifteen knots and a range of six thousand nautical miles. A crew of sixteen."

With upkeep at something like half a million dollars a year: Harry had seen the piece in *Business Week*. And since *L'Arlésienne* was both office and home, it probably came off Gimpel's taxes—assuming he paid any taxes. The same article had suggested that Count Gimpel was financial advisor to the Vatican, though not a Catholic. The Pope's own money man—perhaps he could give Harry a tip on the market, or advise him on his sex life. "And you keep her—*L'Arlésienne*—always at Marseilles?"

"In winter and spring, yes," said Schröder-Devrient. "But in the hot weather of summer we prefer the Aegean Sea, the Greek Isles, occasionally the Balearics."

"And the Count lives aboard?"

"This is so. We keep a large house and a business office, of which I am privileged to be manager, in Gstaad, as you know. But that which you see beneath you is Count Gimpel's true home."

"Who would want to live on a boat?" Frankie commented.

Harry considered pushing her out the hatch, but apparently Schröder-Devrient was not offended. "I think you will find her suitable," he said with a wink in Harry's direction. "She is half the size of *Christina* but larger than *Deo Juvante*, and I believe it accurate to say that both Mrs. Onassis and Princess Grace have found *L'Arlésienne* to be more comfortable than their own vessels—more intimate, more seaworthy and in better taste."

Ma Mère l'Oye set down with much crashing of the sea against her aluminum hull. Within minutes they were transferred to *L'Arlésienne's* launch and then to *L'Arlésienne* herself. Apparently they were the last to come aboard: as soon as the launch and seaplane were craned to the upper deck, the crew cast off.

The first to greet them was that useful Swiss, Klaus König. "Harry, dear Miss Tree—and how do you like our little toy? Is she not a beauty? But then you, Harry, will have sailed in her before."

"My first opportunity, actually," Harry admitted.

"Come—it is the champagne hour. Luncheon will be served when we clear the harbor. You will wish to meet your fellow travelers. . . ."

The first friendly face was that of Jean-Luc Barraud—the trip could not be entirely unpleasant. But behind him, wearing one of those obscene French bathing suits which hardly cover penis and testicles, was—oh, God—Mihai Florescu, Edith's beautiful boy baritone.

"You know each other, of course. . . ."

Florescu was ebullient. "Of course! We are very best friends! Although, dear Harry, from the way you have treated poor Mihai, we should be fighting the duel, is not so? . . . Ah, Mademoiselle, I have not had the pleasure. . . ."

Harry introduced Frankie. Mihai kissed her hand, then both cheeks. Frankie blushed and attempted to pull back. But the baritone—one of God's most beautiful creatures, with the biceps of a steelworker—refused to let go until she said, with just a slight smile, "You're hurting my arm."

König continued the introductions. "Harry, have you met Guy? Guy, come here a moment, like a good boy." Guy was Guy du

Bonhomme, from Alsace. König introduced him as a *"directeur des artistes."* The boy appeared to be about twenty, with long black hair, very white skin and a shy, diffident manner.

"And of course you know Felicity. . . ." Felicity Kraus, publicity manager for Spitz-Schallplatten: according to rumors—now verified—the current girl friend of Herr König.

"And say hello to Beppe and Paolo. . . ."

"Hello, hello . . ."

"And this is Nikki. . . .

"And this is Monique. . . .

"And this is Aurore. . . ."

Charmed, charmed, charmed, I'm sure. Frankie seemed somewhat less charmed to meet these bikinied beauties, and the girls did not bother to rise from their towels. The smell of sun lotion was intense.

"And finally, dear Harry, our distinguished artists . . ."

Rose and Richard, the duo-pianists Temple & Box, no longer active on the major stages. "Rose . . . Richard . . . Well, this *is* a great surprise. May I introduce Miss Tree?" In their late fifties, Harry supposed: two modest English people who had never quite made the top rank, not as individuals and not as a team. Richard Box had started out to have a reasonably big career, but then he'd married the mousy London lady and the level of his playing had descended to hers. So *this* was where failed artists spent their final days.

"Harry, if I may have a word . . ."

König took Harry to one side while Mihai poured Frankie her champagne. "A matter of some delicacy . . ."

"Oh, yes?"

"Dear Harry, I have assigned you and Miss Tree to the same cabin. I hope that you will not find this—objectionable?"

"Whatever is—most convenient."

"Splendid. Come—Fritz, our chief steward, will show you and your charming companion below. . . ."

Stateroom assignments were posted in the passageway on the cabin deck. The individual rooms were named after composers. Gimpel had a very personal view of musical history, to be charitable about it. Nowhere was Beethoven, Bach, Mozart or Haydn to be seen—no Schubert and no Brahms. There were eight double cabins, and the bedding order was as follows:

Cabin Verdi:	K. König, F. Kraus
" Puccini:	R. Temple, R. Box
" Mascagni:	J-L. Barraud
" Bizet:	
" Donizetti:	G. du Bonhomme, S. Schröder-Devrient
" Zandonai:	H. Chapin, F. Tree

"   Cilèa: G. Podestà, P. D'Eustachio
"   Rossini: M. Florescu

Podestà and D'Eustachio in Cabin Cilèa were apparently Beppe and Paolo, the Roman boys. Bizet must have been saved for the girls Nikki, Monique and Aurore—or perhaps two of the girls were expected to join Rossini and Mascagni while the third shared Count Gimpel's suite on another deck?

"And we're *both* supposed to stay in this one little room?" Frankie complained bitterly.

"It's a ship, after all. Space is at a premium. I'll take the upper bunk. You'll be more comfortable below."

"And this is the *toilet?*"

The bathroom—head?—might have been small, but by the wash-basin were matching sterling-silver soap dishes initialed "H.C." and "F.T." with tastefully engraved presentation cards bearing the legend: "*With compliments of Count Stanislaus Gimpel.*" The soap was Hermès of Paris.

Frankie collapsed onto her bunk and burst into tears.

"Hey, what's wrong? If it's that boorish Florescu . . ."

"I'm so bloody *miserable.* How can I go on deck dressed like *this?* . . . How could you not *tell* me we were going on a *cruise?*"

"I didn't *know.* What about *me?* You think I've got clothes for a thing like this? I thought this was *business.*"

"This is so like you. . . ."

Perhaps it was—but a considerate person would never have said so.

I I

Luncheon was announced over the intercom. Harry climbed up onto his bunk so Frankie could change. She finally settled on a pair of white tennis shorts, white T-shirt with no bra, and white tennis shoes with no socks. The least formal outfit he had with him was chinos and a tennis shirt and his jogging shoes. He, too, omitted socks in an attempt to reflect an air of casual indifference.

"Ah, here's the man at last. Come join us, Harry. What will it be, champagne or a screwdriver?"

An elaborate buffet had been set out on the stern deck, which was covered with a blue awning to keep off the warm Mediterranean sun. A chef in *toque blanche* stood ready to assist in selection of a variety of eggs, meats, several kinds of freshly-caught fish, cheeses of the nearby districts, wines and champagnes, fresh fruit and coffee. On the sun decks to either side, the ladies and gentlemen of *L'Arlésienne* ate and drank, applied Bain de Soleil, read newspapers in five languages and chatted amiably.

"You've heard about Stash and Maserati, of course," said Miss Kraus.

"I don't believe I have."

"Maserati is once more in liquidation. *Finis.* The oil shortage—fatal illness for an automobile designed to run at two hundred kilometers per hour. But Stash has offered to save it—he needs an investment outside the music world, he tells us. What do you think? Or would this be simply another artistic investment, like opera? Ha ha . . ."

The crisp blue canvas flapped gently in the moist breeze. They were headed east, by Harry's calculation. "Quite right," Schröder-Devrient confirmed. "That is Cap de Carqueiranne—and off the bow, the Golfe de Giens. Our destination is Porquerolles in the Iles d'Hyères, where we anchor tonight. We shall go ashore for dinner at the Auberge de l'Arche de Noé, which will, I believe, meet your own high standards."

"Wonderful, I'm sure. And Count Gimpel? He will not be joining us for lunch?"

"I regret not," said Schröder-Devrient. "We have this morning encountered a business problem which will occupy the Count for the remainder of the day. Perhaps tomorrow . . ."

"Nothing serious, I hope."

"You know business, Mr. Chapin. Everything is urgent, yet of no consequence at one and the same time. And so it is with this."

"Yes," Harry said. "I know the feeling. . . ."

". . . Ah, dear Harry," said König, helping himself—and Harry—to another portion of lobster, "and will you join us for a swim after luncheon? We shall pause by the *plage* at Fort de la Gavaresse in order to permit the ladies to show us the latest in Riviera beach fashion."

"Klaus, to be candid, I had no idea that we would be, well, cruising. I expected only a brief business meeting. But now—"

"Ah, but this is Stash's way. Never business alone as in an office, but always in most comfortable surroundings—"

"I'm not complaining, understand. It's quite fabulous. However . . ."

He revealed his awful secret: he had no bathing suit. The useful Swiss was at his useful best. This would be no problem at all for Mme. Rasponi, the housekeeper, who could be found at that moment making up the beds.

Harry went below and found the lady in question, an older woman in severe black attire. He explained his problem. She measured him with her eye. *Non.* Being in charge of the laundry, she knew every piece of clothing aboard. None of the ship's crew was of his girth except perhaps

Captain Waldteufel, who had no use for such a garment.

Harry was mortified. "Never mind," he said. He would wait and buy shorts at the next port of call.

But Mme. Rasponi was not so easily defeated. She made him follow her down to the laundry room. "Take off trousers," she said. Then she had him stand against a roll of blue sailcloth while she traced the pattern. "You wait there," showing him into the dispensary next door.

He weighed himself on the old-fashioned doctor's scale, the kind with sliding weights. When the arm was still not in balance at 190, he got off—he had suffered enough mortification for one day. He could hear Mme. Rasponi's sewing machine. Blue sailcloth swimming trunks. How would he have nerve enough to show himself on deck?

"You put on," she said when she'd finished. She wouldn't leave the room. He turned around and covered himself as best he could.

"Oh, they're just perfect," he said. He had to hold his stomach in as he had when she'd done the measuring. "Oh, yes, just fine."

Mme. Rasponi was so pleased with her handiwork that she called in the valet, a Portuguese, who merely giggled. Harry got his wallet out of the chinos, but Mme. Rasponi wouldn't hear of it: guests paid for nothing aboard *L'Arlésienne*. He kissed her on both cheeks instead. There had been garlic in the crew's mess.

He headed back to Cabin Zandonai—aware that she watched him all the way down the corridor. He soon understood that the crotch was not exactly right, but he was in no mood to be laughed at further. As long as he walked with care, he would be fine. It was a life of constant peril, but then he was used to that.

The *plage* at Fort de la Gavaresse had suffered a most untimely oil spill and *L'Arlésienne* was unable to pause for the ladies' post-luncheon swim, denying Harry an opportunity to show off his new garment. However, in late afternoon they anchored off a sandy beach bordered by pines and briar and a shady forest rich in wild flowers—the Ile de Porquerolles—and Beppe and Paolo, who seemed to be in charge of entertainments, organized a race to shore. Frankie, slim and boyish in her borrowed one-piece swimsuit—she and Aurore were the same size— was the first female to finish; she had been something of an athlete at school. The first male, naturally, was Florescu. Harry did not finish, turning back about midway, exhausted, and finding refuge among the old folk—Temple and Box, Schröder-Devrient and Captain Waldteufel —on the champagne deck. Nobody mentioned Harry's shorts or the fact that they just matched the canvas awning overhead, for which Harry was immensely grateful.

Florescu was managing to spend a fair amount of time at Miss

Frankie Tree's side; Harry kept Captain Waldteufel's binoculars constantly trained on the pair. And what was wrong with Miss Tree's shoulder straps that the big Rumanian imbecile had to spend so much time fingering them?

"Is he promising, would you say? The baritone?"

Poor Box—he was interested in other people's careers, having none of his own these days.

"A smallish voice," Harry judged. "Pleasant enough timbre and quite resonant within a limited range. Going to be a pretty fair Germont if he doesn't abuse himself."

Box smoked a most terrible brand of cigars. Here in the absolute purity of the Mediterranean air Harry found them almost unbearable. The little man—hair mostly gone, cheeks pink from all those whiskies—reminded him of a mock Churchill: greatness which, in this case, had failed.

"You do his records, then, do you?" Box persisted.

"Oh, we've used Mihai a time or two. But nothing important yet."

"I had heard—"

"The Cavalieri *Otello?* Yes, but that didn't work out, I suppose you'd say. You know how these things go."

"I must say I do. Rose and I . . ."

But then the sad little man lost interest, or could not remember the circumstance.

"And your own plans . . . ?" Harry prompted.

"There is some talk of the *Liebeslieder Waltzes.* . . ."

"For Decca, would that be?"

"Hopefully, Decca, yes. But if there were interest in your camp . . ."

Nobody was going to record their *Liebeslieder Waltzes* or anything else; nothing quite so uncommercial as these out-of-fashion duo-pianists playing their irritatingly limited repertoire of arrangements, transpositions and hopeless new pieces written on commission. Bravely they had broadcast their total interdependence: no solo engagements for Temple and Box—you want one, you take the other.

"I believe they're coming back. . . ."

Florescu and Tree won the return leg, too.

"And what do the winners get as their prize?" Klaus König wanted to know. "And what for second place?" He and his own damsel, Miss Kraus, had come in second.

"Why, you get each other!" cried Beppe.

And to cement the bargain, the two couples met in passionate embrace, to the enthusiastic applause of guests and crew alike, with the exception of one.

* * *

Dinner ashore was first-rate, as Schröder-Devrient had predicted. Somehow in the rush for seating Harry found himself between Guy du Bonhomme, who preferred to discuss the theory of artistic collaboration, and Rose Temple, who indulged in an incredibly destructive analysis of her husband's technique. Frankie and Mihai arrived last, Frankie having paused to record the magnificent sunset with her wonderful Nikon, and were thus forced to sit together at the very end of the table, outside the range of Harry's hearing.

Afterward the launch had to make two trips in order to carry everybody back to *L'Arlésienne*. Frankie insisted that Harry go with the first group in order to assist Rose Temple, who had had a bit too much to drink; Richard Box had remained on board and did not witness her undoing. Harry waited atop the gangway for the launch to return, but Frankie and Mihai were not aboard. They had decided to stay behind and dance in the salon of the Grand Hôtel Alycastre.

At a little past three o'clock Harry awoke to the gentle splash of the Mediterranean against *L'Arlésienne's* hull. "Are you asleep?" he whispered to the bunk below. But there was no reply, because the bunk was empty.

I I I

Tuesday was devoted to the Côte des Maures. Harry rose early and took breakfast with the chef and stewards, who were setting the usual spread on the fantail. They wanted to cook eggs for him, but he preferred to stick to juice, toast and coffee: never too late to begin one's diet, even here.

After breakfast he conducted himself on a tour of the ship. The main salon was perhaps twenty by thirty feet—a very large space on a boat—and paneled in exotic African hardwoods. There was a piano—very much out of tune, from the humidity, no doubt—which Harry treated to a little Debussy; and a projection booth for the showing of movies. The decks were of teak, the fittings of well-polished brass. Off the main lounge was a dining room with murals and paintings by celebrated artists of the Mediterranean. Far forward were Count Gimpel's own quarters, consisting (Harry was told by a young crewman) of two bedrooms, a living room, an office and a small cabin for Miss Loose, the German stenographer. All of these were one deck above the guest staterooms. There were also two small salons for letter-writing and card-playing, a marvelous circular bar, the galley and "*Le Snack*," a kind of butler's pantry where you could go for tidbits at any time of day, and a laundry and dispensary. The only thing missing—he had heard Aurore complaining—was a freshwater swimming pool. "You know, they have that on *Christina*," she said, thus lending credence to the rumors that, before she was mistress to then Prince Juan Carlos Alphonso Victor María de Borbón y Borbón, she had been mistress to the late Aristotle Onassis.

Harry substantiated Schröder-Devrient's claim that the crew numbered sixteen; with his own eyes he saw Captain Waldteufel, the engineer, three common seamen, two teenage boys who delivered messages and polished the brass, the Portuguese valet, the Maltese maid, the chef and his helper, two stewards (one of whom tended bar), Miss Loose, Mme. Rasponi and the pilot of *Ma Mère l'Oye*. Sixteen salaries to be paid each month, and very good salaries they would be, given Count Gimpel's reputation. So this was how the other half lived.

While the others were having breakfast, Harry went to the sun deck and lay down with a Simenon paperback he had found in the library, *Maigret et le clochard*. But before he could get two pages into it (an exercise to improve his French as much as anything else) he was joined by Nikki and Monique.

"And what do you do?" Monique, the more animated of the two, asked him.

"Records," Harry said.

"Oh," with disappointment.

He knew how she felt. "And you?"

This was perhaps an unfair question, Harry knowing exactly what she did. Monique was an heiress, according to *Paris-Match*, who had recently been divorced by her German husband and ordered by the court to give the poor boy something like a million Deutsche marks as cash settlement because—though they'd had a long affair before the wedding—she refused to sleep with him afterward.

"What do you think I do?" she replied rather testily.

"Films?" he said.

"Sometimes," she said. "But it's such a bore."

"Have I seen you in anything lately?" Besides this fabulous bikini, of which the top had now been discarded.

"Not lately," she said. "It is so boring," she repeated.

He turned his attention to the other one—Nikki. A French lady, she had the most glorious figure: marvelous breasts, shapely and heavy, a tiny waist, thighs that were full but not too much so, lovely legs of the kind usually bestowed upon girls small in the bust, which Nikki was not. Her bathing suit was sparkling white, modest as to cut, but made of the thinnest possible material so that her nipples stood out as sharply as if she'd been naked. "Are you waiting to see Stash?" she said to him—interrupting his appreciation of her merits.

"Yes. Business, actually."

"Everyone is the same," with resignation.

"Not *you*, surely?"

"Of course. You find that strange?"

"Well—"

"I am going into business for myself," she said.

"Oh?"

In France it was a legitimate business, wasn't it, if you had the proper health card? One learned so much from Simenon novels.

"Fashion," she countered.

"Ah. I'm afraid I know nothing about fashion."

"Designing and modeling. My fiancé is a photographer and my mother is quite marvelous in the cutting and sewing. Originals, you understand. It is really Egon's idea. You should make a note of his name, for he will soon be very famous—Egon Zorn, with a Z. We hope to persuade Stash to supply our capital. Perhaps three hundred thousand francs. I shall pay him back. It is to be a real business. It is not a plaything."

"It sounds very ambitious. Good luck to you."

"And what do you require?"

"Nothing so—grand," Harry said. "Just an understanding, I suppose you could say."

"Ah, but *that* is very difficult. It is you who will need good luck."

This lady was brighter than she first appeared. Perhaps the sight of her pointy nipples had misled him. "Have you seen him? Count Gimpel?"

"Oh, yes. We saw him on Thursday. Or was it Friday? In Ibiza. He was most pleasant."

"And when would you expect to see him again?"

"He is Stash, isn't he? One never knows. . . ."

The plan for the day was luncheon off Le Lavandou followed by swimming beneath the Corniche des Maures; then anchors aweigh again for a brisk sail around Cap Camarat and ashore at St.-Tropez for drinks at L'Escale and supper and a nightclub and back to *L'Arlésienne* by 2:00 A.M. Just before luncheon they stopped and put the faster of the two launches in the water so that Mihai could give a demonstration of water-skiing. When he had performed the usual tricks, he instructed them to put him ashore with Frankie so that she could climb up on his massive shoulders, and then they towed this beautiful young couple at forty miles an hour, first on one side of *L'Arlésienne*, then the other, with Harry Chapin rushing from rail to rail to record the event with Frankie's Nikon.

In truth, Florescu displayed the physique of Adonis. Harry seriously wondered why such a specimen would waste his time with opera, where the incredible torso was inevitably concealed by some ridiculous costume. But now very little of the torso was concealed, and even as Harry thought these envious thoughts Adonis returned to *L'Arlésienne*, his Aphrodite by his side, to accept the exuberant applause of guests and crew. Never had Mihai's Escamillo gained greater approbation. Much that Harry had not understood before—the entire episode with Mme. Cavalieri—now made perfect sense. A body in such condition was not to be taken for granted, especially by a fifty-year-old woman who no longer found love in her public life. A body of steel upon which any woman might find ecstasy . . .

Florescu's body served to arouse Harry's own dormant manhood. He followed Frankie back to Cabin Zandonai, determined to reassert himself where Aphrodite was concerned.

"I suppose you've just come for some dry clothing," he said. "How are things in Cabin Rossini?"

She ignored him: kept right on fishing through her suitcase.

"I don't know," he mused. "Maybe we should take the seaplane back right now. Still no appointment with this fucking Gimpel. I can't understand the man. First he summons us here, and now—"

"I don't see the hurry."

"Oh, you don't, huh?"

"It's not as though we're invited every day to go cruising on a great yacht. . . ." She stripped naked, throwing her borrowed swimsuit into the bathroom and exposing her private parts as though he had no more feelings than the deck beneath her feet. ". . . And, besides, when did *you* start caring so much for the bloody business?"

He followed her example, stripping off the crotch-pinching sailcloth shorts in the most casual manner, pretending to look for dry clothes in *his* suitcase. "I've been talking to Barraud," he said over his shoulder, "and it's a lucky thing we're not stuck with Florescu as our Iago. Jean-Luc says the poor Rumanian boy's never even *seen Otello* and he's only read the play in some terrible German translation, so he thinks Iago is a *comic* role like Figaro."

The bitch wouldn't respond. When was the last time they'd had sex—in Munich? "I hear he's quite a ladies' man," he drawled on. "According to König, he's banged everything from here to Istanbul. Can't tell now whether he's screwing Nikki or Aurore or Monique or—most likely—all three."

"We're almost out of film," she said.

"What? Oh."

Where was he supposed to find film? To think that he'd wasted the Bayerischer Hof's double bathtub on her. Gotten her fill early on, this one had: had all the fucking she wanted from Harry Chapin before leaving England.

"Why don't you ask one of the crew to buy us some at St.-Tropez? I prefer Kodachrome sixty-four, but if they can't get that, then . . ."

She had adapted to luxury living with remarkable speed. "I'll get it myself," he said petulantly. "I'm good for *something*," an afterthought.

"You're a sweetheart," she said. "Now don't you think you should put something on?"

He found some clean underwear; got decent again.

"Have you heard the rumors?" she bubbled with girlish delight.

"No—what?"

"About who's coming on board at Cannes?"

"No—who?"

"Warren Beatty!"

"You're kidding."

"Either Warren Beatty or—Monique thinks—Barbara Walters. Isn't it *kicky!* I'll never forget this trip, Harry. Not as long as I live."

Me, too, lady. "Well—let's hope it's Walters, then."

"But *why?*" squealing.

"Because Mr. Florescu won't welcome any competition."

"That's what I like about you, Harry."

"What?"

"You can be such a total shit. . . ."

I V

Wednesday.

"Take your average Wagnerian soprano," Klaus König was saying.

"Do, whenever I can," replied—quite out of character—Serge Schröder-Devrient.

"She's nothing but an overgrown, brainless, athletic German girl," said the Swiss.

"Trouble with me," said Schröder-Devrient, "that's precisely what I like. Athletic German girls . . ." A twinkle in the eye. A gallant remembering much, remembering many.

They were making less than twenty-five miles a day, by Harry's reckoning, stopping constantly for swimming, sightseeing, shopping in the little boutiques along the coast, games of one kind or another. The pattern was now clear. They remained at anchor till midday to give the guests time to get over their hangovers or get started on new ones. A morning swim and then brunch, with more champagne and screwdrivers. The ladies preferred sunbathing; the men favored games— poker, craps, bezique, bridge. After brunch *L'Arlésienne* moved off slowly in search of the next hospitable cove where the guests might again cool off with a swim in the crystal-clear sea or go snorkeling for fish or water-ski with Mihai. Then back on board to nap, put on some clothes and appear on the champagne deck in time for cocktails. A late dinner, usually on shore, was followed by more drinks and dancing in the main lounge or perhaps a film and then gambling until two or three in the morning. And then the whole cycle would start over again.

Each day's itinerary was posted in the lounge. Today there would be a short sail up the coast past Ste.-Maxime (shopping, if anyone desired), Les Issambres (swimming), St.-Augulf (more shopping), arriving off Fréjus-Plage in time to watch Arthur Ashe play tennis at 4:00 P.M. Following cocktails, an authentic Provençal dinner would be provided at La Voile d'Or in St.-Raphaël.

". . . But there is no air-conditioning at all in Cabin Donizetti." Guy du Bonhomme spoke like a man who had come from the rack.

"I believe it's the central system," Harry said. "An electrical malfunction, according to the pilot who brought us from Toulon."

Harry had taken a strong dislike to this foppish Alsatian, without reason. Or perhaps not: perhaps it was right to dislike these spoiled post-teenagers who said things like, "I have only silk next to my skin. I find any other material intolerable."

"On another occasion," Du Bonhomme said, "I should like very much to discuss with you the artistic ethic."

"Oh, yes?"

"In that I could never myself accept employment in a commercial concern, I am quite fascinated by the idea that a man of your sensibilities should do so."

"Work for a living, you mean?"

"To put it crudely."

"Yes—we must discuss it sometime. . . ."

He escaped to the forward deck, hoping to watch the crew work for a living—only to be trapped by Temple and Box, who had moved their deck chairs to the bow in order to escape *L'Arlésienne*'s diesel smoke, which gave poor Richard, Rose said, a queasy stomach.

"Do join us, Mr. Chapin. We should be most delighted of your company," said Richard.

"Richard is not feeling well today," said Rose. "He is of delicate constitution. I had hoped that the sea air . . ."

The poor bastard. Tyranny came in many forms these days, but none quite so awful as this canny termagant.

"We—all of us aboard—had hoped to hear you play," Harry said, speaking to Box. "But given the condition of the piano . . ."

"Oh, Richard would not be able, on such short notice, to prepare a program," Rose said. "He is not what one terms a 'quick study.' Regrettably, our career has endured some rough patches for just this reason. And when one reaches a certain age . . ."

"Oh, my," Harry said, looking at his watch, "I'm afraid I have business with Mr. Schröder-Devrient. Perhaps later we might continue . . ."

Gratefully, he returned to the stern. "I don't suppose anyone has seen Count Gimpel," he said to the others.

Nobody had. He had never been so bored in his life—truly bored. You see, being rich is not the answer: he would describe all this boredom to Maggie when he got home.

Ah, they were putting *Ma Mère l'Oye* in the water. Harry watched closely in hope of seeing the mythical Stash Gimpel. He would tell Maggie about this, too—on board almost three full days now and still no host. Wait—is *that* Gimpel: a tall, rather elderly man in a business suit? "Who do you suppose . . . ?"

"That is Dr. Weissbrot of Siemens," said König. "Stash is a major shareholder, as you know."

"Ah . . ."

Once or twice a day *Ma Mère l'Oye* flew off to pick up these businessmen who came, had their meeting (apparently) and were then returned to their points of origin. This certainly beat life in the office. Except that right now Harry would have preferred the activity of his own office to this meaningless drift.

"Ah, Mr. Chapin—do sit down and let us get to know each other better."

Felicity Kraus: tall, buxom, with Middle Eastern eyes. By now her nipples were at least as familiar to him as Frankie's: like the other ladies, she tended to begin each day with her bra in place, only to lose it as the sun rose in the sky.

"I understand," Harry said, settling himself to have a more advantageous view, "that you've just published a novel."

"Yes, that is so. You've not read it?"

"I'm afraid not. I just learned—"

"Naughty, naughty. Stash has dozens of copies. There is even one in the library below."

It was hard to believe that this bikinied delight—a little heavy in the thighs: what did they call it, cellulite?—had written a book. "Have you known the Count long?" he asked. "I'm embarrassed to say that I've not met him face to face."

"Stash? Oh, yes. You will like him—and he will like you."

According to Jean-Luc, Felicity had been Stash's mistress for an extended period—which probably accounted for König's present interest, since König never did anything without purpose. "Well, I hope to see him one of these days," Harry said. "In case you run into him, you might pass along that message."

"Oh, I am sure that you will—and soon."

"Are you writing another book?"

"I am hoping to write Stash's biography, if he'll let me. Did you know that he is descended from the kings of Poland?"

"I may have read . . ."

"You must ask Serge. They are very close friends. Did you know that Serge was once conductor of the Warsaw Opera?"

"I didn't, no. That certainly explains . . ."

"And now I wonder if you would be so kind as to put this lotion on my back."

He did as directed. Her skin was substantial to the touch—the female's extra layer of subcutaneous fat?

"And now I believe I shall take a nap."

Meaning that he could go. His services, as usual, were no longer required.

He went below and lay down on Frankie's bunk. It was actually his bunk now that Frankie no longer used it. He shut his eyes and immediately had visions of Felicity Kraus—that enormous brown back, those long brown legs, those fat white breasts. He wouldn't require marijuana or any kinky tricks to combat impotence, not with that female. Incredible that she should settle—having certainly had the best of Stash Gimpel—for that Swiss dumpling Klaus König. Or maybe that was only cosmetic—lurid material for the cabin-occupancy chart and nothing more. Perhaps if he spent more time with the lady . . .

The cabin door opened, scaring him to death.

"Oh, hello. I thought you were on deck. Do you mind?"

In came Frankie, carrying towels and beach bag.

"No, of course not. How have you been?"

"Fine," she said. "I don't suppose you got my film."

He moved to the cabin's one chair so that she could spread out her stuff. "No—sorry. They didn't have any at . . ."

"It's all right. Maybe this afternoon, at the tennis place."

She took off her clothes and began to shave her legs with his razor. He got out his Simenon and pretended to read.

"You really should try the water-skiing," she said. "It's super fun."

"I suppose. Maybe later."

She went to work on her toenails.

He stood up, took off his shirt and bathing suit and wrapped a bathtowel around his waist. The way she sat on the bunk—totally naked—was designed to punish him, he knew. She was applying a sparkling silver polish and he could see directly between her legs. He took off his towel and hung it on the bathroom door, turning around so that she was in close proximity to his erection.

"Oh, oh," she said. "Now, Harry . . ."

He moved the bottle of polish off the lower bunk, setting it on the nightstand, and pulled her to her feet. "This is just ridiculous," he whispered. She tried to reach her robe, but he kept her from it. "I love you," he said. He kissed her with passion and tried to back her onto the bunk.

"*Harry?* I'm *warning* you—"

He had never wanted a woman so much in his life. He forced his tongue into her mouth—a thing she'd once said she liked—and at the same time opened her legs with his hand. He was guiding his member to the opening . . . when she rapped him across the balls with her knuckles. . . .

He missed luncheon and the Arthur Ashe tennis match. Jean-Luc Barraud was sent down by the others to make sure Harry wasn't seasick. "No, fine—just resting," he called through the door. He hadn't seen stars since he was sixteen years old and was struck in the forehead during batting practice at Choate. He crawled around the tiny cabin on his hands and knees taking inventory. The Nikon and all its accessories were gone, as were the clothes in the dresser and her toilet articles and his razor. He felt sick to his stomach for several hours, but couldn't vomit. When he heard the launch leave for St.-Raphaël and the Provençal dinner, he buzzed for the steward and obtained two bottles of the excellent rosé they'd had at dinner Tuesday night. By the time he had finished the second, he was able to vomit.

V

Next morning the winds of fortune began to blow in Harry's direction—though he did not think so at the time. Stepping out of a hot shower, he forgot a lifelong rule and stuck a Q-tip into his left ear, where the warmed wax, instead of sticking to the little cotton ball, found itself pushed farther into the ear canal, thus creating a perfect hydraulic seal and making Harry, for all intents and purposes, deaf in one ear.

For five minutes he ricocheted around the damnable metallic cabin in a heavily listing attitude, banging his head with the palm of his hand on the side opposite to the clogged ear in hopes that the alien substance would obey the feeble laws of gravity—without positive results.

He began to sweat. This kind of personal disability unnerved him more than anything else in life—more even than being smashed in the groin. Harry Chapin, a music man by profession, deaf—like Beethoven, his mentor—in one ear. His panic knew no limits.

"Madame? I wonder if you might . . ."

He pulled Mme. Rasponi out of the passageway and explained his difficulty. Minutes later the Portuguese valet arrived with a piece of wire guitar string. With tweezers Harry fashioned a tiny triangle at one end. Then—sterilizing the wire in the bottle of brandy that adorned each guest cabin—Harry probed the affected ear. The operation was not a success.

". . . Corniche de l'Esterel—yes, there ahead."

"Pardon? I didn't hear what you said."

Felicity repeated her statement.

"Yes, of course. Sorry . . ."

The program for Thursday was sightseeing beneath the great red cliffs of the Corniche de l'Esterel, with arrival at Cannes in time for dinner dancing at Aux Ambassadeurs and gambling in the Municipal Casino. In mid-morning—while Harry was lying under the hot sun in such a way that his left ear would be warmed in preparation for another attempt with the probe—*Ma Mère l'Oye* was again swung out and placed gently in the water, being sent this time to fetch the mystery guest.

"It's definitely Barbara Walters," said Monique. "I'm dying to ask her about her contract."

"Not at all," said Nikki. "It's definitely Paul Newman."

"I have heard," said Felicity, "that it is David Niven, who lives here on the Riviera. I intend to give him an autographed copy of my book, and then perhaps . . ."

Others said it was Ava Gardner, who had been seen on every yacht in the Mediterranean at one time or another. Others said Cary Grant. Or Grace Kelly, and they would sail into Monte Carlo—which the girls called just "Monte" to show they had been there many times—under military escort and would receive the salute of cannon due the Grimaldis.

It was none of these. The guest of honor was the opera star Didi del Campo.

"Didi! Didi! Didi!"

He was *ecstatic* to see his Didi. She looked up to him from the launch and shouted something that sounded like "I love you." But with his ear . . .

On deck she kissed him on the mouth in front of all the others, including Frankie. "Oh, baby," she cried, "I've got so much to *tell* you. Come help me unpack."

She was temporarily assigned to Cabin Mascagni—Jean-Luc agreeing to move in with Mihai, who did not seem entirely pleased. She looked marvelous: no signs of the bruises from New York, and no weeping. A free woman, she said she was. That's what she'd meant about a holiday in Santo Domingo: she'd gotten herself the fabled "pressure cooker" twenty-four-hour divorce.

"I'm *so* happy for you," Harry said, holding her in his arms. "So now then—there's still a chance for old Harry Chapin?"

"Always," she said, kissing him loudly and with disconcerting wetness. "Except for one man in the world," she laughed with that spine-tingling gay giggle of hers, "Harry Chapin is *Número Uno.*"

"But I thought you said—Mr. Bucellatti?"

"Not *Mario,* silly. I'm talking about Stash. We *are* going to be married. Isn't that wonderful?"

"Wonderful's not the word. . . ."

After lunch Didi dragged Harry back down to Cabin Mascagni and made him turn around while she put on her new bathing suit, which she'd just bought at Cannes.

"Well—what do you think?"

It was one of those string bikinis—thongs, he guessed the correct term was—just a small piece of cloth between the legs with two even smaller pieces held by bits of yarn over the breasts. Pulling tight between her buttocks, the bottom looked hellishly uncomfortable—and intended for ladies of more modest dimensions than Didi's. "Don't tell me you're going to wear that on deck? The crew will mutiny."

But she did—ignoring the chorus of oooh's and aaah's which Harry had predicted. "Screw them," she said bravely.

"I believe they have the opposite in mind."

"Here—do me, okay?"

He had become expert with the Bain de Soleil. "And there *is* a Stash Gimpel?"

"You bet your ass."

"Promises, promises . . . Free one minute, and you want to surrender your freedom again the next. I didn't think career girls these days—"

"They don't. It's fucking women's lib—all that Helen Reddy 'I Am Woman' crap. Sure, I want to be independent—have my career while I can. But when the sun goes down, I want to know I've got a man to hold me through the night. Let's face it, Harry, sooner or later we've all got to grow up. A person can't go through life singing opera. . . ."

His dear, foolish Didi. He was in love with her again, naturally—
now that she was no longer available. Ah, to have given *this* lady his
child . . .

They didn't go ashore with the others: Didi had just come from
Cannes and had found it cheap and commercial. Instead, they stayed
behind and took gambling lessons from Captain Waldteufel and the
chief steward, a Russian gentleman called Preferanski, who knew all
there was to know about games of chance. The only other guests aboard
were Temple and Box, who had retired to the grand salon to play the
piano despite its bad state of tune. This came as a surprise to Harry
because the duo-pianists had staged a bitter row during cocktails—to the
point that Klaus König had asked them to return to their cabin.

"If one wishes to learn baccarat," said Captain Waldteufel, "one is
well advised to watch Count Gimpel. For his talent in this regard, as in
others, is of world class."

Harry wanted desperately to learn the game, if only to keep up with
Didi, but games in general escaped him: *jeton*, betting a single number,
en plein, two numbers, *cheval*—paying seventeen to one, was it?—a
transversale, three, *carré* for four, a *sixain*, the *douzaines* and *colonnes*,
manque and *passe*, the *chances simples*—no, no, no, it was just not
simple enough for him.

Didi was quickly $200 ahead: the late lamented Mr. Bucellatti had
taught her in Vegas.

"Now watch, Harry, how I place my bets. . . ."

But just as he was getting the hang of it, they were interrupted by
the junior steward, who burst into the salon with the news that there
had been a violent quarrel in Cabin Puccini.

"Can you come, messieurs? I believe that she has broken his
hands. . . ."

V I

Ma Mère l'Oye went off Friday morning to Grasse, where there was an
excellent hospital. Jean-Luc volunteered to go along as interpreter because Rose and Richard, despite three decades of touring on the Continent, had never learned to say more than *"bonjour"* and *"merci."* One
of Richard's hands was very swollen and had turned black-and-blue
overnight—she had smashed him with a gold "Oscar" which had been
won by a film that Stash produced in the '40s, according to Felicity
Kraus—but there appeared to be no real damage. Of greater interest was
the suggestion that when *Ma Mère l'Oye* returned, she would be bring-

ing with her Count Stanislaus Gimpel, who had been conducting business in Marseilles.

They had reached the Côte d'Azur proper and were anchored now off Juan-les-Pins, where hardly anybody wore any clothes. Ergo, the naked woman off *L'Arlésienne*'s stern.

"Isn't that . . .?"

Yes, it was. Didi del Campo, floating on her back.

They lined the deck rail—Harry, Schröder-Devrient, König, Beppe and Paolo, Mihai, even Guy du Bonhomme, who had never seen anything so vulgar, he said, in his life.

"Oh, *men*," Frankie said, dragging Mihai away to swim off the bow. "What would possess her to *expose* herself like that? It's *disgusting*."

Harry was perhaps the least affected by this display, having cherished the *Playboy* spread for many weeks. Judging now, the artful camera had made certain helpful alterations, minimizing a too comfortably padded derrière while maximizing those gorgeous frontal orbs which, while admirably shaped, were slightly undersized for a lady of such opulent hips.

"What do you suppose she weighs?"

"Eh?" Harry's left ear—just slightly less opaque-seeming than yesterday—made conversation on that side annoyingly dull and distant.

"Her weight?" König repeated. "What would you judge it to be, in kilograms?"

"Oh—hundred and forty pounds? Whatever that is in metric."

Soon the game was on: a pool organized by Beppe and Paolo. Each guest would give his or her estimate, and the one who came closest to the actual weight would win. The ante? To make it interesting, said Beppe, one hundred American dollars.

They had no difficulty in finding entrants. Guy, Felicity, Klaus, Mihai, Beppe, Paolo, Serge, Harry: that made eight. Captain Waldteufel was told and immediately sent down a hundred for himself and a hundred for a pool of the crew. At which point Serge added a hundred for Stash—who enjoyed a good joke, Serge assured them—and Harry put in a hundred for Jean-Luc, who would surely have entered if he had not been in Grasse. That made $1200! This was no longer a joking matter.

"But how will we ever know the winner?" Felicity asked.

Good point. The scale to be used was that in the dispensary. But who would witness the weigh-in?

"Two witnesses," Mihai demanded.

"As I am the oldest," said Schröder-Devrient.

"As I am a woman," said Felicity.

"As I have known her longest," said Harry.

It was quickly agreed. Harry and Felicity were designated a committee of two to perform the judging. And Harry was appointed a committee of one to persuade her to undergo the test.

The estimates were not kind. König thought 150 even. Mihai was a more gallant 138. Frankie, on behalf of Jean-Luc, said 145. The others ranged between 129 and 147. The crew collectively thought 140—"a very beautiful" 140, its youthful spokesman was instructed to say.

Harry waited till last. The number on his slip was met with a general gasp: 155. "And you might as well pay me now," Harry said, "for I have won."

Harry waited until after lunch—when Didi had already had a vodka or two and drunk her part of a bottle of Provençal rosé—to make his approach.

"Oh, shit, Harry—if this is business . . ."

"Business and pleasure all in one."

He described the wager.

"And that's all I have to do—get weighed?"

"Precisely."

"Why should I? What do I get out of it?"

He had anticipated this moment. Didi was notoriously cheap. She had been known to lose an engagement over a difference of $100 in fee. Living the good life with Mr. Bucellatti had taught her the value of the dollar. For six hundred of them, Harry calculated, she would do a great deal more than step on a scale. So he said:

"Assuming that I have guessed correctly, I'll give you half my winnings. But if I've guessed incorrectly—which you can tell me now—then you simply decline to take part in the whole affair."

She smiled with delight. "You *are* a dear man. How much did you guess?"

"I've done an ungentlemanly thing, I'm afraid."

"Come on—how much?"

"Bet against the house, to use a term from baccarat."

"Shit, Harry, how *much?*"

"I have wagered that your present weight—in the off-season, mind you—is somewhat more than others might think."

"*Harry*—"

"Let's keep this in perspective, shall we?"

"A hundred and seventy-five? Something horrible like that, huh?"

"Didi, my love, I may be a cad, but I am not *that* big a cad. One fifty-five."

"You *bastard!* You absolute Harvard *stinker!* . . . But I think you win."

"Then the bet's on?" He was already thinking of ways to spend his half.

"It's on," spoken with admirable resolve. "God—the things I'll do for money . . ."

They stopped by Cabin Mascagni to get Didi's robe. In the passageway, she pointed to the cabin-assignment notice. "I'm a little disappointed in you, Harry."

"Oh? And how is that?"

"Sleeping with that little English number. I thought you had taste."

"To be truthful, I'm not. Sleeping with her, that is. We're just traveling together. Temporarily."

"I didn't really think you'd go for something like that, with no tits."

Mme. Rasponi was still at lunch. Harry locked the dispensary door to ensure privacy. Didi took off her robe and stepped on the scale, wearing only her bikini. Harry handled the sliding weights.

"I make it . . . one-fifty . . . seven . . . and a half. We win! Let me go get our witness, Felicity."

"Hold it," Didi commanded. "God, I haven't been this heavy in ages. Maybe you're not doing it right. Try again."

This time she discarded the bathing suit—both parts.

"Well—" His shaking hand knocked off one of the weights.

"Why, Harry Chapin—you're *nervous.*"

"Not a bit. Actually—I make it . . . one . . . fifty . . . seven . . . even."

"Okay, Buster. Now you."

"What? Oh, no, I don't think so—"

"*Get on.* Without the trunks."

As modestly as he could—pulling in his stomach and hating every bite of the lobster he'd just consumed—he stepped out of his trunks and onto the scale.

She giggled, then laughed. "One ninety . . . *eight!* You fat old man!"

"Satisfied?"

But before he could retrieve his trunks, she kicked them out of reach and threw her arms around him.

"Didi, really . . ." She grabbed him in a delicate place. "*Hey—*"

"I don't excite you, Mr. Chapin?"

"Of course you do. But—"

"But what? You locked the door, didn't you?"

She spread her robe on the deck and pulled him down.

"Didi, I don't think I can—"

"Ssssh—let me, then . . ."

"Oh, God, Didi—I love you. . . ."

When he came, he did so with a bang: the blocked ear canal popped open, enabling him to hear every whisper of wind and sea, every footstep on deck—including (he learned later) those of the Count Stanislaus Gimpel, who had returned to claim his bride.

VII

Dinner was taken at the Eden Roc in Cap d'Antibes—Count Gimpel and Mme. del Campo conspicuous by their absence and Mr. Harry Chapin much relieved. L'Arlésienne made a late start next morning, and Harry put on his good gray flannels, the better of his two tennis shirts and his blue blazer in anticipation of a summons to the bridge.

He was not disappointed. One of the serious young boys found Harry in the library and presented a handwritten invitation on a silver tray. The Count would be pleased to have Harry join him for luncheon in his private quarters at one o'clock.

As Harry entered, Gimpel was seated at an exquisite Louis Quinze desk with Serge Schröder-Devrient on one side and Miss Loose, the German stenographer, on the other.

"If I am disturbing—"

"Ah—my dear Harry—to be face to face at last, after all these years of the telephone."

The Count rose and came forward to shake Harry's hand.

"Count Gimpel—"

"Oh, my, no—Stash, please. You do me a great disservice to rely upon meaningless titles."

Gimpel was younger in appearance than Harry had expected—he was sixty-five, according to Felicity—and more handsome in the flesh than in his photographs, most of which had been taken on the run by frustrated newspapermen. Gently persuasive voice, wavy black hair specked with gray, sharp features, aquiline nose, dark sad eyes surrounded by tiny laugh lines. Except for heavy acne scars on his neck and jaw, Gimpel might have been a distinguished character actor of the Raymond Massey school.

"And the Strausses are well? I remember with great fondness my long association with them. Leonid must be gratified that you have carried on his work in Melos-Doria as you have."

"It's kind of you to say so. I only hope that I don't prove an embarrassment to him."

Miss Loose excused herself to begin transcription of the morning's dictation. Schröder-Devrient promptly cleared away the papers from the desk and opened a bottle of champagne at the sideboard.

"Harry was most helpful," Schröder-Devrient said, serving the champagne, "in rescuing poor Box."

"A tragedy," Gimpel said, his sad eyes sadder still. "You know, he had real talent, that boy. I witnessed his debut in London. But marriage to that woman . . . Ah, but my dear Harry—have you been comfortable? What have you thought of our *L'Arlésienne?* Is she not a dear lady?"

"Perfect beyond description," Harry said. "I can't imagine why you would be interested in the *Christina.*" It had been reported when Onassis died that Gimpel wished to purchase the larger vessel.

"Not for my own use, but as an investment perhaps. But they do not know their own minds in that camp—I do not believe the daughter will ever sell. As for this dear lady"—said with a gentle laugh—"has Didi told you of her desire to bring an interior decorator from New York to refit *L'Arlésienne* from stem to stern? The vanity of women . . ."

"A strong-willed young girl," said Harry, flirting with disaster.

"You are quite correct. And we never seem to learn. The former Countess Gimpel was a soprano, you know. Ah—and I have never thanked you properly for your efforts on my behalf in *l'affaire Villeneuve.* . . ."

Stéphanie Villeneuve, prima donna of the Marseilles Opera. Harry had made a recording of lieder—real German songs from this sweet French bird—in order to please, he thought, his friend Jean-Luc Barraud: an accommodation, he learned later, which had been a favor to Count Gimpel. "It was our pleasure," Harry said modestly. "She possessed rare talent."

"Yes, a shame. She married, and then—poof, end of career. As is so often the case . . . But now, should we not take some nourishment and perhaps afterward discuss *les affaires?* . . . As we shall anchor at Nice this afternoon, I have asked our chef to prepare a true *salade niçoise.* Not as you would have it in your Beverly Hills restaurants, but *très authentique,* for Chef Célestin comes from nearby Villefranche and understands the subtleties of his profession. . . ."

The *salade niçoise* was memorable, served with a substantial white Burgundy and chunks of bread soaked in olive oil and garlic. Gimpel ate little, but talked a great deal. Harry said almost nothing, but stuffed himself with tuna and glass after glass of the delicious chilled wine. At three o'clock Schröder-Devrient excused himself to send cables while there was still plenty of daylight in America.

". . . Being by preference and birth both a Pole and a Jew, dear Harry, I have no difficulty in likening myself to our ancestors of the Old World who bought and sold kingdoms, financed the Crusades, developed trade with the East and ultimately created the code of commercial morality—the Commercial Ethic, as I believe it is called in your Harvard Business School—which governs transactions even today. Of course, I have an advantage over my competitors. My family has had money for twelve centuries—thus, it is unlikely that these nouveaux riches will uncover hidden treasure in this, my own part of the forest."

Harry could only nod in alcoholic agreement.

"Ah," said Gimpel, taking note of Harry's malaise, "but you have been the most gracious of guests, and I the most self-indulgent of hosts. It is simply that I do not have the pleasure of such company, dear Harry, with any frequency. And you have got me talking about myself, which is my favorite topic."

They adjourned to Gimpel's private sun deck overlooking the stern. Below, Beppe was breaking targets with a shotgun, hardly ever missing. Mihai tried his hand, but muscles meant nothing in this sport and he could do no better than two out of ten. Didi and the other girls lazed in the cool Mediterranean, floating on their backs and shouting criticisms to the marksmen above.

"With respect to Benno Toggi," Harry began bravely. This was what he had come for—this simple conversation—but now, in these circumstances, talking to a man whose family had had money for twelve centuries, his business seemed unworthy, even ludicrous. "What terms," he began again, "would we be expected to . . ."

"This is a very simple matter, Harry. Not complicated at all. For providing the services of Signor Toggi we ask nothing in fees, no advance, not even a royalty."

"I'm afraid I don't understand," Harry said.

"You may wish to cover Benno's expenses at Rome," Gimpel continued, "but nothing more. This is, for me, a personal undertaking. Signor Toggi was, in better days, a fine gentleman who was most kind to the first Countess Gimpel—Mme. Rossen—and I am merely repaying a debt of honor. What he requires you cannot afford—a rebuilding of his personal fortunes, a settlement of his present legal problems. In such matters I am most effective."

"Naturally, we would propose to take care of Signor Toggi's expenses at Rome," Harry said.

"Whatever you would do for other artists—yes, that is equitable.

. . . But now, on a more personal basis, I would speak to you of an accommodation."

"An accommodation?"

"A favor, if you like. To me, personally."

"Ah. Well, certainly—if it's in my power to give."

"Why, it is of such simplicity, dear Harry—I am surprised you have not already guessed it. It is simply—*that*. . . ."

That being Miss Didi del Campo, who was just then climbing aboard and beginning to towel off.

"But—I'm afraid I still don't understand. With respect to *Otello* . . .?"

"Not *Otello*, dear boy. I speak of the contract you now hold with Didi. For her exclusive services."

"I'm sorry if I seem dense—the wine perhaps—but—"

"We shall wish to suspend her present contract—or otherwise modify it. Naturally, Didi would continue to offer her services to Melos-Doria on a preferential basis—the *Bohème*, for example, that you and she have talked about. But with regard to other projects—projects in which Melos-Doria could be expected to show little or no interest—we would wish to have freedom to place Didi elsewhere."

"Ah . . ."

Again the hated quid pro quo—Benno for Didi—in this instance, requiring that he surrender a major asset of the corporation. What was an exclusive long-term contract with Didi del Campo worth? Difficult to estimate—but surely more than the temporary services of an aging Benno Toggi.

"We would not abuse this new-found freedom, Harry, I can assure you. If that is your concern . . ."

"In the past," Harry said, thinking aloud, "we have entered into arrangements by which an artist agrees to make one LP for Melos-Doria for each one he or she makes elsewhere. Would such a formula . . .?"

"Let us not encumber ourselves with needless paperwork. This makes only the lawyers happy. Instead, why do we not simply make an addendum to the present contract, to the effect that should Mme. del Campo wish to record elsewhere, she may do so. Would this not be the simplest and, thus, best approach?"

"If we were not able—for one reason or another—to come to such an agreement . . ."

The Count's eyes were even sadder than usual. "In that event, dear Harry . . . No, I would not wish to contemplate such a state of affairs. Nor, I should think, would you. . . ."

"And would it be indiscreet of me to ask, Stash, what you have in mind for Didi? What other projects—for what labels?"

"Not at all, dear boy. To begin, we shall make for my good friend

Dr. Udo Blinn and his company with the strange initials—"

"D-D-R-SCH," Harry said.

"—thank you, yes, in East Germany—we shall make first a series of operatic highlights—the standard works of the Italian and French literature, but in the German language, which they require for their market. And then, by means of tracking, we shall prepare the same recordings, but in the proper languages, for America and the rest of the world."

"It sounds very—ambitious."

"You are kind. No, I realize that such a program must seem ridiculous to you—the plaything of an aging gentleman who has too much money. But I am not a musician like you. I cannot conduct like our colleague Schröder-Devrient. I cannot even play the piano like that poor soul Box. And yet—through Didi—it is within my power to have an artistic career as if it were my own. . . . And so it is that I presume to ask you, as a favor, for this accommodation."

There was no one quite so graceful in defeat as Harry Chapin. Refuse to relinquish Didi's exclusivity and there would be no Benno Toggi at Rome—and thus no *Otello*; no new contract with Vova Slonimsky; and no more Del Campo on Melos-Doria Records. "I shall ask our attorneys to send you the necessary amendment at the earliest opportunity. And, naturally, Stash, you have my best wishes for future happiness with our Didi—she is a most wonderful lady, and you a most fortunate man."

The Count smiled with remarkable warmth. "I accept your good wishes—and your generosity—with infinite gratitude. And 'our Didi,' as you so justly say it, returns your affection tenfold—you have always treated her with respect and equity, and this is rare in our business. . . .

"But now—I have bored you beyond conscience."

"Not at all. But since we have concluded our affairs—and if you don't mind—I shall be leaving tomorrow, when we reach Monte Carlo."

"Must you? Didi will be most disappointed."

"If we are to make this opera at Rome . . ."

"I understand perfectly. Opera—the great compulsion of my life."

"A dying business, I'm afraid. In today's economy . . ."

The Count's cordial manner evaporated with shocking abruptness. "Never—*never* make such a statement. It is false and unworthy of a man of your quality."

Harry experienced a shiver of alarm. "Perhaps I am expressing myself badly. Speaking in a commercial sense—"

"You need not tell me of commercial sense. Why are we committed to opera even now, when so much of the world around us embraces the spiritual poverty of materialism? Because one is inevitably drawn to the aristocracy—this is basic to social order—and opera constitutes the last true aristocracy on this poor earth."

"I had not thought of it in exactly those terms—"

"But, dear boy, it is undeniably *true*. And the last aristocrats? Why, tenors and sopranos, of course. Look at the ladies—Callas, Caballé, Cavalieri, yes, even Del Campo—yachting with royalty (what there is left of it), wearing all the best jewels, commanding the best tables in the best restaurants . . .

"Oh, no, Harry, the fascination of opera does not lie in the music, which hardly counts at all, or in the drama—*La Forza del destino*, now I ask you, a literary dustbin! . . . No, I shall tell you what it is. It is the sinful extravagance . . . the Byzantine intrigue . . . the pathetic narcissism of middle age . . . the morbid classical decadence . . . Yes, *these* are the shameless propositions that command our ultimate romantic surrender . . . that compel us to serve willingly as vassals of Art. . . ."

He fled down the ladder like a thief, his feet barely touching the rungs.

". . . Oh, but I have forgotten to thank you, dear Harry"—called to him from above as he sought refuge among the normal people on the shuffleboard deck—"for my share of yesterday's winnings. Yes, already Didi and I are splitting, what do you say, fifty-fifty? This money was for me the only profit of the week—a very bad time on the Swiss gold market, as you may have heard. . . ."

VIII

Sunday, May 29. *Otello* would begin at Rome in just twelve weeks.

They arrived at Monte Carlo well before noon and moored along the Quai des Etats-Unis, within sight of the Casino. Harry had made no reservation, but at this time of year there wouldn't be a problem. He would go first to the Hôtel de Paris; if no room there, then L'Hermitage. He would stay only one night, then fly to Paris and catch a TWA 747 straight back to the Coast.

He wanted to say goodbye to Frankie, who was making her own travel plans now, but she was not to be found. Perhaps she and Mihai had already gone ashore; he would wait another half-hour and then leave, no matter what. He penned a short thank-you note to Gimpel and then went up on deck to watch the new arrivals. Three young ladies came aboard—Gaby, Dulci and Lisl—replacing Monique, Aurore and Nikki. Nobody seemed to know who they were, but it made no difference: aboard *L'Arlésienne* all were equals. The new girls were in their bikinis even before the crew got ashore, and the crew moved very quickly in port. These weren't the sweet sun-blackened honeys of Laguna and Malibu; these were a harder lot, baked on purpose for the

pleasure of the Riviera set—of which Harry Chapin was definitely not a
member. His blue blazer was wrinkled and stained and smelled of suntan lotion. Perhaps in the hotel he would buy a new one—feed this one
to the fishes.

And then he saw Frankie, moving up the gangway in apparent
distress. She was crying and Mihai couldn't seem to make her stop. To
have a lovers' quarrel so early in the game . . .

Surprisingly, she made straight for Harry and clutched at him,
hugging him as she never had before.

"Babe—hey, *easy*. Everything's going to be all right. . . ."

"No, it isn't," she wept. "It can *never* be all right now. . . ."

She and Mihai had been ashore to get the papers, and she now
made Harry take one—the *Times* of London.

"Well, what is it? What's the problem? It can't be that bad. It—"
But then he saw that it was:

MR. McEVOY
HANGED HIMSELF
IN HIS OFFICE

Theodore Dawes McEvoy, aged 44, the expatriate American public-relations counselor and London restaurant proprietor, hanged himself in his offices on the King's Road, it was
said yesterday at an inquest in London.

According to his executive assistant Miss Patricia Hobson,
Mr. McEvoy had suffered the loss of several important accounts in recent months, principally in the pop music field
which was his specialty, and had become deeply depressed over
the separation from his estranged wife Priscilla, who is resident
in Portland, Oregon, U.S.A. According to Miss Hobson, Mr.
McEvoy informed employees that he intended to work late on
Friday evening, May 20. Nothing more was heard from Mr.
McEvoy, who lived by himself at 12 Eaton Crescent, until
Saturday morning when porters opened the offices and discovered him hanging from a lighting fixture. A large aquarium
in his office had been smashed, and its single occupant, a fish
which was pet to Mr. McEvoy, was dead as well. A letter was
found addressed to a personal friend in America, it was stated.
Police have declined to reveal the contents. Mr. Morris
Finchley, deputy coroner for Knightsbridge, said: "This was an
impulsive suicide during a period of deep depression brought on
by business difficulties." He recorded a verdict that Mr. McEvoy
killed himself.

". . . Oh, Harry—whatever shall we do?" It was as though she
had rapped him again in the balls.

Intermezzo

HOLLYWOOD: *June*

Take but degree away, untune that string,
And hark what discord follows!

Shakespeare

She left the office early, as Mr. Chapin—Harry—had suggested.

Poor man, he never did reach his party in Europe. "Oh, bad luck," the Count's private secretary, Mr. Schröder-Devrient, had said: Count Gimpel was on his honeymoon and could not be reached for another three weeks. Mr. Chapin—Harry—had had so much bad luck lately—especially the death of his friend in England. But now—perhaps she would be able to cheer him up. He was such a *strange* man in many ways—so unpredictable. Still—he *was* attractive and certainly generous and good company, and after three years of working in the same office she definitely preferred him to any of the other bosses she'd ever had.

So that now she went about her preparations with a light heart, unwrapping the frozen rumaki and egg rolls and putting them on a cookie sheet in the oven, ready to turn on as soon as he arrived. She got out the two best wineglasses—because he was sure to bring a nice bottle—and fluffed the pillows in the living room, and then changed into her Chinese lounging pajamas, green silk with matching slippers, and no bra because none was needed. She had herself a healthy jigger of Scotch on the rocks just to be on the safe side—there being nothing wrong with Alix Stern that a little loosening up wouldn't cure, so said they all—and literally let her hair down from the office bun to a far more informal styling—not exactly sensual, perhaps, but complementing her own angular femaleness, which not all the males in the world had disliked.

And, besides, there was nothing serious planned for the evening:

only casual and, above all, *comfortable* sociability with a man she'd known and liked, in intimate office circumstances, for a substantial period of time.

Oops—almost forgot the most important item of all, the envelope of magical white powder which Mr. Chapin had seemed so (playfully) interested in, and which Carlos, her hairdresser, had gotten her on very short notice for the bargain price of just seventy dollars cash.

There now—could any man ask for more?

". . . Good evening, Mr. Chapin, sir. And won't you come in?"

"Hi—I found it, obviously. Am I too early? Or late?"

"Just perfect, as always."

He kissed her in approved older-brother fashion, and she returned the compliment.

"My—like that outfit. Good thing you don't wear it on the lot. Men would kill."

"This? Practically a uniform for us Hollywood working girls. May I take that?"

"Little something to drink, actually."

"Oh, you *are* nice." Two chilled bottles of the Lancers *vinho branco* in the green pottery flask that she'd taken such a fancy to at their last little get-together, the Christmas party in the Art Department bungalow. "And *two* whole bottles . . ."

"I thought we might develop a thirst," he said, gay old dog that he was. He looked a little tired after their long day, but she sensed a letting go now, a genuine relaxation, which dear Mr. Chapin seldom showed in public.

"If you would do the honors . . ." She directed him into the minuscule kitchen and handed him the corkscrew.

"Mmmm—something smells good," he said, removing his jacket and tie, which she quickly hid away in the front-hall closet.

"Rumaki and egg rolls," she called back to him. She wondered if marriage was like this—tired husband coming home to rumaki and egg rolls every night, wife in green Chinese pajamas. "Only frozen, I'm afraid. But maybe they're not too bad." A proper wife, she supposed, would have baked something from scratch—but you, dear Harry Chapin, will have to settle for something in the convenience line.

He came from the kitchen with the bottle open and two glasses poured, balancing the whole works with consummate ease.

"Oh, here, let me help. . . ."

She settled them in the living room. She took the couch from college days (God, Brandeis '62 wasn't *that* long ago), slouching down with her silly long legs askew; he got the canvas director's chair stenciled

HOT SEAT which her kid brother, Bernie, had thought just right for a sister who was going to the Coast to make it big in show business.

"Better put a magazine under the bottle," he said. "It'd be a shame to mark up this nice table."

He was such a polite man; no wonder half the secretaries on the lot went for him, wife and kiddies or no wife and kiddies. But then all the Harvards she'd ever met were nice and polite, even the Jewish ones, which was the only kind she'd known before her boss Harry Chapin. "If that chair's not comfortable . . ."

"No, fine. Fine—really."

He looked as though he'd put on a few more pounds during his European junket: chair would go crashing to the floor any second now, but then they would have a fine laugh. "Mmmm—this goes down like ice water," she said. "If you'll pour me another glass, I'll go see about the rumaki. . . ."

She could hear him prowling around, rummaging through her books, picking at her LPs, taking inventory of this poor working girl's few possessions. Never seen a coffee table made out of an old railway baggage cart, she'd bet. As for the rest—a few sticks of college furniture, bookshelves made from concrete blocks and unfinished pine boards— well, Mr. Chapin, there's nothing wrong with genteel poverty, is there?

"I don't know," she said, returning with her best platter of the things, "but these look pretty ratty compared to your lovely wine."

Mmm, he *ate* them as though they were all right; eat, drink and be merry, definitely his motto.

"And what may I ask," said with that super looking-down-the-nose attitude of his, "is *this?*"

He had this great sense of humor, thank God. "That, my dear, is a pack of what used to be known in the trade, I believe, as condoms. Open it up."

She watched, bemused, as he undid the wrapping.

"I see," he said. "And what is 'Sanctuary Much'?"

"My, you *are* out of touch. Only Honeybee's top new rock group, that's all. Probably paying for these egg rolls, as a matter of fact. 'Sanctuary Much'—get it? Say it fast. Condoms are the group's idea of promotion. Some boys in Merchandising dropped them by. All the single girls got them. Probably a little message there somewhere." Condoms imprinted with the names of new pop groups: surely the worldly Mr. Chapin, famed for his witty nature and liberal leanings, wouldn't be offended?

"I didn't realize that you were on terms of such—familiarity—with the pop types."

"A girl can't exist solely on classics. I don't really know them all that well—just to talk to at parties and things."

The big lug seemed just the slightest bit injured. What did he think—that she sat home alone night after night and lived only for the few words he threw her way at the office? Was there something *wrong* with seeing young men—eating a meal from a young man's pocket? And what business was it of his anyway? She felt just a smidge annoyed—yes, she did. Okay, they were *friends*—but not in any personal sense. "Where are you supposed to be—in case anyone should ask?" Like *Mrs.* Chapin, for instance.

"Meeting, as usual. Always at a meeting, this Chapin," he chuckled.

"I only meant"—might as well ease the pressure—"that we can eat in, if you'd rather not go out to a restaurant. Got a few things in the fridge. Endless supply of rumaki, among other things."

"To tell the truth," he said in that intimate way of his, "I would *love* not to go anywhere. It's so much more—comfortable—here with you."

Go on, Mr. Chapin, sir, keep up the smooth talk. "Your compliments will be conveyed to the chef," she said. "Scrambled eggs it is— just yell when you're hungry. Meanwhile, what about some music? How do you feel about the Stones?"

She didn't wait for his reply—these classical guys didn't know one group from another. Yes, they would begin with the last Stones LP, which *she* liked, to be followed by Fleetwood Mac and her old favorite, Johnny Mathis. "Has a beautiful green taste, this stuff," indicating her empty wineglass, which he quickly filled.

"I don't suppose you were able to get any—"

"As ordered, sir," she interrupted. "There on the desk—in the Melos-Doria envelope."

"God, you're marvelous," he said. "Where does the guy get it? The one you said?"

"My hairdresser. A lovely Mexican boy, naturally, called Carlos. Oh, he has his sources. Got a big movie trade, so he can get all you want—assuming you don't care about money. Grass, too. But his real thing is coke."

"You're a woman of parts, Stern. How much? Here—let me give you a check before I forget."

"Oh, there's no rush. In the office's fine."

"Remind me or I'll forget. A hundred, did you say?"

"Yes, but it was only seventy this time—trade discount, doncha know. That's cheap for a 'G,' which is what this is—a gram, it's called."

"Not bad at all."

No, not for you, Mr. Chapin, with *your* salary. I've seen those bank deposit slips.

"Well—when can we try it? Will the wine make a difference?"

He certainly seemed interested in the white powder. Could it be—as he said—that he'd never had a snort before? "How 'bout now?" she said. You want to know a real Hollywood swinger? Well, now you know one. They finished what was left in their wineglasses, and he quickly refilled.

"Well, this is what *I* do," she said. It was like explaining sandbox to a first-grader. "First we need a dollar bill . . ."

He got one out and gave it to her.

". . . and you roll it, see, into a tight tube . . . like that . . . kind of a straw, you might say . . . and then . . . Are you sure you've never done this before?"

"Never—I swear. Never knew anybody with the connections. Go on, so you've made a straw . . ."

She ran to the kitchen and brought back a saucer and a butter knife. "So then you pour a small amount—that's enough—into the saucer . . ." The powder was damp to the touch and had a greenish tint. She worked the powder back and forth with the butter knife, making it as fine as she could. "It'll go farther this way," she explained to her admiring pupil. "And now you take the saucer in one hand and the dollar bill in the other and you very carefully . . . Here, watch me, I'll go first. . . . Very carefully sniff into the straw . . . first one nostril . . . and then the other. . . . Not too much, or you'll sneeze. . . . And then . . . that's all there is to it. Okay, now you try."

He acted kind of scared, doing as she instructed, but doing it with great care . . . sniffing, finally, with the greatest reluctance . . . until he seemed to get the idea. "That's not so bad," he said at last. "So now what happens?"

"Just wait a few minutes. Here—drink your wine and eat an egg roll. Nothing really *happens*, you know. It just makes you feel good—after a while, usually. . . . There now . . . How's that?"

He joined her on the couch, lying back beside her and shutting his eyes and—she supposed—enjoying it. He had been in a foul mood all morning—God, no wonder he couldn't keep secretaries! Mostly over his *Otello*, which seemed to be the biggest thing in his life at the moment. He went around yelling at everybody until lunchtime, when he and that little shit Maury Wiseman had one of their lunches at St. Germain. The incredible thing was that only Mr. Chapin failed to see what an ass-sucking son of a bitch little Maury was.

"So this is very nice," he said, still with his eyes closed. "I see what you mean. Nothing really happens . . . but I feel very relaxed . . . very good . . ."

He was sniffing, then let her do it, then they had more of the wine.

"I'm going to open the other bottle, do you mind?" he said, struggling to his feet.

Mind? Thought he'd never ask. Followed him into the kitchen for the corkscrew.

Got it open with no cork in bottle or glasses: fabulous performance, Mr. Chapin. Pouring and walking at the same time, they navigated back to the couch; plonked down and toasted again; what was it he said, *Prosit?*

She poured some more of the nice powder into the dish. Their dollar bill had gotten pretty unrolled.

"So what the fuck is the symbolism?" he said rather nastily. "The dollar bill? Why don't you just get a piece of paper? Or a real straw, then? Or—don't they have pipes or something for this shit?"

She had never heard him say the word *shit* before. In the office, his language—at least in front of women—was impeccably correct. "I suppose you could. Look, Harry—"

He suddenly began to cry.

Yes! Really *cry*—a grown man. What was he? forty-some-years old? "Harry, honey—what's the *matter?*" He sobbed, then stopped, pulling out his handkerchief. She had never seen a man cry before, except in the movies. "What *is* it?"

"Oh, God, Alix . . ." He began to sob again. "I'm so ashamed. But my best friend . . ."

"Oh, yes—the one in England?"

"He killed himself—I told you. Without any warning. He just . . ."

She was frightened. He couldn't seem to control himself. She got up her nerve and pulled his head onto her shoulder. "Don't cry, honey," she comforted. "Or do, if it helps you."

"Teedee was his name. Isn't that silly? The names we gave each other . . . He left a note. It was addressed to *me.*"

Oh, *no*—he carried it *with him*, folded in his wallet. "Really, Harry—"

And now he *gave* it to her, for her to read. The paper was soiled and torn from folding and unfolding. Oh, God, did she *have* to?

Dear Harry,

McEvoy's had enough, old man. We made a strong start, didn't we? But then we seemed to go wrong, all of us—oh, maybe not you, but asinine Wiggles with his Madison Avenue tricks, little Billy with his sophomoric musicals—God, we were a terrible Class, weren't we?

Think of McEvoy from time to time, will you, old man? Maybe if McEvoy and Chapin had seen more of each other— but can't afford regrets now. McEvoy's got to stop the pain, and this seems the tried and true method, doesn't it? I feel so sorry for Tom.

Anyway, dear Heck—they don't call you that anymore, do they—I hope you're fucking Tree ten times a day, really I do.

Yours ever,

Teedee

Bizarre! Were they all—so *strange?*

"Harry, honey . . ."

"I'm going to be all right, really I am. I don't know why I'm— boring you with all this. . . . You're the only one I can talk to."

"Oh, Harry . . ."

"I called his wife. . . . She's an American girl I've known a long time. . . . And you know what she was worried about? You'll get a laugh out of this. . . . She was worried about the bad *publicity.* . . . Nobody in her family had ever committed suicide before. . . . That cunt . . . She has the money, of course. . . . She had him on an *allowance.* . . . And the agency—he had a PR agency in London—the agency could just go out of business, as far as she was concerned. . . . He would have been forty-five years old next week. . . . It seems only yesterday we were all in school. . . ."

"Do you want to lie down, honey? Do you want me to get you some water?"

"Hey, I'm fine, really. Isn't this stupid? Jesus, look at me. . . ."

"It's not stupid to have feelings, Harry darling. Really . . ."

"Anyway"—the big shudders had pretty much stopped, and he was taking deep breaths now—"it was all very confused because he'd renounced his American citizenship. . . . He went to the American Embassy—his cunt wife told me this—and asked to see the Ambassador . . . and he just said, hey, I want to stop being an American . . . and he filled out the forms and signed the papers and turned in his passport

. . . and that was that. . . . So they had to have him buried . . . in England, because he wasn't anymore . . ."

"Poor baby . . . cry it out of your system. Go on, cry—I don't mind. . . . Poor Harry . . ."

"Oh, God . . . I loved that man so much . . . and he never knew it. . . . I was such an ass when I saw him. . . . Alix? . . . I should have been there . . . with him. . . . You know where I was instead? . . . I was on a yacht in the Mediterrean making a horse's ass of myself. . . . Life is so unfair sometimes. . . ."

She got him cleaned up with a cold washcloth from the bathroom. He was such a baby. But these little boys never really grew up, did they?—they just got older. "How do you feel?"

"I'm fine. Really. Look—I'm eating again—now you *know* I'm fine. I don't know what happened to me there. Just something I had to get out of my system, I suppose. . . ."

She fixed them a plate of scrambled eggs and tomatoes, toast, garlic butter, with a side dish of creamed corn. They finished the second bottle of Lancers and then she got out the good brandy from Christmas and they had some of that with the rest of the coke. Then they went into the bedroom, where the TV set was, and lay on her bed and watched a documentary on Channel 28.

"What would I do without you?" he said to her in the darkness.

"Oh, you'd think of something." She let him have her best smile in the reflection of Alistair Cooke: the always-loyal-no-matter-how-you-fuck-up doglike secretary smile on which all men of her acquaintance apparently depended.

"You're—a very remarkable woman."

"I'm okay, I suppose," she said, "as far as I go. But now, sir—"

His kiss came as a blow. "Harry," she said, "if we're not going to watch—"

"You're worried about the office, aren't you?"

"I *am* your employee, Harry."

"And what's that supposed to mean? That you and I don't have lives of our own?"

She hated all this intensity. Look, this is fun and games, isn't it? A little rumaki. A little white wine. A little coke. God, he was so *unpredictable*. She saw signs of it on the lot—the way he lost his temper, picked fights in all those stupid negotiations, never liked what people did for him. But, like his dead friend in England, it was that time of life for Mr. Chapin too. "Why don't we find some LPs to play?" she said earnestly.

But he wasn't having any: held her tightly and kissed her again on the lips.

Well, she would just wait him out—sooner or later he would come to his senses, apologize and go.

"I want you very much," he said instead.

"Oh, now Harry." He was scaring her again. "Now we're going to sit up and take a deep breath and . . ." He had very strong arms. He might be fat around the middle, but he was no one for a girl—this girl—to wrestle with. *"Harry—"*

Oh, God, her good jacket: he was working the Chinese puzzles up and down the front, working in the light of Alistair Cooke and—oh, how embarrassing—pulling it apart, *exposing* her. *"Please,* Harry, you're going to tear—"

Well, a little nipple wasn't going to do either of them any harm— he had certainly seen better, though this was the good part, gents . . .

But he obviously didn't want just the tits, he had other ideas, he was kneeling above her and pulling on his own clothes, he was opening . . .

Oh, God, he was *hard,* the poor man. How *embarrassing* for them both. . . . No, she did not *want* this. "Now, Harry, we're going to preserve a certain decorum. *Harry?* Are you listening to me? . . . Really, you are going to be *so* embarrassed Monday morning. . . ."

He was pulling at her trousers now, undoing the funny little bone things, the loops. . . .

"I'm afraid, Harry, that I'm going to have to ask you . . ."

Oh, he had them *off,* he was digging at the waistband of her panties, he was pulling and *scratching* her with his frantic fingernails, he was—

"I don't *want* that, Harry, do you understand me? Now, I am not *kidding.* . . . Oh, please, Harry . . ."

Desperate measures. If only he weren't so strong. She tried to resist by conventional means, drawing her knees together. Oh, her arms and hands seemed so weak. . . .

"Oh, You *bastard.* You're *in* me! . . . My God oh my God oh my God oh my God oh my God . . . You—are—*hurting*—me . . ."

Finally—exhausted—she just gave up. . . . Felt him deposit his seed. . . .

"Are you *through?*"

"Babe . . ."

"Did you *come* in me? I want to know. *Did* you?"

"Alix—"

"You *bastard.* I'll tell you what I want you to do. I want you to get your pants on and I want you to get *out* of here."

"Alix, babe—"

"Because I'm going to sit down now and I'm going to think about

whether I should call the police, or whether I should call Mrs. Chapin
and ask her advice on the matter."

"*Please*, Alix—"

"You *raped* me. You *raped* me. You *raped* me. You *raped* me.
You . . ."

Well, I'm going pretty good now. I'm crying all over the place,
even worse than he did, and I'm really shaking him up—look at the
bastard, he's as white as the sheets on this bed which he couldn't wait to
use. Boy, is he going to remember this day for the rest of his life. And
why *shouldn't* I punish him, the dirty bastard?

". . . Yes, now you get out of here, Harry Chapin, so I can go in
that bathroom and try to wash out the slime that you put in me *against
my will*, you awful bastard. And then I'm going to sit down at that
telephone—yes, I've decided what I'm going to do—I'm going to tell
your darling Maggie what her wonderful husband has done—the
bastard who *rapes* his own secretary and won't even stop if you *beg* him
to. . . ."

Despite her sobs, she felt almost like laughing, felt so *good* now—
having this over him *forever*.

Act Four

ROME: *August-September*

Sir, do never try your hand at anything but opera buffa. You would be doing violence to your destiny by wanting to succeed in a different genre. You see, serious opera does not lie in the nature of the Italians. For the true drama, they know not enough of the science of music. And how should they acquire that in Italy?

Beethoven in conversation with Rossini

1

"Welcome to Rome, Mr. Chapin. I am John Martyn and this is my colleague Sergio Cozzone, whom I believe you know. . . ."

"Of course. Great pleasure to see you both again."

John and Sergio were employees of Dischi La Cima, boys in their mid-twenties who had been particularly helpful during the *Boccanegra* sessions several years back. "But you shouldn't have bothered, especially on a Sunday. I could easily have taken a cab."

Except, they informed him, airport taxis were on strike. Leonardo da Vinci di Fiumicino: the worst airport in Europe. Now—during the last week of August, height of the Roman summer, ninety degrees and stifling—it was arguably the worst in the world: breathtakingly inefficient; grossly populated with rude and ignorant clerks, lazy policemen, venal Customs inspectors; an endless chain of departure lounges reeking of transient Africans and unwashed *paesani romani* who had come for a Sunday outing or to meet a less disadvantaged relative from Naples or Palermo.

"And Dr. Quinzi is well?"

"He sends you his sincerest regards," John Martyn said, "but begs your indulgence, as he will fly to Rome from Milan only tomorrow morning to be present at the start of your sessions in the Opera House."

Quinzi, the aristocrat: too smart by half to do battle with the plebeian hordes on a Sunday.

They saw to his baggage, got him through Customs with a wave of the hand, escorted him to the pride of the Dischi La Cima fleet, a Mercedes *Gran seicento* with seating for eight. Sergio drove while John Martyn joined Harry in the cavernous rear compartment and began

mixing Bloody Marys from the fold-down bar—*"due Bloody Mary"*
being the way Dischi La Cima measured the distance from Fiumicino
into the center of town. Harry didn't care much for Bloody Marys—
he'd have preferred champagne, which he'd been drinking on the plane
from New York—but on this sweaty occasion, and given Sergio's idiomatic driving style, he gratefully accepted.

He drank the mandatory *secondo* and, when they found themselves
stalled in traffic no closer to the Piazza Trinità dei Monti than the
Baths of Caracalla, he agreed to an optional *terzo*. The gin served to
filter Rome's late-afternoon chiaroscuro: projected the fantastic
mascolinità of Roman men along the way in their wonderful shirts and
leather jackets and boots. Men, not women, are the stars in Rome:
Mastroianni, not Loren, commands the attention here. Still, Harry preferred the elegant reserve of the Parisians to the noisy emotionalism of
these Latins. The French were so private, so superior in their tastes; they
were right to despise tourists.

"... *Imbecille!* ... *Idiota!* ... *Cretino!* ..."

On entering the rotary of the Colosseum they collided with a tiny
Fiat 500. It was not much of an accident—Harry did not even spill his
drink—but a layer of luminescent blue paint had been scraped from the
Mercedes's left front fender, and the Fiat's right door bore a crease.
Within seconds a white-helmeted policeman approached, which was
enough for both Mercedes and Fiat: all occupants returned instantly to
their vehicles and fled. No one wished to confront Roman justice. It was
nice to be back in Italy.

They moved up the via Nazionale and passed the Hotel Quirinale
Palace. "You wish to stop now?" Sergio asked, noticing Harry's interest.

"No, no," Harry said. "Perhaps later ... "

Norman and Maury and the principals were all staying at the
Quirinale, which was just around the corner from the Opera House. But
the Quirinale was a little too public, to use Mrs. Renée Blankenhorn's
expression, for what Harry had in mind. Something more remote was
indicated—the Hassler, atop the Spanish Steps and close by the house
in which Keats died in 1821. The Hassler Villa Medici was ideal for a
man like Harry Chapin, who valued his privacy—his and Frankie Tree's.

He said goodbye to the boys from Dischi La Cima and got upstairs
as quickly as possible. He felt very fortunate: they gave him the same
suite he'd had during *Boccanegra* days, No. 521 with refrigerator and a
view of the Borghese Gardens. He only wished that he hadn't drunk the
Bloody Marys because he intended now to drink champagne with Miss
Tree, whom he had not seen since that last awful day in Monte Carlo.
He took three aspirins and sat down at the telephone.

Frankie was not in her room. Probably out soaking up local color—
she had never before been to Rome, she had written him. She was

looking forward to Rome like nothing else in her life except her first trip to America, which she planned for later in the year.

He tried Norman at the Quirinale.

"Greetings," Norman said in his nasal New York way. "Have you ever experienced such heat? And the Opera House . . ."

Yes, yes, there were bound to be problems—let's not get bogged down right at the start, shall we? "And Maury?"

"Down working with the technical crew. Do you want me to call him?"

"No, no. Let's not have any more of young Mr. Wiseman than we absolutely must. What about Frankie—Miss Tree? Seen anything of her?"

"As a matter of fact, she came to breakfast with us. Seems a most charming girl, Harry, and very efficient. Had all sorts of press people in tow, including our old friend Mr. Fink. Showing them around town, I expect."

"Good. Say—why don't you and I have a quiet drink while we still can? My place in, say, thirty minutes?"

"With the greatest pleasure . . ."

After freshening up, Harry left a message for Norman at the front desk, changing their rendezvous to the bar, where Harry ordered a chilled bottle of Piper-Heidsieck. "Yes, a full bottle . . . A friend will be joining me."

They set him up at a table in the lounge, a most spacious and elegant room—Roman reds, marble, Oriental carpets, gold trim—where a sleepy old man was playing Albéniz at an unsympathetic Steinway, repeating the "Tango in D" with its voluptuous triplets, which he interpreted with sly rubato. The champagne went right down, erasing any memory of the in-transit tomato juice.

Then a swarm of Americans buzzed in, ordering their Scotches and rum-and-Cokes, and the old man went straight into songs from "Gigi" and "My Fair Lady"—there was a soiled book of Broadway show tunes on the stand—and the Americans responded with exuberant applause. Soon the place was filled with Americans—perhaps one of the tour buses had returned from the Forum—talking to each other from table to table, introducing themselves and their spouses as they would never have done at home. The Hassler lounge was a great deal friendlier than Akron or Toledo.

The old man soon had enough of Lerner and Loewe—or perhaps there was a request for something *più autentico*—and switched to "Mattinata" and "Aprile" and "L'Ultima Canzone" and "O sole mio," which brought cheers. It was definitely a high-toned crowd: American men in good loafers, light slacks, bold plaid summer jackets, all looking like McLean Stevenson out of *M*A*S*H;* ladies in denim suits and slacks, heavy with fat and diamonds and gorgeous pedicures and just-bought Italian sandals from the via Condotti. The women, it must be said, looked far less plausible than their husbands, less certain of themselves. They sweated too much; Roman air-conditioning wasn't *their* kind of air-conditioning. Their husbands, on the other hand, looked comfortable. They were fiftyish, most of them, men who could afford to be away from their patients or clients, men with excellent bank balances and the right amount of insurance and well-sheltered tax situations. Self-righteous, even belligerent in the face of Roman sloth, they were confident as only Midwesterners can be. Yes—

No. They weren't *all* Midwesterners. Not this smiling little man—middle-aged, one would have said—coming Harry's way. This gentleman was definitely Greenwich, Connecticut, despite the purple suede moccasins. And putting on weight, eh, Billy? Little Billy Bigelow, Harvard '54.

"My God—Harry Chapin!"

"Billy."

"You know Alice. From across the Yard?"

Alice with the green book bag, from Radcliffe—but twenty-odd years older. "Of course. What a grand surprise." Grand surprise, like something out of *Tender Is the Night*.

"Harry produces records," Billy said. "Or, what? Runs the whole shebang now—did I read in the alumni bulletin?"

"You're too kind," Harry said. "Won't you sit down?" He sent for more champagne and wondered where Norman Rose had gotten to. Alice didn't remember Harry from Harvard, which was fine with Harry: she had one of those flat, disinterested faces with sullen mouth and contemptuous eyes.

"So what brings you to town?" Billy asked.

"The usual," Harry said. "Opera."

"Harry was the only student in the whole Music Department with any talent," Billy remarked to Alice.

"Is that so?" Alice said icily.

Billy, as a matter of fact, was the only alumnus of the Music Department who had made good since Lennie Bernstein, Class of '39. Like Lennie, Billy had turned his hand to Broadway shows, doing music, book and lyrics for *And So's Your Aunt*, which got him a Tony Award in the early '60s, plus a half-dozen others, none of which Harry could remember because they were pretty awful, even for a classmate. When they both lived in New York, Harry saw Billy irregularly in places like the Oak Room of the Plaza, where they exchanged small talk—"Hear about Teedee?" "Hear about Wiggles?"—but otherwise had little to say to each other. Despite his success, Billy continued to exhibit the

modesty and winning manner of their schooldays, showing discomfort—
not to say disgrace—at the idea that a grown man, product of Choate
and Harvard, could make his reputation and his personal fortune as a
writer of mawkish popular songs.

But now looking rather shockingly *old*. As thick in the middle as
Chapin, the pink, smiling face now puffy over double chins, aristocratic
features no longer chiseled and distinct but softened and submerged in
excess flesh; wispy, silk-fine hair more gray than blond, eyes watery and
bloodshot, skin shiny and smooth like—Benno Toggi's.

"And what brings *you* to Rome, Billy? But no—you *live* here,
didn't I read?"

"Capri—but no more," Billy said, hitting the champagne almost as
hard as Harry.

"The Americans," Alice said by way of explanation.

"Oh, yes." Not much for conversation, these old classmates.
"Heard from Wiggles?" Harry said. Billy and Wiggles had roomed
together their senior year.

"Not a word, the bastard," said Billy. "You?"

"I was supposed to see him last, oh, April or May, in New York.
The Ford Foundation. But something came up. . . . You've heard
about Teedee, of course."

"Teedee? No, I don't think so. What's he up to now? You remember Teedee, don't you, dear?"

"Teedee's dead," Harry said.

Little Billy lost some color from his cherubic pink countenance.
"You don't *mean* it?"

Even Alice seemed to take interest. "That rather nice-looking boy
who lived in Eliot House?"

"He killed himself," Harry said. "End of May. I thought you might
have seen it in the papers."

"Oh my *God*," said Billy. "But *why*? What made him *do* it?"

"He was depressed. . . ." They couldn't very well discuss it here in
front of Alice—Alice, who hardly remembered any of them.

"Poor, poor Teedee. My God, isn't it *awful*," Billy said. "I wonder
what drives a man . . . He was always a bit—emotional."

"And how did he do it?" Alice inquired in her fascinated-with-the-
human-species-in-all-its-forms way.

"He hanged himself," Harry said as brutally as he could.

"Oh, my. Why would a grown man do such a nasty thing? How
stupid."

But then she couldn't be expected to understand, could she?
Women were probably different. Teedee had made Porcellian, but
failed admission to an even more exclusive club. Did she think getting

to be forty-five years old was some kind of joke? Poor Teedee. Poor
Billy. *Poor all of us, when you come to think of it,* as one of Greene's
policemen says.

". . . Opera—oh what *fun,*" bubbled Alice.

"Business, actually," Harry said. "Recording."

"You're the only one of us," Billy said, "who's ever put to use what
we learned in school. Isn't that so?"

"If you can call it use."

"When do you do this work, Mr. Chapin? And are visitors allowed?
I'd be most interested . . ."

"It's very dull, really."

"Oh, but I'd just *love*—"

"You would be quite welcome, of course. Starting tomorrow in the
Opera House. Four o'clock each afternoon. If you'll go round to the
artists' entrance and mention my name . . ."

"Great fun," Billy said. "We shall drop by, then."

"*Otello,*" Harry said, not that it mattered.

"Oh—not one of my favorites," Alice lamented. "So nasty."

"Alice is not much for sex and violence," Billy lamented.

"I'm sorry," said Harry, "but that's all I can offer at the moment."

"Oh, my," said Alice, happy to change the subject, "what have we
here?"

The sounds of Naples had given way to those of the Billy Bigelow
songbook: the old man at the piano was no fool.

"Public performance," Billy said to Alice. "Be sure to collect our
fee. Alice takes care of business."

Yes, Harry could imagine.

II

". . . You feeling all right?" Norman said.

"It's this fucking heat. And that bastard at the Steinway." Harry
didn't mention the Bloody Marys or the previous bottle of Piper-
Heidsieck.

"He *is* fairly awful. If you'd rather go upstairs—"

"No—hot there, too. What about the effects? The wind machine?
All that crap?"

Norman got out another file folder. "We're in pretty good shape, I
think. The organ pedal at the start—eight minutes of it—we'll overdub
in L.A. It's easier on the technical crew, especially with the portable
twenty-four-track quad rig. They've got enough to play with as it is."

"Whatever you think."

"For the cannon, I've got a tentative okay from the people at West Point. They fire the silly things off once a week for ceremonial purposes, and we can get what we need in a day or two and lay that down during final remix. . . . Storm effects—I'm dubious about the wind machine they've got here. I tried it last night, but the thing's too noisy and unpredictable. I would prefer to borrow one from the Met and do that in New York, too. . . . Mandolin parts in Act Two—I've found a pair of very fine players—we used them on the Respighi set a couple of years back, and, fortunately, they're in town and willing to work. One of them even reads music, which, as you know, is not so common among mandolin-players. . . . Choruses. The resident chorus has only sixty members, but we can flesh that out with amateurs for a bigger effect, especially the opening scene. The children's chorus is an absolute joy, sixteen of the sweetest kids you'll ever meet, and they have their parts letter-perfect right this minute. I just wish the orchestra were half so good."

"And the other personnel? Who's going to give us trouble?"

Norman went to yet another folder. "Luigi Mezzapelle, chorus master, not too bad for a Genovese. . . . Fernando Ricci, assistant conductor, has worked with Gian-Carlo before, seems intelligent. . . . Gianfranco Bonisolli, going to act as the quad stage manager—has some experience with RCA, but seems a bit of a prima donna to me. . . . Salvatore Andreolli, senior mixer, speaks some English, comes highly rated by Beard. . . . And of course Beard himself, something of a nuisance, but he should be able to smooth out any wrinkles with the union."

Toby Beard, LTI's studio manager from Dischi La Cima's home office in Milan. Harry had had a run-in with the old fag during the *Boccanegra* sessions, but what was one to do?—the man came with the territory. "Well, it doesn't sound too bad," Harry said approvingly. "Let's go over the call sheets."

Norman retrieved two charts from the bottom of his large briefcase. "This first one will give you the musical sequence. As you can see, I've broken the score into twenty-six units plus one insert—Zeke's 'Esultate,' which I've a hunch we'll want to overdub."

Harry studied the plan as best he could, considering what he'd had to drink.

"I've worked out the side breaks," Norman continued, "based on timings taken at Gian-Carlo's last performance at La Scala. We've got no real problem except for side three, which could run twenty-nine-twenty, and side six, the whole of Act IV, which could go thirty-four-ten, if we're unlucky."

"What do you mean *if?*"

"I agree. In any case, Harry, we must try to make Gian-Carlo move

Time	Act/Unit		DESD.	OTELLO	IAGO	Emilia	Cassio	Roderigo	Lodovico	Montano	Herald	CHORUS
4:15	I.	1			X		X	X		X		X + offstage
5:00		2		*(X)	X			X				X
3:00		3										X
7:15		4			X		X	X		X		X
3:00		5		X	X		X			X		
11:20		6	X	X								
9:10	II.	1			X		X					
5:00		2		X	X							
1:00		3			X							X offstage
4:15		4	X	X	X							X + children
6:00		5	X	X	X	X						
13:05		6		X	X							
2:50	III.	1		X	X						X	
9:40		2	X	X	X							
5:00		3		X	X							
6:30		4		X	X		X		X			
2:40		5		X	X		X		X			X
5:50		**6										
2:40		7	X	X	X	X				X		
10:40		8	X	X	X	X	X	X	X			X
1:20		9		X	X							X offstage
18:45	IV.	1	X			X						
2:15		2	X									
6:05		3	X	X		X						
1:55		4		X	X	X	X		X	X		
5:10		5		X			X		X	X		

*(X) = 1 min. insert ("Esultate")
** = orchestra only (ballet)

right along in the final scene. He tends to drag it out, which may work in the house but certainly doesn't work on records. Also, we don't really know how Zeke handles Otello's death. Does he stick to things as written, like Martinelli, or does he ham it up?"

"Remind me at the time and I'll speak to Gian-Carlo. What about the session sequence?"

Norman unrolled the second chart. "I hold my breath and say a prayer each time I look at this."

Great genius, Norman, say what you would about his sometimes prissy manner. "A little tight," Harry said.

"Twelve three-hour sessions over ten working days. Giving us in the end, hopefully, one hundred and fifty-four minutes of music—about thirteen minutes per session, which is not really too bad."

"Except at Rome."

Session/Units	DESD.	OTELLO	IAGO	Emilia	Cassio	Roderigo	Lodovico	Montano	Herald	CHORUS
FIRST WEEK:										
8/22 MON										
aft 1–1, 1–2, 1–3		(X)	X		X	X		X		X + offstage
eve 2–1, 2–2		X	X		X					
8/23 TUE										
aft 1–5, 2–6		X	X		X			X		
8/24 WED—OPEN										
8/25 THU										
aft 1–2, insert, 1–4, 2–3, 3–5, 3–9	(Del Campo unavailable)	X	X		X	X		X		X + offstage
eve 3–3, 3–4		X	X		X					
8/26 FRI										
aft 3–1, 4–4, 4–5		X	X		X	X	X	X	X	
SECOND WEEK:										
8/29 MON										
aft 2–4, 3–8	X	X	X	X	X	X	X			X + children
eve 2–5, 3–7	X	X	X	X				X		
8/30 TUE										
aft 1–6	X	X								
8/31 WED										
aft 4–1	X		X							
9/1 THU										
aft 4–2, 4–3	X	X	X							
9/2 FRI										
aft 3–2, 3–6, (1–2)	X	X								

"How true. Now if this were London . . . You'll notice the accommodation to Didi."

Didi nowhere to be seen until the second week, and then five straight days of work. "Let's hope she can still make a noise after two weeks at Salzburg," Harry said.

"Her last performance at the Festival is Friday, the twenty-sixth—she goes straight to Florence Saturday morning for piano rehearsals with Gian-Carlo. It's not ideal, Harry, but it's the best I could do."

"I'm not criticizing, Norman—merely commenting. And what about Zeke?"

"No one's seen him, I'm afraid. He's been closeted with Ponti at Florence for the past ten days. *One* of them is probably somewhat the worse for wear."

"But you've made it easy for him? His workload?" Harry took

another look at the call sheets.

"I know what you're thinking," Norman said. "You're concerned about the double sessions."

"Monday, Thursday and the following Monday. That's a lot of work for an inexperienced singer."

"I realize that, Harry. I tried to get the union to allow a Saturday session at the regular rate, but they said no—no Saturday work at *any* price because it's the vacation period and the players don't want it. As a matter of fact, I'm suspicious of the orchestra membership. I have it on good authority that a number of the regulars are out of town and the replacements aren't any too good."

"Does Ponti know?"

"I suppose he does. I haven't discussed it with him, because you know how temperamental he gets. The fact is, Harry, this is the orchestra that comes with the House, and there's nothing we can do about it now except hope and pray."

"And if we run over? Past the second Friday?"

Norman gave a weak laugh. "Ha. Well—none of that, I'm afraid."

"What do you mean?"

"I mean that I've had to promise to be out by midnight Friday, latest, because Philips moves in on Saturday. A complete *Cavalleria*."

Backs to the wall, which was usual in this business. "Fine," Harry said, cuffing Norman on the shoulder and signaling to the boy for another Scotch for this distinguished gentleman—and yes, keep on with the champagne. "I mean it, Norman. It's a fine plan, which only you could accomplish, given the obstacles. You are to be congratulated."

"Well, thank you, Harry. Coming from you . . ."

"A toast," Harry said, raising his glass for the hundredth time that day. "To Rose and Chapin, who do this work better than anybody."

With sheepish delight, Norman downed his whisky. And Harry meant it: he had begun to sense the first labor pains down deep in his bowels. At last they would be getting on with the real work, putting art on tape. This was the payoff for all the lousy flesh-peddling, the low commercial antics, the detestable quid pro quos, the constant fucking and getting fucked. He could hardly wait to see Zeke and Gian-Carlo, old Benno and especially, later on, sweet-but-crazy Didi—trained animals, overfed on diets of public adulation and personal excess, rare specimens that only Harry Chapin and Norman Rose and a handful of other expert trainers could put through the hoop.

"Otherwise all is well?" from the inebriated Chapin.

"Except maybe for your beloved press representatives," Norman said, obviously feeling better now that he had made a clean breast of matters with his boss. "Your good friend Mr. Herb Fink from New York City hates his room. It overlooks trash barrels, he says, in the alley between the Quirinale and the Opera House. I spoke to the hotel, but they haven't got another room. It *is* August."

"Tell him to go fuck himself. No, on second thought, let *me* tell him to go fuck himself."

"And then there's a very high-powered lady, one Charlotte Sachs, called Charlie, who is something of a famous mischief-maker, apparently, and who is here by command of Signor Toggi."

"She can go fuck herself too." No: better see what she looks like first.

"And then there's Leone Sciascia, a very important critic and inveterate Ponti-watcher who sits in the Quirinale lobby and drinks the foul coffee in that place till the wee hours of the morning."

"The same to him."

"And then there's—ah, but we are about to have company of the most charming sort—the very lady whose job it is to handle these troublesome journalists. The beautiful Miss Tree . . ."

"Well, *hello*, Harry—Norman. This *is* a surprise."

No place for kissing: instead, polite handshakes. Frankie had been out sightseeing, she told them: the Nikon—*his* Nikon—slung over one shoulder; nice floral-patterned skirt, white blouse, Roman sandals on her pretty feet; looking very feminine and almost cool.

"Won't you join us—" Norman started to say, but Harry put a quick end to that. He and Miss Tree had some business to discuss—the troublesome press types?—and perhaps Norman would like to go back to his own hotel, where Harry would call him later?

"Fine idea, yes," Norman said, gathering up his papers. "As a matter of fact, there are some last-minute details . . ."

And now, my girl . . .

". . . I should think you'd want us to be over with the others. At the Quirinale. Shouldn't we be?"

She was leaning out his window, pointing the cursed Nikon at the Borghese Gardens.

"Believe me," he said with growing irritation, "you're going to see enough of those people in the next two weeks—you're going to be sick to death of them. So—I arranged a little privacy for us. Was that so wrong of me?"

"You've got a tub," she said, completing her inspection. "I've only got a shower."

"Which is another reason to move in here. I can't understand why you want to stay in your own room."

"Because I want to," she repeated. "Please don't spoil things, that's a good boy. You'll let me use your nice tub, won't you?"

He had such a headache. Gin didn't agree with him, now that he was older. Gin was a fine drink when you were a sophomore, but not later. "Suit yourself," he said. He lay across the bed to ease the heartburn.

"Besides," she countered, "you're going to be having people up here all the time—Maestro Ponti and the other artists and Mr. Fink and . . ."

"As I say, suit yourself."

She put down the Nikon and surprised him by sitting on the edge of the bed. "Should I take my bath now," she said, "or wait?"

"Suit yourself," he repeated.

"You *know* what I mean, Harry. If we're going to make love, I'd rather do that first and then take my bath, instead of the other way round. I don't want to get all sweaty after taking my bath."

"Shit. Why don't we publish a schedule or something?"

"What's that supposed to mean?"

"So fucking mechanical around here. Not exactly contributing to spontaneous passion, would you say?"

"Well, pardon *me*," she said.

"Take your bath," he said bitchily.

"Thank you."

He'd wait until she got out of the tub, then bang her anyway, wet on the bed. Might as well learn now, lady, what the world is really like.

"Did you say something?" from the bathroom.

"Have a nice soak," he called out.

He struggled out of his clothes and fell back again on the bed, naked and exhausted. Roman heat. A wonderful setting for what he had in mind. He'd make it as much like rape as he could: try to duplicate his session with poor Alix. Only maybe *hurt* this one, the selfish little bitch, because she *deserved* it. . . .

He was awakened by the telephone. It was very dark—the curtains were closed across the French windows—and he had no idea of the time. Before he could find the switch to the bedside lamp, his party was on the line:

"Dear Harry? I hope I have not disturbed you. This is Gian-Carlo. . . ."

He found the light and saw that she had covered him with his bathrobe. The door to the bathroom was open. Perhaps she was in the other bedroom.

". . . I have the greatest reluctance, my good friend, in calling you at this hour, but Marianne has urged me to do so. . . ."

Headache, heartburn, nausea. He lay back on the bed so that he would not have to bear the weight of his head. "Oh, yes?" he said into the mouthpiece. "Is Marianne there? Please give her my regards." He sounded like a bad imitation of Harry Chapin.

". . . And Marianne in return sends you her love. But the matter of my call, dear Harry, is just this—"

"You are in Rome, Gian-Carlo? If you'd like, perhaps tonight—"

"No, I am in *Firenze*, Harry. In my home, where, as you know, we have conducted our rehearsal these past days. . . ."

Then, on the nightstand, he saw her note:

Harry darling,

Kicky bath!—you are too sweet! Covered you up—don't want the maid sharing our secrets—remember Munich! You must be very tired after your trip—the sleep will do you good.

Promised one of the boys in the crew to go for supper to Trastevere, the oldest part of the city, see the ruins, etc.

Sweet dreams,

Frankie

How humiliating. "Yes, go on, Gian-Carlo. I'm listening."

". . . And I am strongly of the opinion that we must postpone, dear Harry, if only for a matter of three or four days."

In the distance, on the bathroom wall, he could see another telephone. If he could sit on the toilet and place a cold washcloth across the back of his neck . . . "If you will excuse me, Gian-Carlo, for only a moment, I shall move to another telephone."

He reached the toilet with great difficulty, but immediately felt better. A center tap over the washbasin gave ice water, which he sponged over his burning forehead and face and then applied to his neck. "I am here, Gian-Carlo."

". . . During our time at the piano, Harry, I regret that many questions of interpretation in Mr. Laframboise's part have made themselves felt to us . . . matters which Signor Toggi and I agree must be reexamined if we are to achieve an artistic result."

"Excuse me, Gian-Carlo, but do I understand that you are speaking now of a postponement of the sessions scheduled to begin tomorrow afternoon at four o'clock? Because if this is so, Gian-Carlo . . ."

In the background Harry could hear the throaty soprano of Marianne Kunz, who suddenly burst onto the line: "Harry? It's me, Marianne. How are you, darling?"

"Hello, Marianne. Fine. But what's this that Gian-Carlo—"

"Yes, isn't it *awful*? Where did you ever find this heavenly black boy? The only trouble is, Harry, he doesn't know *anything* about *Otello!*

But who am I to tell you your business? Ha, ha . . . Oh, oh, Gianni wants to talk. See you soon, sweet . . ."

"Harry? Please excuse Marianne, she is a bit of the child tonight. . . . What I must say, Harry, is that, speaking very frankly, we have not been able, because of the schedules of us all, to have sufficient rehearsal. Do you know that I have been two days with the Santa Cecilia concerts, taking programs at the very last minute for dear Passafiume, who has been taken ill?"

"I had not heard, no. But—"

"So that if we could begin not until perhaps Thursday—not so many days ahead—we would most surely improve our result and avoid the fiasco."

"I understand what you are saying," Harry said, speaking only as loudly as necessary to be heard. "But I'm afraid that such a postponement, Gian-Carlo, is simply impossible. The Opera House is overbooked as it is—Philips will follow the day after we finish—and the orchestra and chorus are on call and, as you know, Del Campo's schedule is extremely tight. For better or worse, Gian-Carlo, we must begin tomorrow afternoon, and we must have every note on tape one week from Friday. If there were any way . . ."

"I knew it would be so," said Ponti, a great sadness seeming to hang on each syllable. "But for the sake of Signor Verdi . . ."

"I understand, Gian-Carlo. Believe me when I tell you that somehow we shall overcome these obstacles. It is always this way—there is never enough time, never enough preparation. But you are a professional and so are your principals, and when the time comes we shall achieve a representative performance. Trust me in this."

He was not certain how much longer he could keep talking. Soon he would have to stand up and use the toilet another way.

"It is understood, dear Harry. Then—tomorrow we shall begin?"

"Absolutely," Harry said.

"In that event—"

"Fine—we'll talk in the morning. Good night, Gian-Carlo . . ."

He got turned around with seconds to spare.

2

Harry hadn't been in the Opera House since the now fuzzy *Boccanegra*—1972?—but little had changed. During the summer recess the House was turned over to the record companies. The *platea*, or orchestra seats, had been ripped out so that the players could be positioned there, in the center of the auditorium, and a special extension of the stage had been built out over the orchestra pit as a platform for the singers. Even now, only minutes before the start of Session No. 1, carpenters were still pounding away. The new lumber looked fragile: would it support *il più gran tenore del mondo?* The platform had been covered with a checkerboard canvas bearing fifty numbered squares which Signor Bonisolli, the quadraphonic stage manager, would use in directing movement of the principals to produce the audible illusion of a stage performance. The chorus risers were placed farther back, and beyond them a small stage had been erected for the offstage band required in several parts of the score. Fortunately, from a recording point of view, the Opera House possessed a marvelous natural acoustic, very warm and round, which made all singers sound better than they probably were, and which suited Verdi to perfection.

But the heat. Some of the players were already down to their undershirts. Gian-Carlo Ponti at the podium, handsome as ever in his black turtleneck, did not seem to notice. Constantly running his elegant long fingers through his marvelously full head of hair, he listened as Norman Rose—cool and collected, too, after all those years of Manhattan living—attempted to coach Gian-Carlo in the mysterious ways of the recording world.

". . . And those mattresses, Gian-Carlo, you see along the back walls, over the boxes—yes, there—they are intended to eliminate what we call slapback—reverberations from floor to ceiling and back again. We want a controlled sound, to which we can add electronic reverb later, if we think it necessary, in the final mix-down to four-channel . . ."

Harry stepped forward. "Gian-Carlo, don't let me interrupt—just wanted to say hello."

"My dear *Harry* . . ." They embraced—Gian Carlo taking care not to contaminate his pristine costume with Harry's perspiration.

"Good afternoon, Harry," Norman said. Norman's expression told him that a private meeting was in order.

"Just let me say hello to our good friends. . . ." Harry moved off smartly to the next music stand, that of Ezekiel Laframboise. "*Buon giorno, mio diletto amico. Come va?*"

"How be you, my man?" The big man looked acutely uncomfortable—subdued yet belligerent—being just then the butt of the orchestra's jokes. It was not every day that Rome enjoyed such marvelous chocolate skin, so monumental an Afro. Zeke was a most imposing figure, wrapped in a red-flowered Hawaiian sport shirt and tan khaki walking shorts. (Harry thought instantly of Mme. Rasponi aboard *L'Arlésienne*: what could Zeke's girth be—fifty inches? Chapin looked svelte by comparison.)

"I'm surprised to find you here," Harry said. "Norman purposely scheduled the 'Esultate' for later, when things have settled down. First session's usually pretty rough."

"I come to play, brother Harry," Zeke replied. "Might as well knock it off now, with the other cats."

"Suit yourself," Harry said. "Looking forward to all those lovely G's and A's—and even a B, isn't there?"

"You'll hear 'em, man. Nothin' to get uptight about."

This worried Harry. Why stand around for three hours in this incredible heat to sing one minute of music—maybe a dozen bars—when you could be resting in your suite at the Quirinale? "Hotel okay?" Harry said.

"I been in worse."

"And how about this?" indicating the auditorium.

"Düsseldorf's better, but, like I say, I been in worse. If this heat keeps up, it's gonna stink like a locker room in here." A steady stream of drips encircled Laframboise's place on the fresh plywood flooring.

"And how did it go with Maestro Ponti? At Florence?"

"Shiiiiiit, man. That turkey?" The big man looked sullen and reserved.

"We'll have a talk," Harry said. "Maybe tonight, after the second session?"

"You're callin' the shots," Laframboise replied.

Harry moved on. People's nerves would settle down during the evening session. The Roman schedules were always built around the idiotic weather. The first session was 4:00 to 7:00, followed by a dinner break. Most orchestras played better on a full stomach, so the second session—8:30 to 11:30—would be easier. Also, during the break the singers usually took a drink or two, which tended to relax their voices, and the singing got better, too.

Ah—Toggi making his entrance, surrounded by friends and attendants, including Raffaele Quinzi and other functionaries of Dischi La Cima. "Dear Harry," Quinzi said. "You know Benno, of course."

Toggi shook hands in a shy, deprecating manner. He looked even older under the harsh working lights; age spots dominated his bald dome and cheeks. Still, he remained an elegant figure in a fabulous sport jacket, ascot and cashmere sweater: he seemed not to notice the heat. His entourage, too, seemed at home in such a setting: an assortment of minor personages, Quinzi explained, including a number of former operatic greats who had come to watch, by special invitation, the return of the legendary Benno Toggi.

They introduced Harry to all the strange faces until finally he came to one he knew: Frankie Tree.

"About last night . . ."

"Oh, don't concern yourself," she giggled. The boy from the crew had no doubt banged her till dawn, so what did she care that she'd had to cover up the disgusting, passed-out Harry Chapin? "Harry, I'd like you to meet . . ."

She brought forward the press people . . . Charlie Sachs of *Il Giorno*, the big Milan daily . . . Leone Sciascia of Rome's *Osservatore Romano* . . . A mousy little man from another Rome paper, the name of which he missed . . . And, thank God, the one and only Herb Fink from *Music Week*.

"Well, the day actually came, didn't it?" Harry enthused.

"Harry, my boy, you are a man of your word. Very unusual in your line of work."

"Later—a dinner or something?"

"Great. But remember, no Italian food. I'm still not recovered from the last time."

Or, if not with Fink, dinner with Miss Sachs, then? Penetrating gray eyes, slim and sophisticated, pretty in an adult way—about thirty-five?

Last and certainly least in his desires of the moment: Marianne Kunz, who embraced him with customary vigor—and with an eye on Frankie, or was he imagining this? "Darling," she cried, "how *marvelous* —to know we'll have two whole *weeks* together." He came away tasting

of lipstick—banana oil or something else repugnant. "Oh, and we were
so sorry to hear about your friend in England," she gushed. "Frankie
told us the whole story—poor baby, you must have been *crushed.* . . ."

These ablutions of sympathy left him sticky with embarrassment;
outpourings of synthetic affection drenched him to the skin. Marianne
had always been a bit lush for the likes of him, simple man of the North
that he was—man at home in spare and rustic emotional surroundings.
"You're very kind," he said. "But now I'm afraid that Norman and I
must go to work."

Harry followed Norman out of the auditorium and up two flights
of stairs to a remote greenroom which Norman and Oscar Poole had
made into a control booth. The room was spacious and reasonably well
air-conditioned, which the House itself was not, Romans preferring to
take their opera out of doors at the Baths of Caracalla during the hot
summer months. What air-conditioning there was in the House was
creaky with age and could not be operated during takes because of the
noise—meaning that the temperature would begin each day at perhaps
seventy-six and then climb into the high eighties as the session wore on.
The booth would eventually heat up, too, Harry remembered, from the
electronics: a huge twenty-four-track master console, four massive tape
machines to handle the two-inch-wide reels, and a pair of closed-circuit
TV monitors giving them a wide-angle view of the hall and a close-up of
Maestro Ponti's podium.

"Harry," said Norman, "I'd like you to meet Sal Andreolli, our
chief mixer . . . and this is Mario, in charge of tapes . . . and Signor
Bonisolli, our quad stage manager . . . and of course Oscar and
Maury . . ."

"Good afternoon, gentlemen."

Oscar Poole had been brought from Burbank to oversee the technical production, which Dischi La Cima bitterly resented on nationalis-
tic grounds. Maury—Maury had come on a bet.

". . . And Signor Podestà and Signor D'Eustachio, representing
Signor Toggi."

The sweet Roman boys Beppe and Paolo from *L'Arlésienne.* Harry
embraced each one with enthusiasm.

"Afterwards," said Paolo in English, "we shoot some clay pigeons
off the first balcony, eh, dear Harry!"

Of course—they were at the sessions to protect the interests of
Count Gimpel: namely, the newly acquired Countess Gimpel, who was
still at Salzburg. "Con *piacere il più grande possibile,*" said Harry glee-
fully.

"Oh," said Norman, very much an afterthought—or unpleasant
duty postponed till last—"you know, I'm sure, Monsieur du
Bonhomme."

"An unexpected pleasure," Harry said without smiling. "You are looking well, Guy."

"And you also, Mr. Chapin. Perhaps before these days in Rome have passed, we shall be able to have the discussion of which we spoke aboard *L'Arlésienne.*"

"Of course."

Everybody resumed his seat, giving Harry an opportunity to take Norman aside and ask, "What the fuck is *he* doing here?" indicating Du Bonhomme.

"Then you haven't heard? Why, he's Maestro Ponti's executive producer."

"Producer of what?"

"Producer of Maestro Ponti's recordings, of course."

"I thought *you* were producer."

"So did I."

"This is ridiculous."

"Yes, isn't it? But that's how Gian-Carlo introduced him. He's on Gian-Carlo's personal payroll, apparently. So I've given him a chair. He's even brought his own score, which I don't believe he can read."

Harry had been hearing about little Guy since their cruise together. He was the son of a prominent industrialist from Mulhouse, near the French-German border. Guy's father had spoiled the boy rotten in the interests of a classical education—had the clout to get Guy into various conservatories whether the schools wanted him or not. Now Guy roved the world on questionable credentials, claiming to be artistic director, producer, pianist and critic, using his family's position to ensure acceptance among the Beautiful People.

"Well," Harry concluded, "as long as he keeps his faggy mouth shut . . ."

II

Gian-Carlo asked for a conference, and Harry and Norman went downstairs, trailed by the detestable Du Bonhomme.

"I am disturbed, dear Harry," Ponti said, "by what I see in the schedule which has been so kindly prepared by Mr. Rose. . . ."

"Norman," Harry quickly corrected.

". . . Ah, yes, dear Norman," said Gian-Carlo. "I have seen here that you are scheduling for tonight the opening of Act Two, whereas . . ."

Harry should have anticipated this objection. Ponti had come to the sessions with the idea of recording the entire score straight through from start to finish in normal sequence. "In this manner, dear Harry," Gian-Carlo lectured, "we ensure the natural flow of the music, with always the correct relationship of one tempo to the next."

A very nice theory, but totally impractical and uneconomic. Harry—functioning now in his role as Executive Producer—stepped forward and explained, in perfect detail and with perfect reasonableness, the way the pros worked. They would begin in correct chronological order, attempting to take down in this first session the opening twelve minutes and fifteen seconds of Verdi's masterpiece. Thus, in the hall at that moment were, in addition to the orchestra, our Montano, Mr. Aldo Curtis, bass; our Cassio, Mr. Vincenzo-Paolo Fanelli, tenor; our Roderigo, Mr. Leopoldo Quercio, also tenor; the chorus; and only one of our three stars, Mr. Benno Toggi, baritone, our Iago. (Mr. Laframboise was present, yes, but he need not have been—his one minute of music being easily obtained at a later session.)

However, for the second session—this evening from 8:30 to 11:30—they would jump ahead to the opening of Act II, which required only Otello, Iago and Cassio. The basic approach—Harry continued with exaggerated politeness, his voice as soft as the summer drizzle outside—was simplicity itself. Do the big stuff first—the scenes requiring the most players, the chorus, the principals. When that's over, excuse everybody not needed (and therefore not paid) and do the duets and big solos. Finally, pick up the bits and pieces, including the purely orchestral stuff. Later still, overdub the special effects: ships' cannon, organ pedal under the opening scene, dagger falling to the floor of Desdemona's chamber in Act IV, etc. Understood?

Not by Monsieur du Bonhomme. "But how is it possible, Mr. Chapin, that our Desdemona is not present to witness the initial jealousy of Otello? And how is Maestro Ponti to judge the effect of Iago's creed in the second act if the first act has not yet been heard in its entirety?"

Harry bit his tongue; resolved to be adult. "You see, Guy . . . Following Norman's call sheet . . . Our Desdemona, for example, is not present simply because she has nothing to sing until the very end of the act, and we would not want her sitting around tiring herself even if she were available, which she is not. We have grouped her music in the second week of our sessions because she is in Salzburg." He spoke as to a child. "I can assure you that there is method behind this apparent madness. Generally, we attempt a chronological sequence, but when this is not possible . . ."

The blithe spirit Du Bonhomme was not impressed. "If you are thinking only of saving money, perhaps. But it is quite wrong, in my opinion."

Nor was Gian-Carlo convinced. "But how am I to gauge, dear Harry, the dramatic effect? I am not accustomed to manufacturing such bits and pieces, but to creating an artistic whole."

Harry increased his volume by several decibels. "You will find, Gian-Carlo, as we get deeper into the work, that this procedure—which is quite customary in opera recording, I can assure you—as strange and uncomfortable as it may seem at the moment, produces results of very high quality. And you need not be concerned about working in bits and pieces. We prefer that you make several long takes—whole scenes, even—from which to choose later, when we are away from the hall and able to concentrate in the peace and quiet of the editing rooms at Burbank. Indeed, we wish to keep splicing to a minimum, twenty-four-track being difficult to splice cleanly. The beauty of the system, Gian-Carlo, is the flexibility it gives us in mixing down to the final four-track. We can bring up each section of the orchestra as desired—a clarinet solo, for example—and the same with the singers, each of the soloists being isolated on a single track of the twenty-four available to us. You will see. The final quad mix will produce an aural perspective that approaches your own viewpoint here in the hall—as though the listener were standing where you stand during recording."

"But dear Harry, are you saying that the editing can only be accomplished in Burbank, California, when I am not present? This is quite impossible."

On the contrary, this was Harry's dream: a hundred fat reels of 24-track quad tape—"A" and "B" duplicate reels being cut simultaneously for security—safely in the can, the $90,000 gone and forgotten—with Harry Chapin and Norman Rose and lovable old Oscar Poole free to return to the peace and quiet of Burbank, California, where, in great privacy and absolute dictatorial splendor, they would select the best takes and manage the assembly of all components into correct order and ultimate artistic perfection.

But he was too exhausted and too drenched in his own sweat to share this dream with amateurs. "Really, Gian-Carlo," he said with finality, "I must ask you to trust us in these matters. Later on . . ."

". . . And I really do think," Norman Rose said in *his* reasonable way, "that we must get started, gentlemen, if we are to adhere to our rather tight schedule."

Which ended it, except that Gian-Carlo felt it necessary to get in the last lick, saying to Harry in his petulant way: "If this were London, dear Harry, and my own orchestra . . . But now, with no air-conditioning during recording . . . How can the men survive?"

Several men in the chorus, noticing the orchestra players, were petitioning to work in their undershirts, or even bare-chested. Which

Harry Chapin would gladly permit, if only the ladies of the chorus
would agree to do likewise . . .

III

"Whenever you are ready, Maestro," said Norman over the squawk box.
"The tape is rolling."

Harry remained out front, where he could watch Ponti.

"If I may ask you, ladies and gentlemen, to watch always my
stick . . ."

Was it Harry's imagination, or was Gian-Carlo's precise and supe-
rior-sounding Florentine accent objectionable to the Roman players?

"And what is it, then?" cried Gian-Carlo with great irritation.
There seemed to be a problem in the basses. "No, it is unquestionably
an F," Gian-Carlo corrected. "If you will kindly mark your parts . . .
And now, ladies and gentlemen—the stick, always the stick."

They began. A trombone slide struck a music stand. The player
cursed, but Ponti kept on, hearing no objection from Norman. Harry
could imagine Norman's anguish upstairs. . . . Trumpets slightly
flat . . . Flutes okay . . . Chorus on cue but very loud: "Una vela!" A
sail in the distance—but then Norman's pinched and faraway voice
interrupted: "Maestro, if we may start again . . . And if everybody
could please check his or her stand for rattles . . . Really, the noise up
here is quite amazing. . . ."

Ponti relayed this information to the union representatives, who in
turn wandered up and down the rows of players looking for sources of
unwanted sound. Several ladies' purses were moved to one side, two
chairs were replaced with stouter ones, and each player was shown the
location of microphones which could give trouble.

They began again. Trumpets still flat . . . Flutes okay . . .
Chorus on cue and even louder (but Norman and Oscar would be able
to handle that) . . . Good solo trumpet . . . Tempo a bit fast? . . .
Strings in tune . . . Basses strong . . . Cymbals too loud . . .
Chorus clean and powerful, but sounding top-heavy without the organ
pedal . . . Also going to sound better when the wind machine was
added . . . French horns late on entrance . . . Bass drum too loud
. . . Everything still a bit fast . . . Basses not together . . . Cymbals
better . . . Brass better . . . Ah, Toggi's entrance . . . Good . . .
But the music ends too low for him . . . Get ready, Zeke . . . Zeke
moving *very* close to his mike . . .

"Esultate! . . ."

A struggle—and the top very bad, very unpleasant. Not at all a good effect—sounded short of breath and sagging and losing the tempo. No, that was not nice at all. . . .

"Maestro, if you'd like to come up and have a listen . . ."

Harry got upstairs before Ponti. "What's it sound like?"

"Shit," said Maury before Norman could answer.

"Norman?"

"The boy happens to be right on this occasion. What we're mostly getting is the noise of those incredibly ancient chairs and music stands. How can anyone make records here? I am beginning to remember why we stopped using Rome."

"I'll have Gian-Carlo speak to them again—"

"That's the real problem," Norman scolded. "Gian-Carlo. Either he takes charge of the orchestra, now, during the first session, or we're finished. Have you ever heard such noise? *Conversation* during a take? You know how Barbirolli handled this outfit. Well, Gian-Carlo's got to do the same—or something equally effective."

The Rome Opera House orchestra was famous for its outrageous behavior and lack of discipline. Barbirolli's trick was to refuse to go to the podium until there was absolute silence; then he would walk very slowly the length of the hall and say "Good afternoon, gentlemen," in his charming Venetian accent and give the downbeat. These Roman players loved a dramatic gesture—but surely Norman didn't think that Gian-Carlo Ponti, who was *proud* to be a Swiss citizen, could bring off the same effect? What was it Bongianchino, Rome's artistic director, had said about Barbirolli's way with the orchestra? "The first thing that struck me was the beauty of the sound when the orchestra was playing, and the second was the silence when it was not!" But then Barbirolli, unlike Ponti, was an old pro—his father and *grandfather,* both violinists, had played in the first performance of *Otello* at La Scala in 1887 within Verdi's hearing—and with a young chap named Toscanini in the cellos!

Ponti arrived. They played back the first take. It sounded better in the control room than it had in the auditorium, but Harry was glad they wouldn't be resting their artistic case on this one example.

"Now let's hear a bit of the Angel set," Harry said, "and then the Decca." It was difficult in a strange audio environment to know what a tape really sounded like; the only thing to do was to compare it with the best of the older recordings.

"The Decca sounds closer up," Oscar Poole declared. "The Angel has more bloom."

Harry agreed. In particular, Laframboise seemed to have less ring, less freedom, than either of the rival Otellos, Del Monaco and Vickers. Also, Angel's strings—the Berlin Philharmonic under Karajan—produced a rich, silky sound: nothing at all like Ponti's band.

"Perhaps if we move the mikes back," Harry suggested, knowing that he shouldn't be butting into Poole's bailiwick. But Poole wouldn't be blamed if the set was a failure: Hurston Eliot Chapin II would. "Yes, Oscar—let's back off a bit and see what happens."

Poole didn't argue. He and Harry had been on dozens of jobs over the years. "If you want my opinion," Oscar said, "that orchestra is tired, and moving the mikes ain't going to fix it. But let's try. Gotta do something. . . ."

The orchestra was tired because it had just completed two weeks for Decca/London and it knew that after two weeks with Melos-Doria it would be doing two weeks with Philips.

"I hope you're learning something," Harry said to Maury Wiseman.

"Oh, yeah, don't worry, boss," said Wiseman. "Oh, God, am I learning. Oh, God, yes—this goes in my book. Oh, God, you bet it does. . . ."

They stood around for the next ten minutes while Poole and Andreolli and Bonisolli and the boy Mario pushed and pulled at mike stands. This experimenting should have been done during the orchestral rehearsal at one o'clock—when the high-priced soloists and chorus hadn't been standing expensively around doing nothing. But Maestro Ponti had been available for only half the rehearsal, Norman now informed him, having spent the other half in the offices of the Santa Cecilia Orchestra—the illness of Maestro Passafiume, remember?—and Gian-Carlo would be sneaking off at odd times throughout the two weeks to conduct rehearsals with that organization, too.

Ah—at last. Not that they had obtained the sound balance they wanted, but the players had been moved backward and forward in the hall so often that the union steward said they could move no more: the effort was producing too much heat. Although the air-conditioning units had been switched on when recording stopped, temperature in the House had climbed to eighty-five degrees and one of the viola ladies had retired for the day.

The tape machines began to roll for Take 2 at precisely 5:21 P.M., the first session being thus almost half wasted.

"He'll settle down after a session or two," Harry said to Norman, meaning Ponti.

"He'd better," said Norman, with unnatural ferocity.

I V

Take 6. Say what you would about conditions in Rome, the chorus knew its business and had a marvelous sound, men better than the women as usual, but all doing well under this very finicky conductor. And now the entrance of Mr. Laframboise . . . Very good . . . Nice soaring line . . . Oh, my . . . How unfortunate . . . Cracked again at the *acciaccatura* B, and not really in tempo, either.

"I am sorry, Ezekiel"—they could hear Ponti's exasperated tones over the already dreaded squawk box—"but I must ask you to sing the music in strict meter. Please do not linger unnecessarily over the first G-sharp. Also the first A, a *minima* only, nothing more . . . moving always forward, as this opera will be long enough without your additions."

All of this in Italian, which had then to be translated for Zeke, who did not understand that *minima* meant half-note, among other niceties.

"Shall we do again, Norman?" came Ponti's voice from the hall. "Yes, I think so—no?"

"We would prefer a five-minute break," Norman replied. "Problems here in the booth, Maestro."

Over the intercom they could hear the scraping of players' chairs and the sudden murmur of conversation as the players broke out cigarettes, sandwiches, bottles of beer. Also, in the background, the heavy rumble of the air-conditioning. Zeke was a pathetic sight on the monitor: ghastly shirt and ridiculous walking shorts soaked through, so that the ladies of the chorus, who stood behind and above him, had excellent sport.

Harry, Norman and Maury caucused out of range of Guy du Bonhomme's hearing. Du Bonhomme, aware of this intentional slight, slammed shut his music case and went out—certain to complain to his principal, Maestro Ponti.

Maury said: "It's the walk that's killing him."

"What do you mean?" said Harry.

"Bonisolli wants him to come down toward the front of the apron—squares forty-six to thirty-six to twenty-six to sixteen, ending up on six for the last line, 'Dopo l'armi lo vinse l'uragano.' But Zeke can't do it. He can't sing and walk at the same time, wouldn't you know?"

"What does he do in performance?" Harry barked.

"Remember *La Juive*? He stands still when he's singing and only moves when it's somebody else's turn."

"I believe Maury's right," said Norman.

"Fine," said Harry, "then tell him to stand still. We'll create the movement electronically during remix." More and more they were counting on the remix.

"Gianfranco?" said Norman over the intercom. "May we have you in the booth, please?"

"He'll scream bloody murder," Maury said. "He thinks *he's* in charge of this mess."

"I'll tell you when you can start calling this a mess," Harry said angrily—immediately regretting his words. "Let's not start losing our tempers just yet, okay?"

"Sorry," Maury added meekly.

Bonisolli arrived.

"Gianfranco, about Mr. Laframboise's move . . ."

Norman did a nice job of breaking the bad news. Bonisolli was insulted, but gave in at once. Nobody wanted to argue in such heat.

"How'd you do that?" said Maury, whose Italian was as rudimentary as Laframboise's.

"Easy," said Norman. "I told him that in exchange for not moving Mr. Laframboise, we'd let him move somebody else an equal number of squares."

"Preferably Ponti," Maury shot back, and everybody had a good laugh.

But not for long. "All right," said Harry. "What's the *real* problem? And what do we do about it? The clock's running, remember."

Norman looked even more thoughtful than usual, then gave his considered opinion: "The 'Esultate,' to be perfectly frank, Harry, lies awfully high for this boy. G-sharps, a couple of A's and the *acciaccatura* B, which he can't seem to get. To get the notes at all, he's got to sing full out, and he can't do that and stay in strict meter. So either Gian-Carlo relaxes his beat or Zeke isn't going to hit the notes in the center. Hence, the awful flatting we've got so far."

As usual, Norman's analysis was sound. Zeke tended to sing all over the lot: sharp when he was fresh and really blowing out, but flat when he was tired, as now, after six shots at the "Esultate." Harry picked up the com himself. "Zeke? If we might have you in the booth for a moment, please . . ."

When Zeke arrived, huffing and puffing from the two staircases, Harry took him outside to the great marble-walled lavatory, where they could talk in private. "Hey," said Harry, "I want to talk to you on a completely personal level, okay? As I did back in those would-be Harvard days . . .?"

"You're my man. Lay it on me."

"What I want to say is—don't try so hard. The first day is always shit, so relax. I know you're not happy with what we've got so far. But really it's not that bad. By the time we add a little reverb . . ."

The marble walls echoed with Zeke's rasping growl. "Hey, man—don't be talkin' to *me*. Talk to that dude Ponti, if you want to do some talkin'. 'Cause him and me, brother Harry, we got ourselves some o' them 'artistic differences' you hear about. And I'm tellin' you now, my man—either we're gonna do this piece *my* way, or we ain't gonna do it. . . ."

He had no better luck with Ponti. "Maestro—again—it is **not** necessary to have Otello's entrance performed perfectly today. Later, when Zeke has settled down . . ."

"I regret, dear Harry, that I cannot tolerate an omission of such consequence at this time. Otello's entrance is a pivotal moment in the drama. . . ."

Harry returned to the control room. Twenty minutes more had been wasted. Ponti gave the downbeat and Take 7 was under way—only to be stalled again at bar 47, the "Esultate."

"He can't *sing* it that slowly," Norman whined in exasperation. "If Ponti would let him take it at his own tempo . . . What's this? What are they saying?"

Harry watched on the TV monitor. Laframboise and Ponti had both moved away from their microphones and were shouting to someone off camera.

"Maestro? If we may begin again . . ."

Ponti ignored Norman's call.

"I'll go down," Harry said at last.

In the auditorium he was met by a tearful Frankie Tree. "What is it?" Harry said. "What's the trouble?"

"It's Ezekiel," she moaned. "He wants the press people and visitors *removed*, Harry. Can you speak to him? He's being extremely—vulgar."

Before Harry could reach Zeke, Ponti intervened: "My dear Harry, it is really quite impossible. These people are my very good friends, personally invited. . . ."

Zeke now exchanged insults with a member of the gallery—apparently one of Toggi's guests. The great baritone himself was on his feet gesturing rudely in Zeke's direction. The chorus members, delighted by this development, applauded Toggi's performance.

Harry moved swiftly between the would-be combatants—like a referee separating linemen, he imagined—and bulldozed Laframboise into a far corner. "Zeke, for God's sake—what's the problem?"

"No *problem*, man. I just don't want them dudes sittin' in here. I want this fuckin' place *cleared*."

"Journalists, well-wishers, just the usual pests," Harry said. "They're harmless. Don't let them bother you."

"This is *private*, man—what do you call it?—a *restricted* session? No *ad-mittance*, you dig? I want cops on the doors just like I was Muhammad Ali, you hear me, brother? I'm *workin'* and I don't fancy all these muhthas watchin' me do it."

Frankie Tree joined them. "Really, Harry, I'm afraid we have a serious problem with Mr. Sciascia, who feels very offended by what Mr. Laframboise—"

"I'll join you in a moment," Harry said, sending Frankie away. "Now, Zeke—"

"*Man*, don't go tellin' *me*—"

"*Zeke.* Now, listen to what I say. This is a very important and very costly undertaking. We're not going to let *anything* jeopardize its success—especially anything as silly and unimportant as visitors in the hall. But at the same time we don't want to create bad feelings among people who can potentially be of help to us. I am speaking of the journalists in particular. We'll *need* their help before we're through, as I'm sure you can appreciate. So—let us say that, beginning tomorrow morning, your own sessions—any sessions in which you are singing—are closed to the public. And that includes the press. Now then—"

"Startin' *today*, man. *Now*."

"That I will not do," Harry said evenly. "These people have been invited here as our guests. We cannot throw them out. I'll close your sessions—as of tonight. That's the best I can do."

The towering black grunted, which Harry took to mean acceptance.

"Frankie?"

"Really, Harry, Mr. Sciascia—"

"Fuck Mr. Sciascia," Harry said for Zeke's benefit. "As of tonight, Mr. Laframboise's sessions are closed. Understand?"

He then walked his sorely distressed publicity manager out of the black man's hearing.

"But according to the call sheet," she persisted, "Otello's in practically *all* the sessions. How can we—"

"Frankie, *please* try to help me with this. All right—when Zeke's actually singing, then. You'll have to make arrangements with the management to have a special room set aside. Talk to Maury about having a TV monitor and loudspeakers installed. Also refreshments—sandwiches, wine, whatever you like. But I don't want Zeke aware, when he's at his mike, that we've got outsiders in the House. As far as anybody knows, the sessions are closed. Can you handle that?"

"I had no idea," she said in a small hurt voice, "it would be like this."

"Artistic temperament, it's called. The press people will understand—Toggi's friends, too. Artists are expected to be obnoxious in their personal deportment. Nobody will be surprised in the least. . . ."

V

Order was restored. Ponti and Laframboise agreed to make only one more attempt at the "Esultate" and then move on, whether they got it or not. Harry would speak to Fink and Sachs and Sciascia. If a special room couldn't be arranged for them by 8:30 P.M., when the second session began, Harry would have Maury sneak them into one of the balconies without Zeke's knowledge.

They moved on. Take 8 of the "Esultate" was better, but still not good; the chorus had begun to sound ragged after so much repetition. Harry instructed Maury to accompany Zeke back to the Quirinale and buy him a good bottle of champagne or anything else he wanted. Zeke's exit brought relief to all concerned. Frankie quickly moved her press people and Toggi's guests to places of prominence and comfort in the auditorium. Miss Sachs wanted to interview Harry, but Harry wasn't in the mood, preferring to hide out with Norman and the technical crew in the booth—especially now that Guy du Bonhomme, who apparently had *some* sensitivity, no longer occupied a place at the console.

Toggi was next. They began with the scene between Iago and Roderigo and continued straight through the chorus's "Fuoco di gioia," making four complete takes. Ponti spoke to the aging baritone with deference, especially when suggesting improvements or making corrections. Toggi had been a great star when Ponti was still at the conservatory. "Professore Toggi, it would help us if you could perhaps pause at the G, a gentle retard, nothing more, and then a little more legato. . . ."

"Of course," Toggi said to everything.

"Dear Harry," Ponti said over the intercom after the fifth take, "would it not be preferable, in keeping with your own philosophy of uninterrupted performance, to proceed directly into the 'Brindisi,' as in stage performance, rather than . . ."

Harry reminded Ponti that the "Brindisi" concluded with the return of Otello, and that their tenor was no longer in the House.

Ponti shook his head in bewilderment; reluctantly went on with the patching up of what Toggi had just done.

"What's wrong with Toggi?" Harry said to Norman when the com was closed. "The voice seems so—unsupported."

"I've been thinking of miking him a bit closer—get more of the voice itself on the tape, which we can smooth out later. What do you think?"

Harry agreed. Oscar Poole and his technicians were dispatched to the hall to make the change.

Norman continued his analysis of Toggi's problems. "The banter with Roderigo—it requires a light tone and there's no cover from the orchestra. . . . See there . . . The voice is awfully exposed—I think it frightens him. It's been some years, remember, since he's been in a studio."

Verdi hadn't thought of that: left the part right out front for everybody to see. Poor Toggi. Unless they had Christmas musicals in Italian prisons, how *could* he have kept in practice?

Maury returned from the Quirinale and took over the clock. "Christ, only fifteen minutes to go," he warned.

"That's fine," Harry said. Without question, the longest session of his life. "What are we doing? Where the hell is Ponti? I don't see him on the monitor."

Ah, because *here* was the Maestro himself, arriving just now with his aide by his side. "If we may listen, dear Harry . . ."

"Pipe it into the hall," Harry directed. "Let the orchestra and singers listen, too."

They played back the two best takes. "The first, I should think," said Harry when they'd finished. "With an insert here and there . . ."

Gian-Carlo continued to shake his head. "I would like Guy's opinion on this point," he said, turning to the slim youth. "You know, dear Harry, I put special value on Guy's ears, as he has very fine—what is the word?—*intrinsic* taste."

Harry and Norman exchanged glances; Maury guffawed behind his hands.

"Dear Maestro," the Alsatian boy began, "my own views must be these: I find it impossible to imagine the effect of the whole of this act in the absence of the vital organ pedal or—total insanity—with the 'Esultate' still unfinished, upon which the entire work rests! And as for tonight, proceeding onward to Act Two before we have established the requisite crescendo of the drama—really, gentlemen, this is surely not a faithful reproduction of Maestro Ponti's interpretation."

This mindless fop, this Alsatian pipsqueak who had never made so much as one bar of opera in his life—this *person* was going to tell Norman Rose and Harry Chapin how to produce great art?

"Gian-Carlo—"

But Harry was unable to complete an expression of his vitriolic thoughts because Maury Wiseman, on behalf of the musicians' union, announced the conclusion of Session No. 1, and Oscar Poole, who had been called into private conversation with Sal Andreolli and Frankie Tree's friend Mario, had an announcement of his own:

"Harry? Norman? I don't know exactly how to tell you this—but the channels on the 'A' machine seem to be out of phase. Let's hope the 'B' is okay—I've got the boys looking at that now—or else we'll be starting all over again tonight. . . .Which is maybe not such a bad idea . . ."

V I

During the dinner break, they retired to Norman's suite at the Quirinale. Harry sent down for a half-dozen bottles of Bolla's '69 Valpolicella and two chilled magnums of Cordon Rouge and a tub of potato chips, the bigger the better, and a fifth of good Scotch for Norman, who would be needing it before they finished. The Quirinale's air-conditioning was even worse than the Hassler's, so they threw open the windows in an effort to capture the *ponentino,* the evening breeze that was supposed to cool off the city after each hellish August day.

Oscar Poole—a very unemotional and sensible person, Harry had always thought—was of the opinion that Dischi La Cima's Italian crew had intentionally recorded the "A" machine out of phase in order to protest Melos-Doria's action in bringing along an American technical supervisor. Oscar volunteered to leave immediately and return to Burbank.

"Well, he's perfectly right," Norman agreed. "These bastards . . ." Even so resolute a figure as Norman Rose grew temperamental in the Roman humidity; Norman too offered to withdraw.

Harry disagreed. These things sometimes happened, especially at Rome. Luckily, the "B" machines were correctly set up, the tapes in phase. "These things always look like disaster at the start," he lectured to them. "But, Christ, Norman—and you, Oscar—with your experience, you ought to know that one way or another we always pull it off in the end. . . ."

His audience was noticeably unresponsive. Even Harry was having trouble swallowing this line—but no other line was acceptable. The evening session would test their resolve further—show what manner of men they were. It was the old story: by the time you got these prize sons o' bitches into the recording studio—usually in one of the most expensive parts of the known world—the prize sons o' bitches could no longer sing the parts you hired them for. You call this fucking great irony, or what?

"Time we headed back," Maury said. "If we're going back . . ."

Harry had drunk the larger part of one of the magnums of champagne and felt better for it. Norman and Maury and Oscar had killed a bottle of the Valpolicella and half a fifth of Scotch and eaten all the potato chips. All four of them seemed sober enough. Too sober, probably, for this line of work . . .

"Oh my God," Norman said.

Harry agreed. The sound was appalling: dry, coarse, with no natural resonance at all. "What do you want to *do*, Norman? Figure out what you want to do, and then let's *do* it," spoken with mounting impatience.

Norman knew what he wanted to do. "If we may take a five-minute break, Gian-Carlo . . ."

Off they went—Norman, Oscar, Maury and the boy Mario, who wasn't so bad, Harry decided, once you get used to his loud gum-popping—to fix up what ailed everybody. What Norman had in mind was to arrange a series of portable baffles—like a reverberant shower stall—around the suffering Toggi, putting him into total isolation and giving him headphones through which to hear the orchestra. Also, they changed microphones, giving him a Neumann that was a little brighter on top, more brilliant than the RCA. "Now then . . ."

The bell sounded, the red light went on, the tape decks rolled. . . . Better. Yes, a smoother sound—until the heavy brass chords, and then Toggi seemed not to hear the orchestra from within his shelter, headphones notwithstanding, and went off on a tempo of his own—slower, then slower still, until the whole structure came tumbling down.

Again. Good . . . especially the contribution of the Cassio, Mr. Vincenzo-Paolo Fanelli, who possessed a superb light tenor and most refined style, and who dispatched his few lines with spirit and intelligence.

"Once again—and if I may be permitted, ladies and gentlemen of the *viole*—at letter B, a bit more *portamento* . . ." Ponti's main concern seemed to be the strings, Gian-Carlo having been himself a viola-player in his student days. However, this quest for perfection was potentially fatal to Signor Toggi, who had begun to sweat with the rest of them. How many takes was he good for, before his ancient instrument packed up altogether?

And again.

And again.

And again.

Even with the support of Norman's cubicle, the Toggi baritone was but a faint echo of the powerful instrument heard in the early '50s.

Traces of his unique histrionic style remained—but, unfortunately, much of this fine acting would not be heard on the tapes.

". . . At that point he is supposed to move to his right, as I have instructed. . . ."

Mr. Bonisolli, the quad man again. Everyone had learned to hate his careful diagrams, like dance steps—first come forward, then move to the left, then move to the right . . . Poor Toggi was intimidated by the quad grid beneath his feet; in *his* day there had been no quad, and just barely stereo.

"Take Seven, please . . . We are rolling. . . ."

More balking at the prescribed movement, more lines fluffed, more bad playing from the orchestra. "What do you want to *do?*" Harry's usual line to poor Norman.

"We put down what we can, and then we retire to Burbank."

"Dear Harry," from Ponti downstairs, "if we may have another conference . . ."

Ponti and Du Bonhomme came up to the control room, and the latest takes were played back. Harry watched old Toggi down in the hall. The old man was not deaf—he knew as well as anyone what the problems were.

The air-conditioning was failing them: the heat from the amplifiers had raised the temperature in the booth into the nineties. Harry had long ago abandoned his jacket; still his sweat dripped across Norman's master score. "So you see," Harry said when the tape ended, "there are still some difficulties."

Ponti buried his head in the score. Yes, the *viole* were still not to his satisfaction.

"The unsupported fortes—yes, there," Norman said, "on the words 'Credo che il giusto è un istrion beffardo'—I realize that this is very tiring for Benno. Perhaps if we asked him to produce less volume . . ."

But then—even to Ponti's astonishment—center stage was commanded by another figure: the fey Guy du Bonhomme.

"With your permission, Maestro, I feel it my duty to state what should be obvious to you all. First, it is quite criminal to expect this very old and distinguished gentleman to perform such arduous tasks at two sessions in the same day. One does not need to have been born in a recording studio to understand this. Secondly, this idiotic jumping about—now in Act One, now in Act Two—is surely not a proper method to achieve an artistic result. And, further, I believe that all of these microphones—this quadraphonic technique you insist upon, which, as we all know, can be simulated after the fact and without the encumbrance of so many technicians and this ludicrous marching about on your silly floor diagram—are totally unnecessary. An approach,

gentlemen, which in my opinion—and I believe you share my sentiments, Maestro Ponti—an approach which can only produce a catastrophe instead of the true masterpiece of which Maestro Ponti is uniquely
capable. Dictating, I think you must agree, that the project as now
organized must be at once abandoned and then conceived under entirely new lines and managed by entirely new and more modern
methods."

Underneath it all, thought Harry Chapin, do you suppose this
Ponti is a raging fag? That this snotty asshole Guy du Whatsit is his
current flame?

But he did not ask his question aloud. Instead—when only the
sound of the air-conditioning units far away could be heard—Harry said
in a calm and well-modulated voice: "Are you quite through, Mr. du
Bonhomme?"

"As advisor and executive producer to Maestro Ponti—"

"*Hold it.* Are you through? Because if you are—"

The boy's normally pale complexion seemed even less robust than
usual. He took a step backward.

"—I must inform you, Mr. du Bonhomme, that your advice in
these matters is neither sought nor welcome, and I must ask that you
absent yourself. Because as of now, this control room is off limits to all
but the working crew and the artists."

Du Bonhomme took a step nearer Maestro Ponti. Norman, Maury,
Oscar and the crew remained frozen in place.

"And what is the meaning of this, dear Harry?" said Ponti. "Guy
was simply—"

"The meaning, Gian-Carlo, is this. I don't want to see Mr. du
Bonhomme in the control booth again for the remainder of the sessions.
I will not tolerate his interference. He is not involved in this project in
any way, has no responsibility for its success or failure, and we certainly
don't need his gratuitous criticisms as we try to accomplish this difficult
work under these trying conditions. Mr. Rose here is producer of these
sessions, and his word is the final word on matters of production, as
yours is final downstairs in the auditorium."

Ponti stared into Harry's eyes for several moments in silence. Harry
obtained no message thereby. "And this policy goes into effect," Harry
added with an almost involuntary smile in Du Bonhomme's direction,
"as of this moment."

Du Bonhomme, mouth agape, backed toward the door.

"Dear Harry," Ponti said finally, "I must take the liberty of informing you that since Mr. du Bonhomme, whose views in these matters I
respect, is here at my request, you cannot banish him without in the
same breath banishing me, too. Is this your desire?"

"My desire," Harry said as quietly as before, "is that you continue to perform as the professional you are, in collaboration with the other professionals who are engaged in this work. But I cannot permit an amateur to interrupt or delay these proceedings for even one minute more."

"Then I regret," said Ponti with great dignity, "that I, too, shall find it necessary to retire."

And with that, Ponti and his ward departed.

"Well—how'd I do?" said Harry.

Both Norman and Maury jumped up to shake Harry's hand. Oscar Poole would have done the same but for the great disparity in rank between him—a mere union technician—and Harry, senior member of Melos-Doria management. Poole displayed a great toothy smile, however, and said, "Mr. Chapin, you are one terrific after-dinner speaker!"

"Ladies and gentlemen, that will be all for today," said Norman over the intercom. "Thank you—and we shall begin tomorrow promptly at four o'clock."

"Tomorrow?" said Maury. "But what if he doesn't come back—Ponti?"

"Why, then *I* shall conduct," said Harry, closing his briefcase and getting the hell out of there.

Marianne Kunz caught him under the porte-cochère. "Harry Chapin!" she cried furiously. "How could you *do* such a thing? To a man like *that?*"

"Believe me," said Harry, "it was easy."

"Oh, you bastard!" But then she had to run to catch up with her loving Gianni, who was rushing off with his loving Guy.

"Harry?" Frankie Tree had also heard the good news.

"Hi, kid," he said. For some reason he couldn't seem to stop smiling, whereas Frankie remained tearful.

"Really, Harry," she said, "that was a bit much, wouldn't you say?"

Mmmm, everybody mad at him now. No bed partner tonight for you, Harry Chapin. "Oh, I don't know," he said. "We'll see."

"But what am I supposed to tell Miss Sachs? And the man from *Osservatore Romano?* It's all right for you to joke about these things, Harry, but—"

"Tell them the truth. Or don't tell them anything—isn't that the rule with the press? Hey, while I think of it—here's my room key, in case you want a nice bath. I'm going to be tied up with Norman for most of the evening, so you won't be disturbed."

"A bath? At a time like this, how can you . . ."

He was tired of pointless conversation and he wanted to get back to the lovely Cordon Rouge in Norman's suite. So he just left the pretty young thing there under the porte-cochère of the Opera House, Rome, knowing perfectly well that a girl of her persuasion, with flaming red hair of a length never seen before in the Eternal City, would have no difficulty in finding companionship for what remained of the evening.

VII

The *ponentino* did its work: the city cooled perceptibly, the boiling asphalt took shape again, the unbearable traffic eased to a stop. The Hassler's dining room on the sixth floor offered a magnificent view of the city, coupled with an admirable kitchen. Harry took Norman there to be away from the others—and, incidentally, so that he could drink to excess and not worry about getting back to his bed.

But not away from other Americans: the buzz of American catch-phrases swarmed from table to table like wayward wasps: set up a droning that made for acute irritation on sensitive eardrums. Even the captains spoke an idiomatic American, the kind learned while on detached service in the restaurants of Manhattan.

"And now," said Harry, toasting Norman when the first bottle of wine came—a soft red Lago di Caldaro from the Alto Adige region—"in addition to a scared-silly tenor and a dried-up old baritone, I give you— no *direttore! Salute!*"

"What do you think? Have we seen the end of him? Ponti?"

"It is my impression," said Harry, "that the Maestro will return tomorrow, on time, and without his protégé."

"I hope you're right. Or do I?"

Harry felt the same. Let the bastard stay away. Or come back, hat in hand. Either way, their troubles were just starting.

"And Zeke?" Norman said. "What do we do about him?"

"Zeke's our mistake."

"What do you mean, Harry? I thought you liked the boy. I thought—"

"I do. Love him. What I mean is, we should never have sent him to Florence for piano rehearsals. It's that bastard Ponti—the way he treats him, always correcting his pronunciation, always telling him how poor his technique is, how much he doesn't know about music. Can you *believe* it—a boy with a voice like *that?* As though he needs to know anything about *music.* One thing we know, Norman, you and I—there are singers and there are musicians, and never the twain shall meet (or whatever the expression is). . . . No, the present mess is entirely our fault—or mine, to be truthful. I've let our friend Ponti bang Zeke's ego all out of shape, and a tenor with a damaged ego is in no position to sing the 'Esulate' or anything else."

"You know—I think you're right, Harry. I really do. But my God—what do we do about it now?"

"That's going to be my job the rest of the time we're here. Shore him up, turn him back into the nasty, belligerent spade son of a bitch he was that day we first auditioned him back in nineteen-sixty-whatever-it-was. So don't worry, Norman. If there's one thing I can do, it's turn people into nasty sons of bitches. . . ."

"I've got some ideas on Toggi," Norman said when he'd had enough of Harry's wine.

"Good. We can use them. What?"

"The quality, Harry, is probably less bad than you and I think."

"That's good. It could hardly be worse."

"No, I'm serious. Naturally, we're critical."

"Shit, Norman, we're *critical* because we do this work for a living and are thus, if you'll pardon the expression, professional in our standards. Thus, we are dissatisfied with what we heard today. If I'm being unfair, please correct me."

"I know what you're saying, Harry. But if you'll stop being a horse's ass for just thirty seconds."

Oh, yes, Norman had had his share of the Lago di Caldaro. "I'll try," said Harry, "but thirty seconds is probably my limit." It was still fun getting smashed with old Norman.

"What I'm saying, Harry, is that with twenty-four tracks to play with, we can lay everything down and when we've got the basic score in the can—bingo, a little overdubbing."

"Another *voice?* You're not thinking—"

"No, Harry—you're not *listening.* I'm talking about overdubbing Benno himself. Later—when everybody else has gone home. I'll take him and the backing tracks and go into some small studio around here, where nobody knows us and where the union can't interfere, and we'll overdub until we get something we like—if necessary, bar by bar, note by note. What do you think?"

It was good. Surely Benno would be available—he had no other engagements, unlike all other singers in the world. "I like it," Harry said. "No—I love it."

"And mainly, Harry," Norman said with new spirit, "it solves Benno's real problem."

"Which is?"

"His friends. The claque that sits out there and watches his every move. It's *them* he's worried about, Harry—not you or me or Ponti or even the orchestra. He knows that *we've* heard everything—there's no way he can shock us. But the others are different. They're his country-

men, and he hates to have them see what's happened to him in prison.
I'm sure that if we can get him alone—just me and old Benno and
Oscar . . ."

"I buy it," Harry said. "We'll do it. Just like the pop boys do."

"I suppose. Yes, exactly the same."

"And so, as always, Norman, we've reduced everything to the
lowest possible common denominator, haven't we?"

"You don't have to put it that way, Harry. Tearing yourself—and
me—down like that. We're *trying*, Harry. That's got to count for something, hasn't it? Anyway, I thought I'd suggest it—give us a little hope."

Thank God for Norman Rose.

Hold it there, cowboy: this pony's just a wee bit unsteady on his
legs, wouldn't you say? *How* many bottles of Lago di Caldaro?

Practically fell into the suite—only to find this naked woman lying
across his bed reading his new Italian-translation Simenon and enjoying
his Hassler air-conditioning. "Well, Jesus Christ, what a surprise."

"Boy, are you smashed. Where have you been?"

"I've been doing company business with Mr. Norman Rose, Scout's
honor. But aren't you in the wrong hotel? I kind of had the idea you
were more or less pissed."

"I am. What you did was very unfair, Harry. But we'll discuss that
later. Now get your clothes off—because if I don't get a good fucking
pretty soon, I'm going to scream."

Harry did as he was told, because nobody in the world was more
likely to carry out a threat than Otto's favorite lady, the mercurial
Marianne Kunz.

3

He awoke alone. Apparently she had not stayed the night, because when she did she liked to try things in the morning, and he had not been disturbed.

After coffee, he phoned Ponti. They enjoyed a most satisfactory conversation. Harry concluded by promising to try to make the orchestral rehearsal at 2:30 P.M.—otherwise he would see Gian-Carlo at the recording session, which would begin at 4:00.

He tried Frankie's room, but there was no answer. She was probably out sightseeing again with the Nikon, or perhaps doing the work Melos-Doria paid her for—shepherding the press types around or trying to get photos of Benno Toggi into the Rome papers, which wouldn't be difficult.

But no—here she was in the Hassler lobby:

"Good morning," she said. "Are you all right? You don't look particularly well."

She probably meant his suit: brown seersucker failed to do his figure justice. "I'm fine," he said. He made a point to kiss her there in public because he knew she disliked it. "What did you do with my key?"

"I gave it to Mrs. Kunz," she replied with annoyance. "Why? Won't she give it back?"

"I just wondered."

"Oh, yes—she says you've been good friends for just ages."

"Mmmm. Let's have some lunch, shall we, and I'll tell you all about it." He felt remarkably well, chatting up this bird.

"I can't," she said. "I'm working. I'm taking Herb and Miss Sachs to watch the rehearsal."

"Rehearsal? Then you expect Maestro Ponti to return?"

"Marianne told me," she said with disgust. "You knew he would, didn't you? You can be horribly smug."

"There are some benefits to age," he said, feeling like her grandfather.

"Really? I haven't noticed any."

"You couldn't just let your press friends go off to the rehearsal themselves, could you? And come along with me?"

"I'm afraid not. It wouldn't be right."

"Well—any time you want a bath . . ."

He stood by the entrance and watched her disappear into a dilapidated Fiat. The driver was Mario, who should have been with Norman and Oscar and Maury in the control room going over yesterday's tapes. He would speak to Oscar about young Mr. Mario.

He took himself out the front door and down the travertine cascade of the Spanish Steps. Several misguided *paparazzi*, watching him come from the Hassler, snapped away with cameras far less sophisticated than Frankie's.

"Your distinguished name, Signor? *Il nome, per piacere* . . .?"

"My name is Charlton Heston," he said, and they left him alone after that.

The House seemed cooler today; there was no chorus—perhaps without all those bodies the air-conditioning would have a chance. "Good afternoon, Gian-Carlo. I trust all is going well."

"Very well indeed, dear Harry. Good afternoon." The players seemed more obedient, less agitated. ". . . Crescendo . . . Not too much . . . Yes, and now! . . . Good . . . Very good . . . And so, like a dream . . ."

"Sounds good to us up here," came the authoritative voice of Norman Rose over the speakers. "We are rolling, Maestro, and you may begin at your pleasure."

Mario was at his place between the two pairs of tape machines. Harry did not acknowledge the boy's smile. "It seems smoother," Harry said. "Without darling Guy."

Norman agreed. "As a matter of fact, Harry, Gian-Carlo seems very much relieved."

On the monitor Harry could see Benno Toggi moving to his microphone. "What do we have?" Harry said. "The Oath Duet, isn't it? How far behind are we as a result of last night?"

Norman took Harry through the score. "The scene beginning 'Olà!

che avvien?' and then Scene Five, Act II, the duet for Zeke and
Benno. But first, Harry, Benno would like to take another shot at the
'Credo.' He feels much better today, and he's confident of a better
result."

"He doesn't warm up enough," Harry said, listening.

"He's afraid to. He doesn't know how much he has in hand—Gian-
Carlo and I both spoke to him about it this morning. He's afraid his
supply of tone will run out—his 'capital,' as singers like to say—and he
wants to use it only for performance. The warm-up tires him, he says."

"And yet he wants to redo the 'Credo'—the most exhausting piece
in the book?"

"He thinks he has enough for that. He's not happy with what he
did yesterday. And I'm not either, Harry, as you know."

Harry shrugged. Toggi was as crazy as all the rest; he devoted
himself to such noble sentiments as:

> *I believe in a cruel God*
> *who has made me like Himself*
> *and whom I invoke in anger.*
> *From the vileness of some germ*
> *or base atom was I born.*
> *I am wicked because I am a man*
> *and I sense the primal mud in me.*
> *Yes! This is my faith!*

"It's fine with me," Harry said, "as long as he thinks he can keep
up with Zeke later on."

"Let's humor him just this once," Norman said. And then over his
mike: "May we have quiet, please, ladies and gentlemen . . . Maestro,
beginning of Act II, and this will be Take 8."

To be followed by 9 and 10.

"He's singing a good deal out of tune, Harry. I'd better—"

"No, let him finish. Let's not discourage him any more than we
have to. God, did you ever hear such a lousy band?"

"Awful, isn't it? Maury—bar one-twenty-two, the celli."

"Already got it. And the trumpets are early in the next bar."

The master score bled over every page with red edit notations and
question marks: Use Take 6 for these four bars, Take 2 or 5 for this
patch here, Take 9 for . . . How would they ever put such a hodge-
podge together to make a performance?

"Ouch—why does he *do* that?" Maury howled.

Toggi had hung on desperately—with his last breath, Harry was
tempted to say—only to have Ponti ignore him and invite the trumpets
to make their ragged attack a half-beat early. Toggi was obviously
furious, but Maestro Ponti did not tolerate lingering over a high note—

such a "distortion" of the musical phrase, as he described it—and there was nothing to be done: the tape was useless.

"And how is it for you?" Ponti inquired. "Is all right? Or would you prefer just one more time, from perhaps Letter—"

"Tell him it's fine," Harry instructed, "and let's move on. This is a long opera."

"Especially the way Ponti does it," Maury added.

Norman complied. "And we shall take our ten-minute break now, if you don't mind, Gian-Carlo, and begin fresh with the duet."

"Is all right for you?" Maury mimicked. "Is all right if you love what I believe was called, in your generation, dear Harry, crooning."

Toggi's exaggerated *mezza voce*. But half a voice was better than none at all.

"Mr. Chapin? If you would join us for a moment . . ."

It was Toby Beard, Dischi La Cima's studio manager from Milan.

"The name is Harry. Save 'Mr. Chapin' for the office—no, not even there. By the way, I have just learned that you and our distinguished soloist Signor Toggi were at one time roommates."

"Yes, that is so," said Beard proudly. "We shared an apartment, to be accurate—in Milan, many years ago."

"Ah. Well, he seems a fine gentleman."

"Oh, quite so," said Beard, offering a cigarette first to Harry and then to a dark-complexioned, sharp-featured gentleman who had been standing nervously to one side. "And now I have the pleasure, Harry, of introducing Signor Pellegrini, who is principal bassist of our orchestra."

Signor Pellegrini's hand was limp and wet with perspiration. "I regret . . . My English . . ."

"Forgive me," Harry said in Italian. "Naturally, in Rome we would expect to speak in your tongue. It is a great pleasure for us to be associated in this important venture with the famous Rome Opera Orchestra."

Signor Pellegrini beamed and immediately adopted a more expansive posture. "Actually, it is in this regard, Professor Chapin, that I wish to speak. . . ."

Harry listened attentively. Signor Pellegrini's Neapolitan accent was at times baffling. "Perhaps I do not understand," Harry said at several points, and each time Toby Beard—who, despite his English name, had lived his whole life in Italy—jumped in with explanations and elaborations.

Eventually, Harry understood Signor Pellegrini's message all too well. According to Signor Pellegrini, the bass-players had been examining the score of *Otello*—which Harry would most certainly know by heart, being a distinguished musician himself—and they had discerned that their parts (which apparently the Orchestra of the Opera

House, Rome, had never seen before) were exceedingly long and of the utmost difficulty.

This being the case, Professor Chapin would understand that certain *compensi supplementari*—bonus payments?—not provided in the formal work agreement between Melos-Doria and the orchestra, but *perfettamente solito, solitissimo*—customary?—with all record companies who use the House—were now in order; and in fact would be necessary if Melos-Doria wished to avoid certain *interruzioni* in its very tight work schedule.

"*Io intendo,*" Harry said in the end, nodding with the same gravity affected by Signor Pellegrini. "I must beg your indulgence while I consult my colleagues. You shall have our response without delay."

"It is quite traditional," Toby Beard consoled when Pellegrini had left to return to his stand. "And, really, what is such a small sum for an American company?"

The red light had come on again; Ponti was issuing final instructions. Harry excused himself and went immediately around the block to the Quirinale, where, as he expected, his yachting pals Beppe and Paolo were at their leisure in the deluxe double suite reserved for, but not yet occupied by, the new Countess Gimpel.

"I have a problem" Harry began.

"Quite impossible!" said Beppe.

"But this is not permitted!" cried Paolo.

Harry repeated his conversation with Signor Pellegrini. The charming countenances of Messrs. Podestà and D'Eustachio were instantly transmogrified into masks of cruelty and vengeance.

"And please to permit this unpleasantness to fly from your *anima*" —soul? mind?—"as clay pigeons fly from our slings," said Beppe through clenched teeth.

They invited him to stay for a glass of wine—French champagne, which they knew to be the beverage of his heart (*cuore?* yes, he knew he was getting *some* of the nouns)—but he explained that he could not, being needed back in the control room. And with further expressions of their great distress over his recent unhappiness, they let him go.

I I

"What take was that?" Harry said. He arrived back in time to hear only the last few bars.

"That was 3," Maury said. "And, believe me, the best so far."

"Not too bad, really," said Norman.

"Timpani's overloading," Oscar Poole said. "If your fellah with the stick down there would choose a level and then live with it . . ."

"Let's hear it back," Harry said.

"We're not due for another break, Harry, until—"

"Never mind the break," Harry said. His experiences with Signor Pellegrini and Beppe and Paolo—or perhaps the Valpolicella at lunch—had provided him with a heightened orneriness. "Waste a few minutes on my account. I want to hear it back."

"If you'd like to take over," Norman said, rising from the console.

They were all permitted to lose their tempers once a day in this heat; this was a Chapin rule. "*Et tu, Brute?*" Harry said. "You going to quit me, too, Norman—like Ponti?"

"What *about* Ponti?" said Maury. "Shouldn't we let him know what's going on up here?"

"Tell him we have a technical problem. Tell him it'll be five minutes or so, if he wants to correct the parts or take a piss."

Norman translated Harry's instructions into acceptable Italian and Ponti seemed glad of the delay; the strings at Letter R . . .

"Come on, Mario" Harry barked. "Cue up that fucking machine."

Finally, they were ready to play it back. Harry let his commentary ride right over the music:

". . . The introductory recitative, good, especially Benno, who obviously knows what the words mean . . . Marvelous, very evil and scheming . . . Now, Zeke's first explosion . . . Awful—the A is awful, hollow, no ring at all . . . Here, in the descending passage . . . He's losing it . . . Doesn't have the slightest idea of what three-sharps means . . . The G's okay . . . But now . . . Christ, those are only E's—if he can't hit an E, he shouldn't be calling himself a tenor . . . *Very* strained, *very* painful . . . Ugh!—the worst four bars in the history of singing . . . The top A horrible . . . The descending scale horrible . . . The bottom C ridiculous . . . Benno's C-sharp very good on 'ancor' . . . Benno very good all along here . . . Excellent . . . Be sure somebody tells him . . .

"And now . . . Oh, *shit*, Norman, do something about those trombones, will you? . . . Okay, now listen to this . . . *Terrible*—not together at all . . . Zeke's lagging—why? . . . Awful at Zeke's A . . . Terrible on 'sterminator' . . . Too slow in here—got to speed Ponti up. Christ, this is the heart and soul of the piece and it sounds like a funeral dirge . . . Toggi out of meter there—got to fix that . . . Slow again . . . Too fucking *slow* . . . Not together . . . Not together . . . *Not together!* . . . Zeke's final A *horrible*. And, Oscar, where are the cymbals? Got to bring them up. And brass very fuzzy in that run—the trombones again, Norman . . . *Jesus Christ* . . ."

"You loved it, huh, boss?" said Maury.

"*Maury,*" cautioned Norman. "Harry, I *know* it's not perfect—"

"Perfect?"

"Not even good, then—"

"Awful. Isn't that the word you're looking for?"

"Some of it's awful, yes. But that's only the third take and—"

"I don't want any more takes until we make some basic changes."

Norman tossed his pencil onto the master score and sat back with resignation. "If you've got any ideas, Harry, we'd be happy to hear them."

"I do. Now listen to what I say . . ."

Afterward Harry accompanied Oscar Poole and the technicians down onto the floor while the changes were made. Norman busied himself with Ponti, and Maury, who had been a brass player at UCLA, went to see the offending trombones.

Harry walked up to Zeke and switched off the tenor's mike. "You feel rested this evening?" Harry said.

"I'm okay, brother Harry. I come to play, like always." Even the speaking voice sounded coarse and gritty. The big man smiled, but nervous sweat poured down his cheeks.

"You're not hearing yourself properly," Harry said. "We're going to make a couple of changes. For one thing, that mike's too close. And for another, you're standing in the wrong spot."

"Hey, man—"

Laframboise argued, but Harry was firm. Tenors never thought the mikes were close enough: wanted the voice to sound absolutely huge— probably with the idea of demanding bigger fees from the Met, which valued big voices. There was no ring to Zeke's top, the voice sounding dry and tight, which in Harry's experience meant two things: the boy was frightened for his life and he was being miked too close—receiving no benefit from the natural "bloom" of the wood-surfaced stage and walls. It was different in Toggi's case—one expected Toggi's old reeds to be dry and squeaky and without volume. The best thing to be done there was to mike him close up and then treat the result with electronic reverberation in the edit room. But for proper effect Zeke had to be well back from the mikes, where the room sound could envelop him. When he'd had more experience, Zeke would know where to stand in each house. Smart singers studied every auditorium and kept book on where to stand on every stage—the spot that provided optimum resonance and maximum natural amplification—and pity the poor stage director who wanted to move them off that beloved spot.

"So how'm I supposed to see what that dude's doin'?" Zeke complained, meaning his duet partner, Toggi. Toggi's stand and mike were left in their original position, around which Oscar Poole was now erecting the "telephone booth" used for Toggi's solos.

"You don't have to *see* him. *Listen* to him instead. He requires a different audio environment, and we don't want his stuff bleeding into yours. Trust me in this, Zeke. You'll like the result."

"Man—"

"And there's one other thing. Just an idea to keep in the back of your head." Harry moved closer to Laframboise so that his words would not be overheard by Ponti, who was now at Benno Toggi's music stand with Norman. "This is *your* Otello we're putting down, not Ponti's. He's only here to wave that stick and try to keep everybody on the same beat. So when the tempo's wrong, or there's something else you don't like—let's do it *your* way, okay? Be polite to Gian-Carlo—he's sensitive, like most Europeans. But always remember that *you're* the dude with the voice, and it's *you* that the buyer's going to be listening to at home with the records, not Ponti. Ponti's contribution is important—I'm not saying that it isn't. He's a fine musician, and he's got lots of what I like to call conservatory skills. But opera's a singer's medium, and let's be sure we get on the tapes what it is that *you* do in this role. Let's not leave this hellhole of a town wishing we'd done things differently. Who knows?—maybe nobody will ever ask us to do this work again. So let's kick the shit out of it now—while we've still got a couple of quarters left to play. If you'll excuse the metaphor . . ."

Laframboise stood sweating in awed and awesome silence for fully a minute. Then—a secretive smile on his great black face—he placed a steely hand on Harry's apprehensive shoulder and said, "You know, for a white dude, you're some kind o' coach. . . ."

Maury was the first to notice. "Don't wake me if I'm dreaming—but do you hear what I hear?"

"Nothing wrong with *that* A," Norman agreed. "Don't worry about the balance with Toggi," he told Oscar Poole. "We'll fix that later. Oh, my, yes—this boy can *sing*. . . ."

It was a great deal closer to Paris: a black-silver blade with a terrific cutting edge on top and a burly longshoreman's bottom, the middle C full and convincing now, with legitimate weight and resonance. All the hoarse shouting was gone, replaced by real volume and a soaring, spine-tingling, blood-curdling ring at the top.

"Jesus, boss," Maury said, "you've given this boy back his fast ball—you really have. So *that's* what you get paid all that bread for—knowing where to put the mikes."

Takes 4 and 5 were uniformly acceptable, requiring only minimal cutting. Another ten-minute break was ordered so that Ponti could familiarize himself with the new audio perspective. The Maestro was duly impressed. "But, dear Harry, now we have no choice—we must abandon our tapes of yesterday and begin again with Mr. Laframboise. For his new sound . . ."

Harry agreed that if time permitted at Thursday afternoon's session, when the chorus joined them again, they would remake certain portions of Monday's work. But the important thing was to move ahead and cover all the ground at least once. Now—with morale audibly improved—they could hope to make more rapid progress.

In this new spirit, they prepared to enter the final hour of work— only to be confronted by still another problem. "It's just ridiculous," Norman said bitterly. "What's the point of rehearsing if the fucking orchestra is never the same from session to session?"

Norman, being of an older and better-mannered generation, did not use the word *fucking* lightly. "What is it now?" Harry said with sweet reasonableness. "Tell me and perhaps I can do something about it."

"If you can, fine. But this is Rome, remember? During the break, one of the basses—the *principal* bass, in fact—went out for coffee and didn't come back. The union contractor says he's been taken suddenly ill and somebody else will be sitting in tomorrow. Meanwhile we're hearing five basses instead of six. How is anyone expected to make music under such conditions?"

Harry sympathized. How, indeed?

I I I

He was on his way to Norman's suite for a drink when Frankie intercepted him in the Quirinale lobby. "We're going to have lots of trouble," she said earnestly, "if Miss Sachs isn't allowed to watch Mr. Laframboise work. She's come all the way from Milan just for this, and she was promised—"

"Who promised her?"

"La Cima's publicity department, I suppose. But—"

"So call Quinzi. Let La Cima handle it. Let's not waste time talking any more business today, all right? Can you have dinner?"

"I can't, Harry. I've made—other plans."

This Mario was a lover in the Latin tradition: very difficult competition. And he accomplished his ends apparently without giving expensive gifts. "I might as well be in Burbank," he said sourly, "and you back in London."

"What about Miss Sachs, Harry? Will you talk to her? She's in the lounge."

Frankie went off to her engagement, and Harry did his duty. "Miss Sachs?"

"It's Mrs. Sachs, actually," she said.

"How nice—may I get you a cocktail?"

"I'm afraid I only have a few minutes."

But he ordered champagne anyway. "I'm sorry about the difficulty with Mr. Laframboise," he began.

"You discovered him, isn't that the case?" she said, making notes.

"I wouldn't say discovered, no. I signed him to a record contract several years ago, but even then—"

"And can you tell me of his progress to this point? Is he, for example, living up to your expectations in this role?"

"Mrs. Sachs—"

"Call me Charlie, won't you? And I'll call you Harry—may I?"

Another pushy business lady. He had made a few inquiries. The lady was New York born and bred; husband a German engineer, but separated now or maybe even divorced. Nice-looking in the Manhattan way: dark, slender, fairly good bust, thinnish legs. "Harry—of course," he said. "In fact, we have hopes of opening up Zeke's sessions beginning, oh, Thursday or Friday. If this will satisfy your requirements . . ."

"Oh, not *requirements!*" she laughed. "Earnest desires, at most. That would be very nice. But let's not leave everything to Mr. Laframboise—your black raspberry, isn't that just the *perfect* name for such a gentleman! Tell me something about Harry Chapin—something beyond what's contained in the corporate bio and the bits of gossip I've been able to glean from your dear little Frankie, who, incidentally, thinks you're a doll. Tell me, for example, why Maestro Ponti persists in addressing you as 'dear Harry'—and tell me how you produced that absolute miracle of sending poor Monsieur du Bonhomme to his final reward while at the same time permitting Maestro Ponti—do you address him as 'dear Maestro' in return? yes, I suppose you must—how you permitted him to retain sufficient self-esteem to remain at his podium."

Precisely his kind of woman: mischief darted about her sparkling eyes as irony fell from her pale pink lips. He smiled with honest admiration. "Mmmm—such a mouthful. To tell all would require . . . What, may I ask, are you doing for dinner this evening?"

"Oh, my," she said with apparent dismay. "If only I'd known . . . But, unfortunately, I have other plans."

Yes, he knew. Such plans were legion here in the Eternal City.

*   *   *

He ended up with Norman and Maury, who had no plans. They remained in the Quirinale, where they'd done their drinking. Naturally, they asked Harry to order, and he brought the usual array. Really, one of these days he was going to cut back. He was now averaging not less than a bottle of champagne and two bottles of red wine per day, plus two heavy meals. He was getting his vitamins and minerals, but he was also getting maybe five thousand calories, better suited to coalminers or three-hundred-pound linebackers like Zeke.

"Hemingway had something about it," Harry went on pontificating between mouthfuls, "but I can't remember which book. He said that opera's like bullfighting—'exceedingly dangerous occupation'—the same drama and sense of ritual, except that the torero ran the chance of being killed every time he couldn't hit high C. Which is a very fine idea, if you stop and think about it. We should be allowed to run them through with a sword any time they can't hit a C. Or, in Zeke's case, an A."

"Fucking right," Maury said. "So, hey, pass the bota bag, eh, Pablo?"

"Still—I'd rather be doing it with Zeke," said Norman, who was also somewhat over the line, "than with Kunz. Which was the alternative, if you'll remember."

"Ach, zo," said Maury. "Yah, yah, ze meister of ze Cherman repertoire. Yah, yah, Otto, zing us zumzing from ze Meistershtinker. Vot about ze Price Zong, verein you tell us your fee for next season?"

"No," said Harry resolutely and with dignity. "It is wrong to make fun of them. Believe me, I don't envy these boys. I sympathize with them and I bleed for them. Because sooner or later they lose their gifts. They forget the tricks. They find one day they can't do the thing they did yesterday that made people stand up and cheer." Crocodile tears, nothing more.

"Oh, shit," Maury said, "change the topic, okay? Let's get back to that other thing. Are you gonna tell us or what?"

"What?" said Harry.

"Come on, don't fuck around, boss. The very penitent Signor Ponti. The very *cooperative* Signor Ponti. Yeah, and what have you done with Du Bonhomme's body?"

"A man can pout in his two-hundred-dollar-a-day hotel suite for only so long," Harry said. "Given the state of Roman air-conditioning."

"*I* know what happened," Maury said.

"You *do?*" from a very irritated Norman.

"You *do?*" likewise from Chapin. "So tell Norman, then."

The others protested, but Harry ordered the third bottle of Chianti Classico. It seemed much smoother now than when they'd started.

"Simple," Maury said. "Money talks, okay? So Mr. Chapin here, our revered leader, goes to sulking Signor Ponti and says, Gian-Carlo, baby, how would you like, one, to get yourself a fantastic lawsuit for non-performance of that keen new Globelektron contract, tying up all those sweet Swiss shekels that are now being channeled into that funny little bank in Curaçao; and, two, Gian-Carlo, baby, how would you like never to work again in this business as long as you live, because the much loved Harry Chapin will put the word on the street that you can't be trusted with any project worth, oh, say one thousand lire, which won't buy you a roll of toilet paper in the Vatican PX. So either you come back first thing tomorrow—Harry tells the wop bastard last night, eh, Harry baby?—and you come back solo, with no fag executive producer or artistic consultant or whatever at your expensive side, and you do *precisely* what Mr. Norman Rose or Mr. Maury Wiseman or even Mr. Mario Whatever, the tape boy, tells you to do, and not one thing more, until this gold-plated turkey is in the can; or else, dear Gianni, you pack up your darling little stick which is shorter than your prick and you look for some other form of employment, like maybe cobblestone-polishing along the Appian Way."

Maury, exhausted by the length and vehemence of his narrative, was now delighted to help Harry with the third bottle.

"Well, I for one don't believe it," Norman said. "That's simply not the way Harry operates. It's not his style. Is it, Harry?"

Harry was most appreciative of Norman's sentiments. "Maury, my boy—yes, thank you, just a drop more—do you *really* think that your own Harry Chapin would put the strong-arm on so sensitive a creature as Gian-Carlo Ponti? Shame on you. On the contrary—it was not at all difficult to convince Gian-Carlo, who is after all a man of some substance, that the project at hand—making a truly first-rate, artistically viable *Otello*—putting it down the way Verdi intended it, bringing Gian-Carlo's unique insights and personal vision to it—that such an undertaking is far more important than any personality conflict or difference of opinion or any other factor that might get in the way momentarily, including a little matter involving our bass-players, which remind me to tell you about some other time. . . . And so, naturally, Gian-Carlo Ponti, being the man I thought he was, saw things just this way and resolved to do his best, working hand in glove with other professionals—especially Norman here, a man he truly admires—to make this recording an artistic entity to be enjoyed and savored and held in esteem by generations as yet unborn."

Maury knocked back his own glass, poured another, topped off Harry's and Norman's. Then, looking straight into Harry's well-reddened eyes, he said: "You know what I think, Harry? Boss? Defender of the Faith?"

"No, what?" Harry said.

"I think this whole great speech you just gave us is pure, unadulterated horseshit. But because I love you, I'm gonna ignore it and congratulate you heartily on scaring the living crap out of Signor Gian-Carlo Ponti. Now then, what's this about the bass-players?"

It was only when staggering to the door that they noticed the others. The Quirinale dining room was swarming with Melos-Doria employees and guests. The engineers had a table headed by Oscar Poole and Bonisolli, the quad man. Charlie Sachs's date for the evening was Herb Fink, a fellow Manhattanite whose style, in Harry's opinion, was completely wrong for so sophisticated a lady. But the principal table was occupied by the Roman boys, Beppe and Paolo, Toby Beard and Beard's former roommate, Benno Toggi.

"My dear Benno," Harry said.

"I suffer profound sorrow, Mr. Chapin," Toggi said in Italian. "My inadequacies this evening . . ."

"Nonsense," Harry said. "You will see—the tapes are really not at all bad."

"You are most kind."

"Not a bit of it. Tomorrow is a day of rest. On Thursday everything will be fine, you'll see."

Fortunately, Maury pulled them along.

"You really *believe* that?" Norman said. "What you told him?"

"I *have* to believe it," Harry said. "And so do you."

He got a cab to the Hassler. In the dark he may have given the driver a ten-thousand-lire note instead of a thousand, but he was too drunk to care. Waiting for the elevator, he felt a hand on his arm and looked around to find Frankie Tree. "Babe—"

She was crying. For an instant he imagined them back at Monte Carlo—tensed himself against the blow.

"It's Mario," she said through her tears. "He has a wife. . . ."

I V

Wednesday was a free day: no sessions scheduled, merely rehearsal for orchestra and chorus. After lunch, tipsy as hell, Harry escorted Frankie down via Condotti into Bugari's, the big jewelry place, where he bought a sterling necklace she absolutely adored.

"Okay, sweet potato, now what'll it be? Basilica di San Pietro? Michelangelo's Moses? No? Okay, then, how 'bout the Colosseo? Get a horse carriage, take a little ride? Janiculum? Fontana di Trevi? Or plonk down on a sidewalk terrace, via Veneto, watch the beautiful people go by? . . . Ah, shit, Frankie—come on, be a *tourist*, for crissakes. . . ."

She was tired and wanted to take a nap *alone*, she said, but he finally got her to the Forum. He was starting to get his afternoon headache, and the ruins depressed him: everything fallen down in sad nobility. To think that the Romans had become—Italians. You want irony, I'll show you irony. What had *he* to do with all this Latin tradition? Nothing except that he was supposed to be perpetuating it—the operatic part anyway. It was a joke, entrusting this sacred legacy to the likes of him, Connecticut prep-school boy. He would surely botch the job—he and his Americans Laframboise and Del Campo and his Swiss boy wonder Ponti and his aging Roman ruin Toggi. Poor Verdi.

They broke into separate cabs, hers to the Hassler, his to the Opera House. Headache or no headache, he would see how his wards were getting along. God, the sun. The whole city had ground to a halt. This was Pompeii on the day Vesuvius erupted: all the Latins baked in clay . . .

Oh, yes, orchestra hard at work, delighted now to be indoors because there was no recording, only rehearsal, and the air-conditioning could be running throughout. "This is good, this is good," Gian-Carlo kept repeating, but behind their scores many of the choristers read paperbacks.

"As for yesterday, Mr. Chapin . . ." The abominable Toby Beard. "I didn't want you to think—"

"I don't know what you're talking about, Mr. Beard."

"The unfortunate affair of Signor Pellegrini? He is nothing to me, you know. They come to me only because they know me, and as I am studio chief at Milano . . ."

You are, you bastard, until I can bring the matter to the attention of Dottore Quinzi. "Think nothing of it," Harry said and went upstairs.

Norman and Maury were playing with the tapes. "We've tried different EQ's, Harry," Norman said. "The new miking is an improvement, but still . . ."

"All right, what do you want to *do?* You want to call it quits? Pack up and go home? Or what?" Drinking on the job certainly helped his disposition.

"I just don't want to build up any false hopes, Harry."

Zeke had taken to wearing his muffler, they now informed him. Despite the change in miking, their star tenor was not pleased with the sound of his voice on the tapes, and—to make things interesting—he had developed a sore throat, probably the start of a cold. He was sucking lozenges and not speaking even when spoken to.

Harry was not alarmed. These idiot tenors were all of a kind. One day they were normal people, and then suddenly they found they could make a noise that other people couldn't, and from that moment on they changed: lived on vitamin C, calculated drafts before sitting down in a restaurant, took their temperatures three times a day, went around shot full of antibiotics. Laframboise was no worse than the rest. "Hey, look," Harry said when he'd heard enough, "we'll do the best we can, all right? What more can we do?"

"It would be helpful," Norman said, "if Zeke and Benno *spoke* to each other, Harry. Here they are, singing a duet in which two men swear revenge on the tenor's supposedly unfaithful wife—yet they never say more than 'good day' to each other off mike—which, in Zeke's incredible Italian, comes out 'bone jor-now.' "

"Like, maybe they don't speak the same language?" popped off Maury Wiseman.

Which, lamentably, was true. Zeke's Italian, phonetic at best, was functionally inoperative, while old Benno apparently had no English.

"I'll talk to Ponti," Harry said. "He speaks both languages—perhaps he can bring them together. Meanwhile, they're getting along okay, right?"

"Not right," Norman corrected. "To begin, Toggi is very unhappy about the Act II duet."

"What in particular?"

"The whole thing—all of Scene Five, in fact. Mainly, he hates Zeke's part—not so much the way it's sung as the way the words are pronounced. Toggi can be very sarcastic, you may have noticed."

"Toggi is a great singer. Or great actor, anyway. He can be as sarcastic as he wants."

"Tell that to Zeke."

"But how would Zeke know Toggi's being sarcastic—not speaking the language?"

"He's not an imbecile, Harry. He can tell when Benno and Gian-Carlo are joking behind his back—putting him down for his terrible accent."

"Mmmmm, yes, I suppose you're right. Anyway, play it back for me, will you—the end of Act II?"

The new miking was a definite improvement: take a bow, Chapin. The long scene is filled with wonderful music, most of it Otello's rather than Iago's, but Toggi made the most of what he had, especially the "Era la notte," in which Iago lies to Otello about overhearing Cassio talking in his sleep of his love for Desdemona. Against this perfect piece of singing—Toggi's crooning quite appropriate to the text here—Laframboise's coarse ranting seemed mindless and amateurish.

"Nothing wrong with the 'Ora e per sempre,' " Harry said, trying to find something positive. "Jesus, what a voice."

"Yes, of course," Norman rejoined, "but 'Della gloria d'Otello è questo il fin' sounds like 'Tell Gloria hello just to begin!' On top of which, Harry, he has no idea what the words *mean*. I know for a fact that he's never read the play, and I seriously doubt whether he's even read an English translation of the libretto. They say Mario Lanza worked the same way, but even so . . ."

"You exaggerate, Norman."

No, you don't. Everything bigger than life around here anyway, especially Ezekiel Laframboise. "Where are they now—Zeke and Benno?"

"Downstairs in one of the rehearsal rooms. Ponti's got them working with his assistant, Fernando Ricci, going over tomorrow's material. Two sessions again. I don't know how we'll ever manage. . . ."

Maestro Ricci was a bright young man, very patient with temperamental singers, having learned his business as a prompter and rehearsal pianist at La Scala.

"Good afternoon, Maestro," Harry said in Italian. "If I may have a brief word with our distinguished artists . . ."

With Latin formality, Maestro Ricci absented himself.

"Well, now, how are things going?"

Toggi was his usual elegant self, dressed in a lovely cashmere sport jacket and contrasting flannel slacks, apparently feeling the heat not at all. Laframboise, too, was his usual self: drenched in sweat, antagonistic on principle, the perfect Moor.

"I thought it might be useful to review the first two days' work, resolve any difficulties that may have arisen, ensure that the remainder of our stay in Rome goes smoothly."

Toggi nodded in agreement.

Laframboise failed to respond.

"Oh, yes . . ." Harry repeated his lofty sentiments in English.

Still no reaction from the glowering tenor.

". . . I've just had the pleasure of hearing yesterday's tapes up in the control room"—back to Italian—"and I must say we've already made enormous progress. . . ." And again in English.

"You are exceedingly kind," Toggi replied. "But, as I have just explained to Maestro Ricci, it is essential that we repeat Scene Five."

"With respect to the new miking?"

"Not at all. I speak now of our young hero. It is not enough to possess this wonderful voice if the meanings of the words are not expressed."

"What's he sayin'?"

"He is suggesting, Zeke, that he is not entirely satisfied with yesterday's work."

"Shit."

". . . And how can it be otherwise," Toggi mused, "when this boy knows nothing of our language or tradition?"

"But, my dear Benno—if I may be permitted—Ezekiel possesses a truly exceptional voice, as you have said, and at his still tender age we cannot expect him to command the deep knowledge or refined sense of style of a Benno Toggi."

"This is so. Yet, to do justice to Father Verdi's creation . . ."

"What's he sayin' now?"

"He says you have a most remarkable voice. He thinks you will develop, eventually, into the greatest of all Otellos."

"He says that, huh? So how come he's always complainin' to Ponti?"

"He thinks that at times you sing too loudly. I must say I agree."

"Hey, man, he don't sing at *all*, you dig? You want me to sing like *him?* No way."

"Zeke, let's be reasonable, all right? Signor Toggi may be past his prime, but he knows *Otello*—he's sung several hundred performances. Therefore, I'm suggesting—"

"He's fuckin' everything up, that's what I know. Maybe he was number one in the Thirties—before I was *born*, man—but today—"

"There's no point in discussing it, Zeke. He's our Iago and that's that. The most distinguished Iago of the Modern Era. . . ." Watch out, Chapin: you're beginning to sound like the tour guides at the Forum.

"Fuck *that*, man. What about Milnes? What about MacNeil? What about . . .?"

Signor Toggi's ears perked up at the competitive references. "Maestro Chapin, if you would perhaps translate . . ."

"My apologies, Benno. Ezekiel is merely reflecting upon other Iagos familiar to him from recordings—an important influence in his own conception of Otello. He has great admiration for your art. His only reservation lies in the matter of the blend of your two voices—the differing timbres. I have asked him not to concern himself in this regard."

Now Zeke awaited translation of *that* translation. Harry wasn't certain how long he could keep up this, what?—*trialogue?*

"Zeke, Maestro Toggi is somewhat concerned about your Italian— that is, the pronunciation of the language. The records will be sold in Italy, of course, and he's afraid that your, well, unidiomatic speech patterns will draw criticism."

"Shit, man, I'm not worried about *Italy*—I'm thinkin' about New Orleans, Louisiana. My accent ain't gonna bother my mama—you tell him that."

"As for Ezekiel's diction, my dear Benno—we are hoping even now to arrange for further coaching in your language. And perhaps you yourself, prior to each session, might give Ezekiel the benefit of your own experience . . ."

"But to sing the words is nothing unless one comprehends . . ."

"I can only ask, my dear Benno, that you support Ezekiel in every way you can—making allowances, as I'm sure you will, for both the positive and negative aspects of age."

The sallow-skinned old baritone shrugged his fallen shoulders and replied in wispy tones: "It has always been thus. Our Creator plays a joke, would you not agree, when He permits Father Verdi to create *Otello?* He gives the voice to these young bulls, but holds back the understanding. And when He permits our Mr. Blackberry the understanding, He will then remove the voice—yes, even as He has taken from Benno Toggi the voice of his youth. . . ."

"Hey," Zeke cried, shattering Harry's appreciation of Toggi's sepulchral pronouncements, "you tell the old dude not to worry about Zeke Laframboise keepin' his voice, you dig?"

"I didn't realize, Ezekiel, that your Italian—"

"Come on, brother Chapin, I ain't *that* stupid. And you tell him knock off that 'Mr. Blackberry' shit or I'm gonna kick his ass! Go on, now—you *tell* him!"

"Do not be alarmed, Benno. Ezekiel is only remarking—"

But Harry needn't have worried. The great baritone wasn't alarmed in the least. "And it is not required that you interpret further, Mr. Chapin"—delivered now in perfectly understandable English—"for when one has appeared as often as Benno Toggi at Covent Garden, one acquires a passable fluency in the language of that country. It would seem that our work for today is thus concluded, wouldn't you agree?"

"So what about dinner tonight, boss? Maybe work out some strategy for tomorrow? Tell us how you made out with our superstars?"

Maury Wiseman was rapidly developing a taste for the kind of life that was second nature to Harry Chapin. "Sorry," Harry said, "but I've got another engagement."

"Oh, yeah? So what's her name? Wouldn't be Miss Sachs, would it?"

On the contrary, what he had in mind was continued revitalization of his relationship with Miss Tree, who, underneath it all—despite her unforgivable conduct aboard *L'Arlésienne*—wasn't such a bad kid. They would wait until 10:00 P.M., he decided, allowing time for lunch to digest and his latest Laframboise-inspired headache to subside, and then he would introduce Frankie to the *real* Rome: Alfredo alla Scrofa, greatest kitchen in Italy. Afterward they'd walk around the corner to

Piazza Navona and have the best ice cream in the world and sit and watch the Fountain of the Four Rivers and the people strolling in the arena where the Roman chariot races had been held, and they'd be just like real lovers—as though he too were twenty again. And he really would *love* her—not just sex, but the other thing, romance, which came easier when you were full of Chianti Classico.

"Hi, Babe," he said coming in the door. "Hey, guess what I thought we'd do this evening . . ."

She had her suitcase up on their bed and was packing away the skirts and blouses and colorful summer dresses that she had just unpacked that morning.

"*Hey,*" he cried. "What are you *doing?*"

"I'm moving," she said. "I'm getting a room over at the Quirinale."

"But *why?* I thought we agreed—"

"They gave me this at the desk."

It was a cable from Los Angeles. He had to read it twice before he understood its meaning:

SANTA CLAUS EARLY THIS YEAR TO WIT LOVELY GIFT THREE ROME
AIR FARES FROM BETTE AND BIG HARRY STOP ARRIVING SATURDAY
PM ALITALIA THREE NINETY TWO STOP HECK AND BEACHIE
THRILLED AS I AM STOP LOVING YOU

MAGGIE

"So you see."

"Yes, I see. I'm—sorry."

She looked at him strangely and laughed. "You're *sorry?* But they're your *family,* aren't they?"

"Oh yes—not about that."

I'm sorry, he meant, because you can have anything in life except what you really want.

4

He awoke alone again. Rivulets of sweat drained through his pajamas, staining the sheets and mixing with traces of Frankie's translucent mauve lipstick and ash from their last joint together. Let's hope the maids do a little cleaning up around here—that's all Maggie would need to find. He called down to the front desk and had no trouble in arranging a nice double room for the twins. Maggie would like the suite: what woman wouldn't?

He drifted, sleepwalking, through the next two days. The heat never let up—ninety degrees and ninety-percent humidity. The basic pattern had established itself. Up at 9:00 A.M., coffee with Norman and Maury, then the long walk to the Opera House, which gave him his exercise and permitted him to stop for an *aperitivo* or two along the way. Then conference with Oscar Poole and Sal Andreolli, the chief mixer, review of the most recent tapes, depression, frantic exploration of alternatives (none), a quick look-in on Ponti's orchestra rehearsal, then a big lunch with plenty of wine, a nap or some half-hearted sightseeing, and then the session at 4:00 P.M. Fall back to the bars during the breaks, hit the champagne from 7:30 to 10:00 P.M., a big Roman dinner at George's or Sans Souci or one of the other terrific and elegant places until maybe 1:00 A.M., then a nightcap and finally, reluctantly, bed. Or, as in the case of Thursday, run a second session from 8:30 to 11:30 and start the festivities a bit later. There were always eight or ten for supper, always 100,000 lire or more to pay, but it was only Melos-Doria play money and nobody worried about the expense.

* * *

"Well, well, Mr. Chapin—I understand you're bringing your family to join you. How sweet. I had no idea you were lonesome. Otherwise . . ."

This from Miss Sachs, whose long-legged femaleness had never before looked so good to him. "A surprise to me, actually," he began to explain, but then he realized that she was putting him on and he turned his back to her and walked away and pretended to assist Maestro Ponti in some profound artistic decision, which, after all, was the nature of his work.

"He should lose weight. God, is that guy *fat.*" Maury, being slim himself, could make such judgments.

"No," Harry countered. "Zeke needs his weight. Look at Melchior, Gigli, Martinelli, Sutherland, Horne, Nilsson—the old Callas, even. All the great singers are big. When, like Callas, they diet and come down to normal proportions, what happens? The voice goes. It's inevitable. If you're going to shout all evening in a house holding three thousand people, you've got to have a big instrument. And that means a big housing, like a grand piano. Have you ever seen a grand piano stuffed into a puny upright case?"

"Is that true, Norman? What Harry says? Or is he putting me on?"

"Don't ask me," Norman said. "I don't know anything about singers—as these tapes are going to prove. . . ."

"We flipped a coin and you lost," Maury said. "And besides, Harry, it's your turn. We ought to have a duty roster or something."

So Harry agreed to host dinner for Zeke that evening, but made Norman and Maury and Oscar Poole come along for protection. Laframboise favored George's, behind the Excelsior: Melos-Doria kept a large table there for him. The prices were outrageous, but the management had endeared itself to Harry's crew on the very first evening, when—finding that Zeke's enormous thighs wouldn't fit beneath the framing of the corner table for twelve that was otherwise perfect for such a noisy, extrovertish group—they immediately brought saws and hammers and others tools from the kitchen and modified the offending piece. Harry, who had not been present but who heard the story from Miss Tree, was charmed and amused by this show of Roman hospitality —until he saw by accident the voucher for that evening's meal (the manager had granted instant credit and was running a general tab, which would be paid off by Norman Rose on the final evening) and found that Melos-Doria had bought the table for 225,000 lire.

* * *

Friday night. More of the same—Otello, Iago, Cassio, Lodovico, Montano—but with two new figures in the House: the Herald, Mr. Raúl Gutiérrez, a Mexican baritone, and the Emilia, the celebrated young mezzo Alberta Lisi-Mettler, hometown Rome but now working out of New York under the personal management of one Giacomo Ferlinghetti.

"Now what?" Harry said in disgust.

"It's her shoes," Norman said. "Those—what are they?—cork wedgies?"

No wonder Maestro Ponti had been keen on auditioning this girl. Were they still wearing skirts this short in Rome? A buxom Italian mezzo, perhaps twenty-eight, mini-skirted but maxi-developed—married, alas, to Herr Mettler. Harry had seen a write-up in *Opera News* or somewhere: girl said to have sung a mean Carmen in Perugia. Mmmm, and a lovely gleam to the eye: invitation to fun and games perhaps? "So? What about it?"

"When she goes from square thirteen to, what is it, square twenty-four?—we're hearing her shoes," Norman said.

More of Bonisolli's foolishness. "Maury?"

Yes, Maury knew: go down and banish the cork wedgies. They watched him on the monitor. Watched Alberta, too, who showed both thigh and bosom in sitting down to remove the proscribed footwear. "Boom-boom," went Sal Andreolli at his tape deck. "Boom-boom is her knockers!" Sal had learned his English as a dock worker in Manhattan while studying electronics at Trade Tech High School at night.

"Knockers?" asked the returning Wiseman.

"An earlier terminology," Harry explained. "No longer relevant."

Like opera, he wanted to say.

During the break before the third hour, Billy and Alice Bigelow arrived with a nice middle-aged couple they had met at the Hassler, Midwesterners called Walt and Mary-Beth Knudsen, who were as keen as Alice to witness the cheapjack of Chapin's latest folly. Frankie volunteered to escort them up to the control room while Harry took Billy around the corner to the bar of the Quirinale and ordered the Dom Pérignon appropriate to a reunion of classmates.

"You were always close, I know," Billy kept saying.

"Oh, yes," said Harry. "I loved that man. I really did." They drank a toast to Teedee, and Harry cried.

"I don't wish to intrude," Billy said.

"What the fuck," Harry said. Harry told Billy the whole Teedee episode, the business with Frankie in London, the bass called Tom. "Working for world disarmament—he even made speeches. He'd found a purpose in his life. And then Prissy . . . That bitch . . ."

"Oh, Christ, yes, I understand," said Billy. "I once tried to write a song . . ."

Harry was embarrassed about his crying, but Billy said think nothing of it—perfectly all right for us men to cry over those we love.

When they'd drunk the bottle, they returned to the Opera House. Alice had already had enough of *Otello.* "I don't know how I could make such a mistake," she said. "I was thinking of *Macbeth*—isn't that silly? I was waiting for the three sisters. But this one—and the hero is *black.* How clever, especially today . . ."

The "Niun mi tema"—extremes of range and long-held notes—and then the "Oh! Gloria! Otello fu" and the *ppp morendo* of page 363 and the very end: "Un bacio . . . un bacio ancora . . . ah! . . . un altro bacio . . ." Harry always cried there anyway, even without the re-minder of Teedee.

"I'm going down to see Zeke," Harry said between takes. "Why don't you call a break?"

Zeke had gotten rid of the Hawaiian sport shirt and now wore a somber black turtleneck similar to Ponti's but ten sizes larger. "How do you feel?" Harry said. "Are you tired? You sound a little tired."

"I'm cool, baby," Zeke said. "I'm cool."

"I just had the idea," Harry suggested in his famous reasonable way, "that maybe you were tightening up. Don't. Think about your sound. That nice open sound—easy, just pouring out, no forcing, no pushing. *Think* your sound before you try to do it."

"Zeke's cool, you dig?" But not spoken with much fire.

Otello's death performed five times in one evening. Not even Melchior would have attempted that; not Martinelli, not Vinay, not King, not Del Monaco, not Vickers, not McCracken. "Look, it happens to the best of them," Harry went on. "Tightening up. Hell, even Gedda does it, and he knows more about the mechanics of singing than any-body else in the world. It's no disgrace. It means you're tired. You're tensing those muscles in the back of your throat—you're trying to *make* the sound come out. Don't. Relax. Let it come out on its own. Don't try to help it. . . ."

Take 6. Still no legato. The voice wouldn't begin to "speak" until a certain volume had been reached, volume just a wee bit too loud for the musical circumstances. But that was all right. Norman would know to take it down in the remix. "Oh, yes—much, *much* better," over the squawk box. Important to keep the boy's morale up, correct the damage done by Maestro Ponti, who would have flunked the boy out of class long ago. In other circumstances they'd have had another tenor standing by (and drawing salary) in another city for the full period of the sessions. The principal tenor would not know this, and if he fell down dead or was otherwise indisposed the whole project wouldn't collapse. But with *Otello*—where would you find a stand-by? If you knew someone who could sing Otello, you'd be recording him.

"Thank you, ladies and gentlemen"—Norman Rose's weary voice perfectly attuned to these terminal sentiments—"and may we ask that you return promptly on Monday, three o'clock, for rehearsal with Maestro Ponti. Also, principals only, piano rehearsals with Maestro Ponti at one. Thank you again . . . Thank you very much . . ."

To which the grateful orchestra called in unison, "*Prego. Grazie a lei . . .*"

In the front lobby, as he was trying to escape from the usual dinner group, Harry ran into Herb Fink. "Harry! Just the man I'm looking for. Remember my last girl friend, Harry? The one I told you about? Great apartment in the village, very cultured mind, reasonable body?"

"Oh, yes, Herb. Obviously, I remember. Who forgets such attributes? Why?"

"Because what would you think of taking her to *dinner*, Harry. Thereafter to have and to hold and to cherish and all the rest of it. Because she's right here in the Eternal City, doing Italy with a female companion, also a teacher at P.S. Six. A companion she would be glad to *ditch*, Harry, for one with a penis. I'd accept this offer myself, only now—thanks to the perversity of life, which I know to be a favorite theme of yours—I can't use her, Harry. 'Cause I've got a new one of my own and my evening's entertainment is thus assured. The lady being, of course—and for which I give you infinite thanks—the charming Miss Tree, which is how come I . . ."

Hardly able to breathe, he allowed himself to be swept along by the rapidly dispersing orchestra members, ducking his head so as not to be seen by Gian-Carlo and Marianne, who were now entering Ponti's Ferrari. "You son of a bitch," Marianne was screaming at her escort, "I'm talking about that cunt Lisi-Mettler, that's who I'm talking about!"

He fled now from that duet, too, Zeke's last rasping "un bacio" still pounding in his ears, and moved with the crowd toward via Nazionale, where he might find a cab. He pounded down the pavement, breaking into a half-run but slowing again, shattered by the heat and a violent pain in his side, propelled mercilessly by the image of Frankie Tree, her beautiful long legs spread wide to accommodate the obscene white city-bred torso of Herb Fink.

At the corner a cripple blocked his way—a pathetic figure on crutches, who would no doubt take his cab.

"*Signor Chapin? Scusatemi, ma—*"

But then he saw that it wasn't. It was Signor Pellegrini, principal bass-player of the Orchestra of the Opera House, Rome, who had apparently broken his leg.

I I

"Norman?"

"Good morning, Harry. Trust you slept well."

"Hah. Time for a council of war."

"Your suite? Twenty minutes or so?"

"Come ahead. And you'd better bring Maury. He might as well learn how it's done. . . ."

"What'll you have? Scotch? Champagne?"

"It's hardly eleven, Harry," Norman said. "Make it—Campari-soda. Or, no, just a Coke. Or perhaps—"

With one week's tapes in the can, Norman seemed incapable of decision. "You better have the Scotch," Harry said. Maury asked to share Harry's champagne; one thing the boy had learned on this trip was to drink champagne. They settled around the marble-topped coffee table in Harry's sitting room.

"All right, Norman. Where do we stand?"

"Well, I couldn't sleep," the older man began. "So I got up with the sun and collected Oscar and we listened to some tapes."

"And?"

"Some of it's not so bad. A little of it is excellent—some real fire at times, especially when old Toggi's croak insinuates itself under Zeke's roar. But then, too, some of it is awful. Even with additional retakes next week—and by the way, Harry, I'm trying to sneak in an extra session on Wednesday and maybe one on Thursday, too—I don't know. Maybe with some editing, add some echo . . ."

"Where did it go?" Harry mused. "The magic the boy showed us in Paris? The steely top on the Saint-Saëns LP, for example? Any ideas?"

Maury, who had originally been such an advocate, now seemed particularly inarticulate on the subject. "You're asking *me?*" he said.

"Hell, yes, I'm asking you. He's *your* Otello, if I may remind you."

"Oh, now wait a minute, Harry. If you're looking for somebody to blame—"

"Not to blame," Harry said. "Scholarly interest, nothing more. He *had* it at Paris—we all heard that. So where has it gone?"

"Studio conditions," Norman said. "If you ask me, he's scared to death, working in front of all these professionals. It's a little bit like Toggi, but for different reasons. And Ponti—Ponti doesn't make it easy for either one of them."

"So what do we do about it?" Harry said.

"What *can* we do?" Norman said. "The orchestra—with so many regulars missing, the overall quality is just not what it should be. This constant repetition just to get the notes right—it's killing the singers, and that's not fair. If we were in London . . ."

But they weren't in London. They were in Rome because—as Toby Beard had explained to Harry on the first day—Signor Toggi, under terms of his parole, could not leave Italy. Harry drained his glass and poured himself another. "The real question to be answered this morning," he said quietly, "is—do we go for another Otello?"

Norman winced. "*Now?* Throw away the whole week? Oh, God, Harry . . ."

"What about Vickers? Assuming he's in Italy and able to start work Monday? What would you say to Vickers–Toggi–Del Campo–Ponti?"

"Now, I *like* the sound of that," Maury said suddenly.

"Vickers has *done* it," Norman rebutted. "Twice, in fact. He's a splendid Otello, no question of that. But would he want to do it again? *Could* he do it again on such short notice?"

"I think we should go for him," Maury said with mounting enthusiasm. "The more I think of it—"

"I don't believe what *I'm* hearing!" Norman protested. "*You*, of all people, Maury. You were Mr. Laframboise's greatest living booster, were you not?"

"Hey, if Zeke can't cut it . . ."

"Do we have any real alternatives?" Harry said. "Is it realistic to think that Vickers would take it over now? And who else is there? Corelli?"

"Absolutely not," Norman said.

"Domingo?"

"Who's done the role only a couple dozen times in his life?" said Norman. "And who would want an arm and leg and two years' advance notice at least?"

"Kunz?" said Harry. "Does anybody want to go back to Otto and say, 'Sorry, Otto, we made a mistake kicking you out of our *Otello* in favor of this new boy—will you please come back?' "

Three glum gentlemen staring into their glasses. "Well, then," Harry said at last, "either we make the best of Zeke or we fold the project. That's the proposition on the table. Either we finish up with Zeke or else we fold our tent, our very expensive tent, and steal quietly out of Italy. Shall we have a vote?"

"Stay with Zeke," Norman said.

"Maury?"

"I say Vickers."

"And if he's not available?"

"Then go with Zeke, I guess."

"Well, thank you for your counsel. The chairman votes Laframboise —and offers a toast: to Giuseppe Verdi, who, though dead these many years, continues to dominate the lives of certain fortunate gentlemen— or unfortunate, depending on your point of view—of a Saturday morning. . . ."

"That boy's certainly getting an education," Norman said after Maury had gone.

"Mmmm, isn't he? I'm afraid I'm going to have to have a little heart-to-heart talk with that lad when we get home. His readiness to abandon Mr. Laframboise—this raises questions of, what, character?"

"He's young, of course."

"Precisely," Harry said. "That's when you're supposed to have artistic conviction, isn't it? It might be okay for old hackers like us— *might* be—to abandon principle in the face of temporal pressure. But I like to see a little more integrity in the freshman class."

"I tend to agree with you."

"Anyway—any other problems?"

"Ponti's cuts," said Norman.

"What cuts?"

"You remember he was going to use his own edition?"

"I thought we killed that."

"We did. He's back to standard Ricordi parts, thank God—though he persists in hacking them up, changing accents, 'correcting errors,' as he likes to say. Most of it is nonsense. But now, Harry—he's talking about cuts."

"For example?"

"Well, the 'Ponti edition,' if I may use that phrase, eliminates the ballet."

The delightful little Act III interlude when Otello goes out to welcome the Venetian ambassadors. "No, out of the question," Harry said. "The ballet stays. What else?"

"He wishes to cut about a dozen pages in the Act II ensemble.

The children's chorus, mainly. And he drops another twenty-five to thirty pages out of the Act III finale. He says the orchestra is accustomed to these cuts, and he doesn't think he can whip the players into shape to play this material anyway."

Incredible. Here was a conductor who killed everybody with his slowness and pedantry; who seemed interested only in details and never did get the main line in some sections; and who now wished to cut out great hunks of the score to suit the orchestra's diminished capabilities. "No. Absolutely not. This recording will be *complete,* just as Verdi wrote it—or as close to that as we can humanly come. Next subject?"

"Mme. del Campo. And some good news, for a change."

"It's about time. What?"

"The lady left Salzburg on schedule by private car and should arrive in Florence this afternoon—piano rehearsals with Gian-Carlo and Zeke this evening and tomorrow. So Monday, for the first time, we'll have all our principals in place."

Harry laughed. "How do you spell that? P-A-L-S or P-L-E-S? No matter—definitely going to need both."

Norman got up to leave. At the door he said: "You know, Harry? Despite all the problems—this is the part I'm going to miss. When I retire, I mean."

"What? Drinking Scotch on Saturday mornings in good Roman hotels?"

"You know what I mean. Making music."

"I suppose. Christ, Norman, you're turning into a sentimental old fool. And you can't retire because if you did I'd be stuck with nothing but Maury Wisemans, and you wouldn't do that to an old friend, now, would you?"

Norman laughed. "Well—we'll see By the way, when's Margaret's plane due?"

"Five. To be on the safe side, I thought I'd go out about four. Care to come along? I've got Quinzi's big Mercedes."

"Thanks, but I'd like to play around with our tapes some more."

Smart.

He finished the rest of the champagne—flat and warm now, which he hated—and then put in a call to Raffaele Quinzi in Milan.

"Good day, Raffaele—and please forgive me for bothering you at home on a weekend. But there is a matter of some delicacy."

"Of course, dear Harry. How can I be of service?"

"I seem to remember, Raffaele, that Jon Vickers was scheduled to sing earlier this month at the Festival of Orange."

"Yes, this is so. *Fidelio* under Maazel, I believe."

"I am wondering whether Vickers is still on the Continent. Or has he already gone home to prepare for the new season?"

"I do not have personal knowledge of this, Harry. But I am certain that I can ascertain the gentleman's itinerary with one or, at the most, two telephone calls."

"To be candid, Raffaele—the matter is not one which I would like to become public."

"It is understood completely, dear Harry. Do not worry. My inquiries shall be most discreet. Let me telephone you tomorrow in the afternoon. If you are not at your hotel, I shall leave a confidential message."

"I shall be very much in your debt."

"Think nothing of it, dear Harry. If I may say so—I am somewhat surprised to hear you ask of a tenor. I would not have been surprised in the least if you had asked of a baritone."

"You are most perceptive, Raffaele. But don't feel disappointment quite yet—my next call may very well concern the need for a baritone. *Arrivederci. . . .*"

III

Harry shaved, cleaned himself up, got the suite in order. Through the *portinaio* he arranged for three large baskets of cut flowers; he had not been a husband all these years for nothing.

At 3:50 P.M. Sergio Cozzone called from the lobby to say that the Dischi La Cima car was waiting. Harry had protested to Raffaele Quinzi that a car and driver weren't necessary, but Quinzi had insisted: Sergio would see to the baggage and circumvent Customs procedures. Harry was most grateful but also disappointed: he had been in Rome a week now, his Italian was back in full gear and he would have enjoyed a good shouting match at the airport. Alas . . .

Fiumicino: as poisonous as ever, temperature at least ten degrees hotter than in town—wasn't it supposed to be the other way around, being closer to the sea?

Sergio went on ahead—he had a special pass to get him into the Customs Hall. Harry waited just outside the sliding doors, intent on that first sight of Maggie and Heck and Beachie. The weary travelers had begun to come through. What would he say? Hi, Mag. Hi, boys. Give Dad a kiss. How's Mutt? Did she cry all the way to the kennels as she usually does?

But the first recognizable face wasn't that of Maggie or Heck or Beachie or even Sergio Cozzone. It was the fabulous all-enveloping grin of—oh, I don't *believe* this—Hoyt Dell.

Dell had arranged his own car, a Rolls, which the boys just loved, so they went with him. Harry and Maggie sat back in the Mercedes and shared a chilled bottle of Dom Pérignon, which Raffaele Quinzi had thoughtfully provided in place of the standard Bloody Marys.

"I just don't *believe* this," Harry repeated when Maggie told him.

"He's just that kind of—fantastic person," Maggie guessed.

It was impossible—but apparently true. Dell, learning of their trip—how? how? *how?*—had arranged to meet them at Kennedy during the layover from the Coast; hustled them into Alitalia's VIP lounge; upgraded their tickets to first class; booked himself onto the flight; and escorted them all—like a great party in the sky—straight to Rome. Who *was* this guy?

"But why do you always question everything, Harry? Why not take him at face value? As someone who—thank heavens—just *likes* you?"

"Because he's a phony. I *know* he's a phony. He's like some kind of overaged groupie—he gets his kicks hanging around the business. He *loves* artists, so I *know* he's a phony.

"But then I find out he's not. He says he studied composition with Milhaud—I check into it and I find out it's true. He says he knows Vova Slonimsky and once auditioned for him—I check *that* and I find out that's true, too. That's what kills me. He's just too good to be true."

"Are you feeling all right, Harry? Have you been getting your sleep? You don't look well to me. You're very red in the face, Harry. You—"

"But you don't seem to *understand*," he cried, "he's only *a guy I met on an airplane*. Can't you *understand* that?"

There was a big party at George's in honor of Frankie Tree's twenty-first birthday. All the Chapins were invited, but Harry declined. Instead, he packed them off—*without* Dell, who understood perfectly—to the Hassler's rooftop restaurant and sent for champagne— and four glasses, *piacere*, none of these childish California regulations about no *vino* for the *ragazzi*.

"A toast, then—to Grandma Bette and Grandpa Heck, for making all this possible."

"And how about Mr. Dell?" said Beachie. "For letting us sit in first class."

"Yes, Mr. Dell, too," said Maggie, who liked to run roughshod over her poor stupid husband.

"And now then," Harry said to the boys, "your very first meal in Rome—meaning that it must be extraordinary and marvelous, just like your mom"—who was not above giving him a kiss at the table. Which made him feel terrific, really terrific. Hadn't felt this good in many, many years. Felt good despite Mr. Laframboise's battered ego and Mr. Toggi's creaky vocal cords and Mr. Ponti's pedantic and inscrutable ways and all the rest of it. Felt good, too, to know that Miss Tree, his employee, was no longer lurking in his bed. "Just great to have you here," he heard himself saying again to Maggie. "Really is."

"I share your sentiments," she said. "But—in front of the boys— let's not go crazy with *le champagne,* what do you say?"

Which was why he'd married the beast, he guessed. Insurance against happiness in his old age . . .

I V

Sunday came in three parts, morning, afternoon and evening. Harry was not aware of part one, being very near death in their bed from the champagne or the several bottles of Valpolicella or the very rich food from the Hassler kitchen. He heard about morning only later when Maggie and the boys returned from their sightseeing with Mr. Dell. Promptly at ten o'clock Mr. Dell had come down the hall from his own suite and, cheery and smiling as ever, collected Maggie and the boys and taken them off to St. Peter's for Sunday mass and then on to the Forum and the Colosseum, the full-day tour.

Shortly after what would have been lunchtime if Harry had been in any condition to eat, Maury Wiseman phoned:

"Boss? You're not up yet? Hey, we got problems."

"Really, Maury, I'm not feeling well. Whatever you and Norman decide—"

"It's bigger than that. It's more money than we can okay, among other things."

"Just a minute—someone at the door."

It was the floor waiter with his coffee and an Italian substitute for Alka-Seltzer, which he drank down at once. ". . . Go ahead, Maury."

"I just got off the phone with guess-who, the great-black-bugger-in-the-sky, who tried to reach you and Norman and couldn't find you even though I told him you could always be reached in the bar of the Hassler."

"What does he *want,* Maury?"

"He says he's feeling real good, real strong, and he loves doing piano rehearsals all day long with this white-assed dude Ponti—you know how he talks—and he's really diggin' his new partner, Mme. del Campo of Dover, Delaware, who must give great head, Harry, from the way he tells it—"

"*Maury*. Please—I'm really not in the mood. What does he *want?*"

"He wants to spend some more of our money."

"How much and what for?"

"Are you ready for this? He wants us to fly his old black mammy out here from New Orleans, Louisiana, 'cause she's the only person on earth, he says, who can tell him how to sing them pretty notes the way saintly old Signor Verdi wants 'em done."

"I don't believe it."

"Cross my heart, boss. Seems this old black mammy gave him his first hand job, cuddled them great black lips against her shriveled old black tits, took care of all his bodily functions from the time he could first puke right up to walkin' and talkin' and fuckin' and even singin'. Says you know the lady's name and address and he'd like you, for old-time's sake, to get her on the next direct flight from her little home in the bayou to Signor Ponti's little villa in *Firenze*. So I says to the great spade—"

Meaning that Zeke was truly desperate now and wanted his Mattie Bush Carter there by his side to tell him how to get his sound back the way she did when he sang in her choir. "Why is it," Harry said with unwarranted bitterness, "that you feel it necessary to bring me absolutely *every* problem, however ridiculous?"

"Look, Harry—I thought you should know, that's all."

"Well, the answer is no."

"Yeah, well, that's what I thought," Maury whined. "So I told him—that you'd talk to him about it."

"You're most generous with my time. But that's fine. I'll call him right now."

"Can't do that, I'm afraid. Ponti's a phone freak—doesn't have one because it cramps his artistic style. So they walk down to the corner drugstore or someplace when they want to call out. Anyway, Zeke's going to try again tonight, your suite, sometime after seven o'clock. If that's okay . . ."

"And if it isn't?"

"Hey, Harry, look, I don't know what I've done, but since we took that vote yesterday—"

"Forget it," Harry said. "I'm just not feeling well. Chalk it up to that." And with great pleasure, he hung up.

*   *   *

"Why can't we have dinner now?"

"Because you can't. Not in Rome," Maggie explained.

"At seven o'clock at night?"

"Nine o'clock earliest. It's the Continental custom."

"It's stupid."

"Beachie, I don't like that kind of talk."

"Well it *is*, Mom. I'm starving. I'm *fainting* from hunger. God, isn't there any room service in this hotel? Can't we at least order a *hamburger*? Until we go to the stupid restaurant?"

"If he says one more word on this topic—"

"They're used to eating earlier, Harry, that's all. Beachie, I don't want to hear the word *stupid* again. Where's Heck?"

"He's on the crapper, as usual."

"And don't say *that* word, either. Sometimes I wonder what good it does to send you boys to private school. . . ."

The telephone interrupted. Harry braced himself. Zeke would use language far stronger than *stupid* or *crapper* or anything else that Heck and Beachie had yet learned in their wonderful private school. Or—looking on the bright side—perhaps it was Quinzi with news on Vickers; Vickers, who might solve the entire Laframboise problem.

"Hello? . . . Yes, operator, this is Mr. Chapin. . . ."

But it wasn't Laframboise and it wasn't Quinzi. It was Leslie Deering calling from his home in Bel Air, California. "Leslie? What a great surprise."

"Got to support our boys on the front lines," said Deering. "Thought I'd let you get a week under your belts before I checked in to see if there's anything I can provide—any help from this end."

"Well, that's awfully good of you, Leslie. No, I think we're pretty self-sufficient as of the moment. Usual problems, of course. Our Otello has a bit of a sore throat—bad luck—but we'll struggle through."

"How unfortunate. That would be the Negro? The American?"

"Yes, Laframboise. French name, but very much American."

"So you expect to carry on?"

"Of course, Leslie. Why would you think—"

"Frankly, Harry, I'm sorry I missed you in those last weeks before you left. Unfortunately, it was either take my holiday then or forget it for this year—you know the pressures we've faced."

"Of course, Leslie. Yes, I'm sorry we missed each other."

"But before that—when you were in, I don't know, New York, I suppose—I did have occasion to chat with your assistant, Mr. Wiseman, and he brought me into the picture. I must say I had no idea of the great problems that had developed in this very, very costly project."

"Maury told you there were problems?"

"Well, the Cavalieri problem, of course—which, naturally, you had briefed me on, for the Board. But also he had reservations, I believe, about the Negro—and an American lady?—who had once appeared in *Playboy?*—could this be right? But I take it you've sorted these out."

"Leslie, let me be sure I understand. You're saying that Maury Wiseman, who's never participated in an opera recording before in his life, was talking to *you* about the singers I have retained for this project?"

"Now, now, Harry—it was all said quite innocently, I can assure you—the sort of conversation one has with a fellow executive in the commissary. Naturally, when Mme. Cavalieri dropped out—as you yourself told me in late spring when you returned from your extended stay in Europe—"

"That is correct, Leslie. When Edith found that she could no longer do the part, naturally other cast changes were required. But I do not understand how such, shall we say, 'technical difficulties' should be brought to the attention of the Chairman of the Board."

"Harry, I had fully intended to discuss these matters with you, as I say—only to be interrupted by the unfortunate vacation schedule. But with so much money at stake, dear chap, it's not entirely inappropriate of me to concern myself, I hope you'll agree."

"I'm not questioning that, Leslie—only what I deem to be improper action on my assistant's part in going around me. In going over my head, to be blunt about it—presenting problems to you which, as a matter of fact, are not problems at all—at least not of the kind one puts to the Chairman of the Board."

"Youth must be served, Harry, as we know. And if he felt—"

"It's not a question of youth, Leslie. It's a question of excessive ambition. Frankly, Mr. Maury Wiseman, who is barely off the UCLA campus, is simply not competent to make such judgments."

"Really? Somehow I got the impression that he's very much involved in the artistic management of this project. Associate producer, I think he said—second to your New York man, Mr. Rose, is it?"

"Norman Rose, yes—one of the most experienced producers in the business. No, Mr. Wiseman is *not* associate producer, Leslie. Mr. Wiseman is a very junior assistant—and is, in fact, employed principally in getting people coffee, making sure artists get to the Opera House for each day's sessions, et cetera. No, Mr. Wiseman is very definitely *not* associate producer or anything else very grand on this project."

"Oh, my. Obviously, I've stumbled in where I'm not wanted."

"On the contrary, Leslie, I appreciate your bringing the matter to my notice. As soon as I return to Burbank, I shall be pleased to give you a full report on our activities here. And when I do, I think you'll agree that we've accomplished what we started out to accomplish, in the Consortium's overall interests. Meanwhile . . ."

"Forget I've spoken, old chap. Really, I feel somewhat victimized—I do hope you'll excuse me. I'm sorry I even bothered to touch base, seeing now that it upsets you quite unnecessarily. We have every confidence in you, as you know. Cheerio . . ."

It took several calls to find the elusive Mr. Wiseman. Harry finally tracked down the son of a bitch in Zeke Laframboise's temporarily unoccupied suite at the Quirinale, where there was apparently a party in progress: Harry could make out the laughing voices of Herb Fink and Frankie Tree in the background.

"Maury? Now listen carefully to what I tell you—"

"Always do, boss. How can I be of service?"

"You can do this. You can leave that suite and go directly back to your room—now, right now. The minute you get there, pack your bags and check out of the hotel and take yourself out to Fiumicino by the most direct route—use the Dischi La Cima limousine if it's not otherwise occupied. Once there, get yourself a seat on the first airplane that goes anywhere near Los Angeles, California. Don't bother waiting for a direct flight; go to Paris or London or New York and wait in one of those airports for a connecting flight to L.A. That way you won't have to hang around Fiumicino, which is a very bad place to wait, and I don't want you coming back into Rome.

"When you get to Los Angeles, go into the office and sit down and prepare a detailed memo, in any length you think necessary, explaining to me why you shouldn't be fired. Please give me any and all information you think appropriate to the subject of your recent meeting with Leslie Deering and your remarks to him on your personal reservations about the cast of the Melos-Doria *Otello*. When you've finished that, simply sit tight until I get home, at which time we'll talk about whether or not your limited usefulness to Melos-Doria Records has come to a premature end. Now then, have you got that?"

"Hey, now, Harry—Jesus Christ, who've you been talking to? 'Cause—"

"It's now—let's see—just past seven thirty. With any luck you can be at the airport by nine, nine thirty latest."

"I wasn't being *critical*, Harry! The man just asked my opinion—"

"And be certain, Maury, of one thing. Be certain that you don't run into me between now and the time you go to the airport. Because if you do, Maury, I may well decide not to wait until I return to Burbank to settle the matter of your continuing employment with this company."

"Now, *look*, Harry—you're not living up to your commitment—that I could be present for the sessions? If you'll remember—"

"Nine thirty, Maury. Let's consider nine thirty as the final deadline, shall we? Goodbye, Maury—and *bon voyage.*"

"And *what,* may I ask," Maggie demanded, "was all that? Do you realize that your face, Harry Chapin, is beet red? And you're absolutely *puffing* with anger? What *was* that?"

He took another slug of champagne. "Nothing important," he said. "Just chatting with a former employee . . ."

Dinner was an incredible, fantastic, miraculous event. Hoyt Dell insisted on taking Harry, Mag (as he called her), the twins and Norman Rose to George's. Harry was too much of a gentleman to mention that he had eaten there almost every night since arriving in Rome. Dell himself had eaten there the previous night, when he'd taken over as host of the Frankie Tree birthday party. They had reservations for nine o'clock, but arrived at eight thirty out of consideration for the boys' stomachs. No matter: the *maître d'*, remembering Dell from the night before, disrupted the entire restaurant to accommodate Signor Dell's party.

The chef came out of the kitchen on three occasions to ensure that Signor Dell was happy with the chain of gastronomical events. Harry ate everything. So did the boys—attacked their plates like goats, delighting patrons on all sides. Dell was more of the small-bites, taste-everything-but-eat-little school, as befitted his professional interest. Maggie, always on a diet, went off her diet. Norman, who ate to live instead of Harry's way, found new pleasure in knife and fork. They drank countless glasses of superb Bardolino from countless bottles. They talked for three hours without ever mentioning Giuseppe Verdi or Ezekiel Laframboise. (Norman mentioned Benno Toggi just once—in connection with an unusual form of pasta said to be native to the town of Toggi's birth, Ancona.) Three quarters of the way through, Harry Chapin kissed his wife.

When they were done—everybody but Dell stuffed like sacks of grain, the twins yawning like cats—Harry tried for the check, but Signor Dell had already made arrangements.

"Hoyt—God, how can we thank you enough?" Harry blathered.

"But *that's* my thanks." Dell beamed. "Good people enjoying themselves . . ."

Fiendishly clever. What does the man *want?* Harry pondered the question all the way back—on foot, for exercise—to the Hassler. Dell's Rolls trailed along behind them the way cars did in early Fellini films. Dell kissed "his Mag" good night at their door: to Harry's knowledge, it was the first time another man had kissed her on the lips since they were married. Dell shook hands with the boys, who were most impressed.

Then he embraced Harry in the Latin manner. Harry was less impressed than the others.

"Quite a day, wasn't it?" Maggie said. She got into bed before he did, and didn't wear a nightgown.

"God, I'm tired," he said. But he went without pajamas anyway, so she wouldn't be angry. He had enough people angry with him.

"Have you been a good boy?" she said. "In my absence?"

"I don't know what you mean."

"No little girls? Someone to help you while away the time?"

"I haven't had to 'while away' any time, as you put it. We're pretty busy out here, in case you haven't noticed. What about the boys? How are they reacting? To Rome, I mean?"

"About the way you'd expect fifteen-year-olds to react. Mixture of excitement and boredom. Afraid of too much grownup sightseeing, I suppose. Too many Michelangelos, too many Canalettos."

"Heck looks like he's finally putting on some weight."

"Yes. Beachie's taken to calling him Fatso, which is all right, I guess."

"Mmmm."

"And what about you? I don't suppose you've been getting any exercise. No jogging in the park?"

"What park? In this heat? Are you crazy?"

"Still, with the pasta that seems to come at every meal—you *should* watch your weight, Harry."

"I'm watching it. It's going up and up and up. Hey, let's get some sleep, huh? Lots of work tomorrow. Didi's first day on the job. Children's chorus. The boys should get a kick. . . ."

"No kiss good night?"

He rolled in her direction; made minimal contact. "Good night."

"That's my Harry. . . ."

5

Monday, August 29. The twins came up from their nice double room and joined the senior Chapins for breakfast in the suite. Harry ordered bacon and eggs all around, which the boys pretended not to like. After five minutes of Flintridge-style bickering, Harry booted Heck and Beachie out, telling them to go loiter on the Spanish Steps or do anything else they wanted as long as they got out of his sight.

"You're in good humor this morning," Maggie said with delicious cool detachment.

"And I want to pay that guy back—Dell—right now, the minute we see him, for the difference in the tickets—tourist to first class. God, the *nerve* of that guy. I just don't want to be *indebted* to that guy." Not to any guy who had kicked around L'Hôtel and knew Solange and the monkey cage off the lobby and . . .

He called down to the front desk for messages. No, nothing from Mr. Laframboise, who knew better than to bug Harry about flying in voice teachers from the States. But there was a cryptic message from Raffaele Quinzi:

The merchandise has already been shipped to America.

Meaning that Vickers was no longer on the Continent. Ezekiel Laframboise was their Otello for better or—more likely—worse.

". . . And what about Didi? What's she got to start?"

"Heavy day for her, I'm afraid," said Norman. "Act II, beginning 'Dove guardi.' Chorus, children's chorus, mandolins. Also, I'd like to repeat the scene just before that, if we have time. Children only

needed for the first half—we'll do them and get them out. The afternoon ends with the denunciation ensemble from Act III—chorus,
Roderigo, Cassio, Lodovico, Otello, Desdemona, Emilia, Iago. By then
we'll know what we've got, I'd say."

"And the evening session?"

"The second-act quartet and then Lodovico's arrival in Act III.
All kinds of trouble for Didi—high B-flats everywhere. It's not an easy
role, Harry, as you know."

"Worth ten thousand dollars, would you say?"

"Ah, well—if you're going to put it like that . . ."

"Listen to this," Norman said. "Go ahead, Mario—roll the tape."

"What is it?"

"Zeke's last 'Esultate' on Friday. We've played around with it
some."

Must have been about Take 15. Not too bad. Big, clean, on pitch,
with more bloom now. "How much reverb?"

"A bit," Norman said. "What do you think?"

"A critic here and there may find it suspicious," Harry judged. "But
let's keep it. If we don't get anything better, that's it."

"Marianne Kunz has departed," Herb Fink informed him. "In
tears, they say."

"But *why?*"

"Maestro Ponti has apparently not been attentive of late. Since the
arrival, in fact, of the Italian superstar Mme. Alberta Lisi-Mettler."

"And how do you know all this crap, Fink?"

" 'Cause I'm a reporter, Harry boy. Finding out crap like this is my
profession."

Which gave Harry pause, as Norman Rose liked to say.

For the first time in these sessions, there was a Desdemona in the
House: Miss Didi del Campo. Or rather, the new Countless Gimpel.

"Harry, darling!"

"Didi, I'd like you to meet my wife, Maggie . . . and our sons,
Heck . . . and Beachie. . . ."

"My God, Harry, they're so—big!"

She gave each a resounding kiss: their first kisses ever from a bona-
fide opera star.

"Harry's told me so much about you," Maggie said.

"He *has?* How embarrassing!"

"Salzburg," said Harry. "Tell us all about Salzburg. Didi's just come from Salzburg, haven't you, Didi?"

"Whenever you're ready, Maestro . . ."

It was a most impressive sight, even for old Harry Chapin. All members of the Melos-Doria *Otello* company were present or accounted for. Maestro Ponti and his orchestra of ninety-four individuals were poised and ready on the floor of the House. The remaining principals— Otello, Desdemona, Iago, Emilia, Cassio, Roderigo and Lodovico (Montano and the Herald having finished on Friday and departed over the weekend)—stood as arranged on the quadraphonic matrix of stage manager Gianfranco Bonisolli. The chorus of forty-eight men and thirty women, being the ladies and gentlemen of the Venetian Republic of the late fifteenth century, crowded together under the watchful eye of chorus master Luigi Mezzapelle. Fifteen brass players under the direction of assistant conductor Fernando Ricci tensely awaited their fanfares at music stands at the very rear of the stage. Studio manager (pro tem) Toby Beard and his stage crew made final adjustments to mikes, stands, risers and sound baffles. In the gallery sat the four Chapins, Hoyt Dell, Frankie Tree, a covey of reporters including Fink and Sachs and Sciascia, friends and admirers of the principals (mostly of Benno Toggi, who was completing his final day's work), Beppe and Paolo, the janitors and clean-up crew who had nothing to do until midnight but who like all Romans took deep personal pleasure from this music—the entire vast enterprise under the firm control of Mr. Norman Rose of New York City. Ah, yes, Leslie Deering, you are quite correct to express your concern. . . .

"Beginning, ladies and gentlemen," announced Maestro Ponti, "at Letter R . . ."

And ending, ladies and gentlemen, only God knows where . . .

"So what do you think" Harry said.

"In general, I'm pleased," Norman said. "In places it's really quite beautiful, wouldn't you agree?"

"Yes. Especially Didi."

"Very beautiful. She's got lots of cream left on top—I don't think Salzburg hurt her at all, except maybe for endurance and we'll know about that soon enough. Oh, and, Harry, she wants to take the optional high B at the end."

"Good for her."

"Yes. And for the meeting with Otello—you may wish to look

here—she handles the appoggiaturas with no trouble at all. Should sound very elegant and courtly. Also the high B-flats there . . . Going along very nicely until—ah, now, this is a problem for her . . . The low B-flats here . . . The descending line from E there right on down . . . You see?"

Didi's famous bad patch. The girl could go as high as you wanted— legacy of her soubrette days, before she tried to go *spinto*. But down there in the chest she had a couple of false tones—like bad notes on a horn, something built into the instrument, a point of false resonance, which all singers had somewhere.

But this was why Harry employed a masterful musician like Norman Rose. "You'll fix it in the editing," he said to Norman and Oscar Poole—and then got out of there before they started to throw things.

Harry wanted to wait to have dinner at eleven, following the second session; but Maggie said she and the boys couldn't last that long, and the ever popular Hoyt Dell volunteered to whisk them away at seven to still more Roman wonders, including supper in a grotto dating from Christ's time, where, naturally, the owner was one of Dell's closest friends.

Leaving Harry to fend for himself—which he did by ducking around the corner to the Quirinale to find a decent bottle of red, only to run into Frankie Tree.

"Oh, Harry, thank *God* you're alone."

"The others have gone to supper. Why?"

"Can we talk for a moment? Privately?"

"Of course. Where would you like to go? Would you like some dinner?"

"Maybe my room would be best. Give me five minutes, will you? And then come up?"

He could hardly believe his good fortune. Frankie had never looked more beautiful. The Roman humidity seemed to agree with her fair English complexion, and her gorgeous red hair had never seemed so full, so lush, so—erotic—falling about her shoulders, resting even upon her shapely bosom.

"Hello," he said stupidly. Immediately he kissed her mouth, which was moist and trying to speak.

"I don't think you'll want to do much kissing after you've read this."

She opened an envelope and passed to him its contents. Quirinale letterhead, handwritten. The writing was familiar to him—Marianne Kunz. He read:

Dearest Harry:

I was surprised last evening to find what a nice woman your Maggie is—tho' I guess "surprise" is the wrong word, as she and I seem to have the same taste in men, wouldn't you agree? When I write "surprise" I really mean vis-à-vis your current interest in the little English tramp Miss Tree, who, I guess you know, is fucking just about everybody in camp. I do not, my dearest Harry, understand how you can share your affection (if that's what it is) with both Margaret Chapin and Frankie Tree—and as a bonus, I guess! with yours truly!! For old-time's sake, dearest Harry—and I hope you think affectionately of your Marianne from time to time, as I have reason to think you did at the Beau Rivage—I strongly suggest that you reconsider your current infatuation (because we both know that's what it is, my dearest) with Miss Tree (what a silly name!) and give proper attention to what should be your first order of personal business, namely Margaret, your wife.

With greatest respect and much love,

Your Marianne

P.S. I just adore your boys—so polite!

P.P.S. I just adore you—and you've *never* been polite to your Marianne!

"Jesus Christ. Where did you get this?"

"Marianne gave it to Maury yesterday with some other letters when she was packing to leave. And then when you fired Maury—does everybody know about Maury, by the way, or is that a secret?—he gave me the letters and asked me to post them. And that's when I found this. It wasn't sealed, Harry, which is why I read it."

"I'm sorry you had to see it. She's a vicious—"

"Look at the envelope."

"My God."

It was addressed not to Harry, but to Mrs. Margaret Chapin.

"What will you do?"

"Destroy it, of course." He tore it into small pieces then and there, depositing them in the wastebasket under the desk.

"What if there are others?"

"There won't be. But I'll keep an eye on the mail. She was just upset, that's all. Because of Gian-Carlo. Apparently they had a quarrel."

"I know. Over the new Italian lady."

"Yes, Mrs. Lisi-Mettler. Marianne just wanted revenge, I suppose—on the whole world. We were lucky."

"I suppose so."

"Now—can't I get you some supper? Someplace private?"

"No. We'd better get downstairs. Before someone sees us."

Quite right. Before somebody else starts sending letters.

II

Tuesday. More of the same, but no Iago: Iago all done except for the forbidden overdubbing, which would be accomplished by Norman on Saturday, when everybody else had gone home. The sessions had been terribly hard on poor Toggi. The intelligence and will were still in evidence, but the instrument refused to obey: the descending chromatic scale in the "Brindisi," for example, was now beyond him. Still, the subtlety of his interpretation would appeal to many listeners: Harry Chapin, for one. It was such a tragedy that Toggi had not been asked to put the part down ten or fifteen years ago, when he was truly the best in the world—maybe the best of all time. Yet the Melos-Doria tapes would hint at this greatness, which was perhaps enough.

"Norman? Good morning. Say, I've been thinking about old Toggi. What about a party—or maybe a special dinner? Just to show our appreciation—"

"Then you haven't seen *Notizie di Roma?*"

"What? No. What do you mean?"

"Only a second-rate tabloid, according to Quinzi, but it's not calculated to help. An item in one of the gossip columns."

"What does it say?"

"Along the lines of 'What former Olympic track star and operatic great, recently released from prison, has been observed keeping close company'—the translation is vague at this point, Harry—'with some sweet young boys from the children's chorus currently recording at the Opera House?' "

"Jesus Christ."

"As though we don't have enough trouble—"

"Where is Toggi now?"

"Don't worry, Quinzi's with him."

"And what about Saturday? The overdubbing?"

"That's still on, as far as I know. Effective immediately, Beppe and Paolo will stay with Toggi around the clock. Look, the item's probably untrue, Harry—when would he have had time? But Quinzi says we can't afford to take chances—this is something not even Gimpel could fix."

"Where do you think the item came from? True or untrue?"

"Raffaele thinks we should have a talk, Harry, with the lady from Milan, Miss Sachs."

MAGGIE: Miss Tree seems a capable young person.

HARRY: Ummmmm.

MAGGIE: I don't suppose she's out of her teens.

HARRY: Twenty-one, I understand. They had a party.

MAGGIE: She's really very good with her camera. Did you see those pictures she took of Laframboise and Mr. Toggi?

HARRY: Ummmmm.

MAGGIE: Well, you don't seem terribly interested. Considering that she's a Melos-Doria employee. She's in publicity, did you say?

HARRY: Seems to be, yes. A recent hire, as I understand it.

MAGGIE: I don't know—at times you're so totally blasé about everything, Harry. I hope your attitude doesn't rub off on the boys.

HARRY: What? Sorry, I wasn't listening. . . .

". . . Norman? It's me, Harry. Say, I'm trying to reach Didi, but she's never in her suite—or else she doesn't answer the phone. You haven't seen her, by any chance?"

"Have you tried Laframboise's?"

"For Didi? Why would—"

Oh. It was inevitable, he supposed. "You don't mean, Norman—"

"Yes, I'm afraid so. . . ."

Thrilling stuff—the Act I love duet, which Harry loved above all other music. "Già nella notte densa s'estingue ogni clamor. . . ." "Now in the dark night every noise is stilled. . . ." Except the rarefied screaming of Ezekiel Laframboise.

"Time?" Norman asked at the end of the take.

"Eleven minutes, twenty-two seconds," reported Herb Fink, who had gratefully absorbed several duties of the departed Maury Wiseman. "Fabulous, no?"

Harry agreed. Almost erotic in feel, the clash of two colors, a blending of disparate timbres. Shut your eyes and you saw them with crystal clarity: the Moorish general and his delicate white lady.

But Ponti was not happy. "Ladies and gentlemen, bottom of page one-oh-two . . . Signor Laframboise, may I be permitted . . ."

"What's wrong?" Harry said to Norman. "How the hell are they ever going to improve on *that?*"

"Gian-Carlo's complaining about the 'E tu m'amavi.' It's marked *dolce* and there is no way, Harry, that this boy can attack that *dolce*. He's very fortunate to get it at all, even *fortissimo*."

But what did Ponti know of such limitations? For him, the human voice was merely another instrument. You pushed down on the key and out came the proper note, like a clarinet.

"Take 4 and rolling . . ."

The expensive two-inch tape flew off the reels, two and one-half feet each second. *Very* flat now, as Zeke grew more and more tired: Otello's last note in Act I, a high A-flat marked *pp*. Which nobody in the world could sing *pp*.

But Ponti wouldn't leave it alone: "This is already a tradition, Mr. Laframboise. Yes, as is well known, Verdi wrote to his conductor for the première and begged him to persuade Mr. Tamagno to sing 'something approximating what I have written.' And so may I beg you . . ."

"Kiss my big fat lips," Zeke said to Didi. They shared a music stand for the final dozen bars, according to Signor Bonisolli's master plan.

Didi obliged, to the loud amusement of the orchestra.

"She'll be kissing something else before he's through with her," said Herb Fink, who had rapidly gotten into the spirit of all this serious music-making.

"I do wish," said Norman Rose angrily, "that you would warn me when you intend to make your smart remarks—so that I will have an opportunity to close the com. Or are your comments intended for the artists also?"

He had not meant to go drinking with Herb Fink, but Herb had been persuasive—or Harry had been compliant. It was almost midnight when he got back to the suite.

"Hi, kiddo."

Maggie let him in, but pulled away from his sloppy kiss. "You're a little late, aren't you?"

"Just put down for posterity the most beautiful Love Duet you ever heard in your life. Sorry you weren't there. Oh, hell, you didn't miss much, really. How was your day? Hot enough for you? How are the boys? I was thinking, for dinner tomorrow, what about some real Roman pizza? The boys might get a kick—"

"The boys are fine. We had a lovely evening with Hoyt. They're down in their room packing."

"Packing? Hey, what's going on here?"

"Hoyt has suggested that we go on to Venice in the morning—

which I've always wanted to see—and perhaps Trieste. He thinks the boys will have more fun traveling than staying here in the city, in this heat. The boys don't find the recording sessions very interesting, as you know. But that's not what I want to talk to you about, Harry. I want to talk to you about this."

"What? What's that?"

"This is a lady's douche bag, Harry. I found it under the sink in the other bathroom. I was cleaning up after the boys had their baths, and I found it."

"So? Left by a previous guest, obviously."

"Yes. Obviously."

"Do you want to complain to the management? Or what?"

"I *am* complaining to the management, Harry."

"Hey, look, wonderful metaphor, but I don't see—"

"And that's just the first part, Harry. The second part is our maid. She speaks excellent English—are you aware of that?"

"I hadn't noticed, frankly. I try to speak Italian as much as I can in Italy. But what—"

"She said to me this evening, very clearly, did I think the other lady would be coming back? Or would it just be the boys and me from now on?"

"Well—I don't know what she could have meant by that. Of course, Mag, I've had all kinds of people trooping in and out of here— Norman, half the cast, the publicity people . . ."

"When I said what young lady, Harry, she was able to describe her very easily, very graphically. She said the lady with the beautiful red hair. Now, who do you suppose that could be? Have you any idea?"

The damned refrigerator had nothing in it but Dom Pérignon, which he didn't feel like opening at this time of night, and two cans of Italian beer. "Look," he said, opening one of the cans, "in the morning—"

"I'm going to go back to my packing, Harry. We're leaving tomorrow morning at nine. I'd appreciate it if you would find someplace else to stay tonight. I'm sure if you call around you'll be able to find another bed without difficulty. Because I don't want to share this bed with you again, now that I know you've been using it with that young girl. Poor Harry—our cable must have been such a bitter blow."

"Mag—"

"What are you going to do, Harry, when this is over? What are you going to do when you've eaten in all the fine restaurants and known all the famous singers and had all the pretty young girls?"

Her tears had begun to splash onto his good suede music case, staining the leather. He retrieved the case and then used the telephone in the other room.

"Norman? Hey, I'm sorry to bother you at this hour—but I wonder if you'd mind putting me up for the night? I'll explain later. . . ."

III

"I wish you'd seen it," Norman told him in the morning. "The way your man Dell stepped into the breach. Ponti was furious—no one had ever spoken to him the way Zeke did. But then Dell appeared out of nowhere, and the next thing we knew, Ponti was happy as a lamb."

"Yes, he's helpful," Harry said with his usual enthusiasm.

"Really, Harry, it's miraculous. Dell is simply *loved* by the artists. Always says the right thing at the right time, no job too menial for him, going for coffee, lighting people's cigarettes, amazing. And now—to have him holding Gian-Carlo's hand. Well, he's saved the day, at least temporarily. . . ."

Harry took a cab to the Hassler and found Dell in the lobby waiting for Maggie and the boys to come down.

"Hoyt—I can't tell you how much we appreciate the way you've jumped into the artist thing—since Maury's departure, especially. Zeke and Gian-Carlo and Didi—well, they just love you."

"Entirely my pleasure, I can assure you, Harry. Say, I hope I haven't stepped over the line in suggesting this little excursion with Mag and the twins. God, I love those boys. And, you know, they seem so unhappy in all this tub-thumpin' heat."

"On the contrary," Harry said, "you've done me a great favor. I'd love to go with you—haven't been to Venice myself in some years. Incidentally, while you're there, you might try to show them Desdemona's house—it's marked, as I remember, on one of the canals. All the *gondolieri* know it. When do you think you'll get back?"

"We kinda thought Sunday morning. If that's okay with you?"

"Yes, fine. Perhaps you and I could then have a chat—about business, actually. Melos-Doria business, I mean. Not that you'd find it very interesting—from where you sit . . ."

"Harry—from my heart, I tell you that nothing in the world would interest me more!"

Mmmm—ludicrous idea, really. How about Director, Artist Relations, at, say, $35,000 per annum? Millionaire Dell would get quite a laugh out of that.

No—*wrong.* Harry shuddered at the idea. Dell was great for hanging around superstars and picking up tabs, but he wasn't meant for slogging through the trenches like Chapin and Rose. Amateurs are different from you and me; yeah, amateurs love their art. You can't mix amateurs and pros: old Chapin axiom. Sure, it was nice having some charming guy telling you all the time how great you are, how important your "contribution" is—but he's an *amateur*, Chapin, can't you get that through your thick skull?

Director, Artist Relations. It was the kind of idea Harry usually had when he'd finished a great lunch and drunk his daily two bottles of red. An idea whose time would never come. . . .

It was to be Didi's night: opening of Act IV, Desdemona's scene with Emilia, followed by the "Willow Song" and "Ave Maria"—eighteen minutes of tape to be gotten in the allotted three hours, minus thirty minutes for union breaks. Contemplative art at its highest . . .

"And where's Didi?" Harry inquired innocently. On the monitor he saw Ponti's current interest, Mme. Alberta Lisi-Mettler, but he did not see Didi.

"Our Desdemona is tardy," Norman said with bitterness.

"Well, we mustn't be too hard on her," Harry said generously. "Salzburg . . ."

Ah, but here she was—ugly dark circles of weariness marring Miss Pretty Bright-Eyes.

"Maestro, if we may have a levels check . . ."

Orchestra sounding remarkably polished for a change—but, oh my, our Desdemona . . .

"What's *wrong* with her?" Harry demanded to know.

"I should think that was evident, Harry," growled old ill-tempered Norman.

Meaning? Meaning that she had spent two days or so in the bed of *il più gran tenore del mondo.*

"Do you want me to speak to her?" Harry said stupidly.

"Why don't you speak to *him?*" said Norman.

Maestro Ponti asked for another take.

". . . Rolling . . ."

Each new take sounded worse than the last.

"She's not supporting her tone," Norman groaned. "That's why she sounds so cloudy."

Oscar Poole had another idea. "You want my opinion? About the change since yesterday? I'd say it's her time of the month."

How absolutely perfect! That would explain *Didi's* incipient sore throat. Because, having her period, she wouldn't want to do it the regular way, which meant doing it the *other* way. Giuseppe Verdi would surely have understood. "Assuming you're right, Oscar . . ."

But Oscar provided diagnosis only: had no remedies in his kit.

"Norman?"

Norman had no ideas. Norman was pissed. Norman was the kind of old fogy who didn't like seeing his prima donna's basic good looks deteriorate just because she never got any sleep and let the tenor do unspeakable things to her and arrived late to sessions with a sore throat.

"I'm going out for a while," Harry said. "Got some things to do."

He didn't, but he wasn't a great watcher of human tragedy. He still had his headache from lunch, but he thought maybe a little dinner and some more red wine might fix that.

In the foyer he ran into Signor Pellegrini, the bassist, who was again to be found regularly in the House. The crippled Neapolitan hobbled from place to place on crutches, but seemed in good spirits; there was talk of "compensation" under Italian law, in that he had been injured in the pursuit of his professional career. Italy is, in many respects, a remarkable country.

He also ran into Charlotte Sachs.

"You're not leaving already, are you, Mr. Chapin?"

"I am, yes," Harry said. It suddenly occurred to him that he wanted this lady, a lady of such beautifully turned ankles. He had always had a weakness for the slim ones: slim tended to mean elegant, *n'est-ce pas?*

"Naughty, naughty," she said with her delightful smile. "Playing hookey—is that still the phrase?"

"I don't suppose you'd like to continue this conversation over a bottle of champagne?" he said. "Either here or perhaps at the Hassler, which I find somewhat more relaxing?"

"In other circumstances, I might," she replied. "But in view of Miss Tree's proprietary rights, I wouldn't dare. . . ."

6

Thursday. Would it *never* end?

He got out of bed at noon and drank a bottle of beer and called the control room, where he knew Norman and Oscar would be working on last night's tapes.

"We missed you," Norman said. "Things improved a bit after you left. The 'Ave Maria' is fairly rough in spots, but at least it's usable. . . . How are you feeling, Harry? Because we've got a problem with Mr. Laframboise. He refused to come to Ponti's piano rehearsal at eleven, and he says he's not going to the orchestral rehearsal either. Didi showed up on schedule, but when she found that Zeke wasn't there, she left, too. They're up sulking in their respective suites and neither one is accepting phone calls, according to the switchboard. At least, they won't talk to me and they won't talk to Ponti."

"Well, they'll talk to *me*," Harry snarled, "or we'll bury the fucking tapes in the ground and put an end to their fucking opera careers right now, this morning."

"Technically, I believe you'll find it's already afternoon, Harry— and only three hours until we're supposed to start recording again. . . ."

Harry tried Zeke's suite, but Zeke refused his call. "You tell Signor Laframboise that this is an *emergency*," he instructed the switchboard girl in Italian. Zeke still refused the call.

Harry got dressed, drinking a half-bottle of champagne in the process, and took a cab to the Quirinale. Herb Fink stopped him in the lobby. "Don't go up," Herb said. "He won't see you. I just came down from there. The only person he'll talk to is Frankie."

"Frankie? Who the hell is Frankie?"

"Come on, I'll buy you a drink. There's something you ought to know."

The Melos-Doria party was now well established with the Quirinale staff: Chapin and Fink were greeted in the lounge with happy salutations and instant bowls of nuts and olives. Harry drank Tío Pepe, Fink gin and tonic. "In confidence," Fink said, "they've had a fight."

"Who?"

"Zeke and Didi, who else? You remember what Norman was crying about last night—'sexual high jinks' spoiling everything? Well, apparently Zeke agrees. He's abstaining, and now Didi's pissed."

"You're making this up."

"God's truth. You know the troubles he's been having? The hoarseness? The way he favors his voice—talks so low you can hardly hear him? Well, now he thinks it's the fucking. Didi's problem yesterday gave him the idea, I guess. So after the session, when they got back to his place, he said 'Nothin' doin'' and the lady went crazy. She's moved back to her suite and he's locked up in his."

"Ponti's right—opera singers are nothing but delinquent children."

"Maybe it's something his old black mammy taught him," Fink went on. "Can't knock off those A's if your *cojones* are squeezed dry. Yeah, sounds ridiculous, but that's what this boy believes."

"Does he know," Harry bristled, "that some of the big boys have intercourse *during* a performance? Who was the Met tenor—Chilean, I think—who used to knock off two or three of the chorus ladies during intermissions? Does Zeke know about *that?*"

Fink put down his glass in apparent surprise. "Why, Zeke Laframboise doesn't know about *anything*, Harry—I thought you understood."

Harry went straight upstairs and pounded on Zeke's door. Eventually the door opened—revealing Frankie Tree.

"Ezekiel's not feeling well, Harry. He's in the bedroom, resting."

"He's going to feel a great deal worse when he hears what I have to say."

"Really, Harry—"

"Leave us now. I want to talk to him privately."

"Harry—"

"Do this. Go down the hall to Didi's suite and tell her I want her over here, dressed and ready to work, in exactly ten minutes. And no excuses."

"What if she refuses?"

"Tell her if she's not over here in ten minutes, she can expect a call from Count Stanislaus Gimpel."

"Zeke? It's me, Harry."

The bedroom was dark and stifling. The black man wallowed in sweat atop one of the beds. He was naked. Had little Frankie seen him in this condition? Harry shuddered. Not even Signor Ponti's famous instrument was larger than *that*. No wonder Mme. del Campo bemoaned its loss—assuming that Fink's story was accurate. Harry said: "Shouldn't you be down in the Opera House strangling Desdemona?"

"I ain't in the mood for jokes, brother Harry." The black man's eyes remained closed as he spoke.

"That's good, because neither am I. What seems to be the problem?"

"I don't feel good."

"I don't either. I've got a hangover. What hurts?"

"Every fucking thing. This heat . . ."

"Awful, isn't it? But then this is Roman summer."

"A man my size . . . Think I must be dehydrated or something. Got to find some salt tablets."

"We should have brought along some Gatorade, you're suggesting? Just like the Eagles?"

The big man grunted, gasped for breath, flopped about in misery.

Harry sympathized. These heavyweights tended to fade in the fourth quarter; just *breathing* took a lot out of them. "I understand you've had a disagreement with our Desdemona."

"*Shiiiiit.* That cunt . . ."

"And the usual difficulties with Maestro Ponti?"

"That turkey . . ."

"So—you're unhappy with venue, leading lady and conductor. Anything else, long as I'm here?"

"Got a sore throat, too. Think I'm getting a cold. I don't feel good."

"Yes, you said that."

The black man opened his eyes, squinted up at Harry. "Shit, man, it's not the way I thought it was going to be. None of it."

Again Harry sympathized. For Zeke it must have been reminiscent of the Met auditions—the low point in his professional career—when he'd expected to blow away all competition but instead choked up in front of the strange judges and sounded just like anybody else. Now he had come to Rome expecting to be awarded the victor's laurel without a fight, only to discover that it wasn't his night, wasn't his town, wasn't even his game. A *crise de nerfs*—wasn't that Ponti's expression?

"Well, here's where Dr. Chapin comes in," Harry said.

"Yeah?"

"Yes. I've got remedies in my bag for all such ailments. First—get some clothes on. Didi's on her way over."

The black man jumped to his feet in alarm. Rolls of fat bounced and jiggled around his midsection. "No *way*, man. No *way* I'm having that cunt in here again."

"Oh, but I'm afraid you must. More to the point, Zeke, resign yourself to the fact that we've got two more sessions—another six hours—in which you and the lady are going to make beautiful music together."

"Man, you are *crazy*. There's no way—"

"Zeke—now listen to me. We've got only two sessions to go. We're *very* close to achieving our goal. In your parlance, let's see—it's third down and five yards to go for a touchdown with ten minutes on the clock. There's no reason for us not to score."

"Bullshit. You're not talkin' to some *kid*, brother—"

"We shall see. Here—put on your shorts."

With further groans, the black man began to dress.

"On personal grounds, I must tell you, Zeke, that I'm profoundly sorry you found it necessary to become involved with Countess Gimpel. It's never smart—I tell you this from my own experience—to dip your pen in company ink."

"That's *private*, brother. Sure ain't no business of yours."

"On the contrary—when your personal affairs threaten the success of a very costly Melos-Doria enterprise, then they become very much my business. Ordinarily, I wouldn't care if you were fucking the whole ladies' chorus—remind me to tell you a story sometime. But now that you're letting your relationship with Didi keep you from 'takin' care of business'—excuse the street talk, won't you?—then I *must* step in. For your good as well as mine." Harry ignored Zeke's muttered obscenities. "Just out of curiosity—what's the trouble between you two?"

"Aw, man—"

"No, really. As your friend I care. Perhaps I can help. To put it another way—just how could you be so stupid as to involve yourself with Didi del Campo in the middle of the most difficult challenge of your entire professional life?"

"Look, brother—"

"Or didn't you know Didi was into black?"

For an instant Harry had the nauseous feeling that Zeke meant to hit him.

But then the black man smiled weakly. "Shit, Harry—where'd you find this cunt, anyhow?"

"Long story. No time now to take you through that saga. Point is, what were you thinking about—to get mixed up with a girl like Didi?"

"Shit, man—I thought she was for *real*, that's all. I messed up."

"Meaning?"

"Meaning—all she cares about is fuckin' and makin' lots of bread and havin' people tell her how good-lookin' she is."

"She can *sing*, Zeke. That's all that matters right now, isn't it?"

The black man shook his head sadly. "Zeke messed up," he repeated.

"Sure," Harry went on, "she's a superficial, egotistical, vain, sexy female. But why let that affect your work? Who *cares* about Desdemona? Isn't it Otello we've come to hear? . . . Wait a minute. You haven't—fallen in *love* with her? . . . Oh, hell, Zeke—I had no idea . . ."

Frankie arrived moments later with a very angry Didi del Campo. Harry left Zeke to finish dressing, closing the bedroom door.

"Harry, darling, what do you *mean*—"

"Just a second, please, Didi. Frankie, do me a great favor, will you? Go around to the Opera House and inform Maestro Ponti that Otello and Desdemona will be joining him for the remainder of the rehearsal in approximately—oh, make it two-thirty."

Frankie obviously didn't want to miss the fireworks. "If I may have a *word* with you, Harry—"

"Not now. See that Maestro Ponti gets my message without delay, won't you?"

Near tears, Frankie departed.

Harry led Didi into the sitting room. "Make yourself comfortable," he said. "Zeke will be out in a minute."

"Hey, look, Buster—"

"No, *you* look, Mme. del Campo—or should I say Countess?"

"Shit, Harry—"

"That's what Zeke says all the time—shit this, shit that, shit Harry. Sounds as though you've been hanging around our star tenor, doesn't it?"

"Well, if you're going to be like *this*—"

"*Sit down*. We're going to have a little talk, you and I. As you have every reason to know, my love, I think of myself as quite liberal in the fucking-around department. I also think of myself as your greatest living admirer—on personal, professional or any other grounds that may appeal to you. But now—I'm going to be your Dutch uncle, yours and Zeke's. Which means I'm going to speak bluntly."

"My God, Harry—"

"So let's begin, shall we? You've had a lovers' quarrel—is that right?"

"*Lovers!* Really, Harry, you can be so old-fashioned!"

"Old-fashioned if you like. But that doesn't answer my question. What seems to be the problem between you and Zeke?"

"I've been having some fun. What's wrong with that? *We* had fun, didn't we? On *L'Arlésienne?*"

"The point is—Zeke's in love with you, isn't he?"

"What do you think?"

"I think we—men—tend to fall in love with you, yes. Given any sort of encouragement . . ."

"You *are* sweet."

"And you *did* encourage him, didn't you?"

"Jiminy! Why so *gloomy*? I've just been having *fun* with him, Harry—the big black baby. He's like you—takes everything so seriously! My God, I'm a married woman—*everybody* knows that."

"So you're saying—"

"I'm saying I like a good fuck. That's all there was to it. You know Stash—at his age, well, *he* doesn't mind if I dig up a little extracurricular action. Why should you?"

"I mind, dear Didi, because I'm in charge of your soul, if you like—your artistic soul. And I can't tolerate anything which threatens—"

"Oh, shit, Harry—"

"No, hear me out, please. My entire interest here in Rome—as far as you're concerned—is Desdemona. I don't care about Didi del Campo, the vamp of the Seventies, really I don't. I love Desdemona and I will not see her defiled."

"Christ, Harry, you sure have lost your sense of humor. Really, you're no fun at all anymore."

Zeke emerged from the bedroom. He wore his khaki walking shorts and a sweat-drenched T-shirt and remained barefoot. His Afro sparkled with drops of perspiration. "You *cunt*," he said. "I been listenin'—"

"Zeke, now *wait* a minute."

"Fucking nigger," Didi replied.

"Cocksucker."

"Spade asshole!"

"Look, you two—"

Didi grabbed up a pitcher of ice water and hurled it at the black man.

Zeke came straight at her.

"Didi!" Harry shouted, stepping between them.

The massive black forearm struck Harry in the chest, sending him crashing to the floor. One corner of the coffee table caught him in the mouth, splitting his upper lip. His teeth remained intact, as far as he could tell.

"Now look what you've done, you motherfucker!" Didi screamed.

They helped him into the bathroom. The blood on his shirt reminded Harry of Hoyt Dell in Paris. "I'm all right," he kept saying. His heart pounded and he was covered in sweat, his and Zeke's.

Zeke was vociferously repentant. "Man, I'm *sorry*—"

"Forget it. Forget it. I'm all right. . . ."

His upper arm was numb; intense pain enveloped his shoulder. He rubbed the injured joint, swinging his arm in a great arc to make sure it still functioned. If Zeke's punch had reached Didi, he estimated, she would now be en route to the hospital and Desdemona's death would remain unrecorded—except by the local authorities.

"Now *sit down*," he commanded when he could, "and don't let me hear a word out of either of you until I give permission."

He stood, working the damaged arm at regular intervals; they sat.

"Frankly, I've never been so disgusted in all my life . . . so *ashamed* of two would-be *adults*. . . . Look at me—*trembling* with rage. . . . I'd like to tell you what I think of you. But then we really would be finished here, and that's not my purpose. That's not *our* purpose, *is* it?

"Okay, so listen to what I'm telling you. I'm only going to say this once. Afterwards, we're not going to have any discussion either.

"Trying to be objective—you're two marvelously gifted artists—no, don't say a *word*, Didi. But, being blessed as you are, you have a choice to make. Either you can go on acting like spoiled brats or you can accept the responsibility that goes with talent.

"Signor Ponti's rehearsal is still in progress. I suggest that you go down there now and prepare for tonight—prepare to make Desdemona's death the thrilling achievement it can be in the hands of first-rate artists. Unless, of course, you don't think you *are* first-rate artists—in which case you can stay right here and kick the shit out of each other, for all I care. . . .

"Now, if you'll excuse me, I'd like to go back to my hotel and put some ice on this lip."

Otello enters by a secret door, places a scimitar on the table, pauses before the torch undecided whether or not to extinguish it. He looks at Desdemona. He extinguishes the torch. The stage is now illuminated only by the candle on the priedieu. Otello, moved by sudden rage, advances toward the bed, but then stops. He contemplates the sleeping Desdemona at length. He kisses her three times. At the last kiss Desdemona awakes.

". . . The F-G passage," Norman was saying to no one in particular, "is almost *impossible* for him—can't Gian-Carlo *hear* that? There is simply no point in repeating and repeating and repeating . . . Oh, hello, Harry—say, what happened to your mouth?"

Penultimate session: the Act IV murder scene with Otello, Desdemona and Emilia. The taping had begun well enough, Herb Fink reported, but Ponti soon had them into retakes and the scene quickly fell to pieces. Still, one had to be thankful, Norman guessed: at least the principals had shown up.

Harry listened intently. Gian-Carlo Ponti to the contrary, it was good. Zeke's shouting had lots of terror to it, lots of menace. For her part, Didi sounded scared: had no trouble imagining, perhaps, Otello's fat black fingers around her pretty white neck.

But immediately after each take Didi was her fun-loving self again, laughing and joking with her new buddy, Mme. Alberta Lisi-Mettler, she of the boom-boom knockers. Those two would be in bed soon enough, if Harry knew anything about Didi—Didi "swinging both ways" and not being above such tricks even with Maestro Ponti's current inamorata.

After the third complete take, Harry relaxed, knowing that they had enough in the can for protection. Ponti began again with the forty-bar orchestral opening, which he'd already done five times, and which was now Harry's signal to cut out.

First he stopped downstairs to see Zeke and Didi. Zeke continued in apologetic mode, seeking sympathy for himself by complaining again of his sore throat; Harry was not touched. Didi was more expansive, kissing his injured lip tenderly and begging, "Oh, you *will* forgive your Didi, won't you, darling? Got the rag on, which always makes me bitchy . . ."

Harry relented. "You sound marvelous tonight—keep it up, okay? Also, Mr. Laframboise seems to have fallen under your spell again. How did you manage that?"

"Easy. I told him if he didn't sing good, the next chance I had I'd bite off his pecker."

I I

"Ah, good morning, Norman. How do you think it went? How are the tapes?"

"Fine, Harry—excellent in spots. Ponti was most gratified. You're to be contratulated, as usual, for working the miracle."

"Oh?"

"Bringing those two—*animals*—back to their senses, if only for the moment. But now, Harry, I'm afraid we have another problem—a very servious problem."

"*Really*, Norman? How unusual." Last day of the sessions: perforce, the problems must now end, *c'est entendu?* "What now, old man?"

"It's Zeke. I've just spoken to Frankie. He's coughed up a bit of blood, and he's asked us to send for a doctor."

"My God. Well, let's get him one."

"I have. The doctor's up there now. I thought you'd want to know."

"I'll meet you in Zeke's suite in thirty minutes."

The doctor, who had been recommended by Quinzi, was a dark, beautifully dressed Milanese named Du Plessix—like Signor Laframboise, of French extraction—who had taken his M.D. degree at Johns Hopkins.

"I would recommend hospitalization," Dr. du Plessix said out of Zeke's hearing. "For complete examination and treatment."

Harry explained the urgent necessity—or, at least, desirability—of having Signor Laframboise available for just one more session: three hours, beginning at 4:00 P.M.

Dr. du Plessix was dubious. "Perhaps if I were to describe Signor Laframboise's condition in greater detail . . ."

The vocal cords were swollen. One of the cords was hemorrhaging —yes, *bleeding*—hence the occasional spots of blood when the tenor coughed. Signor Laframboise's illness was not psychosomatic, as Harry had diagnosed. The tenor's difficulties did not stem from dislike of Maestro Ponti, or even from frequency of sex with Mme. del Campo, but from overuse—or perhaps improper use—of his vocal cords. No doubt he had been insufficiently relaxed at the start of the sessions, and now, after two weeks of controlled shouting, his instrument was worn, frazzled and in danger of collapse.

Cortisone. Harry Chapin had been at this business long enough to know all the tricks. "Perhaps a shot of cortisone, Dr. du Plessix? Just enough to carry him through this evening? Not enough, naturally, to cause any further damage . . ."

The good doctor was familiar with this therapy; had seen it used in America. Shoot Zeke with the same drug used on halfbacks with bad knees; ease the pain until after the Big Game. "Such treatment is possible. Assuming that our patient would be willing . . ."

Harry spoke privately to Zeke, a pathetic figure in tentlike terry-cloth bathrobe. "Of course, you haven't got that much to do tonight—most of the burden is Didi's. And if it hurts—causes you any discomfort—why then, we'll stop."

Eventually, the black man agreed. "You're my man. You tell me I gotta do it . . . I do it. . . ."

"This afternoon, then, Doctor? What time would be convenient? The session begins at four. . . ."

"Harry? I want to talk to you."

Except for the modest English accent, it might have been Maggie. Dear little Frankie, and never looking more beautiful. "Sure. Come on—I'll buy lunch."

"No, I've got to get back upstairs. I want to talk about these shots you think Ezekiel should have."

"What about them?"

"I'm not certain Zeke should do it."

"*You're* not certain?"

She had been talking to Herb Fink, who seemed to know everything. According to Dr. Fink, the cortisone was a bad idea—liable to ruin Zeke's voice forever.

"Frankie, really, I haven't got time right now to explain the whole science of the thing. But the doctor, you'll be glad to know, was trained in America—and besides, what the hell have *you* got to do with Ezekiel Laframboise's vocal cords?"

"Well, you might as well know, Harry," she said with maternal conviction. "I'm staying with Ezekiel now. In his suite . . ."

"Would you like a menu, sir? Or may I bring you another half-bottle . . . ?"

"Just the wine," he said. "I'm not hungry."

He was glad to have the table to himself. How *stupid* of him. Poor *innocent* little Frankie. Her appetite was far greater than he had imagined. She had had enough of Harry Chapin—couldn't blame her for that—but this didn't mean she had sworn off the whole human race. The poor little English *bitch*, all white innocence except where it counted. So grateful for the tutelage of her nice Harry Chapin, for the lessons of love he'd been able to teach her, but mostly for the Nikon, her key to higher learning. Now, baccalaureate in hand, she was ready to

matriculate to bigger stuff—the *biggest* stuff—dying, in fact, to study
the great black cock of Ezekiel Woodrow Wilson Laframboise.

Little Frankie Tree, all one hundred pounds of her, set to tangle
with a three-hundred-pound linebacker of the Philadelphia Eagles . . .
That slim white back, the downlike pink patch between milky-white
thighs, the girlish breasts with their delicate pink crowns, the slender
neck, the finely molded jaw and cheekbones and forehead, the great pile
of burnt-auburn hair—such total beauty, so fragile and childlike, still all
virginal innocence despite brief encounters with the Harry Chapins of
this world, such absolute visual splendor now to be subjected to . . .
My God. My God. She would come away from their first union dripping *blood*: did she have any idea of *that*? She would come away thinking that Harry Chapin and the earlier English lads had been playing an
entirely different game. Now, for the first time—virgin—she would
know what it was to be *fucked*. . . .

". . . Harry? Harry? Are you all right?"

"Hi, Norman. Sorry—I was . . ."

"You feeling okay? You look a little pale."

"Fine, sure. Nerves, you know. The thing with Zeke. Just having a
drink. Join me? Little wine?"

"I'd better not, Harry. The doctor's finished now—gave Zeke the
shot. So I guess there's not much to worry about. Hard on the nerves,
this business."

"Oh, yes, nerves the whole story in this line of work. Come on—
one drink isn't going to kill you. Christ, one session left. Eleven down
and only the one to go. Can't fail now, Norman."

"Well—maybe I will. No disgrace, is there, in needing a drink now
and again?"

Herb Fink, who had kept the clock since Maury's departure, was
accorded the honor of calling takes during the final session:

"Act III, Section Two, Take 1 . . ."

The principal work of the evening was the handkerchief scene
between Desdemona and Otello—nine minutes, forty seconds on
average—to be followed by the lovely little Act III ballet and, if Signor
Laframboise felt up to it, one last attempt at the "Esultate."

The first hour went well. Three full takes of the handkerchief scene
were made, providing sufficient usable material, Norman thought, for
final editing. Then—in Fink's Eighth Avenue argot—"diamonds turned
to shit." Following the break, Ponti insisted that they repeat the great
scene for Otello, "Dio! mi potevi scagliar," which follows directly on
from the handkerchief scene—Ponti indulging his love of chronology—
and in the midst of the first runthrough Zeke stopped singing and

collapsed heavily to the stage. The blood he swallowed had produced nausea. " 'Ecco il Leone!' " Fink wisecracked, which nobody in the booth thought funny, because the Moor was done for the evening.

Five minutes into the second hour—during rehearsal of the ballet—thunder was heard in the distance. The deep rumble grew in amplitude and proximity, and a short time later a heavy summer rain began to beat down upon the roof. Gian-Carlo continued to rehearse, but there was no possibility of recording; the noise was immense.

And so the sessions ended. No great moment of victory: only the unpredictable evaporation of time, vocal resources and, ultimately, weather.

"No ballet, just as Ponti wanted—and we never did get a proper 'Esultate,' " Norman complained. He looked as though he were going to cry.

"A failure of cortisone, I like to think," Harry said. The "Esultate" —thirteen lousy bars, a deadly octave at the top part of the tenor's range—which Zeke simply couldn't manage. Too bad, my boy: your account is drained, capital and interest, and you have no reserves. Very poor fiscal policy, my lad—bankrupt at the age of twenty-nine.

In his most poetic Italian, Norman Rose formally closed the sessions. There was a certain amount of kissing, none of it very enthusiastic. As was the custom at such events, champagne was provided for the entire company—five cases, which Harry hoped would be enough in view of the anticipated budget overage. Toasts were drunk—including one to Dr. du Plessix—and then Harry was asked to make a speech:

". . . An occasion both happy and sad . . . The completion of a momentous and historic work of art . . . Now the reluctant parting of artistic collaborators who must wend their weary ways to other halls, other concert stages around the globe . . . Special thanks to our Maestro, Gian-Carlo Ponti, for his tireless devotion to high artistic purpose . . . Our beloved prima donna, Miss Didi del Campo . . . The premier Iago of our era, the incomparable Benno Toggi . . . And of course our marvelous young hero, Mr. Laframboise, who, despite vocal difficulties, has contributed so brilliantly to our undertaking . . . So until we meet again in the name of Art—Godspeed and *bon voyage* . . ."

There wasn't a dry eye in the house except maybe Frankie's—Miss Tree being anxious to get upstairs in the Quirinale and begin life as the bride of Frankenstein.

Dinner would be served at George's beginning at 10:00 P.M. and running into the wee hours; all principals and the working party were invited. Especially Miss Charlotte Sachs, who looked so good to him now—yes, the most excellent target of opportunity seen in their thirteen working days in Italy. Harry's goal for the evening would be to remain sober enough for sophisticated seduction or, depending on the lady's mood, drunk enough for rape.

"Oh, Harry—I meant to give you this before your very touching speech," said Norman. "A cable of congratulations, I believe, from Mr. Deering."

It was from Deering all right:

MOST DISTURBED CIRCUMSTANCES MR WISEMANS DISMISSAL
FROM ROME STOP KINDLY FORWARD FULL REPORT YOUR EARLIEST
CONVENIENCE STOP REGARDS

DEERING

"What's it say, Harry?"

"Oh, usual congratulations on a job well done. Same old bullshit, to tell the truth . . ."

And he left it right there in one of the boxes of spoiled tape; just another artistic mistake, like all the rest.

III

He was not well when he awoke. The way he felt told him that the party had been a great success. Charlotte Sachs confirmed this impression when she phoned at 11:00 A.M. "After you were so kind as to invite me to your private party, I'm afraid I was just awful."

"I don't remember anything of the kind," he said, trying to remember.

"Oh, but you *must*. I was horrid. I just wasn't in the mood. Will you ever forgive me?"

She was apparently apologizing for not ending up in his bed. "Consider yourself forgiven," he said magnanimously.

"Is our date still on, then?"

"Our date?"

"Oh, my—you *have* forgotten. Our lunch together? The Vatican?"

"Of course I haven't forgotten. I just hadn't thought of it as—a 'date.' Why don't we say one o'clock at the Flora . . .?"

He called for the maid and insisted that she clean up the suite while he shaved. He watched with interest as she put new linen on the bed. The bed was comfortable for a European hotel, and very large. Even with a hippopotamus like Chapin in the middle, there would be plenty of room for Miss Sachs. The maid was the same one who had asked Maggie whether or not the young girl with the beautiful red hair would be returning. No, that lady is never coming back. A new lady—modish slim brunette of a more sensible generation—will be taking her place. But only for the one night, probably. Maggie and the boys and Dell would be returning tomorrow afternoon, and then—well, he didn't know what the sleeping arrangements would be, starting tomorrow. When the maid finished, Harry gave her a thousand-lire note as a tip for doing his suite out of sequence—and to show her there were no hard feelings.

He had chosen the Flora at the top of via Veneto because the food was excellent and nobody he knew was likely to go there on a Saturday afternoon in early September. He walked over from the Hassler, arriving puffing and sweaty. His handkerchief was soaked through from frequent moppings of face and neck along the way, and he dropped the useless rag into a trash receptacle so she wouldn't notice a soggy bulge in his pocket.

She was waiting for him in the lobby. At first he hardly recognized her. She looked prettier, softer, more girlish than he remembered. She wore a sweater and skirt in contrasting shades of brown, with a beautiful silk scarf tied around her neck, and she'd done something with her hair—long and flowing now instead of pulled tightly back.

"Dear girl," he said. He kissed her before she could say anything. "A scarf—on a day like this?"

"For St. Peter's. I didn't bring a hat. Don't say another word until I apologize."

"Don't be silly."

"No, I mean it, Harry. For that *awful* remark about you and—Miss Tree."

"Idiot. Did you *really* think that a girl like that—"

"Let's not talk about her."

"My sentiments exactly. Your husband—was he an imbecile?"

"My husband—"

"To have let you get away?"

"You *are* a charming man."

"Hungry?"

"Famished."

"Then what are we waiting for?"

They swept into the dining room. Unquestionably, he was more effective with these ladies of a certain age—Lady A in London, Marianne, even Didi—and now this wonderful Charlie. Why had he wasted his time with all those young ones, the secretaries? "Everybody's staring at us. Have you noticed?"

"But why? Is something unbuttoned?"

"Not yet," he said without cracking a smile. Mastroianni could not have delivered the line with greater wit.

"No, really—tell me."

"Because you're so beautiful. And because I'm obviously so pleased with myself."

She was very much the mature lover he would soon ask her to be. As they were being seated, she quietly reversed their positions so that—being left-handed as she was—they could hold hands under the table while eating. His admiration of her—and pleasure with himself— grew moment by moment. On such an occasion there was no reason to stint on food, so he got them all his favorites—anchovies and pimientos to begin, *fettuccine,* a crisp green salad and, as the main course, *osso buco.* And the wines: a Verdicchio, cool and sparkling, followed by a Barolo, deep ruby red and calculated to fire the blood.

". . . And poor Mr. Rose, who has worked so hard?" Like a good reporter, she never ceased to probe.

"If everything has gone according to plan, Mr. Norman Rose is right this minute—and I tell you this strictly off the record, my lady, 'deep background' as you journalists like to say, indulging in that forbidden pleasure known as overdubbing. That is, having recorded all of the orchestra's part during the regular sessions, Mr. Rose has now gone to a secret studio somewhere the other side of the Tiber, in the company of our Moor's Ancient—that is, our ancient Iago, Signor Benno Toggi—and the two gentlemen will now re-record bits of Mr. Toggi's part—with Mr. Toggi wearing earphones through which they pipe the orchestral backing already recorded—and later Mr. Rose will synthesize the various takes to make one complete audio performance which will sound, we hope, as though Mr. Toggi had been able to make the proper noises at the proper time. Am I making myself clear? Probably not. And later on, back in the States, Mr. Rose will do the same with Mr. Laframboise, obtaining sooner or later the elusive 'Esultate' with its umpteen A-flats. . . . Hey, but that's all crap." Typical Chapin transition. "It's raining again. If you'd rather save the Vatican for another day, we could simply go back to the Hassler and spend the rest of the afternoon . . . because, as I think you know . . . I want you very much. . . ."

"And you shall have me," she said gaily. "But why can't we do both? The sun's bound to come out and—I know you won't believe this —I've *never* been to St. Peter's."

Whereas she'd spent countless afternoons in gentlemen's hotel rooms; yes, he knew. . . .

*   *   *

The taxi let them out a million paces or so across Bernini's incredible Piazza San Pietro—this at Charlie's request because she wished to take a picture of the Basilica. From her purse she produced a Kodak Instamatic, the very model recently bought for the twins by their doting grandmother. He was momentarily disoriented: these females with male names and cameras always at the ready.

That done, they marched across the square and up the marble steps. She took his photo three times, which he detested. He tried valiantly to pull in his stomach, but in the end failed. He wished now that he had not eaten and drunk so much. Of the two bottles, he had probably had a bottle and a half. Like so many females, she had a birdlike appetite. Probably in bed, too—but there was no point in worrying.

"Hurry up, slowpoke!" she cried.

He hadn't heard that expression in years. She seemed to grow younger before his eyes, as he grew older. Every time he caught up to her, she ran ahead again, leaving him to huff and puff his way through the clusters of tourists fresh from their buses. He wanted to go right to the Sistine Chapel, where they could pause and crane their necks upward and meditate for an hour or so. But the sun had come out and she wanted to go immediately to the top of St. Peter's for the view.

There was an elevator—thank God—which took them to the roof of the Basilica. He found the view breathtaking, but it proved insufficient to Charlie's needs. "Come on," she cried again. "There are steps to the cupola. . . ."

He thought of staying behind—letting her go on ahead to get her pictures while he enjoyed the cooling breeze. But she seemed to be calling his manhood into question, and he would not permit her to think of him as her senior, a middle-aged man.

He had bought a guidebook and now pretended to be absorbed by it:

> . . . The greatest church of Christendom both in the moral and architectural fields, it exceeds the dimensions of every other Christian church and its architecture sums up the experience of Renaissance and Baroque. . . . Through a spiral corridor we reach the roof of the Basilica, from which it is possible to reach the drum of the Cupola (53 meters high) and then the second terrace, where we enter the "panoramic loggia" offering a magnificent vista over the city. The last ascent leads to the copper globe, which can hold sixteen persons. . . .

"It says here, Charlie—"
But before he could protest, she had entered the staircase. By the

time he resigned himself to this torture, a Dutch family had gotten into the staircase ahead of him, and Charlie was lost from sight.

The steps were incredibly narrow, permitting only one person at a time to pass in either direction. Unfortunately, an Oriental family came immediately after him, including two young boys who thought nothing of the steepness of the ascent.

With each turn the passageway grew narrower. The handrail, smoothed by centuries of tourists, was worn and slippery and eventually gave way to a rope with which the pilgrim was expected to pull himself along—leaning ever more toward the center as Michelangelo's dome curved inward toward the horizontal.

At the halfway point he felt panic. The sound of his breath pounded against his eardrums; tears of sweat cascaded from his brow and nose and splashed against flushed cheeks. He forced himself to take ever deeper breaths, expanding and contracting his chest with conscious effort until the pain made him halt, stumble, rest against the cool stones of the dome.

The light faded as the slits in the outside walls diminished, and he found it increasingly difficult to make room for travelers coming at him from above. He thought now of turning back, but suddenly the path ahead parted and he found himself in a single file moving only upward. The Japanese boys (he decided they were) nipped at his heels, goading him onward. Sweat soaked his body, dripped from the ends of his matted hair.

When he could go no farther he stopped abruptly and motioned for the Japanese boys to pass. They did, laughing and springing quickly ahead, out of sight. He began again, but soon the Japanese parents asked to pass, and he gladly flattened himself against the sharply curving wall: they stepped on his feet, but he cared nothing for their apologies. The top was surely near—the worn stone steps had become steeper and narrower, and the rope had begun to burn his hands. Another family closed on him, and he tried desperately to pick up his pace. The drumming in his ears grew louder; he had to push down on his thighs with all the strength left in his arms to heave his bulk from one step to the next.

He thought of Charlotte Sachs, who had run ahead like a young deer, but she weighed only half as much as he did. He thought of the *osso buco* and the Verdicchio and the Barolo and of being sick in a public place—"it exceeds the dimensions of every other Christian church"—just another gluttonous American with too much alcohol in him, the sweat coming through his suit coat, through the seat of his pants.

He could not go on. He would turn around, and others would have to move aside or back down for him; he would feign illness. . . . But then he saw a wedge of light just ahead and knew it must be the landing, the "panoramic loggia." He continued to fall upward toward the light, skinning his shins on the last of the stone steps and, overcome by sudden vertigo, stumbled forward, out the doorway.

Blinded by the sunlight, he found himself on his knees, unable to rise. An iron band encircled his chest. He extended his arms upward; a wall of white seemed to engulf him. "Oh my God . . . Can you help me . . . ?"

"Monsieur? Je ne comprends pas—"

Regrettably—as Dr. du Plessix subsequently determined—the first to reach him were four young Ursuline novices of the Order of St. Agatha—Flemings from Bruges, giddy teenage girls who had run ahead of their Mother Superior—who, upon seeing the gentleman thus fallen to his knees, assumed that he had witnessed a vision; and, recognizing his anguished cry to God, so fell to *their* knees and offered prayers of gratitude to the Holy Father for permitting them to be present at this modern-day miracle in the greatest church of Christendom.

Instead of prayers—as he later remarked in the ironic fashion of the Milanese—Dr. du Plessix would have preferred immediate and vigorous mouth-to-mouth resuscitation.

Act Five

FLINTRIDGE/BURBANK:
December

Appearance should never attain reality,
And if nature conquers, then must art retire.

Schiller

1

Harry Chapin, ninety-seven days since his cardiac event, sixty-one days after his forty-fifth birthday and twenty-two days before expiration of his employment contract with Leisure Time Industries, Inc., awoke to the usual stomach pangs: pangs brought on by still-unaccustomed emptiness, stomach juices dripping down bare stomach walls, walls that saw only occasional bits of broiled fish or chicken, a few leafy vegetables for roughage, never a drop of Tío Pepe or Moët et Chandon or Valpolicella or real coffee or any of the other stimulants and/or depressants that formerly had sustained him in good times and bad.

7:00 A.M. Flintridge time, a dull rainy Friday, the 9th of December. Maggie lay beside him on her back, snoring softly. Harry lay on his back, too, daydreaming in self-conscious contentment and enjoying the soft sprinkle, almost a fog, which barely floated leaves in the gutters and put the garden into mellow soft focus. L.A. has the worst weather in the world, he reflected, typically blah and smog-ravaged, but rain is best: rain keeps people off the streets and gives the place a feeling of privacy that it sorely needs.

Ah, what have we here? Member at least partially erect—*recherche du temps perdu*, perhaps—quite remarkable considering that its master has not indulged its whims in what, three months now? Its last sortie had been a rather joyless early-morning coupling with Miss Frankie Tree after her tearful break-up with the tape boy, what was his name, Mario? He'd come close with Mrs. Charlotte Sachs, before the roof fell in. (He could still see the terrorized Charlie's long, thin Manhattanized face looming over him, as white as his.) Yes, dear Miss Frankie Tree was the last victory on his list—*Der Letzte auf der Liste*, as the Germans said, which was also the name of a super paperback he'd read in the hospital in order to spruce up his always failing German just in case the Kunz *Lohengrin* became a reality, which of course, now, it never would. . . .

The rain had stopped. The garden's pastel haze dissolved into precise Kodachrome rendering, more brilliant than life. He swung his feet down and stood. Most of the vestigial dizziness—attributed first to his long confinement to bed, and later to the 750-calorie diet—had disappeared. He padded easily to the bathroom and rid himself of a modest quantity of urine. He stepped on the scales: 178, down from 210 at St. Peter's. He marked the chart on the back of the bathroom door: thirty-two pounds in ninety-seven days, very good, but still a long way to go to the 158 that was judged appropriate to a man of his height, bone structure and sedentary ways. 158 would be reached, according to the chart, on February 15, meaning another ten weeks of broiled fish, raw greens sprinkled with lemon juice, nothing to drink but Sanka. We shall soon know what manner of man you are, Chapin. . . .

He put on his morning-walk outfit—gray sweat pants and shirt, classy new Adidas track shoes, tennis hat—and got his old raincoat out of the front-hall closet, snagging it momentarily on the tank of oxygen and Red Cross emergency kit that had been his stock in trade since the events of September 3. These things probably wouldn't be needed, the doctors said, but better safe than sorry—at worst, the oxygen would give Maggie something to do while waiting for the ambulance. He went back through the house to the kitchen and got Mutt and went out the back door.

"Morning, Phil," he said to the pool man.

"Mornin', Mr. Chapin. So how's the old ticker comin' along?"

"Just fine, thank you. Feel strong as a horse, actually. . . ." Phil, like everybody else, had been most solicitous—far more impressed, in fact, by Harry's heart attack than by his listing in *Who's Who*, which had been reported in the Pasadena *Star-News*. Practically anybody in a community of over-achievers like Flintridge could get into *Who's Who*, but to stage a full-fledged coronary on the roof of St. Peter's so that your unconscious body had to be lifted off by helicopter—this was true celebrity.

He marched out the driveway at a brisk pace, pulling Mutt along. The doctor had specified 120 paces per minute, and Harry took a fifteen-second count to make sure: yes, thirty good-sized steps and not breathing hard at all. Only walking—no jogging—was permitted: this new doctor was a precise son of a bitch. They'd had to get rid of old Pope, unfortunately; the friendly neighborhood GP was in worse shape than Harry—fat, smoked a pack a day, probably drank, too, judging from the red splotches on his nose and cheeks—and obviously wasn't one to treat a coronary patient with the required strictness. Thanks to Dr. du Plessix and the heart specialists at Huntington Memorial, where they'd put him after his return from Rome, Harry now dealt—if that was the word— with a tough Pasadena internist named Iselin, who immediately invented the ridiculous diet and insisted on regular exercise. "When you feel like eating, go for a walk instead." Fine advice. When Harry got down to 170, he could start tennis again, Iselin said, one set per week, and also a little jogging. When he got down to his "norm," the mythical 158, maybe they'd talk about a little alcohol—one glass of wine a day or something in that neighborhood.

He went as far as the fire station, his regular route, which was basically uphill and gave him an opportunity to work the weakened pump while he was still fresh and then coast back home on overdrive. He was sweating now—the humidity probably—but he wasn't out of breath, which said something about his new condition, he supposed, and (grudgingly) the value of Dr. Iselin's advice. ". . . Fifty pounds overweight, no exercise within memory, eating and drinking like a madman, constant stress, emotional and otherwise—the classic burning-the-candle-at-both-ends coronary case . . . You want to live to be forty-six? Then you'll mend your ways. . . ."

Maggie was on the bedroom floor doing yoga with Dickie Hittleman when he got back. She had lost eleven pounds as a serendipitous side effect of his diet and looked pretty sexy now herself for a forty-four-year-old lady with sixteen-year-old twins to her credit.

"Don't forget your limbering up," she reminded him. "Do you want me to count?"

"No, I can do it," he said with just the slightest hint of the old Chapin impatience. He went through the daily dozen and then stripped naked and walked around the bedroom selecting underwear and showing off his svelte new figure—well, it would be svelte by the time he reached 158. Maggie did not seem particularly impressed; left her sexy blue leotard in place. They weren't *forbidden* to couple, Iselin had said, "but try to use some judgment in the matter." Oh, yes, Doc, judgment was Harry Chapin's forte. Look—no erection, see?

In the shower he opened with "Ombra mai fu" from *Xerxes* (Handel's "Largo" to you), moving rapidly through Leoncavallo's "Mattinata" and the Neapolitan song "Core 'ngrato," finishing strongly with the "Cujus animam" from Rossini's *Stabat Mater* sung in authentic well-pronounced Latin as taught since 1896 at Choate School, Wallingford, Connecticut. Strange how he favored the tenor repertoire, even though this meant bringing everything down a major third to suit his own dry baritone. Probably something Freudian there—subconscious desire for castration perhaps: or maybe the tenors got all the good tunes—probably the latter. But notice: nothing from Giuseppe Verdi's late-period masterpiece *Otello*. Something Freudian there, too. And no complaints from the lady of the house, either. In fact, she complimented him: "You're in awfully good voice this morning. Should I wonder why?"

"No, I don't think so. Sounds of a man on the mend, most likely."

Maggie was naked herself now, for her own weigh-in. 132 and falling—yes, not bad, especially for a mature lady requiring a 36-C bra. But still no reaction down below in this Chapin. Maybe the thing was no longer operative. One could always hope. . . .

Breakfast went with the new smoothness. The place was awash with change. The boys sat down promptly when called, following the rule that family meals would be taken together whenever possible. Gone were the ravishing odors of real coffee and bacon and eggs fried in all that wonderful grease. The new menu featured fresh-squeezed orange juice, Kellogg's Special K, skim milk, Sanka, vitamins for all and an extra pill for Harry to help keep his blood thinned out. The boys, who were thought to be still growing, were permitted one frozen doughnut each, heated in the microwave oven. Gone, too, were the old tensions, the loud bickering, the silent resentments. Beachie, who wasn't as dumb as he looked (yes, a father could have such thoughts), had come to him and said, "Glad you and Mummy are better friends now, Dad." Oh, yes, very good friends. While he was still in the Huntington and it looked as though Harry Chapin might remain an on-going proposition, Maggie had invited him to put aside past animosities and start over again—two mature adults who needed each other to survive in a hostile world. Pending receipt of a better offer, he had accepted.

Heck excused himself early to get in five minutes' practice on his new guitar, one of a pair of matched Gibsons that had recently come into the house. Beachie, less "gifted" but infinitely more practical, took an extra doughnut and retired to the bathroom. Mrs. Wallace, the piano lady, had been terminated after three character-building years (and some $4000 in fees) in favor of a Caltech senior who taught the boys songs by Elton John and the Beatles and Honeybee's own Judas Goat, whose members—the twins rejoiced in hearing—Harry had once met in the flesh.

When the boys had left the house—picked up this morning by a lady whose husband, also at Caltech, had just won a Nobel Prize—Maggie gave him a second cup of Sanka, and they retired to the bedroom and dressed side by side: Maggie putting on her Friday gray jumper with the Volunteer patch on one shoulder, and Harry trying to select one of the three Cardin suits she'd bought him at Saks and had tailored right there in the house so that he wouldn't expose himself to the elements during his period of convalescence.

"You're sure you don't want me to give you a quick trim?" she repeated. "Just around the ears?"

"Oh, I don't think so. Maybe after lunch I'll go see Mario. . . ." The other Mario, with scissors, not tape.

He looked at himself closely in the mirror over the dresser. During his recuperation he had not had a single haircut, so that now his hair was very full and long, curling dramatically around his neck and ears. Even with the increased amounts of gray at the temples and sideburns, he looked—in his opinion—a relatively young forty-five. A good haircut might take off two or three years, but the present shaggy look seemed perfectly appropriate to the lush styling of the French suits.

"The blue looks awfully nice on you. . . ."

She'd get no argument from him; blue it was, complete with silk Cardin handkerchief in the breast pocket. He had worn the blue on Monday, his first day back, and had been met with a chorus of ooohs and aaahs from the many admiring ladies who had (probably) given him up for dead. With his devastating new image—*romantic* was the word that came to mind—he couldn't help feeling some disappointment that the apparatus between his legs hadn't shown more interest. But the regaining of full powers would require time, Iselin had told him, and he supposed he could wait.

Fully attired and carrying his elegant new pencil-slim Cardin diplomat's portfolio (Maggie and the boys had gone crazy at Saks in their ecstasy at having him home), he sauntered to the front of the house—admiring wife trailing behind—and paused before the full-length mirror in the foyer. A very mod executive we've got here, eh Chapin? And when we get down to the promised land of 158—wow! (Saks had been wonderful about his invalid status: bring the suits back when his "permanent" size had been reached and further alterations would be made without charge.) Soon they were going to require more mirrors around here. "Hah!" he laughed aloud.

"What are you laughing at?"

"Nothing in particular. Just feeling good, I suppose. From all this non-eating . . ."

Naturally, he passed right by the sherry decanter on the sideboard: fantastic willpower.

Maggie eyed him with old-style suspicion. "When should we expect you?"

"Oh, four-ish? It depends on how long the Cavalieri business takes."

She escorted him out to the driveway. "And isn't this the day you see Mr. Deering? About your contract?"

"I think so, yes."

"Will you call and tell me what he says?"

"Mmmmm—maybe, if it's good news. Otherwise . . ."

She kissed him on the cheek, then stepped back to admire her man in his lovely silver Mercedes. "Well, I'm sure Mr. Deering appreciates everything you've done for Melos-Doria—and what you've been through."

"We shall see. Meanwhile—go kind of easy on the checkbook, okay . . . ?"

I I

Old Max, the cop on the front gate, gave him a cheery wave. All week people had been exceedingly kind: "Take it easy, Harry boy—job's just not worth killing yourself over. . . ." He liked getting in after ten now and leaving at four. There was less traffic at these privileged hours, and who was to complain of his abbreviated schedule? Back Lot people weren't expected to keep regular hours, especially not a Melos-Doria chief executive who had come through the Battle of Rome.

". . . Alix, love."

"Good morning, Harry. My, you're looking awfully well this morning."

"Feeling fine. No new developments from Personnel, I'm glad to see."

"They called again just a few minutes ago. Mr. Choate would still prefer that you hire someone from inside. Unless you're completely adamant."

He hadn't had a permanent secretary since firing Heidi in April. Dear Alix, always the martyr (and the most forgiving of women, when not under the influence of Debil Cocaine), had volunteered to resume her old role as temp-sec until he found what he wanted, assuming he knew. But inside had little to offer: Maureen in PR, Tina from International, Debbie of the great boobs from Merchandising—in fact, there was hardly a girl on the lot who *wasn't* interested in working for Mr. Chapin, since his attack. Hospitalization had worked a wondrous change in his image. Maybe they thought *that* organ was affected, too: you'd get the free trip to San Francisco, but you wouldn't have to submit to the physical abuse. "I'm absolutely adamant," he said upon reflection.

"I thought so."

"And the other calls?"

"Mr. Ferlinghetti called from New York to ask you to be sure to listen to the Met broadcast tomorrow morning. It's *Lohengrin* with Kunz, and he says there's a wonderful new mezzo as Ortrud."

Dear Alix—such a faithful transcriber of arcane communiqués. How would he *ever* find her equal? "I'll try to remember."

"And Mr. Deering would like to see you at eleven thirty."

"About the luncheon?"

"His girl didn't say."

"Anyway, eleven thirty's fine."

"And Mr. Bull would like to come over at noon with Mr. Musgrove, concerning Mme. Cavalieri. He said you'd know. . . ."

"Yes, fine—assuming that Deering doesn't run on and on."

"And Mr. Canby would like to see you, at your convenience."

Young Ross Canby, flower of the South, recent Ph.D candidate from the University of Texas: a most welcome, soft-spoken replacement for the departed Maury Wiseman. "As soon as I've looked at the mail."

"And, last but not least, would you consent to a haircut? Poor Mario—he calls every day to see how you are. Getting a little shaggy there, aren't we, Chapin?"

God, how could he *ever* hope to replace this fabulous creature? Chapin in love again: usual fatal irony. "No, no," he said brightly, "got to leave it long and sensual to please certain favored ladies. Which reminds me—need some flowers, Stern. What's good in December?"

"Roses are always good, I suppose," spoken with audible curiosity.

"Roses, then. Monday, first thing, send a dozen—no, make it two dozen—to Mrs. Chapin at the house."

Forty-four. Old for a woman. Besides the flowers, he'd get her something nice, maybe a piece of jewelry, because Maggie deserved something nice, putting up with him, forgiving his transgressions over the years. Something from Tiffany's, maybe, if he had time Monday morning.

"And the message?"

"Just say, 'Happy Birthday, love, Harry.' Oh, and while you're at it, order two dozen of those special yellow ones—with the small buds?"

"Yes?"

"And have them sent here to the office."

"Here?"

"Yes. And have the card say, 'For Alix, with gratitude and love, Harry' . . ."

It promised to be a big day. The main event was luncheon with Deering and all the LTI VPs and other members of senior and middle management, the guest of honor being Mme. Edith Cavalieri. Edith was making her first visit to California, passing through from the Orient on her way to a series of "farewell" recitals in the East. Also (as she had written to Harry) she was engaged in a "surprise" project which she would announce over lunch; and she wished to introduce her new manager, E. Jerold Bock, Esq., prominent Manhattan attorney and partner of Harry's good friend Joe Blankenhorn. Mr. Bock would explain to them Edith's recent decision to bring suit against Melos-Doria for breach of contract.

Besides Cavalieri-related matters, Harry faced a second budget review with Deering—the *Otello* overruns, which had surfaced on Tuesday—and later Sidney Jonas would submit his *Otello* cover design for Harry's approval and for the edification of the J. Walter Thompson account exec, who was dying to get started on the ads. Finally, with luck, Norman Rose would be calling with the first of the advance reviews on the album—reviews which might contain some juicy quotes for use in JWT's campaign. A very big Friday by any standard—doubly so for a man with diminished capacities for grief and harassment.

He applied himself to the mail. On top was a cable from Hilary Cairns in London:

RE MANDELBAUM SESSIONS APRIL 12 AND 13 HAVE PERSUADED LONDON SYMPHONY WITH GREATEST DIFFICULTY POSTPONE ON GROUNDS MANDELBAUM INDISPOSITION STOP NOW ESSENTIAL CONFIRM EQUIVALENT PONTI SESSIONS SOONEST STOP LUNCHING WITH LADY A WHO SENDS WARM REGARDS STOP LOVE AND KISSES
HILARY

He scrawled "Ross—please see me" at the top and deposited the item in the Out tray.

There were two bits from the Harvards. The first was a crimson-inked form letter on the subject "The 25th Reunion."

Dear Classmate:

During Commencement week of 1979 our Class will celebrate the 25th Anniversary of its graduation from Harvard College with a Reunion of as many of our Classmates as can come to Cambridge with their families. . . . Like the Classes preceding us, we plan to present Harvard on that occasion with a large 25th Reunion Gift. . . .

Another plea for funds. Christ, hadn't he just *sent* them something? Okay, a hundred dollars—not a penny more.

The second Harvard missive was marked PERSONAL. He sliced it open, using the silver letter-opener that had been presented to him by a grateful (?) staff on Monday—a belated token of affection on his twentieth anniversary with Melos-Doria, which had occurred while he was still *hors de combat*. The blade bore the words of Thomas Carlyle: "Music is well said to be the speech of angels," which Harry no longer found quite so apposite.

The letter, carefully typed on stationery of the Pierian Sodality of 1808, oldest musical organization in America, invited him to conduct the Harvard-Radcliffe Orchestra at Sanders Theatre, Cambridge, on Friday evening, April 21, 8:30 P.M., the program to be of Harry's choosing, though it was suggested that Beethoven's Leonore Overture No. 3, Haydn's Symphony No. 100 ("Military") and Dvořák's Piano Concerto in G Minor, Op. 33, might be in order, as these pieces would be the subject of intensive classroom study during the second semester. Soloist in the Dvořák would be a talented member of the Class of 1978. ". . . The Sodality would be most gratified, Mr. Chapin, if you, as a prominent Alumnus yourself, could accept this engagement. . . . Unfortunately, an Honorarium of Fifty Dollars is all that the Sodality can offer. . . ."

Most tempting. He had last conducted the HRO as an undergraduate, his principal interest then being the first 'cello, who had a fantastic pair of (as Sal Andreolli would say) knockers. But today—yes, it would do him a world of good: serious music-making for a change, with no interest at all in knockers. And in place of the Leonore No. 3 he would suggest an original composition by Hurston Eliot Chapin II, '54, a "mature overture on adolescent themes" which he would get started on this very weekend. . . .

"Ah, Ross—come in, come in," said Harry with honest warmth and anticipation. "Make yourself comfortable. In the old days, before you-know-what, I'd have offered you a glass of sherry. But now . . . What have we got this morning? Anything of intellectual interest?"

Ross Canby had been found and hired by Norman Rose while Harry lay in bed and the paperwork piled up. Like Maury Wiseman before him, Ross was starting as a Melos-Doria Executive Trainee at a salary of $12,000 per annum. Ross was a perfectly serious young man, probably a fag, knowledgeable, polite, with the exaggerated good manners of a Southerner, having been born and raised in Charleston, South Carolina. The boy had a vaguely superior way of speaking, but smiled a great deal, or looked sympathetically serious, and the rest of the staff, including Alix, seemed to like him very much. *Everybody* liked him better than Maury Wiseman.

"First, suh, the final repoht on *Otello* costings, as you requested. I'm sorruh to say that the total, suh, appears to be somethin' ovah one hundred and forty-two thousand six hundred dollahs. Does this seem possible, do you think, suh? Or have I made an errah somewhere along the line?"

Possible, if not desirable. Harry gave the spread-sheet a once-over-lightly. $142,600, with edit-room charges still coming in. The fraudulent billing at Rome, the overtime, the extra sessions, the further overdubbing at New York, the incredible hotel and meal costs, not to mention the outrageous talent fees, Didi's $10,000 among them. Deering would certainly be pleased—Deering, who had already told the angry Board that even with the Rome overruns the total couldn't possibly exceed $110,000—the Board having originally approved $90,000. "You might check the figures one last time with Mr. Rose in New York. Otherwise . . ."

"The Publicity Department called, suh. They want to know if they can go ahead with the news release on Mr. Slonimsky?"

"Hold it a day or two. Until I specifically give them the go-ahead, you'd better say."

"Also, they want to know if you'll be in New York soon, suh, for a photograph. The only picture they have of you and Mr. Slonimsky togethah is one taken last spring, apparently at a cocktail pahty. This one . . ."

My God, how *fat* he looked. "No, kill this one. I don't know when I'll be in New York next—I'm not supposed to do any flying right now. Tell them to use a photo of Slonimsky alone. Nobody cares about me anyway."

Ross looked dubious, but wrote down Harry's instructions. The boy took notes in one of the formal shorthand systems; Harry was impressed.

"Regahdin' Maestro Ponti—"

"Yes?"

"His attorney, Mistah—"

"Blankenhorn. Watch yourself with that gentleman—very tough."

"He's raised a question, suh, concernin' royalty provisions in Maestro Ponti's new contract. Maestro Ponti agrees to accompany Miss Kaufman in the Brahms D-minor. Howevah, he wants to be paid, suh, his regulah ten-percent royalty instead of the five percent specified for concerto accompaniments."

Hard to believe: that the persnickety Maestro Ponti had actually agreed to record with Diana Kaufman, who went braless even at her Alice Tully recital. On the other hand, what more natural collaboration? Ponti, who had sworn off opera and gone back to his monastic studies in the Tuscan hills, there to prepare for his May sessions with the Cleveland Orchestra and continuation of his complete-Beethoven-symphony series for Melos-Doria. "The whole *point* of a contract, Ross, is to memorialize agreement on such points. No. Tell Blankenhorn that either Gian-Carlo accepts the terms agreed in his contract or we shall find another conductor."

"Ah—yes, I see, suh. There's so much to learn—isn't there, suh?"

Hold on, pardner: felt the old blood pressure rising. Couldn't expect these Texas Ph.D.s to know anything about the real world; you weren't hiring them for practical knowledge. It was like having to invent the wheel at the opening of each business day, hadn't he read in *Business Week?*

"A Mistah Bloom called regahdin' some old concerto recordings made by Mistah Slonimsky in St. Louis . . . ?"

"Which he wishes to lease from us for a budget album to be called *Slonimsky Plays the Great Romantic Concertos.* The answer is no—always no. And if he threatens you by using Deering's name—"

"As a mattah of fact, suh, he did mention Mistah Deerin'—"

"Fine. You simply refer the matter to me or, until December thirty-first, Mr. Rose. After that—well, we'll see after that. Meanwhile, Mr. Bloom is to be given *nothing*—not a single master, not even the courtesy of a return telephone call. Do you *understand?*"

"Yes, suh. I—uh—didn't realize—"

Harry was aware of his pulse. When this happened—said Dr. Iselin—he was to stop, drop whatever he was doing, relax. But no Tío Pepe. "Have you very much more?" he asked, nodding toward Ross's neat row of file folders.

"If you'd lack me to come back latuh, suh—"

"Actually, Ross, I *am* beginning to feel a little tired. What would you say to continuing—oh, after lunch some time . . . ?"

"Alix?"

"Yes, Harry?"

"No more mail? Nothing from Norman Rose? I'm expecting—"

"Yes, it came, Harry. But—it's not terribly good news. I thought I'd better hold it until later."

"Let me see it *now*—please."

Mmmmm—triggering a *very* strong pulse. He took another of his 10:00 A.M. pills: if one was good, two were better, right?

"I'm sorry, Harry. I didn't mean—"

"Don't worry about it. Nothing to get upset about. I'll read it in private, if you don't mind."

He was no longer to get upset over things like this—repeated this maxim three times, then read the memo from Norman Rose:

ADVANCE REVIEW: NEWSWEEK

Dear Harry:

As you know, I had preliminary lacquers of our love-child prepared and delivered to TIME, NEWSWEEK, HIGH FIDELITY, SATURDAY REVIEW, MUSIC WEEK, etc., in hopes of obtaining at least one major review for quoting in the "teaser" ads before

national release date (now Feb. 6, to coincide with the new
date of Zeke's Met debut). Murray Teele at NEWSWEEK
phoned a few minutes ago to give us the following (bad)
news:

Murray listened to the set last night. In brief, he feels he
can't give it a "generally positive" notice; and for this reason
he doesn't want to write his formal review from lacquers—prefers to wait for pressings even if his review misses Zeke's Met
debut. What he *means* (I believe) is that he prefers to wait to
see what the other critics have to say! Overall, he thinks the
conducting is slow and lifeless (finicky is the word he used);
Toggi an "interesting disaster"; Del Campo surprisingly good;
and Zeke prematurely cast in the role. Murray went so far as to
ask why Melos-Doria didn't consider doing the part with Otto
Kunz!

Anyway, I share your disappointment in full measure, and
I suggest that, having fired our opening round and missed the
target, we now fall back and await better news from other
quarters.

Onward and upward in the Arts.

NORMAN

P.S. Given the nature of Murray's "notice," I have refrained from disturbing you with a phone call. However, as
soon as I get anything from Kolodin or Schonbaum or one of
the other biggies, rest assured that I shall resort to Ma Bell.

P.P.S. Trust you are enjoying ever-improved health—and
pray that Ross Canby is turning out to be more help than
hindrance.

Civilized fellow, old Norman. Melos-Doria would miss him—
Norman having reaffirmed his intention of jumping ship on December
31 at a mere fifty-five, thus denying them the final decade of pain. His
specific plan was to retire to a cottage in Majorca, "no electricity and no
phonograph," as the catch-phrase now ran.

"Alix? Come in, will you?" Females. They would never learn to
handle their men.

"Harry, I *am* sorry," she said in anticipation.

"Oh, don't be," he said. "But look—you, of all people—you don't
have to protect me from, well, *life.* I can still take *some* punishment. A
little bad news isn't going to *kill* me!"

And at that they both burst out laughing, for no discernible reason.

2

He sought refuge with Oscar Poole in Edit Room No. 3, where the quad mixing was done.

"You sure you want to hear this?" the crotchety Poole asked. "In your condition?"

"Especially in my condition," Harry said. "I'm not allowed to get excited anymore. Doctor's orders."

"I hope you got a good doctor."

Poole cued up the final "Esultate" recorded by Norman in New York just before Zeke went into the hospital to have nodules removed from his vocal cords by a specialist friend of Dr. du Plessix. Harry listened critically—the way Sargeant and Kolodin and Bernheimer and Rich and the other tough guys would listen when they received Melos-Doria's pressings in February. . . . Not bad, really. The timbre a little brighter than the Rome tapes, a little more metallic. Maybe roll off the top a bit, but no more reverb: the damned voice was already beginning to "swim" among the four channels of the quad mix. "It's good," Harry said finally. "Very good. This will be the take we'll use, then."

"Is that my okay?" Poole said skeptically. "Or do I wait around for Ponti and the black boy and Norman and—"

"That's your okay. No—on second thought, you'd better wait to hear from Norman. Norman's the producer. But don't worry about Ponti and Laframboise. Norman will speak for them."

"You wouldn't mind, would you, Mr. Chapin, if I confirm this back to you by memo? Last time I got my ass reamed—"

"Oscar, Oscar, *please*. Do it any way you want. But do it without acrimony."

"Fine by me. So what do you want to do about the side lengths, then?"

Coming to see Oscar had been a mistake. "What about the side lengths?"

Poole pulled out the tape-assembly notice. "You've got two very long sides," the older man explained. "Side three is bad enough— twenty-seven ten. But side six is impossible. It runs over thirty-four minutes and there is no way you can cut a good disc that long, even with the Neumann cutter. On those lacquers we made for Mr. Rose, we broke it onto an extra disc."

"Well," said Harry with studied calm, "we certainly can't break the act. Act IV is always complete on the final side. How do the other companies do it?"

"Other people don't make it run thirty-four minutes, and they don't do it in quad. Oh, you *can* squeeze it on, I suppose. But you won't have any level—you'll be hearing nothing but clicks and pops and back-ground noise. You don't want that, do you?"

He was aware of his pulse again. In the new pared-down Chapin form, even the slightest change in emotional rhythm was noticeable. "No, I don't want that," he said quietly.

"I kicked it around with Mr. Rose," Poole went on, "and he says there's a Victor set that starts Act IV on the fifth side and then runs it on over, making two pretty reasonable running times."

"The act *shouldn't* be broken," Harry said petulantly. "On musical *and* dramatic grounds."

"Okay, then," said Poole.

"Okay, what?"

"Okay, it shouldn't be broken."

"So what do we do?"

"So you tell me where you want it broken."

Harry remained silent for several minutes, fingering through the master score. Oh, yes, this was the new Harry Chapin, who did not become unnecessarily exercised over trivial business decisions. "Oscar?"

"Yeah, Mr. Chapin?"

"Break it after the 'Ave Maria.' You'll have to redistribute sides four and five, too, or else five is going to be too long. Yes, start side six there—right after 'Amen!' "

". . . Are you all right, Harry? Your face seems a little—"

"I'm fine, Alix. Feeling just wonderful."

"May I get you another cup of Sanka? A glass of water?"

"I would like a Tío Pepe."

"But I thought—"

"Just kidding. Instead—why don't you get me Norman Rose in New York, like a good girl . . . ?"

"Good morning, Harry. How are you feeling? Not working too hard, I hope. Ease back in, that's the best way. Put the burden on Ross. Capable young man, don't you find? Got to take it easy, especially at first. I was reading just last night—"

"I'm *fine*, Norman."

"They tell me you're thin."

"Thinner—not thin."

"And your blood pressure? They say . . ."

Back only a week and already he was tired of the constant pampering, the unsolicited medical advice. Monday it had been rather pleasant, hearing from everybody how thin he was and how well he looked and how he should take it easy and not worry about anything, a man in his condition. But now . . . "Hey, Norman?" he barked impatiently. "How 'bout knocking off the daily report on the patient's condition and instead get down to some business, would you mind?"

"I only meant, Harry—"

That's better: Chapin the bastard back in town. "I know what you meant, Norman—and I appreciate your kind thoughts. But what about Kolodin? What about Schonbaum? What about somebody important other than Murray Teele, the son of a bitch?"

"I felt like such a coward—writing you a memo."

"No, you were right. There was no reason to phone."

"As for Schonbaum, I'm stopping by his office at three. If he's finished his review—which I'm sure he has—I'll call and read it to you later today."

"Excellent. And the others?"

"I'm afraid I have some bad news, Harry."

"More bad news, you mean. Who hates us now?"

"The people at *Time*."

"Lederer? *Bill Lederer* rapped us? I don't believe it. This is *his* kind of project, for God's sake. Unorthodox casting—"

"That's the problem, Harry. We didn't get Lederer. Lederer's in Europe, it turns out, and the acetates went directly to a new girl from Barnard who's acting as Lederer's assistant. She's done a 'preliminary evaluation,' as she calls it, in the form of an internal memo. If we're lucky, Lederer will ignore it and start all over again. At any rate, the girl understands there's to be nothing in print earlier than January twenty-sixth—she's agreed to respect our outdate."

How nice. They'd wait years for a few kind words from Bill Lederer, and then Lederer would be on vacation or junketing or otherwise occupied, and some rank amateur would get the assignment, and their collective fates—and an investment of $142,600—would rest in the hands of an unpredictable Barnard girl who'd probably majored in political science and was doing Music while waiting for an opening on Nation or World or Modern Living.

"Do you want me to read it, Harry? What she's written?"

"Sure," Harry said, "why not? I'm dying to know what some ugly-as-sin Barnard girl thinks of our little venture."

"As a matter of fact, Harry, she's rather nice-looking."

"Just *read* it."

"Remember, this is only a memo, Harry—this will never appear in print."

"*Read it!*"

". . . 'Yet another *Otello*, this one from the esteemed Swiss-Italian maestro Gian-Carlo Ponti, with a mixed-bag of performers, two of the leads American. Regrettably, Signor Ponti can't seem to make up his mind about who the star of the set is to be: the campy lady from Dover, Delaware, Miss Didi del Campo, who essays Desdemona; the ancient Italian baritone (Golden Age, but singing now with lesser metal to his voice) Benno Toggi; or—last and, in this company, least—the young New Orleans tenor Ezekiel Laframboise, who has the dubious honor of beginning his international career in the cruelly demanding role of the Moor. Signor Ponti seems more interested in the details of Verdi's masterful score than in his singers, each of whom requires—or, in Mr. Laframboise's case, demands—artistic leadership of a high order. Laframboise, leading tenor of the Deutsche Oper am Rhein of Düsseldorf, has a voice of steel but little idea of the psychological implications of his role, and seems incapable of the legato singing called for by this largely stentorian part. Mr. Toggi, recently released from an Italian prison (*Time*, May 7, 1977), not surprisingly exhibits rusty vocal technique, though his dramatic instincts remain true to Verdi's cause. Mme. del Campo—well, what can one say of Mme. del Campo that hasn't already been said—and offered in full frontal display—by *Playboy*?'

"It goes on in this vein, Harry, mostly criticizing Didi as an example of the 'have voice, will travel' school of modern-day divas. There's no point in my boring you with the rest of it. I'll drop a Xerox in the mail if you'd like. . . .

"Harry? Harry, are you still there? Operator . . . ?"

"I'm still here, Norman."

"Oh, thank God. For a moment I was afraid—"

"Another seizure? Heart attacks are very painful, Norman. Usually the victim will cry out—you'll know he's having it."

"Really, Harry, how you can joke—"

"I'm not joking, Norman. But let's go on, shall we?"

"About Edith, then—"

"What about her? I'm having lunch with her in less than two hours."

"While I realize this is not your favorite topic of conversation—in view of Edith's lawsuit—I feel I must pass along to you, Harry, what Blankenhorn has said."

"If you must."

"The final recital of the so-called 'farewell' series will take place at Avery Fisher Hall. Edith would like us to record it—first at rehearsal, then during the recital itself, then afterwards, inserting anything which may not be acceptable. She'd like the album to include a large booklet filled with photos, memorabilia, et cetera, covering her entire career. I said that naturally we were interested in principle. Which I suppose we are?"

"In principle, yes. But not in practice. One, the New York recital will never take place—she'll find herself 'indisposed' after we've spent a fortune in advertising. Two, even if she *did* go through with it, the tapes would be useless—she would want to re-record things a million times and make an infinite number of edits, which would cost another fortune and eventually produce no album. Three, if she were serious, why would she choose Lincoln Center, which is still inferior acoustically, despite the renovation, to Carnegie Hall? And four, Edith Cavalieri is—or was—an opera singer, not a recitalist, and to avoid a fiasco she'd need an orchestra, not a piano, to support—or hide—her vocalizing. So yes, in principle we want the album. But in practice the entire scheme will die a natural death, with no help from us. By the way, what is this 'secret project' that she's springing on us at luncheon? Nonmusical, she says like all her recent work."

"My God, Harry, you're certainly back in form. I don't know—about the secret project, I mean. Sorry, can't help you on that."

"I'm sorry, too. Because I like to know in advance, whenever possible, just what I'm turning down."

"I've played for Zeke the final mix on the new 'Esultate,' and he seems happy."

"Yes, I've just done the same with Oscar here. It's good—excellent, even. I've told Oscar to go ahead with it, if you agree, and include it in the final assembly. Meaning, Norman, that you must get back all existing acetates—so that later comparisons will be impossible."

"Ah. Good point. Yes, of course."

"And how is he, by the way? Zeke?"

"Fine. In very good form. The operation was apparently a complete success. He won't begin vocalizing again until after New Year's, but he's in very good spirits, as we might expect, vis-à-vis the Met."

Incredibly enough, Sy Gravinius, Esq., had wangled Zeke a Saturday-broadcast matinee for his debut—meaning exposure before millions of potential fans instead of the usual three thousand aficionados. "I still don't know how Gravinius managed that," Harry said.

"Well, as long as we're asking questions, Harry, you might ask Mr. Gravinius how he's persuaded American Airlines to underwrite the new *Pagliacci* for Mr. Laframboise next season. Really, Harry—everybody's treating this boy as though he were a god, and he's yet to sing one single note in Manhattan. Your judgment in choosing Zeke for the *Otello* is certainly being sustained all over this town."

"I'm not interested in having my judgment sustained," Harry responded with heat.

"No, no—I didn't mean—"

"I know what you meant. Anyway—get back those damned acetates, will you? I don't want *Time* magazine, those fuckers, comparing versions of the 'Esultate' and printing a lot of crap about our 'electronic wizardry.' "

"Yes, I heartily concur . . . You've heard about our friend Miss Sachs, of course."

"Charlie? No, what?"

"Oh, yes, she's had her revenge, if that's what it is. In *Der Spiegel*. A full account of our overdubbing activities with Signor Toggi at Rome."

"Incredible! She sent me a string of get-well cards, but never mentioned— my God, the *bitch*."

Easy there, Chapin; remember the pulse. His early impression had been correct: a nasty, evil woman. He should have fucked her while he had the chance. But then he never *did* have the chance, did he, lying there at her feet, gasping for air and praying, with the silly Belgian girls, for his life?

". . . If I may conclude, then, with two pieces of gossip."

"Oh, my yes," said Harry. "Love 'dishing the dirt,' as my parents used to say. What have you got? Something juicy, I hope."

"You be the judge. I saw Maury Wiseman yesterday."

"No."

"Yes. He asked about you, and I told him you were making a speedy and full recovery."

"Which warmed his heart, I suppose."

"He seemed genuinely concerned for you, Harry. We bumped into each other at the Kaufman recital. His wife was with him, a nice young girl from Brooklyn, I believe. They were most cordial and he looked very prosperous—much cleaner and better dressed than he ever was with us."

"Effects of a liberal education gotten at our expense."

"I suppose. Anyway, he sends you his regards and says he's dying to hear how the recording turned out."

"Suggest that he buy one at Sam Goody's or Korvette's."

But that was needlessly harsh. The boy was merely young: his raw ambition would eventually be tempered by experience—and defeat. It was too bad, in a way, that Maury hadn't hung around long enough to witness the complete *Otello* cycle from creation in a Paris hotel room to damnation at the hands of a Barnard girl at Time Inc. But Maury was gone: resigned almost as soon as he got home from Rome, taking advantage of contacts he'd made during the sessions, and working now for RCA in New York. Good luck to him. And good luck to RCA . . .

"You said two pieces of gossip, didn't you? I hope the other one's more exciting than Maury Wiseman."

"Oh, it is—very much so. Guess who else I had occasion to speak to yesterday?"

"Marlene Dietrich."

"Close."

"*Close?*"

"Also German."

"That certainly narrows the range. I give up. Who?"

"Herr Otto Kunz."

"Oh, yeah, I remember him. So what did he want—besides *Lohengrin,* which he can't have?"

"Well—you're aware, I assume, that they're back together? Marianne and Otto?"

"Yes. So what?" He was indeed aware of Marianne's latest maneuvering. She had sent him the most heart-wrenching (by her calculations) letter while he was still in the hospital: *so* sorry about that awful note she'd left for Maggie, and praying that Maggie had not been too vindictive.

"So," said Norman with obvious relish, "they're expecting."

"Expecting? What are they expecting? Certainly not—"

"Precisely."

"A *baby?*"

"They *are* man and wife, Harry."

"Yes—but *whose?* Whose baby?"

"*Precisely,*" said Norman again, with that delicious smugness of his later years. "Or—more to the point, Harry—what color?"

Harry, following doctor's orders ("keep nothing in"), laughed aloud. *Fabulous* stuff! Marianne Kunz having somebody's *baby!* Not Ponti's anyway—too much of an interval for that. Zeke's? Poor

Marianne had ended up (poor choice of words, eh, Chapin?) with the big black crybaby following Rome: held the croaking tenor's hand all through surgery, it was said. But Zeke's *baby?* She *was* a lady of protean habits where all these opera studs were concerned.

"I don't suppose we'll ever know," Norman lamented.

"Perhaps not in Majorca," Harry said, thinking now on the matter. "But we'll most certainly know here in the States."

"You *will?* But how?"

"Simple," Harry said. "If it's born with a foot-long prick, it's Ponti's. If it's chocolate brown, it's Zeke's. If it's got a serial number tattooed on its arm, it's Otto's. And if it's born tone-deaf and dumb— it's definitely mine. . . ."

I I

When he got to Deering's office, Lott's Wife was blocking the entrance: five-girl junk-rock band, of course—even Harry had heard of them. Biggest thing on the Honeybee label since Judas Goat, said *Rolling Stone.*

"Ah, Harry," Deering called out, "give us just a second, can you, like a good chap? Youth must served, wot?"

Lindsay, the Honeybee photographer, was setting up the usual contract-signing shot—Deering at his desk, pen in hand, the greedy manager with a big grin on his idiot's face, the group members hanging idly about, hamming it up for the camera: *Billboard* and *Cash Box* printed dozens just like it every Monday morning—only the names (not even the faces) changed.

Harry stood to one side and paid the girls modest attention. Four of them were thin, sexless waifs with remarkably dirty hair and filthy jeans; the fifth was the chubby drummer, larger but just as dirty and just as sexless. The manager was a middle-aged faggot, bald except for a few long strands brought forward to curl over his forehead, wearing a suit almost as expensive and stylish as Harry's. The latest Lott's Wife single droned away in the background; Deering, who was beginning to learn something of the pop business, had instructed Electronic Maintenance to rewire his amplifier so that the volume couldn't be increased beyond tolerable limits, and even Harry found the sound pleasant, almost sleep-promoting.

"Oh, Gardner," Deering said to the manager, "say hallo to Hurston Chapin, will you?" Bad experiences in the past had taught Deering to eschew "Harry" in front of pop groups. "Mr. Chapin's head of our

classical operations—Melos-Doria? I'm sure you've seen the name. . . .
Gave us quite a scare, this lad—coronary, and so youthful, too. Shows
the need for proper diet, periodic recreation, keeping one's work in
perspective . . ."

"Pleased ta meecha," the manager said without taking his eyes off
the camera. "Geez—that's too bad, about your ticker."

"Whilst Harry—Hurston—is himself a classical musician of note,"
Deering rattled on, "we find that he possesses golden ears in the pop
field, too. Recently brought us the most *marvelous* tapes from England—band of the name Brain Damage—single on the charts this very
moment—*very* heavy airplay on all the stations. Released on our Fools
Gold label, isn't it, Harry? Hurston?"

"I believe so, yes, Leslie." For further details, you will wish to
contact Mimi from Minneapolis.

It was incredible: Deering had been *ecstatic* over Brain Damage—
as though Harry had done nothing else of value in his life. Brain
Damage, a repudiation of Harry's whole career.

Eventually Lindsay got what he wanted and Gardner and Lott's
Wife said a collective goodbye. Deering retained his traditional position
of advantage behind the massive mahogany desk and bade Harry to sit
in the one comfortable chair. "Are you permitted to smoke? May I send
for an ashtray?"

Harry explained that he could but didn't, thanks all the same.
Deering seemed unusually ill at ease. Harry by contrast was a picture of
contentment. He crossed his legs and admired the beautiful workman-
ship of Monsieur Cardin's slacks; also his *soigné* brown boots from Mr.
Bally. Deering's three-piece banker's outfit looked distinctly shabby and
unfashionable by comparison.

"Well, there is no point procrastinating—as painful as this subject
is for me," Deering began.

"Oh—what is that?" Harry said with admirable calm.

"I'm speaking again of the very serious cost overruns on your
Otello, Harry. And, I'm afraid, the consequences thereof . . ."

At least—after countless meetings on the subject during Harry's
absence—Deering had stopped calling the piece *Othello.*

"The commercial prospects for this recording—I'm told this by
your own Sales Department, Harry—simply cannot justify what the
Board regards as unbusinesslike management."

"I can appreciate," Harry said, "how the Board might adopt such
an attitude."

"As a result—and believe me when I say that I speak now with the
greatest personal regret—"

"Of course, Leslie. Please don't be disturbed on my account."

"I regret to advise you that the Board has decided not to offer you a new employment contract—but rather to proceed on a month-to-month basis from January onward."

"Meaning—"

"Simply meaning, dear chap, that you will now serve at the pleasure of the Board—as do, I might add, most other employees of LTI. Your own past employment contracts have been exceptional, shall we say— based, of course, on your long tenure—twenty years, isn't it?—with Melos-Doria."

"Sixteen years under the Strausses," Harry explained for this dodo's benefit, "and four years with LTI—yes, twenty years in all."

"Not to put too fine a point on it, Harry, but I hope you can appreciate the rather painful embarrassment I've suffered personally as a result of all this—the Rome affair, the unfortunate letter from Mr. Wiseman to Board members at the time of his resignation, the recent— and I might say totally unexpected—defection of Mme. Cavalieri from our ranks . . . Well, I shan't belabor matters except to repeat what has been said to me over and over by the Board—art is no excuse for poor cost-control. Mr. Law in particular feels strongly on this point. This is a business, after all—a public corporation—and naturally we must be sensitive to the financial goals and desires of our shareholders. . . ."

Harry smiled—providing yet another sharp contrast, this time to the set of Deering's jaw, the scowl, the worry lines around the older man's eyes—and said as quietly and as calmly as he could: "If it will help, Leslie—with the Board, that is—naturally I shall offer my resignation."

Deering was momentarily speechless. "My dear chap," he sputtered eventually, "oh, my, no—wouldn't hear of it. Out of the question. But—most considerate of you."

"I'm serious, Leslie. I've lived in the corporate world long enough to understand these things. The costs at Rome were—well, regrettable. In fact, I have further news in that regard. According to my assistant, charges to date—those that have shown up on the computer runs through last evening—now total something over one hundred and forty-two thousand."

Poor Deering: the sudden flipflop from good news (offer of Chapin's resignation) to bad (yet *more* cost overruns on this damnable project) threatened to produce the second coronary of LTI's current fiscal year. "But you *assured* me, Harry . . ."

"These things are simply beyond control," Harry said expansively. "Or at least *my* control. If the Board is upset—as it might well be—I suggest that next time, Leslie, you ask the Board to go to Rome, Italy, and produce a work as complicated as *Otello* under conditions as unpredictable as those which apply today in the Opera House."

Chairman Deering took this thought under advisement, said nothing. He worked his jaw with determination, but no words came out. Harry sympathized. The original budget had been $50,000. This, of course, was in the '60s, before the Strausses sold out to LTI. Soon after acquisition the LTI Board, at Harry's request, had blessed a revised plan in the amount of $90,000. Naturally, costs had increased in the interim, and Deering, an experienced executive, would certainly have accepted an actual expense of, say, $100,000, taking into account inflation, union wage scales, etc. However, when Harry's office—during Harry's absence in hospital, for which the Board had expressed sympathy and concern— submitted October estimates amounting to $110,000, the Board had taken umbrage. And now—to hear that the actual total was $142,000 . . .

"And perhaps even more," Harry said in a soothing, almost disembodied voice, "in that we have no idea what edit-room charges are yet to be received by Data Processing. . . . And so I say again, Leslie, I shall be glad to submit my resignation to the Board if this will spare you further embarrassment. Naturally, I regret the matters have turned out as they have. I have paid something of a price myself for these failures, real or imagined. . . ."

"Oh, my dear chap," Deering protested, "no one doubts for a moment your personal sacrifice. You've given your all"—vague gesture indicating Harry's "condition"—"in the line of duty. But in a strictly *business* sense—"

"True," Harry said without remorse, "I never did go to the Business School." There being only the one . . .

The *real* problem, Harry ascertained, was a gentleman who *had* gone to the Harvard Business School: Mr. George Law, a senior vice president of the California Bank in the firm's home office at San Francisco, who was the new outside director on the LTI Board. Harry, flat on his back at the time of the last Board meeting, had not yet met the gentleman. Law possessed, according to Deering, "a profound financial mind." His first official act had been to conduct a brief but penetrating examination of Melos-Doria accounts and to determine that Management—meaning Harry—was at grave fault ("negligence bordering on the criminal" were Mr. Law's words) in failing to control operating budgets—most strikingly "this foolish operatic extravagance in, of all places, Italy."

"When I informed him," Deering said with audible distress, "that the final figure had grown to one hundred and ten thousand, the man wanted *heads* to roll. God knows what he'll want when he hears your new figure."

Mmmm—perhaps a new Chairman of the Board?

"But you'll see for yourself at luncheon—try to get with him, won't

you, during drinks? He's a pianist, did I tell you? Thinks the signing of
this chap, ah—"

"Slonimsky?"

"—Slonimsky, yes—thinks this is the only thing we've done right in
years. . . ."

Such anguish. How sad to find this powerful man—what would a
desk like this cost, two thousand dollars?—reduced to tearful babbling
by yet another Busy School type.

"Well, then," said Harry in a more somber tone of voice, "let's just
hope that Vova—Mr. Slonimsky—signs his contract. Perhaps then Mr.
Law—"

"What? What do you *mean?*" Deering's face was frozen into a
mask of terror. "Surely the contract is *signed?* You told me—"

Harry had never before witnessed such alarm. "What I told you,
Leslie—if you'll think back—was that Vova has expressed his *intention*
to sign. We have, in fact, prepared just this morning the news release
announcing the new contract. But no—he's not actually put pen to
paper."

"My God!" said Deering, falling back in his lovely leather Chairman's chair. "Whatever shall we do?"

". . . About luncheon, Leslie . . ."

"Yes, yes," Deering said, recovering somewhat. "And how should I
address the lady? Is it Miss Cavalieri? Madame . . . ?"

"I would begin with Madame," Harry said, "but she will very
quickly put you onto an Edith basis."

"Is there anything I should know? Her background? I don't want
to say anything—"

"Speaking with candor, Leslie, Edith is a fifty-year-old woman—
older, some say—vain, semi-hysterical, desperate to find happiness while
there's still time—and praying now—fantasizing—that she can somehow manage a string of farewell recitals. She has, in fact, given one
recital already, in Tokyo. After singing two songs she was 'indisposed'
and could not continue. 'Too carried away by the love of her audience,'
I believe she said—but the lamentable fact is that the lady can no longer
sing—a natural result of these years of inactivity and neglect. Still, she
will talk to you of her many plans, which include recitals on all continents of the world except the Antarctic. Edith has proposed that
we—Melos-Doria—record the final recital of the tour, in New York.
This would be an artistic and commercial disaster of the first magnitude.
Fortunately, the tour will never take place—Tokyo is proof of that—so
we need only nod in agreement and the project will eventually go away
of its own accord. The main thing with sopranos, in my experience,

Leslie, is to say 'yes' to everything they propose. The only word that is truly offensive to any diva is the word 'no.' Never, no, never, say 'no.' . . ."

Poor Deering was making notes: yes, *writing down Harry's advice!* "I'm grateful, Harry. . . ." Grateful! Oh, too sad!

"And there's one other matter of which you should be aware, Leslie."

"Yes?"

"The lady is suing us."

"You're not *serious,*" Deering cried sharply.

"Oh, I am. Very serious. She has served us with papers."

"But on what *grounds?* I thought you told me our relations were perfectly cordial?"

"They are. But she feels that we have damaged her professional reputation by making *Otello* with Del Campo—a lady absolutely abhorred by Edith, sopranos commonly detesting each other—and she claims that we materially breached her last contract—which expired, by the way, several years ago—by not giving her the *Otello* or, as a substitute, a *Rosenkavalier* which the Consortium does not wish to make and would not make even if Edith *could* sing the Marschallin, which of course she cannot. I know it sounds complicated, Leslie, but you need remember only one thing: the lady can no longer sing, and any and all projects she mentions are merely thrown up as a smoke screen to cover the basic fact that her public life is over."

"But a *lawsuit,* Harry. Think of the adverse publicity at a time when—"

"Oh, yes, that's the lady's game. She knows that you and the Board will react in just this way. She counts on never going to court, but settling outside. Among other things, she counts on the idea that Harry Chapin, head of mighty artist-oriented Melos-Doria, would never take the stand to testify to the artistic incompetence of a grand lady like Edith Cavalieri."

"And would you? If—God forbid—she brought us into court?"

"Oh, heavens, no, Leslie. Just not done, as our U.K. pals like to say. But, believe me, we shall never go to court. I'm sure I can settle matters amicably."

"But how? And are you *certain* that we can avoid the publicity? I am thinking again of Mr. Law—and the other Board members as well. With the price of our shares already in decline—"

"Oh, yes, I'm positive," Harry said, rising to leave. "By simply promising the lady more records she will never be able to make . . ."

"There *is* one other matter, Harry. . . ."

Harry paused at the door while Deering shuffled through the great stacks of paper on his desk. "Ah, yes, here it is—most remarkable letter from a gentleman who says—extraordinary—that he wants your job. Hints, in fact, that you plan to *retire* in the near future. Nothing to it, I suppose?"

"Retire? At age forty-five?"

"No, I quite agree—ridiculous on its face. Still—this chap seems awfully sure of himself. President of something called D-B Franchising Industries, Chicago, Illinois. Wants an appointment with me, at my convenience. Says he can pull Melos-Doria out of its current 'doldrums.' . . . 'Not adverse to investing my own capital in such a heaven-blessed enterprise' . . . 'Track record of uninterrupted growth and profitability' . . ."

"My, my," said Harry, "obviously someone who doesn't know anything about classics. Who is the gentleman, if I may ask?"

"Fellow's name is . . . Mr. Dell. Mr. Hoyt Dell. Would you know him, by any chance?"

"*Know* him?" Harry said. Not the same Dell who arranged the charter flight home from Rome, paced the hospital corridors with "his Mag" on his arm, promised to see the boys through college if it came to that? Not *that* Dell? "Not really, Leslie. Oh, I've met him socially. But no—I wouldn't say that I know him."

"Well—suppose I should agree to an appointment. Just a courtesy, of course . . ."

"Of course," said Harry with a smile. "Why don't you see him? Should be a fascinating experience . . . for you both. . . ."

III

No contract after the 31st: not exactly a surprising turn of events, eh, Chapin? He was remarkably cheerful as he strolled toward the Back Lot. He would leave promptly on January 1 and they would take an extended vacation—just he and Maggie, with Bette and Big Harry coming up from Balboa to look after the twins. Maybe lie on the beach in Hawaii or do one of those Caribbean cruises: get a super suntan to go with his new figure. Only at the last possible moment would he start thinking about a job. Hell, finding a new association wouldn't be that difficult. Once word got around that Chapin was available, there would be offers galore—DG, Philips, Decca, maybe even one of the domestic labels.

Or maybe not. Maybe—at this advanced time of life—think about a teaching job, with a little composing on the side. Yes—the invitation to conduct Harvard-Radcliffe had touched a nerve. Maybe take up residence at a small but prestigious college in the sticks someplace—Oberlin or Mills or Middlebury—and finish out his days in the groves of academe, working with these gosh-darn bright kids they've got these days. Or—as long as we're dreaming—maybe catch on as Visiting Professor of Music at some place like Harvard—or even Yale, where he'd taken his M.A. Where did Maggie keep that 1956 letter of recommendation from Hindemith? Hindemith bound to have some clout, even now, around New Haven.

Anyway, they had his LTI profit-sharing and the exercisable stock options to fall back on: $160,000 of the one, $70,000 of the other: $230,000 less taxes. They wouldn't starve. The boys would go to college, even without Hoyt Dell.

The only real question now was how to stick it to the bastards with maximum pain—how to shove Melos-Doria up George Law's ass? No Vaseline for you, ole buddy: you take it straight, like a man. Because, naturally, Harry wasn't going to work from month to month at the "pleasure" of any board, especially one dominated by that *soi-disant* piano expert, Mr. George Law.

No, first thing Monday morning—having thought matters over during the weekend: all part of good form—he would submit his resignation. Then, right after the 1st, he'd clean out his desk, make his farewells to the old Melos-Doria staff, kiss Alix and get the hell out. He was not a man to hang around where not wanted.

". . . Oh, Harry, thank heavens. Mr. Bull and the other gentlemen have been waiting in the music library. May I send them in?"

"Let them wait. First, Alix, I want to speak to the Count Stanislaus Gimpel. Or, if he's not available, the Countess."

The call to Gimpel went through almost immediately. The Count was aboard *L'Arlésienne* at anchor in the Baie des Canébiers off St.-Tropez. The line was perfectly clear: Harry did not have to repeat a single word. ". . . I wanted you to be the first to know, Stash. At the end of the month I shall be leaving Melos-Doria."

Gimpel took the news badly. "This pompous fellow Deering, eh, Harry? . . . Yes, we have heard that he lacks the stomach for our business. Vova, of course, will be most angry."

Harry did his best to defend poor Deering—mentioning George Law, in fact, by name. ". . . But Vova need not be concerned," Harry said. "We have a very fine staff, and he will be looked after . . ."

Gimpel was a man of infinite kindness: he had been among the first to call the hospital in Rome following Harry's event. He now offered Harry a job. "I have already made a commitment to Klaus König, but I can use him elsewhere. Obviously, dear Harry, it would give me the greatest pleasure to announce your appointment as general manager of all of our music affairs, worldwide."

A most flattering offer. Harry had heard the gossip: Klaus König
hired away from Globelektron to manage Stash's recording enterprise
with special emphasis on the Countess Gimpel, who would now put on
tape almost the entire soprano literature, French, Italian and German.
Also there would be film projects: Didi had already made a series of
operatic short subjects for Eurovision, and Charles Champlin in the
L.A. *Times* reported that she was being considered for a straight dramatic role in a major TV movie at 20th Century-Fox—with her clothes
on, for once.

But no—as much as he liked Didi, Harry could not see himself
spending the rest of his days—few though they might be—catering to
the whims of yet another soprano. Respectfully, he declined.

"No, I did not think you would accept—or I would, naturally, have
made the offer to you long ago. Well, then, I have my Swiss. Herr
König will do my bidding, that we know."

"But I very much appreciate the thought," Harry said.

"Keep your health, dear Harry," Gimpel concluded. "All else is
meaningless. Please accept my counsel in this. . . . And know that
Didi sends you her love, as always. . . ."

"Gentlemen, gentlemen, *do* come in. I *am* sorry. . . ."

Sorry because he was now experiencing those large growling pre-
luncheon pangs that formerly had been quelled by generous doses of
sherry and champagne. Sorry, too, because he did not care for present
company:

Davis Bull, LTI's General Counsel, trying to fake his way through
those last few years before retirement, and thus inclined to surrender to
any outsider who might be on the attack: Settle, my boy, avoid litigation at all costs.

Young Dan Musgrove, latest in an unending chain of baby-faced
boys fresh from law school who came to LTI to learn the entertainment
business from legendary figures like Harry Chapin before leaving to set
up lucrative practices in Beverly Hills or Century City.

And, thirdly, Harry's least favorite member of a class—lawyers—for
which he felt only contempt anyway, the male half of the prestigious
Washington, D.C., firm of Titcomb and Titcomb, dear Marcus—the
other half being his sister Letitia.

"Marcus, what a pleasant surprise."

"A pleasure, as always, Harry. And how well you look. Davis has
just been telling us of your recent trials and tribulations."

"A minor ailment, I can assure you, Marcus," Harry scoffed. In the
presence of Marcus Titcomb, Harry's own English went all to pieces—

or, rather, took on an English cast: "I can assure you" . . . "Oh, indeed" . . . "Frightfully rude of him" . . .

Marcus was indeed formidable, as was his entire family now and in history. Most of us are mongrels: man and woman coupling at random. The Titcombs were products of an entirely different program. As others breed dogs or horses to secure certain desirable characteristics, so the Titcombs had for at least twelve generations (members of the family having shown papers since 1520) bred for special qualities: a female of high forehead mated to a male of the same condition; a lad of noble, aristocratic nose—finely nostriled, generous of length—wed to a lass of similar refinement; six feet or better always mated to five foot nine or more; clear white noble skin . . . etc. The current specimens were not particularly pleasant to gaze upon: rather too much nostril, too high a forehead, too much Adam's apple even in the females (Marcus more handsome than Letitia, who carried the idea of big-boned a bit far). Yet there were positive qualities too: an intelligence always in the over-135 IQ range, superior mien and demeanor, a balance, a confidence, a superiority so genuine, so absolutely sound, that a place on the executive committee of this corporation or that, a position of responsibility in the arts, was as natural to a Titcomb as fleas to a dog. In fact, the Titcombs possessed such an abundance of aristocratic qualities that Harry Chapin had been moved to ask just how such superior creatures could make their way in a world predicated on Everyman's lowest common denominator. Specifically, now, what would possess so superior a being as Marcus Titcomb to interest himself in the ridiculous affairs of Mme. Edith Cavalieri? It couldn't have been—*money*—could it?

". . . The matter of the TV set," Marcus was saying. "Surely we don't wish to make an issue of so petty—"

"Oh, but we *do!*" Harry interjected savagely. "Oh, yes, very much so. We are not speaking of a TV set, Marcus, but of an elaborate, professional-quality audio-visual home-entertainment center. Included are a very fine color TV set, a Sony videotape recorder, a Sony audio tape recorder with mixing console, and a very expensive Acoustic Research playback system—the value of all this being something in excess of five thousand dollars."

"But isn't the point, Harry—"

"No, no, Davis—let me finish. At my request, our friends at Apogée installed this sophisticated and costly equipment in Mme. Cavalieri's Paris apartment with the clear understanding that the lady was about to enter into a new contract with Melos-Doria. The *loan* of this equipment was made as a gesture of our corporate love and devotion. Whereupon Mme. Cavalieri returned our devotion by marching straight off to Deutsche Grammophon, a major competitor. Thus, we have dutifully asked for the return of our equipment. And now that she has seen fit to sue us, we most certainly want it back. Oh, yes, it's just that simple, Marcus. Surely you see the point."

Titcomb had no rebuttal, but Bull, who lacked Titcomb's brains and good manners, was quick to reply. "Be *reasonable*, Harry. Christ, why argue with the lady? All right, so it's more than a TV set. But it's still peanuts compared to the cost of litigation. And who's to say that she hasn't got a pretty good case—"

"*I'm* to say," Harry countered. "Her suit is garbage, Davis. We don't owe her a thing. The reason we didn't make the *Otello* with her is that she can no longer sing Desdemona—which is her part in the opera, by the way. I was a witness to her inability to sing, as I've told you."

"You're not going into court to testify that you sneaked under the floor of the Paris Opéra and—"

"It wasn't the Paris Opéra, it was the Salle Vauban."

"The principle remains the same."

"Ah, but you lawyers are sticklers for accuracy, Davis: so must I be. No, I don't wish to testify to the lady's vocal inadequacies. But in the same breath I tell you that I won't have her ripping off this company with her fraudulent claims. . . ."

Harry permitted the meeting to go in circles for another half-hour:

". . . She maintains that she was temporarily indisposed. . . ."

". . . I was not alone in Salle Vauban. We shall produce another witness. . . ."

". . . But why, in God's name, Harry, couldn't you just let her come in and do a little singing? . . ."

". . . If I told you how foolish that sounds to a trained ear, Davis, you would never speak to me again. . . ."

". . . But *was* there tortuous interference? . . ."

". . . Which seems to be the gravamen of the case . . ."

". . . Damage to a career which, if I read Harry correctly, was already . . ."

". . . The incalculable harm that such charges might do to our corporate image . . ."

Finally, Alix buzzed to remind Harry that the Cavalieri luncheon would start promptly at 1:00 P.M. and it was now 12:45. They ended as they had begun: in disagreement. Titcomb's best advice—for which LTI was paying him $150 per hour plus expenses—was to acquiesce, agree, accommodate and, finally, concede. "Far cheaper in the long run, Harry—I say this as a friend. . . ."

Davis Bull agreed wholeheartedly: ". . . The specter of a long-drawn-out action at law, Harry . . ."

Even poor Musgrove, twenty years everybody's junior and scared to death to find himself in such high-priced company, thought Edith's case had merit: ". . . Because who's to say, Mr. Chapin?—except the critics, isn't that right?—whether or not she *might* have been able to sing the music if you hadn't signed this other lady, Miss . . ."

But the morning's events had stiffened Harry's resolve. "Thank you, gentlemen, for your counsel. But I've decided to pursue another course."

"*What* course?" Bull said indignantly. "What do you mean *you've* decided—"

"Are you saying," Titcomb inquired with a virtuoso display of patience, "that you do *not* wish us to commence negotiations with her counsel for an out-of-court settlement?"

"What I'm saying," said Harry, feeling as well as he'd felt in maybe his whole life, "is that if this lady wants to meet us in court, we'll be there wearing spurs"—even later he was unable to understand where this totally uncharacteristic metaphor had come from; just genius, he supposed—"and we'll kick the living shit out of her and all her kind, no matter how long it takes or how much money it costs. Now then, gentlemen, shall we go to lunch? We don't want to keep the great lady waiting. . . ."

3

The luncheon had gotten completely out of hand. Edith was in town to do the Tonight Show, and—not having seen Harry since his heart attack—she had been delighted to accept his invitation to visit the lot, meet the Melos-Doria staff, "perhaps have a quiet meal in the Board Room with our Chairman." But then the Chairman had become involved. Harry found Deering's sudden interest in classical matters surprising and a little sad. The Chairman had never before associated himself with any product line exhibiting such questionable profitability. But—having spent the greater part of his adult life in the finance departments of large corporate enterprises (principally home appliances before he was invited to take over at LTI)—Deering was still stage-struck, and he would do almost anything to have himself photographed with major show-business figures, even operatic ones, especially if that same evening the artist might say to Johnny Carson on the air, "Why, just today I was having lunch with Leslie Deering, and he thinks . . ."

The luncheon was organized (Deering's new favorite verb) on Sound Stage No. 9, where the Remy Fontaine Show had once been taped—the comedian having since been dropped from the LTI roster, victim of an unforeseen elevation of public taste. The usually empty hall had been transformed into the Art Department's conception of a Parisian garden in spring. Naturally, it was like no garden ever seen in Paris: all pink and green with freshly painted white trellises festooned with live flowering pear and ivy and, at the base of each vertical member, great gobs of azaleas interspersed with giant tropical ferns. No TV special of the current season would boast a more opulent—or costly—

mise en scène. Later, Harry would learn, the set—which was what it was—would be used for the filming of Chevrolet commercials. Deering was not a man to let corporate resources go to waste unnecessarily. Twenty circular tables for eight were artfully set with pink tablecloths and Abbey Rents' best flatware and genuine Baccarat wineglasses purchased for the occasion but destined for eventual safekeeping in Deering's Bel Air mansion. Loudspeakers hidden under the tables poured forth muffled repetitions of "La Vie en rose" and "April in Paris" and other standards from a stack of Edith Piaf LPs. In the center of the great hall—the interior walls of which had been painted rose, with the ceiling and light racks and miscellaneous piping done in sky blue—the Prop Department had created a grassy knoll, using huge rolls of St. Augustine turf trucked in from Bakersfield and put down in tight-knit sections and then freshly mowed so that not a single point was evident. Here now gathered the 130 most senior LTI managers, representing all branches of Leslie Deering's entertainment empire from A to Y (Archery to Yachting, LTI having no product line in the Z's except maybe zuba-diving, as Burt Moss, Melos-Doria's ranking wag, liked to say).

Harry was the last to arrive, having sent the lawyers on ahead while he checked New York again for word of Schonbaum's verdict on *Otello*. (Still no news—or maybe Norman didn't think he could stand any more news.) Harry was soon sorry he'd come. Bloxom, idiot chief of Field & Stream—as fat and hospital-prone as Harry had been before Rome—spotted him and let out a great roar of welcome which quickly turned into a standing ovation: overwhelming applause (Harry grinning sheepishly in self-defense) for this brave veteran who, like great executives the world over, had fought the Coronary War and lived to tell of it.

". . . By God, you're looking well, Harry . . ."

". . . Atta boy, Mr. Chapin . . ."

". . . Can't keep a good man down, eh, Harry boy . . .?"

He staggered forward, desperate for a drink—no, no, forbidden, of course—or a familiar face he didn't dislike. The commissary's regular waitresses had been supplied with French peasant-girl outfits from Western Costume, colorful skirts and blouses last seen in *Gigi*, and Harry called to a blonde he thought he knew under her pigtailed wig: "Marge? I wasn't sure it was you. . . ."

"Fantastic to have you back, Mr. Chapin—your Tío Pepe . . ."

How thoughtful—and how he hated to disappoint. "Just this once," he said to Marge, "I wonder if you might let me have a gin and tonic—but without the gin? That is, just a glass of quinine water? With a twist of lime, if you have it . . ."

Consternation. She eyed him warily, as so many did nowadays. Oh, yes, very unpredictable since his "accident." He turned, looking for someplace to hide, only to find himself inundated with unwanted hand-shakes (all those germs not good for heart patients) and further rough thumps on the back (hey, watch the kidneys, okay?). Throwing up a barrage of false smiles, he disengaged from the mob, got his tonic from a still-dubious Marge and felt his way along the perimeter—Bowling & Billiards, Snowmobiles, Baseball Bats, Toys & Games—until he reached the Deering party, which stood aloofly to one side and included at its center a regal being who looked every inch "the Queen of Opera" (*Newsweek*).

"My dear Edith . . ."

"Alas, my poor Harry! What has *happened* to you . . .?"

Their loving embrace seemed to delight the very nervous Leslie Deering. "We were worried sick about this boy. No point working oneself into an early grave, as I've tried to tell our senior people . . ."

Why don't you tell her about not renewing my contract? Harry thought. But why be unkind? Deering's own position was not entirely enviable.

"Edith, darling," Harry said, "your return to the recital stage ob-viously agrees with you. You've never looked more beautiful." He was not exaggerating. Fifty-one, did she now claim? But so beautifully gotten up that she could have gone straight out onto any stage and conquered all hearts—unless, of course, she opened her mouth to sing.

"My dear Harry, only you would understand. When art is one's *raison d'être* . . ."

She seemed excessively pleased to see him, but he couldn't blame her: what had she, a *grande artiste*, to do with all these businessmen? "I don't believe I've had the pleasure," Harry said, turning to the short, dark, balding gentleman standing uncomfortably to one side.

"But you have not *met?*" Edith exclaimed. "Oh, how terrible . . ."

The new face belonged—as Harry had assumed—to E. Jerold Bock, Esq., newest partner in Blankenhorn, Ledbetter, Morrison & Rhodes of New York. Harry decided not to smile: let the bastard worry a little before their little post-luncheon get-together. "Oh, yes," he said, "an-other of Joe's merry men."

"Brought in," Bock was quick to say, "to put some life into the old firm."

"Do tell," Harry said tonelessly.

The little man chuckled nervously, then fell back to sipping his Scotch.

"And how is Joe getting on?" Harry probed. "Did he ever buy that Chagall?"

"Chagall? I don't think I heard about that."

Excellent. Harry could hardly wait to sit down and talk lawsuits. Now he remembered where he'd seen Bock before: reincarnation of one of those smart-ass young lawyers who'd surrounded Senator McCarthy during the TV hearings in the early '50s. Good. It was always fun putting down one of those.

But now back to Mme. Cavalieri, who probably didn't want to talk to Deering. "And what's this I've been hearing," Harry said, showing his back to E. Jerold, "about a farewell recital tour?"

Deering, a more considerate chap than Chapin, took Bock's arms and suggested that the two of them mingle. It was just as well, because Edith wanted to talk shop. She was outraged, she said, that Harry Chapin, one of the few men she truly admired, could *suggest* such a thing. She was *not* beginning a "farewell" tour or anything of the kind, as rumored, simply because she was not ready at her still tender age to say farewell to anything. A recital tour, yes, because she had been off the boards entirely too long—almost a decade, if one kept track of such things—and she wished to repay her loyal public for its continued devotion during her recent period of "creative silence." Now that the "distractions" of her personal life had been set aside, she had regained her confidence and was once again prepared to share her art with an adoring public.

"And is it true, dear Edith, that Richard Box will accompany you?"

Incredibly, yes. Edith, like Norman Rose, could dish the dirt. When we last left Richard Box, he was en route to the wonderful hospital at Grasse to have his swollen hand tended to. The damage was minimal, but there had been another "incident" which Harry might have seen reported in the press: What distaff side of what famed duo-piano team went after her partner with a butcher knife in their fashionable Cotswold cottage? The lady had tried to cut off the offending digits one by one, but failed and ended up in a nice sanitorium in Scotland. So dear Richard was now free to ply his old trade, which was accompanying great ladies like Edith Cavalieri in Schubert's "Erlkönig" and Schumann's "Nussbaum" and Ravel's "Trois chants hébraïques"—just perfect for an audience that had come to hear arias from *Macbeth* and *Aïda* and, yes, *Otello*.

The more Edith talked, the more Harry worried. The woman seemed intent on going through with it. "Naturally, Edith, we're mad to record the New York recital. But, as your most ardent fan, I reserve the right to argue for a change of venue—from Lincoln Center, with its still questionable acoustic, especially as pertains to the solo voice—to the house that deserves the honor of presenting Edith Cavalieri's return to the musical capital of America—Carnegie Hall."

Edith was moved to tears by this declaration of professional love. "Oh, Harry . . . To have someone to talk to again . . . Someone who *understands* the artist's dilemma . . ."

More kisses, more mutual admiration. Interrupted—thank God—

by the very nervous Leslie Deering, who returned to say, "I believe we're being asked to take our seats. Mme. Cavalieri, if I may offer you my arm . . ."

The head table, seating only a dozen, was elevated at one end of the "garden" so that assembled executives might have an uninterrupted view of the guest of honor as well as ultimate corporate leadership. Edith occupied a throne chair at stage center—the chair occupied by Faye Dunaway in *The Three Musketeers*. A delicate pink follow-spot, directed from the catwalk above, imitated each pan and tilt of Edith's gorgeous coiffure. Deering and Chapin, who sat to either side, shared in this cosmetic boon: neither man had ever looked quite so beautiful before.

On Harry's other side, looking tired and gray by contrast, sat a tall, rugged-looking individual—a Cal football star of the immediate post-war era, Harry might have known—in a marvelous blue pinstripe with broad shoulders and a disconcertingly narrow waist. "Ah, Mr. Chapin," the fullback said, "this *is* a pleasure. I'm George Law, I guess you know. I've been hoping to have an opportunity . . ."

Harry would have no difficulty disliking Law—disliking, as he did, outside directors anyway, meddling busybodies who took pride in how little they knew about your particular business, "whereas down at the bank . . ." "You've met Edith, have you?" Harry asked. "If not—"

"Oh, my, yes. Leslie was good enough—"

"Leslie?"

"Leslie Deering."

Mmm, knocked nicely off stride with that one: poor Law ain't heard about eccentric old Chapin yet.

"Ah, yes. Got a lot of Leslies around here—mostly females in the typing pool, thank heavens. Would you care to switch chairs? Be nearer to—"

"No, no," Law protested. "I'm sure Mme. Cavalieri would prefer to talk to someone, ah, more closely attuned—you being our opera man, isn't that right? The chap who seems to like Italy so much, eh?" punctuated with gruff and hearty guffaws.

"Oh, yes," Harry said. "Much prefer Rome to say, Burbank." Harry drank down his quinine water, signaled for another.

"And you're the man," Law went on, "who signed up Slonimsky, I'm told."

"Re-signed," Harry corrected. "He has been with our label since the late forties, to be accurate."

"Re-signed, then," Law agreed. "As a matter of fact, I'm something of a pianist myself."

"*Oh?*" Harry acted as though he'd just heard the most shocking news. "You've played in *public?*"—delivered with great earnestness.

"Well, no—not exactly. But—"

"Ah," Harry said, crestfallen. "Sorry—only deal in professionals around here."

"I *might* have been a professional," Law shot back, "if it hadn't been for my career with C.B."

"C.B.?"

Law wasn't believing his ears today. "Why, Cal-Bank, naturally."

"Oh, *banking*," Harry said. Faulty memory, this Chapin. "And had you any talent, do you suppose? For the piano?"

"According to my teacher—"

"Yes, but what do our teachers know? You were probably right to stick with the bank."

"Somehow, Mr. Chapin, I have the feeling that you and I—"

"Will you excuse me for a moment? Someone's trying to get my attention—a rather urgent business matter . . ."

While the first course was being served—*Salade Melos-Doria*, which was avocado and baby shrimps and bits of pineapple bathed in French dressing, which Harry couldn't eat anyway—he circulated among the tables, exchanging greetings on the terrace level until he found Alix, who was sitting with Ross Canby and Burt Moss and the rest of Melos-Doria middle-management. "Alix, love," he said, kissing her cheek, which immediately turned a lovely salmon pink, "if you've got a moment . . ."

This would set tongues a-wagging: Chapin and Stern an item— what could be more natural? He motioned for her to follow him to an empty table where everybody could see them—especially George Law— and where Harry pretended to engage the lady executive in serious business conversation. Alix only got to attend functions like this be- cause she was now carried on the books as Manager, Classical Adminis- tration, a little bonus that Harry had recently sent her way—and well deserved it was, in his opinion. "So what do you think, then?" he said. "Pretty painful, huh?"

"The party? Oh, *no*, Harry—it's *super*. I'm having a wonderful time. Mme. Cavalieri is very beautiful, isn't she?"

"Oh? Do you think so? Mmmm—maybe. At least *you* get a free meal out of all this, which is more than I can say."

"You're in an awfully carefree mood," she said, eyeing him closely.

"Irresponsible, you mean. Yeah, comes from hitting the quinine water too hard." She was right: he *did* feel giddy, and not just from what Deering had told him about his contract either. "Actually," he went on, "I'm drunk as a skunk. It's called *ivresse de vacuité*—rapture of the empty stomach being the technical term. Oh, yes, you can stand anything if it's given a pretty name."

"I thought perhaps it was good news from Mr. Deering—from your meeting this morning."

"Hah! Quite the contrary! Which is probably why I just told our big banking friend up there to go fuck himself. Remind me to tell you about it sometime."

"I shall," she said.

"Oh, Christ, the Chairman's leering at us—probably hot for your body, he's already *had* mine. I'd better be getting back. Hey, you look terrific today—did I tell you that?"

Salade Melos-Doria gave way to chicken in white sauce with mushrooms and artichokes and flecks of imported truffle washed down with Almadén's "Blanc de Blancs" champagne: still nothing that Harry could eat or drink, which the attentive staff immediately noticed. With minimum fuss they sent back to the commissary for a plate of fresh fruit and cottage cheese and an iced Sanka, the same lunch he'd had each day since Monday.

About halfway through—when his tongue would normally have been loosened by alcohol—Harry decided to let up on poor Law and make conversation. Law seemed greatly relieved. "So glad to hear you *say* that!" he said in response to one of Harry's inane suggestions: that all young people be *forced* to take piano lessons between the ages of ten and fifteen. "As a matter of fact, our daughter Melissa . . ."

Melissa was a veritable genius of the keyboard, it seemed: started lessons when she was four and could now sight-read all of Messiaen. What did Harry think of a concert career for girls? Harry thought why not? Women are screwing up all the other professions, why not pianoplaying? Law chuckled; after a rocky start, he was beginning to like this boy Chapin.

"Now about this *Otello* business . . ."

Harry nodded with solemnity. "Mmmmm, *Otello*. Where does one begin . . .?"

Law had never seen *Otello*, the opera. He'd seen *Othello*, the play, of course, while in college—Cal Berkeley followed by Harvard Business, as Harry might have heard. But he was not an opera buff: had seen *Carmen* once and didn't like it. Found *Carmen* too "stylized" for him— meaning that it was unrealistic for people to come out on stage and start singing their dialogue.

Well, then, Harry suggested, he wouldn't like *Otello* either, because that's just what people did, sang their dialogue. As for *recording* these long, boring things . . . "Matter of fact," Harry said between orange slices, "just starting on a new one."

"*Another* one?" the fullback said with alarm. "Requiring, I suppose, another hundred thousand dollars?"

"Oh, no," Harry responded with glee, "more. Much more. This one's twice as long." Law's expression went from alarm to panic, but Harry was not to be slowed. "*Lohengrin,* it's called. A lot like *Carmen,* but in German. No, you probably wouldn't like it. Anyway, in view of your decision not to renew my contract . . ."

Law's features took on a painful cast. "To be fair, Harry, the entire Board—"

"Oh, don't worry about it," Harry said, cutting the bum off in midsentence. "It doesn't worry me, so why should it worry you . . . ?"

You got brandy whether you wanted it or not. Harry, good boy, didn't touch his. While the French peasant maids went around pouring, Chairman Deering got to his feet and delivered the Words of Welcome called for in the Artist Relations Department's "Schedule of Activities."

". . . Not only a great personal pleasure and honor for me, but a source of notable company pride for us all . . ."

Deering spoke for ten minutes, using the words *pride* and *honor* a dozen times each before turning to Harry. Harry, knowing how Deering worked, had taken the liberty of preparing a mental text. In a series of carefully wrought and beautifully phrased paragraphs, he first sketched —mostly for the benefit of the many LTI executives who had never heard of Mr. and Mrs. Leonid Strauss—a brief history of Melos-Doria and Edith's long association with the label; then suggested that artistic merit of the first order like Edith's was seldom—as now—wed to great popular acclaim; and finally put the proposition that presenting Mme. Cavalieri's art to a world hungry for beauty was a responsibility, a profession, nay, a *calling* which few men were privileged to follow, and which provided personal gratification far beyond any that might be measured by a Personnel Department's wage scale.

He sat down quickly—at the precise moment of optimum emotional climax (orgasm was perhaps not too strong a word)—and Mr. George Law led a standing ovation, Harry's second of the day.

Afterward Edith herself—exhibiting great reluctance and almost painful modesty in the wake of Harry's panegyric—was prevailed upon to say a few words. Her hold on the audience was magical; not an eye wandered, not a head nodded off. Her association with Melos-Doria had provided, she said, many of the dearest moments of her life—in particular, her deep personal ties to dear Harry Chapin. . . . But now, contrary to malicious gossip, she had no intention of retiring from public life. Indeed, she was planning a major recital tour which would reach its climax in New York's Carnegie Hall (quick glance of understanding and appreciation in Harry's direction) and would be recorded by Mr. Chapin's peerless crew for early release on the superlative Melos-Doria label.

Harry nodded in accord, triggering appreciative applause and putting a grateful smile on LTI's collective management face.

Further (what? *more* good news? such a bounty!), she was pleased to reveal that she was at that very moment on her way to Gotham, where that dear man David Merrick was waiting to discuss with her the starring role in a fabulous new Broadway musical—in which she would play the madam of a Parisian brothel.

No more agreeable nods from Chapin. Really, it was tragic the way these moribund supernovae found themselves fatally attracted to Broadway—the gravitational effects of cold cash, he supposed. A chagrined Raffaele Quinzi had just informed Consortium members that fragile old Toggi, far from retiring, was about to star in a Roman production of *Man of La Mancha* in the role of Don Quixote!

LTI's enthusiasm knew no bounds. Outside Director George Law was beside himself (he might not know opera, but he certainly knew Broadway musicals). Chairman of the Board, President and Chief Executive Officer Leslie T. Deering was ecstatic. "A fabulous success, Harry," Deering told him afterward. "Incredibly fine—George thinks so, too. Don't know why we don't stage these events more often. Wonderful effect on staff morale . . ."

Deering and Law had their photos taken with Edith, who finally insisted that Harry get in the picture. (But I'm *out* of the picture, Harry wanted to tell her.) He affected his best corporate smile and why not?— his last publicity shots ever as Melos-Doria chief. Law, revealing weakness which Harry had not thought possible, broke down and asked Cavalieri to autograph a menu—for Melissa, his daughter, he said, but Harry knew better: Edith's magic had subdued more formidable foes than George Law.

"Oh, yes, Harry," Deering repeated, "we must make a regular habit of this. Give the employees a chance to see that ours is a business of flesh and blood . . ." Harry made no reply. Perhaps the new man—of course, *Dell!*—would share Deering's newfound enthusiasm for artists. Harry did not.

The Melos-Doria limo was waiting out front. Deering had persuaded Edith to make a brief tour of the lot; he now urged Harry to come along: "Relax, my boy—get away from that desk of yours for an hour." But Harry was able to escape, reminding Deering of the meeting

with E. Jerold Bock and LTI's legal staff in the matter of Edith's
pending lawsuit. "My God, yes," Deering whispered. "Can we settle, do
you think? A shame to spoil such an otherwise *cordial* relationship . . ."
Harry—happy in the knowledge that E. Jerold Bock had been rele-
gated to one of the least-favored tables at the back of the hall with Bull
and Titcomb and Musgrove—pledged that he would do his best.

Edith insisted on having a private word with Harry before she left.
They sat alone in the rose garden while the others cooled their heels.

Harry said: "We missed you, of course—Norman and I—in Rome.
Your Desdemona. I still regret—"

"What's past is past," Edith said. "You are not happy about the
Broadway business, I can tell."

"Let's just say that I am not—enthusiastic."

"And why is that, dear Harry?"

"Mmmm—dilution of one's effort? Like the album of popular
songs?"

"Oh, but *that* was very different. A false start, a lady's vanity, a
mistake in judgment . . ."

"Of course. And who am I to judge? If Broadway will make you
happy . . ."

"Yes, you understand completely, as I knew you would. This
foolish opera charade—I do not wish to pursue it further. And so . . ."

"And what would you have me do, dear Edith, about this new
lawyer of yours—Mr. Bock?"

"A puppy-dog," Edith said. "I have told Joe that I am most
offended."

"Mmmm—sometimes the young ones know their business," Harry
lied. "But if he persists in talking lawsuits—"

"But this is the nature of attorneys, *n'est-ce pas?*" she said impatiently. "They insist on making difficulties."

"They do, yes," Harry agreed.

"But this is not between us—this *business?*" She said *business* the
way another person said *shit.*

"Of course not," Harry said. "No matter what ensues, dear Edith,
the business is not between us. Only the art . . ." (Oh, God, Chapin,
you do your job so well.)

"Dear man. Yet, if Joe insists—with this puppy-dog—on going to
court—"

"Naturally, we must defend ourselves."

"And what does this mean? In practical terms?"

"It means—with great regret, Edith—that there can be no reissue
program, no recording of the New York recital, no flowers in the hotel
rooms, no advertisements in the newspapers. It is not something I can
control, dear Edith, once matters go so far."

"But Joe believes *I* am the injured party. That it is my *right* to expect compensation. He believes that only in court can I—"

"Joe's fees, Edith—if you will forgive me—are proportional to the amount of trouble he can create. He does not wish to go to court any more than we do, but he believes that such threats improve his negotiating position."

"And are you being fair to me? In these negotiations?"

"Would I be otherwise? Am I such a *businessman*"—Harry, too, could say *shit*—"that I would treat Edith Cavalieri unjustly?"

"My dear Harry . . ."

She pressed his head to her bosom. Such a wondrous scent. "My dear Edith . . ."

He delivered the Queen of Opera into Deering's anxious hands. An almost reverent George Law expressed his profound regrets at being unable to accompany Edith on her tour of the lot; but even now he would be lucky to make his return flight to San Francisco.

"Harry," Law said, shaking hands with incredible power, "I look forward to our next meeting. What about over lunch? Maybe up my way?"

"My pleasure, of course," Harry said. "But don't hold your breath, asshole," under *his* breath.

I I

The meeting on Mme. Cavalieri's lawsuit was held in the Melos-Doria conference room, adjoining Harry's office. Harry instructed Alix to offer no coffee and no ashtrays; to interrupt only if Mr. Rose called from New York; and to buzz not later than 3:25 so that he would be on time for his meeting with Sidney Jonas and the man from J. Walter Thompson.

While the others were in the men's room (Harry, having eaten and drunk so little, didn't have to go) he wrote on the blackboard:

> A—reissues
> B—N.Y. recital
> C—audit
> D—pop LP
> E—new contract

"Ah, a man who does his homework," E. Jerold Bock complimented on returning. "We're gonna get along just fine."

Harry said nothing. He took his place at the head of the table while the imperious Bull, the effete Titcomb and the weak-kneed Musgrove found chairs on one side, the unknown Bock across from them. Harry felt a sudden surge of adrenaline: one line manager, four attorneys—he was never happier than when surrounded by these bandits of the law who cared nothing for equity but only for fees and appearances.

"Well, then," Davis Bull rumbled in his pompous bullfrog way. "We all understand, I believe, gentlemen, why we've gathered here this afternoon."

"I certainly *hope* so," Bock said smugly. The balding little New Yorker took from his briefcase (Mark Cross on Fifth Avenue, Harry noted, but not first quality—$100 at most) a sterling-silver cigar case, removing from it a particularly evil-looking brute. "Why don't I kinda lay out for you guys the problem areas and let you know the things we gotta have? Then if you have any questions . . ."

"Fine, fine," said Bull.

"Excellent idea," said Titcomb.

"Very helpful," said Musgrove.

"That won't be necessary," said Chapin.

Bock put down his unlighted cigar. "Not *necessary?*" He continued to look around for an ashtray. "I suppose you got a *better* idea?"

"To save time," Harry said, pulling up his shirt sleeve and making pointed reference to his Otto Kunz Memorial Rolex, "let me summarize our two positions, giving you Melos-Doria's final offer in each case. You may take this down, if you'd like, Mr. Bock, but in any case I'll be sending you a confirming letter on Monday."

Bull, Titcomb of the long nostrils and Musgrove were plainly scandalized. LTI's General Counsel began making notes at a feverish pace for his report to Deering. Titcomb admired Harry's watch. Musgrove helped Bock look for the nonexistent ashtray.

Bock—Bock imploded. And for good reason, Harry knew: because usurping the floor was the greatest punishment any layman could inflict upon these fellows.

"Hey, *look,*" Bock finally sputtered—trying gamely to smile—"it's *your* ballpark. But, man, you start talkin' final offers . . ."

"Thank you," Harry said. "Point A, reissues . . ."

He proceeded down the list with—if he did say so himself— laudable grasp of detail and pellucid exposition of the real issues at hand:

Melos-Doria proposes to reissue all of Mme. Cavalieri's recordings, including even the earliest monophonic ones—some four dozen LPs in all—as part of Melos-Doria's mid-priced Heritage Series. In the face of constantly increasing costs and the resulting squeeze on profits, Melos-Doria has asked Mme. Cavalieri to accept half-royalties on these albums, which would bear a retail list price of $4.98, approximately two thirds of the price of the regular $7.98 line. Mme. Cavalieri, however, insists on full royalty rates and new advances of $10,000 per album. Melos-Doria finds these terms uneconomic. Melos-Doria's "last best" offer: half-royalties plus an advance of $1000 per LP.

"Well, I can tell you right now—"

"Please wait till I've finished, Mr. Bock. . . ."

Point B: Mme. Cavalieri has asked Melos-Doria to record her forthcoming recital in New York, proposing an advance of $50,000 for the master. Melos-Doria would be pleased to record the recital, but could offer an advance of no more than $5000—recitals with piano having a notoriously poor sales history. Also, Melos-Doria could not undertake such a project under threat of a lawsuit or in the absence of a comprehensive new contract with the lady.

Mr. Bock tapped the table nervously with his unlighted cigar, but refrained from interrupting again.

Point C: Mme. Cavalieri has recently undertaken, through the good offices of Mr. Bock, an audit of her royalty account with Melos-Doria; and, according to Mr. Bock's report, Melos-Doria owes the lady more than $250,000 in back royalties. Harry himself has gone over the report with Melos-Doria's VP, Finance; and Melos-Doria is now of the opinion that it owes Mme. Cavalieri $17,400 as a result of having inadvertently applied an incorrect royalty rate to Canadian sales after 1973. A check for the $17,400 will be mailed to Mme. Cavalieri's accountant in due course.

"That's *bullshit!*" Bock erupted. "If you're going to tell me—"

"Point D," Harry said. "The pop LP . . ."

With respect to the album of popular songs recorded by Mme. Cavalieri for the English firm Orb & Sceptre—but not released by them—Mme. Cavalieri proposes that Melos-Doria take over the project, buying the existing tapes from O&S for the amount already invested by them—an astonishing $70,000—and recording or re-recording such material as Melos-Doria might think necessary to complete the album. Regrettably, Melos-Doria declines to involve itself in such a venture, believing that the tapes should be scrapped and that an artist of Edith Cavalieri's stature should not damage her reputation through such lapses of judgment.

And finally, Point E: a new contract. Mme. Cavalieri's last contract with Melos-Doria expired in 1972; and though Melos-Doria has continued to act as though that contract were still in effect—treating Mme. Cavalieri as a première Melos-Doria artist—the lady herself has done otherwise, entering into new contracts with Deutsche Grammophon and O&S. Mme. Cavalieri now alleges that Melos-Doria has caused her career and reputation irreparable damage by denying her the role of Desdemona in the recently completed *Otello*—a role specifically called for in her contract—and demands that Melos-Doria undertake, as a substitute, a complete recording of Strauss's *Der Rosenkavalier,* with Mme. Cavalieri as the Marschallin.

"This final point," Harry explained, "is the most important of all. Therefore, let me choose my words with care. Melos-Doria replies that Mme. Cavalieri herself aborted the *Otello* called for in her last con-tract—in addition to other major projects too numerous to cite—and the company thus declines to contract with Mme. Cavalieri for the recording of any more complete operas. Melos-Doria would agree, how-ever, to undertake an album of songs or arias, the repertoire to be mutually agreed upon, in addition to the aforementioned New York recital album.

"Yes, I believe I've said that correctly. Now, let's see—have I omitted anything? No, I think not. . . . Oh, Mr. Bock, how thought-less of me—you require an ashtray, don't you . . . ?"

The performance had been a total success: Bock was literally speechless at the final curtain. Musgrove ran out to Alix's desk and crashed back with *two* ashtrays. But Bock's hands were shaking too wildly for the little lawyer to think of lighting up. Titcomb, who hated detail, and who had never before heard so much of it in his entire life, excused himself most apologetically to make an "essential" phone call to his Washington office.

Harry sat placidly at the head of the table and waited.

Bull couldn't take the pressure. "Ah, Jerold—let us view these posi-tions," he rumbled, "merely as points of departure—"

"No, I'm sorry, Davis," Harry corrected at once. "Let's not raise false hopes. The positions I have just enunciated are Melos-Doria's firm and final responses to the various points raised in Mr. Blankenhorn's letter of November twenty-first."

Finally, E. Jerold Bock spoke. He hardly knew how to begin, he said. He had never received such an *insulting* proposition in his life— and he was older, he assured Harry, than he looked. As a CPA—as *well* as a lawyer—he had *personally* directed the audit of Edith's account, and he stood by the figure $250,000. If Melos-Doria wanted to go into court—

"Oh, but apparently we must," Harry said lightly.

"Now, *wait* a minute, Harry," Bull cried angrily. "You and I both know—"

"I know only," said Harry in his most infuriatingly reasonable tone of voice, "that Mme. Cavalieri's audit claims are without merit. But then that's the purpose of courts, isn't it? At any rate, Mr. Bock, why don't you put our responses to Mme. Cavalieri?"

"But *how?*" the little man squealed. "How am I gonna get up *nerve* enough to tell her what you're offering? Hey, Mr. Chapin—Harry—man to man, this is bullshit and you *know* it!"

"We don't use that kind of language here," Harry said without smiling.

"Look—sorry. But—"

"Or would you prefer," Harry offered, "that *I* speak to Mme. Cavalieri?"

"Now, *really*, Mr. Bull," Bock begged, "do I have to listen to this . . . ?"

Harry loved it when all these fine legal gentlemen took sides against the common foe, the layman here—and never mind that LTI paid Bull's very handsome salary. He'd never seen it fail: suggest that you'll talk directly to their principals and they shit in their pants—because if the principals reach agreement, what need is there for lawyers?

"Now, *Harry*," Bull said frantically, "I must *insist* that we caucus. Jerold, we'll be just a few minutes—there are some aspects of this which Harry obviously—"

"Sorry, Davis," Harry said, referring once again to his lovely time-piece, "but, regrettably, I'm meeting with the ad agency in a few moments. In any event, we seem to have made as much progress as we're going to make today."

"And you expect to leave everything up in the air?" cried Bock, turning back to Harry now, Bull having failed him. "With nothing *decided?*"

"From our point of view, Mr. Bock, matters *have* been decided. Of course, if you have new proposals to make . . ."

Bock was really sweating now. "Look," he said, softening his voice, trying to control his hands, "the most urgent thing right now is cash flow. In view of the audit—"

"As I've said, Mr. Bock, our check in the amount of seventeen thousand four hundred dollars—"

"Hey, *Harry*—Mr. Chapin—that's just not *enough*," Bock moaned. "In view of our very large audit claim—"

"Which we deny. But then that's a matter for the courts, as you say. In due course—over the next few years, the civil calendars being as crowded as they are . . ."

Bock began again, searching desperately in Harry's direction for some sign of understanding—mercy, even. "Speaking man to man—"

"So you've said."

"If you'll let me *finish*. Certainly you can afford to make *some* advance—just based on her regular on-going sales?"

"We could, of course," said Harry. "But why should we? Put your-self in my place, Mr. Bock. If the lady is going to sue us . . ."

"Your *attitude,* Harry—Mr. Chapin—I've never experienced anything like it in my life!"

"Again—put yourself in my place. You—being a CPA, as you point out, as well as an attorney—you know the cost of money. Why should I lend my company's money unless I can get something in return? Now, if you were to withdraw your suit . . ."

"That's *blackmail!*"

"I *must* object, Harry," Bull cried angrily, "Jerold is quite right when he says—"

"On the contrary, Davis—this is business. We're not a bank. If you wish to borrow money, Mr. Bock, why not go to a bank? And in the meantime you can press your suit against us."

Now Bull was looking at *his* watch.

Titcomb returned in time to hear the discussion of advances and bank loans. "Jerold," he said soothingly, "any further discussion today would seem to be counterproductive to our—"

"I think you're right, Marcus," Harry said brightly. "Why don't we adjourn now, Mr. Bock, and perhaps next week, after you've had an opportunity to talk this over with Joe Blankenhorn—"

"So what you're saying is you'll offer us *nothing* now? No advances of *any* kind? Not a nickel—"

"How much did you have in mind?"

"What? Oh—well—at least fifty thousand dollars. Which, you've got to admit, ain't gonna break the bank."

"Done," said Harry, banging the table loudly.

Bull, Titcomb and the very silent Musgrove came to attention.

"You're saying—"

"I'm saying, Mr. Bock, that we'll provide you with an immediate fifty-thousand-dollar advance—give you a check on Monday morning—on the following conditions:

"One, the lawsuit is dropped and you sign a waiver for any damages or other sums in excess of the audit figure I've given you—seventeen-four, as I remember it.

"Two, you agree to the reissue plan at half-royalties and with a one-thousand dollar advance per LP.

"And three, we proceed with the New York recital album at the terms previously mentioned—five-thousand advance against the usual royalty rate."

Bock added a column of figures on his yellow pad, muttered under his breath, shook his head in frustration and impotence. "Nope—out of the question. For a lousy fifty-thousand advance—"

"In our league," Harry said gently, "that's still considered a sizable amount of money."

"And if we don't agree to your terms?"

"Why, then—'see you in court,' isn't that the expression?"

Bock thought again. "Obviously, we're gonna have to talk to Cavalieri. No—Joe'll *never* go for this. It's just *ridiculous.*"

"Yes, well, I can appreciate that for a man in Joe's circles our numbers are depressingly small," Harry agreed. "But on the off-chance you would like to reconsider our terms, Mr. Bock—may I ask that you reach a decision as quickly as you can?"

Bock was shocked yet again. "Why? You got to be *kidding.* What's the rush, all of a sudden?"

"I agree, Harry," Bull offered gratuitously. "What possible reason can there be—"

"The reason," Harry said, "is that we're out of time with respect to Edith's recital tour—which, as you know, has already begun. If we're not to have another contract, our marketing people will wish to withdraw their advertising support. Though I'm sure, Mr. Bock, you'll have no difficulty in obtaining such support from DG or O-and-S—or will you?"

"You *bas—*"

But Mr. Bock got hold of himself and withdrew that inflammatory sentiment. Instead, he said as nastily as he could: "Well, I'll promise you one thing, Mr. Chapin."

"Oh?"

"Yeah—you can forget all about any special rates on her catalog stuff. Your reissue program is dead, D-E-A-D. You've released your last Edith Cavalieri album."

"Oh, I'm afraid that's not quite true," Harry said even more gently than before.

"What do you mean?"

"We have the right to reissue Edith's recordings any time we want at half-price, if not mid-price—paying her half-royalties, of course."

Bock reacted sharply. "I'm not sure about that. I'd have to look at the old contract."

"Yes, do. I have. Melos-Doria can begin issuing Edith's entire catalog at three ninety-eight tomorrow morning, if we wish, without obtaining any further permission or approval."

"Maybe you can and maybe you can't," Bock spat out contemptuously. "But you guys don't even *have* a three-ninety-eight line—that much I *do* know."

"Mmmm—no, we don't," Harry said, a tinge of melancholy to his voice. "I really wish we did. Because, as things stand, we have to license our half-price material to Rosco Bloom for reissue on one of his many labels, and they're really of such poor quality. In addition to which, we're never certain of a proper accounting."

Bock's eyes narrowed. "You *wouldn't*," he said. "You wouldn't put Edith Cavalieri on one of those—*garbage* labels?"

"Not happily," Harry said. "But—assuming no new contract with Edith—what else can we do? You've tied our hands, Jerold—if I may call you that. Yes, I'm afraid you've outsmarted us again. . . ."

Nuts! Only after they'd gone did he remember Apogée's audio-visual system: forgotten to demand its immediate return. Hell. Well, he'd add that to his confirming letter Monday morning.

"Harry? You've got five minutes until you're expected in Art, and Mr. Bull's on line one—he sounds rather angry."

"Thanks, Alix—yes, I'm just about to leave. . . . Ah, Davis . . . How do you think it went? With our little friend Mr. Bock?"

"Harry, I'll make this short. I have *never* been so ashamed of a company officer. To treat a member of the *bar* with such utter disrespect—to indulge in such *unethical* tactics. You should be aware, Harry, that at the earliest opportunity I intend to relate the entire shameful episode, in full detail, to Mr. Deering."

"Davis? You can't know how pleased I am by your reaction. I shall be delighted to discuss with Leslie your collusion with outside counsel against the interests of this company—and in full detail, as you suggest. Thank you for calling. . . . Oh, and Davis?"

"What is it?"

"Go fuck yourself, won't you?"

III

With a light heart—and stomach—Harry sauntered out back to the last bungalow overlooking the Lakeside Country Club, home of Advertising & Art. Here—drinking gin-and-Fresca of a Friday afternoon and feeling little pain even in the presence of the big boss—gathered the Back Lot Mafia: Joe Kidd, self-proclaimed merchandising genius, Burt Moss, closet novelist and sometime ad manager, Sidney Jonas, art director and father-confessor for wayward husbands, and one interloper, Laughton McNab, JWT's erstwhile supervisor on the Melos-Doria account.

". . . Fuckin' great to have you back, goddammit, boss . . . Sit your ass down . . . Take a load off the ole ticker . . . Get you something to drink? Ah, Jesus, that's right, you can't have it anymore, can you . . . ?"

Harry detected an unwonted note of respect, solicitude, consideration bordering on devotion. They even said they'd liked his little speech at the Cavalieri luncheon. "So what the fuck's going on out here anyway?" he cried in rebuttal. "Boozing on company time. When are you parasites going to start earning your outrageous salaries . . .?"

There had never been much discipline here in the Out Back. His boys. How he would miss them (except McNab, who didn't count). He would probably never attend another meeting like this in his life. If only he could have a drink. It wasn't natural to remain sober in these circumstances. He felt like crying. "Okay, so show me the fucking cover," he said.

"The cover?" said Sidney.

"The *cover*," said Harry.

The stall was on. Harry could see the flats standing in the corner. Nobody had seen the artwork yet, and anticipation ran high, which Sidney liked. Whenever possible, Sidney made you sweat.

Sidney, looking so *old*. The Bronx-bred art director had gray hair on the day they met—in 1958?—but now he had the stoop to go with it. It was hard to look upon Sidney now with the respect formerly accorded this gentleman because—contrary to all forecasts—Sidney had done the unforgivable: returned to darling wife Hannah and kiddies—brought the troops out from East Orange. After three brief years of swinging bachelorhood, he again yearned for home cooking. "Oh, how you *disappoint* me," Harry had said Monday on hearing the news.

"The bachelor life is such a dream, you are thinking," replied Sidney. "Well, a few things I could tell . . ."

But Harry didn't want to hear them. Why lose one's hard-won middle-age misconceptions?

". . . So while you're here," Sidney now ambled along, "maybe you could settle a problem for your old friends and associates?"

"So what kind of problem?" falling into Sidney's patois.

"We are receiving only today a note from your pal Mr. Quinzi in Milan," Sidney related, searching among the papers on his drawing board.

"So what is it saying?"

"And may I quote: 'Contractual commitments concerning the packaging and advertising of *Otello* . . . Mr. Toggi retains the right of approval of all photographs and other likenesses of himself employed in said album, whether cover or booklet, or in print advertising.' If you are expecting us to trust the Italian mail service to make our February release date . . ."

"Ridiculous," Harry said, feeling a little like E. Jerold Bock. "I never agreed to such a thing. Use whatever photos you want and send me the complaints if you get any, which you won't."

"You are one sweet *goy*," Sidney said. "But another letter, which I have misplaced, informs us that a 'use fee' must be paid to the session photographer on any black-and-whites we use in the libretto. May we disregard this instruction also?"

"I don't remember any session photographer."

"Tree, the name was," Burt Moss interjected. Burt, being a writer, remembered words. "Mr. Frank Tree—probably English."

Horrors.

"No," said Harry with practiced calm, "that's a Miss, actually. Miss Frances Tree. But no—there are no fees to be paid on her work."

As a matter of fact, those fees have already been paid, and then some. Dear little Frankie. He'd had a nice letter from her, too. She was no longer employed by Melos-Doria, but was a professional photographer, having joined her brother Kenneth in his studio in New York, where they did fashion stuff for the agencies up and down Madison Avenue. She was abandoning London forever, she said, now that Teedee was gone. Also, Mr. Herb Fink, who had fucked her a number of times in Rome, had made noises about photo assignments he could throw her way if she could get herself to Gotham, which of course (thanks to the world-famous generosity of Mr. H. E. Chapin II) she had. Her photo spread on Zeke and Didi had been bought by *Music Week* and would run in the February issue, when *Otello* would just be hitting the stores—perfect timing. So, little Frankie had prospects.

Harry rose to leave. "Have a nice weekend, all," he said. "See you on Monday, huh?"

Sidney, who had dealt with Chapin down through the ages, wasn't fooled for a second. "You're *dying* to see it, aren't you? You can't *wait* to lay your weary management eyes upon it, isn't this so?"

Ever so slowly, Sidney brought forward the Siamesed cardboard flats.

Harry sat back down. "I do hope it's not too—evocative," he said straight-faced. "My heart . . ."

With artful gesture, Sidney permitted the flats to swing open.

"Mmmm," Harry said. Once again he was aware of his pulse at neck and wrists. "Mmmmmm."

Burt Moss let out a soft whistle. Nobody else uttered a sound.

"Who was the photographer?" Harry said at length.

"Phelps," Sidney said. "Ty Phelps—Didi's boy."

"Mmmmm."

Harry chuckled at the thought of what George Law would say when he saw the album in a store window. Because, oh, yes, every record-store window in America would display this album. "A business of flesh and blood," hadn't the Chairman said in his poetic boardroomese? Flesh and blood—or at least flesh—is what we got here, my man.

"It's a bit—direct—don't you think?" said Laughton McNab with

typical agency prissiness. "At least add a screen? Soften the, ah, percep-
tion of, ah, nudity . . . ?"

Harry had never cared for agency people. They were like the outside attorneys, Titcomb and that crowd: standing comfortably and
safely on the sidelines while the line manager took all the risks. ("You
don't like anybody," Sidney had once told him, "who isn't covered with
our brand of pigshit.")

"If we're gonna use this, we'd better get workin' on our Southern
strategy," said Joe Kidd, who was from Savannah, Georgia. "Integration
we reluctantly accept, but miscegenation . . ."

"They're not fucking," said Burt Moss. "Or are they?"

Harry took a closer look. So did Jonas, Kidd, McNab and Moss.
"How disappointing," said Harry, giving voice to the consensus.

Incredible graphics. The front cover was Didi and Zeke, each nude
to the waist, in what movie people call a clinch, Didi's glistening white
back to the camera, Zeke facing head on, his massive black arms
wrapped tightly around her fragile body, his face half buried in her
neck. The back cover was the reverse of this, Zeke's back to the camera,
Didi's pristine white arms around his waist and her natural pink lips
pressed into his muscular shoulder. The blatant blackness of Ezekiel
Laframboise against the white purity of Didi del Campo. *Dynamite
stuff*. Ten thousand sales on the cover alone.

"Mmmmmmm," Harry mused. "And who's approved it so far?
Didi? Zeke?"

Sidney displayed all his teeth. "They *adored* it," he said modestly.

"What did Zeke say?"

"He didn't say anything."

"*What?*"

"As Jehovah is my witness. He wasn't speaking the day we saw him.
Just had his tonsils out or something—could only nod, being unable to
read and write, as you know. Initial it he did, with our assistance. See,
there . . ."

Huge initials, E.W.W.L., drawn in Pentel red. Even that ass Bull
would agree on the weight of Zeke's scribbling at law. "And Didi?"

"She avowed that it is the greatest example of album art in the
history of the phonograph. Or photograph—I am not certain which.
She said this, Harry, in a letter, which is now out being framed—in case
you want to go to court."

"Fine," Harry said. "Better than fine—magnificent." He reached
across the table and shook Sidney's hand. The others applauded. Nothing more embarrassing than men applauding each other. "Get me
proofs for my office as soon as you can," Harry said, "and a set for my
studio at home."

"Do you want to sign off, then?" said Sidney, pen in hand.

"Why not?"

In one corner he wrote the familiar "H.E.C.—approved" and the date. It was easy enough for him to approve it, but what of Stash Gimpel, the lady's husband? Mmmm—there wasn't anything in particular that required air-brushing, no nipples, no genitalia—but the overall effect was overwhelmingly erotic. Oh, yes, the very finest cover in Melos-Doria history—and the very last to be signed off "H.E.C." Historic moment, eh, boys?

"And now," Harry said, his voice not as firm as he wished, "give me a shot of that fucking Fresca or you're all fired. . . ."

In the midst of their splendid nonsense, the lovely Alix Stern arrived, out of breath, dragging with her two lengths of yellow TWX paper—three-foot sections freshly ripped from the machines over in Mail & Communications.

"I knew you'd want to see this right away," she gasped. "Oh my God"—seeing the *Otello* artwork—"isn't that—*incredible* . . ."

The others put down their gins and looked over Harry's shoulder as he read. It was Morris K. Schonbaum's review for the *New York Times*:

> . . . On records, Otello, the great black role in all Grand Opera (Aïda notwithstanding), has been the exclusive property of white tenors in blackface—the names Melchior, Martinelli, Vinay, Del Monaco, Vickers and McCracken come most quickly to mind. Now, thanks to Melos-Doria, we have an authentic Moor—the young American from New Orleans, Ezekiel Laframboise—and quite simply he makes the role his alone. . . .
>
> Laframboise's interpretation is not merely skin-deep. He has the part in his blood and—as only a young singer can—he dares to expend his total vocal resource, which is immense, to make the Moor live and resound in our minds and hearts. He exhibits a certain roughness in dramatic moments, even a hoarse quality at times—could he have been suffering from a cold?—but the opening "Esultate" is a thing of power and glory, and in the love duet and closing scene he is incontestably a monumental artist. Melos-Doria is to be commended for its imagination and enterprise—and, yes, courage—in presenting so youthful an Otello, whose work here portends a distinguished future career. . . .
>
> Laframboise is by no means the whole show. Melos-Doria's casting is exceptional in many respects. What daring to offer Didi del Campo as Desdemona, a role she has performed on

stage only once (not counting Italian TV), the famous *scandale* at Santa Fe, in which she completed the death scene *sans* nightdress. But—surprisingly enough—her Desdemona is eminently believable, girlish, proud, pathetically doomed from the start by the perfidy of Iago and the jealousy of the Moor. Here is singing of notable grace and purity. . . .

As for the Iago, further magic from Melos-Doria: the greatest Iago of the modern era, Benno Toggi, just now returned from involuntary retirement in Italy. His is a unique conception: evil, yes, but evil predicated on enormous intellectual presumption. Signor Toggi brings tears to this listener's eyes with the elegance and nobility of his work. Alas, the legendary baritone's vocal estate today is precarious at best— the top thin and dry, the bottom wobbly and hollow. Withal, isn't it marvelous to have this fabled characterization in vinyl at last—a living document for the ages, if sometimes only a faint impression of what this great singing actor was able to bring to Shakespeare's (and Boïto-Verdi's) fabulous invention twenty years ago? Again, bravo, Melos-Doria . . .

I cannot say that I have the same affection for Gian-Carlo Ponti's handling of Verdi's miraculous score. It seems to me that the Swiss-Italian maestro is needlessly finicky and narrow-minded in pages which demand sweep, broad lines and panache. However, he is new to this business—this set marks his debut as conductor of opera on records—and he will progress rapidly: he's got all the right instincts, makes music with every breath he draws, and is already expert in the relationship of voice to orchestra—never does he under- or over-support his singers. . . .

The orchestra and chorus of the Rome Opera perform adequately, if not with special distinction, while the odd bits— the children's choir, the cannon and organ point of the opening scene, the mandolins in Act II—are exceptionally well managed. The entire enterprise has been well served by Melos-Doria's engineers, who obviously had some fun with the quadraphonic version. If you have four-channel equipment, by all means close the windows, lock the doors and crank up the volume: the Moor *lives!*

". . . Hey, *easy* boss—you don't want to upset the old ticker again, huh? . . . Get a glass of water, Burt. . . . Hell, it's not like it's your first rave review—you got a zillion of these things to your credit! . . . Yeah, give him a little gin. . . . You feeling better, Harry? . . . Atta boy . . . Come on, now—one lousy drink ain't gonna kill you. . . .

"He's going to be all right—let's just give him a minute to catch his breath. . . . You're feeling better, aren't you, Harry? . . . Here, take another sip. . . . Color's coming back. . . .

"Boy, you had us scared there for a minute, boss. . . . Don't do that anymore, will you, Harry? . . . Remember, we got hearts, too. . . ."

4

Old Max on the front gate gave him a startled wave, signaled for Harry to stop.

"Sorry, Mr. Chapin, but you're wanted back in the Chairman's office—your girl just called."

Deering? Probably about *Otello*. He'd had Alix carry over a copy of the Schonbaum review: set the stage for Monday's dramatic resignation scene—let the bastard know what kind of man LTI was losing.

Almost 4:30 P.M.—strange that Deering was still on the lot. To offset the hardships of Bel-Air living, the Chairman had recently bought himself (through LTI connections, with a great saving in broker's fee) a fantastic fifty-foot Kettenburg sloop, the *Best Revenge*, which had once belonged, so they said, to Tyrone Power; and he liked to head for Marina del Rey no later than 3:00 on Fridays—even the crucial monthly Management Committee meetings had been moved to Thursday as an accommodation. It would take something fairly catastrophic, Harry suddenly realized, to keep Leslie Deering from his appointed rounds.

Harry went first to the Melos-Doria bungalow to find out what Alix knew.

"I'm *so* sorry, Harry," she said with concern. "I told them you'd left, but they said it was urgent and that I should try to catch you at the gate."

"You did the right thing."

"Oh, and you just had a call from Mr. Blankenhorn in New York."

"I can imagine."

"He says that's urgent, too. He left his home number."

"Monday for that. Or maybe Tuesday."

"Oh, but, Harry—"

"If he calls again, tell him I'm with Mme. Cavalieri and can't be disturbed."

"Really, Harry—"

"Hey—one last thing."

"Yes?"

"There's something I want to tell you—confidentially."

"Oh?"

"Nobody knows yet, not even Deering. But I'm leaving Melos-Doria."

"Oh, *Harry*—"

"Yes. I'll give notice on Monday and leave at the end of the month."

"But *why*? What will you *do*? Where will you *go*?"

"Depends. Maybe teach school for a while. Or even write some music—what would you think of that? Or maybe just bum around for a while. Anyway—it's our secret, okay?"

"I hope—you'll be happy," she said. She began to cry.

He held her tightly. "I will be," he said. "Don't worry. You know me, kiddo. Always looking out for *Número Uno* . . ."

"Oh, Harry—thank God."

He had never seen Deering in such a state. There were no rock groups present now, no photographer, and the Chairman looked uncharacteristically vulnerable. The great yellow dispatch from Morris K. Schonbaum snaked in untidy rolls from Deering's In basket. Nodding in its direction, Harry said, "I thought you might be interested—the *New York Times*'s reaction to Chapin's folly."

"What? Oh, the notice. Splendid, absolutely *splendid*. But hadn't you warned me—be prepared for a nasty knock or two, you said?"

"One never knows."

The "one" he had borrowed, he realized, from Hilary Cairns—or, better, Lady A. Still, it seemed fitting under the circumstances, with this bogus Englishman.

"You don't smoke, do you? No, you're very fortunate. Filthy habit . . . Do you mind?" Deering lighted up a cigar similar to that which E. Jerold Bock had been unable to smoke in Harry's office. "I have just been speaking"—puff, puff, puff, this evil-looking brute not drawing well—"with George Law at his home in San Francisco."

Do my eyes deceive me? Are those hands actually *shaking*? "Oh?"

"Yes. And before that"—still puffing away without pleasure—"I had the most extraordinary call from a gentleman who fancies himself"—quick reference to note pad—"Count Stanislaus Gimpel."

"Really?" said Harry. "My—that *is* extraordinary."

"Quite."

"What did Stash have to offer? I'm really quite surprised—"

"Yes, I thought you would be. Getting right to the point, dear chap, he claims to represent this pianist—"

"Vladimir Slonimsky. Yes, he does, in a rather informal way."

"I was afraid so. Well—the Baron—"

"Count. Polish count, actually."

"Count Slonimsky—"

"Count Gimpel—"

"Count *Gimpel*—I don't know what's wrong with me today, my mind . . . At any rate, old chap, this Gimpel takes pleasure in informing us that Mr. Slonimsky will sign his new contract with Melos-Doria *only* if it contains a provision permitting him, Slonimsky, to leave Melos-Doria if for any reason Mr. Harry Chapin should leave Melos-Doria's employ."

Harry tried not to smile, but failed. "I find this very hard to believe, Leslie. The gentleman—well, he's said nothing to *me* along these lines."

"Mmmm. Strange, isn't it, how these classical fellows get such *bizarre* ideas."

"Yes, isn't it?"

"What, then, would your personal view be? Of this proposal?"

"Well—I'm appalled," Harry said. "We have never permitted such a clause in the past. Who is Mr. Slonimsky to restrict me in this way?"

"Quite right. Still—"

"Besides, Leslie—in view of the Board's decision not to renew my contract . . ."

"Oh," said Deering. "Well, on that point, Harry—"

"No, it would be quite wrong," Harry said, thinking now on the full implications of Gimpel's demand, "to saddle my successor with such an onerous clause. To permit Vova to walk away after Melos-Doria has spent thousands of dollars to build up his image in the marketplace—"

"Your *successor*?"

Deering put down his cigar, came from behind his desk, took the chair next to Harry's. "Dear chap, surely there is no talk of a successor?"

"But this morning—"

"These outsiders on the Board," Deering said with biting deprecation, "sometimes develop peculiar notions."

"Mr. George Law—"

"Don't concern yourself with *Law*," Deering protested. "Law is a *banker*. He knows nothing of the entertainment business."

"Still, when it comes to contracts—"

"My dear chap"—the hand which had held the cigar now took Harry's arm—"in the final analysis, Mr. Law, like all the others, will do as he's told. The fact is I have just related to him this entire episode. Naturally, he was extremely upset. You know the value he attaches to this chap—"

"Slonimsky."

"—Slonimsky. And while he was understandably annoyed by this other fellow's tactics—the Count—Law appreciates that ours is a most difficult task, and naturally he will support me, as Board Chairman, in anything I think essential to the well-being of our company."

"In that case—"

"Yes, quite. Well, speaking for myself—I suggest we go ahead, give the man what he wants, write in this new clause and—"

"Oh, but, Leslie," Harry said, "I'm afraid that's simply not possible."

"My dear chap—"

"I was going to wait until Monday to tell you of my decision. But in view of Gimpel's call—"

"What decision, my boy? What could possibly—"

"My decision to leave the company."

"To *leave*—"

"Yes. The Board's action in not renewing my contract constitutes a rather strong signal—wouldn't you agree?—that my value here is effectively at an end. Otherwise—"

"But, my dear *chap*, not at *all!* Don't you *see?* Boards of directors, as I've tried to explain, are *habitually* insensitive to operating managers' needs. Oh, no, boy—believe me when I say—"

"I will not stay on, Leslie, without a contract."

"Of *course* not. Quite *right*. And you shall *have* a new contract. George Law *agrees*. It is but a formality. At the next Board meeting—"

"Still," Harry said—musing now at Deering's expense—"I'm no longer sure. . . . You've got this man Dell to fall back on, remember."

"An *amateur?* In a business like *yours?* Surely you're *joking*, Harry. Not a bit of it. A new contract—three years? Would that be satisfactory? And naturally an appropriate increase in stipend. Let's not have any further talk about—"

"And the presidency," Harry said.

"I'm sorry—what did you say?"

"The presidency," Harry repeated quietly. "Of Melos-Doria. President and Chief Executive Officer. There hasn't been one since Mr. Strauss, and it's time we had one."

"Ah," said Deering, falling away now, returning to his desk, slouching down, his corporate energy nearly expended. "Now, that *is* a problem, Harry. Not that you don't deserve it. But, thinking of your peer group—the heads of the other subsidiaries. If *you* were to have such a title, then what about—"

"I'm really not interested in the others," Harry said matter-of-factly. "And I would not be prepared to stay on, Leslie, without a three-year contract and the title 'President and Chief Executive Officer.'"

"Now *really*, Harry—"

"Perhaps you'll wish to discuss the matter with Mr. Law."

"That reminds me—he wants you to fly up to San Francisco Monday for luncheon with him at the Old Pacific Club. I said you'd meet him there at one o'clock. I hope that's convenient."

"I'm sorry," Harry said, "but I'm not flying anywhere right now. Doctor's orders."

"Oh, dear chap, I had no idea—"

"No, I'm perfectly fine. It's just a precaution. If Mr. Law would like to come down here . . . Otherwise, I'm afraid he'll have to use the telephone."

Harry rose to leave.

"Dear chap," Deering continued to mumble.

"If there's nothing else—"

Deering found strength enough to rise and accompany Harry to the door. "By the way," the Chairman said with delicacy, "I've had several calls regarding the Cavalieri situation."

"Oh?"

"Yes. Davis Bull is—well, tremendously upset, the only phrase I can use—over your tactics with Edith's lawyer. The little fellow whose name I can't seem to—"

"Bock. E. Jerold Bock."

"Yes, Bock. Perhaps at your convenience you could fill me in?"

"Of course. With pleasure."

"Also, Edith herself called."

"*Did* she?"

"An awfully nice woman, wouldn't you agree? I found her most charming company."

"A remarkable lady, yes."

"Obviously, she thinks the world of you—spoke of having you personally produce her recordings. The album of pop songs, for example, which she is keen to do."

"There would be no harm in talking, I suppose."

"But her real purpose in calling was to say that our current offer—and you *must* fill me in on the precise terms at our next get-together, dear chap—she finds our current offer satisfactory and acceptable, and she would be most grateful if the 'new check'—her description—could be sent to her, posthaste, care of the Plaza in New York, rather than to her usual company of chartered accountants. And definitely *not* to Mr. Blankenhorn's office. Does this make any sense?"

"Oh, yes," Harry said. "Makes perfect sense. I shall see to it first thing Monday morning."

"Fine, old chap. Well, then—have a pleasant weekend, won't you? And let's try to get together early in the week, shall we? Perhaps a bite together at my club?"

"I can think of nothing, Leslie," said Harry, lying through his teeth, "that would give me greater pleasure. . . ."

Dear faithful Alix had waited for him. "Was it really—urgent?" she asked warily.

"Hah! Quite routine. I'll tell you about it sometime."

"I haven't said you're here—but there's a call for you on line one. It's Mr. Musgrove from Legal."

"Why not? . . . Yes, Dan? What can I do for you?"

"I'm just calling to say, Mr. Chapin—well, that I appreciated the way you stuck up for our company at the meeting. Of course I'm inexperienced in these things—but it seemed to me that with somebody like this Bock character . . ."

"I'm grateful for your support," Harry said. "If I seemed a little rude—well, in my experience, there are times when it pays to 'hang tough,' as our pop brethren say. Anyway—thanks."

"One question, Mr. Chapin. And you don't have to answer if you don't want to."

"Shoot."

"The business about giving Mme. Cavalieri's old tapes to that guy . . . ?"

"Bloom. Rosco Bloom—called 'The Junk Man' in the trade."

"Right. Well—would you *really* do it? Let him have her old albums for one of those supermarket things?"

"What do you think?"

"I—I think you were bluffing, Mr. Chapin."

"Don't you ever tell that to Mr. Bull."

"Oh, no, sir. But—well, I'm glad."

"Are you, now? Well—I suppose I am, too. Have a nice weekend, Dan."

"You, too, Mr. Chapin. And thanks . . ."

Nice kid, Musgrove—Union counterpart to the Confederacy's Ross Canby. These young fellows would inherit the earth one of these days—run Melos-Doria when the Harry Chapins and Norman Roses and all the other old crocks had been put out to pasture. Harry certainly hoped that Musgrove knew what he was talking about when he said Harry Chapin had been bluffing.

"Alix?"

"Yes, Harry?"

"Go home. But remind me first thing Monday morning to call Stash Gimpel. Also, I'd like you to go down to Tiffany's on your lunch hour and get us a thank-you gift. Token of gratitude, in exquisite taste, for a descendant of Polish kings—but not costing over a hundred and a half, okay? . . . Oh, hell, I'll go with you—got to get Maggie a birthday present anyway—and maybe even find something for ol' Alix Stern, but only if she promises not to cry. . . ."

I I

Maggie and Mutt met him in the foyer with kisses. He embraced the former, petted the latter. "You had your hair done. Who did it—what's his name, Fernando?"

"A new boy—Ronald. Do you like it? Is it too—young-looking?"

"Just right," he said. "Looks—great."

There now, that's better, eh? Considerate son of a bitch, this Chapin.

"Hi, Dad! . . . 'Bye, Dad! . . ."

"Where are *they* going?"

"Back to school. Rehearsal for the Christmas play."

"I still don't think *Death of a Salesman* is a proper vehicle for Christmas. In my day we did *Charley's Aunt* or gave readings from Dickens or, one year, danced *The Nutcracker*."

"That was New England," Maggie said, hanging up his jacket and bringing him his before-dinner pill. "This is California."

He had gone to a rehearsal the previous weekend. Heck and Beachie played Willy Loman's sons, Happy and Biff. This required some artistic license because Happy and Biff are not supposed to be twins. The boys approached *Death of a Salesman* as though it were *Othello*, a gloomy classic from another age. When Harry mentioned that he had seen the original production at the Morosco Theatre during Easter holiday when he was still at Choate, the boys chose not to believe him: more of Dad's famous satiric humor. No boy of sixteen expected ever to be forty-five.

"Are you hungry? Silly question—everything's ready, we can sit right down. Or would you like to take a swim first?"

"Neither one," he said. "Got a whole new idea—compensation for the kind of day I've had."

He marched out back, Maggie trailing along, and picked himself a lemon from the tree beside his studio.

"Oh, Harry, what would Dr. Iselin—"

He was not supposed to have these things—absolutely *forbidden* on his diet—but he went resolutely back to the wet-bar and made himself a very powerful Myers's Rum Collins, which he had not had for months now but which he very much needed. Ninety-seven days since the events of Rome; a man was entitled to a blast of rum once every ninety-seven days, *n'est-ce pas? C'est nécessaire, naturellement!*

Maggie and Mutt looked on dolefully.

"Just the one," he said, testing it for sweetness. Ah, *parfait.* "It's not going to kill me." Probably.

Maggie poured herself a small glass of white wine; she took this conditioning business more seriously than he did. They sat in the living room while whatever it was she'd fixed him for dinner—either the broiled chicken or the broiled fish—got cold in the kitchen and he ran down the day for her. . . . Yes, saw Deering. No, nothing particularly important—well, we'll discuss it later. . . . The luncheon for Cavalieri? Oh, yes, big success: gave a little speech myself, seemed to go over okay. . . . Met the new Board hotshot, George Law. Like all San Franciscans (like Maggie), superior and just a bit dull: wants me to fly up for lunch at the Old Pacific Club. No! Yes. Will you go? No. Oh. Yes, oh . . . Received Schonbaum's advance review of *Otello.* And? Not too bad, actually. Oh, Harry. Got it in my briefcase, show it to you later. . . . Also saw Sidney Jonas's *Otello* cover: quite effective—nudes, you know. You're kidding. No, no—no more kidding from this boy, quite serious. Oh, Harry. Yes, oh, Harry . . . Deering—did he say anything about your contract? Renewing it? Mmmmm, we talked awhile. But it's complicated—let's discuss that later, too, okay? Okay, Harry. Whatever you think best . . . I don't suppose I can have another of these? Absolutely *not.* No, I didn't think so. . . .

After dinner (the broiled fish: Friday, remember?) he left Maggie to watch *Upstairs, Downstairs* and retired to the studio. He didn't feel like going through the mail, bills mostly, so he got out Schonbaum's review and went over it again, savoring every line, even the reservations about Ponti, which Harry shared. For the ads, he would tell Burt Moss to use "Quite simply Laframboise makes the role his alone" or maybe "Incontestably a monumental singer" or—yes, this could be the headline: "Bravo, Melos-Doria . . . The Moor *lives!*" Thank God for Morris Schonbaum; maybe pen him a nice thank-you at an appropriate moment.

He put side one of the new acetates on the turntable and listened to the set's first twenty-two minutes and forty seconds again, this time with the new "Esultate" in place, the one that Schonbaum hadn't heard yet. Mmmm, yes, oh my, yes—stage fright or no stage fright, this boy Laframboise can *sing.* Going to be a *big* star at the Met before he's through. And to think they'd been looking for a replacement, Vickers, *anybody*, after the first week at Rome . . .

The buzzing of the intercom brought him back to reality. It was Maggie, of course, asking him to turn down the phonograph. Ah, that's better: this was the *real* Maggie, not the Pollyanna who'd been tiptoeing around since they shipped him home practically in a box.

He took off the *Otello* and put on the old Deutsche Grammophon *Lohengrin*. The acoustics were awful and the tenor, King, sounded tired. The ironic thing was—as Otto would show everybody tomorrow morning on the Met broadcast—Kunz could sing the Swan Knight better than *anybody*, even now at fifty-seven years of age. So why didn't some brave record man give him the job? Five LPs, that's why. Like all Wagner (except *Dutchman*), the silly piece was ridiculously overlong, filled with padding.

For his part, Harry Chapin was off the hook: DDRSch, the boys from East Berlin, had agreed—after a little gentle persuasion from Count Gimpel—to give Otto his *Otello* in late '79; meaning that Harry owed the little German only one more set, the *Aïda* which the Consortium wanted anyway. An excellent commercial decision, Chapin . . . Still, *Lohengrin* was the role that Otto had in his blood, not Radamès. Might be worth a man's time and energy to put that score down properly for once—get all the notes and bring a little *art* to the subject at the same time. A puzzle: how to do it and not be ruined in the process? . . . What about using the Dresden Orchestra? A co-production with those same boys from DDRSch? Might just get old Dr. Udo Blinn on the phone and see what was what—maybe get their Commie pal Boris Makhov to sing Friedrich of Telramund—but still no Mercedes at Zürich, Boris baby. . . . Mmmm, yes, and try to keep the budget under, say, $200,000, just to please George Law.

He was going to miss campus life, he supposed—all those nubile young music majors dying to know what it was like in the big time.

But if Harry Chapin didn't lay down Kunz's *Lohengrin*, who would . . . ?

For Aria, Brown Meggs has drawn on eighteen years' experience with a major American record company, ultimately as its chief operating officer and member of the board of directors. In 1976 he resigned his corporate post to devote his full time to writing. A Californian by birth and inclination, Meggs was schooled at St. Luke's, New Canaan, Connecticut, and Harvard. He makes his home in Pasadena with his wife, the former Nancy Bates Meachen, and their son, Brook.